Marriage License Affidavits

1861–1921

Sonoma County, California

Volume II: G–M

(Alphabetized by Surname of Groom)

Part One: Groom, Bride, Date of Application, Comments

Part Two: Groom, Bride, Age, Residence, Place of Birth

Sonoma County Genealogical Society

Heritage Books
2011

HERITAGE BOOKS
AN IMPRINT OF HERITAGE BOOKS, INC.

Books, CDs, and more—Worldwide

For our listing of thousands of titles see our website
at
www.HeritageBooks.com

Published 2011 by
HERITAGE BOOKS, INC.
Publishing Division
100 Railroad Ave. #104
Westminster, Maryland 21157

Copyright © 2011 Sonoma County Genealogical Society

All rights reserved. No part of this book may be reproduced or transmitted in any form or by any means, electronic or mechanical, including photocopying, recording or by any information storage and retrieval system without written permission from the author, except for the inclusion of brief quotations in a review.

International Standard Book Numbers
Paperbound: 978-0-7884-5358-8
Clothbound: 978-0-7884-8902-0

Contents: Volume 2: G - M
(Alphabetized by Surname of Groom)

Part I
Groom, Bride, Date of Application, Comments

Part II
Groom, Bride, Age, Residence, Place of Birth

Marriage License Affidavits, 1861 to 1921
Sonoma County, California

Introduction

The information contained in this four volume series is taken from Marriage License Affidavits currently housed at the Sonoma County History and Genealogy Library in Santa Rosa, California. These data originated in the office of the Sonoma County Clerk. The information is contained on eight reels of microfilm and contains approximately 14,000 records.

The volumes consist of:

Volume	Data Alphabetized by Groom's Surname
I	A - F
II	G - M
III	N - Z
IV	Index to Bride's Surname

In 1990, the Sonoma County Genealogical Society published *Sonoma County Marriages, 1847 - 1902*, which was an index to marriage records housed at the office of the Sonoma County Recorder. This current publication, unlike the index, in most cases contains the age, residence, and birth place of both the bride and groom. In addition, the consent of a parent or guardian is noted for brides under the age of 18 and grooms under the age of 21. In a few cases, birth dates or other pertinent information is given.

Affidavits are the application for a marriage license and may well include persons who were never actually married. The date may or may not coincide with the actual marriage date of those who did, in fact, get married.

Condition of the Microfilm

In many cases, the condition of the microfilm is exceedingly poor, and the handwritten entries vary from readable to totally unreadable. Forms often varied from year to year, and in some cases, a handwritten note from the parent(s), guardian(s), or a notary was substituted for the form generally in use during that time period. Many of the parental consent forms were handwritten notes and were not always adjacent to the marriage affidavits to which they belonged. Some notes partially obscure the information written on the affidavits.

A clerk apparently filled in the form in most cases, which was then usually signed by the groom, sometimes by both the bride and the groom, occasionally only by the bride, or occasionally by another person. Not infrequently, the spelling of the name made by the clerk did not agree with the spelling of the person who signed the affidavit. In such cases we used the spelling of the person(s) who signed if it was legible. All affidavits were read by at least two persons, and, in some cases, by three persons to try to resolve the correct spelling. If the issue could not be resolved, a question mark (?) appears beside the name, or other information provided.

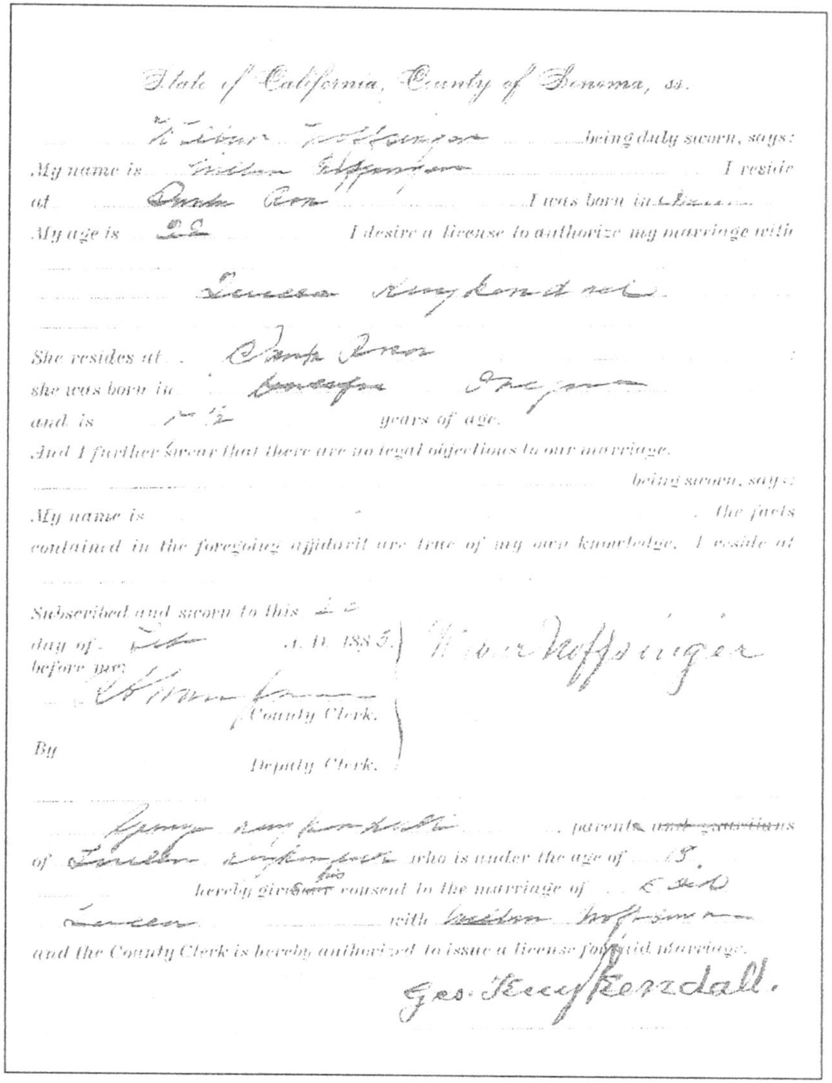

Figure 1: Example of an 1883 marriage affidavit

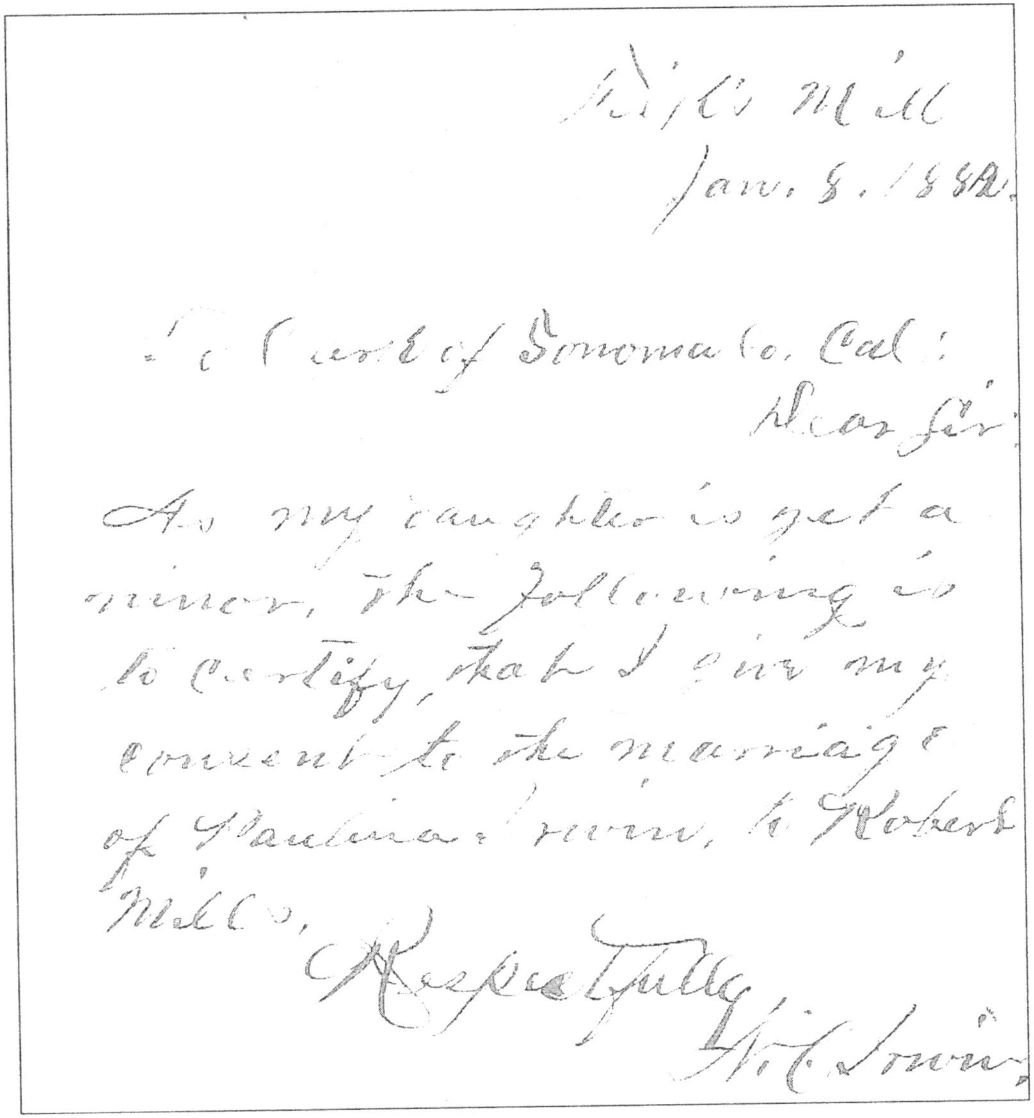

> Mark West Mill
> Jan. 8, 1882.
>
> To Clerk of Sonoma Co, Cal:
>
> Dear Sir:
>
> As my daughter is yet a minor, the following is to certify that I give my consent to the marriage of Paulina Irwin, to Robert Wilds.
>
> Respectfully,
> W. C. Irwin

Figure 2: Example of one of the "better" notes of permission

Description of Data Layout

The data are presented alphabetically by groom's surname in three volumes, each volume having two parts. A fourth volume is an index to the bride's surname.

Part	Data Included
I	Name of groom, bride, date of application, comments (includes name of parent or guardian for males under 21 and brides under 18), and occasionally other notes
II	Detailed information on groom and bride: age, residence, place of birth

Example of Use

If you know the name of the groom, locate the appropriate volume, begin with part I, then go to part II for additional information about both parties. If you know only the name of the bride, go to volume IV and locate the bride's name to find the name of the groom. Then located the groom in parts I and II to find additional detailed information.

For place of residence, the town was most frequently given. The state can be assumed to be California unless otherwise noted (using standard postal codes). State codes may be designated for smaller/lesser known towns in California and other states. State codes are not used for well-known cities (Chicago, New York City, New Orleans, etc.).

Place of birth is most often given as state or country; standard postal codes are used for the USA, as shown in Table 3. A three-character code is used for other nations, as shown in Figure 4. However, some birth places may be given as a city or town, township, county, or region in the USA or in another nation. Those cities or other locations that are most frequently used are also coded to conserve space and are shown in Figure 5.

Table 3: United States Codes

Postal Code	State
AL	Alabama
AK	Alaska
AZ	Arizona
AR	Arkansas
CA	California
CO	Colorado
CT	Connecticut
DE	Delaware
DC	District of Columbia
FL	Florida
GA	Georgia
GU	Guam
HI	Hawaii
ID	Idaho
IL	Illinois
IN	Indiana
IA	Iowa
KS	Kansas
KY	Kentucky
LA	Louisiana
ME	Maine
MD	Maryland
MA	Massachusetts
MI	Michigan
MN	Minnesota
MS	Mississippi
MO	Missouri
MT	Montana
NE	Nebraska
NV	Nevada
NH	New Hampshire
NJ	New Jersey
NM	New Mexico
NY	New York
NC	North Carolina
ND	North Dakota
OH	Ohio
OK	Oklahoma
OR	Oregon
PA	Pennsylvania
PR	Puerto Rico
RI	Rhode Island
SC	South Carolina
SD	South Dakota
TN	Tennessee
TX	Texas
UT	Utah
VT	Vermont
VA	Virginia
VI	Virgin Islands
WA	Washington
WV	West Virginia
WI	Wisconsin
WY	Wyoming

Table 4: International Codes

Code	Country
AFG	Afghanistan
AFR	Africa
ALB	Albania
ALS	Alsace-Lorraine
ARG	Argentina
ASY	Assyria
AUS	Austria
AUT	Australia
AZR	Azores
BAR	Barbados
BAV	Bavaria
BER	Bermuda
BCL	British Columbia
BHS	Bahamas
BLG	Belgium

BOH	Bohemia
BOL	Bolivia
BOR	Borneo
BRA	Brazil
BRG	British Guiana
BUA	Buenos Aires
BUL	Bulgaria
BUR	Burma
BWI	British West Indies
CEN	Central America
CHL	Chile
CHN	China
CLB	Colombia
CLZ	Canal Zone
CND	Canada
COR	Costa Rica
CRT	Croatia
CUB	Cuba
CZH	Czechoslovakia
DEI	Dutch East Indies
DMR	Dominican Republic
DNK	Denmark
EGY	Egypt
EIN	East Indies
ELS	El Salvador
ENG	England
ESI	East India
EUR	Europe
FIN	Finland
FRN	France
FRP	French Polynesia
GAM	Guam
GBR	Great Britain

GER	Germany
GIB	Gibraltar
GRC	Greece
GUA	Guatemala
HAI	Haiti
HIN	Hindustan
HLD	Holland
HND	Honduras
HUN	Hungary
HWI	Hawaiian Islands
ICE	Iceland
IDA	India
IND	Indonesia
IOJ	Isle of Jersey
IOM	Isle of Man
IRL	Ireland
ISR	Israel
ITL	Italy
JAM	Jamaica
JPN	Japan
JVA	Java
KOR	Korea
LAT	Latvia
LEB	Lebanon
LIT	Lithuania
LUX	Luxembourg
MEX	Mexico
MLT	Malta
NAM	North America
NBW	New Brunswick
NRY	Norway
NSC	Nova Scotia
NSW	News South Wales

NTH	Netherlands
NWL	North Wales
NZD	New Zealand
OTT	Ottoman Empire
PAL	Palestine
PAN	Panama
PAR	Paraguay
PEI	Prince Edward Island
PER	Persia
PLD	Poland
PRS	Prussia
PRT	Portugal
PRU	Peru
PUR	Puerto Rico
QUE	Quebec
ROM	Romania
RUS	Russia
SAF	South Africa
SAM	South America
SAX	Saxony
SCT	Scotland
SEA	(born at sea)
SGP	Singapore
SIB	Siberia
SLO	Slovakia
SMI	Santa Maria Islands
SPN	Spain
SRB	Serbia
SWD	Sweden
SWI	Sandwich Islands
SWT	Switzerland
SYR	Syria

TRK	Turkey
URG	Uruguay
VEN	Venezuela
VIE	Vietnam

VRI	Virgin Islands
WIN	West Indies
WLS	Wales

WTS	Western Islands
YUG	Yugoslavia

Figure 5: Cities, Towns, Townships, and Other Areas

Bey	Bayrouth, SYR
Can	Canton Ticino, SWT
Chi	Chicago
Clo	Cloverdale
Clv	Cleveland
Dak	Dakota
Dun	Dundas, Ontario, CND
Hld	Healdsburg
Hon	Honolulu
Lak	Lake Co.
Lon	London, ENG
Mac	Marin Co.
Men	Mendocino Co.
Oak	Oakland
Pet	Petaluma

Pett	Petaluma Twp.
Por	Portland, OR
Saj	San Jose
Sfo	San Francisco
Sab	San Bernardino Co.
Sac	Sacramento
Sar	Santa Rosa
Seb	Sebastopol
Son	Sonoma
Soc	Sonoma Co.
Utt	Utah Territory
Vts	Vallejo Twp., Sonoma Co.
Wat	Washington Territory
Wdc	Washington, D.C.

Acknowledgments

Project Director
Carmen Finley

Data Entry
Maggi Andrews
Kerri Bailey
Kay Clegg
Phyllis Kuehn
Joe Panaro
Helen Strickley

Proofreaders
Anna Conley
Doris Dickenson
Carmen Finley
Lois Nimmo

Editor
Doris Dickenson

Camera Ready Copy
Carmen Finley

Special acknowledgment goes to Anthony Hoskins, head of the History and Genealogy Library in Sonoma County
and Sonoma County Archivist who made the microfilm available for abstraction. Also, thanks to Mairi Barsky, Branch Manager of
the Guerneville Regional Library for the use of their library facilities.

Groom Surname	Groom Given Name	Bride Surname	Bride Given Name	Date	Comments
Gaba	Marks	Kubic	Annie	21 Feb. 1892	
Gabel	W. E.	Peck	Muriel	20 Mar. 1915	
Gaberel (?)	G. W.	Seward	Mollie	17 Apr. 1880	requested by Henry Reynolds
Gaberil	Manuel Joseph	Morel	Mary Caroline	28 June 1898	br: requested
Gables	Chaney R.	Richardson	Ella M.	17 Nov. 1866	
Gabrielsen	William J. A.	Down	Edith	30 July 1910	
Gabrielson	Carl O.	Anderson	Johanna L.	26 Sept. 1910	
Gaffney	William	Walsh	Rose	21 May 1917	
Gage	George S.	Conne	Margaret	3 Sept. 1918	
Gagliando	Andrea	Pierano	Teresa	2 Jan. 1897	
Gaige	Walter Louis	Chance	Mary E.	3 Dec. 1904	
Gaillard	Robert G.	Harrison	Amanda J., Mrs.	23 Nov. 1901	do not publish until 30 Nov.
Gainer	Roland L.	Chelini	Josephine	1 May 1916	
Gaither	William	Chism	Martha	28 Sept. 1914	
Galard	Nicholas	Anglade	Katy	13 Mar. 1891	
Gale	Adelbert Orlando	Grant	Frankie	31 July 1899	Frank C. Jordan duly sworn; neither party divorced within one year
Gale	Archie R.	McAfee	Georgie L.	24 Oct. 1906	
Gale	Archie R.	Dowdall	Mary E.	14 Feb. 1920	
Gale	Cecil H.	Leete	Margaret S.	17 Jan. 1912	gr: W. A. Gale, parent; br: O. R. Leete, parent
Gale	D. R.	England	Carrie	2 Oct. 1888	
Gale	James A.	Barnett	Emma B.	3 Oct. 1891	
Gale	Leander	Conecl (?)	Eva	9 May 1908	
Gale	Milton C.	Taylor	Minnie S.	15 Jan. 1887	br: Carrie Virginia Linebaugh, mother & John Linebaugh, stepfather
Gale	W. S.	Poulsen	Maria Francisca	10 July 1894	br: M. C. Gale says they are of age.
Gale	Wallace P.	Penn	Ida Irene	25 May 1916	gr: Mrs. Marie F. Gale, mother

Groom		Bride		Date	Comments
Surname	Given Name	Surname	Given Name		
Galgani	Guiseppe	Frediani	Katie	11 Aug. 1915	
Galgani	Vincenzo	Dinucci	Julia Katherine	5 Feb. 1910	
Galindo	Joseph Vincent	Manning	Ellen Ida	31 Jan. 1906	
Galindo	Ruperto	Duffey	Mabel G.	5 June 1913	
Gallagher	Dominic	Granger	Carrie E.	7 Nov. 1904	
Gallagher	Edward H.	McIntire	Mary L.	25 Nov. 1919	
Gallagher	Frank George	Struve	Martha Olga	13 June 1910	
Gallagher	James	Donahue	Rena	2 Sept. 1902	
Gallaway	Alfred J.	Nelson	Thyra A.	27 May 1920	
Gallaway	Alfred Russel	Ware	Lilla	31 Dec. 1907	
Gallaway	John C.	Gallaway	Lizzie, Mrs.	9 Feb. 1920	
Gallaway	John W.	Gamble	Bertha V.	16 Mar. 1918	
Galleher	John Harry	Fredericks	Minna	8 Sept. 1906	
Galli	Verginio	Bartolomei	Sabina	15 May 1912	
Galliah	San	Kirmess	Caroline	30 July 1918	
Gallo	Lorenzo	Zandrina	Rosa	20 Feb. 1889	
Galpin	John W.	Hutchings	Susie	5 July 1901	br: Mrs. A. D. Huchings, mother
Galvin	George Jay	Green	Emily Augusta	5 Sept. 1914	
Gamage	Jule Crigden ?	Lewis	Lillian L.	9 June 1896	gr: Mary T. Gamage, mother, gives consent.
Gambarasi	Edward	Notari	Regina	29 Nov. 1909	
Gamber	A. A.	Royce	Mollie T.	6 Dec. 1879	
Gambini	L. P.	Grandi	Ella C.	16 Oct. 1903	
Gambini	William A.	Hockin	Margaret M.	25 Sept. 1913	
Gamble	Charles	Clark	Ella	27 Dec. 1886	
Gamble	Charles Elmer	Lumsden	Martha Louise	29 July 1902	
Gambogi	Amchese	Garborini	Annie	8 Apr. 1899	
Gambogi	Davino	Ronchali	Rosa	13 Feb. 1905	

Groom Surname	Groom Given Name	Bride Surname	Bride Given Name	Date	Comments
Gamboni	William Robert	Menary	Mary Katherine	8 Feb. 1911	
Gambonini	Alfonso Joseph	LaFranchi	Sylvia J.	9 Jan. 1920	
Gambonini	Arnold	La Franchi	Anita E.	30 Sept. 1918	
Gambonini	Silvio G.	Dado	Evelina E.	16 Jan. 1909	
Gammill	Charles F.	Beatty	May V.	21 Sept. 1892	
Gandy	Lemaul J.	Nelsen	Emma G.	15 Apr. 1914	
Gangler	Xaver	Hueber	Regina	22 Dec. 1914	
Ganner	James Edwin	Pierce	Augusta	6 Oct. 1890	
Ganter	Clinton E.	Wyckoff	Maggie	20 Feb. 1899	no previous marriage
Garbini	Angelo J.	Gossage	Rachel L.	7 Aug. 1919	
Garcelon	W. Scott, Jr.	Schibi	Margaret B.	20 Sept. 1919	
Garcia	Agopito P.	Mills	Winifred Alice	22 Oct. 1907	
Garcia	Antonio	Gracia	Ception	19 June 1915	
Garcia	Benigno	Casasnovas	Sara	31 July 1914	
Garcia	Chick	Bones	Alice	12 June 1906	
Garcia	Felix	Mendosiz	Fara	16 Feb. 1866	
Garcia	Firmin	Emeldi	Theodora Marie	7 Sept. 1916	
Gard	James F.	Kopiske	Amelia	30 Apr. 1917	
Gardella	Joseph	Veganogo	Angelo	29 Nov. 1890	
Gardenhire	W. H.	Laymance	Leona	31 July 1915	
Gardenhire	William A.	Rider	Lois E.	24 Dec. 1910	br: L. E. Rider, parent
Gardenshire (?)	S. B.	Lingenfelter	Lucy	2 May 1885	br: W. J. Lingenfelter, guardian
Gardiner	Bevil F.	Wilcox	Edith M.	21 May 1917	
Gardiner	Charles W.	Tramor	Marie A.	3 Sept. 1920	
Gardiner	Waldron R.	Pharris	Alice	27 Nov. 1918	br: 574 8th St., Oakland
Gardner	Albert E.	Weller	Eva U.	16 July 1914	
Gardner	Bernard Rogers	Klink	Vernie Gladys	3 June 1905	
Gardner	Chas. M.	Murbar	Clara	29 Sept. 1885	

Groom		Bride		Date	Comments
Surname	Given Name	Surname	Given Name		
Gardner	Robert Elmer	Cornett	Edith Luella	8 June 1895	
Gardner	Roy Lee	Hart	Delphine Antonia	8 Apr. 1918	
Gardner	Vanness	Crotts	Emily K.	30 Dec. 1907	
Gardner	William H.	Joseph	Mae Vera	9 Feb. 1921	
Garety	Leo J.	O'Brien	Elizabeth V.	22 Oct. 1919	
Garguilo	Fred	Burke	Margaret May	17 Aug. 1912	
Garland	Harry	Burgess	Beatrice	26 May 1915	
Garloff	Henry R.	Finley	Genevieve	24 May 1915	br: Mrs. Carrie Ann Finley, mother
Garloff	John A.	Mapes	Annita G.	4 Nov. 1908	
Garloff	Walter W.	Finley	Bessie	24 May 1915	
Garloff	William F.	McDonald	Jessie F.	12 Jan. 1911	
Garlow	J. A.	Bryant	Della D.	2 June 1914	
Garman	James	Sebring	Sarah E.	31 May 1865	
Garner	Walter A.	Allen	Ethel Mae	2 Dec. 1919	
Garnett	Kennedy Porter	Foote	Edna	20 May 1907	
Garofalo	Bert	Beattie	Friedia	17 Dec. 1915	
Garoni	Guiseppe	Shevoskey	Eva	10 June 1914	
Garratt	Mansfield W.	Ray	Juanita I.	1 Dec. 1920	
Garretson	John D.	Purvine	E. Mae	23 Dec. 1911	
Garrett	Albert Walker	Hall	Cora Pauline	27 Nov. 1894	
Garrett	Edward Lee	Norris	Erma B.	25 Oct. 1897	
Garrett	Thomas	Kanieri	Anna	29 Aug. 1911	
Garrett	Vernon George	Carithers	Gladys Ellen	23 Mar. 1920	
Garrison	Bert L.	Kalen	Charlotte S.	21 July 1897	
Garrison	Charles H.	Brown	Marguerite J.	16 Mar. 1920	
Garrison	Charles S.	Sutherland	Della	30 Dec. 1902	
Garrison	Elmer B.	Doty	Ida H.	19 Sept. 1919	gr: Charlotte S. Garrison, mother
Garrison	James G.	Moran	Blanche E.	29 Apr. 1912	

Groom Surname	Groom Given Name	Bride Surname	Bride Given Name	Date	Comments
Garrison	Nonnie	King	Matilda J.	23 Dec. 1903	br: William King, father
Garrison	Richard William	Langer	Alice G.	22 June 1920	
Garrison	Ross J.	Whitcomb	Annie O.	16 July 1900	
Garrison	Will Robert	Randall	Fannie J.	9 June 1911	
Garrity	Thomas	McFarland	Mary	11 Apr. 1902	
Garside	Thomas H.	Glazier	Mary O.	14 Feb. 1914	
Gartner	Charles Henry	Neal	Rita E.	16 Apr. 1921	
Garvey	John F.	McMartin	Mary J.	12 June 1911	
Garzoli	Alfonso	Dodd	Delfina	25 Nov. 1907	
Garzoli	Joshua	Eraldi	Emma	8 Aug. 1905	br: E. Eraldi, parent, gives consent
Garzoli	William Victor	Pellascio	Lillie Vergie	16 Sept. 1914	
Gashwiler	L. F.	McClellan	Ruth	22 June 1892	license requested by J. W. Oates
Gaspari	Julius	Mecchi	Mary	31 Jan. 1920	
Gasperi	Pietro	Maccario	Katie	7 Dec. 1899	no previous marriage
Gaston	Geo. W.	Sales	Dora A.	20 July 1892	
Gaston	George R.	Anderson	Ruth M.	28 Sept. 1917	
Gaston	John W.	Freeman	Nadien J.	31 Aug. 1881	br: John H. Freeman, father
Gaston	William H.	Winn	Hattie M.	28 June 1911	
Gater	Frank I.	Dana	Emma	10 Nov. 1891	
Gater	J. E.	Smith	Carrie	2 Aug. 1887	
Gater	J. E.	Miles	Mary	23 Dec. 1884	
Gates	Earl J.	Henslee	Marie L.	21 Jan, 1915	
Gates	William Henry	Sikes	Viola Bly	6 Jan. 1908	
Gauldin	Joseph E.	Chamler	Fannie Belle	20 Nov. 1906	br: D. G. Chamler, parent
Gaupp	Edward Philip	Hawthorne	Esther Gertrude	10 Jan. 1917	
Geanskag	John	Sellers	Mattie	23 June 1903	
Gearhart	L. C.	Horgson (?)	Emma	3 Sept. 1881	
Geary	George E.	Ranker	Bernice O.	26 Dec. 1914	

		Bride		Date	Comments
Groom					
Surname	**Given Name**	**Surname**	**Given Name**		
Geary	Michael	Anderson	Alice H.	10 June 1915	
Geary	William W.	Wilson	Emma	25 Mar. 1892	
Gebauer	Charles J.	Selzle	Lena A.	20 Dec. 1893	
Gebharth	Christian	Bollinger	Dora Francis	15 Mar. 1892	
Geiger	Fred	Demetz	Anna	12 Feb. 1889	
Geils	George F.	Druckhammer	Minna	16 Aug. 1893	
Gein	August Carl	Barnes	Ruby Rhomance	21 Apr. 1908	
Geiorvas (?)	Pete D.	Nelson	Mary E.	1 Sept. 1920	
Geisel	Henry John	Peterson	Bertha	21 Aug 1907	
Geisler	Francis Joseph	Journey	Nettie Belle	10 Mar. 1910	
Gellerman	Louis W.	Curtis	Mabel H.	24 Aug. 1914	
Gellissen	Andrew	Rohlfs	Frances	2 Oct. 1913	
Gemetti	Battista	Cotta	Delia	20 Nov. 1900	
Gemmer (?)	John C.	Boehrner	Annie E.		filed between 25 Mar. and 12 Apr. 1881
Genazzi	Charles E.	Bittner	Mary H.	24 Jan. 1902	
Gender	Edward F.	Dwyer	Nellie A.	10 June 1918	
Genelle	Emanuel Ignacio	Stegeman	Julia	11 Jan. 1907	
Generrilli	Albert J.	Gibson	Dorothy Irene	24 Nov. 1919	
Gennette	Rene Even	Shaw	Irene	2 Apr. 1919	
Gensler	G.	Montague	Eleeta	8 Aug. 1911	
Gensler	Goodkind	Swift	Lizzie	21 Jan. 1895	
Genther	Jeremiah	Thompson	Agnes L.	15 Mar. 1913	
Gentis	Camille	Cone	Kathryn A.	4 Sept. 1917	
Gentry	Samuel	DeYoung	Minnie	14 Jan. 1898	
Genung	William L.	Fournier (?)	Alice	4 Feb. 1921	
George	Harmon Alfred	Pierce	Ethel Ruth	27 Dec. 1907	
George	James W.	Jones	Nellie M.	3 Jan. 1902	do not publish for some time
George	John	Green	Lucy	7 Jan. 1905	

Groom Surname	Groom Given Name	Bride Surname	Bride Given Name	Date	Comments
George	Joseph M.	Elton	Gratia	2 July 1918	gr: J. M. George, guardian
George	William Edgar	Burke	Evelyn Lucille	15 June 1918	
Georgi	Ralph A.	Wheeler	Juanita	7 Apr. 1902	br: Geo. W. Wheeler, father
Gerald	James T.	Fairbairn	Martha, Mrs.	23 Mar, 1892	
Gerald	James Thomas	Lowrey	Cerillda (?)	12 Feb. 1881	
Gerberding	Howard R.	Kaufman	Hazel L.	9 July 1914	
Gercar	Josef	Flack	Rosie	23 Apr. 1917	
Gercich	Fred	Bimmerle	Emma	26 Oct. 1914	
Geremia	Massente	Bianchi	Eugenia	28 June 1901	
Gerig	Henry	Schelbert	Marie	13 July 1909	
German	Covington E.	Geezley	Katie	4 Dec. 1890	br: Mike & Katie Geezley, parents
German	Wm. W.	Ridenhour	Ella	16 Nov. 1882	
Gerow	George E.	Jones	Hattie R.	16 Oct. 1899	no previous marriage
Gerstley	M. Louis	Mercer	Elizabeth	31 Dec. 1917	do not publish
Gesse	Giolio	Ponzie	Madelena	29 June 1918	
Gestra	John	Gestra	Maria	22 July 1920	
Ghigliotti	Fred V.	Moresi	Angela	20 Oct. 1913	
Ghiselli	Anacleto	Arrighi	Ernestina	21 Dec. 1911	
Ghisletta	Antone	Pedrotti	Mary Angelina	28 May 1909	
Ghisletta	Antonio	Beretta	Olivia	28 Jan. 1914	
Giacconi	Santi	Vicari	Clara	1 Feb. 1899	br: John H. Vicari, father; John Vicari requested license
Giacomelli	Etalo	Dinnucci	Giula	9 Oct. 1911	br: Earcelia Dinnucci, parent; gr: W. S. Coulter, W. W. Futi, Jr., witnesses to his mark
Giacomini	Michele	Soldate	Mary J.	23 Jan. 1903	
Giaconini	Americo	Lopus	Minnie	3 Apr. 1920	
Giacosa	Luigi	Francia	Maria	31 Jan. 1912	

Groom		Bride		Date	Comments
Surname	**Given Name**	**Surname**	**Given Name**		
Giambruno	Alberto	Consiglieri	Josephine	21 Dec. 1916	
Giannecchini	Aladino	Battaglia	Polissene	30 Nov. 1914	br: Domenico Battaglia, father
Giannecchini	Louis	Passalacqua	Silvia	31 Aug. 1903	
Giannini	Harry	Suchowski	Helen	9 Apr. 1920	
Gibb	James W.	Ogden	Ermon S.	19 Oct. 1912	
Gibbens	John W.	Campbell	Phoebe L.	24 Jan. 1899	no previous marriage; don't publish until 26 Jan. 1899
Gibbens	Robert L.	Leslie	Margaret May	5 Mar. 1900	
Gibbens	Walter Raleigh	Grote	Jennie Estelle	7 Aug. 1905	
Gibbins	Lue Amos	Wiess	Bertha	24 Sept. 1920	
Gibbons	Alfred Sydney	Fowler	Cornelia W.	15 May 1900	
Gibbons	Estell Ellis	Porter	Bertha	19 Nov. 1902	
Gibbs	E. C.	Light	Ella	13 Oct. 1884	
Gibbs	F. H.	Doss	S. N.	13 Aug. 1887	
Gibbs	George D.	Garrett	Retta	9 Oct. 1897	no previous marriage
Giberson	William P.	King	Hollis E.	22 Dec. 1890	
Gibson	Charles W.	Wolfe	Eliza	9 Oct. 1893	br: B. H. Wolfe gives his consent, x mark; J. C. Smith, witness
Gibson	Clifford LaVere	Hunt	Lois Irena	13 Nov. 1915	
Gibson	Clyde C.	Clark	Lottie J. M.	21 Nov. 1916	
Gibson	David L.	Knox	Maud Florence	3 Apr. 1907	
Gibson	Edward E.	Wichman	Ida B.	6 Oct. 1915	
Gibson	Floyd E.	Buckman	Kathleen W.	18 Dec. 1920	
Gibson	Frank Lester	Shaw	Bessie Lurane	18 June 1909	
Gibson	G. W.	Beck	Belle	30 Aug. 1889	
Gibson	Gardie L.	Travers	Emma	10 Sept. 1911	
Gibson	Henry	Butler	Sarah A.	30 July 1883	
Gibson	Henry	Ward	Polly A.	11 Dec. 1893	

Groom Surname	Groom Given Name	Bride Surname	Bride Given Name	Date	Comments
Gibson	Henry Brown	Smith	Adeline F., Mrs.	20 June 1877	
Gibson	Henry Frank	Cadd	Ethel Mae	27 Mar. 1907	
Gibson	Herman W.	McMillen	Helen Martha	28 Dec. 1920	
Gibson	James	Taylor	Cordelia J.	8 Mar. 1888	requested by Godfrey C. Taylor
Gibson	James W.	Justi	Otilda R.	19 Dec. 1896	
Gibson	James W.	Thompson	Myrtle C.	27 Jan. 1900	gr: widower
Gibson	John A.	Prewitt	Mabel A.	12 Mar. 1921	
Gibson	John R.	Garrison	Lena	19 Feb. 1915	
Gibson	Martin R.	Jensen	Lillian H.	5 Aug. 1897	
Gibson	Ora Ray	Smith	Zella	1 May 1915	
Gibson	Robert P.	Wilson	Saidie E.	29 Feb. 1892	
Gies	John J.	Rollins	May	17 Feb. 1890	
Gifford	Francis M.	Stone	Sarah Jane	21 Aug. 1871	
Gifford	John M.	Powell	Marcella	21 July 1916	
Gilardi	Americo	Soldati	Palma E.	3 Sept. 1919	
Gilardi	Andrew Richard	Tomasi	Johanna Mary	20 June 1913	
Gilardi	James J.	Soldati	Adeline	6 Dec. 1913	
Gilardi	Joe P.	Berta	Anna	19 Dec. 1912	
Gilardoni	Attilio	Laurent	Julia	5 Jan. 1901	br: Louis B. Laurent, father
Gilbert	Bret Alexis	Sephton	Grace	22 Apr. 1911	
Gilbert	Charles Robert	Smith	Emma J.	21 Mar. 1908	
Gilbert	David W.	Freshour	Nancy C.	7 Oct. 1865	
Gilbert	Joseph L.	Lachman	Violette	6 Sept. 1914	
Gilbert	Thos. A.	Clark	Fannie E.	5 Nov. 1894	
Gilbert	William J.	Carriger	Margaret F.	14 Nov. 1891	br: Frederick V. Carriger, father
Gilbride	Philip Joseph	Lagomarsino	Katie	3 June 1913	
Gilbride	Rodger James	Thompson	Charlotte	5 Apr. 1900	requested by J. M. Cassin
Gilder	Alfred	Doherty	Gertrude H.	26 Dec. 1911	

	Groom		Bride	Date	Comments
Surname	Given Name	Surname	Given Name		
Gilder	Alfred	Benninghoven	Emma	19 Aug. 1905	
Giles	Grant	Hemseth	Bernardena	15 Oct. 1904	
Gilford	Francis M.	Stone	Sarah Jane	21 Aug. 1871	gr: Francis M. Gilford, father br: Ryland Stone, father
Gilkey	B. H.	Spaulding	Laura B.	13 Mar. 1889	
Gill	Charles W.	Austin	Alice E.	28 Dec. 1910	
Gill	George W.	Krumdick	Jennie, Mrs.	9 Sept. 1899	both widowed
Gill	George Willard	Bonnel	Edith, Mrs.	29 June 1907	
Gill	James W.	Livey	Sarah V.	29 Aug. 1889	
Gill	Robert J.	Walker	Margaret B.	11 Sept. 1920	
Gillespie	Vern B.	Sharp	Hazel R.	31 Mar. 1919	br: Van Sharp, father
Gillespie	William Breese	Russell	Helen Jane	28 May 1920	
Gillett	C. W.	Lumsden	Elizabeth R.	25 Nov. 1911	
Gillett	Charles	Strong	Lizzette W.	20 June 1907	
Gillett	Charles	Forbes	Mary Jane	14 Sept. 1916	
Gillett	Martin	McGee	Kate	10 Dec. 1887	
Gillette	Russell W.	Jenkines	Lida M.	5 Mar. 1921	
Gilliam	David T.	Moore	Sarah	8 Feb. 1897	
Gilliam	David Taylor	Williams	Minerva	20 Feb. 1875	br: Charles Williams, father
Gilliam	George D.	Dei	Aneta	26 Aug. 1912	
Gilliam	James Mitchell	Hansen	Bessie May	22 Apr. 1905	
Gilliam	Samuel Jackson	Loyd	Lillie May	25 Sept. 1906	
Gillogly	William J. S.	Gallagher	Alice Louise	24 June 1920	
Gillon	Charles Mark	Howe	Louise A., Mrs.	17 Oct. 1909	
Gilman	P. E.	Tucker	Harriet E.	24 Dec. 1891	
Gilmer	William M.	Sheldon	Mabel E.	1 June 1889	
Gilmore	Carl F.	Brundige	Bessie M.	19 Dec. 1908	
Gilmore	George	Freeman	Ella	29 Aug. 1877	br: B. S. Freeman

Groom Surname	Groom Given Name	Bride Surname	Bride Given Name	Date	Comments
Ginsti	Angelo	Celeri	Elizabetto	22 May 1886	
Gionnoni	Eugene	Bartolomei	Amelia	19 Nov. 1906	
Giorgi	Alfred	Clark	Ethel Mary	29 Nov. 1916	
Giorgi	Arthur	Lencioni	Carrie	9 Dec. 1907	
Giorgi	Nicola	Buonaccorsi	Penelope	22 Dec. 1900	br: Olinto Buonaccorsi, parent
Giorno	Vincent W.	Lane	Grace A.	2 Apr. 1912	
Giorno	Victor E.	Dorward	Anna G.	1 Feb. 1913	
Giovani	Galliani	Torelli	Pollonia	2 Mar. 1891	
Giovannetti	Domencio	Fregulia	Catherine	5 Aug. 1911	br: Theresa Fregulia, mother; Paul Dimici & Morris Fregulia, witnesses to mother's mark
Giovannini	Romeo J.	Rosenthal	Nettie	30 Aug. 1900	
Giovannoni	Adolph Joseph	Baldocchi	Lizzie Mary	7 June 1906	
Girder	Clyde H.	Burkett	Helen M.	20 July 1917	
Girolo	Gabriele	Albini	Emelia	22 Dec. 1906	
Girolo	Pietro	Perotta	Josephine	22 Apr. 1905	
Girtaner	Alfred	Trotman	Eva Blanche Muriel	3 July 1917	
Gise	Edward	Ryan	Josie	20 July 1891	
Gisel	Herman	Beebe	Stella S.	2 June 1900	
Giulieri	Mansueto	Pellascia	Mary	15 May 1890	
Giusti	Alfred	Lorenzini	Louise	22 July 1911	
Giusti	Omero	Pocai	Clotilde	20 May 1893	
Given	Andrews Logan	Dibble	Avonia	30 Oct. 1909	
Given	Robert H.	Hacker	Edith Amy	17 Aug. 1911	
Givens	Archibald Wills	McReynolds	Virginia	5 Sept. 1906	
Givin	Aneil W.	Lapham	Cornelia E.	19 Oct. 1918	
Gladding	Orman B.	Savercool	Alice	11 Aug. 1919	
Glady	Thomas	Granger	Ethel	12 Aug. 1918	

Groom		Bride		Date	Comments
Surname	Given Name	Surname	Given Name		
Glaister	Middleton P.	Thomas	Sarah A.	27 May 1901	
Glaisty	Skelton D.	Burris	Eudora	16 Oct. 1901	requested by F. T. Duhine (?)
Glaizer	Walter Oscar	Cook	Evelyn	7 Feb. 1914	br: Mary Cook, mother
Glaser	Abe	Feinberg	Lillie	9 Feb. 1915	
Glaser	Albert Ludwig	Ludmann	Sophie	22 Nov. 1902	
Glasgow	Sumner E.	Wright	Eva Pearl	15 Apr. 1905	
Glass	Hugh M.	Keller	Josie E.	17 Apr. 1919	
Glassman	Abraham B.	Jacobs	Amelia A.	28 July 1885	
Glatfelder	Clement	Walker	Addie L.	1 June 1920	
Glazer	Henry	Todfield	Fannie	6 Jan. 1913	
Gleason	Cyrus S.	Tittus	Phebe	14 Jan. 1879	
Gleason	David P.	Carson	Katherine F.	29 Dec. 1902	
Gleason	Guy Strahom	Day	Agnes Nettie	5 Feb. 1907	
Gleason	Leo H.	McLain	Agatha F.	16 Nov. 1917	
Gleason	Walter Raymond	Fitzpartrick	Lillian Gertrude	24 Sept. 1915	
Gledhill	Ernest B.	Von Berg	Annie	30 Aug. 1908	br: Henry Von Berg, father
Glidden	Willard W.	Stympson	Ethel V.	16 Apr. 1902	
Gliddon	William	Folks	Nellie	16 Jan. 1885	br: John Folks, father
Glinden	Harry	Birkenstock	Eleen	14 Aug. 1920	
Gloeckner	Charles	Smart	Tamar Ewen	12 May 1908	
Glover	Albert Carl	Guntly	Irene M.	27 Dec. 1920	
Glover	Harold	Smith	Loretta R.	26 Oct. 1919	
Glynn	Burr Augustus	Bittner	Martha	5 July 1910	
Gnesa	Louis, Jr.	Ramos	Ida A.	7 Feb. 1920	
Goard	W. F.	Esquieu	Louise	18 Nov. 1902	
Goatley	John L.	King	Mabel Ruth	7 Nov. 1919	
Gobbi	Charles W.	Wooster	Carrie A.	22 Jan. 1904	br: requested license
Gobbi	John	Marzoli	Margaret	9 Apr. 1906	br: Teresa Marton?, mother

Groom Surname	Groom Given Name	Bride Surname	Bride Given Name	Date	Comments
Gobbi	Joseph	Croste	Madalina	12 Dec. 1903	
Gobbi	Julius James	Yengling	Ella C.	6 Apr. 1886	
Gobbi	William V.	Spencer	Maude E.	6 Aug. 1920	
Gober	B. F.	Bidwell	Sarah J.	7 Jan. 1886	
Gober	Benjamin F.	Towle	Emma S.	7 Mar. 1881	br: Augustino & Susan Towle, parents
Gober	Charley Van Buren	Breitling	Matilda	23 Nov. 1908	
Goddard	Albert D.	Liscomb	Florence A.	9 Oct. 1891	
Goddard	Daniel N.	Horine	Allie	13 Dec. 1877	
Goddard	Elmer F.	Cadd	Mary I.	18 Dec. 1912	
Goddard	Frank	Smith	Hattie L.		requested by N. H. Cox; filed between 18 and 22 Dec. 1883
Goddard	J. P.	Sturgess	Sarah A.	23 Nov. 1878	
Goddard	Jesse J.	Goddard	Hattie E.	6 Jan. 1914	
Goddard	Wellman	Clifford	Blanch H.	25 Oct. 1890	
Godman	Charles Edwin	Cissell	Mary Annis	26 June 1911	
Godman	George G.	England	Cora May	15 Dec. 1908	
Godman	Robert Edward	Cummins	Loretta Ellen	25 Apr. 1908	
Goeffert	Edward Raymond	Bulotti	Lillian S.	23 Dec. 1910	
Goeller	John	Schnitz	Louisa, Mrs.	10 July 1896	
Goess	Ferdinand Howard	Schwarz	Nellie	18 Nov. 1902	
Goess	George Andrew	Simmons	Jennette Augusta	24 Nov. 1882	from Sonoma
Goethe	William E.	Nau	Barbara E.	11 Mar. 1896	
Goewey	Charles H.	Young	Edith A.	26 Jan, 1915	
Golden (?)	James (?)	Odem	G. A.	21 Apr. 1881	requested by Joseph Childers
Goldman	Leon	Van de Water	Grace M.	27 Mar. 1909	
Golds	John	Johannsen	Emma	16 Nov. 1898	
Goldsam	Matthias G.	Sutherland	Mayme H.	9 July 1919	
Goldsmith	Edwin S.	McClellan	Minnie	7 Sept. 1903	

	Groom	Bride		Date	Comments
Surname	**Given Name**	**Surname**	**Given Name**		
Goldson	William H., Jr	King	Sarah I.	26 Sept. 1891	br: Mrs. John King, mother
Goldspring	Samuel	Loubier	Louise	19 Sept. 1885	
Golsch	Henry	Boechen	Anna	20 June 1913	
Golub	Dave	Sugarman	Fannie	9 Mar. 1911	
Gomes	Antonio E.	Freitas	Rosie E.	3 Nov. 1919	
Gomes	Antonio Jos.	de Freitas	Isabelle	8 July 1896	br: Manuel Jose de Freitas, only living parent, gives consent and signs. Witness: Faureger ?
Gomes	Joseph	Stafford	Alice E.	25 Oct. 1913	br: Mrs. Berdie Stafford, mother; Alvin Stafford, witness
Gonella	Ray N.	Dinucci	Eleanor	3 Mar. 1920	gr: E. Gonella, parent; br: Elsie Dinucci, mother
Gonnella	John	Donati	Teresa	1 Nov. 1909	
Gonnella	Leo	Guidotti	Sarah	27 June 1916	
Gonnella	Zaccheria	Francischi	Rosa	2 Apr. 1904	br: P. Alberigi, guardian
Gonsales	Frank	Jalon	Mary	21 Sept. 1893	
Gonsalves	Frank S.	Ciancao	Mary	4 Sept. 1900	
Gonsalves	George S.	Johnson	Inez A.	3 July 1917	
Gonsalves	Joe P.	Daveiro	Mary C.	6 Apr. 1912	
Gonsalves	Manuel	Cardoza	Mary	28 May 1908	
Gonsolos	Antonio	Lawrence	Katie	22 Aug. 1891	br: Manuel Lawrence, father
Goobi	Julius	Ausseresses	Marie Louisa	14 Nov. 1898	no previous marriage
Goodbrake	Christian H.	Murray	Elizabeth D.	19 Nov. 1890	gr: signed with his mark; no witness
Goodenough	Raymond F.	Weirick	Nellie G.	25 May 1920	
Goodfellow	John	Holland	Nettie B.	6 Jan. 1886	
Goodfellow	Lyle C.	Meeker	Iola	8 Sept. 1911	
Goodfellow	Thomas C.	Williams	Kate D.	6 May 1884	requested by Chas. H. Bane
Goodhart	Lewis E.	Conley	Marion B.	13 July 1904	
Goodman	Daniel O.	Billing	Edith C.	13 Dec. 1888	

Groom Surname	Groom Given Name	Bride Surname	Bride Given Name	Date	Comments
Goodman	Frank	Seeman	Alvina	7 July 1894	
Goodman	Howard W.	Hoar	Fern	20 Mar. 1915	
Goodman	Howard W.	Tenney	Irene J.	19 Mar. 1920	
Goodman	James W.	Arnold	Nellie M.	23 Dec. 1890	
Goodman	George R.	Woodworth	Katie	22 May 1882	
Goodman	Thos. F.	Hoffman	Eva Belle	17 Jan. 1883	
Goodrich	Edwin C.	Cummings	Lizzie	18 June 1898	
Goodrich	Francis M.	Wilcox	Susan, Mrs.	24 May 1909	
Goodrich	Henry P.	Kinloch	Mary	25 June 1917	
Goodrich	Milford	Moore	Nettie	9 Oct. 1900	
Goodsir	Thos. H.	Hawkins	Linda	10 May 1884	
Goodwin	Albert Michael	Price	Lauretta Elizabeth	29 Sept. 1906	gr: Mrs. Jennie Goodwin, mother
Goodwin	Charles W.	Rogers	Lizzie L. F.	2 Nov. 1897	
Goodwin	George M.	Carey	Adeline Helen	22 June 1918	
Goodwin	Henry B.	Dean	Flora Hilton	26 July 1902	
Goodyear	Lloyd S.	Stack	Lydia D.	24 Dec. 1917	
Gookins	Ernest James	Matthias	Frances L., Mrs.	1 Aug. 1900	do not publish ages; br: widow
Gordon	Frank Hendricks	Regan	Mary	10 Apr. 1907	
Gordon	Frank W.	Myers	Josie M.	30 Apr. 1912	
Gordon	James F.	Rose	Susan A., Mrs.	27 Sept. 1902	
Gordon	Reece	Laughlin	Cynthia E.	28 April 1894	
Gordon	William	Terry	Mary Jane	7 Aug. 1886	handwritten; witness John J. Terry
Gore	Alonzo J.	Stemple	Lucretia M.	10 Apr. 1877	
Goree	Ernest B.	Foster	Bessie E.	19 Apr. 1921	
Gori	Adolph	Leonardi	Alphonsa	4 Oct. 1889	
Gori	Bruno	Rabolli	Letitia	16 Aug. 1919	
Gori	Michael	Basaglia	Angeline	10 Apr. 1911	
Gorman	James	English	Margaret M.	10 July 1915	

		Bride		Date	Comments
Groom					
Surname	**Given Name**	**Surname**	**Given Name**		
Gorman	James B.	Behler	Helena	1 Dec. 1892	
Gorman	Timothy J. O.	Corrigan	Bridget M.	16 Sept. 1920	
Gorman	Syrem	Buckland	Jeff	10 Dec. 1917	
Gosney	Charles J.	Badger	Kathryne C.	24 Dec. 1912	
Goss	John	Malone	Ellen M.	25 Nov. 1885	
Goss	William H., Jr.	Farrell	Marjorie J.	26 Mar. 1921	
Gossage	Chas. S.	Allen	Annie	7 Sept. 1887	br: James K. Allen, father
Gossage	H. S.	Mooney	Edna	3 Aug. 1896	
Gossage	Joseph, Jr.	Story	Verinda Belle	14 Dec. 1893	br: J. A. Story, father, gives consent and signs.
Gossman	John	Markham	Susan	29 Sept. 1915	
Gott	William	Bray	Sarah Jane	22 Sept. 1877	witness: Milburn Williams
Gott	William J.	Fewel	Millie C.	26 Apr. 1898	not to be published before Thursday
Gottenberg	Hartley W.	Appleton	Eliza G.	4 Oct. 1900	
Gottlieb	Sam	Lielien (?)	Rose	12 Aug. 1918	
Gotzsek	Albert Henry	Voutron	Bartha Barbra	4 Aug. 1894	
Gough	Leo J.	Robinson	May A.	11 May 1912	
Goulart	Baptist Silveira	Silva	Erminda Adeline	18 Jan. 1916	
Gould	Emerson Weyl	Shelton	Dorothy Day	15 Sept. 1910	
Gould	Emmet F.	Pettis	Annie	5 Nov. 1898	
Gould	Frank H.	Eaton	Nettie, Mrs.	4 Dec. 1897	br: widow
Gould	George F.	Mosman	Jessie M.	7 June 1884	
Gould	James A.	Mitchell	Florence L.	24 Dec. 1901	
Gould	Wm. J.	Robinson	Edith G.	7 Oct. 1911	
Goulder	C. N.	Preston	Mary Louise	16 June 1890	
Gourley	John A.	Dennison	Lucy E.	10 Sept. 1902	
Gow	Aleck W.	Gow	Blanche M., Mrs.	27 June 1903	
Gow	George Buchanan	Atkinson	Irene	21 Apr. 1908	

Groom Surname	Groom Given Name	Bride Surname	Bride Given Name	Date	Comments
Gowan	Francis W.	Bucknell	Hazel	23 Dec. 1919	
Gowans	Andrew, Jr.	Story	Gladys E.	16 Aug. 1915	
Gownig	Clement O.	Stinson	Fannie Barbara	5 Feb. 1919	
Goyette	William Henry	Peterson	Alma Edna	25 June 1906	
Gozzarino	John	Bertoli	Maria	25 Apr. 1908	
Graban	John	Barry	Honora	16 Sept. 1905	
Gracy	Charles	Skivington	Emma	18 Dec. 1907	
Grady	Harry Clarence	Gibson	Laura Lee	23 May 1916	
Grady	W. D.	Uristen	Annie M.	13 Apr. 1885	
Graff	John	Robinson	Anna Catherine	19 May 1914	
Graff	Walter Harold	Hall	Alma Elizabeth	14 Sept. 1917	
Graglia	John	Bonini (?)	Felicita	29 Jan. 1921	
Graham	Albert W.	Morrow	Isabel	7 Nov. 1884	br: Marry J. and J. H. Morrow, parents
Graham	Arthur W.	Edwards	Jennie	31 Oct. 1888	
Graham	James Hunter	Brewitt	Lucille Elviara	14 Nov. 1914	
Graham	James W.	Amos	Villa	22 June 1881	
Graham	Monon	Mills	Ora Anna	24 Aug. 1899	no previous marriage
Graham	Patrick	du Temple	Madeleine	30 July 1904	
Graham	William	Kellog	Ella Francis	23 Nov. 1892	
Graham	William Emerson	Cox	Evalyn Augusta	24 Feb. 1906	
Graham	Robert W.	Freeman	Mary E., Mrs.	1 Apr. 1899	br: divorced more than one year
Graheck	George A.	Penrod	Florence A.	8 Mar. 1917	
Grand	Peter	Lavege	Mary Jane Laragoche	28 Aug. 1895	br: signs with X mark witnessed by R. W. Thompson Justice of the Peace, Analy Twp.; gr: signs as Grand Pieter
Grandi	William H.	Williams	Julia C.	4 Sept. 1915	
Grandin	Edward	Johnson	Hulda	10 Feb. 1912	
Grandy	Henry	Camesi	Diva	2 Nov. 1908	

	Groom	Bride		Date	Comments
Surname	Given Name	Surname	Given Name		
Granice	Harry H.	Bonner	Grace I.	28 Sept. 1914	
Grant	Ben E.	Brown	Catherine	5 July 1892	
Grant	Francis E.	McCappin	Lavina E.	19 Oct. 1915	
Grant	Frederick	Newell	M. A., Mrs.	26 Nov. 1902	
Grant	Frederick T.	Bates	Marion	15 July 1901	
Grant	Henry M.	Eliason	Agnes	9 June 1886	
Grant	Ralph Delano	Beeson	Elva Marie	29 Dec. 1916	
Grant	William C.	Gawler	Pearl	13 Feb. 1905	
Granucci	Angelo	Balducci	Rosa	26 Jan. 1897	Fred P. Conne, Notary Public, and V. Lucchesi, witness to signature.
Granucci	Frank	Muzio	Olivia L.	30 July 1918	
Graper	Elmer B.	Smithers	Ida V.	6 Nov. 1918	
Grassman	Otto	Dannhausen	Alvine	8 Apr. 1902	br: Clemens Dannhausen, father
Gratto	Frank Richard	Mudd	Althea Arline	23 July 1914	
Graumlich	John Y.	Trisse ?	Caroline, Mrs.	13 Apr. 1865	
Graunlick?	John	Walker	Elizabeth H.	29 Jan. 1872	gr: John Cobb, father
Gravatt	Wm.	Foreman	Kate	6 July 1885	
Graves	Bartlette	Hornbuckle	Kittie	30 June 1893	
Graves	Ben F.	Watson	Margaret	8 May 1920	
Graves	Edwin C.	Ogburn	Edith L.	30 Sept. 1916	
Graves	Harry Thomas	Maddocks	Helen Carter	4 Mar. 1919	
Graves	J. H.	Maddux	Lorette	23 Nov. 1891	
Graves	Joseph L.	Dorman	Marjorie W.	5 Dec. 1908	
Graves	Zennie B.	Jonas	Bess B.	7 Aug. 1920	
Gray	Alva C.	Cline	Anna Maria	24 June 1919	
Gray	Alvin A.	Marsh	Adeline J.	29 Nov. 1909	
Gray	Alvin A.	Marsh	Adeline J.	23 June 1910	

	Groom	Bride		Date	Comments
Surname	Given Name	Surname	Given Name		
Gray	Clarence A.	Miller	Alice L., Mrs.	9 Dec. 1899	neither party has been divorced within one year
Gray	Elmer	Thompson	May	20 June 1907	gr: J. W. Ford, witness to his mark
Gray	Frank S.	Cooney	Stacy L.	16 Nov. 1918	
Gray	Fred L.	Rose	Florence L.	15 June 1889	
Gray	Henry Charles	Haskins	Lillie Irene	18 Dec. 1897	no previous marriage
Gray	Isaac	Parmer	Clarissa	11 Dec. 1865	
Gray	James W.	Goode	Lillian	19 Nov. 1902	
Gray	James W.	Harvey	Elizabeth E.	12 Oct. 1865	
Gray	Joseph Allen	Weisshand	Alvina Christina	30 Apr. 1914	
Gray	Robert Floyd	Palmer	Caroline Isabelle	16 Nov. 1917	
Gray	Thos. H.	Torr	Ida May	1 Feb. 1886	
Gray	W. J.	Kelley	S. Z., Mrs.	20 Feb. 1905	
Gray	Woodward Martin	Kohler	Mary Elizabeth	7 Nov. 1908	
Gray (?)	Luster D.	Culu (?)	Ollie		filed between 26 May 1884 and 11 July 1883
Grazini	Emelio	Polloni	Celia	11 Jan. 1907	br: G. Polloni, parent
Greaver	Andrew J.	Minkle	Amelia L.	26 Sept. 1882	
Greaver	Elmer	Osborn	Edith	6 Nov. 1916	
Greaves	Walter	Parkin	Marguerite I.	31 Dec. 1920	
Grebe	William C.	Jacobsen	Constantine	30 May 1891	
Greeley	Benjamin M.	Pancrazi	Minnie E.	4 Sept. 1913	
Green	Charles	Howeth	Daisy	28 Sept. 1896	
Green	David J.	Gregg	Bessie C.	25 June 1901	do not publish until July 22
Green	Geo. E.	Williams	M. J., Mrs.	4 Feb. 1886	
Green	George E.	Wymore	Elaine C.	12 Jan. 1918	
Green	Harvy	Matthews	Edna	1 May 1915	
Green	Henry H.	Butterfield	Carrie	11 July 1883	

| Groom | | Bride | | Date | Comments |
Surname	Given Name	Surname	Given Name		
Green	Ira G.	Randall	Helen Mar	6 Jan. 1917	
Green	Isaac Leander	Overton	Beatrice	24 July 1909	
Green	John	Brewer	Kate	21 May 1896	license requested by Kate Brewer.
Green	John William	Willey	Laura Rosella	4 Nov. 1878	br: Mrs. E. M.? Willey, mother
Green	Jonathan	Symonds	Gertrude J.	28 Oct. 1890	
Green	L. D.	Patterson	Geneva E.	29 Jan. 1916	
Green	Lewis E.	McNeill	Ida E.	25 May 1912	
Green	Lewis Ralston	Covey	Mary M.	14 Sept. 1883	
Green	Louis H.	Ahern	Bella	13 Dec. 1892	
Green	Parley H.	Knight	Mary Augusta	25 Apr. 1898	
Green	Perry W.	Howell	Myrtle L.	17 Aug. 1915	
Green	Raymond L.	Baine	Emma	7 Jan. 1904	
Green	Robert Franklin	Mason	May Augusta	3 July 1909	
Green	Walter Thomas	Swift	Ethelyn Irene	25 Jan. 1910	
Green	William A.	Carter	Mary E.	5 June 1894	br: Mrs. L. W. Carter gives consent and signs
Green	William C.	Glynn	Nellie M.	29 July 1884	
Greene	William N.	Jewett	Olive	16 Sept. 1919	
Greenlee	John D.	Grigsby	Jessie M.	15 Oct. 1892	
Greentree	Charles T.	Shaver	Hattier L.	5 Jan. 1889	
Greenwood	Harry E.	Lentz	May C.	6 June 1903	
Greeott	John	Williams	Sarah	29 Apr. 1899	no previous marriage
Greer	Earl C.	Barnes	Emily L.	10 Dec. 1917	
Gregg	Art A.	Jackson	Ethel	21 Mar.1904	
Gregg	Augustus I.	Wells	Ida	26 Aug. 1899	no previous marriage
Gregg	Edward E.	Atkinson	Laura M.	22 Jan. 1901	
Gregg	Edward E.	Richardson	Polly	20 Nov. 1912	
Gregg	George	Jessen	Marie	10 June 1911	

	Groom	Bride		Date	Comments
Surname	Given Name	Surname	Given Name		
Gregg	George W.	Rudolph	Rose M., Mrs.	14 Dec. 1920	
Gregg	Isaac	Wilkinson	Jane	7 Mar. 1866	
Gregg	John W.	Gossage	Carrie B.	16 Oct. 1899	no previous marriage; don't publish until Saturday
Gregg	Nelson G.	Gray	Marion	5 May 1902	
Gregg	Pleasant Wesley	Charmley	Helen Tilston	25 Sept. 1920	gr: Isaac A. Gregg, father
Gregg	Walter T.	Bryan	Jessie E.	14 July 1909	
Gregganis	James Sargent	Stretch	Mary Ellen	21 Jan. 1918	
Gregoire	Joseph	Winant	Pauline	30 Aug. 1894	br: witness: Emile Deleau
Gregoire	Louis	Mathe	Marie	24 June 1904	
Gregori	Peter	Fiori	Teresa	30 Aug. 1913	
Gregory	Bion S.	Mac	Mabel E.	8 Nov. 1894	
Gregory	Canfield Burrell	Anderson	Catherine Mildred	7 May 1904	license requested by James H. Anderson
Gregory	Edwin Stanley	Hardin	Julia A.	14 Apr. 1900	neither divorced within one year prior
Gregory	Ernest Bernhardt	Marshall	Florence B.	1 Feb. 1896	
Gregory	Harvey	Kniffen	Mary M.	16 Mar. 1897	
Gregory	John Shattuck	Martin	Rebbeca Marilla	12 Nov. 1906	
Gregson	Henry M.	Parks	Maria C.	21 Dec. 1882	
Gregson	John N.	Hoyt	Almah E.	1 Sept. 1882	
Gregson	Luke B.	Surryhne	Alice Mabel	30 Dec. 1898	
Gregson	Paul V.	Button	Eva A.	26 Apr. 1920	
Greig	David	Townsend	Mary Ann	21 Feb. 1918	
Grenache	Harry L.	Farnsworth	Hazel M.	21 July 1910	
Greninger	George Frederick	Christensen	Elizabeth F.	27 May 1905	
Greppi	Louis	Zeni	Fausta	23 Jan. 1920	br: Ed Zeni, father
Greppi	Sylvester	Mattei	Sephina	25 Mar. 1889	
Gresham	Joseph Francis	Adcock	Dora	7 Aug. 1894	

		Bride			
Groom				Date	Comments
Surname	Given Name	Surname	Given Name		
Greves	Thos. N.	Sellers	M. Jane		filed between two licenses dated 28 July 1882
Grewell	E. D.	Marshall	Lottie B.	17 Dec. 1892	
Gribbin	Jack H.	Roberts	Mila M.	2 Aug. 1920	
Gribbin	Thomas H.	Byrne	Lizzie A.	11 Jan. 1899	no previous marriage; don't publish until 18 Jan. 1899
Grider	Loran T.	Hatton	Blanche L.	3 Dec. 1910	br: Carrie S. Hatton, mother
Grieb	Henry Carl	Spencer	Chrystal F.	22 Mar. 1918	gr: Anna Grieb, mother
Griesheimer	Charles	Lynch	Mary Stasia	25 Apr. 1903	
Griest	Peter	Myrick	Eliza	9 Nov. 1883	
Griffin	Gerald A.	Moore	Emily T.	11 Mar. 1921	
Griffin	H. E.	Poat	Minnie L.	30 June 1891	
Griffin	John M.	Bailey	Nellie C.	13 June 1890	
Griffith	Alonzo B.	Wilson	Minnie	18 Oct. 1902	
Griffith	Archer C.	Farmer	Frances M.	16 Dec. 1892	
Griffith	Clyde E.	Allen	Juanita	12 Dec. 1892	
Griffith	Thomas E.	Ormsby	Stella	27 Oct. 1899	
Griffith	Will Samuel	Ross	Pearl S.	6 July 1896	
Griggs	Achilles	Montgomery	Sarah	12 Nov. 1878	
Griggs	Alvan Stanley	Stanley	Blanche	21 Dec. 1908	br: B. Stanley, parent
Griggs	Alvin S.	Elliott	Amy G.	23 Apr. 1917	
Griggs	Arthur O.	Willams	Alma R.	26 Apr. 1915	
Griggs	Justin S.	Stanley	Viola N.	23 Sept. 1905	br: B. Stanley, parent
Griggs	Reno	Standley	Lillie	26 Aug. 1902	br: Burnett Standley, parent
Griggs	Smith M.	Smith	Emily G., Mrs.	11 Apr. 1900	
Griggs	Smith M.	Patterson	Lou, Mrs.	20 Aug. 1896	
Grimm	Frederick W.	Perlet	Mildred B.	24 Jan. 1917	

	Groom	Bride		Date	Comments
Surname	Given Name	Surname	Given Name		
Grimmer	Louis	Murphy	Ida May	2 July 1912	br: R. W. Murphy, parent; witness to parent's mark W. E. Saunders, Mildred Mathews
Grindle	Monroe Woodard	Warner	Henrietta Mary	27 Nov. 1897	no previous marriage
Grissin (?)	W. H.	Carrillo	Isabel ?.	29 Nov. 1879	
Groff	William R.	Kendall	Emma J.	4 Mar. 1882	
Grofmyer	Henry C.	Heisel	Nellie	16 Feb. 1901	
Grogan	Spencer Jordan	Miller	Josephine	14 Dec. 1909	not signed by br. or gr.
Groining	Hyalmar	Johnson	Augusta, Mrs.	8 Oct. 1904	
Grokopf	Frank D.	Breitenbach	Gertrude I.	18 Sept. 1917	
Groom	Joseph	Hall	Mary Juanita	3 Nov. 1906	
Groshong	Hal Willard	Marshall	Ida May	20 Feb. 1907	
Groshong	Sidney	Hiatt	Minnie E.	3 Apr. 1901	gr: Mrs. J. E. Heald, mother
Groshong	Walter E.	Swank	Susie	28 Apr. 1898	
Grosjean	Camille, Jr.	Stevens	Stella M.	27 Feb. 1897	gr: Camille Grosjean gives consent and signs.
Groskoff	Albert, Jr.	Batto	Louise R.	19 Apr. 1921	
Groskofs	Joseph F.	Clements	Lena A.	23 May 1914	
Groskopf	Albert	Miller	Bertha	27 Dec. 1884	
Groskopf	Albert	Gartman	Annie	4 Aug. 1883	
Groskopf	Charles E.	Keechler	Lena K.	10 Sept. 1919	
Gross	Eugene A.	Corbin	Ida	16 Nov. 1911	
Gross	Harry B.	McMellon	Mary S.	25 Feb. 1907	
Gross	Ludwig	Zimmerman	Frances H.	22 Mar. 1886	
Grosse	Guy E.	Gibbs	Lizzie W.	25 July 1888	
Grosse	Guy N.	Yarnell	Eloise I.	16 Apr. 1914	
Grossi	Domengo	Buzzini	Teresa	11 Dec. 1901	
Grossman	Abraham L.	Kern	Josephine	22 Feb. 1913	

		Bride		Date	Comments
Groom					
Surname	**Given Name**	**Surname**	**Given Name**		
Groth	Leopold Frederick	Gibson	Kate	20 June 1916	
Groulx	Albert	Moyer	Eva	26 Oct. 1910	
Grove	Arvil T.	Wentworth	Ida H.	24 Feb. 1885	
Grove	Bert B.	Dalessi	Sophie May	1 June 1904	gr: N. A. & C. C. Grove, parents; br: A.& C. C. Dalessi, parents
Grove	Clarence	Locke	Beryle Evelyn	7 June 1916	
Grove	David	Davis	Elmira	29 Apr. 1882	
Grove	Edward	Sinclair	Ann Jane	7 Aug. 1883	
Grove	Elliot W.	Wilson	E. Marguereitte	23 Sept. 1914	
Grove	George W.	Clark	Emma E.	5 Nov. 1881	
Grove	Jesse Roy	Isaac	Dora	9 Dec. 1907	
Grove	John	Sinclair	Mary Adelaide	20 July 1886	
Grove	Ray S.	Robinson	Jessie	15 June 1907	
Grover	William A.	Wilke	Emma L.	7 Apr. 1909	
Groves	Christopher Columbus	Hopper	Nancy A.	14 Oct. 1875	br: Amos Hopper, father; John Bolin Hopper, witness
Groves	James H.	Wells	May	31 May 1894	
Grubb	Harry Thompson	Ramos	Myrtle Teresa	17 Aug. 1905	
Grubb	Merle M.	DeNye (?)	Freda	2 Oct. 1920	
Grube	Axcel E.	Douglass	Ila T.	29 Dec. 1919	gr: Mrs. Hannah M. Grube, mother
Gruenhagen	Gottfried H.	Hall	Clara	10 Feb. 1919	
Gruenhager	Henry	Borchers	Clara	10 July 1914	
Gschwend	Thomas	Pallady	Nellie G.	10 Dec. 1898	no previous marriage
Guadagno	Pompey	Foley	Josephine	22 May 1917	
Guaspari	Domenico	Gamborini	Amelia	13 Aug. 1898	no previous marriage
Guder	William C. O.	Lingg	Louisa H.	24 May 1909	gr: Mrs. E. C. Linder, mother
Guedet	Joseph Henry	Dabner	Mary Josephine	5 Oct. 1906	
Guenther	C. F.	Mosure	Emma R.	27 Mar. 1894	

Groom Surname	Groom Given Name	Bride Surname	Bride Given Name	Date	Comments
Guerne	A. L.	Smith	Julia	22 Nov. 1877	
Guerne	Alfred Lucian	Coon	Josephine	1 Sept. 1905	
Guernsey	Fred R.	McAbee	Hazel N.	29 June 1911	
Guernsey	Louis E.	Millerick	Mae E.	24 Dec. 1914	
Guffanti	Amedeo	Sturla	Angela	22 Aug 1907	
Guffanti	Domenico	Tollini	Celestina	9 Jan. 1913	
Guffanti	Emilio	Bianchini	Giulia	29 July 1914	
Gugg	Roy I.	Caldwell	Lissie S.	18 Jan. 1921	
Guglielmetti	Alfred J.	Gilardi	Katherine M.	10 July 1917	
Guglielmetti	Cesare	Lafranchi	Olimpia	12 Jan. 1893	br: Joseph Lafranci gives consent; Joseph Lafranchi requests license
Guglielmetti	Noe	Pierucci	Clara	22 Oct. 1915	
Guglielmetti	Marino J.	Jefferies	Sylverine	15 June 1918	gr: Peter Gughelmetti (?), father
Guiberson	Wallace	Goodwin	Agnes L.	19 Dec. 1913	
Guidi	Angelo	Davini	Concetta	13 Feb. 1909	
Guidi	Ismaele	Morchio	Argentina	26 Nov. 1901	
Guidotti	Francesco	Frugoli	Theresa	29 Jan. 1883	
Guidotti	George	Santos	Gussie	15 Nov. 1912	
Guidotti	Giovanni	McReynolds	Lizzie	28 Dec. 1889	
Guidotti	Giuseppe	Peduzzi	Pierina	31 Oct. 1907	
Guidotti	Joseph	Rocchioli	Angeline	24 June 1916	br: Mike Rocchioli, father
Guidotti	Leonardo	Paganini	Carmalita	16 July 1891	
Guild	George	Smillie	Isabell R.	11 Sept. 1918	
Guilfoyle	John	Watt	Agnes	18 Nov. 1899	please do not publish ages
Guilhot	Bernard	Francisco	Amelia A.	21 Sept. 1920	
Guill	Etna E.	Voight	Hannah E.	25 Feb. 1898	
Guillie	Edward H.	Heitz	Ida M.	5 Nov. 1903	
Guinnar	David Andrew	McMahon	Maggie	26 Dec. 1908	

	Groom	Bride		Date	Comments
Surname	**Given Name**	**Surname**	**Given Name**		
Guinnar	Jesse W.	Simmons	May	30 Dec. 1901	br: John P. Simmons, parent
Guirin	Stephen I.	Voigt	Margaret M.	22 Aug. 1914	
Guisler	Edward T.	Cook	Fidella	2 Nov. 1909	
Guisti	Paulo	Campomenosi	Victoria, Mrs.	30 Mar. 1905	
Gularte	George S.	Rich	Ira	24 Dec. 1917	gr: Lucy Showalter, mother
Guldager	Fred H.	Jackson	Bertie Estelle	19 June 1911	
Guldager	George M.	Nourse	Susie L.	11 Oct. 1892	
Guldager	L. C.	Carroll	Agnes J.	13 June 1899	no previous marriage
Guldin	Fred R.	James	Ella	16 Mar. 1889	
Gully	Frank J.	Cook	Elsie M.	2 Nov. 1901	
Gum	William M.	Hiatt	Josie, Mrs.	5 June 1901	
Gunn	Charles A.	Murphy	Myrtle Violet	17 Dec. 1917	
Gunn	George Lucius	Newland	Maude L.	11 Oct. 1907	
Gunn	Robert	Kyle	Beatrice J.	27 Dec. 1887	
Gunther	Frederick A.	Mauch	Katy, Mrs.	2 Apr. 1889	br: widow
Gunther	John Douglas	Robinett	Mary	21 May 1894	Samuel B. Berry, witness
Guntz	Joseph A.	Storey	Grace Dudley	25 Oct. 1910	
Guptill	Roscoe Volney	Bean	Helen A.	6 Apr. 1908	
Guptill	William H.	Lyman	Kate	16 Nov. 1901	
Guptill	William H.	Gray	Cecil D.	10 Nov. 1915	
Gussman	Cass	Nippert	Nancy Frances	14 Mar. 1892	
Gussman	Santo	Jaques (?)	Belinda	21 May 1881	br: Stephen A. Jaques, father
Gustafson	Alfred	Howell	Julia E.	17 July 1911	
Gustafson	Carl G.	Wells	Olive	20 Dec. 1886	
Gustafson	Gustof Sigfrid	Hawkins	Mildred Claretta	17 May 1918	
Gustafson	Howard Paul	Faylor	Florence M.	2 Jan. 1909	gr: Carl G. Gustafson, father; br: Orson C. Faylor, father
Gusti	Albert	King	Effie	22 Dec. 1910	

Groom Surname	Groom Given Name	Bride Surname	Bride Given Name	Date	Comments
Gutenberger	Jacob	Winton	Fannie	24 Oct. 1889	gr: M. & Josephina Gutenberger, parents; R. B. Werner, witness
Gutermute	David	Smart	Cora M.	11 Nov. 1907	
Gutermute	Henry Shauer	Derby	Linda Burr	9 May 1892	
Guth	Gustave John	Walton	Louise Evelyn	15 July 1909	
Gutheil	C. R.	Cummings	A. G.	23 May 1885	
Guthrie	Thomas George	Hansen	Henryetta	3 Aug. 1912	
Guthrie	Vernon Hamilton	Byce	Hazel Irene	7 Oct. 1912	
Gutscher	Joseph	Stewart	Mary A.	22 Sept. 1902	
Guy-Perret	Andrew	Martin	Marie	31 Aug. 1916	
Gwaltney	W. B.	Westwood	Inez V.	21 Feb. 1913	
Gwin	Andrew J.	Bartow	Helen	26 Mar. 1915	
Gwin	Andrew J.	Blake	Maggie		crossed out; appeared among 12 June 1899 licenses
Gwin	Andrew Jones	Blake	Maggie M.	6 Apr. 1900	please send tomorrow a.m.
Gwin	Walter Edward	Rock	Anna Marie	24 Apr. 1916	br: Mary Rock, mother
Gwyn	George P.	Martin	Ella A.	25 Feb. 1902	
Gwynn	Wm. A.	Smith	Mary E.	28 Oct. 1893	
Gwynn	Edward	McMannus	Eunice E.	1 June 1885	
Haag	Michael Peter	Anderson	Meta Catherine	16 Apr. 1913	
Haas	Henry	Standley	Barbara E.	15 Nov. 1878	br: L. R. Standley, parent
Haas	Joseph G.	Riding	Hannah	14 June 1919	
Habenicht	John F.	Oster	Ellen L.	27 June 1910	
Haberfelde	Albert Valentine	Thompson	Elma Pearl	15 Feb. 1918	
Haberhouer	Karl	Colassor	Albertinn	21 Nov. 1898	
Haberman	Charles Henry	Scott	Helen Beatrice	12 Nov. 1908	
Hackmann	William	Burkhardt	Evelyn	4 Oct. 1913	
Hadermann	Carl	Hinrichsen	Annie J.	16 Nov. 1920	gr: Louise Hadermann, mother

	Groom	Bride		Date	Comments
Surname	Given Name	Surname	Given Name		
Hadler	Henry	Rygel	Francisca	29 May 1897	
Hadley	William	Flynn	Ella Marie	28 Feb. 1918	
Hadrich	C. F. Hugo, Jr.	Doggett	Averil Alison	13 Jan. 1917	
Hadrich	Carl F. H.	Haltiner	Babette	22 Apr. 1887	
Haehl	Carl	Sedgley	Mary M.	9 Apr. 1904	
Haehl	Edward Oliver	Adams	Jennie	16 Mar. 1909	
Haehl	Otto	Hanson	Christine	15 Aug. 1906	
Haehl	Walter L.	Thompson	Martha P.	3 Feb. 1917	gr: Rosa Haehl, mother
Haering (?)	Fred	Feeley	Helen, Mrs.	26 Sept. 1878	
Hagans	Alfred H.	Hall	Mary	3 July 1865	
Hagedohm	Herman B.	Staats	Ida	27 Nov. 1899	
Hagedohm	William	Harms	Emma	25 Aug. 1899	no previous marriage
Hageman	Emil H.	Oxtoby	Alice Josephine	23 Aug. 1900	
Hagemann	Gustav Henry	Cutter	Mabel Viola	13 June 1919	
Haggard	Nathaniel	Pritchett	Dollie	12 Mar. 1897	
Hagler	John	Carmichael	Nannie	8 Oct. 1889	
Hagler	John M.	Brining	Margaret M.	23 Feb. 1918	
Haigh	Edwin	Fried	Enmma	8 Dec. 1885	
Haigh	Robert Charles	Lynch	Ella Louise	9 Jan. 1907	
Haigler	Albert Chester	Sweetser	Violet Marda	3 July 1909	
Hakansson	Axel V.	Grace	Edith Emily	27 Dec. 1920	br: Edith E. Grace, mother
Hakes	Dorr	Rutherford	Lyle	2 Apr. 1892	br: widow
Hale	Eugene C.	Herterich	Katherine C.	11 Mar. 1916	
Hale	Leslie Ravone	Nagel	Edna Viola	1 Dec. 1906	
Hale	Peter	Hardin	Margaret	12 May 1911	
Hale	W. D.	Kelso	Ada E.	24 Nov. 1880	br: N. B. Kelso,
Hale	John F.	Bosworth	Mary Etta	15 Aug. 1882	
Haley	Charles F.	Billman	Susie A.	10 Oct. 1892	br: widow

Groom Surname	Groom Given Name	Bride Surname	Bride Given Name	Date	Comments
Haley	James A.	Karn	Mabel Idelle	29 Mar. 1911	
Haley	James Lewis	Monahan	May Elizabeth	16 Apr. 1906	
Haley	Michael E.	Muller	Bettina	24 June 1902	
Haley	Robert	Greyson	Lida	blank	filed between 29 June and 3 July 1905
Haley	William R.	Grohe (?)	Helen S.	30 June 1918	
Halkidis	Sam	Mahan	Genevieve	23 Dec. 1918	
Hall	Adolphus Warren	McCutchan	Minnie May	17 Feb. 1896	
Hall	Albert E.	Starke	Anna Frances	24 Apr. 1915	
Hall	Albert Leroy	Blunden	Violet	7 Oct. 1908	
Hall	Arthur Lipskey	James	Florence Katherine	23 June 1913	
Hall	Charles A.	Hall	Lena H.	13 Dec. 1898	don't publish
Hall	Charles S.	Byrne	Lena C.	18 May 1914	
Hall	Clarence C.	Mead	Alice C.	6 Nov. 1883	
Hall	Eugene F.	Toltschin	Clara	31 July 1913	
Hall	Eugene F.	Burns	Ethel G.	3 May 1919	br: J. B. Burns, parent
Hall	Francis	Jakway	Margaretta	13 Apr. 1883	br: Stephen Jakway, father
Hall	Frank J.	Dunker	Hattie A.	9 Jan. 1915	
Hall	Geo. A.	Morton	Dicie M.	14 Dec. 1889	
Hall	Geo. H.	Gauldin	Laura	24 Nov. 1880	
Hall	George	Washburn	O. E., Mrs.	23 July 1903	
Hall	George A.	Wass	Jessie E. R., Mrs.	28 Sept. 1893	
Hall	George H.	Speers	Josie	29 Apr. 1892	
Hall	George Henry	Pepin	Jeanette Corine	13 Apr. 1908	
Hall	George Herbert	Mauch (?)	Matilda Dorothy	10 Jan. 1908	
Hall	George Morrill	Mayes	Ethelyn Lorena	16 Dec. 1907	
Hall	Granville M.	Francis	Nettie	3 Oct. 1900	gr: E. G. & Rebecca H. Hall, parents
Hall	H. F.	Shuler	Georgiana	23 Aug. 1889	br: S. A. Shuler, mother
Hall	Halbert P.	Stridde	Thyra	7 Jan. 1902	

	Groom	Bride		Date	Comments
Surname	Given Name	Surname	Given Name		
Hall	Harley A.	Feehan	Gladys Lorene	2 Sept. 1916	
Hall	Harry H.	Rego	Mayme A.	20 Feb. 1912	
Hall	Harry L.	Willson	Annie W.	1 Nov. 1890	
Hall	Harry Willson	Kenworthy	Elvira Charity	21 June 1919	
Hall	Henry	Perry	Isabel	20 July 1914	
Hall	Isaac K.	Bryant	Ruth	13 May 1867	
Hall	James	Dameron ?	L. E.	21 Nov. 1866	
Hall	James F.	Lehritter	Annie Louise	18 May 1920	
Hall	James Otto	Cooper	Mary L.	16 Dec. 1908	
Hall	John W.	White	M. Cadona	28 Sept. 1897	
Hall	Lieuallen J., Jr.	Gum	Hazel Nellie	8 May 1907	
Hall	Louis Williard	Early	Cleora A.	17 Mar. 1920	br: Mrs. Alpha Early (also Mrs. J.), mother
Hall	Luke	Miller	Sarah A.	20 Dec. 1877	br: Mrs. Terill (?) Miller, mother; witness: Benjamin F. Wright
Hall	Martin V.	Champlain	Sarah D.	23 Jan. 1867	
Hall	Oliver Perry	Linebaugh	Olivia Fay	24 June 1902	
Hall	Theodore T.	Smith	Aileen F.	14 Mar. 1918	
Hall	Thos. R.	Dodson	Mary	3 Sept. 1901	
Hall	Walter R.	Allenbury	Evelyn	4 Jan. 1882	
Hall	Walter S.	Smith	Alice	29 Aug. 1894	
Hall	Walter W.	Nelson	Alice M.	2 Oct. 1907	
Hall	William Clyde	Vestal	Lena	9 Nov. 1917	
Hall	Wm. S.	Guldager	Annie C.	23 Dec. 1895	
Hallberg	John	Pearson	Louisa	22 Jan. 1886	
Hallberg	Oscar A.	Barlow	Mary Elizabeth	11 Jan. 1918	
Hallenbarter	Frank A.	Huber	Resina A.	9 May 1903	
Halleran	Joseph Francies	Burgess	Sarah Ethel	22 Nov. 1906	

Groom Surname	Groom Given Name	Bride Surname	Bride Given Name	Date	Comments
Halley	James L.	Kroehuke	Clara E.	3 Apr. 1920	
Halliday	William J.	Begbie	Jeanne	12 May 1920	
Hallinan	J. F.	Shea	Kate	28 May 1894	
Halman	William C.	Stone	Stella	24 Dec. 1889	
Halsey	Henry G., Jr.	Randle	Etta M.	26 June 1911	
Halstead	Harry Oliver	Heryford	Jessie Marguerite	8 Oct. 1907	
Halstead	Jesse S.	Purcell	Eunice A.	25 Feb. 1897	not to be published.
Haltiner	John W.	Hadrich	Melani	10 Dec. 1892	
Halvarsen	Herbert T.	Bourgon	Amelia	20 Sept. 1917	
Ham	James T.	Ham	Julia	7 June 1911	
Ham	Whitcomb H.	Lewis	Nellie M.	3 Aug. 1912	
Hamer	Sylvester T.	Suman	Belle, Mrs.	16 Nov. 1895	
Hamersley	Garvin	Gilmore	Grace	26 Apr. 1909	br: Anna Gilmore, mother
Hamersley	Jay	Robinett	Ollie	23 Oct. 1911	
Hamilton	Aymer Jay	Frisbee	Sarah Howland	17 June 1915	
Hamilton	Charley S.	McGrew	Rosella	23 Apr. 1902	
Hamilton	Durley LeRoy	Burgess	Ethna Mae	8 Oct. 1920	
Hamilton	Gilbert S.	Cole	Sylvia G.	11 Dec. 1883	
Hamilton	Henry Liberty	Hubbell	Maysie	8 Nov. 1905	
Hamilton	James W.	Cnopius	Gertrude M.	23 Sept. 1897	
Hamilton	John A.	Grove (?)	Mary F.	17 Aug. 1900	
Hamilton	Lovell Joyce	Hunter	Helen	6 July 1916	
Hamilton	Rush Emmor	Williams	Ethel Maude	10 Jan. 1906	
Hamilton	William A.	Sutton	Etta A.	20 Feb. 1906	
Hamilton	William H.	McDonald	Mabel	11 Aug. 1904	
Hamlin	Charles J.	McKenna	Maggie	14 June 1900	
Hamlin	George O.	Grissim	Lizzie, Mrs.	24 Dec. 1889	
Hamlin	Harry	Coddington	G. W., Mrs.	30 Jan. 1891	br: widow

	Groom		Bride	Date	Comments
Surname	Given Name	Surname	Given Name		
Hamlin	Martin Edward	Hamilton	Georgia Helen	19 Dec. 1905	
Hammeken	George L.	Roberts	Lola, Mrs.	12 Oct. 1901	
Hammel	Chas. P.	Livey	Mary	24 Apr. 1882	
Hammel	Henry	Gist	Lurana	26 Oct. 1866	
Hammel	Walter	Quotis	Jeanette S.	25 Feb. 1889	
Hammell	Charles E.	Doss	Bell	5 July 1892	
Hammell	Fred R.	Benjamin	Penelope F.	24 Aug. 1897	
Hammer	Marquis	Kubie	Katie	29 Sept. 1888	
Hammermann	George B. G.	Meyling	Freda M. E.	20 June 1914	
Hammon	Charles Howland	Scott	Esther Margaret	24 Dec. 1915	
Hammon	William Henry	Brown	Malinda	4 Nov. 1913	
Hammond	Frank	Cooper	Catherine	6 Nov. 1878	br: Mrs. I. ? E. Cooper, parent; H. H. Atwater, witness
Hammond	Grant	Duval	Laura M.	21 June 1899	no previous marriage
Hampton	Robert M.	Kennedy	Annie M.	10 June 1915	
Hampton	William	Maebury	Eva Kenworthy	12 Nov. 1890	br: widow
Hamson	Chris	Carr	Daisy Ethel	5 Sept. 1918	
Hanchette	Edward	Haas	Louise Dorothey	28 Nov. 1916	
Hancock	Henry	Haraszthay	Ida	25 Feb. 1865	
Hancorn	Walter T.	Lindsy	Coney Gunda	18 Oct. 1893	
Hand	Wm. E.	Brown	Emma	30 Sept. 1865	
Handy	Percy W.	Rea	Alice J.	14 Dec. 1896	
Haney	Free	Hellman	Linda	30 Apr. 1887	
Hankins	Samuel S.	Morgan	Mattie	30 Dec. 1903	
Hanks	Geo Lewis	Brooks	Lucy	27 Apr. 1886	
Hanks	J. D.	Staudard	Ceripta A.	15 Feb. 1894	
Hanks	William W.	Briggs	Belle	30 Dec. 1899	
Hanks	William Wallace	Sherman	Mary Anna	1 Dec. 1913	

Groom		Bride		Date	Comments
Surname	Given Name	Surname	Given Name		
Hanley	Frank	Siever	Alice	22 Dec. 1910	
Hanley	Harry	Hewitt	Marry E.	14 Nov. 1918	
Hanlon	Frank	O'Mally	Mary	28 Sept. 1918	
Hanlon	Newton B.	Bosworth	Cora May	29 Dec. 1906	
Hanna	Daniel N.	Aspenwall	Georgiana F.	14 Nov. 1891	
Hanna	J. G.	Frazier	Mary T.	18 Feb. 1888	
Hannah	David Albert	Edwards	Josephine Letitia	24 Jan. 1917	
Hannah	Percy J.	Dexter	Ella B.	25 Oct. 1914	
Hannan	Daniel	Cereghino	Mary	2 Oct. 1893	br: widow
Hannan (?)	Patrick	Sweeny	Ellen A.	10 Apr. 1888	
Hanner	Elmer R.	Kirkland	Daisy Helen	26 July 1920	br: Phoebe A. Kirkland, mother
Hannon	Joseph F.	Edrington	Rhea R.	20 Dec. 1919	
Hanold (?)	Nathaniel Gould	Canepa	Mabel	7 June 1920	
Hansbrow	George Rutlege	Gavin	Margaret Helen	12 Jan. 1907	
Hansen	Adolph N.	Smith	Isabel I.	26 June 1920	
Hansen	Albert	Boning	Marie H.	29 Sept. 1913	
Hansen	Andras	Wedemeyer	Dorothy E.	1 Dec. 1920	
Hansen	Andrew	Feddersen	Inka	6 Sept. 1894	
Hansen	Antone M.	Bostrom	Anna C.	26 Aug. 1920	
Hansen	August	Jepsen	Christina	24 Apr. 1893	
Hansen	Axel O.	Simpson	Luella B.	14 Feb. 1914	
Hansen	Carl	Powers	Catherine	27 Nov. 1886	
Hansen	Carl Christian	Iverson	Elsie	16 Sept. 1910	
Hansen	Carl Emil	Armstrong	Lusettie	20 May 1907	
Hansen	Chris P. F.	Brucher	Hazel G.	3 Sept. 1919	br: Louise Vail, mother
Hansen	Christian	Saunders	Elsie	23 Dec. 1911	

	Groom	Bride		Date	Comments
Surname	Given Name	Surname	Given Name		
Hansen	Christian C.	Brokins	Sarah Jane	10 Mar. 1897	br: C. H. Holmes gives consent and signs; br: lived in his family for past 5 years, and her birthday is 18 Jan. last
Hansen	E. J.	Purcell	Gertrude	17 Nov. 1894	
Hansen	Edward	Brown	Mary J., Mrs.	26 Mar. 1885	
Hansen	Einer C.	Henderlong	Martha V.	26 Aug. 1918	
Hansen	Elmer	Thomsen	Elsie Loraine	14 Mar. 1919	
Hansen	Elmer	Fromell	Anita Mabel	3 Sept. 1919	
Hansen	Frederick E.	Taylor	Georgie A.	24 Dec. 1904	
Hansen	George G.	Speer	May E.	22 Aug. 1912	
Hansen	Hans	Winding	Sina	20 Aug. 1915	
Hansen	Henry	Malchow	Bertha	7 Jan. 1911	
Hansen	Herbert M.	Gray	Goldie Irene	26 Feb. 1921	
Hansen	James G.	Solari	Isola L.	12 Nov. 1906	
Hansen	John G. E.	Adams	Annie Mary	18 Apr. 1919	
Hansen	Louis	Cutts	Olive	3 July 1900	
Hansen	Maurice	Witherspoon	Cornelia E.	8 Dec. 1885	
Hansen	Niels	Jorgensen	Magdalena	15 Oct. 1886	
Hansen	Orin F.	Blake	Ella	31 May 1865	
Hansen	P. B.	Enevold	Maria	23 Oct. 1895	license cancelled. License not issued.
Hansen	Paul B.	Wilson	Florence I., Mrs.	31 Oct. 1901	
Hansen	Peter	Peters	Elene	31 May 1904	
Hansen	Peter	Mugge	Louise Feltz	14 Sept. 1907	
Hansen	Peter E.	Pease	Abba	1 Mar. 1904	
Hansen	Rufus	Loveland	M. J.	27 Mar. 1865	
Hansen	Walter	Andersen	Annie	9 June 1915	
Hansen	William	Payne	Florence E.	9 Aug.1898	no previous marriage
Hansen	William Adolf	Larson	Dora	9 Oct. 1909	

Groom Surname	Groom Given Name	Bride Surname	Bride Given Name	Date	Comments
Hansen	William C.	Kas	Rhoda F.	25 Sept. 1913	
Hanshop	Guy Edwin	Davis	Edna Angie	20 May 1905	
Hanson	Hans	Holgersen	Hedvig	26 Oct. 1895	
Hanson	Hans P.	Moore	Grace Mabel	3 Oct. 1902	
Hanson	John	Hitchcock	Mary Elisabeth	29 Sept. 1891	gr: N. B. Turner, Jr., witness to identity
Hanson	John G.	Pedersen	Annie	26 May 1902	
Hanson	Peter	Lacque	Sarah A.	18 May 1888	
Hanson	William J.	Haberman	Christine	29 Oct. 1898	no previous marriage
Hanssen	Louis O.	Peterson	Ethel	2 Sept. 1914	
Hansten	Herman	Banks	Lenora	30 Dec. 1907	br: Mrs. L. E. Rider, mother
Happersburger	Frank, Jr.	Dawson	Maude E.	26 July 1919	
Happy	Abraham	Tiers	Ethel Maggie	10 Apr. 1891	
Haran	James	Mullen	Ellen	19 Nov. 1889	
Haraszthy	Mariano J.	Simmons	Carrie J.	27 Aug. 1889	license requested by R. D. Emporan
Harbin	Thomas B.	Crabtree	Ella	1 Sept. 1879	
Harbine	James L.	Clark	Alice F.	8 Dec. 1890	
Harbine	N. W.	Pitkin	Nettie J.	29 Dec. 1894	
Harde	Grant O.	Leviston	Elizabeth M.	3 June 1915	
Harder	Oscar C.	Brown	Gladys B.	22 Nov. 1911	
Hardin	Andrew Evan	Eardley	Eliza Fitchford	26 Oct. 1899	
Hardin	Clarence E.	Stegemann	Katherine R.	22 May 1917	
Hardin	Harold Jefferson	Friis	Elene Christine	15 Oct. 1907	
Hardin	Henry	Livingston	Minnie H.	8 Aug. 1903	
Hardin	J. Rolla	Tonini	Nellie C.	2 Aug. 1904	gr: J. M. Hardin, parent
Hardin	James Taylor	Bryan	Marie E.	5 Dec. 1901	
Hardin	John M.	Rhodehaver	Lulu	16 Sept. 1882	
Hardin	Lester B.	McMinn	Mary M.	25 Sept. 1882	
Hardin	Lexter B.	Lindsay	Edna P.	29 Apr. 1920	

	Groom		Bride		
Surname	**Given Name**	**Surname**	**Given Name**	**Date**	**Comments**
Hardin	Robert	Showalter	Victoria	17 July 1882	
Hardin	William Graves	Stout	Clara Edna	24 Aug. 1905	
Hardin	Wm. H.	Hopper	Nancy J.	30 June 1865	
Harding	Edward F.	Smith	Nettie	24 Apr. 1916	
Harding	Reinhardt T.	Holmes	Eunice C.	30 Jan. 1920	
Harding	William A.	Bone (?)	Ellen	14 Nov. 1882	
Hardisty	James A.	Staley	Edna M.	10 Dec. 1904	
Hardy	Orlando B.	MacIntosh	Sara	4 Apr. 1914	
Hare	Stephen	Hoar	Mary L.	7 May 1896	
Harford	Lyman	Ross	Genevieve	20 June 1914	
Hargens	Charles	Bollinger	Maggie	5 Nov. 1897	no previous marriage
Hargreaves	Thomas W.	Lyttaker	Emma M.	21 June 1892	
Hargreaves	Thurlow E.	Richardson	Gladys Mae	10 Nov. 1920	
Harhoe	Christian	Meyer	Rosa	9 Mar. 1878	
Harkness	Raymond L.	Bond	May Emily	1 Nov. 1920	
Harkrader	Albert L.	Gober	Elizabeth	22 June 1910	
Harlan	Carolus	Ellis	Laura C.	12 Nov. 1894	
Harlan	Charles E.	Vaughan	Bertha J.	1 Oct. 1894	
Harlan	James W.	Ellis	Olive I.	19 May 1893	
Harlan	Joel M.	Currier	Kate, Mrs.	27 Apr. 1886	
Harlan	William Christian	Layneance	Charity L.	22 May 1897	
Harlan	William Christian	Cardinet	Elva	15 Sept. 1906	
Harman	Roy	Philbrick	Jean M.	31 Jan. 1916	
Harman	William A.	Anderson	Gussie	25 Sept. 1902	
Harmon	Charles Reuben	McMullen	Margaret	21 July 1896	
Harmon	Frank A.	Kimble	Mary M.	11 Aug. 1900	
Harmon	James E.	Satterlee	Edith G.	4 Sept. 1900	gr: J. P. Harmon, father; C. H. Pond, witness

-36-

Groom Surname	Groom Given Name	Bride Surname	Bride Given Name	Date	Comments
Harmon	Oliver Lewis	Fewell	Kate Florence	5 June 1895	
Harmon	Owen	Briggs	Lizzie	3 July 1903	
Harmon	Peter A.	Pray	Harriet May	1 Aug. 1910	
Harmon	Robert A.	Kimble	Delia	24 Dec. 1900	br: J. W. Kimble, father
Harmon	Robert A.	Allen	Mary C.	1 Oct. 1904	
Harmon	Russell J.	Wedge	Mamie C.	29 Oct. 1919	
Harms	Alvin	Petersen	Elena	7 Sept. 1904	
Harms	Leland	Gonsalves	Emerentia I.	8 Nov. 1920	br: Minnie L. Gonsalves, mother
Harow	Tom	Phinney	Josephine	15 Oct. 1906	
Harper	Charles H.	Winter	Annie M.	12 Dec. 1888	
Harper	John	Watt	Margaret M.	2 Dec. 1889	
Harrigan	G. W.	Treadwell	Sarah E.	30 Jan. 1914	
Harrigan	James Daniel	Jenkins	Clara Louise	9 Oct. 1916	
Harrington	Ambrus	Kise (?)	Etta	29 May 1883	
Harrington	Charles Winfield	Givlin	Margret Ella May	8 Nov. 1906	br: John Giulin, father
Harrington	Daniel	Lowery	Jennie	19 Dec. 1888	
Harrington	James	Stevens	Nettie	1 Dec. 1894	
Harris	Arthur L.	Pickett	Helen S.	8 Dec. 1890	
Harris	Arthur M.	Storey	Bertha A.	24 Nov. 1920	
Harris	Bert A.	Berry	Lelia	7 Sept. 1898	
Harris	Charles C.	Lauz	Lydia (of colour)	17 Feb. 1865	
Harris	Claude	Alexander	Selma	2 Feb. 1916	br: Elizabeth Alexander, mother
Harris	Earl L.	Worms	Alice D.	24 May 1916	
Harris	Edward E.	Young	Maude E.	17 Dec. 1901	
Harris	Eli	Waddell	Isadore Belle	4 May 1878	
Harris	Ephraim D.	Crommett	Sarah A.	10 Oct. 1882	
Harris	George F.	Caito (?)	Belle	15 Mar. 1879	
Harris	George W.	Daniels	Minnie M.	24 Oct. 1889	

		Bride			
Groom				**Date**	**Comments**
Surname	**Given Name**	**Surname**	**Given Name**		
Harris	Granville	Spencer	Nonie	22 Sept. 1885	
Harris	Harry J.	Rich	Nettie May	27 July 1909	
Harris	Henry R.	Sievers	Augusta M.	29 Sept. 1920	
Harris	James W.	Pharris	Ilma	2 Aug. 1913	
Harris	James William	George	Zella	4 Dec. 1909	gr: Mrs. Mattie J. Harris, mother
Harris	Jesse Winfred	Branstetter	Daisy Dean	24 Nov. 1909	
Harris	John W.	Brown	Catherine A., Mrs.	13 Feb. 1889	
Harris	Leon F.	Trent	Maude S.	16 Jan. 1912	
Harris	Paul C.	Crose	Nellie	14 Nov. 1891	
Harris	Ralph W.	Crawford	Nadine E.	21 Oct. 1919	
Harris	Richard A.	Utt	Mary E.	12 Nov. 1884	
Harris	Richard Alexander	Collier	Louisa Jane	19 Dec. 1877	
Harris	Robert E.	Kiser	Agnes C.	27 Apr. 1920	
Harris	William E.	Carpenter	Leah	17 Dec. 1900	
Harrison	Francis Richard	Bartholomew	Yula D.	26 Oct. 1907	
Harrison	Frank M.	Sullivan	Amanda J.	17 Dec. 1888	
Harrison	Fred Kingsley	Fletcher	Ruth Ann	21 May 1907	
Harrison	G. A.	Howard	Lucinda	10 Sept. 1904	
Harrison	Robert H.	Williams	Sarah I.	8 Oct. 1883	br: W. H. Williams, father
Harrison	Wm. H.	Shaw	Hannah M.	1 Dec. 1866	
Harrod	W. W.	Buckman	Mary Jane	11 Mar. 1889	
Hart	Albert Paxton	Jackson	Flora Helen	14 May 1906	
Hart	Albert R.	Irvin	Esther	23 Dec. 1901	br: W. H. Irvin, parent
Hart	Benjamin F.	Hixson	Charlotte J.	26 Dec. 1894	
Hart	Benjamin F.	Moyer	Sybil	19 Sept. 1898	
Hart	Charles E.	DeLude	Martine O.	3 Apr. 1917	
Hart	Chenowith B.	Flinn	Anna	26 June 1908	
Hart	David B.	Mizer	Sarah P.	27 July 1888	requested by H. H. Churchill

Groom Surname	Groom Given Name	Bride Surname	Bride Given Name	Date	Comments
Hart	Ellis O.	Durbin	Susie Loraine	9 July 1906	
Hart	Frank	Cline	Jessie	24 Sept. 1915	
Hart	Harold D.	Day	Lyda Edith	14 July 1906	
Hart	Hubbard	Shackelford	Susan	22 Apr. 1890	br: widow
Hart	Jack E.	McReynolds	Ruth F.	27 May 1914	
Hart	Jesse B.	Moodey	Rose C.	14 Oct. 1916	
Hart	John E.	Carlson	Hilda M.	2 Mar. 1896	
Hart	John T.	Carey	Hettie E.	31 Mar. 1915	
Hart	Leo Blair	Bowles	Veda A.	10 June 1912	
Hart	Robert M.	Smith	Mary E.	18 June 1888	
Hart	Victor E.	Pepper	Lydia E.	2 July 1902	
Hartin	Richard	Aiken	Inez Mabel	27 Dec. 1905	
Hartley	William H.	Roberts	Tillie	14 Feb. 1889	
Hartsock	Freedom E.	Stone	Grace E.	6 Dec. 1917	
Hartwell	George H.	Pendleton	Edna F.	18 Dec. 1912	
Hartzel	Joseph	Hahn	Mary	30 June 1904	
Harvey	Ira B.	Spottswood	Annie	13 May 1908	
Harvey	James H.	Fountain	Minnie	20 July 1886	
Harvey	John F.	Simas	Helen	21 July 1919	
Harvey	Lowell N.	Cooper	Sadie A.	27 July 1889	
Harvey	Marion Wilson	Woods	Ethel Blosom	16 Dec. 1908	
Harvie	Harold B.	Haines	Helen H.	17 Apr. 1920	
Harwell	George O.	Booker	Caroline	20 July 1904	
Harwood	John F.	Beaulieu	Marie H.	23 July 1910	
Haselswerdt	Harry E.	Frey	Annie M.	8 Apr. 1919	
Haselton	C. O.	Ward	Mina B.	28 Dec. 1885	
Hasenberg	William F.	Switzer	Ivy W.	1 Mar. 1897	
Haskell	Greenlief A.	Davies	Harriett C.	21 June 1899	

	Groom	Bride		Date	Comments
Surname	Given Name	Surname	Given Name		
Haskell	Herbert Raymond	Lang	Myrtle Ethel	7 July 1913	
Haskett	Max H.	Winson	Isabelle M.	17 Dec. 1914	
Haskins	Elmond Sterling	Mego	Jennie Angelia	12 Oct. 1905	
Haskins	W. R.	Noble	Frankie L.	9 July 1896	
Haskins	William Joseph	Halley	Ellen Cecelia	30 July 1904	
Hasper	Henry	Bundesen	Marie	8 Jan. 1909	br: H. M. T. Bundesen, parent
Hassett	Adlai V.	LeBaron	Sarah	6 Mar. 1914	
Hassett	James T.	Laughlin	Ella	29 Dec. 1885	
Hassett	Jay Vernon	Ireland	Grace Elizabeth	18 Mar. 1908	
Hassett	Ora T.	Sears	Mary E.	5 Aug. 1891	
Hassett	William Henry	Butler	Annie S.	28 Feb. 1878	
Hasting	Fletcher D.	McClellan	S. F., Mrs.	19 May 1902	
Hasting	Joe C.	Gann	Martha A.	8 Oct. 1891	
Hastings	A. R.	Corrall	Caroline	10 Apr. 1865	
Hastings	Fletcher D.	Cook	Emily	11 May 1908	
Hastings	Nelse	Smith	Nellie, Mrs.	5 Dec. 1910	
Hastings	William Walton	Letold	Alice Mary	20 Sept. 1916	
Hasty	Charles H.	Warren	Addie J.	8 Dec. 1900	
Hatch	Frank R.	Bagley	Amy L.	22 Dec. 1911	
Hathaway	Albert	Kiser	Edith E.	1 Apr. 1893	
Hatler	John P.	Deering	Martha J.	20 Jan. 1914	
Hatler	Joseph E.	Bones	Hila	8 Apr. 1911	br: has been previously married see 26 Nov. 1907
Hatton	Charles B. D.	Gober	Elizabeth C.	16 Dec. 1882	
Hatton	J. E.	Boothby	C. M., Mrs.	23 Apr. 1887	
Hatton	William Henry	Byrne	Mary Agnes	28 Feb. 1893	
Haub	Chester C.	Flewelling	Bessie H.	30 June 1920	
Haub	Theodore G.	Egan	Lena K.	19 Nov. 1919	

Groom Surname	Groom Given Name	Bride Surname	Bride Given Name	Date	Comments
Haubrich	Benjamin F.	Keyes	Mattie	1 June 1897	
Haubrich	Leonard	Ward	Sarah, Mrs.	3 Sept. 1887	
Hauck	Harry E.	Prien	Florentine A.	17 Nov. 1915	
Haukel ?	Herman, Jr.	Gailor	E. B., Mrs.	10 Oct. 1894	gr: name could be Hankel
Haupt	Charles W.	Patten	Julia A.	4 Apr. 1889	
Haupt	Frank L.	Clancy	Anna Estelle	1 July 1920	
Haupt	Louis C.	Parker	Bessie M.	10 Feb. 1917	
Haus	Fred C. H.	Mastrup	M. Sophie	15 April 1901	
Hausmann	John	Harrison	Emma	21 May 1908	
Havard	Laurence S. H.	Capucetti	Rose	29 Sept. 1910	
Haven	Acton	Noble	Maude	26 July 1909	
Havens	Charles I., Jr.	Coutts	Mabel	30 July 1915	
Havenstrite	Reed C.	Marshall	Grace A.	25 Mar. 1920	
Haverlo	Jesse	Drake	Ella	25 July 1879	
Haw	Michael J.	Naughton	Julia M.	21 July 1899	no previous marriage
Hawes	William Henry	Holinsteat	Clara Ella	4 Oct. 1907	
Hawes	William R.	Meek	Tina O.	1 Sept. 1900	
Hawkes	William	Granger	Edith	25 May 1908	
Hawkins	Christian H.	Bacon	Mildred E.	15 May 1920	
Hawkins	J. R.	Harden	Anna B.	2 May 1888	
Hawkins	Louis J.	Mize	Maria	15 Nov. 1871	witness: Albert Mize
Hawkins	Louis J.	Mize	Maria	15 Nov. 1871	br: Albert Mize
Hawkins	W. H.	Burrison	Alice	16 Jan. 1913	
Hawley	George L.	Phillips	Ina	21 Nov. 1904	
Hawley	William Alexander	Johnson	Mary Hattie	14 Jan. 1907	
Haws	Alpheus Peter	Haws	Hannah Eleanor	23 Oct. 1906	gr: W. P. Burke, witness to his mark
Hawthorn	Loyet/Loyel A.	Upson	Lucy	16 Dec. 1878	

		Bride			
Groom				**Date**	**Comments**
Surname	**Given Name**	**Surname**	**Given Name**		
Hayden	John S.	Jones	Estella Pearl	11 Oct. 1892	br: Rachel Ward, sister of bride's mother gives consent; aunt signs with mark witnessed by Henry Crocker; mother dead, wherabouts of father unknown; long note about family situation
Hayden	Richard	Foresti	Dora	11 Apr. 1914	
Hayden	S. R.	Haupt	Mary	14 Apr. 1888	br: Charles Haupt, father
Hayes	Bert J.	Jones	Edna M.	3 Sept. 1901	
Hayes	Charles Ronan	Waller	Eva Myrtle	3 Feb. 1907	
Hayes	Frank	Mann	Ora	16 Oct. 1914	
Hayes	Jacob	McPhearson	Malinda	1 May 1867	
Hayes	James E.	Scudder	Elizabeth	15 Jan. 1898	br: J. S. Scudder, parent
Hayes	John	Grace	Anastasia	16 June 1890	
Hayes	John Henri	Ford	Dorothy Louise	15 Nov. 1919	gr: Charles E. Hayes, father
Hayes	Leroy L.	Grigsby	Lillian L.	26 Nov. 1917	
Hayes	Stanley W.	Burbank	Edna H.	2 Feb. 1907	
Hayne	Harry Henry	Stegman	Helene A. H.	12 May 1917	
Hayner	Ralph Waldo	Landrus	Edith Lily	8 Nov. 1909	gr: May Hayner, mother; br: Hugh McFadden, guardian
Haynie	Wm. M.	Adams	Anna M.	17 Oct. 1911	
Hays	Edwin B., Rev.	Gingery	Mandilla	10 Dec. 1895	
Hays	Ira C.	Partridge	Grace E.	9 July 1888	
Hays	James W.	Brown	Martha J.	3 Dec. 1877	gr: D. H. Rickman, guardian, signs with his mark; witness A. E. Shattuck
Hays	Marmion	Leeth	Myrtle	11 Nov. 1902	
Hays	Walter Daniel	Johnson	Julietta, Mrs.	6 Jan. 1906	
Hayt	William A.	Bower	Emma Katherine	16 May 1903	
Hayward	Harry M.	Carpenter	Sallie P.	19 Nov. 1887	
Hayward	J. B.	Meeks	D. C., Mrs.	18 Apr. 1889	br: widow

Groom Surname	Groom Given Name	Bride Surname	Bride Given Name	Date	Comments
Hayworth	Ruben F.	Miller	Nancy C.	24 Dec. 1879	br: Josh Miller, parent
Hazlett	Emmett M.	DeMartini	Cecilia T.	2 June 1917	
Hazlett	Herman C.	Wilen	Lillian C.	2 Nov. 1917	
Head	Albert P.	Bethel	Dora	27 Apr. 1889	
Head	Clarence Elmore	Bruce	May Lena	26 Mar. 1904	
Head	Robert Calvin	Marsh	Lulu May	23 Nov. 1908	
Head	Walter W.	Van Aukin	Laura	26 Jan. 1892	
Heafey	John J.	McDorley	Mary U.	7 Feb. 1911	
Heald	J. G.	Elliot	Rachael, Mrs.	5 July 1866	
Heald	William T.	Smith	Aurelia Maud	27 Dec. 1894	
Heald	William Thomas	Brighouse	Henrietta C.	22 June 1911	
Healey	Dennis J.	Needham	Maggie	10 Nov. 1886	
Healey	Earl F.	Mendonca	Mary Frances	30 Mar. 1921	
Healey	Joseph M.	Long	Agnes E.	9 Feb. 1920	
Healey	Robert D.	Spencer	Katie R.	25 May 1899	br: R. A. Spencer, parent; no previous marriage
Healey	Thomas James	Wallburg	Edna Elizabeth	8 Sept. 1914	
Healey	Thomas Matthew	Conniffe	Delia Teresa	22 Sept. 1917	
Healey	William E.	Dempsey	Katherine C.	5 Apr. 1912	
Healy	Edwin R.	Gossage	Addie	17 Sept. 1881	
Healy	Frank	Jewell	Annie	19 Oct. 1877	
Hearfield	Harold H.	Menihan	Gertrude	4 June 1915	
Hearns	Charles H.	Pellini	Perry, Mrs.	15 June 1907	
Hearsey	Mason E.	Decker	Josie C.	26 June 1888	
Heason	George W.	Patterson	Hester A.	5 Jan. 1889	br: James T. Patterson, father
Heatley	Lloyd Eldridge	Scott	Anna Catherine	17 Feb. 1906	gr: Eliza Heatley, mother
Heatly	George O.	Martin	Mary E.	14 Aug. 1920	
Heaton	Charles C.	Bryant	Bertha	11 Dec. 1916	

		Bride		Date	Comments
Groom					
Surname	**Given Name**	**Surname**	**Given Name**		
Heaton	Robert Bruce	Lambert	Gussie	20 June 1907	
Heaton	William H.	Heaton	Olive C.	3 May 1919	
Heatzelman	John	Hakemier	Elizabeth	21 Feb. 1865	
Hebbron	Elton Benson	Ulrey	Wava	7 Nov. 1906	
Hebrard	Henry Hepolet	Westwood	Mary Ellen	7 Oct. 1907	
Hebrard	William J.	Gambini	Mary Alice	29 Jan. 1907	
Hecgman	Gustaf	Reidling	Bertha	10 Aug. 1901	requested by Anna C. Straub, friend of groom
Heck	Joseph H.	Schultz	Bertha	8 Jan. 1914	
Heckendorf	August J.	Lindenmeyer	Jeanette O.	28 Feb. 1898	
Heckley	Thomas B.	Beebe	Olive D.	31 May 1900	
Hedden	Donald	Ledford	Vesta V.	25 June 1915	
Hedel	Henry	Albrecht	Hulda	19 May 1906	
Hedges	Benjamin F.	Schug	Rose E.	8 Nov. 1916	
Hedges	Edward D.	Fritsch	Nelly	21 Nov. 1881	
Hedges	S. H.	Rohrer	Nellie	5 May 1883	
Hedin	Sven Thomas	Jacobsen	Hedvig	26 Aug. 1911	
Hedrick	Clyde Warren	Mumma	Lela Maude	3 Aug. 1917	
Hedrick	David M.	Cook	Mary E.	27 Jan. 1893	
Heesche	Henry G. K.	Fricke	Caroline	14 July 1919	
Heezen	G. J.	Gotschalk	Theresa	11 Mar. 1895	gr: Last name could be Steeger?
Heffelfinger	William	Baum	Arvilley K.	4 Feb. 1890	
Hefferman	William H.	Barrett	Mary	18 Mar. 1921	
Heffner	Edward L.	Hoffman	Marie J.	14 Sept. 1916	
Heffron	Fred H.	Wilson	Nancy E.	21 Nov. 1896	
Heffron	George	Cole	Annie	9 Apr. 1898	
Heggie	Norman J.	Aguillon	Gabrielle F.	5 July 1895	
Hegler	Gerhard H.	Skillman	Eva	22 Feb. 1881	

Groom Surname	Groom Given Name	Bride Surname	Bride Given Name	Date	Comments
Heid	Conrad G.	Barrows	Mary J.	20 May 1915	
Heil	Roy P.	Mahoney	Mary Agnes	18 Sept. 1920	
Heimorth	Charles R.	Payne	Hannah J.	20 Jan. 1885	
Heimroth	William Henry	Laymance	Sarah Augusta	7 July 1886	br: Henry Laymance, brother
Heine	Louis William	Webb	Fanny	11 Mar. 1917	
Heinicke	Carl	Scherren	Mathilde	29 July 1915	
Heinkel	Herman Frank	Toomey	Agnes V. D.	22 May 1916	
Heinrich	Frank A.	Looney	Laura	10 Nov. 1886	
Heinshaw	Benjamin P.	Rabe	Edith	9 Oct. 1915	
Heintz	August Henry	Eggers	Hermine	12 Sept. 1914	
Heintz	John H.	Bollard	Marguerite M.	13 Mar. 1920	
Heintz	Victor F.	McGonagill	Eunice R.	24 Sept. 1918	
Heitstuman	Henry	Kempf	Jennie E.	15 Apr. 1901	
Heitter	Henry	Bade	Augusta	24 Dec. 1908	
Heitz	Frank	Nielson	Dorothy E.	20 Dec. 1909	
Heitz	Frederick Charles	Long	Hazel Gertrude	29 Dec. 1910	
Heitz	Howard L.	Warren	Edith G.	27 May 1915	
Heitz	James Louis	Hughes	Lila Dell	20 Oct. 1906	gr: Mrs. Josie Heitz, mother
Heitz	John Louis	Rodgers	Myrtle	26 Nov. 1913	
Heitz	Joseph	Harris	Sarah	23 Oct. 1880	
Heitz	W. F.	Nielson	Grace M.	8 Oct. 1912	
Heitzel	David	Lund	Ovina Sicretta	21 Apr. 1897	
Helberg	William	Krahmann	Amelia	16 Nov. 1894	
Helberg	William	Werner	Meta	12 Apr. 1909	
Helberg	William E.	Thomas	Myrtle	15 May 1918	
Held	H. R.	Coover	Anita B.	17 Nov. 1914	
Helfer	George A.	Hodges	Jessie M.	22 July 1918	
Helin	Charles Edward	Pallady	Ruth Miller	15 Sept. 1917	

	Groom	Bride		Date	Comments
Surname	Given Name	Surname	Given Name		
Heller	William S.	Greening	Nancy Jennie	27 Mar. 1920	
Hellinge	William J.	Ray	Mary Gertrude	19 May 1917	
Hellrich	Paul H.	Murray	Alice	18 Dec. 1902	
Hellrick	Edward Joseph	Henry	La Veda Lucille	7 Oct. 1916	
Helman	Edwin Daniel	Silverthorn	Maude Frances	23 Dec. 1908	
Helman	L. W.	Proctor	Clara L.	16 June 1890	
Helman	Louis W., Jr.	Yeager	Carolyn E.	4 June 1913	
Helmke	F.	Shine	A. E.	16 Nov. 1865	consent
Helton	William A.	Millington	Bessie M.	25 Dec. 1915	
Hembree	Albert Lafayette	Copeland	Josephine	29 Dec. 1877	
Hembree	Atlas T.	McClelland	Clara	12 Nov. 1895	
Hembree	Leon	Murray	Fodie L.	2 Dec. 1904	br: John C. & Leah I. Murray, parents; notary seal
Hemenover	Dudley A.	Bussman	Harriett I.	24 Jan. 1920	
Hemenover	Dudley A.	Rivers	Adah E.	5 May 1915	br: Cora E. Rivers, mother; no one signed for groom
Hemenway	Daniel D.	Ward	Alice I.	20 Oct. 1887	requested by A. Ward
Hemler	George E., Sr.	Herrick	Annie M.	18 Aug. 1919	
Hemma	Harry A.	Johnson	Edna M.	15 Mar. 1909	
Hemmarberg	Edward	Becklund	Olge	23 Mar. 1912	
Hemphill	John H.	Morley	M. J., Mrs.	28 Nov. 1896	
Hemphill	William	Gordon	Lizzie Jane	7 Aug. 1883	requested by Robert Gordon
Hemple	George	Crites	Nan	15 Sept. 1906	
Hemsath	Jack Henry	Stoughton	Elizabeth Carlon	20 Nov. 1908	
Henderson	Fred S.	Winkler	Martha, Mrs.	18 Aug. 1899	br: divorced over one year
Henderson	George P.	Heim (?)	Florence Elizabeth	22 Oct. 1910	
Henderson	H. Seymore	Pomeroy	Ollie A.	16 Feb. 1887	br: Theodoro O. Pomeroy, ?
Henderson	Hardin W.	Mize	Mary	29 Nov. 1879	gr: signs with his mark

Groom Surname	Groom Given Name	Bride Surname	Bride Given Name	Date	Comments
Henderson	Harry H.	Chaffee	Mary S.	31 Oct. 1885	gr: George W. Henderson, father; br: P. M. Chaffee, father
Henderson	James T.	Small	Emma S.	29 Aug. 1914	
Henderson	Vernon E.	Smith	Ora	29 June 1917	
Hendley	Chas. Bacon	Arnold	Katie A.	28 Feb. 1888	
Hendley	Harry L.	Crigler	Lucy	14 May 1904	
Hendrick	James M.	Allen	Lizzie M.	14 Nov. 1877	
Hendrick	Wallace	Heill (?)	Amanda Ellen	14 Jan. 1884	
Hendricks	Geo. L.	Phillips	Maude	6 Nov. 1901	
Hendricks	George L.	Ledford	Anna May	16 Dec. 1904	
Hendricks	J. W.	McElhany	Florence	19 Nov. 1894	
Hendrix	Edwin W.	Peterson	Susan A.	6 Oct. 1880	gr: the consent of his father being given personally
Hendrix	G. L.	Collins	Ella C.	3 June 1903	
Hendrix	Harvey L.	Hall	Mae	26 July 1902	gr: Mrs. S. Hendrix, mother
Hendry	Howard W.	Walters	Audry V.	9 June 1917	
Henelly	Michael J.	Fitzgerald	Ellen A.	16 June 1914	
Henley	Elihu Shields	Robson	Marion Louise	3 June 1916	
Henning	Thomas	Garza	Margareth	21 July 1919	
Henningsen	John P.	Hogedohm	Johanna F.	23 Feb. 1895	
Henningsen	Knudt Theodor	Andersen	Caroline Amalie	22 Jan. 1918	please do not publish, good reasons
Hennisch	Albert G.	Bell	Vivian Phillis	10 July 1920	
Henrichsen	Henry R.	Geertz	Mathilde, Mrs.	17 June 1895	br: widow
Henrichsen	Theodore	Stoeker ?	Emma	29 Aug. 1896	
Henrichson	Harry C.	Heinsen	Letitia R.	19 June 1920	
Henry	Amos	Penick	Mackie Katherine	24 July 1920	
Henry	Charles P.	Bonkofsky	Willamena	15 July 1911	
Henry	George	Payran	Mary	4 Aug. 1875	

Groom		Bride		Date	Comments
Surname	Given Name	Surname	Given Name		
Henry	J. R.	Emerson	S. R.	14 Nov. 1866	
Henry	James	Hiett	Nelia	1 Apr. 1975	br: mother consenting, the father being dead
Henshaw	George M.	Meador	Leanora	9 Jan. 1889	
Henshaw	Iram	Alexander	Hannah	8 Nov. 1878	
Hensley	F. C.	Hughes	Mary G.	10 Aug. 1914	
Hensley	Harry	Hogeboom	Alice B.	8 Sept. 1902	
Henzi	William	Willis	Sylvia I.	21 Oct. 1914	
Hepworth	Albert	Dutcher	Stella V.	8 Oct. 1895	
Herald	E. H.	Bonsell	Ada	blank	br: J. C. Bonsell, stepfather
Herbert	Fred A.	Kaster	Julia	3 Sept. 1904	
Herbert	John	Silvers	Rettice	20 Aug. 1890	
Herbert	John	Silvers	Lizzie A.	18 Oct. 1881	br: Mary E. Silvers, mother
Herbert	Thomas	Robertson	Daisy	8 Oct. 1901	
Herbert	Vanscoy P.	Uttley	Juanita I.	23 June 1920	
Herbert	Victor	Borer	Florence A.		br: John Borer; James March, witness; filed between 11 and 15 Nov. 1879
Herbert	William	Bates	Charlotte	13 Mar. 1897	
Herberts	Harvey	Hutchins	Mabel	5 July 1911	
Herbst	John Frank	Blum	Theresa	21 May 1908	
Herbst	John H.	Demol	Claire	30 Aug. 1898	no previous marriage
Herlitz	Robert	Hachett	Ella	10 Nov. 1902	
Herman	Christopher M.	Ellison	Grace E.	24 Apr. 1911	
Herman	Franklin A.	Cookson	Ruth A.	14 June 1916	
Herman	Fred A.	Fine	Mary E.	16 Aug. 1887	br: J. M. Fine, father
Hermann	Albert	Behrens	Tillie	27 Sept.1904	
Hermansen	Carl Andreas	Petersen	Hansine	2 Mar. 1908	
Herrick	Albert B., Jr.	Dixon	Helen Louise	27 June 1916	

Groom Surname	Groom Given Name	Bride Surname	Bride Given Name	Date	Comments
Herrick	Emerson Brown	Smith	Adah	1 May 1918	
Herring	Elias	Nicholsen	Mary Emily Jane, Mrs.	3 Sept. 1866	
Herrmann	Ino	Mosher	Ella	4 Sept. 1877	
Herron	Frank C.	Stockdale	Lena A.	16 Dec. 1897	no previous marriage
Herron	Joseph H.	Chapin	Ethel	6 July 1909	
Hersey	Merrick C.	Johnson	Florence E.	18 May 1916	
Hershberger	John F.	Whitaker	Rhoda M.	4 Dec. 1893	
Heryford	Bennett, Jr.	Cazerous	Laura	21 June 1890	br: widow
Heryford	David Hilton	Hickey	Cathaleen Violet	18 July 1908	gr: Mrs. Joseph Heryford, mother; br: Thomas D. Hickey, father
Heryford	Hilton	Kirry	Dora	23 Apr. 1913	
Heryford	James W.	Lindemenn	Sarah B.	11 Oct. 1915	
Heryford	Jno. F.	Fraim	Daisy, Mrs.	3 Nov. 1902	
Heryford	Reuben M.	Van Winkle	Alice M.	12 Oct. 1897	no previous marriage
Heryford	Roy	Earnest	Helen Pearl	29 Aug. 1916	br: Mrs. Martha Earnest, mother
Heryford	William B.	Rawlings	Bertha	2 Oct. 1909	
Heseker	Fred W.	Conley	Clara B.	23 Dec. 1891	
Heselschwerdt	Fred	Ping	Kate Lee	16 Jan. 1905	
Heselschwerdt	Vernon W.	Frey	Jennie A.	19 Apr. 1919	gr: Jacob Heselschwerdt, father
Hesketh	George William	Schiman	Marion	18 Oct. 1907	
Hess	Albert	Palmater	Sarah E.	22 June 1914	
Hess	Frank	Nelson	Grace	5 July 1911	
Hesse	Fredderick G.	Scott	Martha E.	7 June 1886	
Hesse	Walter E.	Brown	Bertha E.	17 Mar. 1913	
Hessel	Andrew Conrad	Bean	Jessie May	29 Dec. 1908	
Hessel	Joseph W.	Jasperson	Emma A.	15 Mar. 1909	br: J. Jasperson, parent
Hesseltine	Benjamin L.	Coffer	Addie	6 Sept. 1879	br: W. W. Cofer, parent

		Bride		Date	Comments
Groom					
Surname	**Given Name**	**Surname**	**Given Name**		
Hesser	Herman R.	Phillips	Sarah		filed between 21 and 28 April 1877
Hettinger	Charley	Reed	Laura	2 Sept. 1908	
Hetzel	Carl	Thompson	Lillie	5 Mar. 1891	gr: D. Hetzell, father
Hevel	Wm. T.	Sparks	Minnie	15 Oct. 1894	
Hevel	Christopher	Parr	Barbara	9 Apr. 1917	
Hewett	Clyde A.	Millard	Carrie G.	22 Nov. 1895	gr: C. E. Hewitt gives consent and signs; Carrie G. Millard requests license
Hewitt	Ernest E.	Morrow	Emma	16 May 1891	br: Jas. H. Morrow, father
Hewlett	Lewis Clifton	Monteith	Marie Loomis	15 May 1912	
Hewlett	Louis Clifton	Bell	Alice Ruth	18 Sept. 1916	
Heyneman	David H.	Bata	Grace	25 Jan. 1917	
Heyward	Jesse	Beebe	Christina M.	5 Sept. 1887	
Hiatt	Charles	McDonald	Josie	22 Sept. 1897	br: Mrs. Julia McDonald, mother
Hiatt	Charles G.	Roberts	Ollie May	2 Feb. 1901	br: Mrs. Wm. Ollie Roberts, mother
Hiatt	Lloyd W.	Shelford	M. Effie	3 Oct. 1904	
Hiatt	Ray Isaac	Dickson	Rena M.	7 Nov. 1914	
Hiatt	Robert E.	Porter	Martha Anna	1 Nov. 1916	
Hiatt	T. L.	Cooper	May E.	28 June 1893	
Hiatt	Thos. L.	Stuart	Lydia J.	15 May 1867	
Hibbard	Charles Elbert	Bond	Lola Ethel	1 June 1903	
Hibbard	Earl Francis	Kreps	Minnie Elizabeth	14 Aug.1909	
Hibbard	Lee	Laymance	Suzanne	29 June 1912	
Hickey	Jerry D.	McGuyre	May	24 Apr. 1911	
Hickey	John	Ehmer (?)	Julia	17 Oct. 1900	
Hickey	Maurice	Merritt	Mary A.	15 Oct. 1870	
Hickey	Maurice J.	Howard	Pearl	4 June 1901	
Hickey	William A.	McGrath	Mary	15 Oct. 1904	
Hickey	William Joseph	Breckwoldt	Alma Lillian	17 July 1906	

Groom Surname	Groom Given Name	Bride Surname	Bride Given Name	Date	Comments
Hicklin	Lieuallen A.	Johnson	Callie F.	6 Dec. 1893	
Hickman	M. S.	Parks	Elvira	13 Apr. 1880	
Hickman	Wade H.	Graper	Hazel	2 Nov. 1912	
Hickok	James C.	Smith	Alice L.	4 Aug. 1890	
Hicks	Archibald Lynn	Clark	Hazel Frances	15 Jan. 1910	
Hicks	Edward S.	Sline (?)	Etta M.	10 Apr. 1884	gr: Mrs. E. A. Hicks, mother
Hicks	George M.	Bowers	Eliza M.	21 Jan. 1885	
Hicks	George Milton	Poff	Mary J.	30 Dec. 1910	
Hicks	John H.	Bailer	Honora E., Mrs.	11 July 1898	both parties divorced more than a year ago
Hicks	Moses C.	Bolton	Sallie, Mrs.	23 June 1902	do not publish for a week
Hicks	Walter Eugene	Boyer	Gertrude Emily	11 June 1906	
Hienrichsen	Jurgen T.	Jensen	Catherine Marie Doretha	22 Sept. 1891	
Higby	Earl D.	Fryer	Elizabeth M.	6 Dec. 1920	
Higgins	Raymond J.	Goldman	Edith	19 May 1919	
Higgins	William J.	Solomon	Crescencia Edson	30 Apr. 1910	
High	Arthur Desten	Van Winkle	Lettie	3 Oct. 1908	
Highbee	H. B.	Fairbanks	J. Nettie	3 Nov. 1886	
Higley	John Burdett	Johnson	Elizabeth	16 June 1906	
Hildebrand	Calvin G.	Conne	Josephine M.	30 Sept. 1903	
Hilder	Henry D.	Biddle	Ruth M.	22 Jan. 1920	
Hilderbrand	Walter G.	Wilson	Inez M.	11 Nov. 1915	
Hile	Charles H.	Hanson	Martha	16 Oct. 1907	
Hilgerloh	Sierich	Sewell	Mildred	21 Feb. 1894	
Hill	Alexander B., Jr.	Olmsted	Dorothy J.	26 Dec. 1919	
Hill	Arthur C.	Collins	Loretta M.	9 June 1920	
Hill	C. S.	Willits	Anna	10 Oct. 1883	
Hill	Charles N.	McGrew	Lovila A.	14 Jan. 1905	

	Groom	Bride		Date	Comments
Surname	**Given Name**	**Surname**	**Given Name**		
Hill	Dolph Brice	Maney	Josephine Mason	5 June 1916	
Hill	George O.	Lamburth	Ada E.	14 Oct. 1919	
Hill	Herman Gordon	Stites	Harriett Estelle	23 July 1907	
Hill	James D.	Gibson	Eva L.	6 Sept. 1902	
Hill	James M.	Boyes	Polly H.	20 Apr. 1882	gr: signs with his mark
Hill	Raymond Moffatt	Smith	Frances Elizabeth	31 Mar. 1921	
Hill	Robert	Morris	Delia	2 Sept. 1865	letter from father
Hill	Robert Elmer	Breaks	Blanche Edna	23 Feb. 1906	
Hill	Samuel R.	Chitwood	Mary B.	19 Dec. 1908	
Hill	William	Canevascini	Bena	23 Mar. 1906	gr: Mrs. A. D. Hill, mother; br: Peter Canevascini, father
Hill	William C.	Arnold	Emma	5 Jan. 1885	
Hill	William C.	Luman	Anna Mai	10 Sept. 1890	
Hill	William James	Clark	May Edith	5 Dec. 1908	
Hill	Alexander B.	Fairbanks	Hattie L.	5 Feb. 1887	
Hillam	Frederick J.	Gatter	Elizabeth A.	1 June 1915	
Hillblom	Gottfrid	Soderman	Susanna	3 July 1908	
Hillendahl	Frank J.	Rippin	Doris A.	8 Jan. 1919	please do not publish in local papers
Hillis	John A.	Harp	Emma R.	29 Feb. 1888	
Hillis	William Franklin	Huikston	Annie	20 Aug. 1901	
Hillman	Theodore	Blanck	Annie	7 Sept. 1909	
Hills	Percy J.	Goddard	Hazel M.	20 Oct. 1907	
Hills	Walter J.	Johnson	Marguerite	17 Dec. 1920	
Hills	Winford G.	Marshall	Mabel	15 July 1914	
Hilton	Harry L.	Hardy	Bessie L.	10 Aug. 1908	
Hilton	Melville H.	Setliff	Vida, Mrs.	9 Apr. 1910	
Hinch	William I.	Guerin	Frances M.	30 Apr. 1920	
Hinds	Loring D.	Mulqueen	Lucy M.	blank	filed between 15 and 24 Mar. 1910

	Groom		Bride		Date	Comments
Surname	Given Name	Surname	Given Name			
Hindson	Francis	Bolden	Nettie C.		3 July 1880	br: Samuel Bolden, father
Hinkelmann	Gustav	Mothorn	Lizzie		14 Nov. 1896	
Hinkle	H. C.	Mecham	Loretta		19 June 1888	
Hinkleman	Fred G.	Wright	Neva F.		14 Feb. 1910	
Hinrichsen	Peter M.	Springer	Helena		26 May 1898	
Hinshaw	A. G.	Frederickson	Mary		31 Dec. 1894	
Hinshaw	A. G.	Price	Rose		1 July 1914	
Hinshaw	B. B.	Colby	F. A.		12 Jan. 1895	
Hinshaw	Clyde C.	Aladalo	Sadie M.		30 Nov. 1917	
Hinshaw	Hugh B.	Stevens	Mary E., Mrs.		22 Aug. 1895	
Hinshaw	J. D.	Laufenburg	Ellen		3 Dec. 1888	
Hinshaw	William P.	Hall	Maud M.		8 Mar. 1902	
Hinton	Arthur R.	Gibbs	Mary L.		15 June 1914	
Hinze	Victor A.	Nuhrenberg	Henrietta M.		16 Sept. 1918	
Hipsher	Henry Clay	Perkins	Blanche		9 Dec. 1910	br: Sarah A. Shuler (?), guardian
Hirschman	J. C.	Black	Ada		5 Sept. 1903	
Hirst	Samuel	Kelso	Alice L.		15 July 1886	
Hiscox	Richard A.	Griest	Artie M.		18 Nov. 1891	
Hitchcock	Arthur L.	Salmela	Helza J.		28 June 1920	
Hitchcock	James E.	Ramsey	Mollie		25 Dec. 1890	
Hitchcock	John	Brown	Utilla		28 Aug. 1897	
Hitchcock	John R.	Yager	Birdie L.		2 Oct. 1899	no previous marriage
Hitchcock	LeRoy V.	Woodward	Jessie		29 May 1911	
Hixson	Charles H.	Leavitt	Cecilia W.		1 Apr. 1913	
Hixson	John	Allen	Molly		8 Apr. 1885	handwritten
Hixson	John, Jr.	Pope	Mary Delilah		6 Nov. 1914	
Hixson	Roy H.	Lea	Lola		27 Mar. 1911	note this marriage was annulled by the superior court

	Groom	Bride		Date	Comments
Surname	Given Name	Surname	Given Name		
Hixson	Roy H.	Lea	Lola M.	31 Mar. 1911	br: A. F. Lea, parent
Hixson	W. H.	Ramsey	R. L., Mrs.	4 June 1891	
Hixson	William H.	Faught	Ruth	13 May 1905	
Hixson	William J.	Jaggers	Mayme T.	15 Oct. 1904	br: Mary L. & N. R. Jaggers, parents
Hoadley	Charles W.	Hipsher	Lottie C.	31 Mar. 1905	br: J. W. Hipsher, parent
Hoadley	Mervyn J.	Allen	Ethel Lillian	15 Dec. 1917	
Hoar	Charles A.	Hamlin	Emma	20 Nov. 1900	
Hobbie	John F.	Zimmerman	Therese	21 Mar. 1911	
Hobbs	Charles C.	Adcock	Lois J.	23 Mar. 1918	
Hobbs	Jason	Gilliam	Emily	6 Feb. 1909	
Hobbs	Robert M.	Philbrook	Pearl C.	18 Apr. 1899	
Hoberg	Arthur O.	Martin	Minnie H.	18 Jan. 1911	
Hoberg	James A.	Camfield	Addie	26 Dec. 1919	
Hobson	Frank S.	Evans	Marie H.	17 May 1915	
Hobson	Jerome C.	McMullen	Minnie F.	16 June 1892	
Hobson	Myron	Wilkinson	Mildred	19 July 1919	
Hocker	Will O.	Chiver?	Lena A.	5 July 1893	
Hockey	Albert James	Redmond	Pauline Mary	16 Sept. 1905	
Hockin	William	Totten (?)	E. A. T.	28 Nov. 1878	
Hockin	William Henry	Lee	Margaret L.	10 July 1909	
Hocking	Frank	High	Minnie B.	9 Aug. 1918	
Hocking	James	McKinzie	Eliza Jane	8 June 1887	
Hocking	William Benn	Conley	Daisy	26 Oct. 1907	
Hockney	Byron S.	Doerges	Louise	12 Mar. 1914	
Hodge	Alexander L.	Damon	Eliza A.	2 Sept. 1876	
Hodge	Levi Francis	Weymouth	Corrinne	4 June 1895	
Hodges	Edgar W.	Purvine	Sarah H.	20 Sept. 1919	
Hodges	Henry C.	Foreman	Annie	19 May 1896	

	Groom	Bride		Date	Comments
Surname	Given Name	Surname	Given Name		
Hodghead	William Horace	Field	Emma H.	29 Mar. 1892	
Hodgson	David R.	Winton	Leticia A.	27 May 1889	br: Stephen C. Winton, father
Hodgson	Joseph E.	Stevenson	Mary M.	10 Jan. 1888	
Hodgson	Ralston Winton	Calley	Mildred Madeline	27 Oct. 1920	
Hodgson	Richard	McDonald	Flora	27 Nov. 1888	
Hodgson	W. H.	Luman	Mary A.	30 Dec. 1882	
Hoeck	F. P.	Willey	Mary A.	4 Dec. 1888	
Hoeck	Frederick W.	Thomas	Margaret E.	11 May 1920	
Hoegh	Hans Matzen	Rickerts		1 Feb. 1905	br: Alfred R. Larsen, stepfather, and Catrina Larsen, mother, give consent
Hoerle	Fred	Richers (?)	Dora	29 Dec. 1899	
Hoff	Herman James	Dennison	Maude Pearl	1 June 1904	
Hoffer	Virgil	Thompson	Gertrude	16 Oct. 1900	
Hoffman	Alfred H.	Watson	Sarah	27 Apr. 1867	
Hoffman	Charles	Rundell	Rosa	27 May 1880	
Hoffman	Charles T.	Pantier	Emma May	14 Sept. 1880	br: Cathary Pantier, mother
Hoffman	Fernando	Woodruff	Eva B.	25 Mar. 1876	br: J. G. & ? Woodruff, parents
Hoffman	Freedom W.	Peugh	Jemella G.	22 Aug 1907	
Hoffman	George W.	Trubody	Clara C.	6 Apr. 1918	
Hoffman	John Walter	Barff	Mary Eleanor	18 Mar. 1921	
Hoffman	Walter A.	Westover	Irma L.	6 June 1918	
Hoffman	Walter Roy	Shade	Ida L.	24 Apr. 1917	
Hoffschneider	Arthur P.	Smith	Minnie E.	25 Aug. 1917	
Hogeboom	Robert Percy	Drescher	Lena	29 May 1906	gr: Jane Hogeboom, mother
Hogg	Robert O.	Cunningham	Loura E.	31 May 1907	
Hogg	William G.	Wilson	Jennie M.	29 June 1897	
Holaday	Elon R.	Eckman	Minnie	8 Nov. 1901	
Holchester	Paul E.	Hasting	Clara	19 Apr. 1890	

	Groom	Bride		Date	Comments
Surname	Given Name	Surname	Given Name		
Holcomb	Alfred	Overton	Mattie C.	19 Jan, 1915	
Holcomb	Leonard C.	Holst	Annie	29 Dec. 1914	br: Mrs. Mollie Holst, mother
Holcomb	William	Brucker	Isabella	29 Dec. 1914	br: Mrs. J. H. Vail, mother
Holden	Charles	Ragan	May	28 May 1917	
Holden	John Edwin	Rosenquest	Matilda Estalla	5 Sept. 1913	
Holden	Josiah N.	Norris	Sarah	7 Nov. 1876	
Holding	George	Danterman	Priscilla	31 May 1890	
Holdrich	Hilarius	Glaser	Emma	13 June 1901	
Holdsworth	Miles E.	Maguire	Ann Loraine	2 Oct. 1919	
Holdt	H. Christian	Haugh	Marguerite	11 Oct. 1918	
Holgard	Carl C.	Lampson	Nellie E.	29 May 1920	
Hollar	Henry H.	Gott (?)	Laura	29 Aug. 1881	
Holles	Clayton W.	Cochrane	Clare A.	16 Sept. 1915	
Holliday	James E.	Stone	Hattie L.	14 June 1882	
Hollingshead	Edward	Bond	Lizella Edith	12 Nov. 1896	license requested by J. W. Bond
Hollingsworth	Dale Raymond	Wright	Viola May	29 May 1916	br: Alice Wright, mother
Hollingsworth	Greene	Damon	Maggie A.	27 Aug. 1910	
Hollingsworth	Harry M.	Alexander	Pearl L. G.	10 Nov. 1920	
Hollis	George Lester	Hardin	Edith Lourena	6 June 1904	
Hollister	George C.	McLeod	F. M.	21 Feb. 1903	
Hollister	George S.	Mutschlechner	Mary	23 Aug. 1894	
Holloway	Calvin Walter	Carpenter	Mamie Ellen	18 Apr. 1892	
Holloway	Clarence	Parker	Mildred	4 Apr. 1907	gr: Mrs. Emma Holloway, mother; br: A. L. Parker, parent
Holloway	Isaac Newton	Griffith	Malinda Ann	15 Dec. 1874	br: have consent of her parents
Holloway	James Henry	Albertson	Ella	5 Nov. 1900	
Holm	Jacob F.	Drees	Mary	13 May 1892	
Holman	Charles W.	Smith	Nova N.	19 Oct. 1920	

Groom Surname	Groom Given Name	Bride Surname	Bride Given Name	Date	Comments
Holman	Edward Kingwell	Brians	Nellie Isabelle	23 Dec. 1896	
Holmes	Charles H.	Holmes	Nellie	10 Jan. 1910	
Holmes	Chas. H., Jr.	Ward	Margaret M.	14 May 1888	
Holmes	Lester S.	Houck	Mary L.	4 June 1917	
Holmes	Marvin P.	Austin	Hattie H.	21 Feb. 1901	requested by Marvin T. Vaughan, friend
Holmes	Melvin Leon	Phelps	Mary Agnes	6 July 1908	
Holmes	Neal Arthur	Jones	Lillian Beatrice	17 Nov. 1916	
Holmes	Ovid	Luttrell	Ruth M.	24 Dec. 1914	
Holst	Henry	Fisher	Mollie	4 Sept. 1890	
Holst	Jacob E.	Tuttle	Mary	6 June 1893	
Holst	James	Young	Hazel	31 Dec. 1910	gr: Henry Holst, father
Holst	James P.	Vassar	Etta	12 Sept. 1900	
Holst	Joseph A.	Blank	Grace, Mrs.	15 Aug 1893	
Holst	William	Dutcher	Pearl	1 Dec. 1902	
Holt	Alva Smith	Stahl	Laura B.	11 July 1914	
Holt	John A.	Yarbough	Georgia J.	29 Sept. 1910	
Holt	William T.	Clerve	Helen A.	17 July 1916	
Holtchauer	Louis	Enyisch	Martha	7 Dec. 1912	
Holtz	James H.	Cox	Lulu H.	11 Feb. 1920	
Holtz	Richard Gustav	Hansen	Elene	31 Dec. 1908	
Holxer	Ernest	Shearer	Annie	4 May 1885	
Homer	William Harry	Simmons	Jennette Augusta	31 Jan. 1900	br: requested license; Jennette A. Goess, witness
Hondaa	Emile J. B.	Canale	Elvira S.	3 July 1917	
Honsa	Joseph	Cervinki	Katie	14 May 1900	
Honton	Paul Noel	Vassar	Agnes Aileen	31 May 1917	
Hood	Alexander	McDonnell	Nellie	30 Sept. 1892	
Hood	Benjamin H.	Cook	Daisy D.	22 Nov. 1901	

	Groom	Bride		Date	Comments
Surname	Given Name	Surname	Given Name		
Hood	Frank B.	Doyle	Nellie J.	19 Apr. 1887	
Hood	James G.	Young	Neva	11 Dec. 1902	
Hood	John	Rutledge	Florence	31 May 1900	
Hood	Thomas Bergin, Jr.	Tenter	Fredericka	4 Aug. 1906	
Hooke	H. W.	Gibbons	Mary A.	5 Sept. 1891	
Hooper	Thomas R.	Booth	Eugenie M.	24 Sept. 1892	
Hoosier	Charles Rasmond	Anderson	Mabel J.	13 Oct. 1916	
Hoover	Leo V.	Harben	Jennie E.	2 May 1914	gr: Chas. H. Hoover, father; br: Emma Learn, guardian
Hopcroft	Charles	Baumann	Ida	18 Dec. 1913	
Hope	Earl Paul	Goula	Ismay Josephine	24 June 1920	
Hope	John B.	Menary	Matilda J.	13 Nov. 1883	
Hopkins	Alban David	Stone	Lillian Agnes	24 July 1899	
Hopkins	Oliver Clay	Bryant	Caroline Augusta	19 June 1897	
Hopkins	Osmer Clyde	Ham	Edith L.	6 Oct. 1902	gr: 56A Hancock St., San Francisco
Hopkins	William Hewes	Reid	Louise S.	5 May 1908	
Hoppe	Anton	Frei	Rosa	23 Sept. 1908	
Hoppe	Joseph Edward	Respini	Delia	31 July 1903	
Hopper	David E.	Smith	Wilhelmina L.	29 Jan. 1918	
Hopper	Edward	Grove	Emma B.	23 Nov. 1886	
Hopper	Elmer Merton	Wilson	Loretta	30 Dec. 1908	
Hopper	George R.	Lamb	Mary A.	28 Nov. 1882	
Hopper	Henry	Burris	Mary F.	19 Sept. 1882	requested by L. W. Burris
Hopper	Henry J.	Huffman	Cora	3 July 1891	
Hopper	Henry James	Kimball	Lulu M.	14 Apr. 1906	
Hopper	Thomas	Everly	Julia N., Mrs.	8 Dec. 1892	
Hopper	Walter E.	Harrington	Leila M.	22 Oct. 1919	
Hopper	Wesley L.	Felton	Nellie	8 Mar. 1902	

Groom Surname	Groom Given Name	Bride Surname	Bride Given Name	Date	Comments
Hopper	William Thomas	Adams	Mary Etta	27 Nov. 1901	
Hopper	Zachamiah (?)	Houx	Josephine	22 Sept. 1876	br: Julie Ann (Houx) Cooper, mother; D. B. Morgan, witness; Cloverdale
Horak	Ferdinand	Blodget	Anna	4 Oct. 1895	
Horan	Charles	Cronin	Catherine E.	16 July 1918	
Horgan	Edward Timothy	Ventura	Mary Francis	26 Oct. 1912	
Horgan	Eugene	Keohane	Nellie	23 June 1897	
Horgan	Patrick	Harnett	Johanna	21 Dec. 1914	
Horita	Katsuki	Miyamoto	Shina	30 Aug. 1920	
Horn	Balthasar	Hanekamp	Anna Maria	15 May 1889	
Horn	Frank Charley	Breitling	Matilda	23 Aug. 1905	
Hornberger	Charles	Doyle	Louise	7 July 1882	
Hornbuckle	Thomas J.	Hill	Florence S., Mrs.	12 Mar. 1896	
Horne	David	Walts (?)	Elizabeth	17 Mar. 1879	
Horr	Riley J.	Freeman	Sarah A.	no date	
Horrick	John	Softus	Mary	1 Feb. 1894	
Horrup	Frank J.	Kynoch	Edna I.	6 Oct. 1920	
Horton	Arthur	Blake	Lulu E.	21 Sept. 1901	
Horton	Arthur S.	Fiske	Elizabeth C.	31 Mar. 1919	
Horton	Samuel	Eby	Ida J.	7 Nov. 1901	
Hoskins (?)	Edward Sterling	Fredricks	Ella	8 Sept. 1919	
Hosmer	Raymond J.	Henderson	Violet V.	25 Oct. 1919	
Hosmer	Stanley	Dean	Maybell	27 Jan. 1904	
Hoss	Frank Blair	Allen	Nellie May	8 Jan. 1906	
Hoster	William S.	Malouf	Fifie	31 Oct. 1919	
Hotchkiss	Douglas F.	Hutchinson	Lily E.	9 Feb. 1903	
Hotchkiss	W. J.	Grom (?)	Emma L.	24 Nov. 1880	
Hotle	Charles E.	Litchfield	Cora L.	12 Feb. 1895	

	Groom	Bride		Date	Comments
Surname	Given Name	Surname	Given Name		
Hotle	William Marley	Dickson	Mary L.	15 Oct. 1904	
Hottel	Peter G.	Laughery	Martha E., Mrs.	16 June 1899	
Hottinger	Bernard F.	Stump	Dottie	11 May 1901	br: D. A. & Carrie Stump, parents; Catherine Hottinger, witness
Hotz	Gustave H.	Enslow	Emma A.	15 Jan. 1887	requested by Joseph Childers
Hotz	Ralph O.	Waterman	Ida E.	28 June 1912	
Hough	Martin	Branaum	May, Mrs.	15 Oct. 1904	
Houghton	Albert S.	Shriver	Ethel A.	24 Aug 1907	
Houghton	Grover C.	Mecum	Alice L.	6 Mar. 1917	
Houghton	Wm. H.	Bennett	Ethel A.	31 Aug. 1887	
Hougland	Ira A.	Neasham	Anna Leah	16 Apr. 1921	
Hourcaillon	John B.	Fredinani	Edith	23 Mar.1910	
Hourtani (?)	Alphonse J. P.	Akmann	Lillian G.	3 Sept. 1918	
Houser	Basil L.	Daniels	Ethel I.	7 Feb. 1921	
Houts	Orrie Leonard	Swain	May McConnell	2 Apr. 1908	
Hovey	Albert Theo	Thompson	Mabel B.	3 Apr. 1920	
Hovey	Arthur La Verne	Dempsey	Emogene E.	15 Apr. 1915	
Hovey	Theodore	Hall	Emma J.	18 May 1885	
Howard	Alphonse E.	Howard	Florence L.	5 Oct. 1897	gr: C. S. Howard, father
Howard	Benjamin F.	Shipmon	Mary E.	14 July 1881	
Howard	Benjamin Franklin	Levalley	Lena, Mrs.	2 June 1906	
Howard	Calvin P.	Shafer	Emma E.	16 Feb.1901	
Howard	Carl C.	Young	Blanche	12 June 1911	
Howard	Charles E.	Glenn	Eda, Mrs.	12 Apr. 1905	
Howard	Clarence	Pruitt	Ethel June	22 Nov. 1910	gr: D. M. Howard, father; br: B. F. Pruitt, father
Howard	David Jackson	Cake	Mary Emma	15 Nov. 1905	
Howard	Emmett Robert	Goodwin	Mary Jane	28 Dec. 1904	

Groom Surname	Groom Given Name	Bride Surname	Bride Given Name	Date	Comments
Howard	Frank E.	Solomon	Ruth	27 Oct. 1919	
Howard	Frank M.	Melehan	Mae J.	27 Dec. 1900	
Howard	Frederick W.	Botts	Ethel	28 June 1916	
Howard	Harry	Baine	Dora	18 Jan. 1915	
Howard	Henry Ward	Sellon	Violet Mabel	2 Mar. 1917	
Howard	Horace A.	Corel	Jane	19 Oct. 1888	
Howard	James	Moore	Henrietta	19 Sept. 1881	
Howard	John B.	McCracken	Louisa	28 Sept. 1866	
Howard	John W.	Canell	Nellie Floy	16 Oct. 1907	
Howard	Phillip	Degardin	Clara	8 May 1909	
Howard	Raymond L.	Cofer	Lottie Edith	31 Dec. 1906	br: A. T. Cofer, parent
Howard	Roe Burdett	Saunders	Ada Henrietta	26 Apr. 1906	
Howard	Roeder M.	Randolph	Emma M.	15 Sept. 1917	
Howard	Vernon R.	Gonella	Mary	26 Dec. 1913	
Howard	W. H.	Yarbrough	Virginia J.	15 Jan. 1890	
Howard	William C.	Francischi	Teresa	18 Sept. 1893	
Howard	William W.	Shackelford	Mary Ida	5 Mar. 1921	
Howe	Asa A.	Daggett	Jennie N.	9 Dec. 1904	
Howe	Baxter	Morrison	Eliza A.	17 Apr. 1888	
Howe	Charles J.	Smith	Maud	27 Mar. 1886	
Howe	Chas. W.	Brown	Abbie E.	17 Oct. 1877	
Howe	James Henry	Howe	Frances	11 Sept. 1905	
Howe	Joseph	Miller	Ella L.	17 Dec. 1913	
Howe	Willard Earl	Conner	Jeannette Muriel	2 Oct. 1920	
Howell	Ambrose M.	Gardner	Dela May	1 Feb. 1897	
Howell	Frank M.	Sweetsen	Alice L.	8 Nov. 1906	
Howell	George	McDonald	Mary Jane	28 Aug. 1877	witness: John McClish
Howell	James Myras	Kelly	Mildred Edith	19 Mar. 1920	gr: F. E. Howell, father

		Bride		Date	Comments
Groom					
Surname	Given Name	Surname	Given Name		
Howell	Joseph L.	Ervin	Katie	5 Apr. 1867	
Howell	Louis V. H.	Johnson	Cora L.	19 Jan. 1897	
Howell	Olin Kenneth	Hahn	Lillian Genevieve	4 Nov. 1916	
Howell	Thomas Wm.	Burns	Anna J.	6 Oct. 1884	
Howell	W. E.	Kinner	Harriet B.	21 Sept. 1896	J. T. Coffman, witness
Howell	William	Gage	Laurina B.	10 Oct. 1895	
Howland	Gardiner G.	MacGregor	Jessie C.	20 Oct. 1904	
Howland	Thomas A.	McCloud	Rose, Mrs.	29 May 1901	br: she is widow
Hoyle	George Wilson	Dunn	Maggie Irene	28 Nov. 1906	
Hoyrup	Rasmus Nielson	Martin	Ida Mary	22 Nov. 1902	
Hoyt	Elijah	Jackman	T. A.	30 Sept. 1865	
Hoyt	Franklin Lowe	Barrows	Leah Louise	30 Dec. 1905	
Hoyt	Jesse D.	Wetmur	Olive M.	28 Oct. 1897	
Hubbard	Clyde H.	Steele	Ruth	25 July 1913	
Hubbard	George F.	Yakovleff	Catherine	13 Dec. 1895	
Hubbard	Henry	Moody	A. M., Mrs.	21 Mar. 1887	
Hubbard	James L.	Ray	Marie E.	20 Oct. 1920	
Hubbard	Junius H.	White	Rachel	7 Mar. 1919	
Hubbard	Pearl D.	Scott	Henrietta, Mrs.	8 Sept. 1900	br: widow
Hubbard	William B.	Geary	Helen J.	19 June 1920	
Hubbell	O. B.	Ames	Phebe E.	11 Sept. 1888	
Hubseh	Albin J.	Law	Elmira	9 Oct. 1882	
Hudelson	Warren S.	Long	Edna	8 Mar. 1879	
Huderson	Robert G.	Blair	Mary	19 Aug. 1904	
Hudson	Alvin P.	Hillmon	Katie	11 May 1894	
Hudson	Arthur T.	Johnson	Mary A., Mrs.	5 Aug. 1901	
Hudson	Clarence D.	Gibson	Lenore C.	7 June 1917	
Hudson	Daniel Bertnette	Tarwater	Emma Louisa	11 Oct. 1905	

Groom Surname	Groom Given Name	Bride Surname	Bride Given Name	Date	Comments
Hudson	David Hill	Jones	Abigal Akerley, Mrs.	3 May 1905	
Hudson	George R.	Elphick	Mattie E.	27 Dec. 1900	gr: requested by Kelsey S. Hudson, brother; do not publish until 5 Jan.
Hudson	H. R.	Levicy	Ethel	14 Mar. 1913	
Hudson	Henry F.	Herriford	Henrietta	27 Sept. 1884	
Hudson	James	Stevens	Mamie	13 Nov. 1890	gr: Nathan Sharp, guardian
Hudson	W. T.	Adams	Delcina, Mrs.	25 Feb. 1888	
Hudson	William H.	Brumfield	Priscilla	9 July 1881	br: J. S. Palmer, guardian
Hudson	Kelsey S.	Flecsher	Minnie R.	26 Feb. 1898	no previous marriage
Hudspeth	James M.	Johnston	Ethel E.	27 May 1920	
Huebner	Oscar Constantine	Jones	Ethel May, Mrs.	25 Feb. 1908	
Huff	Henry J.	Miller	Amelia	3 May 1890	
Huffman	Aaron	Peterson	Elsie	1 Apr. 1899	gr: Mrs. A. Huffman, mother; no previous marriage
Huffman	Daniel	Maxwell	Elizabeth Belle	24 Oct. 1907	
Huffman	Daniel	Pastorino	Rose Lee	14 June 1919	
Huffman	Eddie	Brewer	Bertha	15 Aug. 1891	gr: A. Huffman, parent
Huffman	Hezekiah	Stevens	Susie M., Mrs.	26 Apr. 1902	
Huffman	Jacob	Hayes	Clifton Clay	21 May 1904	
Huffman	James R.	Nelson	Violet Rose	17 Feb. 1913	
Huffman	W. H.	Turner	Laura A.	12 May 1894	
Hufner	Franz	Grand	Fannie	21 Feb. 1918	
Hughes	Alfred G.	Meyer	Julia T.	14 July 1899	br: requested license
Hughes	B. C.	Sutluff	Harriett	6 Jan. 1885	
Hughes	Charles T.	Shea	Ada	10 Apr. 1904	
Hughes	David E.	Shaumburg	Belle	17 Oct. 1908	
Hughes	Floyd B.	Luscher (?)	Marie G.	4 Sept. 1920	
Hughes	George	Haskell	Clista	30 Sept. 1905	

		Bride		Date	Comments
Groom					
Surname	**Given Name**	**Surname**	**Given Name**		
Hughes	George G.	Hall	Vista M.	18 June 1910	
Hughes	George W.	Smith	Clara I.	29 Sept. 1913	
Hughes	Henry F.	Boone	Renette Emogene	10 Feb. 1904	
Hughes	Hugh	Petre	Louise V.	6 June 1894	
Hughes	John Franklin	Egler	Anna Reynella	6 May 1912	
Hughes	John S.	Starbuck	Emma Grace	9 Nov. 1908	
Hughes	Judd	Benton	Alice	29 Sept. 1902	
Hughes	Louis D.	Weed	Edna M.	30 Mar. 1918	
Hughes	Michael J.	Brown	Leona	30 June 1913	
Hughes	Thomas M.	Upson	Kathryn	30 June 1920	
Hughes	William L.	Pannell	Frances M.	11 June 1919	
Hughett	Ernest Adolph	Carter	Annie Elizabeth	29 May 1920	
Huittmann	John O.	Lynch	Elizabeth F.	6 Apr. 1901	
Hulbert	Ansel C.	Davis	Bessie Smith	29 Dec. 1893	
Hulbert	Charles P.	Scott	Lola	13 Mar. 1905	license requested by bride
Hulbert	Clarence E.	Toal	Rosanna	15 Aug. 1908	
Hulbert	Harry E.	Martin	Effie, Mrs.	12 Feb. 1917	
Hulbert	Harry E.	Duncan	May Agnes	9 Apr. 1887	br: Noel Duncan, father
Hulbert	Hiram Perry	Hufstoder	Mary Belle	19 July 1877	
Hulbert	Marion O.	Endicott	Edythe E.	28 Oct. 1912	
Hull	Alonzo Clinton	Gifford	Evelyn Barnum	14 Aug. 1915	
Hull	Guy L.	Wilson	Reno	19 Sept. 1910	
Hull	Irving Melvin	Fechter	Esther Ella	19 Apr. 1917	
Hull	Jerome H.	Ross	Jennie	9 Mar. 1892	
Hull	Money Elliott	Hughes	Estella M.	24 Dec. 1918	gr: 572 Grove St., San Francisco; Anna Fleming, mother, she signs Anna Zewissler; br: 1019 King St., Santa Rosa; Nellie Hughes, mother

Groom Surname	Groom Given Name	Bride Surname	Bride Given Name	Date	Comments
Hull	Silas William	Johnson	Velmer Vermeta	23 Aug. 1916	br: Alice Johnson, mother
Hull	Wm. D.	Corey	Augusta	30 Dec. 1865	
Hullen	Peter H.	Elderkin	Edna M.	21 Sept. 1918	gr: 810 5th St., Santa Rosa; br: 919 Monroe St., Santa Rosa
Hulsey	John B.	Tabor	Bessie	21 Dec. 1916	
Hultgreen	Gustaf Olof	Evanson	Josie	27 Dec. 1906	
Hultgren	John A.	Garrison	Jennette J.	11 Jan. 1902	
Humbert	George H.	Davis	Carrie E.	23 June 1910	
Humbert	Charles E.	Hoadley	Ida L.	29 Dec. 1884	br: J. F. Hoadley, father
Hummer	William T.	Spofford	Edith E.	7 Nov. 1914	
Hundley	W. P.	Holland	Mary	24 Dec. 1895	
Huneke	Robert Carlisle	Cox	Irene	23 Sept. 1909	br: Mrs. Anna Eliza Cox, guardian
Hunger	Elmer G.	Anderson	May Etta	10 Nov. 1917	br: Almer P. Anderson, parent
Hunger	F. J.	Thorpe	Anna	4 Aug. 1903	
Hunken	John Carl	Hink	Catrina	21 Mar. 1908	
Hunkins	Lyle D.	McCord	Ruby D.	30 Jan. 1921	
Hunt	Arthur H.	Leeter (?)	Sadie E.	30 Oct. 1919	
Hunt	Avery G.	McDonald	Faith	31 Aug. 1910	
Hunt	B. W.	Harris	Sarah A., Mrs.	28 Jan. 1867	
Hunt	Byrd A.	Adams	Viola, Mrs.	24 Nov. 1890	br: widow
Hunt	Clyde E.	Price	Estella M.	24 June 1916	
Hunt	Edward Rowland	Eyton	Lilia A. C.	23 Apr. 1900	
Hunt	Elmer H.	Bostick	Louise M.	17 Apr. 1920	br: Mrs. Mercie Bostick, mother
Hunt	Eugene Warren	Weaver	Anna Alberta	9 Dec. 1912	
Hunt	Francis Willard	Pierce	Alice M.	14 Dec. 1880	
Hunt	George M.	Carter	Flora, Mrs.	10 Nov. 1904	
Hunt	George Walter	Wadsworth	Alice Maud	11 Mar. 1916	
Hunt	Joseph H.	Mock	Margaretta	28 Jan. 1891	

		Bride			
Groom				**Date**	**Comments**
Surname	**Given Name**	**Surname**	**Given Name**		
Hunt	Milton G.	Seward	Laura I.	8 Oct. 1915	
Hunt	Oscar L.	Davidson	Adele E.	28 Sept. 1916	
Hunt	Paul	Harris	Cora Bell	27 Oct. 1899	
Hunt	W. J.	Griffin	Ida, Mrs.	10 Mar. 1888	
Hunt	Warren E.	Douglass	Julia	27 Nov. 1886	handwritten; witness Chas. Douglas
Hunt	William C.	Litchfield	Anna M.	31 Mar. 1891	
Hunt	William Irvin	Doss	Emma A.	15 Jan. 1883	
Hunter	Eugene W.	Brooks	Leslie E. M.	21 July 1913	br: Mrs. E. R. Brooks, mother
Hunter	Grover C.	Denney	Emma C.	22 Dec. 1914	
Hunter	John J.	Casey	Anna J.	8 Jan. 1886	
Hunter	Rea Baron	Hauger	Perle	4 Oct. 1906	
Hunter	William Crittenton	Waite	Thenia	15 Oct. 1885	requested by Jas. L. Whitton
Huntington	Harry E.	McClellan	Elizabeth L.	8 Sept. 1920	
Huntington	Horace H.	Gregory	Martha M.	12 Dec. 1889	
Huntley	Albert	Bowers	Elizabeth A.	28 July 1906	
Huntley	George W.	Lindsy	Phoebe	21 June 1890	
Huntley	George W.	Fagie	Emma	1 Sept. 1900	
Huntley	John S.	Zumwalt	Dora	17 Oct. 1918	
Huntoon	J. R.	Melson	Josephine	31 July 1912	
Huntt (?)	George E.	Weigel	Esther D.	6 Aug. 1918	
Huph	Henry Philip	Bittner	Ella Emile	22 Apr. 1916	
Hupp	Roscoe E.	Hulbert	Laura Irene	12 Mar. 1921	
Hurlbert	Fred Yale	Curren	Annie	20 July 1907	
Hurlbert	Theron Louis	Jones	Estella Amanda	16 Aug. 1877	
Hurlburt	Robert H.	Prestwood	Delia	30 Mar.1893	
Hurlbutt	Willard A.	Hazelton	Ruth M.	31 Aug. 1918	
Hurley	Joseph	Ericksen	May	9 Oct. 1914	
Hurley	Thomas F.	Dempsey	Mary E.	15 July 1914	

Groom Surname	Groom Given Name	Bride Surname	Bride Given Name	Date	Comments
Hurst	Leslie E.	Roberts	Clara	6 June 1901	
Huskey	Everett	Forgett	Annabel	15 Oct. 1915	
Husler	Edward A.	Myers	Dora M.	26 Nov. 1894	
Huson	Willis O.	Haus	Margaret L. D.	30 June 1915	
Hussa	Walter H.	Donnelly	Elizabeth F.	1 Feb. 1913	
Hussey	Edward Otis	Connolly	Louise Bernidette	20 May 1905	
Hussey	William J.	Fountain	Ethel	27 June 1895	
Hussy (?)	Eugene	Clark	Emma Nettie	10 Oct. 1882	br: Mack C. & wife Clark, parents
Hustad	Paul L.	Kaufman	Elsie M.	29 Sept. 1915	
Hutchings	Edward Thomas	Wilder	Elizabeth Gertrude	16 Oct. 1906	
Hutchins	Horatio	Brown	Mary, Mrs.	30 July 1866	
Hutchins	Jasper Lawrence	Duncan	Bessie	29 Sept. 1906	gr: Mrs. W. H. Priest, mother
Hutchinson	David F.	Hutchinson	Clara D.	29 Oct. 1901	
Hutchinson	David Kyle	Lasher	Sarah Lela	13 Sept. 1910	br: George A. Lasher, father
Hutchinson	Edward Lincoln	Vosilotos	Louisa Agnes	31 Dec. 1910	gr: D. F. Hutchinson, parent
Hutchinson	F. A.	Christian	Mary A.	18 July 1882	
Hutchinson	Lawrence	Rich	Rose	7 July 1911	
Hutchinson	Oliver A.	Cartmel	Alice S.	8 July 1878	
Hutchison	Earnest E.	Carter	Sarah E.	9 Oct. 1901	br: Esther Carter, mother
Hutchison	Lawrence	Hanson	Eva	2 Mar. 1910	
Hutchison	Lawrence	Bone	Maud, Mrs.	28 Jan. 1899	Gr: 264 Golden Gate Ave., San Francisco; br: widow
Hutchison	Lester Earl	Hicks	Mary Nunn	16 Oct. 1907	gr: Wm. S. Hutchison, parent
Hutton	Daniel D.	Gregory	Mary, Mrs.	2 July 1902	
Hutton	George W.	Crutson	Angeline	25 Apr. 1896	witnessed by R. L. Thompson for X mark of groom
Hyatt	Garrett	Henningsen	Johanna, Mrs.	20 Aug. 1904	
Hyatt	John B.	Farmer	Margart, Mrs.		filed between 2 and 15 Jan. 1880

	Groom	Bride		Date	Comments
Surname	Given Name	Surname	Given Name		
Hyatt	Robert Roy	Gaston	Alta Mae	1 Dec. 1919	
Hyatt	Will Carlton	Wheeler	Nellie Ethel	4 Feb. 1907	
Hyde	William H., Jr.	Hope	E. Claire	25 July 1903	
Hyman	Frank J.	Ward	Cleone	24 Dec. 1912	
Hynes	Wm. H.	Gossage	Ellen C.	30 Apr. 1866	
Icanberry	John M.	Ellison	Edith	20 Sept. 1902	
Icanberry	William M.	Gage	Mabel	29 June 1895	br: Watrous A. Gage gives consent and signs.
Ielmorini	Thomas	Gambonini	Adeline	24 Jan. 1914	
Igom	Julius Petersen	Nelson	Christina	4 June 1909	
Ilg	Fred G.	Cardoza	Josephine M.	29 June 1914	
Imlay	Loren	Smith	Helen M.	2 Dec. 1889	
Imperiale	Gianni D.	Francchia	Josephine	3 July 1920	
Imrie	George Nicoll	Cooley	Katherine	20 June 1913	
Ingalls	John C.	Rickman	Amanda J.	21 Dec. 1892	
Ingalls	John C.	Livemach	Mary F.	17 Aug.1909	
Ingersoll	John W.	Frost	Emma M.	30 Dec. 1915	
Ingerson	Lewis Nelson	Mellington	Leoleon S.	15 Aug. 1914	
Ingham	A. H.	Sullivan	Prescella M.	19 July 1884	
Ingham	Arthur Blaine	Rowell	Helen Hale	11 June 1915	
Ingham	Arthur Cleveland	Meisner	Hattie	14 Apr. 1906	br: Mrs. E. H. Meisner, mother
Ingman	John V.	Porter	Katie May	7 Oct. 1914	
Ingraham	Edgar	McCurrie	Madeline E.	17 Sept. 1910	
Ingram	Charles L.	Merritt	Minnie E.	17 June 1885	handwritten
Ingram	Charles W.	Ewing	Gertrude	23 May 1887	
Ingram	Mercer E.	Hiatt	Madge C.	8 Mar. 1913	
Ingram	William F.	Stimmel	Cecelia	12 Apr. 1919	

Groom Surname	Groom Given Name	Bride Surname	Bride Given Name	Date	Comments
Inman	James Thomas	Stump	Carrie Annell (?), Mrs.	16 June 1908	
Insel	A.	Traeger	Mary E.	23 Oct. 1883	
Ireland	Claude C.	Boxold	Margaret E.	30 Oct. 1920	
Ireland	James David	Baker	Annie Elizabeth	18 Mar. 1908	
Irvin	John H.	Christy	Myrtle May	19 Mar. 1919	
Irving	John J.	Grearson	Ada	28 Oct. 1912	
Irving	Joseph O.	Crane	Ella A.	7 Mar. 1883	
Irwin	A. W.	Moody	Clara J.	17 June 1915	
Irwin	Joseph W.	Nobles	Hattie	2 May 1899	
Irwin	Nathaniel	Fan	Lenora	31 Dec. 1889	
Irwin	Robert	Davis	Elma Olive	28 Feb. 1907	
Irwin	Thomas Jackson	Johnson	Sarah Elizabeth	15 Oct. 1889	
Irwin	William M.	Wedde	Henrietta	17 Sept. 1895	
Isaacs	Ernest A.	Archer	Berdena E.	26 Apr. 1911	
Isaksen	Linfred	Peterson	Christine	27 Mar. 1912	
Isbell	Fred E.	Speegle	Lillian	31 Mar. 1909	
Isola	Alphonso	Arsnip	Sarah	10 Aug. 1885	br: John & Susan Arsnip, parents
Itter	William Henry	Mardon	Alta	13 Apr. 1906	
Ivarson	A. G.	Bergersen	Magdalena	16 Dec. 1911	
Iversen	Iver Alfred	Sandborn	Vira Ann	20 Dec. 1909	
Iverson	George	Eliasen	Johanne	9 Oct. 1909	
Iverson	Louis	Christensen	Karen O. M.	25 Apr. 1916	
Ives	Alfred	Nerton	Mattie, Mrs.	5 June 1909	
Ives	Alfred	Muller	Amanda Louise	29 June 1905	
Ives	William S.	Cominos	Johanna	21 Sept. 1907	
Izant	Percy Arthur	Jones	Ethel May	19 Sept. 1905	
Jacks	Lorenzo D.	Byington	Josephine S.	2 Apr. 1896	

		Bride		Date	Comments
Groom					
Surname	**Given Name**	**Surname**	**Given Name**		
Jackson	Amos	Maclath	Mary M.	24 Dec. 1866	
Jackson	Andrew	Jackson	Mina, Mrs.	29 Oct. 1902	gr: 1002 Polk St., San Francisco; br: 1002 Polk St., San Francisco
Jackson	Arthur V.	Bowe	Josephine	8 June 1900	
Jackson	Bernard	Powers	Nora	25 Sept. 1911	
Jackson	Bert	Lamonte	Idella	24 Jan. 1910	
Jackson	Carlisle P.	Conners	Nama V.	25 Apr. 1918	
Jackson	Charles F.	Shelford	Hanna Odessa	24 Dec. 1907	
Jackson	Clarence S.	Bringham	Arvilla May	21 Feb. 1918	
Jackson	E. N. B.	Wilkinson	Eva	19 May 1866	
Jackson	Elmer	Smith	Inez L.	12 Feb. 1912	
Jackson	Frank	Nay	Martha A.	31 Oct. 1887	
Jackson	Frank	Mason	Tressie B.	22 Sept. 1900	br: H. B. Mason, parent
Jackson	George Samuel	Carrillo	Ramona	23 June 1883	br: Julio Carrillo, father
Jackson	Guy H.	Gwin	Laura M.	10 Sept. 1901	
Jackson	Harry E.	Meeker	Clara E.	22 June 1912	
Jackson	Herbert L.	Salmon	Mabel C.	18 June 1917	
Jackson	Hugh L.	Shader	Nellie	19 Mar. 1894	
Jackson	John B.	Perkins	Cora	10 Mar. 1906	
Jackson	Luther	Wood	Minnie M.	8 Dec. 1886	
Jackson	Matt	Leon	Louise	20 May 1911	
Jackson	Parker L.	Harrington	Elise	6 Sept. 1898	no previous marriage
Jackson	Roy E.	Murray	Maud M.	21 Nov. 1911	gr: John B. Jackson, father
Jackson	W. Edward	Lawson	Dorothy B.	8 May 1915	
Jackson	William G.	Staup	Fannie B., Mrs.	3 Feb. 1917	
Jacob	Thomas	Burnham	Emily L.	11 May 1910	
Jacobs	Cameron	Story	Ida May	1 June 1906	
Jacobs	George	Looney	Alice	27 Mar. 1893	

Groom Surname	Groom Given Name	Bride Surname	Bride Given Name	Date	Comments
Jacobs	James B.	Bailey	Nina E.	1 July 1885	
Jacobs	Norman Francie	Hewald	Elfrida Katherine	30 Mar. 1918	
Jacobs	Price	Hooper	Annie T. ?	13 Nov. 1878	witness: A. M. Low
Jacobs	Walter Wyrt	Weber	Alma Pearl	11 Aug. 1905	
Jacobsen	Frederick	Walker	Katherine E.	31 Jan. 1921	
Jacobsen	Jacob C.	Nielsen	Anna	6 May 1916	
Jacobsen	Jacob E.	Thomsen	Johanna I.	14 Sept. 1909	
Jacobsen	Jacob E.	Martin	Dahmar	3 Oct. 1890	
Jacobsen	Neils L.	Hoirup	Sine C.	2 Oct. 1916	
Jacobsen	Niels	Stieper	Mary	14 Apr. 1914	
Jacobsen	Richard	Jacobsen	Hansine	27 Feb. 1907	filed in middle of Feb. 1908
Jacobsen	Thomas S.	Tronoff	Helena L.	2 July 1919	
Jacobsen	William Robert	Grindell	Hazel Evelyn	31 Oct. 1914	
Jacobson	Jens	Strome	Hilma	24 Nov. 1919	
Jacobson	Peter N.	Guerne	Grace E.	24 Nov. 1913	
Jacobson	Roy	Bressman	Genevieve	10 July 1917	
Jacquot	Alexander C.	Lineard	Louise I.	6 May 1919	
Jaeger	Jacob	Geisbuhler	Ida	29 May 1908	
Jahn	Henry	Morrison	Lulu	9 June 1896	
Jakober	Carl	Kiser	Matilda	20 Sept. 1907	
James	Burnie Edgar	Church	May Adeline	4 Dec. 1912	br: C. E. Church, parent
James	Charles G.	McCord	Henretta	7 Apr. 1888	
James	George A.	O'Callaghan	Mary	8 May 1916	
James	Henry W.	Doggutt	Georgie W.	5 May 1896	
James	John P.	Eichler	Ella, Mrs.	17 Dec. 1901	San Francisco papers please copy
James	Orie (?) Edward	Burgess (?)	Maud Stella	20 Nov. 1919	
James	R. L.	McDougall	Annie	10 Aug. 1887	
James	Thos. J.	Ward	Julia Ann	9 May 1885	

		Bride		Date	Comments
Groom					
Surname	**Given Name**	**Surname**	**Given Name**		
James	William A.	Harding	Jennie L.	15 Apr. 1904	
Jameson	Arthur Roy	Dahlmann	Georgia Wilma	15 Sept. 1917	
Jamieson	B. T.	Watson	Alvania	10 Dec. 1887	
Jamieson	Daniel J.	Moller	Thora A.	15 June 1907	
Jamieson	James	McQuade	Anna	14 June 1905	gr: I. F. McQuade, Thomas Cadden, witnesses to mark
Jamieson	John A.	Ehrhardt	Elvesta I.	7 Sept. 1914	
Jamison	H. H.	Shaver	Carrie I.	29 Sept. 1896	
Jansen	Martin H.	Hansen	Rosa L.	2 Nov. 1914	
Jansen	Philip R.	Scott	Cecilia Esther	31 July 1914	don't publish
Janssen	George	Brown	Lillie	28 Sept. 1901	do not publish [illegible date]
Jardin	Antonio Fernadis	Pereria	Carrolina Amaro	12 May 1913	gr: Allan Mollison, Manuel M. Barretto, witnesses to his mark
Jarred	George Carl	Butler	Clara	19 Dec. 1899	
Jarvis	Eugene L.	Berger	Ruth E.	19 Mar. 1907	
Jarvis	L. B.	Berger	Hattie E.	27 Dec. 1915	
Jarvis	Morgan	Nilansen	Hansine Helene	22 May 1886	
Jason	Anton	Switzer	Beryl	1 Dec. 1909	
Jason	Frank	Alves	Amelia	22 Sept. 1906	br: J. W. Ford, witness to mark
Jasper	Gustavus A.	Wells	Alice Maud	2 June 1890	br: S. Wells, parent
Jasper	Joseph John	Rasmussen	Sigris	29 Aug. 1913	
Jauke	Carl August	Reubold	Emma Antoinette	25 Apr. 1915	
Java	M. Murin (?)	Schultz	Anna	22 Jan. 1883	
Jayer (?)	Mentin (?)	Fouts	Emma A.	29 Jan. 1881	
Jeans	Newton	Baird	Mary	11 Dec. 1901	
Jeffery	Renaldo J.	Gould	Gladys V.	6 Sept. 1919	
Jeffress	James V.	Paget	Lulu G.	22 Aug. 1881	
Jeffress	John K.	Paget	Susie H.	22 Aug. 1881	

Groom Surname	Groom Given Name	Bride Surname	Bride Given Name	Date	Comments
Jeffreys	Thomas Leland	Schoonover	Ethel Verda	21 Oct. 1907	
Jelbert	Richard H.	Alves	Gladys Clark	30 Sept. 1919	
Jenkines	James H.	Weeks	Anna M.	5 Dec. 1891	
Jenkins	Allen	Pickens	Mary	1 Sept. 1920	
Jenkins	Arthur G.	Dunbar	Carrie B.	14 July 1908	
Jenkins	Charles Francis	Jones	Hazel Ann	5 Oct. 1915	
Jenkins	Edgar W.	Eslick	Ida B.	20 Aug. 1919	
Jenkins	Frederich G.	Glatfelder	Lenora M.	3 June 1912	
Jenkins	Gilbert C.	Watkins	Nellie	4 Sept. 1894	
Jenkins	Gilbert C.	Grodhauser	Mary	23 Feb. 1916	
Jenkins	Gilbert C.	Bergmann	Mary R.	18 Oct. 1911	
Jenkins	Henry	Liggett	Ora May	9 Oct. 1914	br: Zella Liggett, mother
Jenkins	Henry R.	Kimes	Ethel A. (Mandy)	3 Nov. 1902	gr: Gilbert C. Jenkins, father; br: Samuel C. Kines, father
Jenkins	Joseph	Folts	Kathryn Laura Frances	7 Apr. 1918	
Jenkins	Joseph L.	Moore	J. Maud	13 May 1893	
Jenkins	Joseph Warren	Platt	Blanch Elizabeth	21 May 1906	
Jenkins	William L.	Lafferty	Mary E.	19 Dec. 1903	
Jenne	Christian J.	Unger	Daphne E.	6 Oct. 1911	
Jennet	Newel	Jones	Rhoda L.	23 Dec. 1911	
Jennings	C. S.	Belgum	Marie	14 Mar. 1913	
Jennings	Edward B.	True	Eliza W.	11 Dec. 1909	
Jennings	John	Brennan	Florence M.	26 Apr. 1920	
Jennison	Alfred M.	Boswell	Clara J.	9 Oct. 1907	
Jensen	Alexander	Patton	Edna	1 Apr. 1892	
Jensen	Alfred J. P.	Kricke	Louisa Mary	9 July 1908	
Jensen	August Adolph	Wilson	Ethel Claire	24 July 1906	

	Groom	Bride		Date	Comments
Surname	**Given Name**	**Surname**	**Given Name**		
Jensen	Christ.	Christophersen	Josephine	22 Sept. 1896	
Jensen	Creston H.	Millerick	Helen E.	9 Sept. 1911	
Jensen	Fred P.	Geertz	Willhelmine C.	6 Oct. 1890	
Jensen	Fred Peter	Parkinson	Rosa L.	30 Dec. 1908	
Jensen	George P.	Ross	Lottie J.	17 Sept. 1901	
Jensen	Hans P.	Fairbanks	Loretta Louise	15 Jan. 1918	
Jensen	John P.	Gilson	Frieda L.	2 June 1917	
Jensen	Niels	Kjar	Helene	15 Feb. 1886	
Jensen	Peter	Hansen	Ingeborg Marie	20 Sept. 1916	
Jensen	Victor	Decker	Emma J.	1 Nov. 1911	gr: N. Jensen, parent
Jenson	Albert L.	Carsin	Margaret L.	4 Sept. 1911	
Jentzsch	Carl Waldemar	Murphy	Mabel Mary	10 Nov. 1894	br: age given as eighteen and two thirds.
Jepsen	Otto A.	Robinson	Irma G.	25 Nov. 1916	
Jepsen	Peter	Mattison	Mary	17 June 1885	
Jepson	Hans Alfred	Jensen	Lillian Johanna	10 July 1913	
Jerden	Arthur G.	Monsees	Jessie L.	14 June 1920	
Jessen	Adolph	La Vallee	Archange	8 Oct. 1912	
Jessen	Christopher B.	Latson	Rosilla	28 Aug 1907	
Jessen	Emil Thomas M.	Wilson	Margaret Jane	19 July 1909	
Jessen	Frank Edward	Clawsen	Minnie Josine	19 Oct. 1904	
Jessen	Julius Theodore	Clausen	Magdalena	7 Mar. 1901	
Jessen	Paul Frederick	Towner	Myrtle June	27 Sept. 1909	
Jessup	Charlie W.	Lloyd	Hattie F.	10 Aug 1907	
Jewell	Jesse I.	Brackett	Fannie E.	3 Jan. 1893	
Jewell	John Francis	Schulz	Elsie Anna	12 Aug. 1916	
Jewett	Augustus Leroy	Torliatt	Theresa	24 May 1909	
Jewett	Frank W.	Kennedy	Eva G.	24 Dec. 1894	
Jewett	Joseph Carl	Cooper	Hazel Grace	15 May 1909	

Groom Surname	Groom Given Name	Bride Surname	Bride Given Name	Date	Comments
Jinks	William Woods	Bartlow	Mary Elizabeth	17 Aug. 1912	br: Emma C. Bartlow, mother
Jobe	Alfred Ewing	Hillyer	Lillian Belle	3 Sept. 1904	
Jobe	Thomas F.	Tomasi	Linda O.	3 Jan. 1918	
Jobe	Thomas Frederick	Dabney	Rose Zelma	7 Mar. 1910	
Johannes	Herman	Koegler	Elisabeth	23 Oct. 1915	
Johannsen	Clyde M.	Williams	Ethel	29 Mar. 1920	
Johannsen	Edward Henry	LaVine	Adelaide	4 Nov. 1895	br: Mrs. M. R. Cady, aunt, gives consent and signs on behalf of deceased mother and unnamed father who lives in NY.
Johannsen	George Henry	Pedersen	Meta Marien	10 Oct. 1904	
Johansan	Axel A.	Cohn	Anna	19 Dec. 1919	
John	Charley	Youh (?)	M.	1 Sept. 1880	
John	Gregory	Casey	Catharine	13 Nov. 1866	
Johns	Cecil D.	Wilson	Bertha L.	11 Oct. 1901	
Johns	Frank M.	Coon	Stella L.	8 May 1911	br: Harriet Coon. mother
Johns	Frederick	Blanck	Katherine M.	10 Apr. 1916	
Johns	Harvey Raymond	Banks	Helen Grace	1 Nov. 1905	
Johns	Robert C.	Jensen	Alma C.	6 Jan. 1917	
Johns	Watson L.	Collister	Vivienne E.	25 June 1917	
Johnson	A. R.	Burger	Alta	24 Dec. 1912	
Johnson	Adolph	Cole	Elsie Rachel	16 July 1904	
Johnson	Alfred R.	Shooks	Sarah	29 Jan. 1894	
Johnson	Andrew E.	Bidwell	M. Callie	20 Feb. 1893	br: consent given by father, John Bidwell
Johnson	Archibald M.	Clover	Minnie C.	26 Jan. 1892	
Johnson	Charles D. G.	Graeter	Emma	21 June 1890	
Johnson	Charles L.	Coffer	Lucy A.	15 Feb. 1885	
Johnson	Charles W.	Reynolds	Ida M.	3 Apr. 1919	
Johnson	Claude E.	Cheney	Clara	4 June 1898	

	Groom	Bride		Date	Comments
Surname	Given Name	Surname	Given Name		
Johnson	Cornelius M.	Cox	Alice Almira	27 June 1903	
Johnson	D. W.	Banks	Emma A.	18 July 1888	
Johnson	David A.	Miller	Julia	21 Dec. 1882	br: divorced from David Miller; Sonoma Co.
Johnson	David E.	McReynolds	Delia	29 May 1897	
Johnson	David Q.	Ballou	Margaret J.	27 Nov. 1899	
Johnson	Demus Gale	Hanlon	Mae Elizabeth	29 Mar.1910	
Johnson	Dudley H.	Blank	Ismpie (?)	24 (?) May 1884	
Johnson	Edwin L.	Saylor	Fern L.	14 Apr. 1916	br: Mrs. C. E. Saylor, mother
Johnson	Elmo A.	Daniels	Lula M.	28 Nov. 1902	
Johnson	Ernest	Lauteren	Gertrude C.	27 Sept. 1919	
Johnson	Frank Eugene	Park	Edith Rae	3 July 1907	
Johnson	Frederick	Kemper	Josephine	10 Dec. 1914	
Johnson	Geo. A.	Matthews	Frances B.	8 Oct. 1888	
Johnson	George C.	Bona	Annie E.	30 June 1920	
Johnson	George W.	Guntly	Lizzie	25 Apr. 1892	
Johnson	Glen	Wilson	Helen	30 Nov. 1918	
Johnson	Gus Charles	Schrub	Evlyn Violet	23 Mar. 1914	
Johnson	Gus Charles	McCutcheon	Elizabeth	2 Sept. 1918	
Johnson	Harrick T.	Baker	Ethel F.	22 July 1914	
Johnson	Harry	Johns	Stella	6 June 1919	
Johnson	Henry	Wagenblast	Alice E.	24 June 1895	
Johnson	Henry Lee	Shreeve	Angie	5 Sept. 1906	br: Ben Shreeve, father
Johnson	Howard B.	Smith	Sadie V.	29 Sept. 1911	
Johnson	James	McIntosh	Clara	14 Sept. 1908	
Johnson	James E.	McGlynn	Alice A.	6 Sept. 1890	
Johnson	James F.	Rose	Clara I.	19 Sept. 1919	
Johnson	James George, Jr.	Rosetta	Alice	27 Oct. 1877	

	Groom	Bride		Date	Comments
Surname	Given Name	Surname	Given Name		
Johnson	James W.	Lee	Emma	20 Aug. 1888	
Johnson	John	Crilly	Anna Francis	28 Oct. 1880	br: N. & Ellen Crilly, parents; Ellen signed with her mark
Johnson	John A.	Phelps	Bessie E.	14 July 1888	
Johnson	John Berger	Bond	Jessie Mae	31 May 1912	
Johnson	John Christian	Gardener	Edith Luella	23 Aug. 1913	
Johnson	John F.	Fredricks	Carrie	16 Nov. 1900	
Johnson	John H.	Gunner	Anna	5 May 1920	
Johnson	John Leroy	Roberts	Lucy M.	19 Dec. 1919	
Johnson	John P.	Murroy	Mary R.	2 Oct. 1880	
Johnson	John W.	Jacobson	Marie E.	17 Sept. 1914	
Johnson	Karl V?klar (?)	Smith	Nellie E.	16 Mar. 1918	
Johnson	L. M.	Marshall	Elizabeth Ann	11 Nov. 1875	br: Henry & Mary J. Marshall, parents, Analy, Sonoma County
Johnson	L. M.	Marshall	Elizabeth Ann	11 Nov. 1871	br: Mary J. & Henry Marshall
Johnson	Louis Webseter	Hull	Edna Odell	28 Mar. 1913	gr: Emma Johnson, mother
Johnson	Martin	Barnett	Nettie J.	23 Dec. 1895	
Johnson	Martin L.	Ruddock	Kittie M.	14 Oct. 1913	
Johnson	Milton H.	Andrews	Lucile M.	12 Jan. 1921	
Johnson	Nels A.	Wheeler	Vera	7 June 1916	
Johnson	Ober J.	Barry	Alice E.	24 June 1915	
Johnson	Okey	Robbins	Myrtle	23 Oct. 1909	br: Florence Robbins, mother
Johnson	Omar H.	Daniels	Myrtle A.	29 Mar. 1915	gr: W. M. Johnson; parent br: Siles Daniels, parent
Johnson	Otto H.	McQuart	Emily	21 June 1879	requested by Robert McGeorge
Johnson	Otto Henry	Seabright	Elice	29 Apr. 1905	
Johnson	Peter S.	Miller	Emma C.	23 Aug. 1919	
Johnson	Phillip F.	Gilmore	Cassie B.	7 Feb. 1893	

		Bride			
Groom				Date	Comments
Surname	Given Name	Surname	Given Name		
Johnson	Ray I.	Ristan	Edna M.	13 June 1914	br: Irene E Ristan, mother
Johnson	Raymond	Kriedell	Elsie	19 Feb. 1903	
Johnson	Robert N.	Cavanough	Nettie A.	15 Apr. 1918	
Johnson	Samuel K.	Johnson	Evie, Mrs.	8 Oct. 1901	br: widow
Johnson	Thomas J.	Crawford	Sarah J.	14 Dec. 1889	
Johnson	Vernon L.	Kennedy	Ethel L.	7 Apr. 1915	
Johnson	Walter J.	Comaich	Louise	17 Jan. 1899	
Johnson	Webster	Smith	Sylvia Lee	9 Dec. 1916	
Johnson	Will E.	Heinrich	Matilda C.	4 Nov. 1896	
Johnson	William	Lusk	Kate	18 Apr. 1877	
Johnson	William A.	May	Delia A.	14 June 1888	
Johnson	William B.	Carle (?)	Catherine R.	11 July 1883	
Johnson	William R.	Ross	Viola A.	14 June 1916	
Johnson	Williard H.	Chevalier	Marguerite	28 May 1920	
Johnston	Alexander C.	Nutter	Lizzie A.	14 Nov. 1889	
Johnston	Charles B.	Goodspeed	Georgia, Mrs.	26 Dec. 1883	
Johnston	Richard I.	Ballard	Effie E., Mrs.	8 Dec. 1902	
Johnston	Wm. F.	McCorkle	Mary M.	3 Oct. 1865	
Johnstone	Ralph S.	Ross	Sue A.	25 Sept. 1920	
Johnstone	Thomas Henry	Mills	Anna Margrett	25 June 1878	
Johr ?	Carlton	Gott	Nancy	18 May 1865	
Jones	Alfred Benoia	Mothorn	Herma Booth	18 July 1916	
Jones	Alvie N.	Makee	Alvia C.	26 Aug. 1919	
Jones	Brainerd	Gibson	Jeanette S.	21 Nov. 1900	
Jones	Cethil	Day	Laura	21 Oct. 1916	
Jones	Charles	Dorman	Sarah Ada	15 Aug. 1876	witness: W. C. Crane
Jones	Charles H.	Morter	Hattie	25 Jan. 1878	
Jones	Charles W.	Warden	Ella M.	11 Sept. 1920	

Groom Surname	Groom Given Name	Bride Surname	Bride Given Name	Date	Comments
Jones	Claude O.	Hall	Georgia May	18 Apr. 1919	
Jones	Clifford W.	Shaw	Gertrude M.	7 Aug. 1915	
Jones	Earl Petwin	Shinn	Annie	16 Nov. 1906	
Jones	Edward Robert	Adams	Iva May	31 Aug. 1906	
Jones	Edward T.	Darden	Rosa Belle	31 Dec. 1883	br: George Darden, father
Jones	Ervon	Olts	Myrtle	19 Oct. 1912	
Jones	Evan	Yager	Barbara	23 Apr. 1888	
Jones	George B.	Reilly	Zel G.	15 June 1920	
Jones	George F.	Wood	Alta L.	6 May 1898	no previous marriage
Jones	George H.	Lowe	Jennie E.	30 Jan. 1889	
Jones	George H.	Isenburg	Hazel G.	25 Nov. 1914	
Jones	George Richard	Davison	Bertha Olive	28 Jan. 1907	
Jones	Harlold M.	Shaw	Ella L.	25 Nov. 1895	
Jones	Henry	Derrick	Lydia	6 Sept. 1906	
Jones	Henry M.	Yeager	Eulalia M.	18 Sept. 1902	
Jones	Homer A.	Allen	Mattie M.	16 July 1883	
Jones	Houston	Reynolds	Bertha	31 May 1893	
Jones	James L.	Brown	Leatha M.	10 Aug. 1920	
Jones	James Lloyd	Peterson	Elizaabeth Cordelia	25 Apr. 1917	
Jones	John P.	Burke	Mabel P.	24 May 1900	
Jones	Joseph C.	Lynch	Frances A., Mrs.	25 Oct. 1901	
Jones	Josiah	Barnes	Sarah Baronetta	15 Oct. 1874	
Jones	Lester	Purrington	Ethel	15 June 1915	
Jones	Lewis E.	Cook	Daisy M.	3 Dec. 1910	
Jones	Lewis Eugene	Upson	Ella Evaline	6 July 1897	
Jones	Lucas M.	Hollingsworth	Mabel	26 Aug. 1918	
Jones	Lyman C.	Hollar	Harriet Ethel	27 June 1896	br: Iradell W. Hollar gives consent. Witnessed by R. L. Thompson

	Groom	Bride		Date	Comments
Surname	**Given Name**	**Surname**	**Given Name**		
Jones	McMillan	Gilbert	Caroline	2 Mar. 1907	
Jones	Milton	Hansen	Mary C.	4 Jan. 1897	
Jones	Nathan H.	Atkinson	Mary M.	18 Oct. 1913	gr: J. H. Jones, parent
Jones	Noah	Beedle	Bella	22 Dec. 1884	
Jones	Oscar R.	Clos	Rose L.	26 Apr. 1919	
Jones	Parker W.	Peachey	Julia H.	17 July 1919	
Jones	Patrick C.	Mullally	Catherine E.	25 Oct. 1890	
Jones	Richard	Burgess	Mary Alice	17 Oct. 1891	
Jones	Richard H.	Jones	Martha, Mrs.	26 Apr. 1897	br: widow; gr: widower
Jones	Samuel	Koch	Kate Anna	10 June 1905	
Jones	Seth W.	Minch	Marguerite W.	18 Mar. 1918	
Jones	Smith Petitt	Gilmer	Eulalia	2 Jan. 1920	
Jones	Thomas A.	Cozine	Charlotte M.	5 Sept. 1910	
Jones	Thomas W.	Lee	Helen L.	17 Oct. 1891	
Jones	Walter	Knapp	Alice B., Mrs.	1 Feb. 1899	both widowed
Jones	William	Hansberg	Catherine	10 Apr. 1883	
Jones	William Farrington	Irwin	Mettie M.	29 June 1889	
Jones	William H.	Keiser	Lena M.	6 Nov. 1915	
Jones	William H.	Dabney	Melissa M.	6 May 1912	
Jones	William L.	Armstrong	Elizabeth	19 Mar. 1901	
Joosten	Fred W.	Maas	Helene	10 Jan. 1896	
Joppini	Joseph	Rhigetti	Velina	25 Nov. 1893	br: last name could be Velina and first name Rhigetti
Jordan	Harvey S.	O'Meara	Julia A.	13 July 1898	
Jordon	Addison D.	Westenhaver	M. E.	14 Dec. 1865	
Jorgensen	Anton M.	Schroeder	Anna M.	6 May 1918	
Jorgensen	Harry I.	Uhlenberg	Catherine M.	8 Apr. 1920	
Jorgensen	John	Rasmussen	Nell	6 May 1914	

Groom Surname	Groom Given Name	Bride Surname	Bride Given Name	Date	Comments
Jorgensen	Julius	Clark	Eva R.	8 Apr. 1898	
Jorgensen	Robert	Giesen	Elsa	17 Jan. 1917	
Jorgenson	Peter C.	Sinclair	Clara M.	18 Aug. 1899	gr: widower
Joseph	Alfred Peter	James	Hattie	1 Nov. 1902	
Joseph	Joe William	Chandler	Ethel	10 May 1907	
Joseph	Tony Peters	Williams	Mary	23 Feb. 1906	
Joseph	William	Irwin	Gladys	7 Mar. 1914	
Josephson	Frederick	Madsen	Emelie	9 Jan. 1897	
Josselyn	Joel S.	Andrews	Carrie E.	8 Sept. 1903	
Jossler	Chris	Davaz	Agnes	9 Feb. 1894	
Jouker (?)	G. G.	Lambert	Nevada	26 July 1883	
Joy	William H.	Wieberts	Kate, Mrs.	28 Feb. 1900	
Joyce	George E.	Regli	Frances	4 June 1919	br: Elizabeth Jones, mother
Judd	Charles A.	Wheeler	Julie	16 June 1910	
Judd	Percy L.	Fredericksen	Laura B.	30 Sept. 1918	
Judsen	George Franklin	Menefee	Victoria	21 Sept. 1876	br: witness: J. S. Menefee
Juler	George Albert	Bond	Bertha Elizabeth	27 Oct. 1906	
Julin	Adolf	O'Neil	Susan, Mrs.	24 May 1901	
June	H. J.	Vestal	Blossom	18 July 1911	
Junge	Walter Frederick	Bischoff	Albertine Louise	24 Nov. 1920	
Junge	Albert Frank Henry	Rust	Madeval Pearl	25 Apr. 1914	
Junker	Clarence M.	Payne	Mary	30 June 1919	
Jurd	Andrew J.	Adams	Rose A.	25 Sept. 1889	
Jurs	Louis	Wollitz	Leopoldine Christine	3 July 1911	
Justi	William Alfred	Roberts	Laura Lavina	21 July 1896	
Justice	Augustus Lorenzo	Stevens	Emma Edith	8 May 1896	
Justine	Frank	Perry	Gussie	3 Oct. 1894	br: Joseph M. Perry, father, consents to marriage and signs

	Groom		Bride	Date	Comments
Surname	Given Name	Surname	Given Name		
Juzix	Chester L.	Nunes	Mary A.	26 Oct. 1914	
Kaelin	Edward	Huber	Amalia	23 Oct. 1900	
Kahler	William T.	Moseley	Lilly Olive	12 June 1899	
Kahrs	Leander A.	Lind	Alma B.	10 July 1893	
Kahrs	Lee A.	Gully	Ibie	15 Nov. 1900	
Kaiser	Frank M.	Schwab	Clare L.	20 Feb. 1909	
Kaiser	William Henry, Jr.	Starke	Agatha Augusta	2 Sept. 1916	
Kalb	August L.	Parsons	Mary E., Mrs.	17 Aug. 1895	
Kalish	William G.	Husler	Lena M.	20 Apr. 1911	
Kammeyer	Erich M.	Luttrell	Leita Lorine	17 Jan. 1914	
Kamp	Daniel W.	Wergand	Loretta M.	17 Aug. 1912	
Kane	John J.	Ross	Julia	16 Sept. 1891	
Kane	John W.	Stone	Judith A.	13 May 1876	br: Rilen & Rachel Stone, give permission
Kane	Thomas	Bauer	Valesea C.	8 Sept. 1917	
Kanode	John O.	Stouder	Helen M.	4 Sept. 1917	
Karcher	Myron M.	Thompson	Cecile C.	15 Sept. 1920	please do not publish
Karnes	Ernest	Steger	Daisy	6 Oct. 1897	
Karnes	Forest V.	Johnson	Lizzie May	5 Dec. 1896	gr: Parents J. C. Karnes and Francis L. Karnes give consent; Witness: Frank S. Rhoads
Karnes	Percy	Ward	Nellie Lorain	16 May 1903	gr: J. E. Karnes, parent
Karpfenstein	Jacob	Schatz	Magdelena	17 Jan. 1890	
Karr	Bert M.	Snyder	Carrie	11 May 1904	
Kastens	Herman J. C.	Pfile	Clara A.	29 May 1908	
Katen	William L.	Tozer	Iva M.	1 Mar. 1917	br: Albert B. Tozer, father
Kathriner	Paul	Kiser	Josephine	19 Oct. 1912	
Katterfield	Julius Charles Peter	Cunningham	Jennie	7 May 1906	

Groom Surname	Groom Given Name	Bride Surname	Bride Given Name	Date	Comments
Katz	Harry H.	Murphy	Frances M.	14 Apr. 1915	license not issued; want to be married in San Francisco
Katz	Robert	Pinkus	Tillie	14 Apr. 1915	
Kauffman	John	McPhee	Kattie	31 Oct. 1884	
Kavanagh	James	Morrisey	Margaret	7 Dec. 1891	
Kaye	Charles Ivan	Thompson	Thelma Gertrude	9 May 1913	
Kayser	Albert H. L.	Seeman	Bertha	8 Nov. 1900	
Kean	J. B.	Wilson	Serena A.	1 Oct. 1884	
Keane	Frederick J.	Kenyon	Alice	24 Nov. 1915	
Kearns	James	Hespe	Mabel Augusta	11 Jan. 1908	
Keating	William Joseph	Brown	Cecilia Frances	16 Oct. 1920	
Keaton	John J.	Phinney	Harriet	10? July 1877	
Keaton	Wheeler M.	Clover	Martha J.	7 Feb. 1885	
Kee	George Hamilton	Dodge	Alice Mae	20 Oct. 1915	
Kee	James H.	Patterson	Tony	14 Nov. 1891	
Kee	James Hamilton	Banks	Maud Eveline	15 Feb. 1909	
Keechler	Bloss F.	Alexander	Lily M.	28 Oct. 1920	
Keefe	Jack S.	Kaiser	Grace	22 Nov. 1919	
Keefe	Thomas	Lenihan	Elsie Mae	31 Aug. 1909	
Keegan	William D.	Payne	Adelia M.	26 Dec. 1919	
Keeler	Nedwyn	Stearns	Edythe Belle	8 June 1911	gr: Margaret Keeler, mother
Keeley	Thomas H.	Norris	Celia E.	4 Dec. 1894	
Keeling	Frederick	Temple	Mary Hutton	18 May 1906	
Keenan	George	Ansbro	Sabrina	9 June 1886	
Keenan	Peter	McGoldrich	Mary T.	22 June 1912	
Keenan	Walter H.	Clement	Loma (?)	5 June 1920	
Keener	John E.	Lewis	Rachal E.	28 June 1879	gr: Mrs. Elen Keener, mother
Keig	William C.	Ackerman	Harriet B.	29 Aug. 1902	

	Groom		Bride		
Surname	Given Name	Surname	Given Name	Date	Comments
Keig	William C.	Graham	Alice G.	10 Jan. 1912	
Keig	William S.	Zeller	Stella R.	31 Mar. 1921	
Keim	Frederick C.	Rider	Marie	2 Oct. 1916	
Keir	Sherwin	McNabb	B. M.	2 July 1903	
Keirn (?)	Henry W.	Stump	Martha E.	29 Jan. 1881	br: Conrad Stump, father
Keiser	Joseph	Garzoli	Dora H.	21 Oct. 1919	
Keithly	Seth T.	Pugh	Sarah A.	21 Feb. 1865	
Keleher	Wm. Thomas	O'Connor	Nora	23 Apr. 1878	
Kelleher	Cornelius	Foley	Mary Josie	9 Jan. 1906	
Keller	Charley C.	Brisino	Mabel	4 Aug. 1903	
Keller	J. Bryant	Ward	Gertrude	14 Mar. 1911	
Keller	John	Burgett	Laura	13 July 1903	
Keller	John Claus	Clanton	Victoria Alice	31 July 1909	br: Lottie M. Tipton, mother
Keller	Peter	Albers	Emma	10 July 1897	license requested by D. E. Albers
Keller	Vernon E.	MacUrton	Ethel	14 Dec. 1920	
Kelley	George F.	Nelson	Violet	8 May 1907	
Kelley	John Asbery	Rupprecht	Mary Annie	30 June 1906	
Kellner	Harold C.	Chapman	Martha	1 Oct. 1919	
Kellogg	Edward L.	Barringer	Matilda	16 Nov. 1920	
Kellogg	Grant L.	Covert	Gladys	4 Oct. 1913	gr: Lillian Kellogg, mother; br: George W. Covert, father
Kellogg	Harold G.	Cooper	Zella R.	1 May 1920	
Kellogg	W. L.	Holcomb	F. M.	10 Apr. 1883	
Kelly	C. E.	Cook	Neva	29 Jan. 1920	br: R. F. Cook, parent
Kelly	David	Kirkland	Lizzie	30 Aug. 1904	br: W. J. Kirkland, parent
Kelly	George Thomas	Lawler	Elsie Margaret	5 Aug. 1915	
Kelly	Henry Clay	Ashcraft	Edith	21 May 1895	
Kelly	James H.	Leck	Alis	30 Sept. 1908	

Groom Surname	Groom Given Name	Bride Surname	Bride Given Name	Date	Comments
Kelly	James P.	Matthews	Myrtle	19 Dec. 1896	
Kelly	John H.	Philbes	Margaret J.	24 Aug. 1887	
Kelly	Joy	Jones	Edith Margarette	2 Dec. 1905	
Kelly	Mark P.	Nichols	Ida C.	7 Sept. 1895	
Kelly	Mark P.	Bellah	Viola N.	12 Oct. 1900	
Kelly	Michael F.	Mackinnon	Grace May	20 Dec. 1915	
Kelly	Thomas Lamb	Bice	Sarah	4 Jan. 1878	
Kelly	William S.	Bell	Maggie E.	3 Nov. 1888	
Kelsey	Earl Ellsworth	Wilson	Austie Lea	14 Jan. 1918	
Kelsey	Edwin Joseph	Light	Emily Hida	10 Feb. 1915	
Kelso	Edgar Clayton	McDougall	Louise	23 July 1910	
Kelton	Clarence F.	Abraio	Marie K.	14 Nov. 1910	
Kemler	Andrew C.	Maxwell	Lillian J.	10 Dec. 1919	
Kemp	Harry Walter	Schendel	Maude Alice	7 Apr. 1916	
Kemp	Joseph	Johnson	Julia	18 Apr. 1903	br: Elisha Johnson, parent
Kendall	Albert Kuy (?)	Melson	Mary Ann	9 Aug. 1875	
Kendall	James	Warren	Bessie E.	4 June 1888	br: William Warren, father
Kenna	Richard	Findlay	Katherine Mary	25 Jan. 1917	
Kenneally	James	Meyers	Addie	8 July 1904	
Kenneally	William Joseph	McClure	Neva	13 Nov. 1905	
Kennedy	C. A.	Emmerson	Delia M.	1 July 1893	
Kennedy	Charles	Hartin	Mary	1 Mar. 1879	br: consent of father
Kennedy	Charles E.	Adams	LaVerne I.	11 Feb. 1921	
Kennedy	Charles W.	Wood	Allie S.	25 Apr. 1888	
Kennedy	Charles Warren	Ingram	Addie Bell	14 Sept. 1889	
Kennedy	David S.	Hicks	Hattie	4 May 1882	
Kennedy	Ebert L.	Hunter	Lola	4 June 1892	

		Bride		Date	Comments
Groom					
Surname	**Given Name**	**Surname**	**Given Name**		
Kennedy	Edward H.	Herman (?)	May Rose	3 July 1913	gr: W. E. Saunders, H. W. Sliler, witnesses to his mark
Kennedy	Elbert L.	Edwards	Lizzie	15 Aug. 1898	gr: divorced more than one year
Kennedy	Floyd	Manning	Evelyn L.	12 Apr. 1921	
Kennedy	Joseph Edward	Ingram	May	4 June 1906	
Kennedy	Willard B.	Perrin	Alice Hollcroft	5 May 1920	
Kennedy	William A.	Werner	Nora, Mrs.	4 Nov. 1907	
Kennedy	William H.	Brown	Mary		filed between 11 and 14 July 1879
Kenney	Martin G.	Soedler	Emma B.	26 Nov. 1920	
Kent	William Charles	Dolan	Maria	5 Apr. 1876	witness: Joseph K. Porter (?)
Kent	Wm. C.	Curtman	Emily	12 May 1865	
Kentzell	James	Murphy	Francis	5 Jan. 1900	gr: 132 1/2 Broadway, San Francisco; requested by J. M. Cassin
Keown	George W.	Ort	Rosa H.	26 Nov. 1889	
Keppel	Fred E.	Cook	Gertrude	30 Sept. 1902	
Ker	Robert M.	Heath	Maude Blanche	7 Dec. 1901	
Keran	J. N.	Torance	Sarah	22 Mar. 1878	requested by A. P. Keran
Kerbey	S. A.	Paulsen	Gwinna M. J.	30 Aug. 1915	
Kerfoot	Lester R.	Sheffer	L. Etta	10 Dec. 1919	
Kerman	Arthur Thomas	Smith	Minnie Alice	24 June 1916	do not publish in San Francisco
Kern	Harry A.	Gilkey	Esther F.	23 Mar. 1915	
Kern	Wm.	Morrow	Maria A.	9 Feb. 1881	
Kerner	Albert G.	Fisher	Louisa	17 Sept. 1891	
Kerner	Henry R.	DuCommun	Lillian E.	10 June 1916	
Kerney	Joseph J.	Redmond	Loretta M.	17 Nov. 1897	no previous marriage
Kerr	James A.	Wuthrich	Antoinette L.	15 Apr. 1917	
Kerr	Newton	Wesson	Justice O.	27 July 1914	
Kerrick	Walter Armstead	Carlson	Lillian Emma	29 July 1915	

Groom Surname	Groom Given Name	Bride Surname	Bride Given Name	Date	Comments
Kerrison	W. W.	Risk	Sarah	28 May 1896	
Kertz	Herbert Joseph	Searey	Laura Joseph	27 June 1909	
Kesler	Jackson	Lamb	Nora	28 Apr. 1871	br: Mrs. Lamb, mother; father being dead
Kessack	John Douglas	Pedrotti	Mary Olivia	10 Feb. 1908	
Kessing	Clemens	Hornbeck	Catherine, Mrs.	17 Apr. 1889	br: widow
Ketcham	Clarence S.	Muller	Marie B.	6 July 1908	gr: Julia A. Ketcham, mother
Ketcham	Lona I.	Harris	Ivy	10 Jan. 1903	br: Richard Alexander Harris, father
Ketcham	Orven C.	Ward	Katie E.	30 Sept. 1901	
Ketelsen	Ocke	Crogan	Elizabeth	15 Oct. 1887	
Kettendorff	Otto J.	Dayton	Pearl	15 Apr. 1914	gr: Max Catendo aka Max Kettendorff, father
Ketterlin	Auguste D.	DeBolt	Lucy H.	1 Aug. 1908	
Kettlewell	Benjamin	Mallory	Edith M.	18 Mar. 1914	
Kettlewell	Richard S.	Duncan	Estelle	19 Dec. 1903	
Kettlewell	William W.	Goodman	Idell L.	20 Oct. 1900	
Kevan	Frank Charles	Pauly	Helen	13 Aug. 1915	
Keyes	John M.	Luebberke	Dora	11 Feb. 1896	
Keyes	Ralph E.	Muthall	Bernice Josie	22 Sept. 1911	
Keykendall	Henry Clay	Thrush	Nettie	22 Sept. 1877	
Keys	Samuel H.	Torrence	Mary E.	18 Oct. 1893	
Kidd	David W.	Black	Mary M.	6 Aug. 1892	
Kidd	Edward Martin	Williams	Maud Jeannette	30 July 1903	
Kidd	Joseph L.	Pickle	Bernice E.	17 Apr. 1912	don't publish
Kidd	William H.	Aldridge	Lulu G.	22 July 1899	gr: widower
Kidwell	Henry C.	Hawes	Estella M.	14 Sept. 1920	
Kidwell	Paul M.	Strahan	Emily A.	17 July 1916	
Kiester	Charles C.	Butler	Rosa E.	4 Oct. 1888	br: James H. & Sarah M. Butler, parents
Kietsinger	George W.	Annike (?)	Minnie	13 Dec. 1882	

Groom		Bride		Date	Comments
Surname	**Given Name**	**Surname**	**Given Name**		
Kilcourse	John Martin	Jessup	Juanita	27 Jan. 1902	not to be published
Killits	George H.	Kamp	Nellie N.	25 Apr. 1905	
Kimball	Heman A.	McDonald	Dora D., Mrs.	29 Sept. 1894	br: widow
Kimball	Jerry Whitney	O'Leary	Mary	4 Aug. 1877	br: Thomas O'Leary, father, Santa Rosa
Kimball	William N.	Schlam	Grace M.	7 Oct. 1912	
Kimble	Thomas H.	Clarke	Sibyl G.	26 Dec. 1900	
Kimes	A. L.	Ross	Alice	21 Dec. 1887	
Kimes	D. M.	Hanson	Cora	29 Apr. 1885	br: Sarah Hanson, mother
Kimes	Edward Thomas	Tomblinson	Hazel Loreta	17 Oct. 1907	
Kimes	Rufus Lee	Jones	Georgana	9 Nov. 1904	
Kimes	Walter H.	Meredith	Blanche P.	30 Oct. 1911	
Kimura	Tokizo	Kimura	Sakae	17 Jan. 1921	
Kincaid	Edwin J.	Smith	Genevieve	13 Aug. 1904	
King	Albert Roy	Cordes	Ethel Lucy	6 June 1918	
King	Andrew	Gollnik	Lizzie	20 Feb. 1909	
King	Cecil Ray	Meade	Edna	18 June 1918	
King	Charles W.	Browning	Catherine L.	24 June 1911	
King	Chester James	Starrett	Anna Letta	7 Dec. 1912	
King	David	Barnes	Annie	2 Dec. 1899	no previous marriage
King	E. Manuel	Emeral	Mary	29 May 1906	
King	Ernest F.	Sales	Geraldine	2 Feb. 1901	
King	Fred	Yates	Francis	26 Oct. 1905	
King	George	Culver	Katherine	11 Dec. 1906	
King	Horace Constable	Daniels	Zella	12 Nov. 1913	
King	James	Dahlmann	Augusta	19 Nov. 1888	
King	James	Willis	Mabel	1 Aug. 1891	br: John Willis, father
King	John	Moore	Amy L.	25 Apr. 1901	br: Eudora E. Moore, mother
King	John	Gibson	Nancy	6 Nov. 1884	

Groom Surname	Groom Given Name	Bride Surname	Bride Given Name	Date	Comments
King	John	Bahr	Bertha	30 Aug. 1905	
King	John F.	Merryfield	Kittie	14 Jan. 1892	
King	Joseph B.	Cowles	Eva M.	22 June 1885	
King	Joseph G.	Borges	Mary	12 Nov. 1900	
King	Lochiel M.	Wadsworth	Anna M.	27 Nov. 1899	
King	Theodore G.	Sales	Ida M.	15 Dec. 1891	
King	Thomas Riley	Strode	Theresa E.	30 Oct. 1908	
King	W. E.	Gardner	Flora	4 Feb. 1887	
King	William	Adams	Lora Z.	4 Nov. 1881	
King	William	Blakley	Mary E.	28 Feb. 1879	br: Mrs. Elizabeth Blakley, mother; Thomas S. Blakley, witness
King	Willis James	Perry	Gertrude M.	16 Oct. 1920	
King	Charles W.	Campion	Kate	2 Oct. 1896	
Kingman	Ralph Elmer	McNally	Ella	21 June 1905	
Kingsbury	De Witt	Pretorious	Mary	7 May 1891	
Kingwell	Alfred Leslie	Weythman	Lucretia Elizabeth	19 Feb. 1913	gr: B. R. & Josephine Kingwell from Contra Costa Co.; br: Annie L. Weythman will be 21 4 May 1913; br Lucy N. Crabtree, mother
Kingwell	B.	Beedle	Josephine	25 Sept. 1886	
Kingwell	William I.	Collins	Clara E.	23 Sept. 1901	
Kinley	Basil E.	Gumes	Bessie V.	11 June 1909	
Kinley	Fielden	Fassoth	Courdadena	3 Feb. 1910	
Kinley	Newton B.	Severy	Edna A.	2 May 1907	
Kinne	Albert B.	Dechenne	Rosa	13 Jan. 1886	
Kinner	William G.	Runyon	Annie	31 Oct. 1875	
Kinney	John H.	Bueno	Maria	31 May 1889	
Kinney	William S.	Kittler	Rose J.	11 Feb. 1907	
Kinsey	Harvey C.	Wyckoff	Emma	10 Nov. 1897	no previous marriage

		Bride		Date	Comments
Groom					
Surname	**Given Name**	**Surname**	**Given Name**		
Kinyon	Reuben H.	Wheatley	Besse Maude	13 Mar. 1909	
Kirby	Charles F., Jr.	Baron	Julia Adeline	2 Nov. 1904	
Kirby	Duncan J.	Lesser	Anita T.	16 May 1917	
Kirkland	David J.	Blake	Effie M.	20 Feb. 1903	gr: William J. Kirkland, father
Kirkland	Harry B.	Nowlin	Lula L.	19 Sept. 1914	br: E. C. Nowlin & Mary Nowlin, parents
Kirkland	Henry B.	Mays	Helen J.	15 June 1912	
Kirkland	Joseph B.	Wilson	Ettie Sarah	30 July 1904	
Kirkman	Claude J.	Perry	Elizabeth G.	16 Nov. 1909	
Kirkpatrick	Josiah M.	Moore	H. C., Mrs.	25 June 1898	gr: divorced 8 June 1897; br: divorced from John 18 Dec. 1895?
Kirkpatrick	Josiah M.	Calbreath	Maggie A.	16 July 1890	
Kirkpatrick	Virgil	Louk	Katie	25 Sept. 1911	
Kirsch	Henry	Henrahan	Effie H.	25 Apr. 1893	
Kirstein	Max	Vogel	Camilla A.	8 July 1918	
Kirwan	Louis J.	Davis	Georgia M.	19 Apr. 1918	
Kirwan	Thomas D.	Mosher	Lucile Ruth	9 Apr. 1917	
Kise	Philip	Myers	Emily	14 Feb. 1882	
Kise	Philip A.	Myers	Katie	25 Nov. 1878	
Kiser	Antone	Stevens	Catherine M.	15 Nov. 1901	
Kiser	Nicklaus	Jakoba	Christina	17 Oct. 1892	
Kiser	William	Infield	Josephine	5 June 1894	br: Alois Infield, father, gives consent and signs; Herman Ludy, witness
Kisling	Frank	Geary	Florence	20 Aug. 1910	
Kissam	William A.	Hussey	Anita	2 June 1917	
Kistler	Ray S.	Stowe	Anna F.	10 Feb. 1921	
Kistner	Lester Alfred	Bever	Cleo Maud	26 Oct. 1908	
Kistner	Loren T.	Hicklin	Evelyn M.	21 Mar. 1918	
Kivett	David W.	Miller	Minnie	5 Aug. 1903	

Groom Surname	Groom Given Name	Bride Surname	Bride Given Name	Date	Comments
Kivett	Walter L.	Johnson	Rolla May	30 July 1910	
Kivi	Newton M.	Capella	Corinne M.	31 Oct. 1914	
Kjeldsen	Vernon Edward	Gibbons	Rose Elliot	7 Mar. 1919	gr: Christian R. Kjeldsen, father
Klaus	Charlie	Filion	Mary	3 May 1902	
Klaustermeyer	Charles F.	Hefty	Amelia M.	20 July 1910	
Kleeman	John	Sper	Rosa	21 Nov. 1876	witness: P. Lowrey
Klein	Christian	Weishand	Margaretta	21 Sept. 1891	br: Carl F. August Weishand, father
Klein	Ernest E.	Johnson	Cassie B., Mrs. (?)	8 Oct. 1900	
Kleiser	James H.	Armstrong	Fannie	26 Nov. 1901	
Klemgard	James G.	Eardley	Gladys	19 June 1917	
Kline	S. R.	More	Lena	28 Aug. 1888	
Klingler	George Adolph	Gale	Ellen E. (per signature)	16 Apr. 1921	
Klintworth	Edward	Michaelsen	Mary W.	19 Sept. 1899	gr: 1225 Chestnut St., Oakland
Kloustermeyer	Wm. J.	Block	Lora	22 July 1890	
Knaak	August	Funk	Lena	24 July 1876	
Knack	Frederick	McGregor	Agnes, Mrs.	25 Apr. 1891	br: widow
Knaff	Henry Richard	Tryon	Elizabeth	5 Apr. 1887	
Knapp	Charles Houry (?)	McAlister	Martha Ann	9 Oct. 1876	
Knapp	Gen W.	Hamilton	Alice B.	21 June 1877	
Knapp	Marion O.	Brown	Mary E., Mrs.	19 Apr. 1892	br: widow
Knapp	Wm. D.	Hawkins	Maud	20 Feb. 1894	
Knecht	Frederich	Hunger	Maria, Mrs.	3 Feb. 1896	
Knecht	Tony	Frey	Anna	10 Jan. 1920	
Kneiss	Gilbert H.	Rayburn	Hannah E.	12 Feb. 1920	
Kneppler	George H.	Roberts	Lulla G.	10 Apr. 1915	
Knight	Bert P.	Arkland	Mabel E.	10 Nov. 1914	
Knight	Francis Marion	Baker	Roxie Dell	17 Apr. 1897	

	Groom	Bride		Date	Comments
Surname	Given Name	Surname	Given Name		
Knight	George W.	Barnes	May E.	26 Sept. 1893	
Knight	Reginald S.	MacKenzie	Blanche	22 May 1907	
Knight	Russell H.	Cornish	Shirley F.	4 Oct. 1911	
Knipp	Ruscher A.	Wheeler	Harriet S.	10 Oct. 1892	
Knock	Malcolm A.	Moon	Carrie	5 June 1912	
Knoles	Rollin C.	Hulbert	Fannie O.	19 May 1900	
Knolle	Frans J. B.	Soderberg	Alice	28 Mar. 1916	
Knott	Warren T.	Allen	Rebecca H.	21 Mar. 1878	
Knott	William	Perry	Alice L.	25 June 1913	
Knowles	Albert William	Palmer	Lou	3 July 1906	
Knowles	D. C.	Menefee	Marinda I.	22 Oct. 1866	
Knowlton	Cyrus Dexter	Dahlmann	Alba Flora	20 Jan. 1916	
Knox	Josiah N.	Cooper	Ella J.	16 May 1894	
Knudsen	Conrad	Hansen	Josie	17 Apr. 1913	
Knudson	Arthur J.	Powers	Zelma V.	11 May 1918	
Knudtsen	Sophus	Nissen	Henrietta	15 Nov. 1907	
Knutsen	Isaac	Miller	Rae	15 Oct. 1900	br: Daniel E. Miller, father
Knutsen	Iver	Clawsen	Cynthia A.	18 Dec. 1865	
Koch	John J.	Morris	Anna M.	11 Apr. 1914	
Koch	Leroy	Norris	Emma	12 June 1907	
Koch	William B.	Nichols	Lillian Edith	17 Sept. 1910	
Kock	George A.	DuBois	Hazel M.	15 July 1912	gr: August Kock, parent
Koebeli	Rudolph	Bech (?)	Elisabeth	5 Nov. 1908	
Koeboom	John Henry	Slade	Alma, Mrs.	24 Apr. 1905	
Koenig	Charles	Costigan	Mary Louise	30 Jan. 1908	
Koenig	Frank	Livernash	Elizabeth A.	18 June 1900	
Koenig	Frank	Strickirt	Martha F.	21 Dec. 1914	don't publish
Koenig	William	Schwartz	Margaretha	28 May 1902	

Groom Surname	Groom Given Name	Bride Surname	Bride Given Name	Date	Comments
Koffenstein	Jacob	Sauer	Carrie	30 Nov. 1895	
Kohl	Stanley E.	Nalley	Marion	2 July 1907	
Kohr	Robert L.	Rose	Eldora	3 Feb. 1897	
Kolb	August L.	Johnson	Belle	17 May 1888	
Kolb	Clifford A.	McDowell	Hazel E.	26 Dec. 1913	
Kolliker	Fred	Young (?)	Minnie E.	15 Apr. 1885	
Kolm	Robert	Huston	Estella	30 Mar. 1897	
Konig	John	Isaak	Helena	23 Feb. 1889	
Kopf	August J.	Quinn	Frances M.	17 May 1900	do not give ages
Kopf	Carl L.	Fick	Emma M.	15 Apr. 1896	
Korbel	Frank	Blaha	Catherine	27 Oct. 1883	
Korbel	Leo V.	McNear	Miriam	30 Aug. 1912	
Kornmuller	Wilhelm	Wenger	Selma	20 July 1916	
Koski	Matt	Frandell	Mandi	14 Aug. 1911	
Koster	James	Martin	Alma	21 Oct. 1901	
Kothgassner	Joseph M., Jr.	Reger	Marie A.	25 Sept. 1920	
Kozminsky	Nicholas	Duffey	Cassandra	29 May 1911	
Kraemer	Herman	Combs	Frances	2 July 1914	
Kraft	Emil C.	Perkins	Fay K.	21 Mar. 1914	br: Mrs. Eva Kingman, mother
Kragel	Adam H.	Belden	Grace A.	9 May 1914	
Kraimer	Isaac	Hecht	Helen	21 Aug. 1877	
Kraus	Albert	Moody	Viola	17 Oct. 1899	
Krauss	Frederick G.	Hilmer	Lizzie	12 Oct. 1897	no previous marriage
Krayenbuhl	John F.	Rebscher (?)	Louise M.	5 Dec. 1918	
Kreidler	Carl W.	Bettencourt	Elvira S.	5 Aug. 1916	
Kreis	Harry Gailord	Jackson	Myrtle P.	7 Dec. 1920	
Kreiss	Frederick W.	McCormick	Alice	5 Sept. 1911	
Kreitler	John H.	Cornwell	Bessie Agnes	13 Feb. 1920	

	Groom	Bride		Date	Comments
Surname	Given Name	Surname	Given Name		
Krenzer	Thomas C.	White	Loma A.	25 Aug. 1919	
Kretzmer	William J.	Carberry	Josephine M.	4 Aug. 1917	
Kreutzberg	Robert	Mangers	Ester May		br: letter to Chief of Police S. F. from D. V. O'Brien, acting chief, for Mr. Peter N. Mangers, resident of S. F. to prevent marriage of underage daughter; 2 Aug. 1917; presumption marriage for military exemption
Kriedell	Fred W.	Hayes	Freda M.	12 June 1900	
Kroncke	Henry Carl	Staley	Ada Lavonia	4 Aug. 1906	
Kronke	Edward J.	Gibson	Gladys J.	6 June 1914	
Krough	Martin L.	Combs	Genevieve	8 Feb. 1911	br: A. R. & Mary Combs, parents
Krueger	Oscar Feasco	Cook	Cassie	19 July 1877	
Kruse	August W. T.	McLean	Katie G.	11 Nov. 1896	gr: L. A. Kruse, brother, gives consent and signs
Kruse	Charles C.	Willey	Mamie E.	19 Sept. 1911	br: Thomas & Margaret Willey, parents; gr: Thomas Willey, J. Elmer Mobley, witnesses to his mark
Kruse	Charles G.	Baagoe	Carrie	12 Nov. 1894	
Kruse	Fred G.	McCombs	Luetta A.	8 Dec. 1911	br: C. M. McCombs, parent
Kruse	Frederick Antonio	Hobson	Louise Jane	13 July 1891	
Kruse	H. A.	Davis	Gertrude L.	22 Dec. 1915	
Kruse	Herbert M.	Pfister	Nellie M.	27 Dec. 1910	
Kruse	Herbert M.	Bullen	Clara J.	3 July 1914	
Kruse	James H.	Ingalls	Emma	12 Sept. 1892	
Kruse	James H.	McNeeley	Eva	14 May 1898	
Krutzberger	Fred	Short	Louise Amelia	2 Apr. 1910	
Kryst	Charles	Reichlin	Anna	22 July 1919	please do not publish
Kuchmann	Henry, Jr.	Waterman	Wylda S.	29 May 1915	

	Groom	Bride		Date	Comments
Surname	Given Name	Surname	Given Name		
Kuck	Hans A.	Hansen	Helga A.	11 Dec. 1920	
Kuechler	Harold J.	Mackey	Verda E.	31 Dec. 1907	
Kuhi	Henry	Brava	Edith	31 May 1913	
Kuhn	Michael	Miller	Sophie	21 July 1903	
Kuhule	Perry	Eades	Nellie	21 May 1894	
Kulberg	Andrew John	Walsh	Sarah Jane	30 Jan. 1896	
Kunde	Kurt G.	Cook	Alice Emme (?)	1 Feb. 1918	
Kunz	George E.	Mason	Mary C.	6 Feb. 1893	
Kunzler	Edward Theodore	Reynolds	Edna May	28 Oct. 1920	
Kunzler	Ora Archibald	Donahoo	Ilma	8 Sept. 1917	
Kurlander	Maurice Aaron	Griffith	Juanita	1 June 1899	br: divorced more than one year
Kurlander	Sidney	Lawrence	Georgie May	23 Nov. 1904	
Kuster	Gerhard	McDowell	Elsie	2 Apr. 1921	
Kuykendall	J. O.	Noffsinger	Melvina E.	19 Apr. 1884	
Kuykendall	James O.	McCoy	Dollie	26 May 1891	
Kuykendall	William Stark	Ingram	Emma	3 July 1888	
Kyburz	Alfred A.	Holloway	Florence M.	22 Aug. 1903	
Kyle	John G.	Cauckwell	Nancy M.	22 Mar. 1890	
Kynoch	Ransom	Rodeck	Louise	10 Oct. 1887	
La Bossure	Louis	McCreagh	May	3 Oct. 1913	
Labat	Jean	Bonnemazon	Catherine	13 July 1904	
Lacey	William F.	Rose	Bessie Pearl	20 Sept. 1920	
Lackmann	H.	Hollahan	Iva	24 Nov. 1913	
Lacoste	George J.	Hautot	Marthe A.	8 June 1920	
Lacque	Clarence Andrew	Beach	Jeannette	19 June 1909	gr: Mrs. B. F. Lacque, mother; filed by F. Sewigh ?
Lacque	Edward F.	Ducker	Ella Mae	14 Nov. 1907	
Lacque	Frank	Weeks	Effie	29 Oct. 1883	

	Groom	Bride		Date	Comments
Surname	Given Name	Surname	Given Name		
Laddish	H. J.	Songey	Harriet M.	16 Dec. 1914	
LaDue	Earl Francis	Leith	Kathleen Laurence	27 Mar. 1920	
LaDue	Valloise A.	Wilson	H. Isabella	2 Oct. 1920	
Lafferty	Daniel H.	Leddy	Lillian Ruth	22 Jan. 1907	
Lafont	Walter Thomas	Sturgeon	Irene	2 July 1904	
Lafranchi	Alfonso	Garzola	Lena Frances	5 Oct. 1907	
Lafranchi	Edward	Piezzi	Lucy	29 Aug. 1899	gr: Joseph Lafranchi, father
Lafranchi	Frank	Forni	Josephine	18 May 1911	
Lafranchi	Fred L.	Dolcini	Zelma D.	2 Aug. 1920	
LaFranchi	Henry G.	Scott	Hattie	27 Dec. 1906	
Lafranchi	John	Confette	Eufemia	26 Sept. 1914	
Lafranchi	Joseph	Spaletta	Erminia	3 Oct. 1895	
Lafranchi	Marino Joseph	Peterson	Emily	9 Feb. 1904	
LaFranchi	Robert	Albini	Ersilia	19 July 1919	
Lafranconi	Frank	Scaroni	Adelina	29 Aug. 1914	
Lafranky	Morris	Piezzi	Eliza	18 May 1891	
Lafrenz	Henry	Teaby	Leonnora	16 Feb. 1892	
Lager	Phillip	Manuck	Minnie	26 Dec. 1912	
Lagger	Cesare	Kreutzer	Kate	12 Aug. 1893	
Lagomarsino	George J.	Cassini	Carrie	4 May 1907	gr: Natalina Pilich, mother
LaGrant	Lucon	Carmady	Maggie	11 May 1878	
Lahue	E. D.	Gross	Ida J.	8 Mar. 1916	
Laird	Fred J.	Kelley	Caroline L.		
Laird	H. Spencer	Logan	Harriet	28 May 1866	
Laird	Thomas F.	Aiken	Mary Edith	23 May 1884	
Lake	Alfred Edwin	Shelford	Susie Blanche	7 Aug. 1912	
Lake	D. Delos	Good	Helen	21 Aug. 1894	
Lalanne	John	Hulbert	Julia A.	18 Mar. 1920	gr: Louis Lalanne, father

Groom Surname	Groom Given Name	Bride Surname	Bride Given Name	Date	Comments
Lalanne	Laurence Marius	Dutil	Jeanne Harriette	22 Sept. 1904	
Lalanne	Louis	Mauregard	Marguerite	9 June 1894	
Lamay	Alfred	McDonald	Isabelle		
Lamb	George H.	Moranzoni	Edith A.	20 July 1907	
Lamb	Louis	Fruitt (?)	Ellen	22 Oct. 1878	
Lambert	Charles A.	Leclerc	Emily	3 Apr. 1882	br: Alphonso Leclerc, father
Lambert	Edward	King	Jennie N.	2 Jan. 1886	br: J. Hamp King & Mrs. Mary E Rosinbum,
Lambert	Frank	Moore	Sarah Inza	3 Jan. 1906	br: Thomas B. Moore, father
Lambert	Henry A.	Moore	Zilla C.	23 Aug. 1912	br: Eudora E. Watson, mother
Lambert	John W.	Rodgers	Julia	29 Apr. 1885	
Lambert	Lewis A.	Bowers	Bertha Blanche	8 June 1910	
Lambert	Richard	Long	Minnie A., Mrs.	23 Nov. 1877	
Lambert	Robert Franklin	Niles	Lavania A.	23 Sept. 1878	
Lambert	William A.	Vadon	Bertha E.	17 Apr. 1915	
Lameneth	Jacob F.	Priestly	Sophia	21 Jan. 1897	
Lamore	Joseph Verrell	Morse	Marie L.	30 June 1919	
Lampson	Augustus	Warren	Mary L.	23 Dec. 1887	
Lampson	Chester William	Parrott	Marguerite Marion	17 May 1909	
Lampson	Everett D.	Caldwell	Ora Helena	12 Dec. 1918	
Lampson	Walter A.	Kirkland	Frances M.	25 Nov. 1914	
Lancaster	John	Truitt	Eva	15 Oct. 1894	
Lancaster	William	Daly	Maria	19 Jan. 1865	
Lance	Ora L.	Miller	Beulah G.	26 Dec. 1917	
Landelin	Frank W.	Ula Page	Cora M.	27 Jan. 1921	do not publish
Lander	Eugene	Arnold	Margaret Elizabeth	25 Sept. 1890	
Landgrebe	Milton William	Lanpher	Ruth Louise	5 Sept. 1917	

	Groom	Bride		Date	Comments
Surname	**Given Name**	**Surname**	**Given Name**		
Landi	Enrico	Lencioni	Emma	24 Mar.1910	br: Domenico Lencioni, father; John Petotte ?, witness to his mark
Landis	Arthur L.	Barnes	Cora	31 May 1894	
Landis	William A.	Sericano	Julia A.	8 Sept. 1906	
Lando	Frank	Treadwell	Alicia E.	13 Oct. 1913	br: Irene Kennedy, mother
Landree	Roy	McCulloch	Eva	26 Oct. 1907	gr: C. W. Landree, father, 14 Oct., Tehama Co. note; br: J. M. McCulloch, parent
Landresse	Charles Paul	Kripp	Clara Betts	6 Jan. 1917	
Lane	Allen S.	Harding	Edith M.	24 May 1915	
Lane	Carlton A.	Brooks	Edith Nellie	28 Sept. 1897	
Lane	Thomas	Harris	Laura Jane	19 Apr. 1909	
Lane	Ernest	St. Clair	Lettye	3 June 1919	
Lane	Ernest	Bailey	Hester Drew	13 Dec. 1920	
Lane	F. J.	Rogers	Mamie	23 Sept. 1891	
Lane	Frank J.	Gossage	Jessie	11 Sept. 1909	
Lane	Howard A.	Bozza	Phyllis Leigh	30 June 1919	
Lane	J.	Conklin	E. C.	23 June 1887	
Lane	James Albert	Toomey	Mary Ellnor	28 May 1906	
Lane	Joseph W.	Robertson	Nellie	9 Oct. 1911	
Lane	Lonnie	Cunningham	Alice M.	19 Nov. 1898	requested by E. C. Carter
Lane	Louis M., Jr.	Blanchard	Lizzie Eveline	27 July 1887	
Lane	Richard E.	Montgomery	Frances	2 May 1913	
Lane	Walter J.	McNally	Mary A.	25 Aug. 1913	
Lane	William J.	Williams	Clara C.	25 July 1914	
Lanfear	James A.	Gilbert	Eleanor M.	16 Apr. 1915	
Lang	August B.	Burgess	Mary Ann	21 Nov. 1898	br: A. B. Burgess, parent; no previous marriage
Lang	Henry A.	Morgan	Grace E.	6 Jan. 1916	

Groom Surname	Groom Given Name	Bride Surname	Bride Given Name	Date	Comments
Lang	Herman Charles	Gwin	Carrie Elizabeth	31 July 1899	
Lang	Robert A.	Turner	Frances A.	6 June 1917	
Lange	Niels Frederik	Latell	Elsie Elizabeth	17 June 1916	
Langensand	Melchior	Daschwander	Francisca	17 Oct. 1892	
Langero	Giovani	Bonfigli	Nazarena	10 May 1915	
Langlois	Robert Franklin	McFarlane	Elizabeth Robina	23 Nov. 1912	
Langon	Michael O.	Riddle	Marvele O.	24 June 1920	
Langpaap	Max	Traeger	Orah Dell	12 Sept. 1917	
Langsdorf	Charles	Dellenbaugh	Madge	14 Aug. 1920	
Lankant	Carl M.	Schumacher	Carrie Theresa	13 Nov. 1909	
Lanker	Albert	Schumacher	Mary	16 Apr. 1906	
Lannom	Clarence Worton	Westover	Minnie Merle	25 July 1916	
Lantz	George F.	Newbert	Della	30 Dec. 1899	
Lapham	Matthew	Welch	Effie C.	30 Apr. 1895	
Lapham	William C.	Bones	Elsie D.	15 May 1900	
Lapum	Oscar Edwin	Livings	Flora Estella	24 Nov. 1897	no previous marriage
Large	Arthur R.	Quinn	Addie	26 July 1893	br: John Quinn, father, consents to marriage and signs.
Larimer	Robert E.	Berger	Clara Lee	14 May 1918	
Lark	Newton Allen	Rich	Bernise Irene	22 Mar. 1911	
Larsen	Albert O.	Anderton	Gertrude A.	30 Jan. 1920	
Larsen	John	Gibbs	Martha	29 May 1912	
Larsen	Jorgen	Larsen	Maria Christine	26 June 1889	
Larsen	Julius Anton	Barnes	Eliza Lownes	27 Nov. 1905	
Larsen	L. P.	Nielsen	Tine	29 July 1892	
Larsen	Peter L. N.	Henrichsen	Anna M.	7 Oct. 1910	
Larsen	Thomas A.	Tunsen	Edith L.	28 June 1912	
Larson	Carl	Nilson	Pauline	29 Dec. 1893	

		Bride		Date	Comments
Groom					
Surname	**Given Name**	**Surname**	**Given Name**		
Larson	John Benjamin	Wittkowski	Frieda	25 Apr. 1914	
Larson	Rudolph Otto	Clavey	Dorothy Louise	8 June 1905	
Larson	Sven	Lussier	Minnie I.	31 July 1913	
Larsson	Gustaf Adolf	Johnson	Lillian May	1 Dec. 1916	
Lascuola	Frank P.	Cordes	Wanda H.	9 Mar. 1917	
Lass	Peter	Friedrichs	Mariechen	19 Oct. 1912	
Lassen	Chris	Hansen	Frieda Elsie	10 Mar. 1917	
Latell	Harry	Fair	Helen	2 Sept. 1913	
Latimer	Hugh N. N.	Kingsbury	S., Mrs.	9 Oct. 1890	br: widow
Latimer	Lorenzo P.	Phelps	Jennie E.	27 June 1893	license requested by Jennie Evelyn Phelps who signs.
Laton	Edward Lee	Flarity	Sadie M.	3 July 1889	
Lattanzi	Emil C.	Dal Poggetto	Elena	3 Oct. 1918	
Lattin	Perry Raymond	Combs	Clara Edna	31 July 1906	
Laufenburg	George	Byce	Eveline	18 Dec. 1916	
Laufenburg ?	George	Hinshaw	Mattie	6 Feb. 1892	
Lauge	Walter Harry	Moore	Ruby Freeman	20 Apr. 1911	
Laughlin	A. P.	Yarbrough	Mattie	19 May 1886	
Laughlin	Gail Everil	Wilson	Mildred Irma	15 Sept. 1917	
Laughlin	Glen P.	Mitchell	Margaret E.	12 Dec. 1914	
Laughlin	Grant A.	Finley	Abbie J.	23 Apr. 1912	
Laughlin	John M.	Hall	Sara C.	7 Apr. 1898	
Laughlin	Joseph P.	Beardin	Mary E., Mrs.	14 Feb. 1903	
Laughlin	Joseph W.	Litton	Mary L.	27 Nov. 1895	
Laughlin	Lester	DeWitt	Ruby Ruth	16 Nov. 1918	br: Mary DeWitt, mother
Laughlin	Merton	Tarwater	Ida	8 Dec. 1897	
Laughlin	Merton	Laughlin	Maesota	29 June 1909	
Laughlin	Perry Raymond	Archer	Grace Dorothy	25 Nov. 1910	

Groom Surname	Groom Given Name	Bride Surname	Bride Given Name	Date	Comments
Laughlin	R. L.	Lafferty	Lola F.	22 Dec. 1888	gr: L. Laughlin, father?
Laughlin	Samuel McKendry	Laughlin	Josephine	14 July 1882	
Laugridge	Leo J.	Hoffman	Nell M.	3 Jan. 1921	
Lauman	John	Gesel	Anne	29 Apr. 1887	
Laumann	Arthur H.	Thomas	Florence L.	9 Dec. 1913	
Laumann	Frank E.	Meyer	Dorothy S.	24 Feb. 1914	
Laurance	George A.	Thomas	Cora	20 Sept. 1902	br: Mrs. Mattie Storothoff, mother, witness to mark M. G. Hall
Laurence	John H.	Jewett	May	29 Mar. 1886	
Laurent	Ernest	Nonnon	Marie	17 June 1905	
Laurent	Julius B.	AFrancard	Julia	4 Feb. 1903	
Laurin	Robert	Phillips	Martha	23 Dec. 1892	
Lauritano	Edward	Perazzo	Julia	31 Oct. 1906	
Lauritzen	Chrisitan	Dahlmann	Clara	6 Jan. 1888	
Lauritzen	Jesse C.	Claassen	May	12 Sept. 1884	
Lauritzen	Knudt Broder	Harms	Edith Johanna	23 Sept. 1907	
Lauritzen	Lewis	Ayers	Veryl D.	20 June 1913	gr: May Lauritzen, mother
Lauritzen	Kundt	Zamaroni	Jennie	25 Oct. 1909	
Laursen	Peter C.	Fredericksen	Anna K.	20 Dec. 1911	
Lausten	Louis Mitchell	Caltoft	Mary	17 June 1905	
Lauteren	Ferdinand	Cnopius	Antoniette Maria	6 Oct. 1879	
Laux	John Frances	Burns	Nellie T.	29 Mar. 1910	
LaValley	Elmer R.	Nydegger	Anna C.	13 Aug. 1914	
Lavell	William T.	Newlin	Laura D., Mrs.	20 Aug. 1899	neither party has been divorced within one year
Laveroni	Dave	Bassi	Julia	1 Nov. 1906	
Lavin	Joseph E.	Doran	Josephine E.	20 May 1893	
Lavio	Dazio	Stefenoni	Maria	15 Jan. 1921	

		Bride			
Groom				**Date**	**Comments**
Surname	**Given Name**	**Surname**	**Given Name**		
Lawford	William E.	Sprague	Blanche	14 Jan. 1902	requested by George W. Skidmore, friend
Lawler	Howard T.	Hoffmann	Verona	19 July 1920	
Lawler	James	Hoover	Louise Booth	29 May 1917	
Lawler	John Gardner	Burns	Carrie Mable	28 Oct. 1903	license requested by Herbert Slater
Lawler	John, Jr.	Poehlmann	Helen Mary	27 May 1910	
Lawrason	Dinnie Fred	Drake	Clarica	9 Aug. 1912	gr: Fred A. Lawrason, father; br: Katie Drake, mother
Lawrence	Bert M.	Kimble	Annie M.	26 June 1908	
Lawrence	Chester Earl	Smyth	Edith	18 Sept. 1912	
Lawrence	Frank	Olivera	Margaret	15 Nov. 1910	
Lawrence	Frank	Bean	Harriet Newell	4 June 1879	
Lawrence	George	Green	Frances	5 July 1895	
Lawrence	George Edwin	Elmore	Lois Merrill	14 June 1916	
Lawrence	Henry E.	Falkner	Amelia, Mrs.	17 Mar. 1902	br: widow; requested by Lyman Green, friend
Lawrence	Horace	Riley	Mary	5 May 1884	
Lawrence	James W.	Clayton	Alice	21 Feb. 1912	
Lawrence	James W.	McPeek	Mary I.	16 Apr. 1902	
Lawrence	Joseph G.	Lawrence	Francis Green	1 Feb. 1902	
Lawrence	William H.	Diaz	Isabelle E.	5 Mar. 1921	
Lawry	William	Cameron	Lottie	16 Oct. 1906	
Lawson	Charles Garfield	Freitas	Edna Lillian	17 July 1916	
Lawson	Grover E.	Adams	Mary L.	21 Sept. 1910	
Lawson	Grover Edward	Ruggs	Ola	25 Nov. 1907	gr: E. I. Lawson, parent
Lawson	Ivan G.	Linscott	Hazel	9 Feb. 1916	
Lawson	J. P.	Rima	Tina L.	12 Apr. 1888	br: Mrs. H. A. Rima, mother
Lawson	Jesse Herbert	Akers	Blanche Louisa	27 Dec. 1915	
Lawson	Oliver Lester	Young	Mattie Isadora	20 June 1905	

Groom Surname	Groom Given Name	Bride Surname	Bride Given Name	Date	Comments
Lawson	Perry Alexander	Wagner	Mazie	1 Oct. 1910	
Lawson	Thomas	Lewis	Cora	4 Oct. 1913	
Lawson	Z. Bert	Rees	Nettie	10 May 1905	
Lay	Henry D., Jr.	Mulligan	Ellen J.	25 Nov. 1865	
Laymance	F. W.	Robinson	Mary E.	16 Oct. 1914	
Laymance	Francis M.	Clark	Leona	30 June 1882	
Laymance	George Ebin	Hatch	Blanche	2 Feb. 1877	gr: I. C. Laymance, parent
Laymance	Henry J.	Bruner	Ada B.	18 Feb. 1891	
Laymance	Henry J.	Morris	Emma Allice	21 Dec. 1882	from Healdsburg; license signed by E. K. Baughn
Lazier	Donald C.	Gould	Mabel	12 Aug. 1895	
Lazzaroni	Peter	Esaia (?)	Jennie	19 Sept. 1918	
Lea	Clarence F.	Wright	Daisy A.	18 July 1907	
Leabo	Benjamin	Stoetz	Louisa	8 Aug. 1906	
Leach	John W.	Marall	Christine M.	22 Apr. 1915	
Leach	Roy H.	Knipp	Winfred	20 Aug. 1918	gr: L. F. Leach, parent
Leachman	Ream S.	Muller	Anna	1 Sept. 1906	
Leahey	Martin E.	ERichey	Ella E.	3 Nov. 1885	
Leahy	John	Hoyne	Bessie E.	22 Sept. 1912	
Leal	Frank Avila	Silva	Annie	29 Oct. 1902	license requested by Joseph Silver, friend
Leaner	Maurice	Kronich	Hannah	14 Feb. 1911	
Leard	Charles M.	Bale	Loletta	17 June 1898	no previous marriage
Leard	J. B.	Nooland	A. A.	24 Apr. 1878	
Leard	Robert B.	Miller	Effie C.	10 June 1895	
Leathe	Frank C.	Tobin	Alice M.	8 June 1907	
Leathers	G. N.	Winters	Theresa I.	3 Sept. 1892	
Leathers	Harry Allison	Morrill	Julia Marie	25 Nov. 1919	
Leavenworth	Randolph J.	McBrown	Marie M.	17 Apr. 1900	

	Groom	Bride		Date	Comments
Surname	Given Name	Surname	Given Name		
Leavitt	Albert Henry	Gotterba	Leona Inez	13 Nov. 1915	br: Hattie B. Gotterba, mlother
LeBallister	Thomas W.	Sander	Ida D.	27 June 1904	
LeBaron	Adelbert J.	Forsyth	M. Margaret	3 Nov. 1903	
LeBaron	C. A.	Johnson	Annie	26 Sept. 1903	
LeBaron	Harrison M.	Palmer	Sarah Emily		filed between 21 and 23 Aug. 1879
LeBaron	Harrison M.	Davis	Helen, Mrs.	28 Aug. 1902	
LeBaron	Harrison M., Jr.	Slattery	Frances	7 Aug. 1913	
Lebech	Andreas	Ketelsen	Freda	15 Jan. 1907	
Leber	Albert L.	Savage	Laura I.	16 Feb. 1887	
LeCarn	F.	Torre	A. C.	23 Dec. 1914	
Lecchetti	Tony	Gargini	Zaira	1 Aug. 1905	Mrs. E. DeBernardi & L. A. Preasley, witnesses to their marks
Leclileiter	Joseph A.	Bowen	La Verne	8 Dec. 1917	
Lecost	William A.	Stewart	Emeline E.	4 Oct. 1865	
Ledford	Clayton A.	England	Mary	16 Dec. 1878	br: Angeline Bates (?), mother
Ledford	Frank M.	Johnson	Ina B.	16 Dec. 1913	
Ledford	George Lee	Caughey	May	3 Sept. 1909	
Ledford	J. H.	Hayes	Mae	25 May 1911	br: Mrs. T. J. Burris, mother; as per notary
Ledford	John Irvin	Capell	Ethel Pauline	18 June 1904	gr: G. Ledford, parent; br: C. M. Capbell, parent
Ledford	Leonard Dowler	Hixson	Mildred Janette	1 Aug. 1904	gr: C. A. Ledford, father; br: John Hixon, father
Ledford	William F.	Larsen	Stella M.	30 Oct. 1918	
Ledger	Guy Wallace	Darr	Lena	11 Mar. 1909	
Lee	Alban	Jones	Myrtle A.	8 Apr. 1921	
Lee	Charles A.	Perry	Ellen, Mrs.	25 May 1897	br: widow
Lee	Charles E.	Schutts (?)	Teresa L.	14 Aug. 1880	
Lee	Edward P.	Blindhein (?)	Alma	29 Aug. 1918	

	Groom	Bride		Date	Comments
Surname	Given Name	Surname	Given Name		
Lee	George S., Jr.	Shaul	Velma Jessie	24 Nov. 1919	
Lee	Olaf	Gotrig	Stella Marie	14 Sept. 1912	br: Anna Gotrig, mother
Lee	Richard A.	Voss	Anna K.	23 June 1913	
Lee	Rollen M.	McHarvey	Mary	14 Nov. 1888	
Lee	W. H.	Casto	Mamie	10 Oct. 1883	
Lee	Walter	Wood	Clara Edith	21 July 1917	
Leech	Albert Ernest	Jacobs	Nettie Ellen	16 Dec. 1895	Geo. H. H. Cornelius, witness
Leedy	Chester Clyde	Maupin	Olive Pearl	27 Feb. 1918	
Leek	Charles E.	Van Winkle	Olive	5 Apr. 1886	
Leephart	James H.	Anderson	Nellie V.	11 July 1901	
Leete	Orton R.	Peddrazzi	Margaret	18 June 1891	
LeFebvre	Eugene O.	Adams	Jennie M.	22 Nov. 1892	
LeFever	Eugene	Alonso	Ruth C.	24 May 1917	
Leffler	Herman V.	MacGregor	Mabel C.	3 June 1912	
Leffmann	Julius W.	Sykes	Lillian R.	14 July 1915	
Legg	Edward T.	Pallady	Viola E.	12 Nov. 1903	
Legg	Samuel M.	Wall	Ella	25 Mar. 1884	
Legg	Samuel M.	Pallady	Ida M.	18 Jan. 1899	gr:divorced 17 Jan. 1898, Sonoma Co.; br: widow
Legg	W. H.	McIntosh	Mary Ellen	15 Nov. 1879	
Leggett	A. E.	Ballou	Althea L.	16 Feb. 1888	
Leggett	Charles F.	Wendt	Mollie	11 Feb. 1893	
Leggett	Elmer E.	Wiley	Minnie H.	5 Dec. 1890	
Leggett	Henry B.	Fulkerson	Nora C.	17 Feb. 1893	br: consent given by father, S. T. Fulkerson
Leggett	Raford Wesley	Lukas	Lavana Ruth	18 Aug. 1916	
Leggett	William Alexander	Willey	Fannie B.	23 Dec. 1902	
LeGoullon	L. C.	Remer	Bertha A.	23 Nov. 1915	

		Bride		Date	Comments
Groom					
Surname	Given Name	Surname	Given Name		
Lehman	George	Bumford (?)	Mary I.	15 Dec. 1882	
Lehn	Charles	Adams	Emma	26 Feb. 1881	
Lehn	Charles	Strother	Joanna	12 Aug. 1865	
Lehn	Louis	Kennedy	Maggie	10 Nov. 1892	
Leib	Jacob	Pugni	Ida	5 Nov. 1888	
Leibert	Robert E.	Lelouarn	Celestine	17 May 1898	
Leiby	George	Roberts	Katie, Mrs.	27 May 1893	br: widow
Leich	James L.	Virgil	Martha E.	13 Oct. 1866	
Leichter	Paul F.	Hastings	Johnietta B.	10 July 1901	
Leighton	Fred H.	Hall	Grace E.	23 June 1920	
Leininger	Daniel W.	Cordevant	Lilly	10 Nov. 1887	
Leisen	William C.	Leisen	Jennie, Mrs.	9 Jan. 1897	gr: Frank Leisen,gives consent and signs; do not publish
Leiser	George	Breitenbach	Emma Anita	15 Sept. 1916	
Leisinger	George Henry	Proctor	Kate	24 June 1896	
Leithman	Louis L.	Williams	Lottie E.	16 July 1917	
Leithold	John V.	Moreland	Esther	27 Jan. 1892	gr: W. W. Moreland, parent
Lelinger	August C.	Murphy	Mary Elizabeth	18 Sept. 1901	
Lelounarn	John	Terry	Della	19 Nov. 1909	br: Mrs. C. Shaffer, mother
Lemaihe (?)	Louis	Murphy	Myrtle	31 Oct. 1909	
Lemay	Josiah	Adams	Ellen	17 June 1882	
Lemon	Joseph P.	Ramos	Mary E.	7 Nov. 1902	
Lemos	J. F.	Marshall	E. E.	2 Jan. 1903	gr: Joseph L. Perry, witness to his mark
Lemos	John B.	DeBorba	Mary L.	4 Feb. 1919	br: Mary Agujar, mother
Lencioni	Agostino	Sbragia	Nanziata	3 Jan. 1898	don't publish
Lencioni	Henry	Alberigi	Ancilla	8 Jan. 1898	
Lencioni	Domenico	Puccioni	Lena	15 Dec. 1920	
Leneve	Edward	Cozad	Bertha M.	18 Aug. 1920	br: S. L. Cozad, parent

	Groom	Bride		Date	Comments
Surname	Given Name	Surname	Given Name		
Lenhart	Lee R.	Morse	Mary	25 Nov. 1914	
Lennard	Edward	Downs	Annie	29 Aug. 1914	
Lennon	Edward Francis	Lewis	Annie A. Walter	1 Aug. 1904	
Lent	D. A.	Gregory	Susie	20 Apr. 1886	
Lentz	Walter Edward	Bedford	Elise	2 June 1917	
Leona	Frank J.	Peck	Henerietta	20 Sept. 1915	
Leonard	James M.	Hobart	Jessie Margaret	28 Apr. 1899	don't publish until Tuesday
Leonardi	Joseph	Burlando	Amelia	13 Feb. 1904	br: Luigi Burlando, father
Leonardini	Paolo (Paul)	Paravinni	Maria	3 July 1900	
Leonesio	Frank	Silva	Lydia	9 Mar. 1914	
Leoni	Placido F.	Zanoni	Lena	6 Jan. 1908	
Lepori	Peter	Lafranchi	Mary	3 Feb. 1913	
Leppo	David Harrison	McNear	Clara	13 Oct. 1902	
Leppo	O. Frank	Spottswood	Minerva Belle	3 Feb. 1897	
Lerouge	Stephen A.	Deputy	Isabelle	25 Mar. 1921	
Leroux	Arthur	Cottle	Ella	6 July 1907	
Leroux	Robert	Peterson	Elsie	21 Dec. 1905	
Leroux	Walter George	Hall	Marion Belle	22 Dec. 1902	
Leslie	Charles W.	Hotchkiss	Anna	20 June 1918	
Less	Alexander S.	Searl	Lotta	15 July 1912	
Lester	B. W.	Rooney	Mary	12 Oct. 1889	
Lestingue	Jean	Bertres	Marie, Mrs.	13 Apr. 1916	
Leva	Leo Frank	Meineri	Edith A.	26 Aug. 1912	
Levansaler	Russell J.	Clarke	Agnes T.	14 Apr. 1921	
Levens	Harry Stocking	Barboni	Celestina	25 Oct. 1899	no previous marriage; gr: requested by Mrs. Josephine M. Stocking, mother
Leveroni	Victor L.	Bremer	Elmira G.	17 Nov. 1917	
Levey	Morris	Bosch	Katherine	5 Feb. 1912	

		Bride		Date	Comments
Groom					
Surname	**Given Name**	**Surname**	**Given Name**		
Levich	George	Ruebenack	Ella A.	22 Mar. 1920	
Levine	Abraham	Schachter	Mary	28 Oct. 1920	
Levy	Alexander	Von Pokrzywnicki	Hattie	7 July 1898	gr: 504 Andover St., San Francisco; br: 1118 Market St., San Francisco
Levy	Harold Walter	Creighton	Elizabeth M.	9 Aug.1909	
Levy	Joseph	Heine	Helen	24 Oct. 1916	
Levy	Robert	Miller	Minnie D.	3 Apr. 1909	
Lewell	Luther Enloe	Rambo	Esther Irene	4 Aug. 1917	
Lewis	Albert Ray	Daniels	Nellie Estella	9 May 1904	
Lewis	Calvin Mc M.	Dodson	Minnie M.	25 Jan. 1917	
Lewis	Charles Wadsworth	Goodwin	Mary Elizabeth	24 Mar. 1904	
Lewis	Edwin	Skinner	Pearl Ethel	23 Nov. 1899	gr: Mrs. C. B. Lewis, mother; br: Mrs. Oliver Skinner, mother; no previous marriage
Lewis	Harry D.	DeRose	Lenora	10 June 1916	
Lewis	J. F.	Van Allen	Emeline C., Mrs.	13 Nov. 1866	
Lewis	J. Hall	Bartlett	Frances Gertrude	1 May 1906	
Lewis	Jere	Wetherbee	Elizabeth C.	19 Nov. 1889	
Lewis	John F.	Fisher	Florence M.	28 Apr. 1904	
Lewis	Joseph Walter	Pfost	Alice May	13 Aug. 1907	
Lewis	Ralph	Robbins	Cora	14 Dec. 1904	
Lewis	Ray A.	Wheeler	Alta	2 Jan. 1920	
Lewis	Saml. R.	Williams	Mary E., Mrs.	23 June 1866	
Lewis	Samuel B.	White	May E.	25 Sept. 1902	
Lewis	Washington J.	Towner (?)	Adeline	26 Feb. 1877	
Lezzeni	Joseph Andrew	Raphael	Hazel Evelyn	29 Aug. 1918	
Libbey	William S.	Willet	Nora M.	20 Dec. 1919	
Libby	George W.	Brown	Leila Emma	15 May 1893	

Groom Surname	Groom Given Name	Bride Surname	Bride Given Name	Date	Comments
Lichan	Arthur Lincoln	Sutherland	Annie Beulah	5 Jan. 1921	
Lichau	Charles Fabian	Farrer	Jessie Catherine	10 Nov. 1906	
Lichau	Edward P.	Esler	Della	4 May 1914	
Lichau	Ernest A.	Whitaker	Julia H.	26 Nov. 1919	br: William H. Whitaker, father
Lichau	George	Riebli	Annie	20 Oct. 1909	
Lichau	Henry P., Jr.	Keithly	Lucy B., Mrs.	23 May 1904	
Lichau	Henry Peter	Stackhouse	Mary Elizabeth	10 July 1905	
Licht	George J.	Underwood	Pearl Alphia	21 Feb. 1920	
Liddle	W. J.	Green	Mary A.	24 Mar. 1891	
Liddle	William S.	McVean	Martha M.	5 Mar. 1912	br: Duncan A. McVean, father
Liggett	Thomas, Jr.	Jenkins	Hulda	11 Aug. 1917	
Light	Elisha	Schlake	Lizzie	16 Dec. 1890	
Light	Wm. R.	Smith	Rosetta (?) J.	18 Sept. 1880	
Lightner	Raymond J.	Vascaressa	Henrietta M.	7 Sept. 1920	gr: Mae Kaiser, mother
Ligore	David Claude	Cooney	Mary Eleanor	20 Apr. 1921	
Likins	James L.	Stapp	Dovey	8 May 1886	
Lile	Joseph A.	Ingram	Bell E.	29 Apr. 1903	
Lincoln	Ulysses G.	Adams	Abbie Mary	16 Nov. 1899	
Lind	Aogost	Giles	Lizzie	14 Feb. 1889	
Lind	Charles W.	Quackenbush	Luella D.	5 June 1894	
Lindenbaum	Louis	Siegle	Sarah	18 Mar. 1915	
Linderman	Clyde E.	Leef	Edith F.	11 Oct. 1920	
Lindig	Charley D.	Kramer	Regine	3 Oct. 1883	
Lindley	Charles	Lewis	Nellie	13 Sept. 1897	
Lindner	John D.	Maule	Lucinda, Mrs.	1 May 1866	
Lindon	Harvey J.	Magnani	Eugenia M.	22 July 1916	
Lindsay	Adin Arthur	Shuster	Ivy Irene	3 Mar. 1908	
Lindsey	Calvin	Barney	Ophelia	12 Feb. 1867	

Groom		Bride		Date	Comments
Surname	**Given Name**	**Surname**	**Given Name**		
Lindsey	Elon	Lange	Catherine	3 Mar. 1907	
Lindsey	Frank	Keenan	Anna	22 Aug. 1889	
Lindsey	William A.	Elden	Helena	24 Sept. 1900	
Lindsley	Alfred	Rowan	Albertine	14 Sept. 1916	
Lindstrom	Charles Otto	Miller	Lois	30 Oct. 1907	
Lindstrom	Henry F.	Johnson	Mary Caroline	10 Dec. 1903	
Linebaugh	Abraham	Millingtin (?)	Ollie	13 Feb. 1882	
Linebaugh	Charles A.	Cunningham	Lillian N.	23 Jan. 1899	br: requested license
Linebaugh	Columbus	Hervey	Katie		br: N. B. Hervey, father
Linebaugh	Francis Elmer	Driver	Edith Katherine	26 July 1905	
Linebaugh	Robert	Berry	Gertrude	21 Dec. 1907	
Linebaugh	Robert A.	Robertson	Rose	7 Sept. 1897	
Linebaugh	Robert A.	Lloyd	Emma May	23 Aug. 1875	
Linebaugh	Robert F.	Dunn	Daisy B.	10 Dec. 1881	gr: John Linebaugh, father; Petaluma
Linebaugh	William A.	Nisson	Anna	30 Dec. 1907	
Lingenfelter	Charles H.	Stearns	Ethel A.	31 Dec. 1914	
Linn	Allen McLeod	Dakin	Eunice I.	10 Oct. 1907	
Linoberg	Montague L.	Kahn	Estelle	11 June 1895	
Linse	C. F.	Quade	Martha L.	21 Nov. 1914	
Linser	Frederick W.	Bloom	Anna M.	25 Nov. 1914	
Linsley	Winfield S.	Hocker	Alice	19 Mar. 1889	
Linthicum	J. F.	Peterson	Annie F.	9 June 1888	
Linton	T. S.	Davis	Lydia A.	11 Sept. 1888	
Linville	Clement R.	Pocock	Eva	13 May 1892	
Linz	Adelbert G.	Ward	Rosine T.	20 Feb. 1912	
Lippi	Dean Orlando	Scatena	Eda Norma	11 June 1919	
Lippitt	Frank K.	Lysnar	Edith E.	12 Feb. 1907	
Lippold	Alfred E.	Andrews	Lilian Grayce	19 Feb. 1921	

Groom Surname	Groom Given Name	Bride Surname	Bride Given Name	Date	Comments
Lires	Ramon	Garcia	Marie Blasa	21 June 1912	
Liston	Van Wyck	Stewart	Edith J.	27 Sept. 1902	
Litchfield	Frank S.	Haas	Vera R.	18 Oct. 1919	
Lithwin	August	Wilson	Iva Selina	31 Aug. 1917	br: Lillie M. Wilson, mother
Little	Wilbert James	Ward	Hattie May	24 Dec. 1906	gr: Elizabeth Little, mother
Litton	A. P.	Keys	Nellie	22 Dec. 1885	
Litton	Bearse A.	Featherly	Fannie	11 July 1885	
Litton	H. B.	Yarbough	Saddie	16 Nov. 1880	
Litton	Roy Burton	Hildebrand	Lena Rivers	2 June 1905	
Litton	William	Rackliff	Ella C.	21 Nov. 1887	
Livernash	Edward J.	Overton	Jessie	5 Feb. 1891	
Livernast	John J.	Schultz	Elizabeth	22 July 1893	
Livingston	Charles	Dougherty	Lillian E., Mrs.	15 Feb. 1909	
Livingston	Charles S.	Taylor (?)	Elizabeth	29 June 1881	
Livingston	Edward Perry	Nobles	Minnie Frances	23 Oct. 1896	
Livingston	Harry Henry	Russell	Isabelle Adelaide	15 Jan. 1907	
Livingston	William Jesse	Crow	Luella Rains	18 June 1906	
Lloyd	Hubert T.	Cline	Jennie	10 Nov. 1894	license requested by Henry C. Cline
Lloyd	Louis A.	Purvine	Jeannette D.	5 Oct. 1912	
Lloyd	Walter A. L.	Lake	Grace E.	9 July 1895	
Lobb	Lewis	Gordon	Ruby Ethel	14 Feb. 1906	
Locatelli	Antonio	Figini	Margherita	28 Mar. 1914	
Locatelli	Luigi	Locatelli	Teresina	9 Apr. 1913	
Lochmer	Joseph K.	Johnson	Emma	5 Dec. 1898	no previous marriage
Lock	Charles	Cauckwell (?)	Mary E. C.	16 Oct. 1879	
Lock	Ernest Lawrence	Buhl	Dorothy Inez	22 Aug. 1917	
Lock	William H.	Norris	Julia	8 Aug. 1889	
Lock	Wm. H.	Hornbuckle	Lulu J.	18 Mar. 1893	

		Bride		Date	Comments
Groom					
Surname	**Given Name**	**Surname**	**Given Name**		
Lockard	Joseph H.	Batten	Sarah, Mrs.	8 Aug. 1902	br: widow
Locke	Albert	Butler	Lillian R.	28 May 1889	
Locke	Augustus Caldwell	Loveland	Inez Lillian	27 Apr. 1910	
Locke	George	Smith	Ada	21 Nov. 1877	
Locke	J. B.	Feehan	Lizzie	4 Nov. 1886	
Lockhart	Archie	Reid	Esther B.	3 May 1913	
Lockhart	Robert	Ritchie	Maggie J.	22 Dec. 1884	
Lockie	James S.	McEwan	Maggie	18 Nov. 1912	
Lockwood	Frank B.	Dodenhoff	Edythe W.	22 Oct. 1915	
Lockwood	Harry E.	Rivers	Mabel	25 May 1918	
Lockwood	James Otis	Sharp	Sara M.	20 Apr. 1912	
Lodge	David E.	Noble	Lizzie	30 June 1887	br: Thomas Noble, father
Lodovico	Morgantine	DeGiorgi	Giuseppina	17 Nov. 1896	
Loftus	Thomas M.	Harrison	Viola M.	2 Jan. 1918	br: Eleanor Harris, mother
Loftus	William	Murphey	Margarett L.	7 June 1890	
Logan	Howard	Cashdollar	Algie B.	10 Aug. 1885	
Logan	John F.	Richey	Ellen May	19 May 1919	
Logan	Roy Sylvester	Dawkins	Lillian E.	21 May 1907	
Logan	Walter	Shulman	Lillie	11 Jan. 1912	
Logue	James P.	Rushton	Coovaa Oral	31 Jan. 1910	
Loiser (?)	Gustave A.	Conger	Antoinette Isabel	6 Dec. 1880	br: consent of mother given in person
Lomax	Walter B.	Langenour	Irma R.	1 Feb. 1919	
Lombardi	Guiseppe	Bertoli	Carmella	20 Aug. 1904	requested by her
Lombardi	Joseph Augustus	Paolini	Mary Innocentia	17 Jan. 1918	
Lombardi	Peter	Bonaccorsi	Mary	2 Jan. 1919	
Londen	Melville Charles	Fields	Margaret	18 June 1910	
Loney	David M.	Busher	Marion Gladys	30 Dec. 1919	
Long	Alfred G.	Hoffman	Louise A.	19 Jan. 1916	

Groom Surname	Groom Given Name	Bride Surname	Bride Given Name	Date	Comments
Long	Charles H.	Willis	Mary Elizabeth	16 Feb. 1905	
Long	Charles H.	Long	Mary E.	23 May 1914	
Long	D. W.	Mallen	Kate F.	3 Jan. 1888	
Long	Geo. W.	Davis	Mary E.	6 Nov. 1878	gr: Isaac Long, father
Long	George	Leathe	Alice May	9 July 1917	
Long	Harold C.	Garrison	Bertha B.	18 Dec. 1919	
Long	James N.	Johnson	Della A.	15 Dec. 1906	
Long	John Suoddy? Beach	Copple	Mary	6 Apr. 1875	
Long	R. H.	Offuit	Ella	5 Mar. 1886	
Long	William Lile	Napper	Maude Ethel	11 Jan. 1910	
Longley	John A.	Dale	Clara E.	23 Dec. 1897	no previous marriage
Longsine	William M.	Scott	Lottie	6 July 1903	
Lonkey	Lloyd C.	Young	Ivy M.	17 Aug. 1916	
Loomis	Denton W.	Fenner	Sarah C.	8 Apr. 1895	
Lopera	Rafael Riviera	Martines	Maria Lopes	8 Mar. 1911	br: witness to mark Frank C. Loomis
Lopez	Charles Paul	Burke	Anna Matilda	8 Jan. 1906	
Lopus	Frank R.	Peters	Mary	24 Sept. 1895	
Lopus	George E.	Young	Cora B.	3 July 1920	
Lopus	Joseph	Herbert	Frances H.	20 June 1914	
Lorange	John	Norsworthy	Hattie F.	9 Dec. 1865	
Lorenze	Albert D.	Ludwick	Elma	7 Apr. 1909	
Lorenzen	Philip S.	Rörden	Ricke G.	15 Oct. 1902	
Lorenzi	Luigi	Antonietti	Angelina	18 Sept. 1919	
LoRomer	J. B.	Raab	Minnie G.	27 Aug. 1889	
Lotti	A.	Fienili	Rosa	16 Sept. 1911	
Lottman	W. B.	Eagleson	Anna May	13 Mar. 1885	
Loukemann ?	Richard	Robinett	Mary J.	21 Sept. 1894	

	Groom	Bride		Date	Comments
Surname	Given Name	Surname	Given Name		
Loukes	Harris Fisk	Baldwin	Cora B.	8 Nov. 1904	gr: E. O. & Ida M. Loukes, parents; dated Stockton 21 Oct. 1904
Louvis	Steven	Avila	Mary Ruth	29 Nov. 1920	
Love	Francis	Donahue	Margaret	21 July 1915	
Love	Wm.	Adams	Margaret, Mrs.	21 May 1866	
Lovejoy	George P.	Bryant	Effie Lyle	23 Dec. 1901	
Lovejoy	Robert T.	Ells	Inice R.	15 Dec. 1919	gr: Geo. E. Lovejoy, father
Loveland	E. A.	Hancock	Mary	12 Sept. 1891	
Lovell	David J.	Bones	Elizabeth A.	19 July 1865	
Lovell	Frank P.	Gathergood	Della Clyde	30 Oct. 1901	
Lovell	James T.	Hopper	Eva Elizabeth	29 June 1900	br: G. R. & Mary A. Hopper, parents; Mrs. J. R. Hitchcock, witness
Lovell	John	Cox	Mary Catherine, Mrs.	17 Nov. 1893	license requested by David Miller
Lovell	John M.	Lovell	Sarah	6 May 1901	
Lovell	Kenneth Henry	English	Norma Beulah	9 Apr. 1914	
Lovell	Walter G.	Hill	Mae	25 June 1900	
Lovell	William Ferdinand	Thompson	Lucy Myrtle	30 Mar. 1908	
Lovell	William I.	Williams	Daisy Dean	1 Sept. 1910	
Lovinggood	Harmon G.	Musser	Edith E.	14 Aug. 1912	
Lovotti	F.	Lagomarsino	Rosa E.	1 Jan. 1894	
Low	William R.	Palmer	Jennie, Mrs.	25 Nov. 1899	both widowed
Lowary	Joseph F.	McMenamin	Rosa	20 June 1889	
Lowe	Dawson	Linebaugh	Mary Jane	28 Dec. 1876	
Lowe	George W.	Herges	Celia K.	7 Dec. 1896	
Lowe	Herbert E.	Dryer	Bessie L.	4 Aug. 1913	
Lowe	Hugh O.	Whitney	Mabel L.	29 Nov. 1919	
Lowe	James Garrett	Shaughnessy	Margaret A., Mrs.	6 Jan. 1906	
Lowell	George R.	Weber	Sophie A.	28 Apr. 1911	

Groom Surname	Groom Given Name	Bride Surname	Bride Given Name	Date	Comments
Lower	John	Doremus	Florence M.	16 Sept. 1907	gr: Mrs. Emma Lower; Herbert Slater, witness to her mark
Lowery	James N.	Hatfield	Mary J., Mrs.	16 Nov. 1897	br: divorced more than one year
Lowery	Mansfield B.	Phillips	Henrietta C.	20 Nov. 1920	
Lowery	Robert D.	Fisher	Etta E.	1 Oct. 1894	
Lowrey	Thomas J.	Wyllie	Beatrice	29 June 1896	
Lownes	John	King	Irene	24 Aug. 1911	
Lowrey	Frederick D.	Parsons	Leila A.	14 Feb. 1911	
Lowrey	George A.	Patton	Lillian E.	6 Dec. 1911	
Lowrey	George W.	Black	Jessie F.	15 Aug. 1896	
Lowrey	Leroy	Dennis	Sarah E.	12 June 1880	
Lowrey	Robert L.	Cameron	Martha M., Mrs.	1 Feb. 1896	
Lowry	Chas. E. C.	Perrier	Katheen	7 Apr. 1887	
Lowry	Herbert L.	Armstrong	Florence	18 Aug. 1910	
Lowry	J. W.	Farmer	Rebecca W.	6 Mar. 1893	
Lowry	Nicholas M.	Hensley	Mary E.	7 Feb. 1865	
Lowry	Patrick Joseph	Elias	Margaret Josephine	26 May 1910	
Lucas	Jacob	Johnson	Allie	20 Apr. 1907	
Lucas	Joseph	Reese	Emma, Mrs.	22 Dec. 1902	
Lucchesi	Alberto	Petrini	Lena Lizzie	16 Apr. 1917	br: Theodoro Petrini, father
Lucchesi	Enrico	Del Fava	Gina	28 Apr. 1921	
Lucchesi	Francisco	Paccini	Italia	8 Nov. 1894	br: Giovanni Paccini, father, consents to marriage.
Luce	Chas. F.	Martin	Amy	27 Oct. 1885	
Luce	Elmer E.	Dickey	Bessie	18 Nov. 1916	
Luce	Elmer E.	Lawsen	Cherrosette	6 Feb. 1914	
Luce	George Liddle	McPeak	Edna Carl	24 Dec. 1905	
Luce	Guy R.	Trunz	Josephine A.	8 Oct. 1919	

	Groom		Bride	Date	Comments
Surname	Given Name	Surname	Given Name		
Luce	Hughbert S.	Coy	Ethel A.	6 Aug. 1908	
Luce	Jirah	Matheson	Nina R.	8 Mar. 1886	
Lucero	Gilbert E.	Marshall	Mary I.	22 Sept. 1914	
Luchesi	Angelo	Dinelli	Nonziatina	20 Oct. 1910	
Luchetti	Agostino	Cerruti	Rosi	9 Apr. 1895	
Luchetti	Giovani	Cerruti	Dominica	9 Apr. 1895	
Luchsinger	Peter	Katharin	Agnes	16 Sept. 1912	
Luciani	Pete	Vannucci	Algi	26 Mar. 1914	witness to her mark Julius Ferroni
Ludtke	John Emil	Tomka	Meta Martha	6 Oct. 1914	
Ludwig	J. Elmer	Hopper	Rosa B.	10 Feb. 1885	gr: Thomas J. Ludwig, father
Ludwig	Peter H.	Albee	May Edith	12 May 1887	
Ludwigs	George	Hunziker	Emma	29 Aug. 1890	
Ludy	Herman	Griess	Caroline	18 Feb. 1893	
Luebberke	Benjamin H.	Cooper	Margaret E.	18 Jan. 1902	
Lueger	Ernest	Horn	Anna	3 July 1911	
Luff	Caleb B.	Dalton	Eva C.	10 Oct. 1888	
Lugo	John A.	Babcock	Sylvania E.	19 Feb. 1921	
Luhr	Lawrence E.	Glavin	Carmelita	22 Nov. 1911	
Luisi	Leonardo	Gandola	Mary A.	20 Jan. 1921	
Lukas	Chris A.	Hadrich	Elsa Barbara	23 Sept. 1910	signed by Eugene B. Bailey
Lukas	Israel	Pahud	Heloise	16 Sept. 1893	
Lukeer	Charles R.	Archer	Nellie	22 Sept. 1911	br: Orbie Archer, parent
Lum	Tsai Yan	Ming	Jennie Woo	15 Dec. 1915	
Luman	William E.	Cuyler	Anna H.	2 July 1896	License requested by Vernon Goodwin.
Lumsden	Alexander Henry, Jr.	Crawford	Mary Anderson	29 Sept. 1903	
Lumsden	Charles William	Ducker	Lottie Alice	20 Sept. 1906	gr: A. H. Lumsden, parent
Luna	Frank	Dugan	Linda	13 Oct. 1906	br: J. W. Ford, witness to her mark
Lunardi	Giovanni	Vitali	Eleda	27 Nov. 1905	

Groom Surname	Groom Given Name	Bride Surname	Bride Given Name	Date	Comments
Lund	Aage F.	Werenberg	Dorthea	1 Dec. 1909	
Lund	August	Cooper	Lillie May	16 Apr. 1890	
Lund	Charles	Green	Carrie	10 Nov. 1896	
Lund	John Oscar	Hayes	Lillian	25 July 1908	
Lundholm	Charles E.	Bryan	Maud R.	21 Nov. 1904	
Lundin	Carl Arthur	Poppic	Sarah Anna	5 June 1913	
Lundy	Harry	Steele	Jennie	9 Dec. 1920	
Luney	William	MacDonald	Vestina	24 Dec. 1909	
Lunger	Elmer S.	Bones	Ella Bessie	2 Feb. 1917	br: Francis M. Bones, father; Hattie M. Brians, guardian
Lunger	Walter E.	Weber	Ruth B.	15 June 1918	
Lunn	Fred C.	Karry	Alice M.	26 Sept. 1914	
Lunney	Phillip	Walters	Sianea (?)	22 Apr. 1878	
Lunt	Arnold E.	O'Leary	Isabella	16 Mar. 1907	
Lupton	Earl L.	Denman	Nellie A.	14 Dec. 1920	
Luque	Peter	Labastorde	Jennie	19 Nov. 1901	
Lusk	William	Coe	Nannie T.	28 Dec. 1907	
Lutgens	Henry Chas.	Backer	Elizabeth	17 Dec. 1887	br: Lewis & Martha Alder, guardians
Luth	Frederick Henry	Fairclo	Carrie Martha	7 Nov. 1895	
Luttrell	Frank M.	Weise	Hattie A.	24 May 1883	
Luttrell	H. L.	Law	Nettie M.	19 Dec. 1888	
Lutz	Carl	Jorden	Mary A.	24 July 1920	
Lyman	Chas.	Thompson	Mattie M.	26 Dec. 1882	
Lyman	Eugene	Jacobs	Myrtle	3 June 1911	
Lyman	James H.	Stephens	Oma E.	17 Aug. 1909	
Lyman	James H.	Lyman	Owa (?) E.	19 June 1920	
Lyman	William J.	Robertson	Bessie	29 Mar. 1902	
Lyman	William Wickam	Gordon	Edna Isma	2 Dec. 1915	

	Groom	Bride		Date	Comments
Surname	Given Name	Surname	Given Name		
Lynch	Bernard C.	Sills	Rhoda M.	14 Jan. 1909	
Lynch	George L.	Tripp	Grace A.	1 July 1907	
Lynch	James M.	Mizer	Sarah P.	24 Dec. 1879	
Lynch	Robert Newton	Riley	Elizabeth	16 Apr. 1907	
Lynch	William Allen	Frahm	Hertha	30 Aug. 1913	
Lyon	Arthur J.	Ware	Margaret	25 Dec. 1911	
Lyons	Cornelius P.	Shadburne	Julia A.	24 Jan. 1911	
Lyons	James A.	Nutting	Mable L.	16 May 1919	
Lyons	John Joseph	Silva	Mary E.	25 Sept. 1912	
Lyons	Thomas J.	Kelso	Eunice O.	11 Sept. 1918	
Lytjen	Ludwig M.	Navoni	Johanna I.	21 June 1917	
Lyttaker	Albert	Garrison	Ellen M.	6 Jan. 1900	
Lyttaker	E. V.	Dillon	Sarah M.	6 June 1885	
Lyttaker	Will	Dearing	Josie	14 Oct. 1899	
Lytte	George W.	Abrams	Nettie L.	28 Oct. 1882	
Maas	William George	McNeil	Myrtle Adell	19 Oct. 1907	
Mabee	John	Richardson	Nettie Gertrude	15 Apr. 1895	br: Mrs. Vernetta Charles, sister of the bride's father, swears that Jerome R. Richardson and Mrs. Theresa Richardson, the bride's parents, separated about 1882. The children were deserted and taken in by Mrs. Charles, who raised Nettie Gertrude since she was four. The bride will be seventeen on Sept. 11, 1895. Mrs. Charles considers herself guardian and gave testimony and consent. Witnessed in Humboldt County by P. T. Senteney, J.O. Peace.
Mac	M. B.	Littell	Nellie, Mrs.	6 May 1907	

Groom Surname	Groom Given Name	Bride Surname	Bride Given Name	Date	Comments
Maccagno	Joseph	Bocca	Clementina	1 Dec. 1894	L. Modini who signs as Lorenzo Modini, witness
Maccario	Tony	Pasero	Christine	26 Mar. 1913	
MacDonald	Gilbert	Piotrowski	Elizabeth M.	10 Sept. 1920	
Macdonald	Leonard C.	McDermott	Marie L.	20 July 1914	
Macdonald	William	Spurr	Grace J.	17 Mar. 1913	
Macedo	Antone Domingos	Furtado	Emma	3 May 1912	
Macerida/Macida	Marcallo	Robba	Malgerita	25 Aug. 1900	
MacFarlane	Earl R.	Thibadore	Jean M.	24 Aug. 1920	
MacGowan	Henry	Brown	Edna	15 July 1915	
MacGowan	Henry	Brown	Edna Catherine	8 Sept. 1916	
MacGregor	Allan Peter	Keaton	Martha Jane	6 June 1894	
Mache	John A.	Albini	Mary	25 Aug. 1902	br: Donati Albini, father
Mache	Steve A.	Silacci	Dora L.	3 Sept. 1918	
Mack	Charles Westly	Charnock	Amy	6 Sept. 1878	
Mack	John	Nance	Grace A.	30 Apr. 1900	br: A. K. Nance, parent
Mack	Richard	Conelly	May	5 June 1897	
Mack	William E.	Du Commun	Lucille	12 Sept. 1914	
Mack	William, Jr.	Church	Linnie	24 Apr. 1906	
MacKay	William	McFadyen	Isabel	22 May 1918	
MacKenzie	Hugh Fraser	Wisnom	Margaret	9 Feb. 1918	please don't publish, good reasons
Mackey	Edward	Howard	Ruby S.	26 June 1914	
MacKillop	David V.	Isaak	Emma V.	27 Nov. 1914	
Maclay	Thomas	Wickershaw	Lizzie C.	22 July 1901	
MacLean	Hector	Gilooly	Rose May	7 Feb. 1905	
MacMurdo	Willis	Riffe	Hazel Idella	13 Feb. 1920	
Macnair	Douglas	Glaszer	Gertrude J.	10 Oct. 1920	do not publish in local papers
MacNevin	Wm. V.	Denton	Carrie M.	23 Nov. 1912	

		Bride		Date	Comments
Groom					
Surname	**Given Name**	**Surname**	**Given Name**		
Macphail	John R.	Munro	B. F.	15 Aug. 1865	
MacPherson	Stuart	Jones	Jeannette, Mrs.	11 Mar. 1905	
MacQuiddy	Oscar Lee	Dunn	Anna M.	7 June 1907	
Macrina	Leo D.	Poncetta	Rosie	12 May 1919	
Macy	William C.	Looney	Nellie	12 Jan. 1895	
Macy	William C.	Philpott	Helen Alzina Lordell, Mrs.	29 Aug. 1903	
Maddalena	Charles J.	Leibert	Lorraine E.	12 Jan. 1921	
Maddalena	John H.	White	Isadora M.	30 Nov. 1894	
Maddelena	Fred	Sartori	Rina	10 Sept. 1912	
Madden	Edward	Richardson	Mary, Mrs.	8 May 1888	
Madden	William	Davies	Rose E.	24 Dec. 1917	
Maddocks	Fred W.	Marshall	Irene P.	5 Sept. 1891	
Maddocks	Harold F.	King	Dorothy I.	3 Nov. 1920	
Maddocks	Louis A.	Johnson	Hattie C.	29 Nov. 1884	
Maddox	Samuel W.	Thompson	Laura M.	19 June 1880	gr: W. H. & S. A. Maddox, parents; br: T. Thompson, parent; license signed by Joseph Wright
Maddrell	Lepolde S.	Zell	Martha S.	31 May 1919	
Maddux	Burt	Wallin	Eva M.	21 Dec. 1915	
Maddux	Harry W.	Clarke	Maybelle	11 June 1913	
Maddux	Joe Ferreira	Curry	Lizzie	22 July 1897	
Maddux	Preston	Sprague	Elsie L.	31 Dec. 1900	br: Mrs. E. Sprague, mother; do not publish until Saturday
Madeira	George D.	Fenno	Minnie	1 Feb. 1893	
Madeira	George Madison	McLean	Ella A.	8 Apr. 1893	
Madeira	W. R.	Ward	Mary J.	2 Feb. 1894	
Madero	Alvin	Nelson	Mary	16 Mar. 1914	
Maderous	Antone	Moniz	Marie Eugenia	21 Nov. 1919	

Groom Surname	Groom Given Name	Bride Surname	Bride Given Name	Date	Comments
Madison	J. Harry	Rice	Charlotte L.	26 Mar. 1890	
Madison	James	Blain	Audrey Jane	21 Dec. 1904	br: Robert E. Lee Blain, father
Madison	John Harold	Silva	Alice May	23 July 1914	
Madsen	Herbert H.	Kyle	Mildred Baxter	27 Mar. 1920	
Madsen	Neils G.	Franzen	Augusta	8 Mar. 1906	
Maffei	Gaetano	Barella	Elena	31 Oct. 1908	
Maffei	Italo	Marcucci	Angelina	28 Jan. 1901	
Maffei	Luigi	Michalini	Corina	31 Dec. 1884	
Maffia	Emilio	Moreschi	Maria	11 Nov. 1913	
Maffini	Ernest	Barsi	Della	20 Mar. 1915	
Mafia	Antoni	Albini	Maria	10 Oct. 1911	gr: Margheta Piezzi, mother; J. W. Ford & W. W. Futi, Jr., witnesses to her mark
Magatelli	Antonio	Malogani	Sereno	13 Apr. 1912	
Magatelli	Domenico	Paroli	Domenica	31 Dec. 1915	
Magee	Thomas Wm.	Mobley	Anna Dorothea	23 Feb. 1906	
Magetti	Robert	Baccala	Carrie	8 Nov. 1893	br: Peter Baccala, father, gives consent; F. Pergzaglia and A. Baccala, witnesses
Maggart	Edward F.	Aitken	Elenor M.	21 Dec. 1894	license requested by Elenor M. Aitken.
Maggiora	Costantino Delbi (?)	Benedetti	Charlotte M.	27 July 1918	
Maghetti	Henry A.	Mehegan	Margaret U.	15 Nov. 1917	
Magona	Peter F.	Filippini	Rose A.	5 Dec. 1911	
Magoon	Edward Oliver	Gentry	M. Alice		gr: H. K. Magoon, parent; filed between 2 and 14 Jan. 1879
Magoon	Wm. H.	Bock	Kate	26 Apr. 1884	
Magri	Guiseppe	Cia	Antoinetta	26 Aug. 1912	br: W. E. Saunders, A Bacci, witnesses to her mark
Maher	William M.	Mason	Rossaline L.	10 Dec. 1919	
Mahler	Henry J., Jr.	Leahy	Lillian	20 June 1916	
Mahlstedt	August	Fochetti	Theresa	17 June 1900	

Groom		Bride		Date	Comments
Surname	**Given Name**	**Surname**	**Given Name**		
Mahoney	David I.	Roche	Annie J.	6 Oct. 1887	
Mahoney	John M.	Robinson	Pearl	2 Apr. 1907	
Mahoney	William	Geaney	Mary	12 Feb. 1897	
Mahony	H. C.	Sexton	Marie A.	16 Dec. 1913	
Mailer	John A.	Lewis	Katherine E.	6 Apr. 1901	
Maitoza	Manuel P.	Rose	Julia	22 Oct. 1910	
Makee	George William	Beckman	Emma Lena	27 June 1917	
Maker	Archie	Ellis	Mary Jane	18 Apr. 1908	
Maksente	Victor S.	Scaramella	Rosie Rena	4 Jan. 1919	
Malandra	Mauro	Verzasconi	Clotilda	15 Aug. 1889	
Malaspina	Gustavo	Rossi	Iside	1 Apr. 1919	
Malfante	Victor	Buschini	Maria	8 Feb. 1917	
Maliard	Edwin	Perry	Violet	17 Sept. 1913	
Mallory	George Brown	Wade	Juniatta, Mrs.	18 Aug. 1906	
Mallory	Herbert W.	Steger	Betty	9 Apr. 1921	
Mallory	Jacob T.	Magnam	Anneta Estella	23 Nov. 1911	
Malm	Arthur Marian	DeWitt	Mary Lauvira (?)	23 Dec. 1919	
Malm	Carl	Johnson	Betty	8 Aug. 1917	
Malmgren (?)	Carl C. M.	Harper	Margaretta W. V.	25 Aug. 1918	
Malnati	Carlo	Giovanni	Clara M.	1 June 1920	
Malnburg	Ira C.	Rinker	Elizabeth	6 Dec. 1917	
Malof	John	Matos	Minnie L.	13 (?) Sept. 1902	
Malone	James H.	Johnson	Rebecca	14 Oct. 1887	requested by John Goss
Malone	Joseph	Carrigan	Agnes	18 Sept. 1919	
Maloney	James	Marmori	Stella	31 Aug. 1912	
Maloof	Charles	Panini	Carmelina	19 Mar. 1904	
Maloof	John	Morchio	Eva	13 July 1911	
Maloof	John	Matus	Lena	31 Dec. 1904	

Groom Surname	Groom Given Name	Bride Surname	Bride Given Name	Date	Comments
Maltman	Francis D.	Bell	Amanda Lydia, Mrs.	19 Feb. 1904	
Manch	Gottfried	Bollinger	Catherine	21 July 1888	br: Mrs. Catherine Bollinger, mother
Mancini	Massimo	Ginsti	Julia	2 Nov. 1905	br: Mrs. Elizabeth Ginsti, mother
Mancini	Pietro	Rossi	Angelina	1 Aug. 1910	
Mane	Paul	Vogel	Olga T.	13 Aug. 1917	
Maner	Marcellus	Paxton	Emza E.	25 Sept. 1897	
Mangiantini	Narciso	Catelani	Conchetta	17 Nov. 1917	
Mangili	Henry G.	McLaughlin	Mary T.	21 Aug. 1890	
Mangin	Eugene Louis	Peloquin	Marie Louise	5 Oct. 1909	
Mangin	Eugene Louis	Fancher	Gladyst Maud	12 June 1906	
Mangini	Jack	Ponzo	Margherita	25 Sept. 1920	
Mangini	Louis J.	Hyland	Elizabeth J.	20 Mar. 1916	
Manies	Morrison	Kelsey	Florence	15 Sept. 1920	
Mankins	Daniel E., Jr.	Johnson	Juanita Ruth	30 Dec. 1917	
Mann	Edward H.	Penning	Mary	30 Sept. 1889	br: Mrs. R. Diebold, mother
Mann	Frank B.	Bedwell	Annie Alberta	3 July 1905	br: Mattie Bedwell, mother, gives permission
Mann	Guy Chester	Todd	Ruby Angeine	10 Dec. 1915	
Mann	Ned Frase	McNamee	Lenora Margarete	5 Jan. 1917	
Mann	Robert J.	Critchfield	Lulu B.		filed between 13 and 20 Mar. 1885
Mann	T. W.	Dolet	Helen A.	18 July 1914	
Mann	Thomas L.	Temple	Anna	3 Sept. 1904	
Manney	James F.	Roach	Jennie E.	9 Jan. 1882	
Manning	James C.	Cropley	Adella C.	27 Dec. 1887	requested by S. J. Allen
Manning	John	Quinlan	Sarah	25 Sept. 1876	
Manning	Lincoln	Bennett	Freda, Mrs.	26 Oct. 1904	
Manouk	Charles	Harenisch	Agnes D. M.	3 Oct. 1889	
Mansfield	Col. L.	Whitlock	Sophia, Mrs.	6 Apr. 1867	

	Groom	Bride		Date	Comments
Surname	Given Name	Surname	Given Name		
Manter	Benjamin H.	Kidd	Alta S.	15 Dec. 1920	
Mantua	Jiulius	Righetta	Elia	4 June 1901	
Manuel	George S.	Krepps	Jennie L.	25 Aug. 1902	
Manuel	H. S.	Baettge	Sophia	7 Nov. 1888	
Mapes	Ira C.	Hall	Sarah F.	8 May 1867	
Mapes	L. Percy	Hansen	Sadie M.	18 Sept. 1909	
Maple	Geo. M.	Mapel	Belle	20 Nov. 1888	
Marall	Henry R.	Delmue	Mary J.	17 Dec. 1901	
Marando	Frank Harry	Fowler	Della	1 Sept. 1905	
Marble	Edward R.	Allen	Hattie W.	14 Jan. 1897	
Marble	John H.	Garrison	Grace E.	6 Dec. 1902	
Marcell	N. E.	Donoven	Mally (?)		filed between 20 Jan. and 6 Feb. 1882
Marchant	Frederick R.	Saul	Sallie Belle	22 Dec. 1902	
Marchetti	Nicoderro	Viviani	Georgia	14 Aug. 1917	
Marchisio	Delfino	Wernecke	Katie	18 Feb. 1889	
Marchisio	Enrico F.	Wiser	Macel	7 May 1917	
Marci	Jerunoz	Malugani	Martina	7 Dec. 1908	
Marci	Luca	Pomi	Anonziata	8 July 1911	
Marcollo	John	Fochetti	Caterine	27 Feb. 1904	
Marcucci	Abromo	Gaddini	Elisabeth	7 June 1911	
Marcucci	Faustino	Bertossi	Teresa	24 June 1911	
Marcucci	Oreste	Monticelli	Emma	7 Dec. 1907	
Marcucci	Paul	Sani	Marie	1 June 1907	
Marcus	Carl Ralph	Matzen	Ella	8 Dec. 1920	
Mardis	John Harvey	Porcher	Marion Louise	25 Oct. 1898	gr: John H. & Martha Mardis, parents; William T. Breenwood, witness
Mari	Ernesto	Domeniconi	Matilde	17 July 1913	
Maria	Jose	Souza	Mary	29 Mar. 1897	

Groom Surname	Groom Given Name	Bride Surname	Bride Given Name	Date	Comments
Marier	Edmund L.	Hoffman	Gertrude L.	10 Aug. 1910	
Marin	George	Bin	Lena	6 Jan. 1919	
Marin	Louis	Martin	Aurore	24 Jan. 1918	
Maringo	Steven	Baker	Lillian Emma	18 Nov. 1911	
Marino	Filippo	Pozzi	Caterina	29 Aug. 1914	
Marinoni	Gaetano	Coregliano	Domencia	26 June 1911	
Marion	Angelo Nickoles	Martin	Sarah Matilda	7 Apr. 1917	
Marion	Vernal Kennet	Summ	Erna Georgia	12 July 1916	
Mariotte	Paul A.	Law	Myrtle H.	6 Apr. 1907	
Markham	Henry C.	Brodie	Annie, Mrs.	8 Nov. 1897	both widowed
Markley	Albert E.	Palmer	Nirma	11 May 1907	
Markley	Thomas Cox	Smyth	Jennie Elizabeth	blank	
Markopulos	Antonio	Root	Hilda	25 Jan, 1915	
Marks	Harry	Keller	Dora	14 July 1920	
Marks	Thomas F.	Piezzi	Catherine D., Mrs.	26 June 1902	
Marks	Walter Randolph	Washburn	Catherine Faith	12 Jan. 1921	
Marks (?)	Julian	Cordova	Rosie	10 Nov. 1911	
Marlatt	Al	Heather	Lizzie	14 Mar. 1910	
Marlatt	Charles E.	McConihe	Ethel M.	31 July 1916	
Marlatt	Frank	Heather	Kate	30 June 1908	
Marlatt	Perry Edward	Udall	Lola Maud	28 Nov. 1906	
Maroni	George Joseph	Lencioni	Theresa Josephine	28 Apr. 1917	
Maroni	Louis	Cassani	Ricca	24 Nov. 1897	br: A. Cassani, guardian
Maroni	Peter	Gomberina	Rosa	9 Feb. 1889	br: Tomaso Gomberina, father
Marple	Robert J	Roberts	Daisy E.	2 Dec. 1899	no previous marriage
Marquis	Thomas C.	Schulz	Gertrude E.	27 May 1919	
Marr	Clyde H.	Martin	Mildred Mae	18 July 1912	
Marr	John A.	McMinn	Rosa	22 May 1886	

	Groom	Bride		Date	Comments
Surname	**Given Name**	**Surname**	**Given Name**		
Marra	Battista	Maggini	Catterina	26 Aug. 1890	
Mars	Charles	Poe	Ethel	25 Nov. 1912	
Marsh	Arthur	Cullen	Mary	18 Aug. 1899	
Marsh	Charles E.	Green	Lida	17 Nov. 1894	
Marsh	Clarence Joseph	Sleeper	Ruth Severne	21 July 1905	gr: Joseph Marsh, father, gives consent
Marsh	Ira M.	Gelhart	Mattie J.	21 Aug. 1884	
Marsh	John P.	Lagan	Katherine J.	26 June 1920	
Marsh	Robert Linus	Mayfield	Flora	16 Jan. 1888	
Marshall	A. F.	Abario	Rose S.	13 Sept. 1913	gr: W. W. Felt, Jr.; G. Brittain, witnesses to his mark
Marshall	Adam, Jr.	Mullikin	Arrilla J.	11 May 1918	please don't publish
Marshall	Aretus	Plum	Elsie	27 Oct. 1909	br: Mrs. C. E. Plum, mother
Marshall	Charles Wilson	Bruce	Ruth Helen	18 Apr. 1914	
Marshall	Cleveland H.	Davis	Pearl	10 Dec. 1902	gr: Mrs. M. Marshall, mother; note about death of bride's mother
Marshall	Frank L.	Turner	May M.	16 Apr. 1887	
Marshall	H. M.	Smith	Gertrude E.	27 Dec. 1911	
Marshall	Harry Lee	Fisher	Lora Etta	6 July 1907	
Marshall	James M.	Steele	Margaret Mae	24 Dec. 1906	
Marshall	Joseph Gilbert	Mitchell	Susan	10 Sept. 1895	
Marshall	Manuel J.	Walters	Pearl	5 Aug. 1916	
Marshall	Robert	Haupt	Louisa	29 May 1888	
Marshall	Thomas	Bryn	Carrie	11 Apr. 1913	
Marshall	Thomas H.	Winkler	Hattie L.	19 Dec. 1898	gr: divorced from Blanche Marshall, Sonoma Co., 12 May 1896
Marshall	Thos. H.	Pickle	Blanche	7 Nov. 1894	
Marshall	William	Ames	Annie L.	26 May 1883	
Martell	Joseph A.	Ford	Lettie F.	1 Dec. 1892	

Groom Surname	Groom Given Name	Bride Surname	Bride Given Name	Date	Comments
Marten	John Edward	Rosewarne	Elizabeth Serretta	24 Apr. 1917	
Martens	Dietrich W.	Kelly	Emma M.	15 May 1919	
Marties	Joseph F.	Dyozenz?	Maria	1 June 1893	
Martignoni	Walter	Lafranchi	Ollie	27 Oct. 1913	
Martin	Andrew William	Court	Ida Belle	29 Jan. 1918	
Martin	Arthur J.	Newbert	Margaret B.	18 Jan. 1905	
Martin	Charles J.	Cummings	Hattie E.	18 Nov. 1896	
Martin	Charles L.	Jorgensen	Evelyn L.	15 Feb. 1918	
Martin	Christian J.	Daniels	Lorena F.	12 July 1897	gr: Christian S. Martin of Oakalnd gives consent and signs
Martin	Dock	Higgins	Minnie E.	26 Aug. 1920	
Martin	Dorchester E.	Rutledge	Mary E.	29 Aug. 1878	
Martin	Edgar	McGaughey	Fannie G.	27 May 1876	
Martin	Edgar Laurens	Gailor	Ima Edna	12 Aug 1907	
Martin	Eugene E.	Brown	Hallie B.	14 May 1883	
Martin	Frances W.	Zumwalt	Berenice I.	27 Apr. 1918	gr: Ethan A. Martin, mother
Martin	Frank F.	Cadd	Lillian Rebecca	27 June 1907	
Martin	Frank M.	Litchfield	Mary E.	22 June 1897	no previous marriage
Martin	Frederick	Cook	Beatrice Bidwell	23 Mar. 1915	
Martin	George A.	Pohley	Mary L.	18 Dec. 1896	
Martin	Ira P.	Bellah	Mildred M.	4 Jan. 1911	
Martin	J. E.	Leard	Nettie A.	27 Dec. 1884	
Martin	James	Kane	Minnie	7 Oct. 1914	
Martin	James C.	Bryant	Susan F.	28 Apr. 1887	br: Mrs. D. Helrevling
Martin	James Delea	Buchanan	Effie	23 Dec. 1909	
Martin	Joe	Smith	Mary	12 Aug. 1910	
Martin	John	Mathison	Ida E. J.	9 Oct. 1865	
Martin	John A.	Shields	Susan	18 May 1888	

	Groom	Bride		Date	Comments
Surname	Given Name	Surname	Given Name		
Martin	John M.	Meyers	Sussie	16 Feb. 1918	
Martin	John Milton	Turner	Minnie L.	22 Aug. 1899	gr: Mrs. Mary Martin, mother; br: Mrs. Agnes Turner, mother; no previous marriage
Martin	John S., Jr.	Brown (?)	Nellie	26 Apr. 1879	
Martin	Josiah	Lewis	Rebecca	24 Dec. 1881	gr: J. B. Martin, parent
Martin	Lauren M.	Peterson	Edith V.	22 Nov. 1904	
Martin	Leopold	Zanini	Maria	11 Sept. 1897	
Martin	Lewis	Brown	Marian	8 Sept. 1910	
Martin	Louis	Dormeau	Albertine	20 July 1912	
Martin	Manuel	Cuadro	Mary	16 May 1889	
Martin	Merwin	Gano	Maud	25 Sept. 1889	
Martin	Milo ?	Mathis?	Emma	21 Nov. 1866	
Martin	Milton	Frost	Corda	21 Dec. 1881	
Martin	Oscar J.	Kenison	Mabel E.	23 Nov. 1910	
Martin	Paul C.	Gravatte	Katheryn F.	21 Dec. 1914	
Martin	Rasmus	Thompson	Annie	25 Mar. 1893	
Martin	Robert A.	Nichols	Sade Jane	5 Nov. 1920	
Martin	Robert Edward	Berger	Flora Helen	19 Apr. 1919	
Martin	Russel Sage	Lyman	Francian V.	24 Apr. 1920	gr: Van Martin, father
Martin	T. J.	Wall	Jennie	22 Dec. 1892	
Martin	Van T.	Proctor	Laura Jane	20 Nov. 1888	gr: J. B. Martin, father
Martin	Walter	Deacon	Martha	18 Sept. 1890	
Martin	William Ira	Stark	Rebecca Marilla	15 Sept. 1897	gr: Ezekiel & Mary Martin, parents; H. C. Weber, J. C. Ingalls, witnesses
Martin	William S.	Esterman	Elsa	10 July 1915	
Martinelli	Fortunato	Chintelli	Jennie	27 Aug. 1910	br: Joe Chintelli, father
Martinelli	Gildo P.	Spottswood	Ada	7 Nov. 1900	

Groom Surname	Groom Given Name	Bride Surname	Bride Given Name	Date	Comments
Martinelli	Ulesse	Casini	Emma	23 May 1891	
Martinelli	Ulysses J.	Fillippini	Silvia O.	2 May 1903	
Martinetti	Gabriele	Guenza	Carmelina	17 Oct. 1911	
Martinez	Leonardo	Remesal (?)	Maria	19 Dec. 1919	
Martinez	Sylvester	Francisco	Mariana	31 Oct. 1893	
Martini	Adolfo	Davini	Antonietta	22 May 1915	
Martini	Narciso	Vannucci	Florinda	13 May 1908	
Martino	Giovanni	Amavisca	Matilda	16 Jan. 1911	
Martinoni	A. H.	Barboni	Mae	12 June 1911	
Martola	H. A.	Fox	Adeline M.	21 Oct. 1915	
Martz	Roy	Badger	Blanche H.	14 Sept. 1920	
Martz	Samuel Anderson	Allen	Cornelia	29 May 1906	
Marval	John	Rivera	Inocencesia	3 Oct. 1912	br: W. E. Saunders, John Marval, witnesses to her mark
Marvin	John F.	Owen	Mary M.	19 Feb. 1912	
Marx	Bert Franklin	Dowling	Anna Katherine	22 May 1914	
Marzolf	Charles Joseph	Offutf	Ella May	30 Sept. 1916	
Marzolf	Frederick George	Furlong	Kathryn A.	14 Feb. 1917	
Masa	Joe	Molf	Minnie, Mrs.	24 Dec. 1900	both widowed; gr: his mark witnessed by F. G. Nagle
Maschetti	Ben	Esaia	Julia	17 June 1911	br: Peter Esaia, father; W. H. Pete, Jr., & L. J. ?, witness to mark
Mascho	Leland H.	Jensen	Caroline	6 Oct. 1920	
Masciorini	Henry T.	Petersen	Hattie	23 Dec. 1917	
Masconi	Pasquale	Belli	Marguerite	23 Nov. 1907	br: E Belli, parent
Masgado	Jose	Werano	Wisenta, Mrs.	22 Feb. 1867	
Masher	John Ed	Mathews	Evy	30 Oct. 1866	
Masini	Sante	Barzi	Angelina	5 May 1914	

	Groom	Bride		Date	Comments
Surname	Given Name	Surname	Given Name		
Maslin	Woolsey	Saunders	Emma	20 Apr. 1894	license requested by H. J. Rogers
Mason	Chas. O.	Cofer	Mary	18 Nov. 1899	
Mason	Craig M.	Hendricks	Sadie D., Mrs.	6 Mar. 1909	
Mason	Ernest	Field	Kate	18 Apr. 1891	
Mason	Frank L.	Hitchcock	C. Elizabeth	6 Apr. 1891	br: Mrs. Mary E. Hitchcock, mother
Mason	Fred B.	Barham	Hattie L.	8 Jan. 1884	
Mason	George B.	Baldwin	Mollie Dell	23 Dec. 1904	
Mason	George C.	Hassett	Carrie J.	26 Dec. 1901	do not publish until Monday
Mason	James S.	Greensmith	Emily R. M.	30 Dec. 1885	
Mason	James W.	Parkin	Josie, Mrs.	1 Oct. 1902	gr: 220 3rd St., San Francisco; br: same address
Mason	Marshall E.	Staples	Viola B.	23 Aug. 1899	no previous marriage; don't publish
Mason	Robt. A.	Tombs	Nellie M.	8 Dec. 1898	no previous marriage
Mason	Troy F.	Fiefer	Della E.	29 Apr. 1919	
Mason	William C.	Howard	Maud C.	8 Feb. 1897	
Mason	William C.	Shohoney	Ethel, Mrs.	6 Nov. 1902	
Mason	William H.	McGinnis	Mary	11 Oct. 1898	no previous marriage
Massaini	Guiseppe	Pensa	Linda	8 Nov. 1913	
Massei	Guido	Marcucci	Iris Marie	18 Sept. 1915	br: Giselda Marcucci, parent
Massie	Fred B.	O'Brien	Annie	22 Apr. 1921	
Massimo	George	Asnip	Ellen	22 Mar. 1889	br: Susan Asnip, mother
Massini	Giuseppe	Scatina	Margherite	14 Oct. 1914	
Massler	George	Messerle	Rosa	8 Nov. 1902	
Massoni	William J.	Davini	Bruna N.	26 June 1913	gr: Eugenio Massoni, mother
Mast	C. I.	Smith	Kittie E.	10 Apr. 1893	gr: consent given by parent Posmelia Mast
Mastai	Battista	Ballati	Ursula	30 Oct. 1893	
Mastrado	Angelo	Benelli	Rosa	11 Apr. 1921	
Mastrup	Andrew	Hutchins	Violet	28 Dec. 1914	

Groom Surname	Groom Given Name	Bride Surname	Bride Given Name	Date	Comments
Mastrup	Christian Theodore	Bruhn	Nandina Rosina	3 Feb. 1906	br: Peter Bruhn, father
Matazzoni	Armando	Ottoboni	Lena Helen	30 Mar. 1918	
Matazzoni	Guiseppe	Baraldi	Leontina	27 Apr. 1912	
Mates	George Adams	Peters	Anna Marie	20 July 1905	
Mateson	Hans	McKean	Mary, Mrs.	24 May 1888	
Mather	William	Allen	Catherine	25 Nov. 1887	
Mather	William Henry	Daywalt	Elizabeth	26 July 1920	
Mathers	Wesley	Schultes	Florence G.	29 Nov. 1920	
Matheson	Charles J.	Brown	Erma B.	28 July 1917	br: Florence B. Brown, mother
Mathews	Alfred F.	Manning	Mary F.	13 Oct. 1866	
Mathews	Alvaro Brown	Veira	Mary Agnes	27 Apr. 1907	
Mathews	George I.	Hall	Eliza	30 June 1883	
Mathias	Antoni B.	Dutro	Josephine M.	13 July 1914	
Mathias	John B.	Raymond	Annie	15 Oct. 1913	
Mathiesen	Fred	Wiegand	Mary	30 Aug. 1902	
Mathiesen	Jesse C.	Hoban	Ida N.	16 Aug. 1920	
Mathiessen	Henry A.	Andersen	Theresa M.	7 Mar. 1897	license requested by Charles W. Stolker
Mathis	Ephraim R.	Drake	Pearl A.	29 Nov. 1904	
Mathis	Henry F.	Leek	Cyntha	20 Sept. 1865	
Mathisen	Dudley	Haigh	Ethel	26 June 1909	
Mathisen	Henry	Mason	Clarrisa	2 Oct. 1906	
Mathisen	Jesse	Dollar	Elsie Elma	27 July 1920	br: Grace E. Dollar, mother
Mathison	Hans Peter	Nilousen	Hanna M.	4 Dec. 1888	
Mathorn	Perry D.	Lewis	Cashia S.	28 Nov. 1885	
Matison	Frank M.	Howard	Mabel C.	21 Oct. 1914	
Matlock	Walter J.	Stiles	Bertha M.	1 May 1900	br: Mrs. Fannie Stiles, mother; R. L. Thompson, witness to mother's mark
Matson	Arthur C.	Kowski	Johanna Witt	16 Nov. 1908	

		Bride		Date	Comments
Groom					
Surname	Given Name	Surname	Given Name		
Matson	Carl E.	Smidberg	Ellen V.	21 July 1910	
Matson	Hjalmar	Bentsen	Carola	24 July 1907	
Mattei	Richard C.	Winchell	Laura A.	4 May 1912	
Mattei	Valenti C.	Fredericks	Ida L.	13 Sept. 1913	
Matteri	Gottardo	Poncia	Mary	28 Mar. 1919	
Matteri	John	Mazzucchi	Giuseppina	24 Apr. 1913	
Matteri	Paolo	Motti	Maddalena	5 Sept. 1896	
Matteri	Peter	Mazzucchi	Giovanna	2 Dec. 1902	
Matteucci	Laurence	Simoncini	Emma	6 Apr. 1911	br:Emilio Simoncini, father
Matthes	Charles C.	Ramsner	Marie R.	30 Aug. 1917	
Matthews	Alvin Wesley	Barnett	Minnie Della	28 Feb. 1907	
Matthews	Charles H.	Clark	Selina C., Mrs.	28 Feb. 1903	
Matthews	Charles W.	Wallace	Annie E.	24 July 1918	
Matthews	Charles W.	Barth	Mary E.	24 June 1891	
Matthews	Fred R.	Estes	Fannie E.	4 Feb. 1899	
Matthews	Frederic Hamilton	Bowman	Estella May	14 Feb. 1918	
Matthews	Hiram Walker	Cusick	Helen Winifred	17 Oct. 1895	
Matthews	James L.	Bassett	Lillian E.	27 Mar. 1915	
Matthews	James Overton	Levilt	Mary Ward	12 Sept. 1887	
Matthews	John E.	Parmeter	Mary L.	24 Jan. 1894	
Matthews	John W.	Johnson	Mattie E.	5 Dec. 1887	
Matthews	O. P.	Hardesty	Susie	29 June 1915	
Matthews	Oscar F.	Woodcock	Maud	3 Oct. 1907	
Matthews	W. C.	Finley	Leora M.	17 June 1915	
Matthews	Winfield Scott, Jr.	Comstock	Cornelia	17 Mar. 1911	
Matthias	Henry G.	Wheeler	Frances L.	15 Oct. 1889	
Matthias	Manuel C.	Rodgers	Catherine M.	8 Sept. 1920	
Matthiesen	Anton Ludwig	Nielsen	Else Christine	2 June 1896	

Groom Surname	Groom Given Name	Bride Surname	Bride Given Name	Date	Comments
Mattiesen	Hermann	Paul	Mabel	11 May 1907	
Mattley	George	Rodeck	Margaret	8 June 1892	
Mattos	Arthur G.	Gomes	Alexandrina A.	5 Sept. 1914	
Mattos	Joseph	Barba	Joaquinna	12 Oct. 1900	
Mattos	Manuel B.	Segueira	Maria	23 Apr. 1914	
Mattson	Laurence A.	Henderson	Myrtle May	3 Apr. 1920	gr: Christina C. Mattson, mother
Mattson	Martin	Pihl	Jennie N.	7 Oct. 1889	
Matzen	Edward	Schlinkmann	Marie	1 Oct. 1914	
Mauck	Carl August	Nessen	Ana	30 Oct. 1866	
Mauerhan	John P.	Johnson	Carolyn	10 Apr. 1920	
Maurer	Ed	Caldwell	Georgia	22 Nov. 1913	
Max	Albert	Martin	Susie	24 Aug. 1889	
Maxwell	Ernest Edgar	Taft	Georginia ? A.	15 Apr. 1908	
Maxwell	Frank Lawrence	Hicks	Grace J.	2 Oct. 1907	
Maxwell	Frank Washington	Gaskins	Minnie Maud	24 Oct. 1907	
Maxwell	John R.	Burns	Carrie Virginia	18 May 1895	
Maxwell	Michael	Wittmann	Maria	28 Nov. 1914	
Maxwell	Watson B.	Wagner	Frances M.	31 Dec. 1913	br: Frances Geezley, mother
Maxwell	William	McCarthy	Tillie	8 Aug. 1908	
Maxwell	William Albert	Rodgers	Alvina Maria	22 Sept. 1906	
Maxzenti	Amanezio	Canepa	Clementina	21 Oct. 1916	
May	Ernest Clarke	Driver	Emma Sarah	28 Nov. 1910	br: Mrs. E. Driver, mother
May	Henry C.	Bach	Adeline W.	1 June 1891	
Maybee	F. E.	Peterson	Sophia	11 Dec. 1895	
Maybee	Frank E.	Johnson	Kitty	23 May 1881	
Mayer	Edmond A.	Olsen	Ruth N.	27 Oct. 1920	
Mayer	Frederic D.	Weyl	Nellie	27 Aug. 1877	gr: Jacob F. Mayer
Mayers	Irving	Mills	Sadie Florence	14 Oct. 1905	

	Groom	Bride		Date	Comments
Surname	**Given Name**	**Surname**	**Given Name**		
Mayes	Ernest E.	Beach	Della E.	16 Sept. 1898	gr: John Mayes, father; br: Mrs. M. Beach, mother; Ollean Moore, witness
Mayes	Ernest E.	Pezzie	Ethel	27 June 1911	
Mayes	John H.	McMinn	Mary Frances	1 July 1878	gr: signed with his mark; br: R. Froger, guardian
Mayfield	George W.	Manville	Minnie E.	5 Sept. 1919	
Maynard	Harry H.	Ficker ?	May	1894	br: nativity is Mo. Could be Montana or Missouri. Date of marriage not given.
Mayo	Larry G.	Williamson	Dorothy E.	20 June 1912	
Mays	John Burton	Berry	Anna Belle	12 Oct. 1896	don't [publish] notice.
Mays	Larkin B.	Carrie	Anna B.	8 Nov. 1884	
Mayze	Joseph	Peterson	Mabel Violet	11 Dec. 1906	
Mazza	Domenico	Proletti	Giovanna	17 Aug. 1896	
Mazza	John	Arata	Angela	15 Aug. 1914	
Mazza	Joseph H.	Filippini	Elvira Leretta	20 Feb. 1908	
Mazza	Ralph	Shepard	Oliva	10 Apr. 1914	br: Mrs. Mary Shepard, mother
Mazza	Romildo Louis	Soldati	Jennie Ida	18 Oct. 1906	
Mazzeri	Enrico	Ferraris	Annetta	15 May 1920	
Mazzoni	John	Lafranchi	Giema	29 Aug. 1895	
Mazzoni	Peter	Mazzurchi	Angiolina	20 May 1914	
Mazzotti	Ralph	Donati	Dosola	28 Oct. 1915	
Mazzucchi	Adorno	Bellotti	Mary	24 Sept. 1919	
Mazzucchi	Martino	Albini	Angela	24 May 1919	
Mc?ammon	Joseph	Hendren	Rebecca	5 Nov. 1900	requested by Alex Hendron, friend
McAbee	Frank	Lile	Ethel	27 Aug. 1906	
McAfee	Lorn Charles	Wade	Bernice	28 June 1916	
McAfee	Vernon	Menne	Mary	16 Dec. 1916	
McAllaster	Anson D.	Nielsen	Mattie	28 June 1913	

Groom Surname	Groom Given Name	Bride Surname	Bride Given Name	Date	Comments
McAllaster	Fred Shelby	Lowrey	Florence E.	27 Dec. 1916	
McAllister	Floyd Stanley	Hall	Evelyn Louise	3 July 1911	
McAllister	Kieth (?) M.	Phillips	Gertrude E.	7 Nov. 1917	br: Mrs. Dolly Phillips, mother
McAlpine	J. K.	Smith	Florence A.	17 June 1911	
McAnally	Robert W.	Meredith	Gladys L.	19 Sept. 1919	
McAnear	Saml. F.	Towne	Florence	23 June 1896	
McAninch	Harry	Wilson	Ella G., Mrs.	4 Apr. 1902	br: widow
McAskell	Angus H.	Koch	Dorothy B.	7 Nov. 1911	
McAuley	George W.	Rhodes	Clara M.	10 June 1914	
McAuley	George William	Wirts	Elizabeth Bernice	10 Dec. 1905	
McBee	Nathan	Newton	Jennie, Mrs.	20 Sept. 1877	br: birthdate, 29 September; H. S. Epperley, witness
McBrayer	Arthur Lewis	Hale	Samantha Anise	5 Dec. 1905	
McBride	David	Willard	Susan Alice	10 Feb. 1877	br: born 1 January 1852; Laura Willard, mother; Fulton; Frank Howell, witness
McBride	Murrie J.	Bell	Mary E.	21 Oct. 1892	
McCabe	Arthur D.	Ehly	Lucile E.	22 Oct. 1911	
McCabe	John D.	Pollard	Jean	17 June 1902	
McCabe	W. H.	Peugh	Erba M.	21 Feb. 1914	
McCallum	Alphonso	Day	Lizzie	2 Feb. 1897	
McCammon	Robert	Nichols	Sarah Margaret	20 Feb. 1917	
McCan	Francis A.	Watkins	Annette A.	18 Feb. 1896	do not publish
McCandless	Robert	Zearns	Mary	6 Feb. 1893	
McCann	George	Lytaker	Anna	23 Nov. 1866	
McCann	Thomas F.	Chambaud	Sadie	11 Aug. 1891	
McCann	William Charles A.	Danhansen	Louise	19 Nov. 1908	
McCappin	John A.	Staley	Ethyle M.	31 Dec. 1906	
McCarcy	Harry	Gwaltney (?)	Myrtle Alice	1 Mar. 1910	

		Bride		Date	Comments
Groom					
Surname	**Given Name**	**Surname**	**Given Name**		
McCargar	H. S.	Warner	Minnie E.	22 Oct. 1894	
McCarter	William Ernest	Alden	Priscilla B.	31 July 1916	gr: Joseph A. McCarter, father; br: John F. Alden, father
McCarthy	A. Marden	Frank	Marie L.	22 Aug. 1908	br: requested license
McCarthy	David A.	McGuire	Mary Jane	21 Aug. 1890	
McCarthy	Eugene G.	Fewel	Addie J.	19 Apr. 1893	
McCarthy	Geo. J	Hyde	Annie E.	10 Nov. 1887	
McCarthy	Timothy	Grabs	Lila B.	25 Oct. 1919	
McCarthy	Will	Farrar	Theo	20 Nov. 1891	
McCarty	Eugene G.	Burger	Jessie	22 June 1898	br: no previous marriage; gr: divorced 21 May 1897
McCaslin	Reo W.	Crist	Wilma L.	7 Nov. 1918	
McCaughey	Howard Cyril	Tibbetts	Elsie Maude	5 Oct. 1903	
McCaughey	James	Carsen	Nancy	18 Mar. 1867	
McCauley	Thomas P.	Church	Alice C.	9 June 1913	
McCausland	James	Kidder	Lizzie	2 Nov. 1877	
McCawley	L. E.	Irvin	Maggie	14 Jan. 1895	
McCawley	Lucien E.	Lukas	Emilie	12 Nov. 1904	
McChesney	Robert S.	Davis	Ona M.	24 Apr. 1920	
McChristian	Owen A.	Greening	Nellie E.	4 June 1902	
McChristian	Wm. E.	Chenoweth	Viola T.	23 Feb. 1895	gr: Owen McChristian, father, gives consent.
McClary	David Reid	Pedersen	Christine Jensine	10 June 1905	
McClellan	Albert R.	Lynch	Tillie	8 Feb. 1898	no previous marriage
McClellan	J. A. S.	Johnson	Lizzie	14 Oct. 1880	br: Margaret Johnson, mother
McClelland	Buchanan	Hudson	Elizabeth, Mrs.	23 Nov. 1881	
McClelland	Robert Henry	Myers	Alice R.	8 May 1917	
McClendon	William J.	Carter	Alice M.	18 Jan. 1896	

Groom Surname	Groom Given Name	Bride Surname	Bride Given Name	Date	Comments
McClish	James B.	Lodge	Hazel K.	10 Mar. 1913	
McClish	James Blaine	Mothom	Claudia Alice	25 Oct. 1906	gr: John N. McClish, father
McClish	John M.	Hamilton	Georgia	12 Nov. 1900	
McClish	Ralph	Thurman	Nellie	27 Oct. 1894	
McClool	Thomas A.	Cargile	Lucina	31 Oct. 1883	
McCloskey	R. M.	Nicholson	Catherine A.	12 July 1915	
McCloud	Louis Clifford	Clark	Mary E.	29 June 1904	
McCloud	William Elbert	Samuel	Dorothy Viola	22 July 1908	
McClude	Roland R.	Harman	Elizabeth	7 Aug. 1919	
McClure	Isaac	Grasso	Mary	9 Mar. 1914	
McClure	Walter	Hansen	Frances	11 Dec. 1901	
McClymonds	Vance	Ellis	Treasure Sterling	7 Feb. 1910	
McCoffrey	Bernard	Wilson	Agnes	5 Oct. 1918	
McCollam	William	Friend	Mary E.	28 July 1882	
McColloch	Wilson	Stainin (?)	Anie	14 July 1879	
McCollum	William	Friesia (?)	Mary E.	7 Mar. 1882	
McComb	Barron N.	Bailey	Clara V.	28 Apr. 1879	
McComb	George B.	Griffith	Lucille M.	16 June 1913	
McCombs	Aaron Cecil	Sandberg	Olga Olivia	20 June 1906	
McCombs	Charles W.	Gillett	Elizabeth A.	18 Sept. 1902	
McCombs	Edward O.	Vivarelli	Minnie	7 Nov. 1900	
McCombs	John F., Jr.	Barrett	Luella B.	26 Nov. 1913	
McCombs	Joseph Franklin	Crowder	Erma May	13 Nov. 1915	br: James William Crowder, father
McCombs	William H.	Rich	Eula S.	30 Nov. 1900	
McConnell	Frederick William	Hall	Gladys	18 June 1915	
McConnell	Hugh	Svenson	Anna D.	23 July 1912	
McConnell	Jesse C.	Hammerlund	Ada C.	8 Sept. 1887	
McConnell	Joseph P.	Wilt	Carolyn J.	20 Nov. 1920	

	Groom	Bride		Date	Comments
Surname	**Given Name**	**Surname**	**Given Name**		
McConnell	Mark	Woodward	Lillian Pearl	9 Jan. 1904	
McConnell	William S.	Alton	Mary Agnes	13 Nov. 1893	br: John L. Alton, father, gives consent
McConochie	Thomas S.	Emmick	Minnie	12 May 1909	
McCord	Arthur	Gray	Minnie M.	5 Mar. 1914	
McCord	Charles	Carrillo	Lulu	23 Mar. 1882	br: Joaquin Carrillo, father
McCord	Charles	McDonnell	Florence Evelyn	14 July 1920	
McCord	David C.	Combs	Leonore	16 Mar. 1899	no previous marriage
McCord	Robert B. M.	Bones	Electa Z.	5 June 1896	
McCord	Rollin Burdette	Tully	Louise B.	24 Feb. 1908	
McCord	Smith	Davidson	Zidana	31 May 1904	
McCormack	Philip	Norton	Ellen	11 Apr. 1891	
McCormack	William H.	Stover	Lillian D.	10 May 1920	
McCormack	Percival W.	Purvine	Lena Aletha	18 Dec. 1917	
McCormick	Chalmers	Hendrickson	C. Maud	3 June 1893	
McCormick	Charles E.	Bradbury	Eva	1 June 1899	
McCormick	Rodney	O'Hara	Emma E.	25 Sept. 1900	
McCory	Gene L.	Fine	Caroline, Mrs.	6 June 1865	
McCown	Albert E.	McCaughey	Edith	19 Apr. 1898	
McCown	George M.	Boyd	Elizabeth L.	13 Apr. 1892	
McCoy	Clyde	Harrison	Margaret	30 Apr. 1920	
McCoy	David A.	Dill	Matilda S.	28 Mar. 1905	
McCoy	Hugh	Combs	Amnada M. F.	25 Sept. 1876	br: A. R. Combs, father; Healdsburg
McCoy	John M.	Young	Emma	10 Mar. 1880	
McCracken	Frank B.	McClish	Jennie C.	8 Dec. 1899	br: divorced more than one year
McCracken	Geo. F.	Capell	Margaret E.	19 Apr. 1886	
McCracken	Marshal N.	Thurman	Alice	7 Nov. 1900	
McCracken	William J.	Archer	Nellie R.	25 Oct. 1897	br: John H. Archer, father; no previous marriage

Groom Surname	Groom Given Name	Bride Surname	Bride Given Name	Date	Comments
McCraken	Alexander	Anthony	Anna M.	19 Apr. 1915	
McCraney	Harrie E.	Condy	Mae E.	2 Jan. 1913	
McCray	Armund W.	Welley (?)	Nora	23 Oct. 1882	
McCray	David W.	Maddux	Gertrude E.	20 Dec. 1911	
McCray	Logan	Sinn	Carrie M.	5 Nov. 1894	
McCray	William Lloyd	Johnson	Ella F.	7 Dec. 1899	
McCray	William Lloyd	Collins	Marie	3 Mar. 1917	
McCrea	James Walter	Goodfellow	Thelma Marie	15 June 1914	
McCready	Thomas	Black	Marie	2 Oct. 1918	
McCready	Thomas C.	Cockrill	Lora T.	27 Nov. 1900	
McCrystle	Arthur B.	Winslow	Geraldine M.	25 Apr. 1914	
McCue	Herbert E.	Rossi	Alice M.	7 May 1917	
McCulley	T. A.	Brockmann	Agnes M.	21 Apr. 1913	
McCulloch	Irvin Scott	Dovin	Elizabeth	4 Mar. 1916	
McCulloch	James Henry	Barham	Lucy	7 July 1891	
McCulloh	Frank	Laughlin	Lizzie	5 Jan. 1888	
McCune	William M.	Dickey	Parmelia	1 Jan. 1866	
McCustion	Bert James	Trowbridge	Grace Tyler	5 Oct. 1907	
McCutchan	Fred E.	Lucas	Metta	27 Oct. 1914	
McCutchan	Geo. F.	Pohley	Margaret	9 Jan. 1884	br: Wm. C. McCutchan, her parents are deceased and she has no guardian
McCutchan	George F.	Meek	Mary L.	6 Feb. 1894	
McCutchan	George Francis	Sorden	Mary	9 Oct. 1906	
McCutchan	William H.	Ward	Ada E.	8 Dec. 1893	
McCutchen	James B.	Bell	Geneva	10 Sept. 1890	br: Henry Bell, father
McCutchen	Stanley S.	Stout	Lizzie	1 Apr. 1905	
McDaniel	Albert Edwin	Cramer	Nettie Louisa	11 Aug. 1915	
McDaniel	Edgar A.	Reihl	Marie Madeline	17 Dec. 1915	

	Groom	Bride		Date	Comments
Surname	**Given Name**	**Surname**	**Given Name**		
McDaniel	Levi J. M.	Griggs	Hattie C., Mrs.	15 Dec. 1881	
McDaniel	Victor G.	Wright	Ruth E.	29 Aug. 1919	
McDermed	Joseph E.	Lewis	Lydia Mary M.	21 Sept. 1894	B. F. Sargent requests license.
McDermott	Charles Henry	Denny	Sadie Mae	20 June 1919	
McDermott	William, Jr.	Barnes	Mildred	10 Sept. 1912	gr: Nora McDermott, mother; br: Mary Barnes, mother
McDevitt	Edward	Murphy	Hannah	7 Jan. 1907	
McDill	S. F.	James	Allie	12 Feb. 1887	
McDonald	Albert S.	Laffey	Rose	28 Apr. 1920	br: Mary C. Laffey Viera, mother
McDonald	Alexander	Mortimer	Anna May	3 Dec. 1919	
McDonald	Bernard John	Noli	Olymipia M.	7 Feb. 1920	
McDonald	Casey	Butts	Nellie	23 Dec. 1908	
McDonald	Daniel	Gilbert	Amelia	29 Aug. 1871	
McDonald	Daniel	Gilbert	Amelia	29 Aug. 1871	
McDonald	Frank Andrew	Catlin	Beatrice Lenore	14 Sept. 1912	
McDonald	George Alfred	Swadeling	Josephine Alden	4 Sept. 1915	
McDonald	Glen	Bugghard	Minnie	29 Apr. 1907	
McDonald	J. R.	Cooper	Emma J.	21 July 1879	
McDonald	James P.	Brown	Lida E.	6 Sept. 1916	
McDonald	John	Kelley	Maggie	21 Dec. 1886	
McDonald	Joseph F.	Snieckpeper	Lillian D.	6 Mar. 1918	don't publish
McDonald	Mark L.	North	Ralphina	15 Jan. 1866	
McDonald	Mark L., Jr.	Juilliard	Florence Isabelle	15 Dec. 1896	license requested by L. W. Juilliard
McDonald	Marshall Bell	Vier	Clara Ellen	27 Oct. 1907	
McDonald	Robert J.	Quant	Minnie Myrtle	25 July 1908	gr: witness to his mark T.? P. Tighe
McDonald	Thomas J.	Brittain	Ora C.	27 June 1911	
McDonald	W. L.	Hayden	A. A.	24 Dec. 1880	
McDonald	William	Miller	Edith Maria	2 Feb. 1888	

Groom Surname	Groom Given Name	Bride Surname	Bride Given Name	Date	Comments
McDonald	William M.	Moretti	Stella I.	31 Jan. 1921	
McDonald	William Vincent	Coul	Annie Laura	26 Dec. 1903	
McDonald	Winthrop G.	Moss	Minnie P.	13 Apr. 1886	
McDonnell	Charles P.	Hodgins	Kathyrn M.	13 Nov. 1920	
McDonnell	John Joseph	Hickey	Ella Berniece	11 Jan. 1919	
McDonnell	Joseph A.	Ruffe	Pauline	19 Aug. 1915	
McDonough	Joseph P.	Powell	Mabel W.	8 July 1893	
McDonough	Michael	Stites	Sarah Effie	18 May 1891	
McDonough	Michael	Baker	Susie R., Mrs.	6 Jan. 1898	license not issued, one party not qualified
McDougall	Edwin J.	Streeter	Myrtle R.	17 Mar. 1920	
McDowell	Frank	Craig	Ethel	10 Nov. 1908	
McDowell	Harry E.	Thompson	Ineaz M.	27 Jan. 1920	
McDowell	James	Hoar	Addie E.	25 Oct. 1882	br: B. F. Hoen, parent; Petaluma
McDowell	William A.	Craig	Bessie	19 Mar. 1915	
McDowell	Wm. J.	McLeod	Amy	11 Jan. 1866	
McElheny	Roy	Fawcett	Margaret	10 Oct. 1913	
McElwain	Arthur E.	Whitcomb	Lelia A.	10 Jan. 1907	
McEntire	Ernest J.	Bullard	Iva Irene	14 Sept. 1920	
McEowen	John W.	Wade	Daisy E.	18 Sept. 1911	
McFadden	George Reuben	Coll	Edna G.	6 Dec. 1907	
McFadden	Joseph	Birks	Elizabeth Richmond	18 Dec. 1920	
McFadden	Sandy	Seiss	Marie Martha	16 Aug. 1913	
McFadden	William H.	Doherty	Sadie M.	3 Dec. 1919	
McFall	Frank	Brown	Martha E.	28 Nov. 1892	
McFarland	James	Morris	Lizzie		not issued; James' divorce in Sacramento May 1897
McFarlane	Frederick George	O'Connor	Eleanor Inez	14 Sept. 1912	
McFarlane	James D.	Broderson	Anna P.	14 Jan. 1887	

Groom		Bride		Date	Comments
Surname	Given Name	Surname	Given Name		
McFarlane	Reginald L.	Seawell	Alice A.	18 Apr. 1914	
McFarlane	Walter C.	Williams	Edna Merle	14 Nov. 1913	gr: Olive O. McFarlane, mother
McFarling	Clarence H.	Bruner	Edith M.	14 Dec. 1901	
McFarling	John Stanley	Cook	May Adeline	7 June 1906	br: Carrie Belle Cook, mother
McFeely	John	Bishop	Effie		undated; filed between 27 and 28 Oct. 1903
McGarr	Frank	McFarland	Dora M.	18 Nov. 1896	
McGarvey	Laurence Thurman	Yates	Pearl	25 July 1904	ge: Mrs. S. S. McGarvey, mother; requested by Smyth, Oscar A.
McGavin	William	McDonald	Erma Eunice	30 Sept. 1919	
McGawim (?)	Frank P.	Norton	Laura A.	30 Mar. 1918	
McGee	Edward William	Gambini	Edith Gladys	15 Feb. 1909	
McGee	Thomas J.	Donnelly	Kate	23 Apr. 1887	
McGeein (?)	Roland J.	Dietz	Gladys N.	24 Jan. 1921	
McGeorge	Le Roy	Hesseltine	Stella C.	6 Apr. 1917	
McGhaney	Edward Jasper	Johnson	Mae	13 July 1916	
McGillwray	William	Donair	Helen E.	17 June 1916	
McGimsey	Charles L.	Murray	Melinda O.	2 Mar. 1889	
McGimsey	Charles L.	Keithley	Nora	5 July 1911	
McGimsey	John Milton	Morris	Katherine Rice	25 Oct. 1903	
McGimsey	Charles R.	Trondsen	Emily Rowena	5 Aug. 1919	
McGlauflin	Hallam C.	Bond	Frances G.	25 Sept. 1919	
McGowan	James E.	Staples	Charleen G.	23 June 1919	
McGowen	A. L.	Evans	Ruby F.	24 Dec. 1912	br: E. R. Evans, parent
McGrath	Basil William	Heselschwerdt	Amy Lillie	20 June 1913	
McGrath	Patrick J.	Bradley	Margaret	11 Dec. 1916	
McGrath	Peter J.	Clanton	Rebecca, Mrs.	11 Dec. 1902	
McGregor	Franklin D.	Cooper	Elanor A.	1 Nov. 1878	

Groom Surname	Groom Given Name	Bride Surname	Bride Given Name	Date	Comments
McGrew	Francis H.	Cole	Arcadia F.	25 Mar. 1907	gr: Sophia McGrew, mother
McGrew	James Gale	Dabney	Lida E.	31 Oct. 1896	
McGrew	Samuel	Wilsey	Sarah	25 Aug. 1890	br: widow
McGroghegan	John Thomas	Hihu (?)	Kathryn Bothwell	28 Aug. 1918	
McGuire	I. N.	Horsley	Annie, Mrs.	7 May 1888	
McGuire	Jacob	McHall	Mary Ellen	19 Jan. 1906	
McGuire	Laurence B.	Vitale	Louisa	20 Nov. 1915	
McGuire	Nathaniel	Wilhoit	Mary Ellen	5 Apr. 1865	
McGuire	Oscar Alonzo	Parsons	Lavina J.	30 Apr. 1910	
McGuire	William J.	O'Leary	Blanche A.	19 Dec. 1914	
McGuire	William J.	Yancey	Laura Russell	17 July 1909	
McGuire	Bert	Bradshaw	Meita	25 Dec. 1908	gr: Nancy E. McGuire, mother
McGuyre	William	McLeod	Margaret	14 Oct. 1912	
McHale	William Anthony	Doughty	Margaret Elizabeth	18 May 1912	
McHatton	Robert L.	Hood	Eva L.		filed between 2 and 11 September 1883
McHugh	George	Martin	Josephine G.	3 Oct. 1916	
McHugh	John	McAlpine	Alice M.	25 Aug. 1915	
McIlree	Alexander	Russell	Eliza F.	15 Nov. 1889	
McIlwain	Alexander	Long	Maud R.	11 June 1889	
McIntosh	Andrew	Wood	Hellen	15 Jan. 1908	
McIntosh	Charles	Regan	Elizabeth	31 May 1898	
McIntosh	D.	Clark	Lennie	17 Dec. 1891	
McIntosh	E. A.	Jones	Veta	25 June 1914	
McIntosh	John O.	Henderson	Mamie	13 Oct. 1900	
McIntosh	Richard Robert	Hemsath	Jewel Hermina	1 Sept. 1905	
McKay	Loran	Wilson	Elizabeth Ellen	5 Oct. 1914	
McKean	George F.	Pool	Elizabeth	12 Sept. 1896	
McKeand	William J.	Benner	Etta M.	12 Oct. 1920	

		Bride		Date	Comments
Groom					
Surname	**Given Name**	**Surname**	**Given Name**		
McKee	Harry B.	Bird	Emma L.	14 Apr. 1917	
McKee	Samuel	Bowse	Nellie F.		filed between 24 Nov. and 6 Dec. 1880
McKee	William A.	Collins	Maud	28 Oct. 1910	not signed by br or gr
McKenzie	James	Banks	Susan R.	27 June 1905	
McKenzie	William H.	Harie (?)	Carrie E.	21 Apr. 1879	
McKibbin	Edward L.	Baker	Alma E.	10 May 1892	
McKibbin	George M.	Wanaka	Leona E.	10 May 1919	
McKillap	Dugald	Allen	Huldah	3 Dec. 1912	
McKillop	Dugald	Ingrim	Delia	1 July 1878	
McKillop	Harry C.	Gibbons	Myrtle M.	5 Nov. 1903	
McKillop	William D.	England	Elma L.	28 Nov. 1906	br: Mrs. J. B. England, mother
McKinlay	D. E.	Hendley	Nannie V.	15 Dec. 1885	
McKinlay	James M.	Glenn	Luella	3 July 1894	
McKinley	Charles C.	Utman	Hazel E.	4 Sept. 1912	
McKinna	Frank	Sheridan	Alice	6 July 1914	
McKinney	George B.	Murray	Annie E.	31 May 1910	
McKinney	John H.	McPeak	Dora	4 May 1895	
McKinney	Joseph Edward	Senteney	Roxie May	6 Oct. 1914	
McKinnon	Alexander W.	Wilson	Elizabeth Elsie	2 Sept. 1916	
McKinstry	George D.	Finley	Carrie Ann	14 Oct. 1916	
McKinstry	Henry H.	Fleming	Nancy M.	17 Mar. 1866	
McKnight	John	Grimley	Eva	14 Nov. 1881	br: T. S. Fulkerson, guardian
McKune	Otis E.	Head	Lulu M.	11 Sept. 1909	
McLaren	Duncan T.	Willard	Nellie C.	5 Feb. 1907	
McLaren	Henry Havelock	DeCarly	Annie	16 Dec. 1903	
McLaren	Richard	McMillen	Cora	25 Feb. 1893	
McLaughlin	Alexander Douglas	Julian	Victoria Susan	1 Sept. 1906	br: Julius Julian, mother
McLaughlin	Bernard H.	Wolf	Marie	31 Mar. 1905	

Groom Surname	Groom Given Name	Bride Surname	Bride Given Name	Date	Comments
McLaughlin	Clarence Joseph	Gillians	Alice	7 July 1919	
McLaughlin	Oswald R.	Parkins	Harriett E.	2 Oct. 1919	
McLaughlin	William Joseph	Shea	Alice Jane	23 Nov. 1909	
McLean	George Graham	Washburn	Rose May	19 June 1905	
McLean	Hector	Carr	Ursula A.	15 Nov. 1884	
McLean	Walter N.	Piutt	Bertha F.	6 Oct. 1884	
McLellan	David T.	Reading	Lizzie	2 Sept. 1885	
McLennan	James	Batt	Faith Ray	24 Apr. 1905	
McLeod	Alfred W.	Temple	Ruth	4 Feb. 1907	
McMahan	Grover Cleveland	Linkogel	Ledona Beatrice	3 July 1916	
McMahon	James	Osborne	Katherina	13 Jan. 1904	
McMahon	John Henry	Spencer	Mabel M.	5 Nov. 1902	
McManus	George E.	Hopper	Bertha S.	29 July 1911	
McMath	Ernest Burwell	Harrow	Della	17 May 1913	gr: Robert F. McMath, father
McMath	Sanford	Renstrom	Ida M.	3 Mar. 1921	
McMichael	John William	Covey	Cashia Mary	19 Nov. 1895	br: George Covey gives consent and signs
McMichael	Rice F.	Yarbrough	Ethel B.	24 Feb. 1899	no previous marriage; don't publish until 4 Mar. 1899
McMillan	Alexander	Palm	Hilda A.	8 Aug. 1914	
McMillan	Harmon D.	Cloer (?)	Vada	18 Mar. 1903	
McMillan	Wm. S.	Garrison	Carrie	22 Nov. 1887	
McMillen	Edd	Johnson	Myrtle	21 Jan. 1908	
McMillen	Hiram	Miller	Sarah B.	27 Dec. 1899	
McMillen	James William	Boyd	Ella Vinora	1 June 1896	
McMillen	John J.	Miller	Daisy M.	2 Aug. 1901	
McMinamin	John	Fitzgerald	Annie	18 Oct. 1907	
McMinn	J. A.	Crisp	Sarah J.	28 Feb. 1885	gr: R. Ferguson, parent
McMinn	Joseph	Carlton	Ada B.	1 Feb. 1897	

		Bride		Date	Comments
Groom					
Surname	**Given Name**	**Surname**	**Given Name**		
McMullen	John	Myers	Phoeby	30 Oct. 1895	br: John B. Meyers gives consent
McMullen	Russell McGarvey	McGovern	Clara Josephine	7 Apr. 1917	
McMullin	Joseph E.	Bates	Pauline C.	17 Nov. 1896	
McMullin	Thomas F.	Johnson	California I.	13 July 1909	
McMurray	R. W.	Gardanier	Carol	14 May 1915	
McNab	Gavin	Davidson	Wilma	20 July 1887	
McNabb	James Henry	Carpenter	Adelia E.	26 Apr. 1898	neither party divorced within one year
McNair	Elmer A.	Conyers	Iva	1 Nov. 1905	
McNair	James	Peters	Ada May	24 June 1909	
McNally	Oscar	Clark	Ella	8 July 1889	
McNally	Raymond Gregory	Meyers	Carleen Marie	21 Nov. 1916	
McNally	Thomas Charles	Camm	Charlotte Shepard	19 Aug 1907	
McNamara	Bernard	Loughead	Maggie	13 Oct. 1879	
McNamara	Dan	Silvia	Frances	8 Mar. 1905	
McNamara	James E.	Trembley	Evelyn A.	13 Jan. 1913	
McNamara	James J.	Sweitzer	Audrey M.	3 Dec. 1920	
McNamara	Thomas	Cullahan	May A.	3 July 1913	
McNeal	William E.	Conne	Annie, Mrs.	24 Dec. 1902	
McNear	George Plummer	Denman	Ida Belle	31 May 1887	
McNear	John A., Jr.	Egan	Nellie V.	23 Sept. 1901	
McNeil	James F.	Krohn	Joeliene E.	13 Apr. 1912	gr: Eliza McNeil, mother
McNeil	James J.	Nelson	Vera A.	27 July 1914	
McNeil	John	Butteer	Henriette	27 Mar. 1916	
McNeil	John	Copperelmann	Laura	9 July 1906	
McNeil	Justin Louis	Barnes	Edna Gay	6 Feb. 1909	
McNeil	Wilbur J.	Barlow	Elizabeth L.	25 June 1901	
McNeill	Wm. J.	Foley	Pearl O.	21 Feb. 1914	
McNiel	James F.	Parrish	Eliza Jane	24 Dec. 1887	br: D. F. Parrish, parent

Groom Surname	Groom Given Name	Bride Surname	Bride Given Name	Date	Comments
McNulty	Charles Augustus	Barnes	Myrtle Blanche	30 Mar. 1907	
McNutty	Edward Francis	Olstad	Gunhild	18 Dec. 1907	
McPeak	Charles E.	Henry	Lucile E.	26 Sept. 1893	
McPeak	Harmon P.	Sinclair	Tenia	19 Nov. 1892	
McPeak	Jefferson P.	Critchfield	Lulu	21 Oct. 1890	
McPeak	Mathew A.	McBee	Fetnie A.	9 Mar. 1866	
McPeak	William H.	White	Jennie L.	9 Dec. 1889	
McPeak	William H.	Mendenhall	Carrie P.	2 June 1900	
McPhail	A. J.	Gale	Mary Ella	26 Feb. 1889	
McPherson	August	Hoe	Elsie	10 July 1915	
McPherson	Bert	Smith	Rose	12 Oct. 1901	
McPherson	Charles W.	Hale	Nannie	6 Feb. 1895	
McPherson	Early	Ferguson	May	23 June 1890	
McPherson	Ernest I.	Baker	Atlanta	3 Jan. 1903	
McPherson	Hal	Johnson	Cora F.	26 Jan. 1915	
McPherson	Harry Moore	Beeson	Ella Frances	6 June 1906	gr: L. McPherson, parent
McPherson	Leon	Capell	Elsie Aline	1 June 1907	
McPherson	Perry Lewis	Brumfield	Margaret Jenette	29 June 1907	
McPherson	Thomas	Harden	Lucinda, Mrs.	21 Oct. 1865	
McPherson	Walter	Allen	Belle	19 June 1896	
McPike	William F.	Hopley	Juno Clarice	2 June 1909	
McProud	Oscar C.	Jackson	Delia	30 Dec. 1910	
McReynolds	Arthur	Clegg	Grace	14 Oct. 1905	br: Mary Silva, mother
McReynolds	Charles Newton	Gregory	Mary Elizabeth	15 Aug. 1879	
McReynolds	Dennis H.	Hinshaw	Amanda	18 Nov. 1893	
McReynolds	Lewis M.	Phariss	Alice	24 May 1879	
McReynolds	Melvin J.	Clegg	Alice	17 Nov. 1900	
McReynolds	R. E. L.	Dunwoody	Lizzie	31 May 1888	

Groom		Bride		Date	Comments
Surname	Given Name	Surname	Given Name		
McReynolds	Samuel W.	Haley	Emma E.	2 Jan. 1886	
McReynolds	Stephen	Olison	Georgianna, Mrs.	27 Nov. 1866	
McReynolds	Thos. A.	Harris	Ellen M.	13 Oct. 1865	
McSweeney	Daniel	McKay	Margaret	22 Apr. 1904	br: requested license
McVay	Clarence L.	Dudley	Daphne A.	9 July 1907	br: I. J. Dudley, parent
McVay	John A.	Iffland	May L.	10 Sept. 1919	
McWilliams	Arthur C.	Reeves	Caroline Helena	30 July 1909	
McWilliams	Eslie B.	Long	Lucy A. M.	26 Feb. 1880	
McWilliams	George S.	Seeman	Dora	8 July 1899	no previous marriage; requested by O. B. Read, friend
McWilliams	Hugh	Shaw	Georgie P.	26 Sept. 1894	
Meacham	Charles S.	Collins	Mary A.	15 Dec. 1899	neither party has been divorced within one year
Mead	Albert Miller	Surryhne	Barbara Stuart	12 Aug. 1916	
Mead	Charles S.	Reed	Mary	24 Oct. 1891	
Mead	Fred Ryland	Gist	Fannie Irene	16 June 1906	
Mead	Wilson Henry	Hewit	Rosanna	26 May 1887	
Meador	Bert L.	Farmer	Agnes	2 June 1906	
Meador	George Frank	Schindler	Lena Olive	29 Feb. 1908	
Meads	Willia C.	Howard	Eleanor Adella	28 Jan. 1918	
Meagher	John F.	Hardin	Nancy	26 Mar. 1891	
Meagher	Thomas	Lowe	Annie	31 July 1890	
Meaney	John	Kaiser	Laura Teresa	17 Nov. 1920	
Means	Thomas Jefferson	Bones	Lillie	10 Aug. 1898	no previous marriage
Mecchi	Costantino	Passalacque	Amelia I.	19 Mar. 1888	
Mecham	Harrison Carlos	Peerman	Alice Elizabeth	26 May 1906	
Mecham	Sherman A.	Noonan	Alice R.	25 Jan. 1908	
Meck	William Edward	Hall	Laura Alice	14 Nov. 1907	

Groom Surname	Groom Given Name	Bride Surname	Bride Given Name	Date	Comments
Medeira	William	Cummings	Kate	23 Dec. 1889	
Mediros	Frank	Haraldson	Elizabeth	16 Dec. 1911	
Mee	Thomas H.	Lewis	Mary Elisabeth	5 Sept. 1911	
Meek	Nathan T.	Young	Flora E.	10 Feb. 1899	no previous marriage
Meek	Thomas Barney	Cavers	Margaret I.	17 Oct. 1907	
Meeker	Alexander H.	Dodge	Florence H.	22 Nov. 1897	
Meeker	Godfrey Hinkley	Dearborn	Ethel	14 June 1902	
Meeker	John V.	Petersen	Clara	28 Apr. 1909	gr: J. P. Meeker, father
Meeker	John V.	Rieck	Mable M.	25 June 1912	please don't publish
Meeker	Robert T.	Lapham	Ethel	6 Dec. 1895	
Meeker	Stephen A.	Menary	Kate G., Mrs.	25 Jan. 1904	
Meeker	William J.	Smith	Carrie B.	31 May 1895	
Meeks	Everett	Petersen	Margaret Marie	15 Mar. 1921	
Meeks	George Lawson	Palmer	Maud Elizabeth	29 Jan. 1907	
Meeks	Robert G.	Branscomb	Sarah L.	6 Mar. 1880	
Meeks	Walter B.	Woodworth	Rose E.	18 Apr. 1907	
Meeks	Walter H.	Harttrodt	Hilda J.	27 Apr. 1907	
Meese	Henry	Mangold	Frederika	21 Feb. 1894	
Meeth	Paul J. W.	Redding	Eva Lee (?)	31 Aug. 1917	
Mego	Edward	Sullivan	Ella	15 Feb. 1898	no previous marriage
Megonigil	Eli	Wahrman	Augusta	25 Apr. 1908	
Mehl	Walter A.	Lawson	Marion E.	7 Oct. 1915	
Mehl	Carl Frederick	Doelling	Eliza	9 Nov. 1909	br: Hugh Mcfadden, guardian
Meilicke	Carl H.	Stickel	Katie	10 Aug. 1917	
Meincke	Herman F.	Vincent	Irene	27 Sept. 1918	
Meineri	Guy	Costa	Lizzie	27 Nov. 1907	gr: Thomas Meineri, father
Meisner	Frank Gustave	Sawtell	Winifred	24 May 1917	
Meissner	Walter Charles	Smither	Ruby Pearl	9 Apr. 1908	

	Groom	Bride		Date	Comments
Surname	Given Name	Surname	Given Name		
Meldi	Paul E.	Thorgood	Vera G.	10 Feb. 1919	
Melehan	Daniel John	Wiers	Mattie Theresa	24 Dec. 1900	requested by F. A. Meyer, friend
Mell	A. William	Duncan	Helen	6 May 1918	
Mell	John W.	Duncan	Vella I.	24 Mar. 1915	
Meller	Reginald D.	Chauvet	Henrietta M.	24 Apr. 1913	
Mellette	Randolph H.	Mantle	Susie L.	6 Sept. 1912	
Mello	Frank	Owens	Leeta	13 Jan. 1906	
Mello	Joseph	Green	Lenora	12 May 1900	
Mello	Louis	Holmes	Minnie M.	18 Aug. 1900	
Mello	William B.	Nielson	Lenora M.	28 Oct. 1911	
Mellow	Frank	Silva	Isabel	15 Nov. 1913	
Melson	J. R.	Swenson	Gyda S.	12 Oct. 1885	
Melton	Newton	Dervin	Eliza	30 Apr. 1880	br: Mrs. Frances Dervin, mother; Mary Roberson, witness
Melton	Thomas	Bean	Zella	10 Jan. 1911	
Melton	William	Barton	Nellie	2 Jan. 1865	written consent
Mendelson	Isador	Clunan	Esther	6 Oct. 1920	kindly do not publish
Mendenhall	Roy D.	Branstetter	Sylvia S.	24 May 1917	
Mendonca	Antonio	Green	Clara	24 Nov. 1899	no previous marriage
Mendonca	Joseph J.	King	Mary F.	24 Jan. 1896	
Menefee	Campbell A.	Hall	M. Isadora	18 Nov. 1906	
Menefee	John Wesley	Smith	Sarah Eliza	19 Dec. 1882	
Menefee	Roderick E.	Mattaini	Mae Isabel	14 June 1912	
Menefee	William Alfred	Zeigler	Minnie Florence	14 June 1910	
Menetrey (?)	Charles Louis	Huffam	Hazel May	2 Mar. 1918	
Mengelt	George	Hemmy	Maria Ursula	11 Apr. 1896	
Menihan	Thos. M.	Hyde	Alicia A.	23 Jan. 1900	no previous marriage
Mentasta	Giovanni (John)	Meineri	Adelaide	30 Nov. 1901	

Groom Surname	Groom Given Name	Bride Surname	Bride Given Name	Date	Comments
Mentch	Hiram A.	Seyfferth	Ida	16 Nov. 1904	
Mentz	Jack F.	Cromwell	Florence	27 Dec. 1909	
Meranda	Howard E.	Blakesley	Lillie Maud	23 Feb. 1901	br: Wm. T. Blakesley, father
Meranda	Robert	Morris	Bessie	22 Dec. 1903	
Merchant	Thos. S.	Hobson	Mary L.	31 July 1882	
Meredith	Cyrus N.	German	Margaret E.	26 Nov. 1877	
Meredith	Laurence Milton	Dibble	Jennie	8 Nov. 1916	
Meredith	Milton L.	Greaver	Jennie	10 Apr. 1889	
Merga	Ambrose C.	Rovera	Marie T.	16 Oct. 1907	br: Mrs. Lucy Rovera, mother
Merga	Antonio	Perottini	Rosa	20 May 1905	br: John B. Perottini, father; signed Giovini B. Perottini
Mergo	Charley	Marenghi	Mary	7 May 1908	
Merlo	John	Garbarini	Louise	14 Oct. 1913	
Mero	Hedly L.	Kahl	Bertha M.	31 May 1919	
Merrill	George D.	Holman	Annie	28 Oct. 1916	
Merrill	Grant P.	Stacey	Angie T.	29 Sept. 1919	
Merrill	John L.	Newman	Nita Claire	10 July 1907	
Merrit	Edson C.	Olson	Edyth W.	14 Dec. 1901	
Merrithew	Robert	Stevens	Helen E.	16 June 1917	
Merritt	Carl B.	Hetzil	Mable K.	19 Sept. 1917	
Merritt	Edson C.	Brush	Mame E.	7 Nov. 1894	license requested by Vernon Goodwin.
Mersereau	Paul, Dr.	Gregg	Mary P., Mrs.	13 Apr. 1886	
Mersfelder	William	Hamilton	Nettie	20 Aug. 1889	
Mesa	Joseph	Allen	Annie K.	8 Apr. 1896	gr: sign with mark
Meschi	Ostiglio	Buchignani	Fannie	23 Oct. 1919	
Messerer	Joseph R.	Schadt	Marjorie	11 Sept. 1918	
Messner	Jacob F.	Eperson	Fannie	6 Feb. 1891	
Metcalf	John W., Jr.	Murk	Mabel	7 Oct. 1913	

		Bride		Date	Comments
Groom					
Surname	**Given Name**	**Surname**	**Given Name**		
Metzger	Alfred V.	Leard	Dora	27 Apr. 1886	
Metzger	George V.	Bowen	Elenore C.	17 Dec. 1920	
Metzger	Joseph E.	Horner	Wilmos E.	22 Nov. 1880	
Metzler	J. A.	Williams	Mary L.	30 June 1886	
Metzzer	Alfred E.	Lundan (?)	Rose	23 Apr. 1920	
Meulenbrock	Leonard	Evans	Lydia L.	1 Sept. 1916	
Meyer	Benedikt	Gisler	Kathrina	17 Oct. 1911	
Meyer	Bruno	Hanks	Alice C.	2 Apr. 1896	
Meyer	Conrad N.	Keller	Winifred W.	30 Aug. 1919	
Meyer	Friedrich Wilhelm	Kurtz	Henricki	12 Aug.1909	
Meyer	Fritz	Brannum	Myrtle E.	28 Apr. 1900	
Meyer	George Homer	Menefee	Sarah Bell	14 June 1883	
Meyer	Henry C.	Silver	Veris A.	22 Aug. 1914	
Meyer	Jakob	Gisler	Emma	14 Nov. 1913	
Meyer	Lawrence	Smith	Bertha G.	6 July 1897	
Meyer	Lorenz	Miller	Elizabeth	3 June 1867	
Meyer	Louis C.	Schifferli	Anna N.	4 Dec. 1898	no previous marriage
Meyer	Theodore	LeMester	Lula A.	1 June 1920	
Meyer	Walter	Barker	Ruth	20 Apr. 1914	
Meyer	William J.	Urton	Elsie S.	28 Mar. 1893	
Meyer	William Jacob	Powers	Adelia	18 Apr. 1899	
Meyers	Charles F.	Mastin	Mary L.	9 May 1919	gr: Fred A Meyers, father
Meyers	Chas. H.	Young	Maggie J.	8 June 1891	
Meyers	Clarence M.	Spiro	Fannie J.	30 May 1908	
Meyers	Henry	Abramsky	Katie	6 Jan. 1901	
Meyers	Herman C.	Davidson	Alice L.	6 July 1920	
Meyers	John C. E.	Pedraita	Clara Irene	19 Feb. 1908	
Meyers	Ranie I.	Ingram	Kezia	4 Sept. 1913	

Groom Surname	Groom Given Name	Bride Surname	Bride Given Name	Date	Comments
Mezger	Adolph	Steinhorst	Amelia	17 Nov. 1894	
Mezzera	Paul P.	Zanoni	Elvezia F.	29 Aug. 1917	
Mich	Mike, Jr.	Smith	Fannie	8 June 1917	
Michael	David Benj.	Boud	Effie	27 Apr. 1893	br: surname could be Bond
Michael	George W.	Crewdson	Dobey	7 Mar. 1896	
Michael	George W.	Miller	Nannie	20 Dec. 1877	
Michaelson	Otto Emil	Christoferson	Dina Marie	1 Dec. 1905	
Micheletti	Stefano	Buffi	Gina	9 Dec. 1916	br: Emilio Buffi, father
Micheli	Adamo	Micheli	Pia	8 Sept. 1910	
Micheli	Alfredo	Picchi	Pasquina	10 Nov. 1913	br: Pasquino Picchi
Micheli	Alfredo	Franceschi	Colomba	21 Dec. 1916	
Micheli	Charles	Miller	Margaret	31 July 1866	
Micheli	Eisani	Buffi	Rosaria	13 Aug 1907	
Micheli	Giovani	Bertolucci	Lieta	24 Nov. 1909	
Michelson	George L. F.	Grove	Edna M.	12 Sept. 1903	do not publish
Michelson	Andrew P.	Ryan	Gertrude K.	29 May 1912	
Michener	William Lewis	St. John	Florence Marion	18 Feb. 1896	
Mickelsen	Mads Peter	Nisson	Christine Anna	19 Nov. 1918	br: Nickleus S. Nisson, father
Mickelsen	Madsen	Nisson	Mary	25 May 1914	
Middagh	Ezra Sypes	Lane	Mary C.	5 Jan. 1892	
Middagh	John R.	Milton	Elizabeth May	21 Feb. 1910	br: Hilda Milton, mother
Middagh	Samuel	Doss	Laura	7 Mar. 1887	
Middagh	William A.	Bellingham	Maggie	7 Jan. 1885	
Middleton	Walter V.	Sutton	Annie	20 May 1877	br: Mrs. Frances West, guardian
Middling	Casper	Fisher	Fannie	29 July 1908	
Miebach	Hans	Woodard	Helen E.	27 Jan. 1920	
Mietzech	Charles E.	Quinn	Margaret A.	31 Dec. 1903	
Mihan	Leo B.	Schudsan	Amalia	9 Mar. 1918	

		Bride		Date	Comments
Groom					
Surname	**Given Name**	**Surname**	**Given Name**		
Milanesio	Virgilio	Vianesi	Angelina	22 Nov. 1919	gr: witness to his mark Mercer H. Farrar
Miles	Elmer Alfred	Goss	Pauline M.	14 Nov. 1908	
Miles	William J.	Van Winkle	Evalena	15 Aug. 1902	
Mill	Clarence J.	Quintero	Florence	10 Jan. 1920	
Millar	John W.	Koch	Anna E.	11 Nov. 1896	
Millar	S. Arthur	Simpson	Ivah	16 Apr. 1904	
Millee	C. T.	Bolton	Emma M.	15 Mar. 1905	
Miller	Addison Charles	Cheesborough	Mable Teresa	9 Apr. 1908	
Miller	Benjamin F.	Tunstall	Annie	15 Nov. 1897	
Miller	Carl L.	Yangling	May	12 June 1899	no previous marriage; please don't publish
Miller	Cecil Jesse	Taylor	Orlean Martha	29 May 1912	
Miller	Charles C.	Gehlken	Anna	16 June 1906	
Miller	Charles R.	Leigh	Jennie	29 Jan. 1901	
Miller	Charlie V.	Harris	Maud	23 Dec. 1911	
Miller	Chas. S.	Benson	Martha E.	18 Nov. 1890	
Miller	Clarence A.	Palmer	Edith B.	13 Nov. 1903	
Miller	D. P.	Clements	Maude H.	26 Sept. 1913	
Miller	Daniel Erskin	Ayer	Lizzie	13 Aug. 1879	
Miller	David	Beeson	Kate	20 Oct. 1894	
Miller	David A.	Orr	Ora A.	24 Mar. 1898	
Miller	David W.	Pound	Jennie G.	11 Jan. 1893	
Miller	E. H.	Mayse	Mary E.	28 Sept. 1865	
Miller	Elmer F.	Allen	Maggie E.	17 Apr. 1891	
Miller	Emerson Paris	Hanke	Beryl Andes	23 Feb. 1906	
Miller	Francis W.	Blonquist	Amanda	6 June 1919	
Miller	Frank B.	Clark	Annie	26 Aug. 1904	
Miller	Frank J.	Petersen	Carrie S.	11 Oct. 1904	
Miller	Frans Oskar Gustafson	Martin	Lauriana Vieira	18 Sept. 1913	

Groom Surname	Groom Given Name	Bride Surname	Bride Given Name	Date	Comments
Miller	Fred	Hart	Nora	20 Oct. 1904	
Miller	Fred H.	Ferguson	Nora	2 Apr. 1896	don't publish until after April 9
Miller	Frederick H.	Gonzalez	Margaret F.	22 Oct. 1890	
Miller	Frederick William	Pedigo	Retha Rosalie	30 July 1910	
Miller	Garnet W.	Boehm	Annie	21 May 1913	
Miller	Geo. F.	Tiede	Mary	20 Mar. 1911	
Miller	George	Greenslade	Ada Louise	27 July 1896	
Miller	George	Jones	Carrie May, Mrs.	22 Aug. 1899	gr: divorced more than one year; br: widow
Miller	George	Canway	Mary E.	15 Oct. 1878	
Miller	George B.	Sheffer	Delpha	4 Sept. 1900	
Miller	George E.	Johns	Stella L.	7 Mar. 1921	
Miller	George R.	Meyer	Caroline L.	26 Oct. 1900	gr: E. E. Miller, parent
Miller	George W.	Peters	Maggie J.	14 Mar. 1879	
Miller	Harold K.	Comstock	Eleanor W.	22 Jan. 1920	gr: John F. Miller, father
Miller	Harry J.	Richards	Ellen B.	4 Jan. 1911	
Miller	Henry H.	Mitchel	Sarah	13 Aug. 1878	
Miller	Henry Maurice	Whitaker	Elsie Day	6 Dec. 1919	
Miller	J. F.	Hudspeth	Exor	7 Oct. 1903	br: Mrs. M. A. & W. W. Hudspeth, parents
Miller	J. S., Dr.	Patten	Elizabeth	29 Nov. 1865	
Miller	Jacob B.	Feltz	Elsie	13 Jan. 1908	
Miller	James Jesse	English	Sadie, Mrs.	13 June 1901	
Miller	James M.	Miller	Martha M., Mrs.	15 July 1896	
Miller	James P.	Meeks	Sarah L.	4 Mar. 1911	
Miller	James Pierce	Brown	Birdie Estella Neva	21 Oct. 1882	
Miller	James R.	Barnes	Ida M.	16 Oct. 1883	
Miller	James Z.	Mosely	Edith P.	4 Oct. 1894	
Miller	John	Tate	Feliciatadad, Mrs.	23 Nov. 1892	

		Bride		Date	Comments
Groom					
Surname	Given Name	Surname	Given Name		
Miller	John	Swan	Dora	28 Apr. 1881	
Miller	John J.	Lawrence	Louise A.	1 May 1896	
Miller	John W.	Naughton	Annie		
Miller	Joseph James	Schoonover	Alice Edna	2 June 1903	
Miller	Leffler B.	Porter	Dorothy Nell	2 Nov. 1917	
Miller	Louis E.	Gummeson	Grayce M.	12 Apr. 1920	
Miller	Melvin Stanley	Wheeler	Grace Gertrude	13 Nov. 1916	
Miller	Oscar Paul	Scott	Nora Edna	4 Dec. 1902	
Miller	Rasmus J.	Hansen	Margretha S.	3 Apr. 1893	
Miller	Raymond F.	Beattie	Edith I.	28 June 1919	
Miller	Raymond J.	Berndt	Gladys	18 May 1920	
Miller	Robert Lee	Ellingwood	Bertha May	23 June 1906	
Miller	Thomas B.	Espey	Jessie L.	20 Oct. 1892	
Miller	Walter	Gemmill	Lillian J.	25 June 1913	
Miller	Will Henry	Palmer	Clara May	8 Mar. 1898	
Miller	William	Eckman	Emma May	5 July 1902	
Miller	William	Reeves	Maud	11 Feb. 1902	gr: 54 Shipley St., San Francisco; br: 112 Junipero St., San Francisco
Miller	Wm. R.	Kelley	Emma A.	30 Apr. 1866	
Millerick	David	Hollenbarter	Mary	5 Oct. 1901	no previous marriage
Millerick	James G.	Focha	Annie	28 July 1908	
Millerick	John	Connell	Lizzie	14 Nov. 1885	
Millerick	John	Landgren	Teresa	30 Dec. 1902	
Millerick	Phillip	Summ	Amelia	16 Apr. 1908	
Millerick	William Dennis	Brown	Hazel Violia	8 Apr. 1911	br: Mae Brown, mother
Millett	William H.	Curter (?)	Mary J.	5 Mar. 1881	
Millington	Ira	Cook	Susan	17 Nov. 1866	

Groom Surname	Groom Given Name	Bride Surname	Bride Given Name	Date	Comments
Mills	Allen Davis	Brady	Julia May	6 Oct. 1914	gr: Elizabeth H. Strong, mother; br: Mary Ann Brady, mother
Mills	Asa H.	Scudder	Hattie L.	21 Sept. 1894	
Mills	Charles E.	Hodge	Minnie C.	13 Jan. 1902	
Mills	Don	Hudson	Mary E.	8 Mar. 1893	
Mills	Easton	Singley	Gertrude E.	2 Nov. 1888	
Mills	Edward C.	Morris	Annie	19 Oct. 1891	
Mills	Ernest M.	Austin	Gula B.	14 Mar. 1914	
Mills	Fredrick W.	Gerow	Elsie E.	16 Oct. 1899	no previous marriage
Mills	G. W.	Hatfield	Sarah M.	1 Oct. 1866	
Mills	Henry J.	Shatto	Jennie	28 Apr. 1909	
Mills	Hiram B.	White	Mary Ellen	26 Nov. 1896	gr: Mrs. Jennie Mills, mother, gives consent and signs; gr: address is 123 Turk St. SF
Mills	Jas. Byron	Tennant	Rose Anna	28 June 1911	
Mills	John	Dodge	A. C., Mrs.	2 Mar. 1889	
Mills	Robert	Irwin	Paulina	8 Jan. 1882	br: N. C. Irwin, parent; from Fisk's Mill
Mills	Robt.	Irwin	Paulina A.	9 Jan. 1882	
Mills	Roy Hudson	Nagle	Helen Catherine	11 Feb. 1916	
Mills	William J.	Jones	Mary C.	11 Feb. 1884	
Mills	William Leslie	Winton	Flora A.	15 Oct. 1898	
Mills	Wm.	Kohle	Minnie	10 Aug. 1885	
Millstead	Silas Augustus	Stevens	Virginia Francis	6 Apr. 1904	
Milne	Donald	Lapus	Marie	5 Feb. 1919	gr: Mrs. Flora Milne, mother
Milne	Henry Clinton	Moxley	Roberta Blanche	17 Aug. 1911	
Milner	Joseph B.	Dahlmann	Gladys Marie	8 Dec. 1919	
Milton	John L.	Hamerlund	Hilda	22 June 1891	
Milty	Nicholas	Middleton	Emma	2 Oct. 1865	

	Groom	Bride		Date	Comments
Surname	Given Name	Surname	Given Name		
Minaglia	John	Bachman	Sophia	5 June 1909	
Minahan	William T.	Millerick	Mary	17 Sept. 1901	
Minelli	Cesare	Decanini	Amanda	28 Dec. 1908	
Miner	E. E.	Buller (?)	A.	28 Nov. 1881	
Miner	Edward P.	Stinson	Elizabeth	12 Feb. 1891	
Minetti	Charles L.	Moran	Vola B.	1 July 1908	
Minghi	Guiseppe	Pigoni	Assunta	6 Nov. 1913	
Mini	Olindo	Binggeli	Rosa	3 Nov. 1920	
Minkel	William J.	McIntyre	Ella F.	9 June 1892	
Minor	William Peter, Jr.	Lebaron	Laura Mabel	8 Apr. 1911	
Minsky	Nathan	Sekolsky	Rose	14 May 1914	
Minto	Lloyd R.	Ford	Alice L.	23 Oct. 1920	
Minton	Wm. M.	Levy	Felice	23 Mar. 1889	
Minyard	Thomas D.	Reed	Jessie L.	11 Dec. 1901	
Miranda	John	Noriel	Lydia Bell	5 May 1902	do not publish until Friday
Miranda	William Melvyn	Hollister	Anna Laura	30 Oct. 1903	br: requested license
Misener	Albert F.	McPeak	Minnie	5 Feb. 1895	
Misner	Horace W.	Cardoza	Alice J.	1 Oct. 1920	
Mitchell	Benjamin F.	Isham	Tolitha Elizabeth	5 July 1865	
Mitchell	Charles	Sander	Mary	12 Aug. 1899	gr: widower; br: requested license
Mitchell	Claude D.	Elliott	Marion G.	2 Aug. 1919	
Mitchell	F. M.	Bray	Louisa J.	12 June 1886	
Mitchell	Floyd H.	Dean	Sylvia G.	17 Aug. 1912	
Mitchell	Frank S.	Weller	Margaret	31 July 1917	
Mitchell	Harry	Wiedemann	Minna Margaret	17 Dec. 1907	
Mitchell	Harry T.	Jones	Geneva A.	4 Jan, 1915	
Mitchell	J. Wright	Wood	N. Pheobie	12 Jan, 1915	
Mitchell	James H.	Loe	Elvira R.	5 Nov. 1896	

-158-

Groom Surname	Groom Given Name	Bride Surname	Bride Given Name	Date	Comments
Mitchell	John	Equi	Teresa	17 May 1902	
Mitchell	John H.	Bonham	Mattie	21 Dec. 1881	
Mitchell	Joseph	Webster	Charlotte E.	1 June 1867	
Mitchell	L. W.	Dunbar	M. A.	15 Mar. 1883	
Mitchell	Merle Ellsworth	Stone	Genevieve Amelia	17 June 1916	
Mitchell	Ralph Brown	Clark	Grace Pitkin	8 Sept. 1906	
Mitchell	Robert A.	Dickson	Adela	24 Jan. 1913	
Mitchell	Robert Henry	Russell	Lena	23 Dec. 1897	gr: Baertling Hotel, San Francisco; br; B St., Santa Rosa; no previous marriage
Mitchell	W. J.	Kennedy	Annie E.	19 Nov. 1885	
Mitchell	Wm. H.	Hays	Anna M.	13 Nov. 1880	br: Mat Hays, father
Mize	Cyril F.	Homerhouse	Alma Margaret	28 July 1920	
Mize	Frederic	Mize	Adeline N.	22 Oct. 1892	
Mize	Frederick	MacDonald	Nellie M.	20 Sept. 1909	
Mize	Thompson	Edmiston	Annie	11 Nov. 1879	
Moad	Marshall M.	Harden	Edna Ursula	13 June 1911	
Mobley	John Elmer	Burger	Pearl J.	18 Dec. 1897	
Mobley	William H.	Arnold	Lucile Frances	4 Aug. 1900	gr: requested by J. E. Mobley, brother
Modesto	Rovere	Frusendi	Mary	10 Aug. 1918	gr: his mark; Josephine Paolini, witness
Modini	D.	Campini	Carolina	20 Jan. 1913	
Modini	James Laurence	Livernash	Margaret Theresa	11 Dec. 1916	
Moe	William	James	Addie Virginia	21 July 1904	
Moenning	George	Frontier	Clara	8 Sept. 1911	
Moffett	L. L.	Chinnock	Jessie May	27 June 1919	
Moffit	Lewis	Howard	Mignonette	19 Oct. 1895	
Mohl	Emil	Goetz	Lena	1 Apr. 1901	
Moiles	Theodore	Risk	Nancy	7 Dec. 1886	
Molinari	Giocommo	Maggioro	Maria Della	12 June 1913	

		Bride		Date	Comments
Groom					
Surname	**Given Name**	**Surname**	**Given Name**		
Moll	Albert Eugene	Hardin	Esther Jimella	13 July 1906	
Moller	Harry H.	Hickey	Lulu	8 Oct. 1902	
Moller	Henry, Jr.	Mills	Sadie	23 May 1885	br: Mrs. Sarah Mills, mother
Moller	Michael C.	Jorgensen	Christina	17 Sept. 1900	
Molne	Cuthbert E.	Jewell	Eleanor F.	1 Apr. 1920	
Moltzen	Albert Christian	Rodgers	Anna Belle	6 Feb. 1917	
Moltzen	Axel	Ekman	Sigrid	11 July 1891	
Moltzen	Thomas	Yockey	Bessie	30 Sept. 1908	
Momsen	Charles F.	Clausen	Anna D.	11 Mar. 1897	
Monett	Chauncey D.	Houx	Edith Pearl	7 Sept. 1912	
Monez	Manuel P.	Rodgers	Mary Edna	16 July 1910	
Mong	George William	DeGroot	Flora	27 Nov. 1916	
Moni	Frank	Buzzini	Kate	7 June 1909	
Moniz	Frank P.	Silva	Frances M.	11 Dec. 1920	
Moniz	Joseph S., Jr.	Felciano	Mary C.	31 Dec. 1914	
Moniz	Manuel Joseph	Ramos	Josephine Matilda	4 Aug. 1914	
Moniz	Tony G.	Moore	Alta	22 Apr. 1914	
Monk	Hans Julius	Simansen	Gertrude Marie Dagmar	11 Nov. 1909	
Monks	John	King	Bertha F., Mrs.	7 Nov. 1898	gr: divorced abt 6 years ago, Alameda; br: widow
Monotti	Eugene	Baldi	Amelia	19 Mar. 1920	
Monroe	Harold H.	McDonald	Mary Elizabeth	28 Sept. 1899	
Monroe	Peter	Taylor	Annie	16 Apr. 1885	
Monroe	Raymond	Leggett	Della Z.	31 Dec. 1917	
Monroe	William Henry	Waugh	Armina	30 Sept. 1905	
Monsen	Martin	Shibbetts	Grace Knick	20 Jan. 1896	
Monson	John C.	Lemley	Laida F.	6 July 1915	

Groom Surname	Groom Given Name	Bride Surname	Bride Given Name	Date	Comments
Montague	Frank P.	Hoagland	Nellie A.	30 Dec. 1915	
Montalon	Paul	Sabia	Camela	15 Nov. 1906	
Montano	Constantin	Sermet	Marie L.	5 Feb. 1920	
Monte	Tiziano	Luiebberke	Flora	27 Apr. 1896	
Montessoro	Pietro	Perazzo	Mary	7 Mar. 1896	
Montgomery	Elmer J.	McCanse	Margaret F.	3 Mar. 1909	
Montgomery	George French	Keener	Raphaella Acosta		filed between 7 and 10 July 1905
Montgomery	Raleigh Claude	Silva	Louise Dalphine	14 May 1917	
Montgomery	Robert B.	Cave	Freda Marie	2 July 1912	
Montgomery	Samuel M.	Scheiderer	Helen M.	5 Feb. 1914	
Monti	Chester H.	Wilson	Iris V.	8 Dec. 1919	gr: T. Monti, parent
Montijo	Daniel	Otterbeck	Evelyn M.	13 July 1917	
Montna	Henry Lewis	Pina	Theresa	21 July 1865	
Moodey	Ross Clarence	LeBaron	Grace Eleanor	27 Nov. 1907	
Moody	Arthur W.	Pitts	Ethel S.	30 Dec. 1912	
Moody	Clyde L.	Hansen	Bertha	6 Jan. 1898	br: Mrs. E. J. Hansen, mother
Moody	Edward Elmer	Warren	Sarah B.	6 Nov. 1889	
Moody	Frank L.	Kubala	Rose A.	21 July 1914	
Moody	Harry E.	Bartlett	Ella M.	6 Oct. 1920	
Moody	Logan	Eslick	Daisy Belle	22 Aug. 1916	
Moody	Wilfrid	Petray	Mary E.	17 Mar. 1892	
Mooney	J. William	Ray	Elsie K.	24 Nov. 1902	
Mooney	William O.	Olson	Mabel B.	27 July 1918	
Moore	Benjamin	Murphy	Minnie A.	30 Jan. 1885	br: William Murphy, father
Moore	C. A.	Morgan	S. J.	20 Sept. 1865	
Moore	C. P.	Vassar	N. J., Mrs.	24 Nov. 1890	br: widow
Moore	Charles	Brown	Fannie	12 Dec. 1879	gr: L. McPherson, guardian
Moore	Charles M.	Keyes	Mary	7 June 1911	

	Groom	Bride		Date	Comments
Surname	Given Name	Surname	Given Name		
Moore	Clement J. B.	Carr	Mary T.	24 Sept. 1880	
Moore	Francis M., Jr.	Clark	Frances H.	4 Nov. 1912	gr: Francis M. Moore, Sr., father
Moore	Frank E.	Malipeide	Rosie	31 Oct. 1911	
Moore	Fred T.	Blair	Huldah	27 Dec. 1907	
Moore	Friend Francis	Ives	Amanda Louise Muller	23 Oct. 1909	gr: 323 Second St., Santa Rosa
Moore	Geo. W.	Mize	Amanda	25 Nov. 1865	
Moore	George Henry	Campbell	Ida Cynthia	4 Apr. 1910	
Moore	Gideon J.	Ashley	Mary A.	24 Nov. 1881	br: Wm. F. Ashley, father
Moore	Harley La Verne	Shelford	Wilda Mabelle	16 June 1905	
Moore	Harold S.	Linebaugh	Anna G.	8 Nov. 1919	
Moore	Harvey	Mitchell	May A.	13 Dec. 1915	
Moore	James E.	Butler	Bettie	24 Nov. 1897	br: previously married, obtained divorce in Yuba, Co. abt Nov. 1893
Moore	James Henry	Powell	Elizabeth	3 Sept. 1915	
Moore	Jesse R.	Saylor	Florence M.	20 Jan. 1899	no previous marriage
Moore	John	Cawley	Maria	18 Oct. 1887	
Moore	John T.	Hammond	Caroline	14 June 1889	
Moore	Joseph H.	Williams	Lucy	9 Feb. 1914	
Moore	Leo A.	Highlander	Irma M.	14 Feb. 1921	
Moore	Lewis? D.	Sheffield	Cora	23 Oct. 1899	br: G. E., M.D. & Mrs. J. E. Sheffield, parents
Moore	Oliver C.	Holmberg	Hilda A.	14 Feb. 1917	
Moore	Ray	Duncan	Vella Irene	16 Aug. 1914	
Moore	Ray D.	Ross	Lodema O.	21 Sept. 1918	gr: Mrs. Arlena Moore, mother
Moore	Robert W.	McIntosh	Annie	9 Oct. 1894	
Moore	Saml. C.	Carrillo	Mary Agnes	15 Apr. 1867	
Moore	Thomas B.	Richardson	Emogene	24 Oct 1879	br: L. Richardson, mother

Groom Surname	Groom Given Name	Bride Surname	Bride Given Name	Date	Comments
Moore	Thomas B.	Richardson	Emogene	20 Oct. 1877	
Moore	Thomas W.	Moore	Elizabeth	3 July 1896	Notation: Not to be published.
Moore	Walter Shelby	Hagmayer	Beatrice Urania	26 June 1905	
Moore	Warren B.	Huggard	Etta	10 Oct. 1895	
Moore	William	Parker	Ella	18 Feb. 1881	br: T. M. Leavenworth, guardian; born 15 April; orphan
Moore	William J.	Foster	Blanche	12 Nov. 1883	
Moore	William Washington	Roberts	Edith	26 Feb. 1906	
Moorehead	Lee	Hendrickson	Clara	12 May 1905	
Moose	Edward Henry	Blankstein	Belle	18 Apr. 1917	
Mora	Antone	Lopes	Mary L.	18 Feb. 1911	
Mora	Laurence	Ariasi	Rose	5 Aug. 1914	
Morais	John P.	Brazil	Vetra A.	31 May 1919	br: Margaret Brazil, mother
Moralli	Bernardo	Poncia	Mary	9 Dec. 1915	br: Celesto Poncia, mother
Moran	Alexander	Lewis	Eva	24 Nov. 1908	
Moran	Jack Willis	Thompson	Heneretta	13 Aug. 1917	
Moran	James	Ross	Georgia N.	31 July 1919	
Moran	Joseph	Poole	Hattie	6 Feb. 1886	
Morand	Charles Harrison	Robertson	Lizzie	3 Nov. 1906	
Moranda	Charles S.	Fees	Mattie Grace	24 Sept. 1904	br: Mary M. Fees, mother
Moranda	Silva	Criteser	Ella	16 Dec. 1915	
Mordecai	William B.	Gould	Hannah C.	4 Aug. 1908	gr: Eva Mordecai, mother
More	E. R.	Mills	Gertrude	18 July 1914	
Morehouse	Arthur L.	Glass	Sarah, Mrs.	4 Dec. 1909	
Morehouse	J. W.	Murbar	Mattie	27 Mar. 1888	
Morelli	Antonio	Mazza	Josephine	21 Oct. 1905	
Morelli	Giuseppe, Jr.	Vanoni	Ermine	13 Sept. 1902	
Morelli	Lee G.	Ferrari	Angelica	8 Dec. 1897	

	Groom	Bride		Date	Comments
Surname	Given Name	Surname	Given Name		
Morelli	Morvin Ulysses	Gonella	Florence Marie	27 Oct. 1920	gr: Angelica Morelli, mother; br: Theresa Gonella, mother
Morelli	Orlando	Canaveri	Louise	31 Aug. 1914	
Morenzoni	Joseph	Mache	Minnie L.	1 June 1920	
Moret	Elie H.	Chevallier	Marie	30 Aug. 1913	
Moretti	Camillo P.	Ramatici	Linda B.	21 Mar. 1917	
Moretti	Joseph	Giaconi	Geovanina	23 Apr. 1907	
Morey	Charles H.	Wood	Mae R.	10 Nov. 1906	
Morey	Robert G.	Rainier	Ida M.	12 Oct. 1918	
Morford	Edward Elmore	Huntley	Birdie J.	4 May 1894	
Morgan	Carey	Barth	Mae	5 Aug. 1918	
Morgan	Hugh	Warner (?)	Madova (?)	17 Oct. 1876	br: Mrs A. S. C?lter, mother
Morgan	John Albert	Barr	Maysel	26 Dec. 1906	
Morgan	John Franklin	Collins	May Caroline	29 May 1905	
Morgan	Patrick H.	Boyle	Sara Hilarita	27 Sept. 1920	br: Ida M. Boyle, mother
Morgan	Ross	Bodwell	Charlotte Elizabeth	29 Oct. 1897	no previous marriage
Morgan	Samuel Henry	Howard	Mary E.	28 Mar. 1904	
Morgan	Samuel M.	Holst	Mary C.	13 Oct. 1909	
Morgan	Thomas P.	Christie	Isabella J.	26 June 1902	br: John H. Christie, father
Morillo	Peter C.	Hooker	E. C., Mrs.	28 Dec. 1894	witness: Fred P. Conner
Morin	Frank L.	Cochran	Mattie J.	2 Nov. 1908	
Morini	Frank	Shoemaker	Leonarda	24 July 1886	
Morini	Ubaldo	Pacini	Ida	31 Jan. 1910	br: Frank Pacini, father
Morion	Louis	Orilley	Nellie	23 Feb. 1889	
Moritz	Meyer	Stewart	Elizabeth	27 June 1913	
Morley	Virgil	Greco	Immaculate	24 June 1918	
Morniga	Lugi	Burnardi	Magareta	6 July 1914	
Morrell	Leonard	Smither	Wanda	26 Aug. 1909	br: Mrs. Emma Smither, mother

-164-

Groom Surname	Groom Given Name	Bride Surname	Bride Given Name	Date	Comments
Morrell	William L.	Stone	Grace E.	27 Nov. 1901	
Morrice	Edward	Lee	Ada A.	9 May 1914	
Morris	Alfred	Cook	Salome	4 June 1895	
Morris	Anton	Smith	Marie	31 May 1902	N. V. V. Smyth, witness to mark of Morris
Morris	Edward	Rodric	Carrie	14 Aug. 1911	
Morris	Ernest	Wagner	Alma	23 Dec. 1911	
Morris	George F.	Kinsel	Dorothy	9 June 1897	gr: resides 6455 Ogelsby Ave. Chicago
Morris	Harry B.	Howell	Albrnia C.	15 Dec. 1887	
Morris	Henry	Messing	Rebecca	8 Dec. 1894	
Morris	J. E.	Partington	Mary Ellen Frances	4 Oct. 1892	br: Elizabeth Partington, mother and widow gives consent
Morris	James	Covert	Emma H.	24 May 1901	
Morris	John	Gallagher	Nellie Mae	20 Sept. 1901	signed by D. A. Cornwall, friend
Morris	John	Stewart	Lydia	25 Sept. 1900	
Morris	John Reuben	Archer	Rubie Isalene	22 Nov. 1915	
Morris	Leslie Lenore	Potter	Hattie Isabel	10 Dec. 1913	
Morris	Roy	Elder	Emma	29 Aug. 1912	
Morris	Rudolph A.	Finale	Josephine	20 Apr. 1914	
Morris	Walter	Mason	Eva	31 Dec. 1912	
Morris	Walter C.	Easter	Lucy J. (?)	13 Aug. 1898	gr: Isaiah B. Morris, father; no previous marriage
Morris	Wm. H.	Franklin	Blandine L.	19 Oct. 1916	br: Daniel B. Franklin, father
Morrison	Alvah Herbert	Hesse	Rachel Elizabeth	8 Apr. 1916	
Morrison	Burk Guy	Davis	Mary Warren	8 Jan. 1916	
Morrison	Francis George	Totton	Ella	7 Jan. 1878	
Morrison	George W.	Steele	Etta	30 June 1898	gr: I was divoced more than one year previous to 30 June 1898
Morrison	Guy Bryan	Doyle	Mary Ellen	27 Jan. 1908	

| | Groom | Bride | | Date | Comments |
Surname	Given Name	Surname	Given Name		
Morrison	John H.	Wagner	Julia	20 Oct. 1890	
Morrison	John J.	Smith	Carrie	10 Mar, 1890	br: widow
Morrison	John M.	Monroe	Madalene	12 June 1915	
Morrison	Lester	Garrett	Ida Hazel	31 May 1917	
Morrison	Thomas	Redenbaugh	Lydia E.	29 Apr. 1893	
Morrison	William	Williams	Daisy P.	17 Apr. 1915	
Morrison	William L.	Roberts	Ella G.	10 Mar. 1914	
Morrow	Harrison E.	Blake	Ruth W.	19 Oct. 1920	
Morrow	Harrison E.	Griffin	Mamie R.	8 Mar. 1913	
Morrow	James	McKee	Hattie Bailey	17 July 1882	br: John & Sara A. D. McKee, uncle, guardian; parents now dead
Morrow	John	Rochford	Jennie	25 Feb. 1881	
Morrow	John A.	Ritz	Ada E.	8 Mar. 1918	
Morrow	Joseph A.	Yancey	Emma B.	17 Nov. 1883	br: O. H. & Sarah C. Yancey, father and mother
Morrow	Thomas J.	Moore	Ellen C.	10 Feb. 1888	
Morrow	Wilford E.	Fagan	Cora A.	1 Aug. 1914	
Morrow	Wm. H.	Hinkle	Katherine Dillon	28 Apr. 1891	
Morse	Daniel G.	Young	Flora M.	30 Sept. 1902	br: Flora E. Darr, mother
Morse	Harry S.	McFarlin	Lottie V.	19 Nov. 1916	
Morse	James Grant	Elphick	Annie M.	5 Feb. 1907	
Morse	Stephen C.	Weeks	Frances E.	20 Mar. 1894	
Morten	A. J.	Morton	L. Permilia Louisa	16 Nov. 1889	
Mortenson	Hans	Peterson	Etta	14 Sept. 1903	
Mortenson	Nicholas	Hewitt	Mary Jane	22 Nov. 1910	
Mortimer	John K.	Brady	Anna, Mrs.	27 July 1910	
Mortimer	John K.	Grant	Elizabeth	5 Dec. 1901	
Morton	Charles	Brown	Della Louise	29 Sept. 1906	

Groom Surname	Groom Given Name	Bride Surname	Bride Given Name	Date	Comments
Morton	Claude C.	Gregory	Louise V.	5 Aug. 1920	
Morton	Dudley D.	Wendt	Katherine B.	13 July 1901	
Morton	Harris M.	Schuhrer	Wilhelmine	23 Dec. 1920	
Morton	Henry	Stack	Lotta, Mrs.	17 Dec. 1917	
Morton	John J.	Brennan	Hetty	5 June 1911	
Morton	Martin Tuller	Caldwell	Martha H.	24 Nov. 1886	
Morton	Nathaniel T.	Pomeroy	Eda	14 Oct. 1878	
Morton	Raymond A.	Speyer	Catherine A.	14 June 1915	
Moseley	William W.	Graves	Mary A.	19 Jan. 1903	
Mosely	Gus	Calcote	Eva Ethel	10 Apr. 1906	gr: A. P. Mosely, parent; br: J. D. Calcote, parent
Mosely	Irve Clyde	Patterson	Pearl Elizabeth	9 Feb. 1906	br: Mrs. Alex Walls, guardian
Moser	Charles E.	Tew	Clara N.	18 Nov. 1914	
Moses	Isaac Newton	Breakes	Katie A.	29 Jan. 1880	
Moses	Meyer	Cochran	S.	22 Mar. 1897	
Moses	Robert T.	Olney	Mary Louise	13 Dec. 1898	no previous marriage
Mosher	Frank	Gay	Mary E.	26 Mar. 1894	license requested by C. J. Porter
Mosier	Francis L.	Johnson	Anne	4 Nov. 1907	
Mosna	Ezekiele	Reinero	Mary Elenar	6 Dec. 1909	
Mosna	John	Mitchell	Elisabeth	20 Oct. 1910	gr: Ezekiel Mosna, father
Moss	George W.	Maguire	Ethel Adella	25 Apr. 1918	
Moss	James Marion	Kelly	Ida C., Mrs.	10 July 1906	
Moss	Lemuel A.	Dahse	Johanna Dorothy	12 Apr. 1917	
Moss	Reginald G.	Heath	Budella W.	12 Oct. 1919	
Mossi	Achille	Bassetti	Amelia	20 Nov. 1920	
Mossi	Emilio	Dado	Guilietta C.	14 June 1920	
Mossler	Frederick A.	Denner	Fulvia M.	2 Dec. 1902	do not publish
Mothern	Fernando C.	Lewis	Sarah A.	13 Dec. 1884	gr: William Mothern, father

	Groom	Bride		Date	Comments
Surname	Given Name	Surname	Given Name		
Mothersole	Thomas H.	Durkee	Caroline A.	9 Oct. 1894	
Mothorn	Pressley Perry	Luce	Marie Antoinette	24 Feb. 1910	
Motroni	Herbert J.	Bertoli	Stella M.	11 Apr. 1910	
Moulton	Page H.	Graham	Ivy E.	4 Mar. 1895	
Mount	John Clayton	Bowman	Bertha May	27 June 1906	
Mountain	Floyd	Peyser	Amelia Augusta	27 Dec. 1916	
Mouyer	Louis	Lourdeaux	Aline	11 May 1916	
Mowberry	Francis Walter	Fisher	May Stella	15 July 1896	
Moy	John Daniel	Vanoni	Ynez Dorothy	14 Oct. 1920	
Muat	William F.	Weinberg	Emma A.	11 June 1918	gr: Amalia Muat, mother
Much	Herbert N.	Cnopius	Gertrude M.	7 June 1916	
Muchway	Peter S.	Miller	Ruth M.	10 Jan. 1921	
Mudget	Charles Austin	Steele	Cora Lovina	19 June 1918	
Mueller	Charles	Pullen	Minnie, Mrs.	30 May 1900	
Mueller	Frank	Frese	Irene A.	5 June 1909	
Muenzer	Anton	Schalid	Julia	30 June 1886	
Muenzer	John P.	Schoningh	Marie A.	11 Oct. 1919	
Mueting	William F.	Taylor	Effie J.	8 Sept. 1917	
Muff	John	Luckenbill	Elise	8 Nov. 1890	
Mugler	Albert Miller	Mugler	Frances Helen	14 July 1916	
Muheim	Adolph A.	Gomzenbach	Elizabeth I.	26 May 1917	
Muir	Guy Edward	Murphy	Dorothy Marie	31 Dec. 1919	
Mulford	George N.	Forsythe	Margaret	25 Feb. 1898	no previous marriage
Mulhall	Henry John	Woodson	Pearl Alphia	26 Dec. 1919	
Mulhall	Thomas J.	Bolle	Sopha M.	27 Apr. 1891	
Mullan	Felix George	Nelson	Jennie	3 Mar. 1920	
Mullen	James J.	Kuehne	Clara	21 May 1914	
Muller	Daniel L.	Allen	Luella Rebecca	7 Dec. 1915	

	Groom	Bride		Date	Comments
Surname	Given Name	Surname	Given Name		
Muller	Frank M.	Thistle	Lizzie	12 May 1885	
Muller	Frederick	Schuster	Barbara	11 Apr. 1879	
Muller	George A.	Engdol	Mabel E.	22 Oct. 1915	
Muller	John	Bryant	Mary	28 July 1882	br: Elzabeth Bryan, mother; Petaluma
Muller	Joseph	Kieser	Agnes	18 Aug. 1890	
Muller	Martin	Nelson	Agnes	8 Oct. 1889	
Mulligan	George Julian	Feltes	May Caroline	24 Apr. 1917	
Mullikin	Andrew Frederick	Saxe	Vella	14 Sept. 1912	
Mullin	Edwin F.	Morrison	Alice J.	29 May 1914	
Mullins	Robert W.	Grosgebaur	Louise A.	12 June 1919	
Mumay	William	Beebe	Maggie	17 June 1892	br: George W. Beebe, Mrs. S. Beebe give consent
Munday	Martin E. C.	Linville	Pemelia	12 Dec. 1876	gr: Elizabeth Munday, mother, only surviving parent
Munday	Thomas O.	Connelly	Mary K.	20 Jan. 1905	
Mundee	George E.	Thomas	Grace E.	27 Feb. 1915	
Mundell	Jackson W.	Procise	Sarah J.	30 Aug. 1866	
Mundell	Oliver A.	Bernardi	Inez M.	24 June 1912	
Mundkowski	Clements Vincent	Jacquet	Rosa Celestine	21 Dec. 1916	
Mundkowski	Hans A.	Guilfoyle	Margaret	21 June 1920	
Munfrey	William Osmund	Dunn	Lillie Caroline	26 Sept. 1898	
Munk	William N.	Barnwell	Gail	27 June 1914	
Munn	Joseph L.	Ray	Robert M., Mrs.	19 June 1900	
Munoz	Mariano	Martinez	Adoracion	19 Dec. 1912	
Murbar	George	Kinlock	May	19 May 1900	
Murchie	William T.	Bale	Caroline	4 May 1905	
Murdock	J. W.	Rickett	Clara	24 Jan. 1885	
Murphey	Harry Bruton	Offutt	Rieta J.	17 July 1909	

		Bride		Date	Comments
Groom					
Surname	**Given Name**	**Surname**	**Given Name**		
Murphey	John J.	Mould	Ella E.	14 Jan. 1903	
Murphey	William H.	Redoine	Edith V. A.	24 Dec. 1917	
Murphy	Albert E.	Cox	Florence M.	15 Oct. 1910	
Murphy	Dennis	Carter	Mary	16 Mar. 1909	
Murphy	Frank Edward	Doss	Wilma Eloise	5 July 1918	
Murphy	Frank J.	Button	Theodosia C.	4 Feb. 1888	
Murphy	George B.	Purvine	Alice	3 May 1913	
Murphy	Henry	Turner	Bettie, Mrs.	24 Feb. 1891	br: widow
Murphy	Herman N.	Polhemus	Louisa M.	5 Oct. 1899	no previous marriage
Murphy	J. R.	Early	Mary L.	23 Nov. 1896	
Murphy	James E.	Grimm (?)	Jeannie M.	31 July 1920	
Murphy	John	Tucker	Mona E.	11 Apr. 1901	
Murphy	Lewis T.	Finerty	Katherine L.	6 May 1911	
Murphy	Osbort Louis	Dovey	Minnie Henrietta	5 Nov. 1894	gr: license signed by B. L. Murphy
Murphy	Ralph Everett	Thomas	Mabel Clare	3 June 1905	
Murphy	Robert M.	Jurgensen	Hermina F.	19 Jan. 1918	
Murphy	Wallace	Hiatt	Meta May	13 Jan. 1912	gr: Richard W. Murphy, father; J. Elmer Mobley, John Burroughs, witnesses to his mark
Murphy	Walter Lewis	Granice	Celia Celeste	20 Nov. 1905	
Murphy	William G.	Bush	Lillian P.	12 July 1900	
Murphy	Wm.	Sensibaugh	Armodale	29 Jan. 1886	
Murphy	Wm. A.	McLaughlin	Mary	24 Aug. 1891	
Murray	Archibald Benjamin	Warner	Maud	25 June 1898	gr: I was divorced more than one year ago; not issued
Murray	Byrd B.	Drake	Ada Verlina	5 Dec. 1918	gr: Leah Isabell Murray, mother; br: George Drake, Sr., father, signs with mark
Murray	Charles L.	Burns	Mae	28 July 1917	
Murray	Cleve	Capell	Lula Romona	20 June 1906	

Groom Surname	Groom Given Name	Bride Surname	Bride Given Name	Date	Comments
Murray	Elmer J.	Lombardi	Lillien B.	1 Feb. 1912	
Murray	George Willis	Johnson	Evelyne Marjorie	12 Feb. 1916	
Murray	Howard E.	Hall	Alice M.	8 Feb. 1907	
Murray	James H.	Perks	Lilly Bevins	10 Feb. 1902	
Murray	John	Clark	Hattie	14 Oct. 1897	
Murray	John A.	Stump	Jessie M.	23 Dec. 1899	no previous marriage
Murray	Joseph	Scott	Ruth	29 Oct. 1890	
Murray	Joseph	Murphy	Sallie	10 Sept. 1895	
Murray	Paul	Archer	Laura	12 Dec. 1914	
Murray	Perry L.	Drake	Maude A.	3 Oct. 1901	gr: John C. Murray, father; br: Mrs. George Drake, mother
Murray	Perry Leland	Howard	Juanita V. R.	5 May 1920	gr: Perry L. Murray, Sr., father; br: J. C. Howard, parent
Murray	Ruby E.	Vanderkarr	Daisy M.	24 Dec. 1902	br: Aaron Vanderkarr, father
Murray	Thomas	O'Brien	Hattie	18 Oct. 1905	
Murray	Thomas Elmer	Crigler	Sally E.	31 Oct. 1903	
Murray	Thos. B.	Capell	Ruby I.	6 Oct. 1910	
Murray	William	Dowdall	Katie	8 Oct. 1886	witness G. W. Sparks
Murray	William	Dwane	Agnes	2 Aug. 1920	
Murray	William Henry	Wing	Belle	19 Jan. 1920	
Murrel	Sylvanus B.	Little	Beatrice G.	21 Oct. 1913	
Murry	John P.	Morris	Leah Isabelle	2 June 1877	br: J. P. Morris, parent
Murskey	Frederick A.	Hary	Louise M.	16 June 1917	
Musante	Louis S.	Walker	Evelyn I.	24 May 1917	
Muse	George W.	Stump	Katie	1 Dec. 1884	br: Mrs. B. Stump, mother
Musgrave	Albert	Findlay	R. Christina	5 July 1918	
Musgrave	Benjamin F.	Whitechurch	Julia E.	7 Feb. 1895	
Musselman	William T.	Moore	Lulu E.	21 May 1890	

	Groom	Bride		Date	Comments
Surname	Given Name	Surname	Given Name		
Mussleman	Jesse A.	Beckner	Carrie O.	28 Feb. 1889	
Mustain	Terry	Kelleher	Rose C.	5 Oct. 1915	
Muther	Frank, Jr.	Ewald	Frances	16 Sept. 1898	no previous marriage
Myer	Anthony R.	Hall	Nellie	23 Apr. 1917	
Myers	Arthur W.	Pratt	Amy	26 June 1896	
Myers	D. P	Bostick	Mary	14 Jan. 1888	
Myers	Frank H.	Brownlee	Ida Mabel	20 Apr. 1892	
Myers	George	Woodcock	Lee	29 Dec. 1896	
Myers	Henry	McNeill	Viola	2 June 1908	
Myers	Henry J.	Hannan	Margaret Grace	6 Feb. 1896	
Myers	Joseph J.	Harris	Grace J.	26 June 1895	
Myers	Joseph S.	Goodwin	Alma R.	15 June 1910	
Myhre	Olaf A.	Koller	Sanne H.	9 Jan. 1917	
Myrick	H. R.	Purvine	Alice	19 Feb. 1895	
Myring	W. H.	Taylor	Emily B.	4 Oct. 1866	
Myron	William	Dowdall	Genevieve	15 Oct. 1907	

Part II

Groom, Bride, Age, Residence, Place of Birth

Groom					Bride				
Surname	**Given Name**	**Age**	**Residence**	**BP**	**Surname**	**Given Name**	**Age**	**Residence**	**BP**
Gaba	Marks	37	San Francisco	PLD	Kubic	Annie	30	Petaluma	CA
Gabel	W. E.	25	Cloverdale	MS	Peck	Muriel	18	Cloverdale	CA
Gaberel (?)	G. W.				Seward	Mollie			
Gaberil	Manuel Joseph	22	Iowa Hill, Placer Co.	PRT	Morel	Mary Caroline	21	Petaluma	For
Gables	Chaney R.				Richardson	Ella M.			
Gabrielsen	William J. A.	30	San Francisco	DNK	Down	Edith	26	Santa Rosa	CA
Gabrielson	Carl O.	32	San Francisco	FIN	Anderson	Johanna L.	27	San Francisco	FIN
Gaffney	William	48	Bodega	CA	Walsh	Rose	22	Bodega	RUS
Gage	George S.	79	Novato	OH	Conne	Margaret	56	Petaluma	GER
Gagliando	Andrea	34	Healdsburg	ITL	Pierano	Teresa	22	Healdsburg	ITL
Gaige	Walter Louis	27	Glen Ellen	KS	Chance	Mary E.	26	El Verano	CA
Gaillard	Robert G.	37	Sebastopol	SC	Harrison	Amanda J., Mrs.	31	Sebastopol	CA
Gainer	Roland L.	24	San Francisco	FL	Chelini	Josephine	22	San Francisco	CA
Gaither	William	31	Santa Rosa	IN	Chism	Martha	33	Tompkinsville, KY	KY
Galard	Nicholas	31	Los Guilicos	FRN	Anglade	Katy	27	San Francisco	FRN
Gale	Adelbert Orlando	45	Geysers, Sonoma Co.	MA	Grant	Frankie	26	Denver	WI
Gale	Archie R.	21	Santa Rosa	SD	McAfee	Georgie L.	22	Bellevue	CA
Gale	Archie R.	34	Sonoma	SD	Dowdall	Mary E.	28	El Verano	CA
Gale	Cecil H.	20	Santa Rosa	NE	Leete	Margaret S.	16	Santa Rosa	Sar
Gale	D. R.	33	Santa Rosa	MO	England	Carrie	23	Santa Rosa	CA
Gale	James A.	28	Petaluma	MO	Barnett	Emma B.	20	Green Valley	CA
Gale	Leander	42	Santa Rosa	MO	Conecl (?)	Eva	32	Santa Rosa	MA
Gale	Milton C.	21	Petaluma Twp.	TX	Taylor	Minnie S.	17	Analy Twp.	MO
Gale	W. S.	21	Petaluma	CA	Poulsen	Maria Francisca	19	Petaluma	CA
Gale	Wallace P.	20	Petaluma	CA	Penn	Ida Irene	21	Petaluma	MO
Galgani	Guiseppe	37	Santa Rosa	ITL	Frediani	Katie	35	Hilton	ITL
Galgani	Vincenzo	25	San Francisco	ITL	Dinucci	Julia Katherine	20	Forestville	CA

	Groom					Bride			
Surname	**Given Name**	**Age**	**Residence**	**BP**	**Surname**	**Given Name**	**Age**	**Residence**	**BP**
Galindo	Joseph Vincent	30	Oakland	CA	Manning	Ellen Ida	24	Petaluma	CA
Galindo	Ruperto	26	Oakland	CA	Duffey	Mabel G.	22	Berkeley	CA
Gallagher	Dominic	23	Petaluma	CA	Granger	Carrie E.	18	Petaluma	CA
Gallagher	Edward H.	44	Eldridge	CA	McIntire	Mary L.	36	Eldridge	IL
Gallagher	Frank George	31	Petaluma	CA	Struve	Martha Olga	21	Petaluma	CA
Gallagher	James	38	Fresno	IRL	Donahue	Rena	25	Santa Rosa	CA
Gallaway	Alfred J.	31	San Francisco	CA	Nelson	Thyra A.	29	San Francisco	SWD
Gallaway	Alfred Russel	22	Sacramento	CA	Ware	Lilla	21	Santa Rosa	CA
Gallaway	John C.	60	San Francisco	ENG	Gallaway	Lizzie, Mrs.	54	San Francisco	CA
Gallaway	John W.	35	San Francisco	ENG	Gamble	Bertha V.	34	San Francisco	OR
Galleher	John Harry	22	San Francisco	CA	Fredericks	Minna	21	Petaluma	CA
Galli	Verginio	22	Santa Rosa	ITL	Bartolomei	Sabina	19	Santa Rosa	ITL
Galliah	San	34	Petaluma	BRA	Kirmess	Caroline	25	Petaluma	OR
Gallo	Lorenzo	32	Healdsburg	ITL	Zandrina	Rosa	20	Healdsburg	ITL
Galpin	John W.	24	Tehama	CA	Hutchings	Susie	17	Santa Rosa	IA
Galvin	George Jay	23	Centralia, WA	WA	Green	Emily Augusta	24	Preston	CA
Gamage	Jule Crigden ?	20	San Francisco	CA	Lewis	Lillian L.	19	Petaluma	CA
Gambarasi	Edward	34	San Francisco	SWT	Notari	Regina	26	San Francisco	SWT
Gamber	A. A.	26	Santa Rosa		Royce	Mollie T.	18+	Santa Rosa	
Gambini	L. P.	21	Santa Rosa	SWT	Grandi	Ella C.	21	Valley Ford	CA
Gambini	William A.	22	Santa Rosa	CA	Hockin	Margaret M.	18	Santa Rosa	CA
Gamble	Charles	30	Merced	IRL	Clark	Ella	23	Lytton Springs	CA
Gamble	Charles Elmer	41	Santa Rosa	CA	Lumsden	Martha Louise	25	Santa Rosa	CA
Gambogi	Amchese	29	Santa Rosa	ITL	Garborini	Annie	18	Santa Rosa	CA
Gambogi	Davino	36	Santa Rosa	ITL	Ronchali	Rosa	31	Santa Rosa	ITL
Gamboni	William Robert	22	Petaluma	Mac	Menary	Mary Katherine	18	Petaluma	Gold Hill
Gambonini	Alfonso Joseph	25	Marshall	CA	LaFranchi	Sylvia J.	25	Petaluma	CA
Gambonini	Arnold	30	Marshall	CA	LaFranchi	Anita E.	30	Petaluma	CA
Gambonini	Silvio G.	26	Petaluma	CA	Dado	Evelina E.	26	Petaluma	CA

	Groom					Bride			
Surname	Given Name	Age	Residence	BP	Surname	Given Name	Age	Residence	BP
Gammill	Charles F.	27	Glen Ellen	IL	Beatty	May V.	18	Glen Ellen	CA
Gandy	Lemaul J.	29	Sebastopol	NE	Nelsen	Emma G.	18	Sebastopol	MO
Gangler	Xaver	30	Oakland	GER	Hueber	Regina	20	San Francisco	CA
Ganner	James Edwin	22	Sebastopol	CA	Pierce	Augusta	24	Sebastopol	IL
Ganter	Clinton E.	23	Ukiah	WI	Wyckoff	Maggie	18	Ukiah	CA
Garbini	Angelo J.	21	Daly City	CA	Gossage	Rachel L.	18	San Francisco	SD
Garcelon	W. Scott, Jr.	28	San Francisco	MN	Schibi	Margaret B.	22	San Francisco	CT
Garcia	Agopito P.	23	Oakland	CA	Mills	Winifred Alice	18	Oakland	CA
Garcia	Antonio	38	Santa Rosa	SPN	Gracia	Ception	30	Santa Rosa	SPN
Garcia	Benigno	30	Santa Rosa	SPN	Casasnovas	Sara	18	Santa Rosa	SPN
Garcia	Chick	24	Sausalito	CA	Bones	Alice	19	Occidental	CA
Garcia	Felix				Mendosiz	Fara			
Garcia	Firmin	23	San Francisco	CA	Emeldi	Theodora Marie	20	San Francisco	ITL
Gard	James F.	35	Petaluma	MT	Kopiske	Amelia	23	Santa Rosa	CA
Gardella	Joseph	21	Santa Rosa	ITL	Veganogo	Angelo	19	Santa Rosa	ITL
Gardenhire	W. H.	64	Sebastopol	IL	Laymance	Leona	64	Windsor	MO
Gardenhire	William A.	24	Duncans Mills	CA	Rider	Lois E.	17	Santa Rosa	CA
Gardenshire (?)	S. B.	27	Fulton	IL	Lingenfelter	Lucy	17	Fulton	MO
Gardiner	Bevil F.	23	San Francisco	CA	Wilcox	Edith M.	19	San Francisco	CA
Gardiner	Charles W.	40	Santa Rosa	MI	Tramor	Marie A.	42	Tomales	CA
Gardiner	Waldron R.	26	Oakland	Oak	Pharris	Alice	18	Oakland	CA
Gardner	Albert E.	37	Santa Rosa	CA	Weller	Eva U.	30	Sebastopol	IA
Gardner	Bernard Rogers	25	San Francisco	NY	Klink	Vernie Gladys	20	Guerneville	CA
Gardner	Chas. M.	25	Merced	CA	Murbar	Clara	21	Santa Rosa	CA
Gardner	Robert Elmer	21	Santa Rosa	CA	Cornett	Edith Luella	19	Santa Rosa	CA
Gardner	Roy Lee	23	Mare Island	CA	Hart	Delphine Antonia	20	San Francisco	NV
Gardner	Vanness	37	Sebastopol	PA	Crotts	Emily K.	21	Sebastopol	CA
Gardner	William H.	21	Oakland	CA	Joseph	Mae Vera	19	Oakland	CA
Garety	Leo J.	40	San Francisco	CA	O'Brien	Elizabeth V.	40	San Francisco	CA

	Groom					Bride			
Surname	**Given Name**	**Age**	**Residence**	**BP**	**Surname**	**Given Name**	**Age**	**Residence**	**BP**
Garguilo	Fred	21	Oakland	CA	Burke	Margaret May	20	Montreal, CND	CND
Garland	Harry	23	Oakland	IL	Burgess	Beatrice	21	Healdsburg	CA
Garloff	Henry R.	24	Sebastopol	MN	Finley	Genevieve	16	Bodega	CA
Garloff	John A.	25	Sebastopol	MN	Mapes	Annita G.	19	Sebastopol	CA
Garloff	Walter W.	23	Sebastopol	MN	Finley	Bessie	19	Santa Rosa	CA
Garloff	William F.	30	Sebastopol	GER	McDonald	Jessie F.	19	Sebastopol	CA
Garlow	J. A.	49	Petaluma	PA	Bryant	Della D.	40	San Francisco	ME
Garman	James				Sebring	Sarah E.			
Garner	Walter A.	36	Hayward	IA	Allen	Ethel Mae	28	Hayward	CA
Garnett	Kennedy Porter	36	Berkeley	CA	Foote	Edna	26	Kellogg	CA
Garofalo	Bert	21	San Francisco	CA	Beattie	Friedia	18	Petaluma	CA
Garoni	Guiseppe	41	Agua Caliente	ITL	Shevoskey	Eva	26	Agua Caliente	RUS
Garratt	Mansfield W.	26	Cloverdale	OR	Ray	Juanita I.	19	Geyserville	CO
Garretson	John D.	40	San Francisco	CA	Purvine	E. Mae	26	Petaluma	CA
Garrett	Albert Walker	29	Healdsburg	CA	Hall	Cora Pauline	22	Healdsburg	CA
Garrett	Edward Lee	24	Calistoga	CA	Norris	Erma B.	20	Stockton	CA
Garrett	Thomas	48	San Francisco	WIN	Kanieri	Anna	41	San Francisco	IRL
Garrett	Vernon George	27	San Francisco	OR	Carithers	Gladys Ellen	25	Santa Rosa	CA
Garrison	Bert L.	21	Santa Rosa	KS	Kalen	Charlotte S.	20	Santa Rosa	MO
Garrison	Charles H.	21	Santa Rosa	MO	Brown	Marguerite J.	20	Santa Rosa	CA
Garrison	Charles S.	47	San Rafael	CA	Sutherland	Della	20	Guerneville	CA
Garrison	Elmer B.	20	Sebastopol	CA	Doty	Ida H.	20	Sebastopol	CA
Garrison	James G.	31	Marysville	CA	Moran	Blanche E.	21	Sebastopol	CA
Garrison	Nonnie	21	Santa Rosa	CA	King	Matilda J.	16	Petaluma	CA
Garrison	Richard William	49	Sonoma	TX	Langer	Alice G.	27	Berkeley	RUS
Garrison	Ross J.	22	Freestone	KS	Whitcomb	Annie O.	18	Sebastopol	CA
Garrison	Will Robert	23	Santa Rosa	CA	Randall	Fannie J.	20	Santa Rosa	CA
Garrity	Thomas	41	Vallejo	NY	McFarland	Mary	33	Vallejo	IRL
Garside	Thomas H.	28	Petaluma	ENG	Glazier	Mary O.	22	Petaluma	CA
Gartner	Charles Henry	25	San Francisco	CA	Neal	Rita E.	24	San Francisco	UT

	Groom					Bride			
Surname	**Given Name**	**Age**	**Residence**	**BP**	**Surname**	**Given Name**	**Age**	**Residence**	**BP**
Garvey	John F.	43	San Francisco	MA	McMartin	Mary J.	33	Oakland	OH
Garzoli	Alfonso	34	Nicasio	CA	Dodd	Delfina	26	Petaluma	CA
Garzoli	Joshua	30	Sonoma	SWT	Eraldi	Emma	15	Sonoma	CA
Garzoli	William Victor	32	Petaluma	CA	Pellascio	Lillie Vergie	18	Petaluma	CA
Gashwiler	L. F.	50	San Francisco	MO	McClellan	Ruth	32	Healdsburg	CA
Gaspari	Julius	55	Santa Rosa	ITL	Mecchi	Mary	37	Santa Rosa	ITL
Gasperi	Pietro	38	Rocklin, Placer Co.	AUS	Maccario	Katie	18	Melita	ITL
Gaston	Geo. W.	32	Two Rock	CA	Sales	Dora A.	22	Two Rock	CA
Gaston	George R.	22	Petaluma	CA	Anderson	Ruth M.	23	Petaluma	CA
Gaston	John W.				Freeman	Nadien J.	16		
Gaston	William H.	40	Petaluma	Pet	Winn	Hattie M.	33	Petaluma	Tomales
Gater	Frank I.	33	Geyserville	PA	Dana	Emma	31	Geyserville	CA
Gater	J. E.	28	Geyserville	PA	Smith	Carrie	24	Geyserville	CA
Gater	J. E.	25	Geyserville	PA	Miles	Mary	19	Healdsburg	CA
Gates	Earl J.	27	Sacramento	CA	Henslee	Marie L.	18	Sacramento	CA
Gates	William Henry	21	Oakland	IL	Sikes	Viola Bly	18	Santa Rosa	PA
Gauldin	Joseph E.	27	Rincon Valley	CA	Chamler	Fannie Belle	17	Santa Rosa	TX
Gaupp	Edward Philip	22	San Francisco	CA	Hawthorne	Esther Gertrude	20	San Francisco	CA
Geanskag	John	29	Fort Bragg	FIN	Sellers	Mattie	20	Fort Bragg	Fort Bragg
Gearhart	L. C.	34	Healdsburg	OH	Horgson (?)	Emma	37	Healdsburg	
Geary	George E.	24	Camerio	MN	Ranker	Bernice O.	20	Glen Ellen	CA
Geary	Michael	59	San Francisco	IRL	Anderson	Alice H.	39	San Francisco	CA
Geary	William W.	39	San Rafael	PA	Wilson	Emma	36	Santa Rosa	ENG
Gebauer	Charles J.	21	Healdsburg	CA	Selzle	Lena A.	18	Healdsburg	IL
Gebharth	Christian	26	San Francisco	RUS	Bollinger	Dora Francis	19	Santa Rosa	RUS
Geiger	Fred	33	Santa Rosa	GER	Demetz	Anna	41	Santa Rosa	SWT
Geils	George F.	28	Chileno Valley	GER	Druckhammer	Minna	23	Petaluma	GER

	Groom					Bride			
Surname	Given Name	Age	Residence	BP	Surname	Given Name	Age	Residence	BP
Gein	August Carl	21	Santa Rosa	GER	Barnes	Ruby Rhomance	23	Santa Rosa	WA
Geiorvas (?)	Pete D.	30	San Francisco	GRC	Nelson	Mary E.	39	San Francisco	UT
Geisel	Henry John	24	San Francisco	GER	Peterson	Bertha	23	Healdsburg	CA
Geisler	Francis Joseph	33	Martinez	AUS	Journey	Nettie Belle	27	Petaluma	IA
Gellerman	Louis W.	41	Healdsburg	IA	Curtis	Mabel H.	37	Healdsburg	CA
Gellissen	Andrew	37	Santa Rosa	GER	Rohlfs	Frances	27	Santa Rosa	GER
Gemetti	Battista	29	Petaluma	SWT	Cotta	Delia	21	Petaluma	CA
Gemmer (?)	John C.	24	Santa Rosa		Boehrner	Annie E.	19	Santa Rosa	
Genazzi	Charles E.	25	Bodega Bay	Soc	Bittner	Mary H.	20	Occidental	Hon
Gender	Edward F.	53	Santa Rosa	CA	Dwyer	Nellie A.	50	Santa Rosa	CA
Genelle	Emanuel Ignacio	37	Piedmont	CND	Stegeman	Julia	29	Cloverdale	CA
Generrilli	Albert J.	28	Oakland	ITL	Gibson	Dorothy Irene	20	Oakland	NV
Gennette	Rene Even	26	San Francisco	KS	Shaw	Irene	26	San Francisco	CA
Gensler	G.	36	San Francisco	CA	Montague	Eleeta	36	San Francisco	IL
Gensler	Goodkind	25	San Francisco	Sfo	Swift	Lizzie	20	San Francisco	Alameda Co.
Genther	Jeremiah	45	Santa Rosa	NJ	Thompson	Agnes L.	21	Santa Rosa	CA
Gentis	Camille	33	Oakland	PA	Cone	Kathryn A.	32	Oakland	CA
Gentry	Samuel	21	Christine, Mendocino Co.	CA	DeYoung	Minnie	19	Christine, Mendocino Co.	CA
Genung	William L.	68	Vallejo	OH	Fournier (?)	Alice	62	Vallejo	CND
George	Harmon Alfred	35	Petaluma	IA	Pierce	Ethel Ruth	24	Petaluma	CA
George	James W.	34	Petaluma	IA	Jones	Nellie M.	22	Guerneville	CA
George	John	30	Merced	AZR	Green	Lucy	19	Sebastopol	CA
George	Joseph M.	19	Santa Rosa	PRT	Elton	Gratia	21	Formey (?)	CA
George	William Edgar	25	San Jose	MO	Burke	Evelyn Lucille	25	Salinas	CA
Georgi	Ralph A.	21	Jamestown, NY	NY	Wheeler	Juanita	17	Santa Rosa	CA
Gerald	James T.	39	Windsor	MA	Fairbairn	Martha, Mrs.	39	Ione, Amador Co.	CA

	Groom				Bride				
Surname	Given Name	Age	Residence	BP	Surname	Given Name	Age	Residence	BP
Gerald	James Thomas	27	Russian River Twp.		Lowrey	Cerillda (?)	28	Russian River Twp.	
Gerberding	Howard R.	22	San Francisco	PA	Kaufman	Hazel L.	19	San Francisco	NE
Gercar	Josef	42	Petaluma	AUS	Flack	Rosie	39	Petaluma	AUS
Gercich	Fred	28	Fresno	CA	Bimmerle	Emma	22	San Francisco	CA
Geremia	Massente	29	Petaluma	ITL	Bianchi	Eugenia	27	Petaluma	SWT
Gerig	Henry	25	Petaluma	CA	Schelbert	Marie	23	Petaluma	MO
German	Covington E.	26	Guerneville	CA	Geezley	Katie	16	Guerneville	CA
German	Wm. W.	22	Guerneville	CA	Ridenhour	Ella	18	Guerneville	CA
Gerow	George E.	21+	Healdsburg	CA	Jones	Hattie R.	18+	Healdsburg	CA
Gerstley	M. Louis	21	Philadelphia	CA	Mercer	Elizabeth	21	San Francisco	TX
Gesse	Giolio	33	Petaluma	ITL	Ponzie	Madelena	42	Petaluma	ITL
Gestra	John	28	Petaluma	ITL	Gestra	Maria	20	Petaluma	ITL
Ghigliotti	Fred V.	47	San Jose	NY	Moresi	Angela	23	Oakland	CA
Ghiselli	Anacleto	25	San Francisco	CA	Arrighi	Ernestina	21	Santa Rosa	ITL
Ghisletta	Antone	30	Duncans Mill	SWT	Pedrotti	Mary Angelina	23	Duncans Mills	CA
Ghisletta	Antonio	30	Petaluma	SWT	Beretta	Olivia	32	Petaluma	CA
Giacconi	Santi	30	Fulton	ITL	Vicari	Clara		Fulton	CA
Giacomelli	Etalo	23	San Francisco	ITL	Dinnucci	Giula	17	Healdsburg	CA
Giacomini	Michele	50	Petaluma	SWT	Soldate	Mary J.	45	Petaluma	Pet
Giaconini	Americo	29	Penngrove	CA	Lopus	Minnie	21	Penngrove	CA
Giacosa	Luigi	32	Kennett, Shasta Co.	ITL	Francia	Maria	27	Petaluma	ITL
Giambruno	Alberto	28	Stockton	ITL	Consiglieri	Josephine	19	Santa Rosa	CA
Giannecchini	Aladino	22	Forestville	ITL	Battaglia	Polissene	16	Forestville	ITL
Giannecchini	Louis	26	San Francisco	ITL	Passalacqua	Silvia	21	Healdsburg	CA
Giannini	Harry	21	Nendling (?), CA	CA	Suchowski	Helen	18	Tormey, Contra Costa Co.	CA
Gibb	James W.	40	San Francisco	CA	Ogden	Ermon S.	31	San Mateo	LA
Gibbens	John W.	50	Walla Walla	IN	Campbell	Phoebe L.	50	Healdsburg	IL

	Groom					Bride			
Surname	Given Name	Age	Residence	BP	Surname	Given Name	Age	Residence	BP
Gibbens	Robert L.	35	Fulton	NV	Leslie	Margaret May	25	Windsor	CA
Gibbens	Walter Raleigh	29	San Francisco	CA	Grote	Jennie Estelle	28	San Francisco	OR
Gibbins	Lue Amos	34	Marysville	CA	Wiess	Bertha	36	San Francisco	NRY
Gibbons	Alfred Sydney	31	Santa Rosa	CA	Fowler	Cornelia W.	26	Santa Rosa	CA
Gibbons	Estell Ellis	30	Cloverdale	Men	Porter	Bertha	22	Healdsburg	Soc
Gibbs	E. C.	24	Petaluma	CA	Light	Ella	22	Marin Co.	CA
Gibbs	F. H.	26	Two Rock	CA	Doss	S. N.	19	Sebastopol	CA
Gibbs	George D.	23	Oakland	George-town, CA	Garrett	Retta	18+	Santa Rosa	Calis-toga
Giberson	William P.	25	Petaluma	NJ	King	Hollis E.	20	Petaluma	NV
Gibson	Charles W.	21	Dry Creek	CA	Wolfe	Eliza	15	Healdsburg	CA
Gibson	Clifford LaVere	21	Palo Alto	CA	Hunt	Lois Irena	21	Palo Alto	AZ
Gibson	Clyde C.	26	Petaluma	CA	Clark	Lottie J. M.	21	Petaluma	CA
Gibson	David L.	57	Kenwood	IL	Knox	Maud Florence	31	Santa Rosa	CA
Gibson	Edward E.	45	Ukiah	IL	Wichman	Ida B.	38	San Mateo	CA
Gibson	Floyd E.	25	Albion	CA	Buckman	Kathleen W.	25	Hopland	CA
Gibson	Frank Lester	25	Petaluma	WA	Shaw	Bessie Lurane	24	Petaluma	NE
Gibson	G. W.	21	Ukiah	CA	Beck	Belle	19	Ukiah	OH
Gibson	Gardie L.	21	Ukiah	CA	Travers	Emma	18	Sebastopol	IL
Gibson	Henry	63	Petaluma	IRL	Butler	Sarah A.	60	Santa Rosa	NY
Gibson	Henry	71	Santa Rosa	IRL	Ward	Polly A.	70	Santa Rosa	NY
Gibson	Henry Brown	28	Bolinas		Smith	Adeline F., Mrs.	26	Bolinas	
Gibson	Henry Frank	21	Healdsburg	CA	Cadd	Ethel Mae	21	Healdsburg	CA
Gibson	Herman W.	26	San Jose	CA	McMillen	Helen Martha	18	Gualala	CA
Gibson	James	26	San Francisco	IRL	Taylor	Cordelia J.	26	Occidental	CA
Gibson	James W.	40	Glen Ellen	CA	Justi	Otilda R.	35	Glen Ellen	CA
Gibson	James W.	43	Glen Ellen	CA	Thompson	Myrtle C.	22	Glen Ellen	CA
Gibson	John A.	34	Los Angeles	CA	Prewitt	Mabel A.	35	Santa Rosa	NJ
Gibson	John R.	38	Santa Rosa	MO	Garrison	Lena	28	Ukiah	CA

Groom					Bride				
Surname	Given Name	Age	Residence	BP	Surname	Given Name	Age	Residence	BP
Gibson	Martin R.	29	San Francisco	CA	Jensen	Lillian H.	26	Oakland	CA
Gibson	Ora Ray	25	Healdsburg	CA	Smith	Zella	19	Healdsburg	CA
Gibson	Robert P.	29	Glen Ellen	AUT	Wilson	Saidie E.	27	Glen Ellen	KS
Gies	John J.	37	Reese, Tuscola Co., MI	MI	Rollins	May	22	Santa Rosa	KS
Gifford	Francis M.				Stone	Sarah Jane			
Gifford	John M.	34	San Francisco	CO	Powell	Marcella	31	Sonoma	IRL
Gilardi	Americo	31	Petaluma	CA	Soldati	Palma E.	27	Petaluma	CA
Gilardi	Andrew Richard	27	Petaluma	CA	Tomasi	Johanna Mary	21	Petaluma	CA
Gilardi	James J.	21	Petaluma	CA	Soldati	Adeline	21	Petaluma	CA
Gilardi	Joe P.	28	Sebastopol	ITL	Berta	Anna	20	Santa Rosa	ITL
Gilardoni	Attilio	29	Glen Ellen	ITL	Laurent	Julia	16	Melita	OR
Gilbert	Bret Alexis	35	Santa Rosa	CA	Sephton	Grace	28	Alameda	CA
Gilbert	Charles Robert	25	Santa Rosa	CA	Smith	Emma J.	35	Santa Rosa	CA
Gilbert	David W.				Freshour	Nancy C.			
Gilbert	Joseph L.	27	San Francisco	TX	Lachman	Violette	20	San Francisco	CA
Gilbert	Thos. A.	64	Petaluma	NY	Clark	Fannie E.	48	Petaluma	MI
Gilbert	William J.	25	San Francisco	NY	Carriger	Margaret F.	25	Sonoma Twp.	CA
Gilbride	Philip Joseph	44	Healdsburg	BCL	Lagomarsino	Katie	38	Healdsburg	CA
Gilbride	Rodger James	25	Healdsburg	CA	Thompson	Charlotte	24	Healdsburg	CA
Gilder	Alfred	45	Healdsburg	ENG	Doherty	Gertrude H.	36	San Francisco	CA
Gilder	Alfred	37	Occidental	ENG	Benninghoven	Emma	35	Occidental	NY
Giles	Grant	36	Petaluma	CA	Hemseth	Bernardena	25	Cloverdale	Clo
Gilford	Francis M.				Stone	Sarah Jane			
Gilkey	B. H.	24	Santa Rosa	VT	Spaulding	Laura B.	24	Santa Rosa	MN
Gill	Charles W.	44	Sacramento	CA	Austin	Alice E.	38	Santa Rosa	GA
Gill	George W.	43	Santa Rosa	MA	Krumdick	Jennie, Mrs.	43	Santa Rosa	MO
Gill	George Willard	50	Petaluma	MA	Bonnel	Edith, Mrs.	28	Petaluma	CA
Gill	James W.	24	Geyserville	CA	Livey	Sarah V.	21	Geyserville	CA
Gill	Robert J.	29	San Francisco	CA	Walker	Margaret B.	29	Long Beach	IN

	Groom					Bride			
Surname	**Given Name**	**Age**	**Residence**	**BP**	**Surname**	**Given Name**	**Age**	**Residence**	**BP**
Gillespie	Vern B.	21	Geyserville	CA	Sharp	Hazel R.	17	Geyserville	OK
Gillespie	William Breese	34	Gardnerville, NV	NY	Russell	Helen Jane	21	Santa Rosa	CA
Gillett	C. W.	26	Santa Rosa	CA	Lumsden	Elizabeth R.	24	Santa Rosa	PA
Gillett	Charles	68	Santa Rosa	OH	Strong	Lizzette W.	50	Santa Rosa	CND
Gillett	Charles	75	Santa Rosa	OH	Forbes	Mary Jane	65	Santa Rosa	MA
Gillett	Martin	49	Occidental	MA	McGee	Kate	18	Occidental	CA
Gillette	Russell W.	57	San Francisco	MI	Jenkines	Lida M.	54	San Jose	CA
Gilliam	David T.	46	Cloverdale	CA	Moore	Sarah	47	Cloverdale	MO
Gilliam	David Taylor	24	Green Valley		Williams	Minerva	16	Green Valley	
Gilliam	George D.	21	Sausalito	CA	Dei	Aneta	18	Duncans Mills	CA
Gilliam	James Mitchell	29	Monte Rio	CA	Hansen	Bessie May	23	Occidental	CA
Gilliam	Samuel Jackson	47	Santa Rosa	OR	Loyd	Lillie May	25	Santa Rosa	MO
Gillogly	William J. S.	38	Alameda	UT	Gallagher	Alice Louise	35	Portola	CA
Gillon	Charles Mark	46	San Francisco	CA	Howe	Louise A., Mrs.	38	Petaluma	CA
Gilman	P. E.	32	Santa Rosa	Houl-ton, ME	Tucker	Harriet E.	18	Santa Rosa	Pet
Gilmer	William M.	37	Sebastopol	OH	Sheldon	Mabel E.	23	Green Valley	CA
Gilmore	Carl F.	23	Port Costa	CA	Brundige	Bessie M.	20	Santa Rosa	CA
Gilmore	George	28	Analy Twp.		Freeman	Ella	17	Santa Rosa	
Ginsti	Angelo	27	Windsor	ITL	Celeri	Elizabetto	20	Windsor	ITL
Gionnoni	Eugene	25	Cloverdale	ITL	Bartolomei	Amelia	19	Cloverdale	CA
Giorgi	Alfred	22	San Francisco	CA	Clark	Ethel Mary	19	Healdsburg	CA
Giorgi	Arthur	24	Healdsburg	ITL	Lencioni	Carrie	18	Healdsburg	CA
Giorgi	Nicola	28	Cazadero	ITL	Buonaccorsi	Penelope	17	Cazadero	ITL
Giorno	Vincent W.	27	Ukiah	ITL	Lane	Grace A.	36	Ukiah	PA
Giorno	Victor E.	22	Petaluma	TX	Dorward	Anna G.	29	Petaluma	CA
Giovani	Galliani	27	Duncans Mills	ITL	Torelli	Pollonia	22	Duncans Mills	SWT
Giovannetti	Domencio	26	Healdsburg	ITL	Fregulia	Catherine	16	Graton	ITL
Giovannini	Romeo J.	26	San Francisco	CA	Rosenthal	Nettie	25	San Francisco	CA
Giovannoni	Adolph Joseph	21	Glen Ellen	ITL	Baldocchi	Lizzie Mary	18	Glen Ellen	CA

Groom					Bride				
Surname	Given Name	Age	Residence	BP	Surname	Given Name	Age	Residence	BP
Girder	Clyde H.	23	Cazadero	CA	Burkett	Helen M.	21	Cazadero	NJ
Girolo	Gabriele	27	Kenwood	ITL	Albini	Emelia	18	Santa Rosa	ITL
Girolo	Pietro	29	Santa Rosa	ITL	Perotta	Josephine	21	Santa Rosa	ITL
Girtaner	Alfred	29	San Francisco	NE	Trotman	Eva Blanche Muriel	24	Healdsburg	NZD
Gise	Edward	24	Sonoma	OH	Ryan	Josie	19	Sonoma	CA
Gisel	Herman	24	Guerneville	SWT	Beebe	Stella S.	18	Guerneville	CA
Giulieri	Mansueto	23	Bodega	SWT	Pellascia	Mary	19	Bodega	SWT
Giusti	Alfred	25	San Francisco	ITL	Lorenzini	Louise	25	Santa Rosa	CA
Giusti	Omero	28	Guerneville	ITL	Pocai	Clotilde	28	Guerneville	ITL
Given	Andrews Logan	26	Forestville	IA	Dibble	Avonia	19	Forestville	CA
Given	Robert H.	30	San Francisco	WV	Hacker	Edith Amy	29	San Francisco	MI
Givens	Archibald Wills	26	Merced	CA	McReynolds	Virginia	26	Santa Rosa	CA
Givin	Aneil W.	45	Occidental	CA	Lapham	Cornelia E.	21	Occidental	CA
Gladding	Orman B.	26	Oakland	OR	Savercool	Alice	25	San Leandro	CA
Glady	Thomas	36	San Francisco	CA	Granger	Ethel	21	San Francisco	CA
Glaister	Middleton P.	23	Sonoma	AUT	Thomas	Sarah A.	21	Sonoma	CND
Glaisty	Skelton D.	25	Sonoma	AUT	Burris	Eudora	22	Sonoma	CA
Glaizer	Walter Oscar	21	Petaluma	CA	Cook	Evelyn	17	Santa Rosa	CA
Glaser	Abe	21	San Francisco	CA	Feinberg	Lillie	18	San Francisco	RUS
Glaser	Albert Ludwig	25	Dry Creek	GER	Ludmann	Sophie	24	Dry Creek	GER
Glasgow	Sumner E.	25	San Francisco	IL	Wright	Eva Pearl	19	San Francisco	MI
Glass	Hugh M.	34	San Francisco	CA	Keller	Josie E.	22	Santa Rosa	IA
Glassman	Abraham B.	27	San Francisco	GER	Jacobs	Amelia A.	19	Healdsburg	PA
Glatfelder	Clement	61	Santa Rosa	IL	Walker	Addie L.	62	Santa Rosa	PA
Glazer	Henry	27	Petaluma	RUS	Todfield	Fannie	23	San Francisco	AUS
Gleason	Cyrus S.	45	Santa Rosa		Tittus	Phebe	37	Santa Rosa	
Gleason	David P.	31	Bodega	CA	Carson	Katherine F.	26	Sea View	CA
Gleason	Guy Strahom	21	Mechanicsville, Cedar Co., IA	IA	Day	Agnes Nettie	22	Healdsburg	IA

	Groom					Bride			
Surname	Given Name	Age	Residence	BP	Surname	Given Name	Age	Residence	BP
Gleason	Leo H.	28	Bodega	CA	McLain	Agatha F.	18	Freestone	CA
Gleason	Walter Raymond	24	Bodega	CA	Fitzpartrick	Lillian Gertrude	21	Bodega	CA
Gledhill	Ernest B.	21	Sacramento	KS	Von Berg	Annie	17	Santa Rosa	TX
Glidden	Willard W.	23	San Francisco	CA	Stympson	Ethel V.	20	San Francisco	CA
Gliddon	William	22	Guerneville	CA	Folks	Nellie	17	Guerneville	CA
Glinden	Harry	38	Petaluma	MN	Birkenstock	Eleen	22	Cotati	AR
Gloeckner	Charles	45	Sebastopol	NY	Smart	Tamar Ewen	32	Sebastopol	SCT
Glover	Albert Carl	27	Navarro	NY	Guntly	Irene M.	21	Philo	CA
Glover	Harold	21	Tracy	WA	Smith	Loretta R.	19	Tracy	CA
Glynn	Burr Augustus	34	Del Mar	CA	Bittner	Martha	26	Occidental	CA
Gnesa	Louis, Jr.	24	Santa Rosa	CA	Ramos	Ida A.	20	Sebastopol	CA
Goard	W. F.	24	El Verano	Ser	Esquieu	Louise	20	Petaluma	Sfo
Goatley	John L.	31	Petaluma	CA	King	Mabel Ruth	27	Petaluma	CA
Gobbi	Charles W.	24	Healdsburg	CA	Wooster	Carrie A.	24	Fruitvale	CA
Gobbi	John	25	Bodega	ITL	Marzoli	Margaret	17	Bodega	ITL
Gobbi	Joseph	26	Valley Ford	ITL	Croste	Madalina	21	Valley Ford	ITL
Gobbi	Julius James	27	Healdsburg	ITL	Yengling	Ella C.	24	Healdsburg	CA
Gobbi	William V.	25	Healdsburg	CA	Spencer	Maude E.	21	Healdsburg	CA
Gober	B. F.	26	Healdsburg	TN	Bidwell	Sarah J.	36	Healdsburg	MO
Gober	Benjamin F.	22	Alexander Valley		Towle	Emma S.	17	Alexander Valley	
Gober	Charley Van Buren	24	Alexander Valley	MO	Breitling	Matilda	21	Alexander Valley	IL
Goddard	Albert D.	25	Healdsburg	CA	Liscomb	Florence A.	18	Healdsburg	MI
Goddard	Daniel N.	23	Healdsburg		Horine	Allie	22	Healdsburg	
Goddard	Elmer F.	23	Healdsburg	CA	Cadd	Mary I.	20	Healdsburg	CA
Goddard	Frank				Smith	Hattie L.	18	Healdsburg	CA
Goddard	J. P.	23	Healdsburg		Sturgess	Sarah A.	20	Healdsburg	
Goddard	Jesse J.	23	San Francisco	AZ	Goddard	Hattie E.	18	Healdsburg	CA
Goddard	Wellman	26	Healdsburg	CA	Clifford	Blanch H.	18	Healdsburg	NV

Groom					Bride				
Surname	Given Name	Age	Residence	BP	Surname	Given Name	Age	Residence	BP
Godman	Charles Edwin	29	Santa Rosa	CA	Cissell	Mary Annis	23	Santa Rosa	IN
Godman	George G.	23	Santa Rosa	CA	England	Cora May	20	Santa Rosa	IL
Godman	Robert Edward	25	Santa Rosa	CA	Cummins	Loretta Ellen	23	Santa Rosa	CA
Goeffert	Edward Raymond	21	San Francisco	CA	Bulotti	Lillian S.	18	Sonoma	CA
Goeller	John	45	Petaluma	GER	Schnitz	Louisa, Mrs.	48	Petaluma	GER
Goess	Ferdinand Howard	22	Sonoma	Agc	Schwarz	Nellie	22	San Francisco	Sfo
Goess	George Andrew	24		CA	Simmons	Jennette Augusta	28		Pom
Goethe	William E.	25	near Sonoma	NY	Nau	Barbara E.	23	near Glen Ellen	CA
Goewey	Charles H.	46	Boyes Springs	CA	Young	Edith A.	31	Boyes Springs	MI
Golden (?)	James (?)	39	Santa Rosa		Odem	G. A.	36		
Goldman	Leon	48	San Jose	MA	Van de Water	Grace M.	34	San Jose	IL
Golds	John	27	Napa	CA	Johannsen	Emma	22	Sonoma	CA
Goldsam	Matthias G.	32	Albion	CA	Sutherland	Mayme H.	29	Albion	CA
Goldsmith	Edwin S.	37	San Francisco	CA	McClellan	Minnie	28	San Francisco	CA
Goldson	William H., Jr	23	Oakland	MS	King	Sarah I.	17	Healdsburg	NV
Goldspring	Samuel	33	Milpitas	ENG	Loubier	Louise	23	Santa Rosa	Oak
Golsch	Henry	28	San Francisco	GER	Boechen	Anna	22	San Francisco	GER
Golub	Dave	23	Santa Rosa	RUS	Sugarman	Fannie	20	Santa Rosa	RUS
Gomes	Antonio E.	56	San Rafael	AZR	Freitas	Rosie E.	52	Petaluma	AZR
Gomes	Antonio Jos.	24	Lovelock, NV	AZR	de Freitas	Isabelle	15	Petaluma	AZR
Gomes	Joseph	23	Santa Rosa	PRT	Stafford	Alice E.	16	Santa Rosa	CA
Gonella	Ray N.	20	Santa Rosa	CA	Dinucci	Eleanor	17	Healdsburg	CA
Gonnella	John	32	Occidental	ITL	Donati	Teresa	35	Occidental	ITL
Gonnella	Leo	23	Occidental	ITL	Guidotti	Sarah	18	Monte Rio	ITL
Gonnella	Zaccheria	24	Occidental	ITL	Francischi	Rosa	16	Occidental	CA
Gonsales	Frank	24	Petaluma	CND	Jalon	Mary	22	Petaluma	Mac
Gonsalves	Frank S.	31	Petaluma	PRT	Ciancao	Mary	19	Petaluma	PRT
Gonsalves	George S.	23	Petaluma	NY	Johnson	Inez A.	18	Petaluma	CA

	Groom					Bride			
Surname	**Given Name**	**Age**	**Residence**	**BP**	**Surname**	**Given Name**	**Age**	**Residence**	**BP**
Gonsalves	Joe P.	21	Sebastopol	BER	Daveiro	Mary C.	18	Sebastopol	CA
Gonsalves	Manuel	22	Sebastopol	BER	Cardoza	Mary	20	Sebastopol	CA
Gonsolos	Antonio	26	Two Rock	PRT	Lawrence	Katie	21	Two Rock	Brook-lyn, CA
Goobi	Julius	39	Duncans Mills	ITL	Ausseresses	Marie Louisa	26	Sebastopol	FRN
Goodbrake	Christian H.	32	Guerneville	IL	Murray	Elizabeth D.	18	Guerneville	AR
Goodenough	Raymond F.	38	Lincoln, CA	IA	Weirick	Nellie G.	38	Lincoln	OH
Goodfellow	John	23	Santa Rosa	CND	Holland	Nettie B.	19	Santa Rosa	MO
Goodfellow	Lyle C.	21	Santa Rosa	CA	Meeker	Iola	20	Santa Rosa	BCL
Goodfellow	Thomas C.	23	Santa Rosa	CND	Williams	Kate D.	22	Santa Rosa	CA
Goodhart	Lewis E.	36	San Francisco	PA	Conley	Marion B.	20	Ukiah	CA
Goodman	Daniel O.	26	Santa Rosa	IA	Billing	Edith C.	22	Santa Rosa	SCT
Goodman	Frank	22	Healdsburg	CA	Seeman	Alvina	22	Healdsburg	GER
Goodman	Howard W.	23	Healdsburg	CA	Hoar	Fern	19	Healdsburg	CA
Goodman	Howard W.	28	Healdsburg	CA	Tenney	Irene J.	27	Healdsburg	CA
Goodman	James W.	22	Santa Rosa	CA	Arnold	Nellie M.	24	Santa Rosa	CA
Goodman	George R.	45	Santa Rosa	KY	Woodworth	Katie	41	Santa Rosa	ME
Goodman	Thos. F.	25	Santa Rosa Twp.	IA	Hoffman	Eva Belle	23	Santa Rosa	
Goodrich	Edwin C.	27	Geyersville	CA	Cummings	Lizzie	23	Healdsburg	CA
Goodrich	Francis M.	33	San Francisco	IL	Wilcox	Susan, Mrs.	42	San Francisco	NJ
Goodrich	Henry P.	33	Vallejo	CA	Kinloch	Mary	28	Ukiah	CA
Goodrich	Milford	24	Healdsburg	CA	Moore	Nettie	20	Healdsburg	CA
Goodsir	Thos. H.	41	Santa Rosa	ENG	Hawkins	Linda	27	Fulton	CA
Goodwin	Albert Michael	19	Petaluma	CA	Price	Lauretta Elizabeth	18	Petaluma	CA
Goodwin	Charles W.	28	Healdsburg	CND	Rogers	Lizzie L. F.	20	Healdsburg	IA
Goodwin	George M.	29	Alameda	CA	Carey	Adeline Helen	23	San Francisco	OR
Goodwin	Henry B.	51	Santa Rosa	MA	Dean	Flora Hilton	36	Santa Rosa	WI
Goodyear	Lloyd S.	26	Healdsburg	OR	Stack	Lydia D.	25	Cotati	CA
Gookins	Ernest James	26	Petaluma	IA	Matthias	Frances L., Mrs.	29	Santa Rosa	IL

Groom					Bride				
Surname	Given Name	Age	Residence	BP	Surname	Given Name	Age	Residence	BP
Gordon	Frank Hendricks	26	Santa Rosa	CA	Regan	Mary	25	Santa Rosa	CA
Gordon	Frank W.	42	Hopland	NJ	Myers	Josie M.	32	Hopland	CA
Gordon	James F.	38	Fort Bragg	MO	Rose	Susan A., Mrs.	38	Ukiah	MI
Gordon	Reece	30	Windsor	IL	Laughlin	Cynthia E.	21	Windsor	CA
Gordon	William	24	Sonoma	NY	Terry	Mary Jane	21	Sonoma	CA
Gore	Alonzo J.	25	Santa Rosa		Stemple	Lucretia M.	19	Tomales	
Goree	Ernest B.	22	Petaluma	TX	Foster	Bessie E.	21	Petaluma	CA
Gori	Adolph	28	Guerneville	ITL	Leonardi	Alphonsa	23	Guerneville	ITL
Gori	Bruno	23	San Francisco	ITL	Rabolli	Letitia	20	Cotati	CA
Gori	Michael	21	Sonoma	ITL	Basaglia	Angeline	19	Sonoma	CA
Gorman	James	37	San Francisco	IRL	English	Margaret M.	36	San Francisco	IRL
Gorman	James B.	39	San Francisco	IRL	Behler	Helena	20	Glen Ellen	CA
Gorman	Timothy J. O.	31	Agua Cailente	IRL	Corrigan	Bridget M.	23	Agua Caliente	IRL
Gorman	Syrem	48	Oakland	CA	Buckland	Jeff	46	San Francisco	CA
Gosney	Charles J.	34	San Francisco	OH	Badger	Kathryne C.	29	Graton	KS
Goss	John	35	Santa Rosa	ENG	Malone	Ellen M.	26	Santa Rosa	OR
Goss	William H., Jr.	38	Hammonton	ENG	Farrell	Marjorie J.	25	Hammonton, CA	CA
Gossage	Chas. S.	23	Duncans Mills	IA	Allen	Annie	15	Duncans Mills	CA
Gossage	H. S.	27	Petaluma	CA	Mooney	Edna	23	Petaluma	CA
Gossage	Joseph, Jr.	23	Petaluma	CA	Story	Verinda Belle	16	Santa Rosa	CA
Gossman	John	60	Philo	NV	Markham	Susan	59	Philo	PA
Gott	William	40	San Bernardino Co.		Bray	Sarah Jane	21	near Santa Rosa	
Gott	William J.	31	Windsor	CA	Fewel	Millie C.	29	Windsor	CA
Gottenberg	Hartley W.	27	Sonoma	CA	Appleton	Eliza G.	20	Sonoma	CA
Gottlieb	Sam	35	Los Angeles	AUS	Lielien (?)	Rose	24	San Francisco	AUS
Gotzsek	Albert Henry	37	Timber Cove	GER	Voutron	Bartha Barbra	29	Timber Cove	GER
Gough	Leo J.	29	San Francisco	CA	Robinson	May A.	24	San Francisco	CA

	Groom					Bride			
Surname	**Given Name**	**Age**	**Residence**	**BP**	**Surname**	**Given Name**	**Age**	**Residence**	**BP**
Goulart	Baptist Silveira	24	Sebastopol	PRT	Silva	Erminda Adeline	20	Sebastopol	CA
Gould	Emerson Weyl	28	Ukiah	MO	Shelton	Dorothy Day	25	Stony Point	CA
Gould	Emmet F.	26	Healdsburg	CA	Pettis	Annie	20	Healdsburg	CA
Gould	Frank H.	42	San Francisco	IA	Eaton	Nettie, Mrs.	29	Santa Rosa	CA
Gould	George F.	23	Santa Rosa	[illegible]	Mosman	Jessie M.	18	San Jose	[illegible]
Gould	James A.	31	Willits	WV	Mitchell	Florence L.	25	Santa Rosa	IL
Gould	Wm. J.	26	San Rafael	IL	Robinson	Edith G.	26	San Rafael	CA
Goulder	C. N.	29	Petaluma	TN	Preston	Mary Louise	24	Petaluma	CA
Gourley	John A.	25	Hartford, IN	IN	Dennison	Lucy E.	25	Santa Rosa	CA
Gow	Aleck W.	28	Petaluma	IA	Gow	Blanche M., Mrs.	28	Petaluma	OH
Gow	George Buchanan	22	Petaluma	MO	Atkinson	Irene	22	Petaluma	CA
Gowan	Francis W.	32	Ukiah	CA	Bucknell	Hazel	25	Ukiah	CA
Gowans	Andrew, Jr.	24	Santa Rosa	CA	Story	Gladys E.	20	Duncans Mills	CA
Gownig	Clement O.	42	Seattle	MA	Stinson	Fannie Barbara	26	Nacogdoches, TX	TX
Goyette	William Henry	21	San Francisco	NV	Peterson	Alma Edna	23	Petaluma	HWI
Gozzarino	John	30	Santa Rosa	ITL	Bertoli	Maria	18	Santa Rosa	ITL
Graban	John	40	San Francisco	GER	Barry	Honora	33	Boston	IRL
Gracy	Charles	27	Napa	MO	Skivington	Emma	24	Napa	CA
Grady	Harry Clarence	24	Oakland	CA	Gibson	Laura Lee	26	Oakland	CND
Grady	W. D.	31	Fresno	TN	Uristen	Annie M.	20	Fresno	CA
Graff	John	33	Berkeley	CA	Robinson	Anna Catherine	36	Berkeley	CA
Graff	Walter Harold	26	Bolinas	CA	Hall	Alma Elizabeth	24	Petaluma	CA
Graglia	John	43	Santa Rosa	ITL	Bonini (?)	Felicita	37	Santa Rosa	ITL
Graham	Albert W.	24	Guerneville	CND	Morrow	Isabel	16	Guerneville	CA
Graham	Arthur W.	21	Petaluma	Pet	Edwards	Jennie	19	Petaluma	Soc
Graham	James Hunter	36	Sebastopol	MO	Brewitt	Lucille Elviara	23	Sebastopol	CA
Graham	James W.	39	Windsor	at sea	Amos	Villa	20	Windsor	OH

	Groom					Bride			
Surname	Given Name	Age	Residence	BP	Surname	Given Name	Age	Residence	BP
Graham	Monon	29	Vacaville	CA	Mills	Ora Anna	21	Vacaville	CA
Graham	Patrick	34	Santa Rosa	SCT	du Temple	Madeleine	23	San Francisco	ENG
Graham	William	30	Sebastopol	IA	Kellog	Ella Francis	29	Santa Rosa	CA
Graham	William Emerson	23	San Francisco	IA	Cox	Evalyn Augusta	18	Ukiah	CA
Graham	Robert W.	22	Santa Rosa	CA	Freeman	Mary E., Mrs.	31	Santa Rosa	
Graheck	George A.	40	Los Angeles	KS	Penrod	Florence A.	39	Oakland	WI
Grand	Peter	33	Sebastopol	FRN	Lavege Laragoche	Mary Jane	28	Sebastopol	FRN
Grandi	William H.	22	Valley Ford	CA	Williams	Julia C.	18	Bodega	CA
Grandin	Edward	22	Berkeley	SWD	Johnson	Hulda	21	Oakland	SWD
Grandy	Henry	28	Riverside	SWT	Camesi	Diva	20	Petaluma	SWT
Granice	Harry H.	64	Sonoma	NY	Bonner	Grace I.	38	San Francisco	CA
Grant	Ben E.	21	Healdsburg	CA	Brown	Catherine	18	Healdsburg	CA
Grant	Francis E.	50	Willow Ranch	IA	McCappin	Lavina E.	46	Santa Rosa	CA
Grant	Frederick	39	Occidental	ENG	Newell	M. A., Mrs.	39	Camp Meeker	CA
Grant	Frederick T.	23	Wheatland, CA	CA	Bates	Marion	22	Healdsburg	CA
Grant	Henry M.	43	Berkeley	RI	Eliason	Agnes	25	Santa Rosa	CA
Grant	Ralph Delano	28	Healdsburg	CA	Beeson	Elva Marie	24	Healdsburg	CA
Grant	William C.	22	Santa Rosa	MA	Gawler	Pearl	20	Santa Rosa	OR
Granucci	Angelo	30	Mendocino Co.	ITL	Balducci	Rosa	26	Mendocino Co.	ITL
Granucci	Frank	24	Sonoma	ITL	Muzio	Olivia L.	20	Sonoma	CA
Graper	Elmer B.	21	Windsor	CA	Smithers	Ida V.	20	Windsor	CA
Grassman	Otto	29	Santa Rosa	GER	Dannhausen	Alvine	17	Mark West	HWI
Gratto	Frank Richard	25	San Francisco	CA	Mudd	Althea Arline	19	Oakland	NV
Graumlich	John Y.				Trisse ?	Caroline, Mrs.			
Graunlick?	John	20	Healdsburg		Walker	Elizabeth H.	19	Healdsburg	
Gravatt	Wm.	39	St. Helena	IN	Foreman	Kate	27	Healdsburg	OH
Graves	Bartlette	21	Santa Rosa	MO	Hornbuckle	Kittie	19	Santa Rosa	IA
Graves	Ben F.	44	Santa Rosa	CA	Watson	Margaret	43	Santa Rosa	CA
Graves	Edwin C.	25	Santa Rosa	CA	Ogburn	Edith L.	20	Hilton	CA

	Groom					Bride			
Surname	Given Name	Age	Residence	BP	Surname	Given Name	Age	Residence	BP
Graves	Harry Thomas	37	Ferulay, NV	CA	Maddocks	Helen Carter	27	Sebastopol	CA
Graves	J. H.	25	Hanford	CA	Maddux	Lorette	24	Santa Rosa	CA
Graves	Joseph L.	30	Suisun	CA	Dorman	Marjorie W.	23	Sonoma	CA
Graves	Zennie B.	24	Santa Rosa	CA	Jonas	Bess B.	23	Santa Rosa	CA
Gray	Alva C.	73	Fresno	OH	Cline	Anna Maria	52	Fresno	AUS
Gray	Alvin A.	22	San Luis Obispo	WA	Marsh	Adeline J.	20	Santa Rosa	CA
Gray	Alvin A.	23	Santa Rosa	WA	Marsh	Adeline J.	20	Santa Rosa	CA
Gray	Clarence A.	32	Newville, Glenn Co.	CA	Miller	Alice L., Mrs.	35	Healdsburg	CA
Gray	Elmer	23	Sacramento	MO	Thompson	May	32	Sacramento	CA
Gray	Frank S.	51	San Francisco	WI	Cooney	Stacy L.	45	San Francisco	CA
Gray	Fred L.	31	Lakeville	PA	Rose	Florence L.	25	Lakeville	CA
Gray	Henry Charles	26	Petaluma	MO	Haskins	Lillie Irene	24	Petaluma	CA
Gray	Isaac				Parmer	Clarissa			
Gray	James W.	31	Healdsburg	CA	Goode	Lillian	24	Healdsburg	ENG
Gray	James W.				Harvey	Elizabeth E.			
Gray	Joseph Allen	26	Petaluma	IRL	Weisshand	Alvina Christina	19	Petaluma	CA
Gray	Robert Floyd	23	San Pedro	CA	Palmer	Caroline Isabelle	18	Alameda	CA
Gray	Thos. H.	25	Petaluma	ENG	Torr	Ida May	18	Petaluma	CND
Gray	W. J.	25	Petaluma	IRL	Kelley	S. Z., Mrs.	35	Petaluma	CA
Gray	Woodward Martin	32	Santa Rosa	TN	Kohler	Mary Elizabeth	23	Santa Rosa	CA
Gray (?)	Luster D.	21	Santa Rosa	CA	Culu (?)	Ollie	19	[illegible]	CA
Grazini	Emelio	26	Agua Caliente	BRA	Polloni	Celia	16	Agua Caliente	ITL
Greaver	Andrew J.	23	Guerneville	CA	Minkle	Amelia L.	20	Healdsburg	TX
Greaver	Elmer	24	Healdsburg	CA	Osborn	Edith	25	Healdsburg	CA
Greaves	Walter	49	Alameda	WLS	Parkin	Marguerite I.	37	Oakland	ENG
Grebe	William C.	31	Oakland	MI	Jacobsen	Constantine	23	San Francisco	GER
Greeley	Benjamin M.	24	San Diego	MA	Pancrazi	Minnie E.	18	Glen Ellen	CA
Green	Charles	23	Santa Rosa	CA	Howeth	Daisy	18	Santa Rosa	CA

Groom					Bride				
Surname	Given Name	Age	Residence	BP	Surname	Given Name	Age	Residence	BP
Green	David J.	32	Petaluma	CA	Gregg	Bessie C.	21	Petaluma	CA
Green	Geo. E.	54	Lakeport	MA	Williams	M. J., Mrs.	36	San Francisco	MA
Green	George E.	21	Santa Rosa	TX	Wymore	Elaine C.	18	Santa Rosa	CA
Green	Harvy	32	Santa Rosa	TX	Matthews	Edna	26	Healdsburg	CA
Green	Henry H.	28	Guerneville	OH	Butterfield	Carrie	18	Guerneville	CA
Green	Ira G.	35	Santa Rosa	TX	Randall	Helen Mar	33	Santa Rosa	CA
Green	Isaac Leander	26	Santa Rosa	CA	Overton	Beatrice	23	Santa Rosa	CA
Green	John	25	Santa Rosa	CA	Brewer	Kate	18	Santa Rosa	CA
Green	John William	24	Cloverdale	CA	Willey	Laura Rosella	19	Cloverdale	CA
Green	Jonathan	24	San Francisco	CA	Symonds	Gertrude J.	23	Petaluma	CA
Green	L. D.	51	Santa Rosa	MI	Patterson	Geneva E.	51	Santa Rosa	OR
Green	Lewis E.	23	San Anselmo	OR	McNeill	Ida E.	20	Healdsburg	CA
Green	Lewis Ralston	25	Paisley, OR	CA	Covey	Mary M.	25	Healdsburg	CA
Green	Louis H.	26	Sonoma	CA	Ahern	Bella	20	Sonoma	CA
Green	Parley H.	43	Willows	IN	Knight	Mary Augusta	36	Sonoma Co.	MI
Green	Perry W.	26	Santa Rosa	CA	Howell	Myrtle L.	21	Kenwood	CA
Green	Raymond L.	22	Caisley, OR	OR	Baine	Emma	19	Healdsburg	CA
Green	Robert Franklin	29	Cloverdale	IA	Mason	May Augusta	20	Cloverdale	CA
Green	Walter Thomas	24	Healdsburg	TX	Swift	Ethelyn Irene	26	Napa	CA
Green	William A.	25	Santa Rosa	CA	Carter	Mary E.	17	Santa Rosa	OR
Green	William C.	23	Sonoma	CA	Glynn	Nellie M.	19	Sonoma	CA
Greene	William N.	24	Oakland	NY	Jewett	Olive	18	Guerneville	CA
Greenlee	John D.	23	Calistoga	CA	Grigsby	Jessie M.	21	Calistoga	CA
Greentree	Charles T.	21	Santa Rosa	CA	Shaver	Hattier L.	18	Santa Rosa	CA
Greenwood	Harry E.	29	San Francisco	OH	Lentz	May C.	21	Santa Rosa	CA
Greeott	John	30	Santa Rosa	ITL	Williams	Sarah	20	Santa Rosa	CA
Greer	Earl C.	23	St. Helena	CA	Barnes	Emily L.	27	St. Helena	CA
Gregg	Art A.	22	Schellville	CA	Jackson	Ethel	18	Schellville	MO
Gregg	Augustus I.	26	Rincon Valley	MO	Wells	Ida	24	Rincon Valley	CA
Gregg	Edward E.	24	Petaluma	CA	Atkinson	Laura M.	21	Petaluma	CA

	Groom					Bride			
Surname	Given Name	Age	Residence	BP	Surname	Given Name	Age	Residence	BP
Gregg	Edward E.	35	Petaluma	CA	Richardson	Polly	29	Petaluma	ENG
Gregg	George	37	Petaluma	MO	Jessen	Marie	34	Petaluma	CA
Gregg	George W.	46	Petaluma	MO	Rudolph	Rose M., Mrs.	31	Petaluma	CA
Gregg	Isaac				Wilkinson	Jane			
Gregg	John W.	29	Petaluma	MO	Gossage	Carrie B.	23	Petaluma	CA
Gregg	Nelson G.	24	Rincon Valley	CA	Gray	Marion	23	Rincon Valley	CA
Gregg	Pleasant Wesley	20	Sebastopol	CA	Charmley	Helen Tilston	21	Santa Rosa	IA
Gregg	Walter T.	23	Petaluma	CA	Bryan	Jessie E.	23	Petaluma	AZ
Gregganis	James Sargent	21	San Francisco	CA	Stretch	Mary Ellen	21	San Francisco	CA
Gregoire	Joseph	26	San Francisco	BLG	Winant	Pauline	22	San Francisco	BLG
Gregoire	Louis	50	Petaluma	FRN	Mathe	Marie	40	Petaluma	FRN
Gregori	Peter	34	Sebastopol	ITL	Fiori	Teresa	27	Santa Rosa	ITL
Gregory	Bion S.	24	San Francisco	IA	Mac	Mabel E.	21	Santa Rosa Twp.	UT
Gregory	Canfield Burrell	24	Point Richmond	CA	Anderson	Catherine Mildred	22	Geyserville	CA
Gregory	Edwin Stanley	30	Petaluma	CA	Hardin	Julia A.	22	Lakeville	CA
Gregory	Ernest Bernhardt	31	Healdsburg	LA	Marshall	Florence B.	24	Cloverdale	CA
Gregory	Harvey	63	Santa Rosa	NY	Kniffen	Mary M.	47	Santa Rosa	IA
Gregory	John Shattuck	31	Petaluma	CA	Martin	Rebbeca Marilla	21	Santa Rosa	OR
Gregson	Henry M.	26	Green Valley	CA	Parks	Maria C.	19	Bloomfield	CA
Gregson	John N.	30	Green Valley	CA	Hoyt	Almah E.	19	Green Valley	MN
Gregson	Luke B.	30	Trenton	CO	Surryhne	Alice Mabel	22	Trenton	CA
Gregson	Paul V.	36	Sebastopol	CA	Button	Eva A.	42	Sebastopol	IA
Greig	David	55	San Francisco	IRL	Townsend	Mary Ann	55	San Francisco	NY
Grenache	Harry L.	21	Petaluma	WA	Farnsworth	Hazel M.	19	Petaluma	CA
Greninger	George Frederick	38	Sacramento	CA	Christensen	Elizabeth F.	37	Sacramento	ENG
Greppi	Louis	26	Navarro	SWT	Zeni	Fausta	17	Fish Rock, CA	CA
Greppi	Sylvester	32	Marin Co.	SWT	Mattei	Sephina	25	Petaluma	SWT
Gresham	Joseph Francis	23	Cloverdale	CA	Adcock	Dora	18	Cloverdale	CA

	Groom					Bride			
Surname	Given Name	Age	Residence	BP	Surname	Given Name	Age	Residence	BP
Greves	Thos. N.	31	Lake Co.	MO	Sellers	M. Jane	19	Sonoma Co.	
Grewell	E. D.	40	Ellensburg, WA	IL	Marshall	Lottie B.	24	Santa Rosa	CA
Gribbin	Jack H.	23	Petaluma	CA	Roberts	Mila M.	19	Petaluma	IN
Gribbin	Thomas H.	27	Garfield, WA	CA	Byrne	Lizzie A.	27	Valley Ford	CA
Grider	Loran T.	22	Cazadero	CA	Hatton	Blanche L.	17	Cazadero	CA
Grieb	Henry Carl	18	San Francisco	CA	Spencer	Chrystal F.	20	San Francisco	CA
Griesheimer	Charles	29	Ukiah	OH	Lynch	Mary Stasia	29	Petaluma	CA
Griest	Peter	61	Healdsburg	PA	Myrick	Eliza	53	Healdsburg	CND
Griffin	Gerald A.	43	San Francisco	CA	Moore	Emily T.	43	San Francisco	NY
Griffin	H. E.	23	Santa Rosa	ME	Poat	Minnie L.	20	Santa Rosa	PA
Griffin	John M.	26	Madera	IRL	Bailey	Nellie C.	21	Sonoma	KS
Griffith	Alonzo B.	26	Windsor	IA	Wilson	Minnie	25	Windsor	CA
Griffith	Archer C.	22	Santa Rosa	CA	Farmer	Frances M.	21	Santa Rosa	CA
Griffith	Clyde E.	23	Santa Rosa	IN	Allen	Juanita	21	Santa Rosa	OH
Griffith	Thomas E.	33	Santa Rosa	MN	Ormsby	Stella	19	Santa Rosa	CA
Griffith	Will Samuel	22	Sebastopol	CO	Ross	Pearl S.	19	Sebastopol	MN
Griggs	Achilles	25	Santa Rosa		Montgomery	Sarah	23	Santa Rosa	
Griggs	Alvan Stanley	21	Healdsburg	TX	Stanley	Blanche	17	Healdsburg	CA
Griggs	Alvin S.	30	Sebastopol	TX	Elliott	Amy G.	25	Sebastopol	CA
Griggs	Arthur O.	33	Santa Rosa	CO	Willams	Alma R.	27	Santa Rosa	CA
Griggs	Justin S.	24	Healdsburg	IA	Stanley	Viola N.	16	Healdsburg	CA
Griggs	Reno	23	Healdsburg	IA	Standley	Lillie	17	Healdsburg	CA
Griggs	Smith M.	63	Alexander Valley	NY	Smith	Emily G., Mrs.	57	Healdsburg	NY
Griggs	Smith M.	59	Alexander Valley	NY	Patterson	Lou, Mrs.	48	Seattle	NY
Grimm	Frederick W.	21	San Francisco	CA	Perlet	Mildred B.	20	Oakland	CA
Grimmer	Louis	23	Geyserville	WI	Murphy	Ida May	17	Geyserville	CA
Grindle	Monroe Woodard	36	Petaluma	OH	Warner	Henrietta Mary	22	Santa Rosa	CA
Grissin (?)	W. H.	25	Santa Rosa		Carrillo	Isabel ?.	20	Santa Rosa	
Groff	William R.	23	Lincoln, Placer Co.	CA	Kendall	Emma J.	24	Petaluma	CA

	Groom					Bride			
Surname	Given Name	Age	Residence	BP	Surname	Given Name	Age	Residence	BP
Grofmyer	Henry C.	30	Stockton	IN	Heisel	Nellie	24	Santa Rosa	CA
Grogan	Spencer Jordan	42	Santa Rosa	IL	Miller	Josephine	42	Santa Rosa	CA
Groining	Hyalmar	44	San Francisco	SWD	Johnson	Augusta, Mrs.	47	San Francisco	SWD
Grokopf	Frank D.	21	Sonoma	CA	Breitenbach	Gertrude I.	22	Sonoma	CA
Groom	Joseph	27	Quicksilver, Lake Co.	ENG	Hall	Mary Juanita	18	Santa Rosa	MO
Groshong	Hal Willard	29	Beatty, Nye Co., NV	CA	Marshall	Ida May	21	Cloverdale	CA
Groshong	Sidney	20	Cloverdale	Men	Hiatt	Minnie E.	21	Yorkville	Yorkville
Groshong	Walter E.	21	Santa Rosa	CA	Swank	Susie	19	Santa Rosa	CA
Grosjean	Camille, Jr.	19	Santa Rosa	Sfo	Stevens	Stella M.	18	Santa Rosa	CA
Groskoff	Albert, Jr.	32	Sonoma	CA	Batto	Louise R.	20	Sonoma	CA
Groskofs	Joseph F.	28	Vineburg	CA	Clements	Lena A.	18	El Verano	CA
Groskopf	Albert	30	Glen Ellen	Alsace	Miller	Bertha	23	Glen Ellen	GER
Groskopf	Albert	29	Glen Ellen	GER	Gartman	Annie	19	Napa Co.	SWT
Groskopf	Charles E.	31	Sonoma	CA	Keechler	Lena K.	22	Schellville	CA
Gross	Eugene A.	43	Sebastopol	IL	Corbin	Ida	29	Petaluma	CA
Gross	Harry B.	30	Oakland	MD	McMellon	Mary S.	20	San Francisco	MO
Gross	Ludwig	28	Petaluma	GER	Zimmerman	Frances H.	22	Petaluma	CA
Grosse	Guy E.	49	Santa Rosa	SWT	Gibbs	Lizzie W.	33	Santa Rosa	OH
Grosse	Guy N.	23	Santa Rosa	CA	Yarnell	Eloise I.	19	Santa Rosa	TX
Grossi	Domengo	26	Olema	SWT	Buzzini	Teresa	22	Olema	SWT
Grossman	Abraham L.	36	Bakersfield	IL	Kern	Josephine	33	Wichita	MO
Groth	Leopold Frederick	38	Briceland	CA	Gibson	Kate	36	Ukiah	CA
Groulx	Albert	28	Petaluma	CND	Moyer	Eva	19	Oakville	WY
Grove	Arvil T.	36	Windsor	IL	Wentworth	Ida H.	20	Windsor	CA
Grove	Bert B.	20	Fulton	CA	Dalessi	Sophie May	17	Fulton	CA
Grove	Clarence	25	Santa Rosa	CA	Locke	Beryle Evelyn	23	Santa Rosa	CA
Grove	David	67	Windsor	VA	Davis	Elmira	47	Windsor	OH

	Groom					Bride			
Surname	Given Name	Age	Residence	BP	Surname	Given Name	Age	Residence	BP
Grove	Edward	34	Healdsburg	ENG	Sinclair	Ann Jane	22	Healdsburg	IRL
Grove	Elliot W.	26	Santa Rosa	CA	Wilson	E. Marguereitte	21	Santa Rosa	CA
Grove	George W.	25	Windsor	CA	Clark	Emma E.	23	Forestville	Soc
Grove	Jesse Roy	22	Windsor	CA	Isaac	Dora	18	Willits	CA
Grove	John	35	Healdsburg	ENG	Sinclair	Mary Adelaide	22	Healdsburg	IRL
Grove	Ray S.	21	Fulton	CA	Robinson	Jessie	20	Santa Rosa	CA
Grover	William A.	26	Ukiah	CA	Wilke	Emma L.	21	Everett, WA	GER
Groves	Christopher Columbus	21	near Windsor		Hopper	Nancy A.	17	Windsor	
Groves	James H.	23	Healdsburg	MO	Wells	May	20	Santa Rosa	OH
Grubb	Harry Thompson	34	Sebastopol	CA	Ramos	Myrtle Teresa	34	Sebastopol	Chile, SAM
Grubb	Merle M.	27	Healdsburg	IL	DeNye (?)	Freda	20	Healdsburg	CA
Grube	Axcel E.	20	Cotati	CA	Douglass	Ila T.	18	Oakland	CA
Gruenhagen	Gottfried H.	28	Santa Rosa	SD	Hall	Clara	23	Santa Rosa	CA
Gruenhager	Henry	22	Santa Rosa	SD	Borchers	Clara	19	Santa Rosa	MN
Gschwend	Thomas	27	Christine, Mendocino Co.	CA	Pallady	Nellie G.	18	Windsor	KS
Guadagno	Pompey	32	San Francisco	ITL	Foley	Josephine	28	San Francisco	IRL
Guaspari	Domenico	31	Healdsburg	ITL	Gamborini	Amelia	20	Santa Rosa	CA
Guder	William C. O.	20	Petaluma	MN	Lingg	Louisa H.	18	Petaluma	CA
Guedet	Joseph Henry	26	San Francisco	CA	Dabner	Mary Josephine	24	Petaluma	CA
Guenther	C. F.	23	Santa Rosa	MN	Mosure	Emma R.	22	Santa Rosa	NY
Guerne	A. L.	38	Guerneville		Smith	Julia	23	Guerneville	
Guerne	Alfred Lucian	26	Guerneville	CA	Coon	Josephine	23	Guerneville	CA
Guernsey	Fred R.	30	Petaluma	CA	McAbee	Hazel N.	19	Petaluma	CND
Guernsey	Louis E.	21	Petaluma	CA	Millerick	Mae E.	18	Petaluma	CA
Guffanti	Amedeo	31	Sonoma	ITL	Sturla	Angela	18	Sonoma	ITL
Guffanti	Domenico	26	Kenwood	ITL	Tollini	Celestina	19	San Francisco	ITL
Guffanti	Emilio	31	Boyes Springs	ITL	Bianchini	Giulia	20	Sonoma	ITL

	Groom					Bride			
Surname	**Given Name**	**Age**	**Residence**	**BP**	**Surname**	**Given Name**	**Age**	**Residence**	**BP**
Gugg	Roy I.	28	Sebastopol	CO	Caldwell	Lissie S.	28	Santa Rosa	OR
Guglielmetti	Alfred J.	44	Petaluma	CA	Gilardi	Katherine M.	24	Petaluma	CA
Guglielmetti	Cesare	34	Bloomfield	SWT	Lafranchi	Olimpia	16	Santa Rosa Twp.	Prescott, AZ
Guglielmetti	Noe	22	Santa Rosa	ITL	Pierucci	Clara	18	Santa Rosa	CA
Guglielmetti	Marino J.	19	Santa Rosa	CA	Jefferies	Sylverine	18	Santa Rosa	CA
Guiberson	Wallace	22	Petaluma	CA	Goodwin	Agnes L.	21	Petaluma	CA
Guidi	Angelo	26	San Francisco	ITL	Davini	Concetta	20	Healdsburg	ITL
Guidi	Ismaele	42	Healdsburg	ITL	Morchio	Argentina	36	Healdsburg	ITL
Guidotti	Francesco	30	Santa Rosa	ITL	Frugoli	Theresa	33	Santa Rosa	ITL
Guidotti	George	23	Petaluma	CA	Santos	Gussie	18	Petaluma	CA
Guidotti	Giovanni	26	Cloverdale	ITL	McReynolds	Lizzie	23	Santa Rosa	CA
Guidotti	Giuseppe	27	Santa Rosa	ITL	Peduzzi	Pierina	30	Santa Rosa	ITL
Guidotti	Joseph	22	Monte Rio	ITL	Rocchioli	Angeline	16	Forestville	ITL
Guidotti	Leonardo	31	Napa	SWT	Paganini	Carmalita	18	Sebastopol	SWT
Guild	George	31	Oakland	SCT	Smillie	Isabell R.	27	Santa Rosa	SCT
Guilfoyle	John	41	Shellville	AUT	Watt	Agnes	21	Shellville	
Guilhot	Bernard	29	Sebastopol	FRN	Francisco	Amelia A.	21	Sebastopol	CA
Guill	Etna E.	30	Oakland	KY	Voight	Hannah E.	24	Sonoma	CA
Guillie	Edward H.	21	Healdsburg	CA	Heitz	Ida M.	20	Healdsburg	CA
Guinnar	David Andrew	24	Kelseyville	CA	McMahon	Maggie	23	Visalia	
Guinnar	Jesse W.	27	Calistoga	CA	Simmons	May	17	Franz Valley	CA
Guirin	Stephen I.	22	San Francisco	CA	Voigt	Margaret M.	19	San Francisco	CA
Guisler	Edward T.	44	Geyserville	CA	Cook	Fidella	45	Geyserville	OH
Guisti	Paulo	35	San Francisco	ITL	Campomenosi	Victoria, Mrs.	28	San Francisco	CA
Gularte	George S.	19	Petaluma	CA	Rich	Ira	20	Vallejo	MO
Guldager	Fred H.	32	San Francisco	WI	Jackson	Bertie Estelle	25	San Francisco	CA
Guldager	George M.	28	San Rafael	CA	Nourse	Susie L.	18	Chicago	IA
Guldager	L. C.	30	Tomales	Mac	Carroll	Agnes J.	24	Bloomfield	Soc
Guldin	Fred R.	27	Petaluma	SWT	James	Ella	27	Petaluma	CA

	Groom					Bride			
Surname	Given Name	Age	Residence	BP	Surname	Given Name	Age	Residence	BP
Gully	Frank J.	21	Santa Rosa	CA	Cook	Elsie M.	18	Healdsburg	MI
Gum	William M.	33	Healdsburg	CA	Hiatt	Josie, Mrs.	21	Healdsburg	CA
Gunn	Charles A.	28	Oakland	IL	Murphy	Myrtle Violet	26	San Francisco	CA
Gunn	George Lucius	26	Healdsburg	CA	Newland	Maude L.	18	Healdsburg	CA
Gunn	Robert	29	Santa Rosa	CND	Kyle	Beatrice J.	23	Santa Rosa	CND
Gunther	Frederick A.	42	Santa Rosa	GER	Mauch	Katy, Mrs.	19	Santa Rosa	RUS
Gunther	John Douglas	29	Sebastopol	MI	Robinett	Mary	23	Sebastopol	CA
Guntz	Joseph A.	32	San Francisco	CA	Storey	Grace Dudley	23	San Francisco	CA
Guptill	Roscoe Volney	30	Lakeport	ME	Bean	Helen A.	31	Guerneville	CA
Guptill	William H.	28	Santa Rosa	CA	Lyman	Kate	27	Bloomfield	CA
Guptill	William H.	42	Santa Rosa	CA	Gray	Cecil D.	38	Sebastopol	MO
Gussman	Cass	30	Guerneville	CA	Nippert	Nancy Frances	38	Guerneville	MO
Gussman	Santo	35 ?	Guerneville		Jaques (?)	Belinda	16	Guerneville	
Gustafson	Alfred	31	Graton	SWD	Howell	Julia E.	28	Graton	Chi
Gustafson	Carl G.	23	Santa Rosa	SWD	Wells	Olive	18	Santa Rosa	
Gustafson	Gustof Sigfrid	29	San Francisco	SWD	Hawkins	Mildred Claretta	23	Oakland	CA
Gustafson	Howard Paul	20	Santa Rosa	CA	Faylor	Florence M.	17	Santa Rosa	CA
Gusti	Albert	22	Fulton	ITL	King	Effie	24	Petaluma	CA
Gutenberger	Jacob	20	Oakland	GER	Winton	Fannie	18	Santa Rosa	MO
Gutermute	David	51	Petaluma	PA	Smart	Cora M.	41	Petaluma	MN
Gutermute	Henry Shauer	26	Petaluma	PA	Derby	Linda Burr	21	near Petaluma	CA
Guth	Gustave John	44	Mountain View	CA	Walton	Louise Evelyn	19	Sebastopol	CA
Gutheil	C. R.	34	Petaluma		Cummings	A. G.	25	Petaluma	
Guthrie	Thomas George	27	San Francisco	SCT	Hansen	Henryetta	21	Occidental	CA
Guthrie	Vernon Hamilton	22	Petaluma	NE	Byce	Hazel Irene	19	Petaluma	CA
Gutscher	Joseph	43	Santa Rosa	CND	Stewart	Mary A.	29	Occidental	CA
Guy-Perret	Andrew	35	El Verano	FRN	Martin	Marie	31	El Verano	FRN
Gwaltney	W. B.	21	Santa Rosa	MO	Westwood	Inez V.	21	Santa Rosa	CA
Gwin	Andrew J.	46	Healdsburg	CA	Bartow	Helen	42	Healdsburg	CA
Gwin	Andrew J.	29	Windsor	CA	Blake	Maggie	19	Windsor	CA

	Groom					Bride			
Surname	**Given Name**	**Age**	**Residence**	**BP**	**Surname**	**Given Name**	**Age**	**Residence**	**BP**
Gwin	Andrew Jones	30	near Healdsburg	CA	Blake	Maggie M.	19	near Healdsburg	CA
Gwin	Walter Edward	22	Santa Rosa	CA	Rock	Anna Marie	17	Glen Ellen	MN
Gwyn	George P.	24	San Francisco	IN	Martin	Ella A.	18	Geyserville	CA
Gwynn	Wm. A.	27	Santa Rosa	CA	Smith	Mary E.	19	Healdsburg	NE
Gwynn	Edward	53	Santa Rosa Twp.	CND	McMannus	Eunice E.	43	Oakland	MI
Haag	Michael Peter	31	Petaluma	NY	Anderson	Meta Catherine	23	Petaluma	GER
Haas	Henry				Standley	Barbara E.			
Haas	Joseph G.	37	Streater, IL	NY	Riding	Hannah	30	Chicago	IL
Habenicht	John F.	26	San Francisco	CA	Oster	Ellen L.	21	San Francisco	CA
Haberfelde	Albert Valentine	21	Bakersfield	CA	Thompson	Elma Pearl	20	Bakersfield	OR
Haberhouer	Karl	29	Bellevue	AUS	Colassor	Albertinn	20	Petaluma	GER
Haberman	Charles Henry	25	Healdsburg	CA	Scott	Helen Beatrice	19	Ukiah	CA
Hackmann	William	22	San Francisco	CA	Burkhardt	Evelyn	20	San Francisco	CA
Hadermann	Carl	19	Petaluma	CA	Hinrichsen	Annie J.	18	Petaluma	CA
Hadler	Henry	35	Petaluma	GER	Rygel	Francisca	36	Petaluma	GER
Hadley	William	45	San Francisco	PA	Flynn	Ella Marie	32	San Francisco	Ontario
Hadrich	C. F. Hugo, Jr.	23	Santa Rosa	CA	Doggett	Averil Alison	18	Santa Rosa	CA
Hadrich	Carl F. H.	25	Santa Rosa	GER	Haltiner	Babette	23	Santa Rosa	GER
Haehl	Carl	28	Cloverdale	CA	Sedgley	Mary M.	21	Cloverdale	CA
Haehl	Edward Oliver	22	Cloverdale	CA	Adams	Jennie	22	Cloverdale	CA
Haehl	Otto	29	Cloverdale	CA	Hanson	Christine	27	Cloverdale	CA
Haehl	Walter L.	20	Cloverdale	CA	Thompson	Martha P.	18	Cloverdale	CA
Haering (?)	Fred	47	Santa Rosa		Feeley	Helen, Mrs.	31	Santa Rosa	
Hagans	Alfred H.				Hall	Mary			
Hagedohm	Herman B.	27	Petaluma	CA	Staats	Ida	20	Petaluma	CA
Hagedohm	William	24	Petaluma	CA	Harms	Emma	18	Petaluma	CA
Hageman	Emil H.	33	San Mateo Co.	WI	Oxtoby	Alice Josephine	32	San Mateo Co.	MI
Hagemann	Gustav Henry	35	San Francisco	CA (?)	Cutter	Mabel Viola	25	San Francisco	CA

	Groom					Bride			
Surname	Given Name	Age	Residence	BP	Surname	Given Name	Age	Residence	BP
Haggard	Nathaniel	42	Healdsburg	OR	Pritchett	Dollie	22	Geyserville	CA
Hagler	John	22	Healdsburg	CA	Carmichael	Nannie	18	Healdsburg	CA
Hagler	John M.	22	San Francisco	CA	Brining	Margaret M.	21	Oakland	KS
Haigh	Edwin	28	Healdsburg	CA	Fried	Enmma	21	Healdsburg	CA
Haigh	Robert Charles	29	Healdsburg	CA	Lynch	Ella Louise	27	Healdsburg	CA
Haigler	Albert Chester	25	San Francisco	KS	Sweetser	Violet Marda	25	Santa Rosa	CA
Hakansson	Axel V.	34	Napa	SWD	Grace	Edith Emily	17	Napa	ENG
Hakes	Dorr	53	Valley Ford	NY	Rutherford	Lyle	44	Petaluma	CND
Hale	Eugene C.	21	San Francisco	CA	Herterich	Katherine C.	18	San Francisco	NY
Hale	Leslie Ravone	23	Santa Rosa	CA	Nagel	Edna Viola	19	Santa Rosa	CA
Hale	Peter	43	Ukiah	CA	Hardin	Margaret	42	Napa	CA
Hale	W. D.	23	Geyserville		Kelso	Ada E.	19	Yorkville	MO
Hale	John F.	21	Geyserville	CA	Bosworth	Mary Etta	22	Geyserville	CA
Haley	Charles F.	21	Sebastopol	MN	Billman	Susie A.	28	Sebastopol	CA
Haley	James A.	29	Sebastopol	IA	Karn	Mabel Idelle	24	Sebastopol	IL
Haley	James Lewis	27	Glen Ellen	CA	Monahan	May Elizabeth	22	Glen Ellen	CA
Haley	Michael E.	40	San Francisco	CA	Muller	Bettina	18	Healdsburg	CA
Haley	Robert	27	Green Valley	IA	Greyson	Lida	20	Green Valley	CA
Haley	William R.	24	Healdsburg	CA	Grohe (?)	Helen S.	22	Santa Rosa	MO
Halkidis	Sam	26	Eureka	GRC	Mahan	Genevieve	19	Eureka	CA
Hall	Adolphus Warren	36	Healdsburg	CA	McCutchan	Minnie May	19	Healdsburg	CA
Hall	Albert E.	26	Petaluma	IL	Starke	Anna Frances	34	Petaluma	WA
Hall	Albert Leroy	25	Sebastopol	MT	Blunden	Violet	23	Sebastopol	ENG
Hall	Arthur Lipskey	28	Petaluma	CA	James	Florence Katherine	27	Petaluma	CA
Hall	Charles A.	25	Petaluma	CA	Hall	Lena H.	23	Petaluma	CA
Hall	Charles S.	32	Two Rock	CA	Byrne	Lena C.	28	Two Rock	CA
Hall	Clarence C.	28	Healdsburg	CA	Mead	Alice C.	22	Santa Rosa	CA
Hall	Eugene F.	21	Santa Rosa	MO	Toltschin	Clara	18	Santa Rosa	CA
Hall	Eugene F.	26	Santa Rosa	MO	Burns	Ethel G.	17	Santa Rosa	OR

	Groom					Bride			
Surname	Given Name	Age	Residence	BP	Surname	Given Name	Age	Residence	BP
Hall	Francis	28	Redwood Twp.	CND	Jakway	Margaretta	15	Redwood Twp.	CA
Hall	Frank J.	30	San Francisco	CA	Dunker	Hattie A.	30	San Francisco	CA
Hall	Geo. A.	28	Petaluma	ME	Morton	Dicie M.	22	Petaluma	CA
Hall	Geo. H.	31	Santa Rosa		Gauldin	Laura	18	Santa Rosa	
Hall	George	29	Santa Rosa	PA	Washburn	O. E., Mrs.	30	Santa Rosa	CA
Hall	George A.	26	Cloverdale	ENG	Wass	Jessie E. R., Mrs.	25	Cloverdale	ENG
Hall	George H.	43	Santa Rosa	KY	Speers	Josie	32	Healdsburg	CA
Hall	George Henry	40	Cloverdale	CA	Pepin	Jeanette Corine	28	Cloverdale	KS
Hall	George Herbert	21	Santa Rosa	CA	Mauch (?)	Matilda Dorothy	20	Santa Rosa	KS
Hall	George Morrill	26	Healdsburg	MA	Mayes	Ethelyn Lorena	24	Healdsburg	CA
Hall	Granville M.	19	Healdsburg	CA	Francis	Nettie	18	Healdsburg	CA
Hall	H. F.	25	Windsor	GA	Shuler	Georgiana	16	Windsor	IA
Hall	Halbert P.	36	Santa Rosa	MN	Stridde	Thyra	32	Santa Rosa	SWD
Hall	Harley A.	21	Santa Rosa	IA	Feehan	Gladys Lorene	18	Santa Rosa	CA
Hall	Harry H.	34	Sebastopol	MT	Rego	Mayme A.	26	Sebastopol	CA
Hall	Harry L.	23	Santa Rosa	CA	Willson	Annie W.	21	Sebastopol	CA
Hall	Harry Willson	24	Sebastopol	CA	Kenworthy	Elvira Charity	19	Santa Rosa	CA
Hall	Henry	32	Bloomfield	CA	Perry	Isabel	24	Bloomfield	PRT
Hall	Isaac K.				Bryant	Ruth			
Hall	James				Dameron ?	L. E.			
Hall	James F.	58	San Francisco	CA	Lehritter	Annie Louise	40	Oakland	CA
Hall	James Otto	24	Windsor	CA	Cooper	Mary L.	21	Windsor	CA
Hall	John W.	37	Pt. Arena	NY	White	M. Cadona	28	Santa Rosa	CA
Hall	Lieuallen J., Jr.	28	Healdsburg	CA	Gum	Hazel Nellie	23	Healdsburg	CA
Hall	Louis Williard	25	Healdsburg	OR	Early	Cleora A.	17	Healdsburg	CA
Hall	Luke	22	Healdsburg		Miller	Sarah A.	17	Healdsburg	
Hall	Martin V.				Champlain	Sarah D.			
Hall	Oliver Perry	24	Bloomfield	CA	Linebaugh	Olivia Fay	19	Bloomfield	CA

	Groom					Bride			
Surname	Given Name	Age	Residence	BP	Surname	Given Name	Age	Residence	BP
Hall	Theodore T.	29	Sussex, MT	MO	Smith	Aileen F.	20	Bodega	CA
Hall	Thos. R.	41	Red Bluff	KY	Dodson	Mary	40	Red Bluff	AR
Hall	Walter R.	28	Santa Rosa	MO	Allenbury	Evelyn	23	Santa Rosa	CA
Hall	Walter S.	25	Healdsburg	CA	Smith	Alice	19	Healdsburg	CA
Hall	Walter W.	24	Seattle	MN	Nelson	Alice M.	21	Kansas City, MO	UT
Hall	William Clyde	46	San Francisco	CA	Vestal	Lena	36	Santa Rosa	CA
Hall	Wm. S.	29	Bloomfield	CA	Guldager	Annie C.	25	Tomales	CA
Hallberg	John	34	Sebastopol	SWD	Pearson	Louisa	34	San Jose	SWD
Hallberg	Oscar A.	24	Sebastopol	CA	Barlow	Mary Elizabeth	26	Sebastopol	CA
Hallenbarter	Frank A.	23	Petaluma	CA	Huber	Resina A.	19	Petaluma	CA
Halleran	Joseph Francies	29	Santa Rosa	NJ	Burgess	Sarah Ethel	24	Santa Rosa	CA
Halley	James L.	26	San Francisco	CA	Kroehuke	Clara E.	26	San Francisco	NE
Halliday	William J.	50	San Francisco	IRL	Begbie	Jeanne	45	San Francisco	SCT
Hallinan	J. F.	38	IA	OH	Shea	Kate	25	IA	IA
Halman	William C.	28	Ukiah	IL	Stone	Stella	21	Ukiah	CA
Halsey	Henry G., Jr.	22	Oakland	CA	Randle	Etta M.	20	Oakland	MO
Halstead	Harry Oliver	26	Mare Island	IN	Heryford	Jessie Marguerite	23	Vallejo	CA
Halstead	Jesse S.	29	San Francisco	IL	Purcell	Eunice A.	24	San Francisco	CA
Haltiner	John W.	31	Santa Rosa	SWT	Hadrich	Melani	19	Santa Rosa	GER
Halvarsen	Herbert T.	24	San Francisco	CA	Bourgon	Amelia	19	San Francisco	CA
Ham	James T.	60	Verona, MO	TN	Ham	Julia	55	Santa Rosa	OH
Ham	Whitcomb H.	24	Santa Rosa	CA	Lewis	Nellie M.	19	Santa Rosa	IA
Hamer	Sylvester T.	42	Petaluma	IN	Suman	Belle, Mrs.	41	Seattle	CA
Hamersley	Garvin	23	Geyserville	OR	Gilmore	Grace	17	Geyserville	CA
Hamersley	Jay	28	Santa Rosa	OR	Robinett	Ollie	22	Santa Rosa	OR
Hamilton	Aymer Jay	39	Berkeley	PA	Frisbee	Sarah Howland	28	Glen Ellen	CA
Hamilton	Charley S.	26	Sebastopol	CA	McGrew	Rosella	23	Sebastopol	CA
Hamilton	Durley LeRoy	26	Anacortes, WA	WA	Burgess	Ethna Mae	21	Cloverdale	CA

	Groom					Bride			
Surname	Given Name	Age	Residence	BP	Surname	Given Name	Age	Residence	BP
Hamilton	Gilbert S.	49	Santa Rosa	PA	Cole	Sylvia G.	33	Santa Rosa	MI
Hamilton	Henry Liberty	23	Bodie, Mono Co.	CA	Hubbell	Maysie	25	Petaluma	CA
Hamilton	James W.	36	Petaluma	IL	Cnopius	Gertrude M.	30	Santa Rosa	HLD
Hamilton	John A.	40	Healdsburg	SCT	Grove (?)	Mary F.	19	Healdsburg	WA
Hamilton	Lovell Joyce	21	Point Arena	CA	Hunter	Helen	19	Point Arena	CA
Hamilton	Rush Emmor	24	Healdsburg	CA	Williams	Ethel Maude	22	Healdsburg	CA
Hamilton	William A.	22	San Francisco	Sfo	Sutton	Etta A.	23	Bloomfield	UT
Hamilton	William H.	30	San Francisco	CA	McDonald	Mabel	21+	Santa Rosa	CA
Hamlin	Charles J.	31	Petaluma	SWD	McKenna	Maggie	25	Bloomfield	IRL
Hamlin	George O.	28	San Francisco	WI	Grissim	Lizzie, Mrs.	31	Santa Rosa	CA
Hamlin	Harry	32	Preston	IL	Coddington	G. W., Mrs.	41	Preston	KY
Hamlin	Martin Edward	33	Tomales	CA	Hamilton	Georgia Helen	30	Sebastopol	CA
Hammeken	George L.	27	Healdsburg	IN	Roberts	Lola, Mrs.	36	Healdsburg	CA
Hammel	Chas. P.	31	San Francisco	IRL	Livey	Mary	20	Healdsburg	MO
Hammel	Henry				Gist	Lurana			
Hammel	Walter	21	Petaluma	Soc	Quotis	Jeanette S.	18	Petaluma	CA
Hammell	Charles E.	22	Petaluma Twp.	CA	Doss	Bell	18	Petaluma Twp.	CA
Hammell	Fred R.	24	Petaluma (near)	CA	Benjamin	Penelope F.	21	Petaluma	CA
Hammer	Marquis	29	San Francisco	PLD	Kubie	Katie	24	Petaluma	CA
Hammermann	George B. G.	26	Petaluma	GER	Meyling	Freda M. E.	25	Petaluma	GER
Hammon	Charles Howland	29	San Francisco	IL	Scott	Esther Margaret	23	Santa Rosa	NE
Hammon	William Henry	25	Petaluma	NY	Brown	Malinda	23	Petaluma	CO
Hammond	Frank	21	Petaluma		Cooper	Catherine	16	Petaluma	
Hammond	Grant	30	San Francisco	CA	Duval	Laura M.	23	Petaluma	CA
Hampton	Robert M.	42	Carrara, NV	PA	Kennedy	Annie M.	38	Oakland	CA
Hampton	William	36	St. Helena	TN	Maebury	Eva Kenworthy	27	Healdsburg	CA
Hamson	Chris	40	Healdsburg	NRY	Carr	Daisy Ethel	28	Healdsburg	MA
Hanchette	Edward	35	Oakland	CA	Haas	Louise Dorothey	34	San Francisco	CA
Hancock	Henry				Haraszthay	Ida			

Groom					Bride				
Surname	Given Name	Age	Residence	BP	Surname	Given Name	Age	Residence	BP
Hancorn	Walter T.	40	Guerneville	MI	Lindsy	Coney Gunda	37	Guerneville	CA
Hand	Wm. E.				Brown	Emma			
Handy	Percy W.	29	Covelo	CA	Rea	Alice J.	24	Covelo	CA
Haney	Free	22	Petaluma	IL	Hellman	Linda	22	Stony Point	MN
Hankins	Samuel S.	40	Healdsburg	IA	Morgan	Mattie	26	Healdsburg	TN
Hanks	Geo Lewis	23	Dixon	CA	Brooks	Lucy	22	Windsor	CA
Hanks	J. D.	56	Santa Rosa	IL	Staudard	Ceripta A.	38	Santa Rosa	MO
Hanks	William W.	26	Santa Cruz	CA	Briggs	Belle	22	Sebastopol	CA
Hanks	William Wallace	39	Sebastopol	CA	Sherman	Mary Anna	40	Sebastopol	CA
Hanley	Frank	46	Santa Rosa	NY	Siever	Alice	46	Santa Rosa	KY
Hanley	Harry	46	Oakland	NY	Hewitt	Marry E.	36	San Francisco	CA
Hanlon	Frank	22	San Francisco	CA	O'Mally	Mary	20	San Francisco	IRL
Hanlon	Newton B.	28	Sacramento	CA	Bosworth	Cora May	18	Geyserville	CA
Hanna	Daniel N.	24	San Francisco	CA	Aspenwall	Georgiana F.	23	Vallejo	CA
Hanna	J. G.	57	Petaluma	MO	Frazier	Mary T.	25	Petaluma	KS
Hannah	David Albert	34	San Francisco	CND	Edwards	Josephine Letitia	26	Chico	WLS
Hannah	Percy J.	26	San Francisco	CND	Dexter	Ella B.	20	San Francisco	CA
Hannan	Daniel	24	Petaluma	CA	Cereghino	Mary	33	Petaluma	MA
Hannan (?)	Patrick	29	Petaluma	IRL	Sweeny	Ellen A.	25	Petaluma	CA
Hanner	Elmer R.	34	Point Arena	IA	Kirkland	Daisy Helen	16	Point Arena	CA
Hannon	Joseph F.	32	San Francisco	MA	Edrington	Rhea R.	23	Glen Ellen	IL
Hanold (?)	Nathaniel Gould	31	Berkeley	CA	Canepa	Mabel	28	Berkeley	CA
Hansbrow	George Rutlege	45	San Francisco	CA	Gavin	Margaret Helen	22	Oakland	CA
Hansen	Adolph N.	21	Cupertino	CA	Smith	Isabel I.	20	Cupertino	CA
Hansen	Albert	29	Berkeley	CA	Boning	Marie H.	21	San Francisco	CA
Hansen	Andras	30	Penngrove	GER	Wedemeyer	Dorothy E.	32	Penngrove	CA
Hansen	Andrew	30	Penngrove	GER	Feddersen	Inka	20	Petaluma	IL
Hansen	Antone M.	26	Petaluma	DNK	Bostrom	Anna C.	22	Petaluma	SWD
Hansen	August	24	Mark West	GER	Jepsen	Christina	22	Santa Rosa	GER

	Groom					Bride			
Surname	**Given Name**	**Age**	**Residence**	**BP**	**Surname**	**Given Name**	**Age**	**Residence**	**BP**
Hansen	Axel O.	28	Sacramento	CA	Simpson	Luella B.	24	Santa Rosa	ID
Hansen	Carl	41	San Francisco	DNK	Powers	Catherine	40	Petaluma	IRL
Hansen	Carl Christian	32	Stony Point	DNK	Iverson	Elsie	24	Petaluma	DNK
Hansen	Carl Emil	44	Korbel Mills, Sonoma Co.	DNK	Armstrong	Lusettie	35	Forestville	CA
Hansen	Chris P. F.	23	Cotati	GER	Brucher	Hazel G.	16	Santa Rosa	CA
Hansen	Christian	24	Napa	CA	Saunders	Elsie	24	Sebastopol	MN
Hansen	Christian C.	29	Kellogg	DNK	Brokins	Sarah Jane	18	Kellogg	CA
Hansen	E. J.	24	Santa Rosa	GER	Purcell	Gertrude	22	Santa Rosa	CA
Hansen	Edward	45	Petaluma		Brown	Mary J., Mrs.	27	Petaluma	
Hansen	Einer C.	24	Geyserville	DNK	Henderlong	Martha V.	26	Geyserville	CA
Hansen	Elmer	21	Stockton	IA	Thomsen	Elsie Loraine	18	Lathrop	CA
Hansen	Elmer	24	Oakland	IL	Fromell	Anita Mabel	20	Oakland	CA
Hansen	Frederick E.	26	Occidental	CA	Taylor	Georgie A.	20	Occidental	CA
Hansen	George G.	23	Oakland	DNK	Speer	May E.	23	Berkeley	CA
Hansen	Hans	27	Petaluma	DNK	Winding	Sina	20	Petaluma	DNK
Hansen	Henry	50	Vineburg	DNK	Malchow	Bertha	49	Vineburg	IL
Hansen	Herbert M.	23	Vallejo	CA	Gray	Goldie Irene	20	Santa Rosa	MO
Hansen	James G.	27	Petaluma	CA	Solari	Isola L.	28	Petaluma	CA
Hansen	John G. E.	61	Santa Rosa	NRY	Adams	Annie Mary	47	Santa Rosa	MN
Hansen	Louis	21	Santa Rosa	NRY	Cutts	Olive	21	Santa Rosa	IA
Hansen	Maurice	31	Guerneville	DNK	Witherspoon	Cornelia E.	23	Guerneville	AR
Hansen	Niels	34	San Antonio Twp., Marin Co.	DNK	Jorgensen	Magdalena	23	Bloomfield	DNK
Hansen	Orin F.				Blake	Ella			
Hansen	P. B.	43	Petaluma	DNK	Enevold	Maria	23	San Francisco	DNK
Hansen	Paul B.	48	Petaluma	DNK	Wilson	Florence I., Mrs.	30	Petaluma	IL
Hansen	Peter	34	San Francisco	GER	Peters	Elene	23	Petaluma	CA

	Groom					Bride			
Surname	Given Name	Age	Residence	BP	Surname	Given Name	Age	Residence	BP
Hansen	Peter	34	San Francisco	CA	Mugge	Louise Feltz	34	San Francisco	GER
Hansen	Peter E.	24	Fruitvale	WI	Pease	Abba	24	Fruitvale	MA
Hansen	Rufus				Loveland	M. J.			
Hansen	Walter	40	San Francisco	DNK	Andersen	Annie	28	San Francisco	DNK
Hansen	William	22	Santa Rosa	Soc	Payne	Florence E.	18	Santa Rosa	CA
Hansen	William Adolf	28	Sebastopol	DNK	Larson	Dora	38	Sebastopol	SWD
Hansen	William C.	27	San Francisco	CA	Kas	Rhoda F.	26	San Francisco	CA
Hanshop	Guy Edwin	25	Santa Rosa	CA	Davis	Edna Angie	19	Santa Rosa	CA
Hanson	Hans	34	Cazadero	DNK	Holgersen	Hedvig	44	Cazadero	DNK
Hanson	Hans P.	31	Healdsburg	DNK	Moore	Grace Mabel	27	Healdsburg	CA
Hanson	John	41	Guerneville	SWD	Hitchcock	Mary Elisabeth	43	Guerneville	AR
Hanson	John G.	31	Kenwood	WI	Pedersen	Annie	24	Kenwood	NRY
Hanson	Peter	33	Santa Rosa	NRY	Lacque	Sarah A.	32	Santa Rosa	CA
Hanson	William J.	28	Lytton	ID	Haberman	Christine	20	Lytton	CA
Hanssen	Louis O.	28	Berkeley	SWD	Peterson	Ethel	21	Berkeley	CA
Hansten	Herman	33	Santa Rosa	FIN	Banks	Lenora	17	Santa Rosa	CA
Happersburger	Frank, Jr.	26	San Anselmo	CA	Dawson	Maude E.	22	San Anselmo	CA
Happy	Abraham	26	Guerneville	CA	Tiers	Ethel Maggie	18	Santa Rosa	MO
Haran	James	40	Fulton	IRL	Mullen	Ellen	25	Santa Rosa	IRL
Haraszthy	Mariano J.	24	Sonoma	CA	Simmons	Carrie J.	20	Sonoma	CA
Harbin	Thomas B.	29	Middletown		Crabtree	Ella	18	Middletown	
Harbine	James L.	31	Forestville	IA	Clark	Alice F.	28	Forestville	CA
Harbine	N. W.	30	Largo, Mendocino Co.	CA	Pitkin	Nettie J.	27	Forestville	IA
Harde	Grant O.	39	Oakland	NY	Leviston	Elizabeth M.	32	Oakland	MO
Harder	Oscar C.	27	San Francisco	CA	Brown	Gladys B.	19	San Francisco	CA
Hardin	Andrew Evan	27	Sebastopol	CA	Eardley	Eliza Fitchford	26	Anaconda, MT	ENG
Hardin	Clarence E.	24	Petaluma	CA	Stegemann	Katherine R.	21	Petaluma	CA
Hardin	Harold Jefferson	23	Petaluma	CA	Friis	Elene Christine	22	Petaluma	CA
Hardin	Henry	29	Santa Rosa	CA	Livingston	Minnie H.	24	Santa Rosa	CA

	Groom					Bride			
Surname	**Given Name**	**Age**	**Residence**	**BP**	**Surname**	**Given Name**	**Age**	**Residence**	**BP**
Hardin	J. Rolla	20	Petaluma	CA	Tonini	Nellie C.	19	Petaluma	CA
Hardin	James Taylor	24	Petaluma	Pet	Bryan	Marie E.	19	Petaluma	Benson, AZ
Hardin	John M.	24	Petaluma	CA	Rhodehaver	Lulu	18	Petaluma	CA
Hardin	Lester B.	21	Petaluma	CA	McMinn	Mary M.	19	Santa Rosa	CA
Hardin	Lexter B.	58	Petaluma	CA	Lindsay	Edna P.	32	Petaluma	CA
Hardin	Robert	22	Petaluma	CA	Showalter	Victoria	19	Sebastopol	MO
Hardin	William Graves	22	Petaluma	CA	Stout	Clara Edna	19	Petaluma	MI
Hardin	Wm. H.				Hopper	Nancy J.			
Harding	Edward F.	35	San Francisco	KS	Smith	Nettie	32	Santa Rosa	PA
Harding	Reinhardt T.	59	San Francisco	CA	Holmes	Eunice C.	54	San Francisco	NJ
Harding	William A.	35	Petaluma	ENG	Bone (?)	Ellen	42	Petaluma	ENG
Hardisty	James A.	26	Santa Rosa	MT	Staley	Edna M.	23	Santa Rosa	OR
Hardy	Orlando B.	65	San Francisco	NY	MacIntosh	Sara	48	San Francisco	NY
Hare	Stephen	26	St. Helena	NZD	Hoar	Mary L.	24	Sonoma Co.	Soc
Harford	Lyman	45	Sebastopol	KS	Ross	Genevieve	18	Forestville	CA
Hargens	Charles	27	Santa Rosa	GER	Bollinger	Maggie	20	Santa Rosa	RUS
Hargreaves	Thomas W.	38	Oakland	NY	Lyttaker	Emma M.	26	Santa Rosa	CA
Hargreaves	Thurlow E.	25	Santa Rosa	CA	Richardson	Gladys Mae	19	Santa Rosa	CA
Harhoe	Christian	38		DNK	Meyer	Rosa	20		CA
Harkness	Raymond L.	28	San Francisco	CA	Bond	May Emily	26	San Francisco	KY
Harkrader	Albert L.	48	Healdsburg	CA	Gober	Elizabeth	48	Geyserville	MO
Harlan	Carolus	26	Geyserville	MO	Ellis	Laura C.	25	Geyserville	CA
Harlan	Charles E.	42	Willow Glenn, Colusa Co.	OH	Vaughan	Bertha J.	23	Geyserville	MI
Harlan	James W.	24	Geyserville	MO	Ellis	Olive I.	23	Geyserville	CA
Harlan	Joel M.	31	Santa Rosa	CA	Currier	Kate, Mrs.	32	Santa Rosa	LA
Harlan	William Christian	36	Healdsburg	CA	Layneance	Charity L.	25	Healdsburg	CA
Harlan	William Christian	40	Santa Rosa	CA	Cardinet	Elva	29	Santa Rosa	CA
Harman	Roy	25	Petaluma	CA	Philbrick	Jean M.	18	Petaluma	CA

	Groom					Bride			
Surname	Given Name	Age	Residence	BP	Surname	Given Name	Age	Residence	BP
Harman	William A.	26	Fort Bragg	KS	Anderson	Gussie	abt. 27	San Francisco	SWD
Harmon	Charles Reuben	23	Freestone	CA	McMullen	Margaret	23	Freestone	CA
Harmon	Frank A.	22	Healdsburg		Kimble	Mary M.	21	Sebastopol	AR
Harmon	James E.	20	Healdsburg	AR	Satterlee	Edith G.	18	Healdsburg	NY
Harmon	Oliver Lewis	26	Healdsburg	IA	Fewell	Kate Florence	23	Windsor	CA
Harmon	Owen	23	Cloverdale	CA	Briggs	Lizzie	20	Santa Rosa	OH
Harmon	Peter A.	32	San Jose	CA	Pray	Harriet May	19	Petaluma	OK
Harmon	Robert A.	24	Sebastopol	AR	Kimble	Delia	17	Sebastopol	CA
Harmon	Robert A.	28	Santa Rosa	AR	Allen	Mary C.	20	Trenton	CA
Harmon	Russell J.	29	Sebastopol	CA	Wedge	Mamie C.	28	Sebastopol	CA
Harms	Alvin	44	San Francisco	GER	Petersen	Elena	19	San Francisco	CA
Harms	Leland	22	Petaluma	CA	Gonsalves	Emerentia I.	17	Petaluma	CA
Harow	Tom	42	Mercury	CA	Phinney	Josephine	47	Rincon Valley	CA
Harper	Charles H.	23	Alameda	ENG	Winter	Annie M.	25	Cloverdale	ENG
Harper	John	58	Sonoma	IRL	Watt	Margaret M.	42	Sonoma	SCT
Harrigan	G. W.	23	San Francisco	CA	Treadwell	Sarah E.	19	San Francisco	ENG
Harrigan	James Daniel	27	Woodside	CA	Jenkins	Clara Louise	25	Woodside	CA
Harrington	Ambrus	24	Davisville, Yolo Co.	CA	Kise (?)	Etta	25	Santa Rosa	CA
Harrington	Charles Winfield	35	Santa Rosa	IL	Givlin	Margret Ella May	15	Santa Rosa	CA
Harrington	Daniel	24	Knights Valley	CA	Lowery	Jennie	22	Knights Valley	OH
Harrington	James	26	Piela, Mendocino Co.	CA	Stevens	Nettie	25	Healdsburg	CA
Harris	Arthur L.	26	Santa Rosa	MA	Pickett	Helen S.	23	CA	CA
Harris	Arthur M.	31	Lodi	CA	Storey	Bertha A.	31	Healdsburg	CA
Harris	Bert A.	21	Santa Rosa	CA	Berry	Lelia	18	Santa Rosa	CA
Harris	Charles C.				Lauz	Lydia (of colour)			
Harris	Claude	23	Santa Rosa	ND	Alexander	Selma	16	Santa Rosa	CA

	Groom					Bride			
Surname	**Given Name**	**Age**	**Residence**	**BP**	**Surname**	**Given Name**	**Age**	**Residence**	**BP**
Harris	Earl L.	29	San Francisco	NE	Worms	Alice D.	22	San Francisco	CA
Harris	Edward E.	25	Sonoma	IN	Young	Maude E.	24	Sonoma	IL
Harris	Eli	25	Calistoga		Waddell	Isadore Belle	18+	Calistoga	
Harris	Ephraim D.	22	Hermitage, Mendocino Co.	CA	Crommett	Sarah A.	18	Analy Twp.	ME
Harris	George F.	22	Vallejo		Caito (?)	Belle	21	Santa Rosa	
Harris	George W.	25	Petaluma	CA	Daniels	Minnie M.	22	Petaluma	VA
Harris	Granville	26	Sonoma	CA	Spencer	Nonie	21	Sonoma	CA
Harris	Harry J.	43	Santa Rosa	MI	Rich	Nettie May	43	Bronson, MI	MI
Harris	Henry R.	39	St. Helena	CA	Sievers	Augusta M.	42	St. Helena	OR
Harris	James W.	24	Petaluma	KS	Pharris	Ilma	20	Petaluma	CA
Harris	James William	20	Santa Rosa	CA	George	Zella	18	Santa Rosa	OR
Harris	Jesse Winfred	32	Berkeley	ND	Branstetter	Daisy Dean	26	Santa Rosa	KY
Harris	John W.	53	Petaluma	ME	Brown	Catherine A., Mrs.	40	Petaluma	AUT
Harris	Leon F.	21	Santa Rosa	CA	Trent	Maude S.	20	Fresno	MO
Harris	Paul C.	23	Santa Rosa	IL	Crose	Nellie	22	Santa Rosa	CA
Harris	Ralph W.	21	Oakland	CA	Crawford	Nadine E.	18	Oakland	CA
Harris	Richard A.	28	Santa Rosa	CA	Utt	Mary E.	25	Santa Rosa	MO
Harris	Richard Alexander	21	Santa Rosa		Collier	Louisa Jane	18 +	Santa Rosa	
Harris	Robert E.	25	Napa	CA	Kiser	Agnes C.	20	Sonoma	CA
Harris	William E.	41	Healdsburg	IL	Carpenter	Leah	39	Cloverdale	CA
Harrison	Francis Richard	31	San Francisco	CA	Bartholomew	Yula D.	18	Occidental	HWI
Harrison	Frank M.	23	Green Valley	MN	Sullivan	Amanda J.	18	Green Valley	CA
Harrison	Fred Kingsley	25	Sebastopol	CA	Fletcher	Ruth Ann	23	Sebastopol	CA
Harrison	G. A.	21	Healdsburg	KS	Howard	Lucinda	19	Healdsburg	CA
Harrison	Robert H.	26	Santa Rosa Twp.	CA	Williams	Sarah I.	17	Santa Rosa	CA
Harrison	Wm. H.				Shaw	Hannah M.			
Harrod	W. W.	37	Hopland	MS	Buckman	Mary Jane	22	Hopland	MO

	Groom					Bride			
Surname	**Given Name**	**Age**	**Residence**	**BP**	**Surname**	**Given Name**	**Age**	**Residence**	**BP**
Hart	Albert Paxton	29	Santa Rosa	CA	Jackson	Flora Helen	23	Santa Rosa	CA
Hart	Albert R.	26	Windsor	AR	Irvin	Esther	17	Windsor	AR
Hart	Benjamin F.	21	Healdsburg	IA	Hixson	Charlotte J.	20	Healdsburg	CA
Hart	Benjamin F.	24	Healdsburg	IA	Moyer	Sybil	18	Healdsburg	CA
Hart	Charles E.	25	San Francisco	KY	DeLude	Martine O.	20	Los Angeles	CA
Hart	Chenowith B.	69	Santa Rosa	VA	Flinn	Anna	65	Santa Rosa	OH
Hart	David B.	55	Santa Rosa	VA	Mizer	Sarah P.	55	Santa Rosa	TN
Hart	Ellis O.	23	Petaluma	CA	Durbin	Susie Loraine	20	Glen Ellen	CA
Hart	Frank	42	Detroit	MI	Cline	Jessie	43	Detroit	MI
Hart	Harold D.	28	San Francisco	CA	Day	Lyda Edith	24	Petaluma	MN
Hart	Hubbard	48	Lyons, Bixet Co., NE	NY	Shackelford	Susan	32	Santa Rosa	WI
Hart	Jack E.	25	Santa Rosa	CA	McReynolds	Ruth F.	19	Santa Rosa	CA
Hart	Jesse B.	38	Red Bluff	IA	Moodey	Rose C.	34	Santa Rosa	IL
Hart	John E.	39	Windsor	NY	Carlson	Hilda M.	27	Windsor	AUT
Hart	John T.	59	Sebastopol	MO	Carey	Hettie E.	49	Sebastopol	MO
Hart	Leo Blair	23	Petaluma	Sfo	Bowles	Veda A.	22	Petaluma	CA
Hart	Robert M.	36	Santa Rosa	CND	Smith	Mary E.	30	Santa Rosa	RI
Hart	Victor E.	21+	Santa Rosa	CA	Pepper	Lydia E.	21	Santa Rosa	MI
Hartin	Richard	27	San Francisco	IRL	Aiken	Inez Mabel	22	San Francisco	CA
Hartley	William H.	29	San Francisco	ENG	Roberts	Tillie	21	Santa Rosa	CA
Hartsock	Freedom E.	32	Healdsburg	CA	Stone	Grace E.	20	Healdsburg	CA
Hartwell	George H.	25	Oakland	CA	Pendleton	Edna F.	25	Oakland	CA
Hartzel	Joseph	51	Healdsburg	OH	Hahn	Mary	42	Healdsburg	WI
Harvey	Ira B.	32	Bloomfield	CA	Spottswood	Annie	32	Petaluma	CA
Harvey	James H.	27	Healdsburg	NY	Fountain	Minnie	29	Santa Rosa	OR
Harvey	John F.	36	Martinez	KS	Simas	Helen	40	Martinez	CA
Harvey	Lowell N.	32	San Francisco	ME	Cooper	Sadie A.	32	Santa Rosa	OR
Harvey	Marion Wilson	33	Montrose, CO	MO	Woods	Ethel Blosom	22	Healdsburg	CA
Harvie	Harold B.	31	Sacramento	CA	Haines	Helen H.	25	Santa Rosa	CA

	Groom					Bride			
Surname	Given Name	Age	Residence	BP	Surname	Given Name	Age	Residence	BP
Harwell	George O.	24	Clovis, Fresno Co.	AR	Booker	Caroline	24	Santa Rosa	CA
Harwood	John F.	40	Cloverdale	AR	Beaulieu	Marie H.	38	San Jose	CA
Haselswerdt	Harry E.	22	Santa Rosa	CA	Frey	Annie M.	22	Kenwood	CA
Haselton	C. O.	22	Santa Paula	VT	Ward	Mina B.	22	Petaluma	CA
Hasenberg	William F.	27	Portland, OR	CA	Switzer	Ivy W.	23	near Sonoma	CA
Haskell	Greenlief A.	24	Santa Rosa	CA	Davies	Harriett C.	23	Santa Rosa	CA
Haskell	Herbert Raymond	22	Oakland	TN	Lang	Myrtle Ethel	22	Suisun	CA
Haskett	Max H.	26	Willets	CA	Winson	Isabelle M.	26	Oakland	ENG
Haskins	Elmond Sterling	28	Petaluma	CA	Mego	Jennie Angelia	25	Petaluma	CA
Haskins	W. R.	34	Petaluma	OH	Noble	Frankie L.	29	Petaluma	CA
Haskins	William Joseph	28	Stockton	CA	Halley	Ellen Cecelia	25	Stockton	NE
Hasper	Henry	27	Petaluma	GER	Bundesen	Marie	16	Petaluma	CA
Hassett	Adlai V.	21	Healdsburg	CA	LeBaron	Sarah	19	Healdsburg	AZ
Hassett	James T.	21	Healdsburg	Hld	Laughlin	Ella	18	Healdsburg	Hld
Hassett	Jay Vernon	21	Healdsburg	CA	Ireland	Grace Elizabeth	28	Healdsburg	CA
Hassett	Ora T.	28	Healdsburg	CA	Sears	Mary E.	28	Healdsburg	MO
Hassett	William Henry	39	Santa Rosa		Butler	Annie S.	34	Santa Rosa	
Hasting	Fletcher D.	68	Santa Rosa	TN	McClellan	S. F., Mrs.	68	Santa Rosa	IL
Hasting	Joe C.	23	Santa Rosa	CA	Gann	Martha A.	23	Santa Rosa	CA
Hastings	A. R.				Corrall	Caroline			
Hastings	Fletcher D.	70	Santa Rosa	TN	Cook	Emily	53	Healdsburg	ENG
Hastings	Nelse	37	Guerneville	CA	Smith	Nellie, Mrs.	34	Guerneville	CA
Hastings	William Walton	27	Vallejo	NE	Letold	Alice Mary	24	Santa Rosa	CA
Hasty	Charles H.	30	San Francisco	CA	Warren	Addie J.	30	San Francisco	CA
Hatch	Frank R.	27	Healdsburg	CA	Bagley	Amy L.	21	Guerneville	CA
Hathaway	Albert	22	Santa Rosa	IA	Kiser	Edith E.	19	Santa Rosa	CA
Hatler	John P.	57	Healdsburg	MO	Deering	Martha J.	51	Healdsburg	OR
Hatler	Joseph E.	25	Santa Rosa	CA	Bones	Hila	17	Santa Rosa	IA

	Groom					Bride			
Surname	Given Name	Age	Residence	BP	Surname	Given Name	Age	Residence	BP
Hatton	Charles B. D.	30	Healdsburg	MO	Gober	Elizabeth C.	18	Alexander Valley	TN
Hatton	J. E.	31	Sea View	CA	Boothby	C. M., Mrs.	29	Sea View	CA
Hatton	William Henry	28	Bloomfield	CA	Byrne	Mary Agnes	26	Bloomfield	IRL
Haub	Chester C.	25	Healdsburg	CA	Flewelling	Bessie H.	25	Healdsburg	CA
Haub	Theodore G.	48	San Jose	CA	Egan	Lena K.	45	San Jose	CA
Haubrich	Benjamin F.	22	Healdsburg	CA	Keyes	Mattie	18	Healdsburg	CA
Haubrich	Leonard	50	Petaluma	PRS	Ward	Sarah, Mrs.	45	Petaluma	IL
Hauck	Harry E.	31	San Francisco	CO	Prien	Florentine A.	22	Petaluma	CA
Haukel ?	Herman, Jr.	26	Santa Rosa	WI	Gailor	E. B., Mrs.	28	Santa Rosa	NY
Haupt	Charles W.	22	Stewart's Point	CA	Patten	Julia A.	18	Stewarts Point	CA
Haupt	Frank L.	40	San Francisco	CA	Clancy	Anna Estelle	30	San Francisco	CA
Haupt	Louis C.	27	Stewart's Point	CA	Parker	Bessie M.	25	Marshall	CA
Haus	Fred C. H.	24	San Francisco	Sfo	Mastrup	M. Sophie	20	Petaluma	Pet
Hausmann	John	43	Occidental	WI	Harrison	Emma	30	Occidental	CA
Havard	Laurence S. H.	26	San Francisco	ENG	Capucetti	Rose	22	San Francisco	CA
Haven	Acton	32	San Francisco	CA	Noble	Maude	32	San Francisco	KS
Havens	Charles I., Jr.	25	Kenwood	CA	Coutts	Mabel	24	Kenwood	CND
Havenstrite	Reed C.	25	Petaluma	OK	Marshall	Grace A.	20	Sebastopol	CA
Haverlo	Jesse	55	Lakeville		Drake	Ella	34	Lakeville	
Haw	Michael J.	30	San Francisco	IL	Naughton	Julia M.	20	San Francisco	PA
Hawes	William Henry	27	Sebastopol	CA	Holinsteat	Clara Ella	19	Middletown	CA
Hawes	William R.	21	Windsor	KS	Meek	Tina O.	22	Windsor	WY
Hawkes	William	45	Fulton	NY	Granger	Edith	33	Fulton	IL
Hawkins	Christian H.	23	Oakland	IL	Bacon	Mildred E.	21	Eureka	CA
Hawkins	J. R.	28	Hollister	CA	Harden	Anna B.	19	Santa Rosa	IN
Hawkins	Louis J.	23	Santa Rosa		Mize	Maria	23	Santa Rosa	
Hawkins	Louis J.	23	Santa Rosa Twp.		Mize	Maria	23	Santa Rosa Twp.	

	Groom					Bride			
Surname	Given Name	Age	Residence	BP	Surname	Given Name	Age	Residence	BP
Hawkins	W. H.	51	Santa Rosa	CND	Burrison	Alice	46	Bellingham, WA	OH
Hawley	George L.	25	Madera	IA	Phillips	Ina	22	Forestville	NE
Hawley	William Alexander	29	San Francisco	VT	Johnson	Mary Hattie	20	San Francisco	OH
Haws	Alpheus Peter	81	Berkeley	CND	Haws	Hannah Eleanor	65	Oakland	IA
Hawthorn	Loyet/Loyel A.	23	Glennbrad, Ormsby Co., NV		Upson	Lucy	20	Healdsburg	
Hayden	John S.	41	Geyserville	CA	Jones	Estella Pearl	15	Geyserville	TX
Hayden	Richard	22	Duncans Mills	CA	Foresti	Dora	18	Duncans Mills	CA
Hayden	S. R.	35	Fisherman's Bay	TX	Haupt	Mary	16	Fisherman's Bay	CA
Hayes	Bert J.	21+	Healdsburg	CA	Jones	Edna M.	18+	Healdsburg	CA
Hayes	Charles Ronan	31	San Francisco	CA	Waller	Eva Myrtle	35	San Francisco	CA
Hayes	Frank	45	Petaluma	IL	Mann	Ora	31	Petaluma	KS
Hayes	Jacob				McPhearson	Malinda			
Hayes	James E.	21	Sebastopol	CA	Scudder	Elizabeth	16	Sebastopol	CA
Hayes	John	31	Santa Rosa	IRL	Grace	Anastasia	25	Santa Rosa	NY
Hayes	John Henri	19	Alameda	CA	Ford	Dorothy Louise	18	Santa Rosa	CA
Hayes	Leroy L.	30	Madison	CA	Grigsby	Lillian L.	21	Madison	CA
Hayes	Stanley W.	41	Geneva, Ontario Co., NY	OH	Burbank	Edna H.	24	Geneva, NY	NY
Hayne	Harry Henry	30	Oakland	PA	Stegman	Helene A. H.	36	Oakland	GER
Hayner	Ralph Waldo	19	Petaluma	NE	Landrus	Edith Lily	17	Petaluma	IL
Haynie	Wm. M.	24	Santa Rosa	CA	Adams	Anna M.	19	Santa Rosa	CA
Hays	Edwin B., Rev.	32	Modesto	Il	Gingery	Mandilla	27	near Fulton	IA
Hays	Ira C.	21	San Francisco	TN	Partridge	Grace E.	18	San Francisco	MO
Hays	James W.	20	Healdsburg		Brown	Martha J.	20	Healdsburg	
Hays	Marmion	23	Santa Rosa	IN	Leeth	Myrtle	23	Healdsburg	CA
Hays	Walter Daniel	31	Middletown	CA	Johnson	Julietta, Mrs.	27	Middletown	CA

	Groom				Bride				
Surname	Given Name	Age	Residence	BP	Surname	Given Name	Age	Residence	BP
Hayt	William A.	21+	Riverside	NY	Bower	Emma Katherine	21+	Petaluma	CA
Hayward	Harry M.	25	Cloverdale	NH	Carpenter	Sallie P.	24	Cloverdale	WV
Hayward	J. B.	68	Analy Twp.	NY	Meeks	D. C., Mrs.	40	Petaluma	OH
Hayworth	Ruben F.	28	Ukiah		Miller	Nancy C.	18+	Healdsburg	
Hazlett	Emmett M.	25	San Francisco	IA	DeMartini	Cecilia T.	24	San Francisco	CA
Hazlett	Herman C.	23	Petaluma	NE	Wilen	Lillian C.	20	Petaluma	CA
Head	Albert P.	29	Santa Rosa	MS	Bethel	Dora	27	Santa Rosa	OR
Head	Clarence Elmore	22	Bodega	CA	Bruce	May Lena	20	Occidental	NE
Head	Robert Calvin	21	Bodega	CA	Marsh	Lulu May	21	Santa Rosa	CA
Head	Walter W.	26	Santa Rosa	CA	Van Aukin	Laura	29	Santa Rosa	WI
Heafey	John J.	29	Oakland	IRL	McDorley	Mary U.	30	San Francisco	CA
Heald	J. G.				Elliot	Rachael, Mrs.			
Heald	William T.	26	Cloverdale	CA	Smith	Aurelia Maud	19	Healdsburg	KS
Heald	William Thomas	43	Healdsburg	Soc	Brighouse	Henrietta C.	48	Healdsburg	Soc
Healey	Dennis J.	25	Donahue, CA	IRL	Needham	Maggie	20	Petaluma	MN
Healey	Earl F.	25	Petaluma	CA	Mendonca	Mary Frances	24	Petaluma	CA
Healey	Joseph M.	26	Petaluma	CA	Long	Agnes E.	22	Petaluma	CA
Healey	Robert D.	28	San Francisco	CA	Spencer	Katie R.	16	Santa Rosa	CA
Healey	Thomas James	24	Santa Rosa	CA	Wallburg	Edna Elizabeth	ill.	Santa Rosa	CA
Healey	Thomas Matthew	30	Sacramento	CA	Conniffe	Delia Teresa	25	Sacramento	IRL
Healey	William E.	28	Santa Rosa	CA	Dempsey	Katherine C.	25	Santa Rosa	ENG
Healy	Edwin R.	25	Oakland	IA	Gossage	Addie	21	Petaluma	CA
Healy	Frank	25	Tyrone Mills, Sonoma Co.		Jewell	Annie	21	Petaluma	
Hearfield	Harold H.	25	San Rafael	CA	Menihan	Gertrude	21	Cloverdale	CA
Hearns	Charles H.	36	Santa Rosa	MI	Pellini	Perry, Mrs.	40	Santa Rosa	CA
Hearsey	Mason E.	34	San Francisco	MI	Decker	Josie C.	22	Healdsburg	CA
Heason	George W.	23	Guerneville	ENG	Patterson	Hester A.	17	Santa Rosa	IL
Heatley	Lloyd Eldridge	20	Santa Rosa	CND	Scott	Anna Catherine	18	Santa Rosa	WA

	Groom					Bride			
Surname	**Given Name**	**Age**	**Residence**	**BP**	**Surname**	**Given Name**	**Age**	**Residence**	**BP**
Heatly	George O.	23	Santa Rosa	CA	Martin	Mary E.	20	Santa Rosa	IL
Heaton	Charles C.	38	Healdsburg	CA	Bryant	Bertha	29	Geyserville	CA
Heaton	Robert Bruce	26	Dry Creek	CA	Lambert	Gussie	21	Dry Creek Valley	CA
Heaton	William H.	34	Blaine, WA	SD	Heaton	Olive C.	30	Raymond, WA	CO
Heatzelman	John				Hakemier	Elizabeth			
Hebbron	Elton Benson	22	Salinas	CA	Ulrey	Wava	21	Santa Rosa	IA
Hebrard	Henry Hepolet	31	San Francisco	CA	Westwood	Mary Ellen	21	Santa Rosa	CA
Hebrard	William J.	28	San Rafael	CA	Gambini	Mary Alice	21	Sebastopol	CA
Hecgman	Gustaf	42	Santa Rosa	PRS	Reidling	Bertha	32	Santa Rosa	GER
Heck	Joseph H.	63	Guerneville	GER	Schultz	Bertha	49	Guerneville	GER
Heckendorf	August J.	24	Santa Rosa	IA	Lindenmeyer	Jeanette O.	19	Santa Rosa	CA
Heckley	Thomas B.	31	Santa Rosa	ENG	Beebe	Olive D.	23	Guerneville	CA
Hedden	Donald	25	Caspar	CA	Ledford	Vesta V.	19	Stewarts Point	CA
Hedel	Henry	34	Petaluma	GER	Albrecht	Hulda	23	Petaluma	GER
Hedges	Benjamin F.	48	San Francisco	PA	Schug	Rose E.	30	San Francisco	IA
Hedges	Edward D.	23	Petaluma	CA	Fritsch	Nelly	19	Petaluma	Pet
Hedges	S. H.	28	Santa Rosa	NY	Rohrer	Nellie	21	Santa Rosa	CA
Hedin	Sven Thomas	21	Penngrove	DNK	Jacobsen	Hedvig	23	Petaluma	DNK
Hedrick	Clyde Warren	27	Turlock	OH	Mumma	Lela Maude	21	Healdsburg	CA
Hedrick	David M.	62	Santa Rosa Twp.	IN	Cook	Mary E.	38	Santa Rosa Twp.	CA
Heesche	Henry G. K.	29	San Francisco	GER	Fricke	Caroline	21	San Francisco	GER
Heezen	G. J.	28	Kuckatine ?, IA	HLD	Gotschalk	Theresa	26	Petaluma	IA
Heffelfinger	William	42	Santa Rosa	PA	Baum	Arvilley K.	29	near Santa Rosa	CA
Hefferman	William H.	42	Sacramento	CA	Barrett	Mary	38	Sacramento	CA
Heffner	Edward L.	30	Healdsburg	NY	Hoffman	Marie J.	21	Healdsburg	MO
Heffron	Fred H.	23	Sebastopol	CA	Wilson	Nancy E.	21	Sebastopol	CA
Heffron	George	26	Guerneville	CA	Cole	Annie	18	Guerneville	NE

Groom					Bride				
Surname	Given Name	Age	Residence	BP	Surname	Given Name	Age	Residence	BP
Heggie	Norman J.	28	Agua Caliente	SCT	Aguillon	Gabrielle F.	27	Sonoma	Son
Hegler	Gerhard H.	22	Santa Rosa		Skillman	Eva	19	Santa Rosa	
Heid	Conrad G.	45	Bakersfield	IL	Barrows	Mary J.	38	Bakersfield	NY
Heil	Roy P.	26	Petaluma	OR	Mahoney	Mary Agnes	19	Petaluma	CA
Heimorth	Charles R.	26	Healdsburg	IN	Payne	Hannah J.	21	Healdsburg	IA
Heimroth	William Henry	26	Sonoma Co.	IN	Laymance	Sarah Augusta	19	Sonoma Co.	CA
Heine	Louis William	23	San Francisco	CA	Webb	Fanny	28	San Francisco	KS
Heinicke	Carl	68	Healdsburg	GER	Scherren	Mathilde	51	Healdsburg	GER
Heinkel	Herman Frank	22	San Francisco	CA	Toomey	Agnes V. D.	19	San Francisco	ENG
Heinrich	Frank A.	25	Santa Cruz	AUT	Looney	Laura	18	Fulton	CA
Heinshaw	Benjamin P.	35	Petaluma	CA	Rabe	Edith	25	Petaluma	CA
Heintz	August Henry	43	Agua Caliente	GER	Eggers	Hermine	43	San Francisco	CA
Heintz	John H.	23	Occidental	SD	Bollard	Marguerite M.	21	Healdsburg	CA
Heintz	Victor F.	33	San Jose	MO	McGonagill	Eunice R.	25	Seattle	OR
Heitstuman	Henry	26	Union Town, WA	IL	Kempf	Jennie E.	21	Healdsburg	KS
Heitter	Henry	28	Santa Rosa	RUS	Bade	Augusta	23	Santa Rosa	WI
Heitz	Frank	25	Healdsburg	WA	Nielson	Dorothy E.	24	Healdsburg	CA
Heitz	Frederick Charles	21	Healdsburg	CA	Long	Hazel Gertrude	21	Geyserville	CA
Heitz	Howard L.	21	Healdsburg	CA	Warren	Edith G.	21	Healdsburg	CA
Heitz	James Louis	20	Alexander Valley	WA	Hughes	Lila Dell	18	Healdsburg	CA
Heitz	John Louis	28	Healdsburg	CA	Rodgers	Myrtle	20	Healdsburg	CA
Heitz	Joseph	28	Santa Rosa		Harris	Sarah	19	Santa Rosa	
Heitz	W. F.	23	Healdsburg	WA	Nielson	Grace M.	22	Healdsburg	CA
Heitzel	David	57	Guerneville	GER	Lund	Ovina Sicretta	35	San Francisco	CA
Helberg	William	30	Shellville	GER	Krahmann	Amelia	23	Shellville	GER
Helberg	William	45	Shellville	GER	Werner	Meta	47	Sonoma	GER
Helberg	William E.	24	Shellville	CA	Thomas	Myrtle	23	Sonoma	CA
Held	H. R.	36	St. Louis	MO	Coover	Anita B.	36	San Francisco	CA
Helfer	George A.	37	Alameda (?)	NY City	Hodges	Jessie M.	38	Alameda	NY
Helin	Charles Edward	30	San Francisco	CA	Pallady	Ruth Miller	23	Duncans Mills	CA

	Groom					Bride			
Surname	**Given Name**	**Age**	**Residence**	**BP**	**Surname**	**Given Name**	**Age**	**Residence**	**BP**
Heller	William S.	65	Santa Rosa	PA	Greening	Nancy Jennie	54	Ukiah	IL
Hellinge	William J.	39	Sacramento	CA	Ray	Mary Gertrude	36	Sacramento	CA
Hellrich	Paul H.	28	Belvedere	CA	Murray	Alice	20	San Francisco	CND
Hellrick	Edward Joseph	36	San Francisco	NY	Henry	La Veda Lucille	19	San Francisco	CA
Helman	Edwin Daniel	29	Healdsburg	IL	Silverthorn	Maude Frances	18	Healdsburg	IA
Helman	L. W.	25	Healdsburg	IL	Proctor	Clara L.	18	Healdsburg	CA
Helman	Louis W., Jr.	21	Sebastopol	CA	Yeager	Carolyn E.	23	Sebastopol	AZ
Helmke	F.				Shine	A. E.			
Helton	William A.	29	Petaluma	MO	Millington	Bessie M.	20	Petaluma	CA
Hembree	Albert Lafayette	21	Forestville		Copeland	Josephine	19	Forestville	
Hembree	Atlas T.	25	Windsor	CA	McClelland	Clara	23	Windsor	CA
Hembree	Leon	27	Windsor	CA	Murray	Fodie L.	17	Windsor	CA
Hemenover	Dudley A.	25	Santa Rosa	CA	Bussman	Harriett I.	20	Windsor	CA
Hemenover	Dudley A.	20	Santa Rosa	CA	Rivers	Adah E.	17	Santa Rosa	IL
Hemenway	Daniel D.	56	Petaluma	NY	Ward	Alice I.	26	Petaluma	CA
Hemler	George E., Sr.	59	Petaluma	IL	Herrick	Annie M.	57	Petaluma	OH
Hemma	Harry A.	23	Vacaville	PA	Johnson	Edna M.	23	Santa Rosa	CA
Hemmarberg	Edward	30	Seattle	SWD	Becklund	Olge	26	Seattle	SWD
Hemphill	John H.	27	Oakland	TX	Morley	M. J., Mrs.	23	San Francisco	NY
Hemphill	William	28	Oakland	IRL	Gordon	Lizzie Jane	20	Valley Ford	CA
Hemple	George	37	Monte Rio	GER	Crites	Nan	28	Berkeley	KS
Hemsath	Jack Henry	22	Cloverdale	CA	Stoughton	Elizabeth Carlon	19	Petaluma	CA
Henderson	Fred S.	23	Healdsburg	OR	Winkler	Martha, Mrs.	22	Healdsburg	CA
Henderson	George P.	30	Santa Rosa	CA	Heim (?)	Florence Elizabeth	24		WI
Henderson	H. Seymore	23	Santa Rosa	CA	Pomeroy	Ollie A.	18	Santa Rosa	ME
Henderson	Hardin W.	26	Santa Rosa		Mize	Mary	46	Santa Rosa	
Henderson	Harry H.	20	Oakland	OH	Chaffee	Mary S.	17	Petaluma	IA
Henderson	James T.	47	Chico	MO	Small	Emma S.	32	Berkeley	CND

	Groom					Bride			
Surname	**Given Name**	**Age**	**Residence**	**BP**	**Surname**	**Given Name**	**Age**	**Residence**	**BP**
Henderson	Vernon E.	30	Marshfield, OR	NE	Smith	Ora	18	Geyserville	CA
Hendley	Chas. Bacon	25	Santa Rosa	CA	Arnold	Katie A.	20	Santa Rosa	CA
Hendley	Harry L.	24	Santa Rosa	CA	Crigler	Lucy	19	Cloverdale	CA
Hendrick	James M.	28	Mendocino Twp.		Allen	Lizzie M.	23	Mendocino Twp.	
Hendrick	Wallace	29	Healdsburg	CA	Heill (?)	Amanda Ellen	23	Healdsburg	KS
Hendricks	Geo. L.	23	Geyserville	CA	Phillips	Maude ?.	20	Geyserville	CA
Hendricks	George L.	26	Healdsburg	CA	Ledford	Anna May	23	Yorkville	CA
Hendricks	J. W.	34	Healdsburg	CA	McElhany	Florence	25	Healdsburg	CA
Hendrix	Edwin W.	18	Fulton		Peterson	Susan A.	18	Santa Rosa	
Hendrix	G. L.	21	San Francisco	CA	Collins	Ella C.	20	Santa Rosa	CA
Hendrix	Harvey L.	20	Santa Rosa	CA	Hall	Mae	19	Santa Rosa	CA
Hendry	Howard W.	24	Crockett	CA	Walters	Audry V.	25	Healdsburg	CA
Henelly	Michael J.	43	Petaluma	CA	Fitzgerald	Ellen A.	37	Petaluma	MO
Henley	Elihu Shields	60	Sacramento	TN	Robson	Marion Louise	55	Windsor	
Henning	Thomas	52	Sebastopol	IL	Garza	Margareth	48	Sebastopol	AUS
Henningsen	John P.	28	Petaluma	GER	Hogedohm	Johanna F.	25	Petaluma	CA
Henningsen	Knudt Theodor	35	Petaluma	GER	Andersen	Caroline Amalie	35	Petaluma	GER
Hennisch	Albert G.	36	San Francisco	CA	Bell	Vivian Phillis	26	Oakland	CA
Henrichsen	Henry R.	44	Petaluma	GER	Geertz	Mathilde, Mrs.	38	Petaluma	GER
Henrichsen	Theodore	32	Petaluma	GER	Stoeker ?	Emma	28	Petaluma	GER
Henrichson	Harry C.	23	Petaluma	CA	Heinsen	Letitia R.	21	Petaluma	CA
Henry	Amos	27	Santa Rosa	MA	Penick	Mackie Katherine	25	Alameda	KY
Henry	Charles P.	49	San Francisco	GER	Bonkofsky	Willamena	50	San Francisco	GER
Henry	George	38	Petaluma		Payran	Mary	19	Petaluma	
Henry	J. R.				Emerson	S. R.			
Henry	James	30	Salt Point Twp.		Hiett	Nelia	15+	Salt Point	
Henshaw	George M.	22	Vekol Mine, A.T.	CA	Meador	Leanora	20	Santa Rosa	TX
Henshaw	Iram	41	Petaluma		Alexander	Hannah	25	Santa Rosa	

	Groom					Bride			
Surname	Given Name	Age	Residence	BP	Surname	Given Name	Age	Residence	BP
Hensley	F. C.	52	San Francisco	ENG	Hughes	Mary G.	40	Daly City	CA
Hensley	Harry	21	Santa Rosa	CA	Hogeboom	Alice B.	20	Santa Rosa	CND
Henzi	William	27	San Francisco	IA	Willis	Sylvia I.	26	San Francisco	KS
Hepworth	Albert	22	Woodland	ENG	Dutcher	Stella V.	18	Santa Rosa	IA
Herald	E. H.	27	Forestville		Bonsell	Ada	18	Forestville	
Herbert	Fred A.	24	San Francisco	CA	Kaster	Julia	18	San Francisco	CA
Herbert	John	33	Paris, San Diego Co.	OH	Silvers	Rettice	20	Santa Rosa	CA
Herbert	John	23	Timber Cove	OH	Silvers	Lizzie A.	17	Timber Cove	CA
Herbert	Thomas	41	Bloomfield	IRL	Robertson	Daisy	30	Santa Rosa	CA
Herbert	Vanscoy P.	26	San Jose	CA	Uttley	Juanita I.	26	Petaluma	NV
Herbert	Victor	23	Albion River, Mendocino Co.		Borer	Florence A.	16	Santa Rosa	
Herbert	William	27	Healdsburg	CA	Bates	Charlotte	26	Healdsburg	CA
Herberts	Harvey	22	San Francisco	MA	Hutchins	Mabel	20	San Francisco	AL
Herbst	John Frank	49	San Francisco	GER	Blum	Theresa	56	Santa Rosa	GER
Herbst	John H.	37	San Francisco	CA	Demol	Claire	36	San Francisco	FRN
Herlitz	Robert	42	Port Costa	Sfo	Hachett	Ella	30	San Francisco	Nev
Herman	Christopher M.	31	Cloverdale	CA	Ellison	Grace E.	23	Guerneville	CA
Herman	Franklin A.	25	St. Helena	CA	Cookson	Ruth A.	20	Sebastopol	MN
Herman	Fred A.	21	Petaluma	PA	Fine	Mary E.	17	Petaluma	MO
Hermann	Albert	28	Petaluma	CA	Behrens	Tillie	22	Corona	CA
Hermansen	Carl Andreas	39	Dawson, AK	DNK	Petersen	Hansine	34	Cotati	DNK
Herrick	Albert B., Jr.	27	Santa Rosa	ND	Dixon	Helen Louise	25	Santa Rosa	CA
Herrick	Emerson Brown	25	San Francisco	CA	Smith	Adah	25	Santa Rosa	CA
Herring	Elias				Nicholsen	Mary Emily Jane, Mrs.			
Herrmann	Ino	30	Marysville		Mosher	Ella	23	Geyserville	
Herron	Frank C.	30	Petaluma	IA	Stockdale	Lena A.	25	Petaluma	Pet
Herron	Joseph H.	33	Healdsburg	TN	Chapin	Ethel	29	Healdsburg	ID

	Groom					Bride			
Surname	Given Name	Age	Residence	BP	Surname	Given Name	Age	Residence	BP
Hersey	Merrick C.	31	Oakland	CA	Johnson	Florence E.	21	Redwood City	CA
Hershberger	John F.	31	Santa Rosa	CA	Whitaker	Rhoda M.	23	Santa Rosa	CA
Heryford	Bennett, Jr.	28	Freestone	CA	Cazerous	Laura	28	Freestone	CA
Heryford	David Hilton	20	Santa Rosa	CA	Hickey	Cathaleen Violet	17	Santa Rosa	CO
Heryford	Hilton	25	Santa Rosa	CA	Kirry	Dora	23	Santa Rosa	CA
Heryford	James W.	31	Eagleville	OR	Lindemenn	Sarah B.	25	Santa Rosa	CA
Heryford	Jno. F.	24	Santa Rosa	CA	Fraim	Daisy, Mrs.	27	Boonville	PA
Heryford	Reuben M.	26	Colusa	IA	Van Winkle	Alice M.	26	Santa Rosa	CA
Heryford	Roy	21	Santa Rosa	CA	Earnest	Helen Pearl	16	Santa Rosa	CO
Heryford	William B.	40	Pickering, MO	MO	Rawlings	Bertha	29	Santa Rosa	CA
Heseker	Fred W.	30	Petaluma	LA	Conley	Clara B.	26	Petaluma	CA
Heselschwerdt	Fred	24	Santa Rosa	MI	Ping	Kate Lee	21	Glen Ellen	CA
Heselschwerdt	Vernon W.	18	Santa Rosa	CA	Frey	Jennie A.	24	Kenwood	WA
Hesketh	George William	30	San Francisco	CA	Schiman	Marion	25	San Francisco	CA
Hess	Albert	44	San Francisco	SWT	Palmater	Sarah E.	48	Sacramento	IL
Hess	Frank	30	Redlands, CA	Chi	Nelson	Grace	22	Seattle	Preston, MN
Hesse	Fredderick G.	60	Oakland	PRS	Scott	Martha E.	29	Oakland	GER
Hesse	Walter E.	25	Santa Rosa	Sar	Brown	Bertha E.	22	Santa Rosa	Sar
Hessel	Andrew Conrad	29	Windsor	IL	Bean	Jessie May	20	Sebastopol	NE
Hessel	Joseph W.	30	Sebastopol	IL	Jasperson	Emma A.	17	Sebastopol	CA
Hesseltine	Benjamin L.				Coffer	Addie	17		
Hesser	Herman R.	46	Santa Rosa		Phillips	Sarah	38	Santa Rosa	
Hettinger	Charley	27	Santa Rosa	CT	Reed	Laura	37	Santa Rosa	CA
Hetzel	Carl	20	Guerneville	KS	Thompson	Lillie	18	Guerneville	CA
Hevel	Wm. T.	24	Woodland	CA	Sparks	Minnie	21	Healdsburg	MO
Hevel	Christopher	71	Santa Rosa	IL	Parr	Barbara	58	Santa Rosa	CND
Hewett	Clyde A.	20	Lytton Springs	CA	Millard	Carrie G.	20	Lytton Springs	NY
Hewitt	Ernest E.	24	Guerneville	IA	Morrow	Emma	17	Guerneville	CA

	Groom					Bride			
Surname	Given Name	Age	Residence	BP	Surname	Given Name	Age	Residence	BP
Hewlett	Lewis Clifton	21	San Francisco	CA	Monteith	Marie Loomis	18	San Rafael	CA
Hewlett	Louis Clifton	24	Oakland	CA	Bell	Alice Ruth	19	Oakland	CA
Heyneman	David H.	46	San Francisco	CA	Bata	Grace	33	San Francisco	KY
Heyward	Jesse	21	Guerneville	CA	Beebe	Christina M.	18	Guerneville	CA
Hiatt	Charles	22	Yorkville	KS	McDonald	Josie	17	Healdsburg	CA
Hiatt	Charles G.	26	Guerneville	KS	Roberts	Ollie May	17	Guerneville	CA
Hiatt	Lloyd W.	27	Lytton	CA	Shelford	M. Effie	24	Cloverdale	CA
Hiatt	Ray Isaac	28	Petaluma	SD	Dickson	Rena M.	18	Petaluma	CA
Hiatt	Robert E.	28	Santa Rosa	OR	Porter	Martha Anna	18	Santa Rosa	OR
Hiatt	T. L.	25	Yorkville	CA	Cooper	May E.	19	Santa Rosa	CA
Hiatt	Thos. L.				Stuart	Lydia J.	20		
Hibbard	Charles Elbert	21	Healdsburg	PA	Bond	Lola Ethel	20	Healdsburg	NV
Hibbard	Earl Francis	26	Petaluma	KS	Kreps	Minnie Elizabeth	21	Petaluma	CA
Hibbard	Lee	40	San Francisco	WV	Laymance	Suzanne	25	Windsor	CA
Hickey	Jerry D.	22	Windsor	CA	McGuyre	May	21	Windsor	CA
Hickey	John	21	Petaluma	CA	Ehmer (?)	Julia	22	Petaluma	KY
Hickey	Maurice		Petaluma		Merritt	Many A.	18+	Petaluma	
Hickey	Maurice J.	22	Petaluma	Pet	Howard	Pearl	22	Petaluma	Sar
Hickey	William A.	35	San Francisco	PA	McGrath	Mary	26	Santa Rosa	CA
Hickey	William Joseph	30	Petaluma	CA	Breckwoldt	Alma Lillian	22	Petaluma	CA
Hicklin	Lieuallen A.	23	Healdsburg	MO	Johnson	Callie F.	19	Healdsburg	MO
Hickman	M. S.	36	Salt Point Twp.		Parks	Elvira	24	Analy Twp.	
Hickman	Wade H.	29	Windsor	OR	Graper	Hazel	19	Windsor	WA
Hickok	James C.	23	Healdsburg	OH	Smith	Alice L.	21	Healdsburg	MO
Hicks	Archibald Lynn	23	Forestville	CA	Clark	Hazel Frances	18	Forestville	CA
Hicks	Edward S.	20	Guerneville	IL	Sline (?)	Etta M.	18	Sebastopol	CA
Hicks	George M.	25	Sebastopol	IL	Bowers	Eliza M.	21	Sebastopol	NY
Hicks	George Milton	51	Healdsburg	IL	Poff	Mary J.	45	Plantation	CA
Hicks	John H.	44	Oakland	CA	Bailer	Honora E., Mrs.	30	Eureka	MO

	Groom					Bride			
Surname	Given Name	Age	Residence	BP	Surname	Given Name	Age	Residence	BP
Hicks	Moses C.	80	Green Valley	OH	Bolton	Sallie, Mrs.	56	Guerneville	VA
Hicks	Walter Eugene	31	Geyserville	CA	Boyer	Gertrude Emily	24	Geyserville	CA
Hienrichsen	Jurgen T.	26	Petaluma	GER	Jensen	Catherine Marie Doretha	18	Petaluma	GER
Higby	Earl D.	49	Santa Rosa	NV	Fryer	Elizabeth M.	41	Santa Rosa	CA
Higgins	Raymond J.	40	San Francisco	IL	Goldman	Edith	31	San Francisco	KY
Higgins	William J.	34	San Francisco	MN	Solomon	Crescencia Edson	25	Oakland	CA
High	Arthur Desten	24	Santa Rosa	MT	Van Winkle	Lettie	21	Santa Rosa	CA
Highbee	H. B.	32	Petaluma	IL	Fairbanks	J. Nettie	24	Petaluma	CA
Higley	John Burdett	24	San Gregorio, San Mateo Co.	IL	Johnson	Elizabeth	24	Santa Rosa	CA
Hildebrand	Calvin G.	28	Oakland	CA	Conne	Josephine M.	23	San Francisco	CND
Hilder	Henry D.	30	San Francisco	CA	Biddle	Ruth M.	26	San Francisco	MO
Hilderbrand	Walter G.	22	Healdsburg	WI	Wilson	Inez M.	23	Healdsburg	CA
Hile	Charles H.	40	Duncans Mill	OH	Hanson	Martha	40	Guerneville	CND
Hilgerloh	Sierich	27	Healdsburg	Sfo	Sewell	Mildred	26	Healdsburg	Hld
Hill	Alexander B., Jr.	23	Petaluma	CA	Olmsted	Dorothy J.	20	Petaluma	CA
Hill	Arthur C.	35	Detroit	CND	Collins	Loretta M.	31	San Francisco	CA
Hill	C. S.	22	Guerneville	OR	Willits	Anna	18	Guerneville	IN
Hill	Charles N.	29	Sebastopol	CA	McGrew	Lovila A.	23	Sebastopol	CA
Hill	Dolph Brice	22	Petaluma	CA	Maney	Josephine Mason	24	Santa Monica	TN
Hill	George O.	35	Petaluma	NV	Lamburth	Ada E.	21	Santa Rosa	CA
Hill	Herman Gordon	22	Tiburon	TX	Stites	Harriett Estelle	22	Geyserville	CA
Hill	James D.	29	Willits	CA	Gibson	Eva L.	18	Ukiah	CA
Hill	James M.	72	Forestville	KY	Boyes	Polly H.	56	Forestville	
Hill	Raymond Moffatt	32	Petaluma	CA	Smith	Frances Elizabeth	19	St. Louis, MO	IN
Hill	Robert				Morris	Delia			
Hill	Robert Elmer	31	Sebastopol	MA	Breaks	Blanche Edna	20	Sebastopol	NE

	Groom					Bride			
Surname	Given Name	Age	Residence	BP	Surname	Given Name	Age	Residence	BP
Hill	Samuel R.	63	Santa Rosa	CND	Chitwood	Mary B.	40	Windsor	OR
Hill	William	19	Petaluma	NE	Canevascini	Bena	17	Petaluma	SWT
Hill	William C.	26	Santa Rosa	OH	Arnold	Emma	23	America	CA
Hill	William C.	31	Santa Rosa	OH	Luman	Anna Mai	21	Santa Rosa	CA
Hill	William James	37	Cazadero	CA	Clark	May Edith	35	Cazadero	CA
Hill	Alexander B.	23	Petaluma	Soc	Fairbanks	Hattie L.	23	Petaluma	Pet
Hillam	Frederick J.	34	Oakland	CA	Gatter	Elizabeth A.	28	Oakland	MA
Hillblom	Gottfrid	25	San Francisco	SWD	Soderman	Susanna	21	San Francisco	FIN
Hillendahl	Frank J.	22	Oakland	TX	Rippin	Doris A.	24	Santa Rosa	IL
Hillis	John A.	39	Santa Rosa	WI	Harp	Emma R.	34	Santa Rosa	MI
Hillis	William Franklin	21+	Petaluma	IN	Huikston	Annie	18+	Petaluma	CA
Hillman	Theodore	31	San Francisco	MN	Blanck	Annie	24	San Francisco	CA
Hills	Percy J.	28	Healdsburg	ENG	Goddard	Hazel M.	22	Healdsburg	CA
Hills	Walter J.	31	Vallejo	NE	Johnson	Marguerite	25	Santa Rosa	KS
Hills	Winford G.	45	Oakland	MI	Marshall	Mabel	31	San Francisco	CA
Hilton	Harry L.	26	Oakland	PA	Hardy	Bessie L.	26	Oakland	CA
Hilton	Melville H.	36	Santa Rosa	ME	Setliff	Vida, Mrs.	35	Santa Rosa	MS
Hinch	William I.	21	Eureka	CA	Guerin	Frances M.	19	Lytton	CA
Hinds	Loring D.	32	Alameda	CA	Mulqueen	Lucy M.	29	Alameda	MN
Hindson	Francis	26	Salt Point Twp.		Bolden	Nettie C.	15	Salt Point Twp.	
Hinkelmann	Gustav	25	Windsor	GER	Mothorn	Lizzie	20	Mill Creek	CA
Hinkle	H. C.	29	Oakland	IN	Mecham	Loretta	29	Stony Point	CA
Hinkleman	Fred G.	22	Cotati	GER	Wright	Neva F.	24	Cotati	CA
Hinrichsen	Peter M.	30	Petaluma	GER	Springer	Helena	22	Petaluma	CA
Hinshaw	A. G.	21	Sebastopol	CA	Frederickson	Mary	23	Sebastopol	CA
Hinshaw	A. G.	40	Petaluma	CA	Price	Rose	36	Sebastopol	IA
Hinshaw	B. B.	27	Petaluma	CA	Colby	F. A.	23	Petaluma	VT
Hinshaw	Clyde C.	32	San Francisco	KS	Aladalo	Sadie M.	21	San Francisco	WY
Hinshaw	Hugh B.	54	Hollister	NC	Stevens	Mary E., Mrs.	45	Cloverdale	IL
Hinshaw	J. D.	41	Petaluma	NC	Laufenburg	Ellen	38	Bloomfield	

	Groom					Bride			
Surname	Given Name	Age	Residence	BP	Surname	Given Name	Age	Residence	BP
Hinshaw	William P.	33	Bloomfield	CA	Hall	Maud M.	26	Petaluma	CA
Hinton	Arthur R.	37	Bakersfield	CA	Gibbs	Mary L.	46	Auburn	CA
Hinze	Victor A.	47	Stockton	KY	Nuhrenberg	Henrietta M.	33	San Francisco	CA
Hipsher	Henry Clay	22	Windsor	WA	Perkins	Blanche	17	Windsor	CA
Hirschman	J. C.	30	San Francisco	GER	Black	Ada	22	Santa Rosa	CA
Hirst	Samuel	37	Santa Rosa	ENG	Kelso	Alice L.	32	Santa Rosa	MO
Hiscox	Richard A.	24	Oakland	CA	Griest	Artie M.	25	Healdsburg	CA
Hitchcock	Arthur L.	36	Cazadero	CA	Salmela	Helza J.	18	Cazadero	CA
Hitchcock	James E.	29	Santa Rosa	CA	Ramsey	Mollie	19	Cloverdale	CA
Hitchcock	John	67	Santa Rosa	MO	Brown	Utilla	46	Santa Rosa	IL
Hitchcock	John R.	30	Guerneville	CA	Yager	Birdie L.	23	Guerneville	CA
Hitchcock	LeRoy V.	23	Santa Rosa	CA	Woodward	Jessie	24	Santa Rosa	MN
Hixson	Charles H.	27	Cloverdale	CA	Leavitt	Cecilia W.	20	Cloverdale	CA
Hixson	John	24	Cloverdale Twp.		Allen	Molly	22	Cloverdale Twp.	
Hixson	John, Jr.	21	Healdsburg	CA	Pope	Mary Delilah	18	The Geysers	CA
Hixson	Roy H.	21	Cloverdale	CA	Lea	Lola	18	Cloverdale	CA
Hixson	Roy H.	20	Cloverdale	CA	Lea	Lola M.	17	Cloverdale	CA
Hixson	W. H.	37	Cloverdale	CA	Ramsey	R. L., Mrs.	40	Cloverdale	MO
Hixson	William H.	50	Hopland	CA	Faught	Ruth	48	Hopland	CA
Hixson	William J.	21	Healdsburg	CA	Jaggers	Mayme T.	17	Healdsburg	KY
Hoadley	Charles W.	38	Timber Cove	CT	Hipsher	Lottie C.	16	Santa Rosa	OR
Hoadley	Mervyn J.	23	San Francisco	CA	Allen	Ethel Lillian	28	San Francisco	CA
Hoar	Charles A.	30	Penngrove	CA	Hamlin	Emma	23	Stony Point	CA
Hobbie	John F.	29	Petaluma	CA	Zimmerman	Therese	30	Petaluma	CA
Hobbs	Charles C.	26	Cloverdale	CA	Adcock	Lois J.	20	Cloverdale	CA
Hobbs	Jason	38	Oakley	IN	Gilliam	Emily	39	Oakley	CA
Hobbs	Robert M.	27	Vallejo	CA	Philbrook	Pearl C.	21	Vallejo	CA
Hoberg	Arthur O.	28	San Francisco	WI	Martin	Minnie H.	25	San Francisco	CA
Hoberg	James A.	31	Vallejo	IN	Camfield	Addie	25	Santa Rosa	MI

	Groom					Bride			
Surname	**Given Name**	**Age**	**Residence**	**BP**	**Surname**	**Given Name**	**Age**	**Residence**	**BP**
Hobson	Frank S.	30	San Francisco	CA	Evans	Marie H.	30	San Francisco	CA
Hobson	Jerome C.	24	Healdsburg	CA	McMullen	Minnie F.	23	Healdsburg	CA
Hobson	Myron	26	Napa	CA	Wilkinson	Mildred	23	Calistoga	CA
Hocker	Will O.	23	Santa Rosa	CA	Chiver?	Lena A.	21	Petaluma	CA
Hockey	Albert James	30	San Francisco	ENG	Redmond	Pauline Mary	30	Occidental	NY
Hockin	William	30	Timber Cove		Totten (?)	E. A. T.	22	Santa Rosa	
Hockin	William Henry	21	Santa Rosa	CA	Lee	Margaret L.	21	Santa Rosa	CA
Hocking	Frank	25	Grass Valley	NV	High	Minnie B.	22	Santa Rosa	CA
Hocking	James	38	Sea View	ENG	McKinzie	Eliza Jane	20	Sea View	NY City
Hocking	William Benn	32	San Francisco	CA	Conley	Daisy	31	Petaluma	MO
Hockney	Byron S.	33	Santa Rosa	OR	Doerges	Louise	31	Santa Rosa	MO
Hodge	Alexander L.	47	Santa Rosa		Damon	Eliza A.	18+	Santa Rosa	
Hodge	Levi Francis	34	Sycamore, DeKalb Co., IA	MI	Weymouth	Corrinne	24	Santa Rosa	OH
Hodges	Edgar W.	30	Oakland	NE	Purvine	Sarah H.	30	Petaluma	CA
Hodges	Henry C.	61	Healdsburg	KY	Foreman	Annie	33	Healdsburg	CA
Hodghead	William Horace	30	Ukiah	VA	Field	Emma H.	22	Cloverdale	CA
Hodgson	David R.	24	Santa Rosa	OR	Winton	Leticia A.	16	MO	MO
Hodgson	Joseph E.	27	Santa Rosa	UT	Stevenson	Mary M.	23	Santa Rosa	CND
Hodgson	Ralston Winton	22	San Francisco	CA	Calley	Mildred Madeline	19	San Francisco	OH
Hodgson	Richard	30	Eureka	UT	McDonald	Flora	23	Santa Rosa	CND
Hodgson	W. H.	42	Butte City	PA	Luman	Mary A.	33	Santa Rosa	IL
Hoeck	F. P.	35	Mexico City, MEX	DNK	Willey	Mary A.	29	Healdsburg	WI
Hoeck	Frederick W.	23	Mill Valley	MEX	Thomas	Margaret E.	23	San Francisco	CA
Hoegh	Hans Matzen	22	Petaluma	GER	Rickerts		16	Petaluma	CA
Hoerle	Fred	22	Petaluma	GER	Richers (?)	Dora	21	Petaluma	GER
Hoff	Herman James	26	Santa Rosa	CA	Dennison	Maude Pearl	19	Santa Rosa	WY
Hoffer	Virgil	24	Santa Rosa	CA	Thompson	Gertrude	19	Santa Rosa	CA

	Groom					Bride			
Surname	Given Name	Age	Residence	BP	Surname	Given Name	Age	Residence	BP
Hoffman	Alfred H.				Watson	Sarah	22		
Hoffman	Charles	30	Sonoma		Rundell	Rosa	24	Sonoma	
Hoffman	Charles T.				Pantier	Emma May	15		
Hoffman	Fernando				Woodruff	Eva B.	17		
Hoffman	Freedom W.	27	Sebastopol	CA	Peugh	Jemella G.	25	Guerneville	CA
Hoffman	George W.	31	Napa	CA	Trubody	Clara C.	40	Napa	CA
Hoffman	John Walter	24	Little River	CA	Barff	Mary Eleanor	19	Mendocino	CA
Hoffman	Walter A.	32	San Francisco	CA	Westover	Irma L.	27	San Francisco	CA
Hoffman	Walter Roy	30	San Francisco	MT	Shade	Ida L.	30	Oakland	CA
Hoffschneider	Arthur P.	44	San Francisco	CA	Smith	Minnie E.	37	San Francisco	OH
Hogeboom	Robert Percy	20	Santa Rosa	CND	Drescher	Lena	18	Santa Rosa	CA
Hogg	Robert O.	40	Honolulu	IRL	Cunningham	Loura E.	33	Honolulu	MO
Hogg	William G.	31	ND	CND	Wilson	Jennie M.	25	Santa Rosa	MN
Holaday	Elon R.	28	Fresno	IA	Eckman	Minnie	21	Guerneville	CA
Holchester	Paul E.	22	Guerneville	CA	Hasting	Clara	19	Bennett Valley	CA
Holcomb	Alfred	48	Santa Rosa	CA	Overton	Mattie C.	31	Santa Rosa	CA
Holcomb	Leonard C.	24	Santa Rosa	OR	Holst	Annie	16	Santa Rosa	CA
Holcomb	William	22	Santa Rosa	OR	Brucker	Isabella	16	Santa Rosa	CA
Holden	Charles	30	San Francisco	CA	Ragan	May	27	San Francisco	CA
Holden	John Edwin	43	Petaluma	IL	Rosenquest	Matilda Estalla	41	Petaluma	IA
Holden	Josiah N.	24	Rincon Valley		Norris	Sarah	21	Rincon Valley	
Holding	George	40	San Francisco	ENG	Danterman	Priscilla	38	San Francisco	FL
Holdrich	Hilarius	34	Geyserville	GER	Glaser	Emma	19	Geyserville	GER
Holdsworth	Miles E.	40	Oakland	CA	Maguire	Ann Loraine	36	San Francisco	CA
Holdt	H. Christian	21	Vallejo	DNK	Haugh	Marguerite	19	Petaluma	CA
Holgard	Carl C.	27	Oakland	DNK	Lampson	Nellie E.	23	Oakland	CA
Hollar	Henry H.	21	Mendocino Twp.	CA	Gott (?)	Laura	20	Russian River Twp.	CA
Holles	Clayton W.	24	San Rafael	OR	Cochrane	Clare A.	24	San Rafael	CA
Holliday	James E.	23	Ukiah	CA	Stone	Hattie L.	21	Ukiah	CA

	Groom					Bride			
Surname	Given Name	Age	Residence	BP	Surname	Given Name	Age	Residence	BP
Hollingshead	Edward	27	San Francisco	OH	Bond	Lizella Edith	24	Healdsburg	CA
Hollingsworth	Dale Raymond	21	Santa Rosa	KS	Wright	Viola May	15	Santa Rosa	CA
Hollingsworth	Greene	57	Seven Troughs, NV	MO	Damon	Maggie A.	43	Oakland	CA
Hollingsworth	Harry M.	23	Petaluma	CA	Alexander	Pearl L. G.	18	Tomales	CA
Hollis	George Lester	35	Petaluma	MA	Hardin	Edith Lourena	25	Petaluma	CA
Hollister	George C.	26	Valley Ford	CA	McLeod	F. M.	25	San Francisco	MN
Hollister	George S.	28	Merced Co.	CA	Mutschlechner	Mary	32	Cloverdale	IA
Holloway	Calvin Walter	23	Petaluma	CA	Carpenter	Mamie Ellen	22	Petaluma	CA
Holloway	Clarence	18	Healdsburg	CA	Parker	Mildred	17	Healdsburg	ND
Holloway	Isaac Newton	24	Santa Rosa		Griffith	Malinda Ann	18+	Santa Rosa	
Holloway	James Henry	21	Healdsburg	MO	Albertson	Ella	23	Healdsburg	CA
Holm	Jacob F.	48	Petaluma	GER	Drees	Mary	41	Petaluma	GER
Holman	Charles W.	60	San Quentin	OR	Smith	Nova N.	40	Santa Rosa	NE
Holman	Edward Kingwell	23	Occidental	ENG	Brians	Nellie Isabelle	23	Occidental	CA
Holmes	Charles H.	41	Santa Rosa	CA	Holmes	Nellie	21	Santa Rosa	CA
Holmes	Chas. H., Jr.	23	Santa Rosa	CA	Ward	Margaret M.	19	Santa Rosa	PA
Holmes	Lester S.	25	Petaluma	CA	Houck	Mary L.	22	Petaluma	CA
Holmes	Marvin P.	26	Dos Palos	AR	Austin	Hattie H.	26	Santa Rosa	KY
Holmes	Melvin Leon	30	Berkeley	CA	Phelps	Mary Agnes	36	Berkeley	CA
Holmes	Neal Arthur	24	Sausalito	MT	Jones	Lillian Beatrice	23	San Francisco	CA
Holmes	Ovid	21	Kellogg	CA	Luttrell	Ruth M.	22	Santa Rosa	KS
Holst	Henry	21	Santa Rosa	MN	Fisher	Mollie	18	Santa Rosa	Sar
Holst	Jacob E.	27	Santa Rosa	MN	Tuttle	Mary	29	Santa Rosa	PA
Holst	James	20	Santa Rosa	CA	Young	Hazel	18	Santa Rosa	CA
Holst	James P.	28	Cloverdale	CA	Vassar	Etta	19	Cloverdale	CA
Holst	Joseph A.	31	Santa Rosa	GER	Blank	Grace, Mrs.	40	Santa Rosa	GER
Holst	William	21	Santa Rosa	MN	Dutcher	Pearl	18	Santa Rosa	CA
Holt	Alva Smith	36	Chehalis, WA	MO	Stahl	Laura B.	33	Santa Rosa	IA

	Groom					Bride			
Surname	Given Name	Age	Residence	BP	Surname	Given Name	Age	Residence	BP
Holt	John A.	25	Loleta, Humbolt Co.	ME	Yarbough	Georgia J.	20	Healdsburg	CA
Holt	William T.	26	Sonoma	MS	Clerve	Helen A.	26	Sonoma	CA
Holtchauer	Louis	29	San Rafael	GER	Enyisch	Martha	20	San Rafael	GER
Holtz	James H.	42	San Francisco	OH	Cox	Lulu H.	42	Ukiah	CA
Holtz	Richard Gustav	34	San Francisco	GER	Hansen	Elene	28	Petaluma	CA
Holxer	Ernest	24	Santa Rosa	SWT	Shearer	Annie	28	Santa Rosa	SWT
Homer	William Harry	21	San Francisco	Sfo	Simmons	Jennette Augusta	18	Sonoma	Son
Hondaa	Emile J. B.	25	Tracy	CA	Canale	Elvira S.	18	Stockton	CA
Honsa	Joseph	36	Guerneville	AUS	Cervinki	Katie	34	San Francisco	AUS
Honton	Paul Noel	24	Hopland	CA	Vassar	Agnes Aileen	20	Hopland	CA
Hood	Alexander	29	Knights Valley	CA	McDonnell	Nellie	23	Knights Valley	CA
Hood	Benjamin H.	37	Green Valley	CA	Cook	Daisy D.	26	Healdsburg	KY
Hood	Frank B.	24	Santa Rosa	CA	Doyle	Nellie J.	19	Santa Rosa	CA
Hood	James G.	48	Santa Rosa	SCT	Young	Neva	36	Santa Rosa	TN
Hood	John	43	Santa Rosa	CA	Rutledge	Florence	31	Santa Rosa	MN
Hood	Thomas Bergin, Jr.	24	Santa Rosa	CA	Tenter	Fredericka	18	Santa Rosa	NE
Hooke	H. W.	26	Cloverdale	ENG	Gibbons	Mary A.	24	Cloverdale	CA
Hooper	Thomas R.	26	Woody, Kern Co.	IL	Booth	Eugenie M.	18	Santa Rosa	CA
Hoosier	Charles Rasmond	29	Salinas	KS	Anderson	Mabel J.	29	Salinas	CA
Hoover	Leo V.	19	Oakland	TX	Harben	Jennie E.	17	San Francisco	CA
Hopcroft	Charles	52	Penngrove	ENG	Baumann	Ida	41	Penngrove	GER
Hope	Earl Paul	24	Shawmut, CA	CA	Goula	Ismay Josephine	19	Healdsburg	IL
Hope	John B.	31	San Francisco	SCT	Menary	Matilda J.	20	Bodega	IRL
Hopkins	Alban David	30	Tomales	WLS	Stone	Lillian Agnes	19	Tomales	Son
Hopkins	Oliver Clay	25	Petaluma	MI	Bryant	Caroline Augusta	22	Petaluma	CA
Hopkins	Osmer Clyde	21	San Francisco	CA	Ham	Edith L.	18	Sebastopol	CA

	Groom					Bride			
Surname	Given Name	Age	Residence	BP	Surname	Given Name	Age	Residence	BP
Hopkins	William Hewes	27	Sacramento	CA	Reid	Louise S.	23	Santa Rosa	CA
Hoppe	Anton	48	Shellville	GER	Frei	Rosa	43	Shellville	SWT
Hoppe	Joseph Edward	34	Petaluma	CA	Respini	Delia	26	Petaluma	SWT
Hopper	David E.	35	San Francisco	NJ	Smith	Wilhelmina L.	32	San Francisco	CA
Hopper	Edward	23	Windsor	CA	Grove	Emma B.	21	Windsor	CA
Hopper	Elmer Merton	24	Pacific Grove	CA	Wilson	Loretta	21	Sebastopol	CA
Hopper	George R.	22	Santa Rosa	CA	Lamb	Mary A.	20	Cloverdale	CA
Hopper	Henry	22	Santa Rosa	CA	Burris	Mary F.	20	Sonoma	CA
Hopper	Henry J.	26	Windsor	CA	Huffman	Cora	19	Windsor	IA
Hopper	Henry James	31	Windsor	CA	Kimball	Lulu M.	18	Windsor	CA
Hopper	Thomas	71	Santa Rosa	MO	Everly	Julia N., Mrs.	35	Santa Rosa	USA
Hopper	Walter E.	22	Hopland	CA	Harrington	Leila M.	19	Hopland	CA
Hopper	Wesley L.	50	Santa Rosa	CA	Felton	Nellie	25	Santa Rosa	CA
Hopper	William Thomas	21	Santa Rosa	CA	Adams	Mary Etta	20	Santa Rosa	CA
Hopper	Zachamiah (?)				Houx	Josephine			
Horak	Ferdinand	64	Glen Ellen	AUS	Blodget	Anna	24	Glen Ellen	MT
Horan	Charles	50	Eureka	IRL	Cronin	Catherine E.	45	Alameda	CA
Horgan	Edward Timothy	28	San Francisco	CA	Ventura	Mary Francis	23	Sebastopol	CA
Horgan	Eugene	34	Markhams	IRL	Keohane	Nellie	24	Markham	IRL
Horgan	Patrick	30	San Francisco	IRL	Harnett	Johanna	28	San Francisco	IRL
Horita	Katsuki	27	Sebastopol	JPN	Miyamoto	Shina	22	Sebastopol	JPN
Horn	Balthasar	31	Petaluma	GER	Hanekamp	Anna Maria	25	San Francisco	GER
Horn	Frank Charley	40	Healdsburg	GER	Breitling	Matilda	38	San Francisco	GER
Hornberger	Charles	30	Sebastopol	NY	Doyle	Louise	21	Sebastopol	NZD
Hornbuckle	Thomas J.	66	Santa Rosa	IL	Hill	Florence S., Mrs.	37	Knight's Landing	CA
Horne	David	24	Petaluma		Walts (?)	Elizabeth	19	Vallejo Twp.	
Horr	Riley J.	70	Ukiah	NY	Freeman	Sarah A.	58	Fulton	MO
Horrick	John	49	Petaluma Twp.	GER	Softus	Mary	42	Petaluma Twp.	IRL
Horrup	Frank J.	35	Petaluma	MN	Kynoch	Edna I.	29	Petaluma	

\multicolumn{5}{c}{Groom}					\multicolumn{5}{c}{Bride}				
Surname	Given Name	Age	Residence	BP	Surname	Given Name	Age	Residence	BP
Horton	Arthur	28	Ukiah	CA	Blake	Lulu E.	18	Pomo, CA	CA
Horton	Arthur S.	23	Petaluma	TX	Fiske	Elizabeth C.	23	Sausalito	CA
Horton	Samuel	32	Healdsburg	CND	Eby	Ida J.	31	Healdsburg	IA
Hoskins (?)	Edward Sterling	40	Petaluma	Soc	Fredricks	Ella	28	Petaluma	Soc
Hosmer	Raymond J.	22	Santa Rosa	CO	Henderson	Violet V.	20	Santa Rosa	CA
Hosmer	Stanley	25	Santa Rosa	CA	Dean	Maybell	25	Santa Rosa	TX
Hoss	Frank Blair	27	Cloverdale	CA	Allen	Nellie May	23	Cloverdale	CA
Hoster	William S.	34	Santa Rosa	CO	Malouf	Fifie	33	Santa Rosa	SYR
Hotchkiss	Douglas F.	41	Santa Rosa	NY	Hutchinson	Lily E.	38	Santa Rosa	MO
Hotchkiss	W. J.	23	Windsor		Grom (?)	Emma L.	25	Windsor	
Hotle	Charles E.	29	Sebastopol	IA	Litchfield	Cora L.	25	Sebastopol	IL
Hotle	William Marley	31	Sebastopol	CA	Dickson	Mary L.	31	Petaluma	CA
Hottel	Peter G.	56	Napa Valley	IN	Laughery	Martha E., Mrs.	40	Napa Valley	CA
Hottinger	Bernard F.	29	Santa Rosa	Nev	Stump	Dottie	17	Santa Rosa	Soc
Hotz	Gustave H.	33	Sonoma	GER	Enslow	Emma A.	21	Santa Rosa	IA
Hotz	Ralph O.	25	Sonoma	CA	Waterman	Ida E.	25	Sonoma	CA
Hough	Martin	25	Willits	CA	Branaum	May, Mrs.	25	Willits	CA
Houghton	Albert S.	35	Healdsburg	KS	Shriver	Ethel A.	25	Healdsburg	CA
Houghton	Grover C.	26	Madison	CA	Mecum	Alice L.	26	Sacramento	CA
Houghton	Wm. H.	25	Santa Rosa	ENG	Bennett	Ethel A.	22	Santa Rosa	ENG
Hougland	Ira A.	32	Redding	CA	Neasham	Anna Leah	28	Santa Rosa	OR
Hourcaillon	John B.	21	Healdsburg	FRN	Fredinani	Edith	19	Healdsburg	ITL
Hourtani (?)	Alphonse J. P.	36	San Francisco	CA	Akmann	Lillian G.	33	San Francisco	CA
Houser	Basil L.	21	Carlos, IN	IN	Daniels	Ethel I.	21	Cloverdale	CA
Houts	Orrie Leonard	40	Oakland	IN	Swain	May McConnell	35	Santa Rosa	CA
Hovey	Albert Theo	28	Healdsburg	CA	Thompson	Mabel B.	18	Healdsburg	CA
Hovey	Arthur La Verne	37	Camp Meeker	IL	Dempsey	Emogene E.	43	Camp Meeker	MA
Hovey	Theodore	38	Healdsburg	NY	Hall	Emma J.	20	Healdsburg	NV
Howard	Alphonse E.	21	Petaluma	CT	Howard	Florence L.	17	Petaluma	IA
Howard	Benjamin F.	29	Bloomfield	CT	Shipmon	Mary E.	35	Bloomfield	CT

	Groom					Bride			
Surname	**Given Name**	**Age**	**Residence**	**BP**	**Surname**	**Given Name**	**Age**	**Residence**	**BP**
Howard	Benjamin Franklin	32	Green Valley	CA	Levalley	Lena, Mrs.	36	Green Valley	TX
Howard	Calvin P.	65	Petaluma	VT	Shafer	Emma E.	39	Petaluma	PA
Howard	Carl C.	21	Santa Rosa	CA	Young	Blanche	18	Santa Rosa	KS
Howard	Charles E.	40	Bloomfield	CA	Glenn	Eda, Mrs.	30	Sebastopol	CA
Howard	Clarence	19	Healdsburg	CA	Pruitt	Ethel June	17	Cloverdale	AZ
Howard	David Jackson	26	Healdsburg	CA	Cake	Mary Emma	25	Healdsburg	CA
Howard	Emmett Robert	23	Petaluma	MI	Goodwin	Mary Jane	24	Petaluma	CA
Howard	Frank E.	28	Santa Rosa	NH	Solomon	Ruth	26	Santa Rosa	CA
Howard	Frank M.	23	Tacoma, WA	MI	Melehan	Mae J.	22	Petaluma	Pet
Howard	Frederick W.	33	Sacramento	KS	Botts	Ethel	32	Santa Rosa	KS
Howard	Harry	25	Healdsburg	CA	Baine	Dora	19	Healdsburg	CA
Howard	Henry Ward	25	Santa Rosa	CA	Sellon	Violet Mabel	18	Santa Rosa	CA
Howard	Horace A.	52	Sea View	MI	Corel	Jane	35	Chattanooga	TN
Howard	James	21	Ukiah	CA	Moore	Henrietta	19	Geyserville	CA
Howard	John B.				McCracken	Louisa			
Howard	John W.	33	Santa Rosa	CA	Canell	Nellie Floy	19	Santa Rosa	ND
Howard	Phillip	27	Santa Rosa	CA	Degardin	Clara	19	Santa Rosa	CND
Howard	Raymond L.	22	San Francisco	CND	Cofer	Lottie Edith	17	Santa Rosa	CA
Howard	Roe Burdett	26	Santa Rosa	MN	Saunders	Ada Henrietta	22	Santa Rosa	TX
Howard	Roeder M.	21	Oakland	NE	Randolph	Emma M.	22	Oakland	CA
Howard	Vernon R.	22	Occidental	CA	Gonella	Mary	23	Occidental	CA
Howard	W. H.	22	Guerneville	TN	Yarbrough	Virginia J.	21	Guerneville	CA
Howard	William C.	24	Howard Station	CA	Francischi	Teresa	18	Howard Station	ITL
Howard	William W.	66	Graton	KY	Shackelford	Mary Ida	53	Graton	TX
Howe	Asa A.	55	Santa Rosa	PA	Daggett	Jennie N.	52	Santa Rosa	CA
Howe	Baxter	29	Oakland	MI	Morrison	Eliza A.	25	Oakland	IN
Howe	Charles J.	24	Novato	CA	Smith	Maud	22	Marin Co.	CA
Howe	Chas. W.	36	Santa Rosa		Brown	Abbie E.	26	Santa Rosa	
Howe	James Henry	29	Petaluma	CA	Howe	Frances	29?	Petaluma	CA

	Groom					Bride			
Surname	Given Name	Age	Residence	BP	Surname	Given Name	Age	Residence	BP
Howe	Joseph	57	Geyserville	IL	Miller	Ella L.	46	Geyserville	IN
Howe	Willard Earl	22	Santa Rosa	CA	Conner	Jeannette Muriel	21	Santa Rosa	CA
Howell	Ambrose M.	27	Santa Rosa	CA	Gardner	Dela May	21	Santa Rosa	CA
Howell	Frank M.	27	Duncans Springs, Mendocino Co.	CA	Sweetsen	Alice L.	22	Santa Rosa	CA
Howell	George	24	San Francisco		McDonald	Mary Jane	23	Healdsburg	
Howell	James Myras	19	Ukiah	Ukiah	Kelly	Mildred Edith	19	Sebastopol	Seb
Howell	Joseph L.				Ervin	Katie			
Howell	Louis V. H.	30	Sebastopol	CA	Johnson	Cora L.	21	Sebastopol	CA
Howell	Olin Kenneth	23	San Francisco	CA	Hahn	Lillian Genevieve	25	San Francisco	CA
Howell	Thomas Wm.	22	Bennett Valley	MO	Burns	Anna J.	22	Bennett Valley	CA
Howell	W. E.	27	Healdsburg	OH	Kinner	Harriet B.	20	Healdsburg	OH
Howell	William	23	Santa Rosa	CA	Gage	Laurina B.	19	Santa Rosa	CA
Howland	Gardiner G.	40	New York, Kings Co.	NY	MacGregor	Jessie C.	23	Santa Rosa	CA
Howland	Thomas A.	36	Eureka	RI	McCloud	Rose, Mrs.	29	Chico	Che
Hoyle	George Wilson	39	Cloverdale	IL	Dunn	Maggie Irene	18	Cloverdale	IL
Hoyrup	Rasmus Nielson	38	Petaluma	GER	Martin	Ida Mary	26	Petaluma	Pet
Hoyt	Elijah				Jackman	T. A.			
Hoyt	Franklin Lowe	25	Santa Rosa	NY	Barrows	Leah Louise	23	Santa Rosa	CO
Hoyt	Jesse D.	25	Santa Rosa	Sar	Wetmur	Olive M.	21	Santa Rosa	USA
Hubbard	Clyde H.	23	Berkeley	TX	Steele	Ruth	18	Berkeley	MI
Hubbard	George F.	35	Guerneville	NY	Yakovleff	Catherine	28	Glen Ellen	RUS
Hubbard	Henry	46	Cloverdale	CT	Moody	A. M., Mrs.	46	Cloverdale	NY
Hubbard	James L.	48	Yountville	IN	Ray	Marie E.	35	San Francisco	CA
Hubbard	Junius H.	58	Oak Harbor, WA	AR	White	Rachel	50	Berkeley	IN
Hubbard	Pearl D.	22	near Windsor	NE	Scott	Henrietta, Mrs.	36	near Windsor	CA
Hubbard	William B.	29	Los Angeles	MN	Geary	Helen J.	24	Santa Rosa	CA
Hubbell	O. B.	25	Tomales	MI	Ames	Phebe E.	21	Valley Ford	CA

	Groom					Bride			
Surname	**Given Name**	**Age**	**Residence**	**BP**	**Surname**	**Given Name**	**Age**	**Residence**	**BP**
Hubseh	Albin J.	35	Sonoma	BOH	Law	Elmira	19	Sonoma	CA
Hudelson	Warren S.	25	Healdsburg		Long	Edna	18	Healdsburg	
Huderson	Robert G.	27	Skaggs Springs	CA	Blair	Mary	27	Skaggs Springs	KS
Hudson	Alvin P.	24	Sonoma Co.	CA	Hillmon	Katie	18	Sonoma Co.	CA
Hudson	Arthur T.	38	Cotati	MI	Johnson	Mary A., Mrs.	18+	San Francisco	VA
Hudson	Clarence D.	22	Healdsburg	IA	Gibson	Lenore C.	24	Healdsburg	CA
Hudson	Daniel Bertnette	29	Kellogg	CA	Tarwater	Emma Louisa	29	Santa Rosa	CA
Hudson	David Hill	74	Santa Rosa	VA	Jones	Abigal Akerley, Mrs.	52	Santa Rosa	NBW
Hudson	George R.	25	San Francisco	CA	Elphick	Mattie E.	24	Sebastopol	CA
Hudson	H. R.	31	Castella, CA	CA	Levicy	Ethel	26	Cloverdale	CA
Hudson	Henry F.	27	Mark West	CA	Herriford	Henrietta	18	Tulivi (?)	NV
Hudson	James	19	Santa Rosa	CA	Stevens	Mamie	18	Healdsburg	CA
Hudson	W. T.	40	Mark West	MO	Adams	Delcina, Mrs.	47	Mark West	MO
Hudson	William H.	25	Ukiah	MO	Brumfield	Priscilla	17	Healdsburg	CA
Hudson	Kelsey S.	25	Sebastopol	CA	Flecsher	Minnie R.	19	Peachland	
Hudspeth	James M.	26	Sebastopol	CA	Johnston	Ethel E.	26	Santa Rosa	CA
Huebner	Oscar Constantine	54	Healdsburg	GER	Jones	Ethel May, Mrs.	28	Healdsburg	MI
Huff	Henry J.	25	King City	CA	Miller	Amelia	22	Healdsburg	CA
Huffman	Aaron	19	Windsor	CA	Peterson	Elsie	25	Santa Rosa	CA
Huffman	Daniel	27	Healdsburg	NE	Maxwell	Elizabeth Belle	22	Healdsburg	CA
Huffman	Daniel	39	Windsor	NE	Pastorino	Rose Lee	43	Oakland	CA
Huffman	Eddie	20	Santa Rosa	MO	Brewer	Bertha	20	Santa Rosa	ENG
Huffman	Hezekiah	32	Santa Rosa	WI	Stevens	Susie M., Mrs.	32	Santa Rosa	CA
Huffman	Jacob	22	Healdsburg	NE	Hayes	Clifton Clay	20	Healdsburg	CA
Huffman	James R.	25	Windsor	NE	Nelson	Violet Rose	19	Elk	CA
Huffman	W. H.	31	Kern, Kern Co.	IL	Turner	Laura A.	22	Santa Rosa	CA
Hufner	Franz	43	San Francisco	GER	Grand	Fannie	33	San Francisco	PLD
Hughes	Alfred G.	23	Alameda	PA	Meyer	Julia T.	30	Sonoma	CA
Hughes	B. C.	38	San Francisco	NY City	Sutluff	Harriett	26	San Francisco	ENG

Groom					Bride				
Surname	Given Name	Age	Residence	BP	Surname	Given Name	Age	Residence	BP
Hughes	Charles T.	31	San Francisco	CA	Shea	Ada	23	Santa Rosa	ID
Hughes	David E.	27	Suisun	CA	Shaumburg	Belle	20	Santa Rosa	CA
Hughes	Floyd B.	21	Oakland	Hon	Luscher (?)	Marie G.	19	Oakland	CA
Hughes	George	28	Suisun	CA	Haskell	Clista	18	Oakland	TN
Hughes	George G.	30	Sacramento	IA	Hall	Vista M.	25	Petaluma	CA
Hughes	George W.	29	Oakland	CA	Smith	Clara I.	24	Guerneville	CA
Hughes	Henry F.	60	Santa Rosa	NY	Boone	Renette Emogene	58	Santa Rosa	NY
Hughes	Hugh	56	San Francisco	ENG	Petre	Louise V.	34	San Francisco	NY
Hughes	John Franklin	34	Santa Rosa	TX	Egler	Anna Reynella	23	Elko, NV	PA
Hughes	John S.	32	Santa Rosa	CA	Starbuck	Emma Grace	24	San Francisco	NE
Hughes	Judd	24	Lake View, OR	CA	Benton	Alice	25	Lake View, OR	MO
Hughes	Louis D.	40	Lafayette	WA	Weed	Edna M.	36	Lafayette	PA
Hughes	Michael J.	38	Oakland	IRL	Brown	Leona	39	Oakland	CA
Hughes	Thomas M.	63	Healdsburg	MO	Upson	Kathryn	46	Healdsburg	CA
Hughes	William L.	22	Santa Rosa	RI	Pannell	Frances M.	21	Santa Rosa	CA
Hughett	Ernest Adolph	35	Ukiah	WA	Carter	Annie Elizabeth	18	Ukiah	CA
Huittmann	John O.	25	Martinez	CA	Lynch	Elizabeth F.	20	Petaluma	CA
Hulbert	Ansel C.	21	Santa Rosa	CA	Davis	Bessie Smith	21	Santa Rosa	KY
Hulbert	Charles P.	25	Cloverdale	CA	Scott	Lola	19	Cloverdale	CA
Hulbert	Clarence E.	23	Cloverdale	CA	Toal	Rosanna	22	Gilroy	MS
Hulbert	Harry E.	28	Cloverdale	CA	Martin	Effie, Mrs.	28	Boonville	CA
Hulbert	Harry E.	22	Santa Rosa	CA	Duncan	May Agnes	15	Santa Rosa	CA
Hulbert	Hiram Perry	24	Occidental		Hufstoder	Mary Belle	20	Occidental	
Hulbert	Marion O.	23	Cloverdale	CA	Endicott	Edythe E.	20	Cloverdale	OR
Hull	Alonzo Clinton	68	Santa Rosa	NY	Gifford	Evelyn Barnum	43	San Francisco	CA
Hull	Guy L.	23	Berkeley	SD	Wilson	Reno	21	Petaluma	CA
Hull	Irving Melvin	37	Oakland	KS	Fechter	Esther Ella	18	Calistoga	CA
Hull	Jerome H.	42	San Francisco	OH	Ross	Jennie	27	Santa Rosa	CA
Hull	Money Elliott	20	San Francisco	CA	Hughes	Estella M.	16	Santa Rosa	CA

	Groom					Bride			
Surname	**Given Name**	**Age**	**Residence**	**BP**	**Surname**	**Given Name**	**Age**	**Residence**	**BP**
Hull	Silas William	24	Graton	KS	Johnson	Velmer Vermeta	17	Graton	CA
Hull	Wm. D.				Corey	Augusta			
Hullen	Peter H.	29	Santa Rosa	GER	Elderkin	Edna M.	21	Santa Rosa	MT
Hulsey	John B.	25	San Francisco	MO	Tabor	Bessie	23	Santa Rosa	OK
Hultgreen	Gustaf Olof	35	Oakland	SWD	Evanson	Josie	21	Santa Rosa	ND
Hultgren	John A.	32	Guerneville	SWD	Garrison	Jennette J.	23	Guerneville	CA
Humbert	George H.	28	Santa Rosa	PA	Davis	Carrie E.	19	Santa Rosa	NE
Humbert	Charles E.	21	Cloverdale	IL	Hoadley	Ida L.	17	Cloverdale	CA
Hummer	William T.	35	San Francisco	VA	Spofford	Edith E.	29	San Francisco	PA
Hundley	W. P.	28	Oroville	NV	Holland	Mary	21	Tomales	Mac
Huneke	Robert Carlisle	21	Santa Rosa	KY	Cox	Irene	17	Santa Rosa	CA
Hunger	Elmer G.	34	Forestville	CA	Anderson	May Etta	17	Healdsburg	KS
Hunger	F. J.	29	Kansas City	CA	Thorpe	Anna	21	Lawrence, KS	KS
Hunken	John Carl	24	San Francisco	CA	Hink	Catrina	20	San Francisco	Sfo
Hunkins	Lyle D.	28	Healdsburg	MO	McCord	Ruby D.	18	Riverside	CA
Hunt	Arthur H.	50	Napa	ENG	Leeter (?)	Sadie E.	49	Napa	CA
Hunt	Avery G.	43	Carpenteria	MS	McDonald	Faith	25	Petaluma	PA
Hunt	B. W.				Harris	Sarah A., Mrs.			
Hunt	Byrd A.	34	Lower Lake	MO	Adams	Viola, Mrs.	24	Cloverdale	CA
Hunt	Clyde E.	27	Santa Rosa	CA	Price	Estella M.	27	Santa Rosa	CA
Hunt	Edward Rowland	40	Kenwood	ENG	Eyton	Lilia A. C.	38	Kenwood	ENG
Hunt	Elmer H.	22	Graton	TX	Bostick	Louise M.	16	Graton	TX
Hunt	Eugene Warren	25	Martinez	CA	Weaver	Anna Alberta	26	El Verano	CA
Hunt	Francis Willard	22	Sebastopol		Pierce	Alice M.	19	Sebastopol	
Hunt	George M.	38	Santa Rosa	CA	Carter	Flora, Mrs.	37	Santa Rosa	IL
Hunt	George Walter	29	Martinez	CND	Wadsworth	Alice Maud	26	Sebastopol	MI
Hunt	Joseph H.	26	Santa Rosa	CA	Mock	Margaretta	22	Santa Rosa	CA
Hunt	Milton G.	26	Petaluma	CA	Seward	Laura I.	19	Ukiah	CA
Hunt	Oscar L.	29	San Francisco	OR	Davidson	Adele E.	21	Oakland	OR

	Groom					Bride			
Surname	Given Name	Age	Residence	BP	Surname	Given Name	Age	Residence	BP
Hunt	Paul	37	Sebastopol	CA	Harris	Cora Bell	24	Tehama	CA
Hunt	W. J.	51	Sebastopol	MO	Griffin	Ida, Mrs.	28	Sebastopol	NE
Hunt	Warren E.	24	San Francisco	MI	Douglass	Julia	21	Sonoma Twp.	CA
Hunt	William C.	23	Santa Rosa	CA	Litchfield	Anna M.	22	Sebastopol	IL
Hunt	William Irvin	28	Lake Co.	CA	Doss	Emma A.	20	Petaluma	CA
Hunter	Eugene W.	22	Healdsburg	CA	Brooks	Leslie E. M.	16	Healdsburg	CA
Hunter	Grover C.	21	Petaluma	CA	Denney	Emma C.	18	Petaluma	CA
Hunter	John J.	22	Petaluma	CT	Casey	Anna J.	22	Petaluma	CND
Hunter	Rea Baron	23	Sonoma	IA	Hauger	Perle	23	Sonoma	VA
Hunter	William Crittenton	24	Ukiah	CA	Waite	Thenia	19	Cloverdale	CA
Huntington	Harry E.	47	Santa Rosa	MN	McClellan	Elizabeth L.	30	Santa Rosa	CA
Huntington	Horace H.	24	Petaluma	CND	Gregory	Martha M.	24	Petaluma	CA
Huntley	Albert	25	Sebastopol	CA	Bowers	Elizabeth A.	28	Sebastopol	CA
Huntley	George W.	25	Guerneville	ME	Lindsy	Phoebe	19	Guerneville	NV
Huntley	George W.	35	Guerneville	ME	Fagie	Emma	20	Santa Rosa	NY
Huntley	John S.	35	Ukiah	OR	Zumwalt	Dora	18	Ukiah	CA
Huntoon	J. R.	23	Windsor	CA	Melson	Josephine	19	Windsor	CA
Huntt (?)	George E.	25	Los Angeles	MN	Weigel	Esther D.	21	Los Angeles	CA
Huph	Henry Philip	23	Ukiah	Mantanja (?)	Bittner	Ella Emile	24	Ukiah	WI
Hupp	Roscoe E.	29	Santa Rosa	KS	Hulbert	Laura Irene	20	Santa Rosa	CA
Hurlbert	Fred Yale	47	Petaluma	NY	Curren	Annie	42	Petaluma	CA
Hurlbert	Theron Louis	21	Petaluma		Jones	Estella Amanda	21	Petaluma	
Hurlburt	Robert H.	49	Santa Rosa	MA	Prestwood	Delia	39	Guerneville	NC
Hurlbutt	Willard A.	21	Santa Rosa	CA	Hazelton	Ruth M.	21	Santa Rosa	CA
Hurley	Joseph	30	San Francisco	MA	Ericksen	May	21	San Francisco	CA
Hurley	Thomas F.	31	San Francisco	CA	Dempsey	Mary E.	31	Healdsburg	IRL
Hurst	Leslie E.	58	San Francisco	KY	Roberts	Clara	20	Healdsburg	
Huskey	Everett	21	St. Louis	MO	Forgett	Annabel	20	Santa Rosa	CA

	Groom					Bride			
Surname	Given Name	Age	Residence	BP	Surname	Given Name	Age	Residence	BP
Husler	Edward A.	24	Petaluma	SWT	Myers	Dora M.	21	Petaluma	CA
Huson	Willis O.	50	Healdsburg	IA	Haus	Margaret L. D.	36	San Francisco	IL
Hussa	Walter H.	23	Sebastopol	KS	Donnelly	Elizabeth F.	25	Sebastopol	CA
Hussey	Edward Otis	21	Petaluma	CA	Connolly	Louise Bernidette	22	Petaluma	CA
Hussey	William J.	33	Palo Alto	OH	Fountain	Ethel	30	Santa Rosa	KS
Hussy (?)	Eugene	24	Cloverdale	LA	Clark	Emma Nettie	15	Cloverdale	KS
Hustad	Paul L.	40	Mill Valley	NRY	Kaufman	Elsie M.	40	Mill Valley	GER
Hutchings	Edward Thomas	22	Petaluma	CA	Wilder	Elizabeth Gertrude	19	Petaluma	CA
Hutchins	Horatio				Brown	Mary, Mrs.			
Hutchins	Jasper Lawrence	18	Healdsburg	CA	Duncan	Bessie	18	Healdsburg	CA
Hutchinson	David F.	48	Forestville	NSC	Hutchinson	Clara D.	41	Forestville	MO
Hutchinson	David Kyle	24	Petaluma	Sfo	Lasher	Sarah Lela	17	Petaluma	Modoc, CA
Hutchinson	Edward Lincoln	19	Forestville	CA	Vosilotos	Louisa Agnes	19	Fulton	CA
Hutchinson	F. A.	27	Alexander Valley	MI	Christian	Mary A.	28	Windsor	CA
Hutchinson	Lawrence	23	Mark West	CA	Rich	Rose	19	Windsor	CA
Hutchinson	Oliver A.	32	Santa Rosa		Cartmel	Alice S.	31	Santa Rosa	
Hutchison	Earnest E.	24	Petaluma	CA	Carter	Sarah E.	16	Petaluma	CA
Hutchison	Lawrence	60	Fulton	SCT	Hanson	Eva	58	Santa Rosa	DNK
Hutchison	Lawrence	48	San Francisco	SCT	Bone	Maud, Mrs.	48	Victoria, B. C.	ENG
Hutchison	Lester Earl	20	Yuba City	IA	Hicks	Mary Nunn	21	Santa Rosa	KY
Hutton	Daniel D.	42	Pt. Arena	CA	Gregory	Mary, Mrs.	32	Pt. Arena	DNK
Hutton	George W.	26	Santa Rosa	CA	Crutson	Angeline	38	Santa Rosa	CA
Hyatt	Garrett	38	Petaluma	CND	Henningsen	Johanna, Mrs.	35	Petaluma	CA
Hyatt	John B.	52	Cloverdale		Farmer	Margart, Mrs.	51	Cloverdale	
Hyatt	Robert Roy	26	Petaluma	CA	Gaston	Alta Mae	25	Petaluma	CA
Hyatt	Will Carlton	21	Healdsburg	NE	Wheeler	Nellie Ethel	20	Healdsburg	CA
Hyde	William H., Jr.	38	San Francisco	CA	Hope	E. Claire	24	Sonoma	CA

	Groom					Bride			
Surname	Given Name	Age	Residence	BP	Surname	Given Name	Age	Residence	BP
Hyman	Frank J.	23	Fort Bragg	CA	Ward	Cleone	18	Westport	CA
Hynes	Wm. H.				Gossage	Ellen C.			
Icanberry	John M.	22	Sacramento	MO	Ellison	Edith	22	San Francisco	NE
Icanberry	William M.	21	Santa Rosa	Kansas City, MO	Gage	Mabel	17	Santa Rosa	CA
Ielmorini	Thomas	37	Marshall	SWT	Gambonini	Adeline	25	Petaluma	CA
Igom	Julius Petersen	40	San Francisco	DNK	Nelson	Christina	42	San Francisco	SWD
Ilg	Fred G.	28	San Francisco	CA	Cardoza	Josephine M.	30	Petaluma	CA
Imlay	Loren	25	Honolulu	OH	Smith	Helen M.	25	Mt. Vernon, IA	IA
Imperiale	Gianni D.	21	Preston	CA	Francchia	Josephine	18	Preston	CA
Imrie	George Nicoll	33	Cloverdale	CA	Cooley	Katherine	23	Cloverdale	CA
Ingalls	John C.	30	Healdsburg	CA	Rickman	Amanda J.	24	Healdsburg	CA
Ingalls	John C.	40	Healdsburg	CA	Livemach	Mary F.	30	Healdsburg	CA
Ingersoll	John W.	39	Pinole	CA	Frost	Emma M.	33	San Jose	CA
Ingerson	Lewis Nelson	23	Petaluma	SD	Mellington	Leoleon S.	20	Petaluma	CA
Ingham	A. H.	44	Santa Rosa	MD	Sullivan	Prescella M.	22	Santa Rosa	IN
Ingham	Arthur Blaine	30	Berkeley	IA	Rowell	Helen Hale	23	Sonoma	MN
Ingham	Arthur Cleveland	21	Santa Rosa	CA	Meisner	Hattie	17	Santa Rosa	IL
Ingman	John V.	39	Annapolis	FIN	Porter	Katie May	23	Annapolis	CA
Ingraham	Edgar	48	San Francisco	NY	McCurrie	Madeline E.	40	San Francisco	CA
Ingram	Charles L.	29	Lake Co.		Merritt	Minnie E.	19	Sonoma Co.	
Ingram	Charles W.	21	Austin, Sonoma Co.	Sfo	Ewing	Gertrude	20	San Francisco	Sfo
Ingram	Mercer E.	23	Cloverdale	CA	Hiatt	Madge C.	21	Yorkville	CA
Ingram	William F.	26	Fort Winfield Scott	TN	Stimmel	Cecelia	24	San Francisco	CA
Inman	James Thomas	65	Woodland	MO	Stump	Carrie Annell (?), Mrs.	55	Santa Rosa	CA
Insel	A.	34	Occidental	GER	Traeger	Mary E.	20	Occidental	OH
Ireland	Claude C.	32	Madison, WI	WI	Boxold	Margaret E.	25	Woodland	CA

	Groom					Bride			
Surname	**Given Name**	**Age**	**Residence**	**BP**	**Surname**	**Given Name**	**Age**	**Residence**	**BP**
Ireland	James David	27	Healdsburg	CA	Baker	Annie Elizabeth	27	Healdsburg	WY
Irvin	John H.	28	Windsor	AR	Christy	Myrtle May	26	Seattle	WI
Irving	John J.	26	Sebastopol	ENG	Grearson	Ada	24	Appleton, WI	WI
Irving	Joseph O.	29	San Francisco	ME	Crane	Ella A.	23	Santa Rosa	MO
Irwin	A. W.	25	Geyserville	CA	Moody	Clara J.	21	Geyserville	CA
Irwin	Joseph W.	26	Fisk's Mill	CA	Nobles	Hattie	26	Stewarts Point	CA
Irwin	Nathaniel	28	Rumsey, Yolo Co.	CA	Fan	Lenora	18	Santa Rosa	CA
Irwin	Robert	39	Santa Rosa	CA	Davis	Elma Olive	23	Santa Rosa	CA
Irwin	Thomas Jackson	22	Fisk's Mill	CA	Johnson	Sarah Elizabeth	22	Fisk's Mill	CA
Irwin	William M.	35	Santa Rosa	CA	Wedde	Henrietta	22	Santa Rosa	Sfo
Isaacs	Ernest A.	21	Healdsburg	CA	Archer	Berdena E.	19	Healdsburg	CA
Isaksen	Linfred	28	Portland, OR	MN	Peterson	Christine	24	Santa Rosa	IA
Isbell	Fred E.	30	Santa Rosa	OH	Speegle	Lillian	30	Santa Rosa	CA
Isola	Alphonso	28	Healdsburg	ITL	Arsnip	Sarah	15	Healdsburg	New South Wales, AUT
Itter	William Henry	32	Grand Forks, Yale, B. C.	CND	Mardon	Alta	18	Grand Forks, Yale, B. C.	WA
Ivarson	A. G.	54	Petaluma	SWD	Bergersen	Magdalena	44	Petaluma	SWD
Iversen	Iver Alfred	23	Healdsburg	CA	Sandborn	Vira Ann	23	Healdsburg	MI
Iverson	George	37	Petaluma	DNK	Eliasen	Johanne	40	Petaluma	DNK
Iverson	Louis	30	Petaluma	DNK	Christensen	Karen O. M.	25	Petaluma	DNK
Ives	Alfred	31	Santa Rosa	IN	Nerton	Mattie, Mrs.	31	Santa Rosa	CA
Ives	Alfred	27	Sebastopol	IN	Muller	Amanda Louise	19	Santa Rosa	CA
Ives	William S.	62	Sacramento	VA	Cominos	Johanna	49	Sacramento	IL
Izant	Percy Arthur	25	Santa Cruz	ENG	Jones	Ethel May	22	Petaluma	CA
Jacks	Lorenzo D.	30	Sacramento	OH	Byington	Josephine S.	31	Santa Rosa	CA
Jackson	Amos				Maclath	Mary M.			
Jackson	Andrew	57	San Francisco	OH	Jackson	Mina, Mrs.	50	San Francisco	OH

	Groom				Bride				
Surname	Given Name	Age	Residence	BP	Surname	Given Name	Age	Residence	BP
Jackson	Arthur V.	26	Oakland	NY	Bowe	Josephine	18+	Berkeley	CA
Jackson	Bernard	30	Sacramento	CA	Powers	Nora	38	Sacramento	IRL
Jackson	Bert	28	Healdsburg	CA	Lamonte	Idella	19	Monte Rio	CA
Jackson	Carlisle P.	24	Burke	Wdc	Conners	Nama V.	19	Burke	CA
Jackson	Charles F.	26	Cloverdale	ID	Shelford	Hanna Odessa	24	Cloverdale	CA
Jackson	Clarence S.	21	San Francisco	TN	Bringham	Arvilla May	21	San Francisco	OR
Jackson	E. N. B.				Wilkinson	Eva			
Jackson	Elmer	22	Healdsburg	OR	Smith	Inez L.	21	Healdsburg	CA
Jackson	Frank	25	Vallejo Twp.	CA	Nay	Martha A.	24	Petaluma Twp.	CA
Jackson	Frank	25	Healdsburg	CA	Mason	Tressie B.	16+	Healdsburg	Wat
Jackson	George Samuel	25	San Francisco	CA	Carrillo	Ramona	16	Santa Rosa	CA
Jackson	Guy H.	22	Healdsburg	CA	Gwin	Laura M.	19	Healdsburg	CA
Jackson	Harry E.	24	Healdsburg	CA	Meeker	Clara E.	20	Healdsburg	CA
Jackson	Herbert L.	36	Ukiah	MA	Salmon	Mabel C.	31	Ukiah	MA
Jackson	Hugh L.	31	Glen Ellen	IA	Shader	Nellie	24	Petaluma	IA
Jackson	John B.	45	Camp Vacation, Sonoma Co.	WI	Perkins	Cora	28	Petaluma	KS
Jackson	Luther	26	Healdsburg	KS	Wood	Minnie M.	24	Healdsburg	CA
Jackson	Matt	29	Richmond	AUS	Leon	Louise	27	Richmond	SWT
Jackson	Parker L.	21	Colusa	CA	Harrington	Elise	18	Colusa	CA
Jackson	Roy E.	20	Forestville	OR	Murray	Maud M.	20	Forestville	OK
Jackson	W. Edward	30	Santa Rosa	CA	Lawson	Dorothy B.	21	Santa Rosa	CA
Jackson	William G.	56	Petaluma	AL	Staup	Fannie B., Mrs.	50	Petaluma	IL
Jacob	Thomas	57	Visalia	NY	Burnham	Emily L.	36	Healdsburg	UT
Jacobs	Cameron	24	Santa Rosa	PA	Story	Ida May	20	Santa Rosa	CA
Jacobs	George	22	Healdsburg	CA	Looney	Alice	20	Fulton	CA
Jacobs	James B.	26	Healdsburg	CA	Bailey	Nina E.	19	Healdsburg	IA
Jacobs	Norman Francie	44	San Francisco	IL	Hewald	Elfrida Katherine	31	San Francisco	NZD

	Groom					Bride			
Surname	Given Name	Age	Residence	BP	Surname	Given Name	Age	Residence	BP
Jacobs	Price	23	Alexander Valley		Hooper	Annie T. ?	20	Alexander Valley	
Jacobs	Walter Wyrt	26	San Francisco	CA	Weber	Alma Pearl	19	Santa Rosa	CA
Jacobsen	Frederick	24	Healdsburg	CA	Walker	Katherine E.	19	Healdsburg	CA
Jacobsen	Jacob C.	24	Penngrove	DNK	Nielsen	Anna	21	Petaluma	DNK
Jacobsen	Jacob E.	43	Petaluma	GER	Thomsen	Johanna I.	23	Petaluma	OH
Jacobsen	Jacob E.	24	Petaluma	GER	Martin	Dahmar	20	Petaluma	Soc
Jacobsen	Neils L.	64	Petaluma	DNK	Hoirup	Sine C.	57	Petaluma	DNK
Jacobsen	Niels	52	Berkeley	DNK	Stieper	Mary	53	San Francisco	SWD
Jacobsen	Richard	40	Sebastopol	DNK	Jacobsen	Hansine	22	Sebastopol	DNK
Jacobsen	Thomas S.	21	San Francisco	CA	Tronoff	Helena L.	19	San Francisco	CA
Jacobsen	William Robert	30	San Lorenzo	CA	Grindell	Hazel Evelyn	26	Hayward	CA
Jacobson	Jens	30	San Francisco	NRY	Strome	Hilma	30	Santa Rosa	NRY
Jacobson	Peter N.	33	Turlock	IA	Guerne	Grace E.	26	Santa Rosa	CA
Jacobson	Roy	23	San Francisco	CA	Bressman	Genevieve	20	San Francisco	NY
Jacquot	Alexander C.	60	Novato	FRN	Lineard	Louise I.	50	Novato	FRN
Jaeger	Jacob	44	Fruitvale	SWT	Geisbuhler	Ida	40	Fruitvale	SWT
Jahn	Henry	23	San Francisco	CA	Morrison	Lulu	24	Healdsburg	NY
Jakober	Carl	21	Sonoma	SWT	Kiser	Matilda	26	Sonoma	CA
James	Burnie Edgar	22	Mt. Olivet	TX	Church	May Adeline	16	Mt. Olivet	OK
James	Charles G.	31	Forestville	NY	McCord	Henretta	17	Santa Rosa	MO
James	George A.	34	San Francisco	IN	O'Callaghan	Mary	26	San Francisco	CA
James	Henry W.	25	Suisun Valley	CA	Doggutt	Georgie W.	22	Santa Rosa	CA
James	John P.	47	Healdsburg	CA	Eichler	Ella, Mrs.	21	Newark	CA
James	Orie (?) Edward	31	Santa Rosa	CA	Burgess (?)	Maud Stella	31	Santa Rosa	CA
James	R. L.	39	Santa Rosa	OH	McDougall	Annie	29	Santa Rosa	CND
James	Thos. J.	24	Forestville	MO	Ward	Julia Ann	20	Forestville	CA
James	William A.	26	Soledad	OR	Harding	Jennie L.	18	Soledad	KS
Jameson	Arthur Roy	21	Petaluma	CA	Dahlmann	Georgia Wilma	24	Petaluma	CA

Groom					Bride				
Surname	Given Name	Age	Residence	BP	Surname	Given Name	Age	Residence	BP
Jamieson	B. T.	38	Iowa Hill, Placer Co.	SCT	Watson	Alvania	29	Guerneville	CA
Jamieson	Daniel J.	24	San Francisco	OH	Moller	Thora A.	22	Petaluma	CA
Jamieson	James	42	Annadel, Sonoma Co.	IRL	McQuade	Anna	49	Annadel	IRL
Jamieson	John A.	36	Sacramento	CA	Ehrhardt	Elvesta I.	31	Sacramento	CA
Jamison	H. H.	29	Hayward	CA	Shaver	Carrie I.	26	Petaluma	CA
Jansen	Martin H.	25	Petaluma	GER	Hansen	Rosa L.	25	Petaluma	GER
Jansen	Philip R.	26	Alameda	CA	Scott	Cecilia Esther	26	San Francisco	SCT
Janssen	George	27	Sebastopol	CA	Brown	Lillie	27	Sebastopol	CA
Jardin	Antonio Fernadis	26	Healdsburg	PRT	Pereria	Carrolina Amaro	24	Healdsburg	PRT
Jarred	George Carl	22	Knights Valley	CA	Butler	Clara	23	Porter Creek	CA
Jarvis	Eugene L.	29	Berkeley	CA	Berger	Ruth E.	25	Kenwood	IL
Jarvis	L. B.	39	Berkeley	CA	Berger	Hattie E.	32	Oakland	IL
Jarvis	Morgan	30	Petaluma Twp.	WLS	Nilansen	Hansine Helene	26	Petaluma Twp.	DNK
Jason	Anton	24	Petaluma	CA	Switzer	Beryl	20	Sonoma	CA
Jason	Frank	32	Petaluma	CA	Alves	Amelia	18	Petaluma	PRT
Jasper	Gustavus A.	22	Santa Rosa	MA	Wells	Alice Maud	17	Santa Rosa	IL
Jasper	Joseph John	26	Mark West Springs	GER	Rasmussen	Sigris	22	Mark West Springs	NRY
Jauke	Carl August	33	San Francisco	CA	Reubold	Emma Antoinette	24	San Francisco	CA
Java	M. Murin (?)	37	Duncans Mills	IRL	Schultz	Anna	24	Duncans Mills	GER
Jayer (?)	Mentin (?)	23	Petaluma		Fouts	Emma A.	20	Petaluma	
Jeans	Newton	68	Santa Rosa	KY	Baird	Mary	63	Santa Rosa	IA
Jeffery	Renaldo J.	29	Stockton	CA	Gould	Gladys V.	28	Petaluma	CA
Jeffress	James V.	25	Oakland	CA	Paget	Lulu G.	20	San Francisco	CA
Jeffress	John K.	22	Oakland	CA	Paget	Susie H.	19	San Francisco	CA
Jeffreys	Thomas Leland	25	Sycamore, CA	CA	Schoonover	Ethel Verda	20	Santa Rosa	CA
Jelbert	Richard H.	23	Lead, SD	SD	Alves	Gladys Clark	21	Forestville	CA

	Groom					Bride			
Surname	Given Name	Age	Residence	BP	Surname	Given Name	Age	Residence	BP
Jenkines	James H.	33	Valley Ford	WV	Weeks	Anna M.	29	Petaluma	CA
Jenkins	Allen	27	Los Angeles	CA	Pickens	Mary	38	Los Angeles	OH
Jenkins	Arthur G.	34	Santa Rosa	CA	Dunbar	Carrie B.	28	Santa Rosa	NV
Jenkins	Charles Francis	36	San Francisco	CA	Jones	Hazel Ann	26	San Francisco	CA
Jenkins	Edgar W.	22	Healdsburg	WLS	Eslick	Ida B.	19	Healdsburg	MO
Jenkins	Frederich G.	23	Santa Rosa	Soc.	Glatfelder	Lenora M.	21	Santa Rosa	Mon
Jenkins	Gilbert C.	45	Santa Rosa	NSC	Watkins	Nellie	36	Santa Rosa	ENG
Jenkins	Gilbert C.	68	Santa Rosa	NSC	Grodhauser	Mary	58	Chicago	GER
Jenkins	Gilbert C.	62	Santa Rosa	NSC	Bergmann	Mary R.	43	Crocker	WI
Jenkins	Henry	31	Santa Rosa	CA	Liggett	Ora May	16	Santa Rosa	CA
Jenkins	Henry R.	20	Santa Rosa	CA	Kimes	Ethel A. (Mandy)	17	Santa Rosa	CA
Jenkins	Joseph	30	San Francisco	OR	Folts	Kathryn Laura Frances	23	San Francisco	LA
Jenkins	Joseph L.	25	Tomales	KY	Moore	J. Maud	22	Tomales	OH
Jenkins	Joseph Warren	26	Santa Rosa	OR	Platt	Blanch Elizabeth	24	Santa Rosa	NE
Jenkins	William L.	27	Santa Rosa	OR	Lafferty	Mary E.	26	Santa Rosa	CA
Jenne	Christian J.	38	San Francisco	KY	Unger	Daphne E.	21	San Francisco	CA
Jennet	Newel	29	Coalinga	KS	Jones	Rhoda L.	23	Santa Rosa	Occidental
Jennings	C. S.	50	Spokane, WA	OH	Belgum	Marie	36	Welders (?), WI	WI
Jennings	Edward B.	38	San Francisco	CA	True	Eliza W.	28	San Francisco	CA
Jennings	John	34	San Francisco	CA	Brennan	Florence M.	28	San Francisco	CA
Jennison	Alfred M.	29	Santa Rosa	IA	Boswell	Clara J.	29	Santa Rosa	CA
Jensen	Alexander	28	Guerneville	DNK	Patton	Edna	25	Guerneville	IL
Jensen	Alfred J. P.	30	Guerneville	CA	Kricke	Louisa Mary	22	Duncans Mills	CA
Jensen	August Adolph	22	Dry Creek	CA	Wilson	Ethel Claire	26	Windsor	CA
Jensen	Christ.	30	Dry Creek	DNK	Christophersen	Josephine	21	Dry Creek	MN
Jensen	Creston H.	25	Berkeley	DNK	Millerick	Helen E.	26	Shellville	CA

	Groom					Bride			
Surname	Given Name	Age	Residence	BP	Surname	Given Name	Age	Residence	BP
Jensen	Fred P.	31	Petaluma Twp.	GER	Geertz	Willhelmine C.	30	Petaluma Twp.	GER
Jensen	Fred Peter	50	Penngrove	GER	Parkinson	Rosa L.	49	Penngrove	IA
Jensen	George P.	27	Santa Rosa	CA	Ross	Lottie J.	19	Santa Rosa	CA
Jensen	Hans P.	32	Pt. Reyes	MI	Fairbanks	Loretta Louise	27	Petaluma	CA
Jensen	John P.	28	Berkeley	NY	Gilson	Frieda L.	24	Oakland	OR
Jensen	Niels	24	Tomales	GER	Kjar	Helene	20	Petaluma	GER
Jensen	Peter	23	Petaluma	IA	Hansen	Ingeborg Marie	19	Petaluma	CA
Jensen	Victor	20	Petaluma	IA	Decker	Emma J.	20	Petaluma	Sfo
Jenson	Albert L.	23	San Francisco	MN	Carsin	Margaret L.	26	Cazadero	CA
Jentzsch	Carl Waldemar	25	San Francisco	Berlin, GER	Murphy	Mabel Mary	18	Petaluma	Covelo
Jepsen	Otto A.	30	San Francisco	CA	Robinson	Irma G.	25	San Francisco	NV
Jepsen	Peter	27	Glen Ellen	GER	Mattison	Mary	22	Glen Ellen	GER
Jepson	Hans Alfred	29	Boonville	GER	Jensen	Lillian Johanna	18	Petaluma	CA
Jerden	Arthur G.	26	Oakland	CO	Monsees	Jessie L.	22	Oakland	CA
Jessen	Adolph	24	Sonoma	CA	La Vallee	Archange	21	Sonoma	CA
Jessen	Christopher B.	24	Petaluma	OH	Latson	Rosilla	23	Petaluma	CA
Jessen	Emil Thomas M.	23	Petaluma	OH	Wilson	Margaret Jane	22	Petaluma	MN
Jessen	Frank Edward	25	Petaluma	OH	Clawsen	Minnie Josine	20	Petaluma	GER
Jessen	Julius Theodore	23	Petaluma	OH	Clausen	Magdalena	21	Petaluma	GER
Jessen	Paul Frederick	29	Petaluma	OH	Towner	Myrtle June	22	Petaluma	CA
Jessup	Charlie W.	35	Windsor	IN	Lloyd	Hattie F.	30	Windsor	CA
Jewell	Jesse I.	30	Santa Rosa	CA	Brackett	Fannie E.	22	Petaluma	CA
Jewell	John Francis	39	San Francisco	CA	Schulz	Elsie Anna	26	San Francisco	GER
Jewett	Augustus Leroy	22	Santa Rosa	CA	Torliatt	Theresa	18	Petaluma	CA
Jewett	Frank W.	23	Santa Rosa	CA	Kennedy	Eva G.	24	Santa Rosa	NV
Jewett	Joseph Carl	27	Forestville	CA	Cooper	Hazel Grace	19	Santa Rosa	CA
Jinks	William Woods	22	Healdsburg	WA	Bartlow	Mary Elizabeth	16	Healdsburg	CA
Jobe	Alfred Ewing	25	Galt, Sacramento Co.	CA	Hillyer	Lillian Belle	23	Santa Rosa	CA

	Groom					Bride			
Surname	Given Name	Age	Residence	BP	Surname	Given Name	Age	Residence	BP
Jobe	Thomas F.	32	Burke	CA	Tomasi	Linda O.	29	Burke	CA
Jobe	Thomas Frederick	24	Exeter, Tulare Co.	CA	Dabney	Rose Zelma	24	Sebastopol	IA
Johannes	Herman	53	Richland, NE	GER	Koegler	Elisabeth	39	San Anselmo	GER
Johannsen	Clyde M.	23	Vallejo	CA	Williams	Ethel	23	Glen Ellen	CA
Johannsen	Edward Henry	24	Sonoma	Sfo	LaVine	Adelaide	17	Agua Caliente	Son
Johannsen	George Henry	26	San Francisco	CA	Pedersen	Meta Marien	21	Petaluma	CA
Johansan	Axel A.	34	San Francisco	RUS	Cohn	Anna	34	San Francisco	NJ
John	Charley	31	Santa Rosa		Youh (?)	M.	31	Santa Rosa	
John	Gregory				Casey	Catharine			
Johns	Cecil D.	21+	Santa Rosa	CA	Wilson	Bertha L.	18+	Windsor	CA
Johns	Frank M.	24	Sebastopol	OR	Coon	Stella L.	17	Forestville	CA
Johns	Frederick	40	San Francisco	CA	Blanck	Katherine M.	29	Santa Rosa	CA
Johns	Harvey Raymond	28	Sebastopol	WI	Banks	Helen Grace	23	Sebastopol	WA
Johns	Robert C.	31	Oakland	ENG	Jensen	Alma C.	25	Oakland	CA
Johns	Watson L.	29	Healdsburg	CA	Collister	Vivienne E.	20	Santa Rosa	CA
Johnson	A. R.	23	Boonville	CA	Burger	Alta	19	Boonville	CA
Johnson	Adolph	30	San Francisco	SWD	Cole	Elsie Rachel	20	Annapolis	CA
Johnson	Alfred R.	33	Santa Rosa	SWD	Shooks	Sarah	20	Santa Rosa	NV
Johnson	Andrew E.	23	Alexander Valley	MO	Bidwell	M. Callie	17	Alexander Valley	CA
Johnson	Archibald M.	24	San Francisco	IN	Clover	Minnie C.	23	Forestville	CA
Johnson	Charles D. G.	30	Santa Rosa	TN	Graeter	Emma	24	Santa Rosa	CA
Johnson	Charles L.	30	Healdsburg	SWD	Coffer	Lucy A.	25	Healdsburg	ME
Johnson	Charles W.	27	Mare Island	OR	Reynolds	Ida M.	29	San Francisco	KY
Johnson	Claude E.	28	San Francisco	CA	Cheney	Clara	25	Sonoma	CA
Johnson	Cornelius M.	25	Healdsburg	MO	Cox	Alice Almira	21	Healdsburg	CA
Johnson	D. W.	28	Forestville	IN	Banks	Emma A.	25	Forestville	OR
Johnson	David A.	33	Salt Point Twp.		Miller	Julia	23	Salt Point Twp.	
Johnson	David E.	24	Santa Rosa	NE	McReynolds	Delia	24	Sebastopol	CA

	Groom					Bride			
Surname	Given Name	Age	Residence	BP	Surname	Given Name	Age	Residence	BP
Johnson	David Q.	32	Santa Rosa	IL	Ballou	Margaret J.	29	Santa Rosa	CA
Johnson	Demus Gale	22	Petaluma	CA	Hanlon	Mae Elizabeth	18	Petaluma	CA
Johnson	Dudley H.	29	Mendocino Twp.	TN	Blank	Ismpie (?)	21	Mendocino Twp.	CA
Johnson	Edwin L.	21	Sonoma	CA	Saylor	Fern L.	17	Shellville	KS
Johnson	Elmo A.	21	Healdsburg	MO	Daniels	Lula M.	25	Cloverdale	OR
Johnson	Ernest	42	San Francisco	KY	Lauteren	Gertrude C.	37	Guerneville	CA
Johnson	Frank Eugene	22	Petaluma	CA	Park	Edith Rae	23	Petaluma	CA
Johnson	Frederick	30	Petaluma	CA	Kemper	Josephine	18	Petaluma	CA
Johnson	Geo. A.	26	Healdsburg	MO	Matthews	Frances B.	24	Healdsburg	CA
Johnson	George C.	31	San Francisco	ENG	Bona	Annie E.	31	San Francisco	CA
Johnson	George W.	25	Sebastopol	CA	Guntly	Lizzie	21	Guerneville	CA
Johnson	Glen	26	Santa Rosa	CA	Wilson	Helen	24	Ukiah	CA
Johnson	Gus Charles	33	Petaluma	CA	Schrub	Evlyn Violet	18	Petaluma	CA
Johnson	Gus Charles	37	Petaluma	CA	McCutcheon	Elizabeth	43	Petaluma	IN
Johnson	Harrick T.	25	Eureka	CA	Baker	Ethel F.	32	Eureka	CA
Johnson	Harry	21	Sebastopol	CA	Johns	Stella	18	Sebastopol	CA
Johnson	Henry	47	Petaluma	SWI	Wagenblast	Alice E.	29	Petaluma	OR
Johnson	Henry Lee	30	Bloomfield	CA	Shreeve	Angie	17	Freestone	OR
Johnson	Howard B.	22	Forestville	CA	Smith	Sadie V.	18	Guerneville	CA
Johnson	James	21	Sacramento	CA	McIntosh	Clara	22	Oakland	MO
Johnson	James E.	35	Martinez	CA	McGlynn	Alice A.	29	Petaluma	CA
Johnson	James F.	21	Alameda	WI	Rose	Clara I.	19	Oakland	CA
Johnson	James George, Jr.	21	Windsor		Rosetta	Alice	19	Windsor	
Johnson	James W.	44	Santa Rosa	MO	Lee	Emma	24	Santa Rosa	NY
Johnson	John				Crilly	Anna Francis	17		
Johnson	John A.	31	Santa Rosa	SWD	Phelps	Bessie E.	23	Santa Rosa	NZD
Johnson	John Berger	21	Armona, CA	NE	Bond	Jessie Mae	27	Hessel	CA
Johnson	John Christian	31	Santa Rosa	DNK	Gardener	Edith Luella	34	Santa Rosa	CA
Johnson	John F.	33	Sebastopol	UT	Fredricks	Carrie	24	Sebastopol	CA

| | Groom | | | | | Bride | | | |
Surname	Given Name	Age	Residence	BP	Surname	Given Name	Age	Residence	BP
Johnson	John H.	34	Mendocino City	NRY	Gunner	Anna	34	Mendocino	CA
Johnson	John Leroy	24	Healdsburg	CA	Roberts	Lucy M.	25	Healdsburg	CA
Johnson	John P.	23	Bodega Twp		Murroy	Mary R.	19	Bodega Twp.	
Johnson	John W.	22	Santa Rosa	CA	Jacobson	Marie E.	19	Santa Rosa	CA
Johnson	Karl V?klar (?)	32	Petaluma	FIN	Smith	Nellie E.	26	Petaluma	CA
Johnson	L. M.				Marshall	Elizabeth Ann			
Johnson	L. M.				Marshall	Elizabeth Ann			
Johnson	Louis Webseter	19	Forestville	CA	Hull	Edna Odell	19	Forestville	MN
Johnson	Martin	22	Bloomfield	CA	Barnett	Nettie J.	19	Pleasant Hill	CA
Johnson	Martin L.	24	Santa Rosa	CA	Ruddock	Kittie M.	22	Santa Rosa	CA
Johnson	Milton H.	29	San Francisco	OH	Andrews	Lucile M.	25	San Francisco	CA
Johnson	Nels A.	22	Hanford	NE	Wheeler	Vera	20	Healdsburg	CA
Johnson	Ober J.	27	San Francisco	OH	Barry	Alice E.	19	Berkeley	CA
Johnson	Okey	21	Geyserville	WA	Robbins	Myrtle	17	Windsor	CA
Johnson	Omar H.	20	Graton	CA	Daniels	Myrtle A.	17	Sebastopol	KS
Johnson	Otto H.	37	Santa Rosa		McQuart	Emily	35	San Francisco	
Johnson	Otto Henry	61	San Francisco	SWD	Seabright	Elice	34	San Francisco	IRL
Johnson	Peter S.	45	San Francisco	SWD	Miller	Emma C.	42	San Francisco	CA
Johnson	Phillip F.	29	Olympia, WA	WA	Gilmore	Cassie B.	19	Guerneville	CA
Johnson	Ray I.	22	Forestville	CA	Ristan	Edna M.	17	Sebastopol	CA
Johnson	Raymond	23	Santa Rosa	MI	Kriedell	Elsie	21	Santa Rosa	CA
Johnson	Robert N.	46	Cloverdale	MO	Cavanough	Nettie A.	36	Fort Bragg	PA
Johnson	Samuel K.	37	Biggs, Butte Co.	TN	Johnson	Evie, Mrs.	34	Redding	CA
Johnson	Thomas J.	26	Guerneville	IN	Crawford	Sarah J.	22	Occidental	CND
Johnson	Vernon L.	21	Santa Rosa	MI	Kennedy	Ethel L.	21	Hilton	KS
Johnson	Walter J.	23	Sonoma	CA	Comaich	Louise	23	Sonoma	CA
Johnson	Webster	33	Modesto	IL	Smith	Sylvia Lee	31	Modesto	CA
Johnson	Will E.	25	Santa Rosa	CA	Heinrich	Matilda C.	21	Santa Rosa	IA
Johnson	William	39	Salt Point		Lusk	Kate	34	Salt Point	
Johnson	William A.	23	San Francisco	CA	May	Delia A.	19	Cloverdale	IRL

	Groom					Bride			
Surname	Given Name	Age	Residence	BP	Surname	Given Name	Age	Residence	BP
Johnson	William B.	29	San Francisco	MA	Carle (?)	Catherine R.	20	San Francisco	CA
Johnson	William R.	28	Santa Rosa	KS	Ross	Viola A.	20	Santa Rosa	CA
Johnson	Williard H.	29	San Francisco	IL	Chevalier	Marguerite	29	San Francisco	FRN
Johnston	Alexander C.	35	Hamlet, Marin Co.	NV	Nutter	Lizzie A.	22	Petaluma	VA
Johnston	Charles B.	42	Los Angeles	SC	Goodspeed	Georgia, Mrs.	27	Healdsburg	NY
Johnston	Richard I.	43	Santa Rosa	MO	Ballard	Effie E., Mrs.	34	Santa Rosa	CA
Johnston	Wm. F.				McCorkle	Mary M.			
Johnstone	Ralph S.	38	Honolulu	Hon	Ross	Sue A.	35	Santa Rosa	CND
Johnstone	Thomas Henry	28	Eagleville		Mills	Anna Margrett	23	Bloomfield	
Johr ?	Carlton				Gott	Nancy			
Jones	Alfred Benoia	22	Healdsburg	KY	Mothorn	Herma Booth	21	Healdsburg	CA
Jones	Alvie N.	24	Santa Rosa	WA	Makee	Alvia C.	23	Fulton	CA
Jones	Brainerd	31	Petaluma	IL	Gibson	Jeanette S.	25	Petaluma	CA
Jones	Cethil	26	San Francisco	KS	Day	Laura	24	Healdsburg	IA
Jones	Charles	40	Healdsburg		Dorman	Sarah Ada	18	near Healdsburg	
Jones	Charles H.	21	Santa Rosa		Morter	Hattie	19	Santa Rosa	
Jones	Charles W.	28	Sebastopol	TX	Warden	Ella M.	25	Sebastopol	WA
Jones	Claude O.	26	Petaluma	CA	Hall	Georgia May	21	Petaluma	MI
Jones	Clifford W.	26	San Francisco	CA	Shaw	Gertrude M.	18	Cloverdale	CA
Jones	Earl Petwin	24	Santa Rosa	IL	Shinn	Annie	18	Santa Rosa	IL
Jones	Edward Robert	29	Petaluma	NV	Adams	Iva May	26	Petaluma	CA
Jones	Edward T.	26	Santa Rosa	CA	Darden	Rosa Belle	17	Santa Rosa	OR
Jones	Ervon	23	Petaluma	CA	Olts	Myrtle	20	Petaluma	CA
Jones	Evan	45	Hamilton, OH	IN	Yager	Barbara	34	Portland, OR	OR
Jones	George B.	26	Healdsburg	CA	Reilly	Zel G.	34	Healdsburg	CA
Jones	George F.	32	Santa Rosa	CA	Wood	Alta L.	21	Santa Rosa	CA
Jones	George H.	26	Sonoma Co.	IL	Lowe	Jennie E.	32	Whitesboro, Mendocino Co.	CA

	Groom					Bride			
Surname	Given Name	Age	Residence	BP	Surname	Given Name	Age	Residence	BP
Jones	George H.	30	San Francisco	VA	Isenburg	Hazel G.	30	San Francisco	CA
Jones	George Richard	33	Bloomfield	CA	Davison	Bertha Olive	18	Bloomfield	KS
Jones	Harlold M.	31	Cloverdale	Eureka, CA	Shaw	Ella L.	24	Cloverdale	Red Bluff
Jones	Henry	24	Dry Creek	CA	Derrick	Lydia	18	Dry Creek Valley	CA
Jones	Henry M.	42	Santa Rosa	KS	Yeager	Eulalia M.	23	San Francisco	SC
Jones	Homer A.	24	Windsor	WLS	Allen	Mattie M.	22	Petaluma	NY
Jones	Houston	31	Healdsburg	IA	Reynolds	Bertha	19	Healdsburg	IL
Jones	James L.	31	Mountain View	CA	Brown	Leatha M.	28	Healdsburg	SD
Jones	James Lloyd	40	Oakland	KY	Peterson	Elizaabeth Cordelia	31	San Francisco	KY
Jones	John P.	23	Altruria	CA	Burke	Mabel P.	22	Altruria	CA
Jones	Joseph C.	52	Guerneville	NH	Lynch	Frances A., Mrs.	43	San Francisco	WI
Jones	Josiah	21	Suisun		Barnes	Sarah Baronetta	18		
Jones	Lester	26	San Francisco	CA	Purrington	Ethel	25	Graton	CA
Jones	Lewis E.	21	San Mateo	CA	Cook	Daisy M.	20	Santa Rosa	CA
Jones	Lewis Eugene	23	Healdsburg	CA	Upson	Ella Evaline	18	Healdsburg	CA
Jones	Lucas M.	37	Healdsburg	Soc	Hollingsworth	Mabel	38	Willits	CA
Jones	Lyman C.	21	Sacramento	CA	Hollar	Harriet Ethel	17	Sonoma Co.	NE
Jones	McMillan	30	Carlin, Elko Co., NV	IL	Gilbert	Caroline	28	Santa Rosa	IA
Jones	Milton	26	San Francisco	CA	Hansen	Mary C.	21	Vallejo Twp.	CA
Jones	Nathan H.	20	Petaluma	CA	Atkinson	Mary M.	28	Petaluma	KS
Jones	Noah	23	Occidental	ENG	Beedle	Bella	21	Occidental	CA
Jones	Oscar R.	21	Santa Rosa	CA	Clos	Rose L.	18	Santa Rosa	UT
Jones	Parker W.	49	Oakland	OH	Peachey	Julia H.	43	Oakland	Oak
Jones	Patrick C.	30	Freestone	CA	Mullally	Catherine E.	24	Freestone	CA
Jones	Richard	24	Forestville	ENG	Burgess	Mary Alice	24	Forestville	CA
Jones	Richard H.	55	Bloomfield	WLS	Jones	Martha, Mrs.	49	Bloomfield	IRL

	Groom					Bride			
Surname	Given Name	Age	Residence	BP	Surname	Given Name	Age	Residence	BP
Jones	Samuel	43	Santa Rosa	ENG	Koch	Kate Anna	37	Santa Rosa	MO
Jones	Seth W.	26	Petaluma	OR	Minch	Marguerite W.	19	Bloomfield	CA
Jones	Smith Petitt	29	Santa Rosa	CA	Gilmer	Eulalia	23	Santa Rosa	MO
Jones	Thomas A.	25	Windsor	MO	Cozine	Charlotte M.	27	Oakland	CA
Jones	Thomas W.	31	Santa Rosa	OH	Lee	Helen L.	23	Elko, NV	MO
Jones	Walter	40	Bloomfield	CA	Knapp	Alice B., Mrs.	39	Bloomfield	CA
Jones	William	38	Sonoma	WLS	Hansberg	Catherine	39	Sonoma	IRL
Jones	William Farrington	29	San Rafael	CA	Irwin	Mettie M.	29	San Rafael	NY
Jones	William H.	29	Santa Rosa	ENG	Keiser	Lena M.	24	Santa Rosa	CA
Jones	William H.	46	Vacaville	KY	Dabney	Melissa M.	51	Sebastopol	IA
Jones	William L.	73	Pomona	ME	Armstrong	Elizabeth	50	Cloverdale	OH
Joosten	Fred W.	31	Santa Rosa	GER	Maas	Helene	34	Santa Rosa	GER
Joppini	Joseph	35	Santa Rosa Twp.	SWT	Rhigetti	Velina	34	Santa Rosa Twp.	SWT
Jordan	Harvey S.	34	Seattle	ID	O'Meara	Julia A.	26	Santa Rosa	OR
Jordon	Addison D.				Westenhaver	M. E.			
Jorgensen	Anton M.	30	Petaluma	CA	Schroeder	Anna M.	23	Petaluma	CA
Jorgensen	Harry I.	33	Petaluma	CA	Uhlenberg	Catherine M.	22	Petaluma	GER
Jorgensen	John	29	Petaluma	CA	Rasmussen	Nell	21	Petaluma	CA
Jorgensen	Julius	23	Fulton	DNK	Clark	Eva R.	20	Fulton	CA
Jorgensen	Robert	22	Agua Caliente	CA	Giesen	Elsa	21	Fruitvale	CA
Jorgenson	Peter C.	38	Santa Rosa	DNK	Sinclair	Clara M.	33	Oakland	CA
Joseph	Alfred Peter	25	Petaluma	Haf	James	Hattie	21+	Petaluma	IA
Joseph	Joe William	23	Petaluma	CA	Chandler	Ethel	19	Petaluma	CA
Joseph	Tony Peters	26	Petaluma	CA	Williams	Mary	26	Petaluma	CA
Joseph	William	26	Newark	CA	Irwin	Gladys	19	Berkeley	CA
Josephson	Frederick	34	Mare Island	SWD	Madsen	Emelie	24	Santa Rosa	DNK
Josselyn	Joel S.	38	San Francisco	CA	Andrews	Carrie E.	25	Santa Rosa	CA
Jossler	Chris	24	Hopland	SWT	Davaz	Agnes	22	Hopland	SWT

	Groom					Bride			
Surname	**Given Name**	**Age**	**Residence**	**BP**	**Surname**	**Given Name**	**Age**	**Residence**	**BP**
Jouker (?)	G. G.	26	Santa Rosa	CND	Lambert	Nevada	26	Santa Rosa	CA
Joy	William H.	65	Healdsburg	NY	Wieberts	Kate, Mrs.	35	Healdsburg	IL
Joyce	George E.	27	San Francisco	CA	Regli	Frances	17	San Francisco	CA
Judd	Charles A.	57	San Francisco	MA	Wheeler	Julie	25	San Francisco	IL
Judd	Percy L.	30	Santa Rosa	CO	Fredericksen	Laura B.	24	Santa Rosa	CA
Judsen	George Franklin	23	Bloomfield		Menefee	Victoria	18+	Santa Rosa	
Juler	George Albert	26	San Francisco	ENG	Bond	Bertha Elizabeth	25	Santa Rosa	CA
Julin	Adolf	44	near Santa Rosa	SWD	O'Neil	Susan, Mrs.	40	near Santa Rosa	OH
June	H. J.	22	Cloverdale	NE	Vestal	Blossom	20	Cloverdale	CA
Junge	Walter Frederick	24	San Francisco	CA	Bischoff	Albertine Louise	19	San Francisco	GER
Junge	Albert Frank Henry	29	San Francisco	CA	Rust	Madeval Pearl	25	San Francisco	NY
Junker	Clarence M.	25	San Francisco	CA	Payne	Mary	27	San Francisco	CA
Jurd	Andrew J.	23	Healdsburg	IA	Adams	Rose A.	21	Healdsburg	IA
Jurs	Louis	54	Santa Rosa	GER	Wollitz	Leopoldine Christine	45	Santa Rosa	GER
Justi	William Alfred	23	Santa Rosa	Sfo	Roberts	Laura Lavina	18	Santa Rosa	Napa
Justice	Augustus Lorenzo	36	Cloverdale	CA	Stevens	Emma Edith	20	Cloverdale	IA
Justine	Frank	22	Petaluma	CA	Perry	Gussie	17	Petaluma	CA
Juzix	Chester L.	23	San Francisco	CA	Nunes	Mary A.	20	Petaluma	CA
Kaelin	Edward	33	Santa Rosa	SWT	Huber	Amalia	19	Santa Rosa	GER
Kahler	William T.	30	Cazadero	IL	Moseley	Lilly Olive	18	Mercury	CA
Kahrs	Leander A.	23	Santa Rosa	OH	Lind	Alma B.	18	Santa Rosa	CA
Kahrs	Lee A.	28	Healdsburg	OH	Gully	Ibie	27	Healdsburg	CA
Kaiser	Frank M.	27	Oakland	CA	Schwab	Clare L.	26	Healdsburg	CA
Kaiser	William Henry, Jr.	25	San Francisco	AR	Starke	Agatha Augusta	25	Petaluma	CA
Kalb	August L.	30	Healdsburg	MO	Parsons	Mary E., Mrs.	26	Healdsburg	WA
Kalish	William G.	38	Petaluma	CA	Husler	Lena M.	35	Petaluma	SWT

	Groom				Bride				
Surname	Given Name	Age	Residence	BP	Surname	Given Name	Age	Residence	BP
Kammeyer	Erich M.	32	Chula Vista	GER	Luttrell	Leita Lorine	24	Santa Rosa	KS
Kamp	Daniel W.	33	Petaluma	CA	Wergand	Loretta M.	27	Petaluma	CA
Kane	John J.	32	Reno, NV	IRL	Ross	Julia	22	Freestone	IRL
Kane	John W.	27	Giffords Mill, Sonoma Co.		Stone	Judith A.	17+	Giffords Mill, Sonoma Co.	
Kane	Thomas	21	Petaluma	IRL	Bauer	Valesea C.	19	San Francisco	CA
Kanode	John O.	21	Graton	VA	Stouder	Helen M.	22	Graton	CA
Karcher	Myron M.	27	Napa	CA	Thompson	Cecile C.	19	Napa	CA
Karnes	Ernest	22	Santa Rosa	MN	Steger	Daisy	18	Santa Rosa	WI
Karnes	Forest V.	19	Santa Rosa	WI	Johnson	Lizzie May	19	Santa Rosa	CA
Karnes	Percy	19	Santa Rosa	CA	Ward	Nellie Lorain	19	Santa Rosa	MO
Karpfenstein	Jacob	26	Santa Rosa	RUS	Schatz	Magdelena	23	Santa Rosa	RUS
Karr	Bert M.	34	Penngrove	GER	Snyder	Carrie	25	Bennett Valley	IA
Kastens	Herman J. C.	31	San Francisco	GER	Pfile	Clara A.	31	Oakland	CA
Katen	William L.	21	Petaluma	CA	Tozer	Iva M.	17	Petaluma	OR
Kathriner	Paul	29	Petaluma	SWT	Kiser	Josephine	23	Santa Rosa	CA
Katterfield	Julius Charles Peter	30	Healdsburg	GER	Cunningham	Jennie	22	Sebastopol	MD
Katz	Harry H.	24	San Francisco	CA	Murphy	Frances M.	21	San Francisco	CA
Katz	Robert	28	San Francisco	RUS	Pinkus	Tillie	21	San Francisco	NY
Kauffman	John	27	Santa Rosa	IL	McPhee	Kattie	25	Santa Rosa	CND
Kavanagh	James	47	San Francisco	IRL	Morrisey	Margaret	34	San Francisco	GA
Kaye	Charles Ivan	28	Cloverdale	CA	Thompson	Thelma Gertrude	18	Cloverdale	CA
Kayser	Albert H. L.	30	Alexander Valley	GER	Seeman	Bertha	26	Alexander Valley	GER
Kean	J. B.	60	Santa Rosa	NJ	Wilson	Serena A.	39	Santa Rosa	IL
Keane	Frederick J.	23	San Francisco	CA	Kenyon	Alice	32	San Francisco	ENG
Kearns	James	23	Kenwood	CA	Hespe	Mabel Augusta	21	Kenwood	CA
Keating	William Joseph	49	Vallejo	NY	Brown	Cecilia Frances	45	Sacramento	PA
Keaton	John J.	32	Forestville		Phinney	Harriet	19	Forestville	

	Groom				Bride				
Surname	**Given Name**	**Age**	**Residence**	**BP**	**Surname**	**Given Name**	**Age**	**Residence**	**BP**
Keaton	Wheeler M.	27	Forestville	IN	Clover	Martha J.	18	Forestville	CA
Kee	George Hamilton	23	Bodega	CA	Dodge	Alice Mae	19	Occidental	CA
Kee	James H.	26	Bodega	CA	Patterson	Tony	18	Occidental	CA
Kee	James Hamilton	40	Bodega	CA	Banks	Maud Eveline	30	Forestville	WA
Keechler	Bloss F.	39	Sonoma	CA	Alexander	Lily M.	21	Santa Rosa	CA
Keefe	Jack S.	28	San Francisco	MN	Kaiser	Grace	18	San Francisco	CA
Keefe	Thomas	35	Bodega	CA	Lenihan	Elsie Mae	27	Petaluma	IRL
Keegan	William D.	33	Sebastopol	CA	Payne	Adelia M.	27	Santa Rosa	NE
Keeler	Nedwyn	19	Santa Rosa	IN	Stearns	Edythe Belle	18	Santa Rosa	CA
Keeley	Thomas H.	43	San Francisco	NY	Norris	Celia E.	42	San Francisco	VT
Keeling	Frederick	36	Vancouver, B. C.	ENG	Temple	Mary Hutton	31	Santa Rosa	CA
Keenan	George	23	Santa Rosa	CND	Ansbro	Sabrina	21	Santa Rosa	MN
Keenan	Peter	33	San Francisco	CA	McGoldrich	Mary T.	26	Petaluma	Sfo
Keenan	Walter H.	21	San Francisco	CA	Clement	Loma (?)	18	El Verano	CA
Keener	John E.	20	Santa Rosa		Lewis	Rachal E.	22	Santa Rosa	
Keig	William C.	29	Petaluma	CA	Ackerman	Harriet B.	30	Petaluma	CA
Keig	William C.	37	Petaluma	CA	Graham	Alice G.	25	Petaluma	CA
Keig	William S.	43	Berkeley	NV	Zeller	Stella R.	26	Oil City, PA	PA
Keim	Frederick C.	45	Oakland	CA	Rider	Marie	38	Oakland	CA
Keir	Sherwin	28	San Francisco	CA	McNabb	B. M.	32	Los Angeles	CA
Keirn (?)	Henry W.	26	Los Angeles		Stump	Martha E.	17+	Santa Rosa	
Keiser	Joseph	34	Petaluma	CA	Garzoli	Dora H.	27	Penngrove	CA
Keithly	Seth T.				Pugh	Sarah A.			
Keleher	Wm. Thomas	26	Santa Rosa		O'Connor	Nora	22	Santa Rosa	
Kelleher	Cornelius	35	Napa Junction	IRL	Foley	Mary Josie	26	Santa Rosa	IRL
Keller	Charley C.	26	Santa Rosa	CA	Brisino	Mabel	20	Oakland	CA
Keller	J. Bryant	24	Lakeport	SD	Ward	Gertrude	22	Cloverdale	WA
Keller	John	30	Healdsburg	CA	Burgett	Laura	20	Healdsburg	CA
Keller	John Claus	30	Petaluma	CA	Clanton	Victoria Alice	16	Petaluma	CA

	Groom					Bride			
Surname	**Given Name**	**Age**	**Residence**	**BP**	**Surname**	**Given Name**	**Age**	**Residence**	**BP**
Keller	Peter	28	Oakland	Heidelberg, GER	Albers	Emma	25	Santa Rosa	IA
Keller	Vernon E.	21	Santa Rosa	IA	MacUrton	Ethel	18	Santa Rosa	CA
Kelley	George F.	21	Healdsburg	CA	Nelson	Violet	20	Healdsburg	CA
Kelley	John Asbery	29	San Francisco	MO	Rupprecht	Mary Annie	22	Petaluma	IL
Kellner	Harold C.	30	Napa	CA	Chapman	Martha	23	Napa	CA
Kellogg	Edward L.	50	Santa Rosa	CA	Barringer	Matilda	50	Santa Rosa	CA
Kellogg	Grant L.	19	Santa Rosa	CA	Covert	Gladys	16+	Sebastopol	OR
Kellogg	Harold G.	21	Healdsburg	Hon	Cooper	Zella R.	22	Santa Rosa	CA
Kellogg	W. L.	22	Healdsburg	CA	Holcomb	F. M.	23	Healdsburg	IL
Kelly	C. E.	26	Gerloch, NV	MO	Cook	Neva	16	Eagleville, CA	CA
Kelly	David	21	Bloomfield	IRL	Kirkland	Lizzie	17+	Bloomfield	IRL
Kelly	George Thomas	30	San Francisco	CA	Lawler	Elsie Margaret	23	San Francisco	CA
Kelly	Henry Clay	34	Healdsburg	CA	Ashcraft	Edith	20	Santa Rosa	CA
Kelly	James H.	47	NY	MA	Leck	Alis	47	NY	FL
Kelly	James P.	26	Sebastopol	CA	Matthews	Myrtle	21	Sebastopol	CA
Kelly	John H.	24	Guerneville	NY	Philbes	Margaret J.	24	Fulton	CA
Kelly	Joy	33	Santa Rosa	CA	Jones	Edith Margarette	26	Santa Rosa	MN
Kelly	Mark P.	24	Healdsburg	AL	Nichols	Ida C.	30	Freestone	CA
Kelly	Mark P.	29	Healdsburg	AL	Bellah	Viola N.	30	Healdsburg	MO
Kelly	Michael F.	22	New York City	NY	Mackinnon	Grace May	18	Oakland	CA
Kelly	Thomas Lamb	28	Healdsburg		Bice	Sarah	21	Healdsburg	
Kelly	William S.	25	Dry Creek	AL	Bell	Maggie E.	21	Dry Creek	CA
Kelsey	Earl Ellsworth	26	Hayward	CA	Wilson	Austie Lea	25	Hayward	CA
Kelsey	Edwin Joseph	33	Petaluma	CA	Light	Emily Hida	21	Petaluma	CA
Kelso	Edgar Clayton	29	Santa Rosa	CA	McDougall	Louise	30	Santa Rosa	CA
Kelton	Clarence F.	22	Sebastopol	CA	Abraio	Marie K.	19	Sebastopol	CA
Kemler	Andrew C.	32	San Francisco	MD	Maxwell	Lillian J.	30	San Francisco	CA

	Groom					Bride			
Surname	Given Name	Age	Residence	BP	Surname	Given Name	Age	Residence	BP
Kemp	Harry Walter	40	Blue Lakes	OH	Schendel	Maude Alice	30	San Francisco	CA
Kemp	Joseph	32	Healdsburg	MD	Johnson	Julia	17	Santa Rosa	CA
Kendall	Albert Kuy (?)	25	Santa Rosa		Melson	Mary Ann	18	Santa Rosa	
Kendall	James	22	Amador City	ENG	Warren	Bessie E.	17	Healdsburg	MD
Kenna	Richard	49	Oakland	NY	Findlay	Katherine Mary	46	San Francisco	VA
Kenneally	James	27	Petaluma	Pet	Meyers	Addie	27	Petaluma	Pet
Kenneally	William Joseph	21	Petaluma	CA	McClure	Neva	19	Petaluma	CA
Kennedy	C. A.	24	Windsor	NV	Emmerson	Delia M.	22	Petaluma	CA
Kennedy	Charles	21	Bennett Valley		Hartin	Mary	16	Bennett Valley	
Kennedy	Charles E.	24	Occidental	CA	Adams	LaVerne I.	22	Bothell, WA	WA
Kennedy	Charles W.	22	San Francisco	CA	Wood	Allie S.	21	Healdsburg	CA
Kennedy	Charles Warren	23	Santa Rosa	CA	Ingram	Addie Bell	22	Mark West	CA
Kennedy	David S.	33	Santa Rosa Twp.	WI	Hicks	Hattie	25	Analy Twp.	CA
Kennedy	Ebert L.	23	Santa Rosa	CA	Hunter	Lola	19	Santa Rosa	CA
Kennedy	Edward H.	42	Santa Rosa	CA	Herman (?)	May Rose	31	Rincon Valley	CA
Kennedy	Elbert L.	30	Healdsburg	CA	Edwards	Lizzie	22	San Francisco	CA
Kennedy	Floyd	26	Penngrove	MO	Manning	Evelyn L.	18	Penngrove	CA
Kennedy	Joseph Edward	44	San Francisco	PA	Ingram	May	38	Petaluma	CA
Kennedy	Willard B.	36	Santa Rosa	OH	Perrin	Alice Hollcroft	24	Santa Rosa	IN
Kennedy	William A.	35	San Francisco	CND	Werner	Nora, Mrs.	26	Sonoma	NJ
Kennedy	William H.	26	Windsor		Brown	Mary	18	Windsor	
Kenney	Martin G.	28	San Francisco	CA	Soedler	Emma B.	23	San Francisco	CA
Kent	William Charles	36	Petaluma		Dolan	Maria	18+	Petaluma	
Kent	Wm. C.				Curtman	Emily			
Kentzell	James	56	San Francisco	PA	Murphy	Francis	29	Sonoma	IRL
Keown	George W.	33	Sanger	VA	Ort	Rosa H.	28	Santa Rosa	CA
Keppel	Fred E.	24	Tomales	CA	Cook	Gertrude	24	Santa Rosa	CA
Ker	Robert M.	35	Santa Rosa	CND	Heath	Maude Blanche	19	Santa Rosa	NH
Keran	J. N.	28	Redwood Twp.		Torance	Sarah	19	Redwood Twp.	
Kerbey	S. A.	28	Petaluma	CA	Paulsen	Gwinna M. J.	20	Two Rock	OK

	Groom					Bride			
Surname	Given Name	Age	Residence	BP	Surname	Given Name	Age	Residence	BP
Kerfoot	Lester R.	27	San Diego	MO	Sheffer	L. Etta	26	Sebastopol	CA
Kerman	Arthur Thomas	33	San Francisco	CA	Smith	Minnie Alice	37	East New Port, NY	NY
Kern	Harry A.	26	Vallejo	KS	Gilkey	Esther F.	21	Santa Rosa	TN
Kern	Wm.	52	Ione		Morrow	Maria A.	32	Santa Rosa	
Kerner	Albert G.	34	Sonoma	GER	Fisher	Louisa	24	Sonoma	GER
Kerner	Henry R.	24	Fresno	CA	DuCommun	Lillian E.	24	Santa Rosa	CA
Kerney	Joseph J.	28	Sonoma	CA	Redmond	Loretta M.	28	Sonoma	IL
Kerr	James A.	25	San Francisco	CA	Wuthrich	Antoinette L.	19	San Francisco	CA
Kerr	Newton	25	Santa Rosa	ME	Wesson	Justice O.	32	San Francisco	CA
Kerrick	Walter Armstead	21	San Francisco	IL	Carlson	Lillian Emma	18	San Francisco	OR
Kerrison	W. W.	36	Vallejo Twp.	NV	Risk	Sarah	28	Vallejo Twp.	IRL
Kertz	Herbert Joseph	27	San Francisco	GER	Searey	Laura Joseph	26	Petaluma	CA
Kesler	Jackson	35	Salt Point Twp.		Lamb	Nora	17	Bloomfield	
Kessack	John Douglas	21	San Francisco	CA	Pedrotti	Mary Olivia	18	Olema	CA
Kessing	Clemens	50	Santa Rosa	GER	Hornbeck	Catherine, Mrs.	32	Santa Rosa	AUT
Ketcham	Clarence S.	20	Santa Rosa	CA	Muller	Marie B.	18	Santa Rosa	CA
Ketcham	Lona I.	23	Santa Rosa	IA	Harris	Ivy	16	Santa Rosa	CA
Ketcham	Orven C.	29	Santa Rosa	MO	Ward	Katie E.	22	Santa Rosa	MO
Ketelsen	Ocke	30	Petaluma Twp.	GER	Crogan	Elizabeth	30	Petaluma Twp.	ENG
Kettendorff	Otto J.	19	San Francisco	CA	Dayton	Pearl	18	Sebastopol	MN
Ketterlin	Auguste D.	31	Santa Rosa	MO	DeBolt	Lucy H.	23	Santa Rosa	IA
Kettlewell	Benjamin	29	Lakeport	CA	Mallory	Edith M.	21	Santa Rosa	CA
Kettlewell	Richard S.	24	Franz Valley	CA	Duncan	Estelle	24	Santa Rosa	CA
Kettlewell	William W.	26	America	CA	Goodman	Idell L.	20	America	CA
Kevan	Frank Charles	30	Oakland	IA	Pauly	Helen	19	Oakland	IL
Keyes	John M.	22	Healdsburg	CA	Luebberke	Dora	21	Windsor	USA
Keyes	Ralph E.	24	San Francisco	CA	Muthall	Bernice Josie	23	San Francisco	CA
Keykendall	Henry Clay	21	Santa Rosa		Thrush	Nettie	22	Santa Rosa	
Keys	Samuel H.	38	Guerneville	CA	Torrence	Mary E.	32	Guerneville	CA

	Groom					Bride			
Surname	**Given Name**	**Age**	**Residence**	**BP**	**Surname**	**Given Name**	**Age**	**Residence**	**BP**
Kidd	David W.	32	Santa Rosa	AUT	Black	Mary M.	19	Santa Rosa	CA
Kidd	Edward Martin	23	Petaluma	CA	Williams	Maud Jeannette	18	Petaluma	NE
Kidd	Joseph L.	4?	Verano	KY	Pickle	Bernice E.	31	Verano	CA
Kidd	William H.	34	Santa Rosa	CA	Aldridge	Lulu G.	21	Santa Rosa	IN
Kidwell	Henry C.	23	Sebastopol	WA	Hawes	Estella M.	20	Sebastopol	CA
Kidwell	Paul M.	22	Berkeley	MI	Strahan	Emily A.	18	Berkeley	CA
Kiester	Charles C.	28	Healdsburg	MN	Butler	Rosa E.	17	Healdsburg	WI
Kietsinger	George W.	30	Lytton Springs	IL	Annike (?)	Minnie	20	Sherman, Wayne Co., PA	PA
Kilcourse	John Martin	22	Petaluma	Soc	Jessup	Juanita	21	Petaluma	Soc
Killits	George H.	33	San Francisco	IL	Kamp	Nellie N.	23	Petaluma	Pet
Kimball	Heman A.	45	Guerneville	VT	McDonald	Dora D., Mrs.	26	Alpina, MI	MI
Kimball	Jerry Whitney				O'Leary	Mary			
Kimball	William N.	30	Kenwood	WA	Schlam	Grace M.	27	San Francisco	CA
Kimble	Thomas H.	22	Sebastopol	CA	Clarke	Sibyl G.	19	Santa Rosa	CA
Kimes	A. L.	28	Santa Rosa	OH	Ross	Alice	18	Forestville	CA
Kimes	D. M.	24	Forestville	IN	Hanson	Cora	17	Forestville	IL
Kimes	Edward Thomas	25	Forestville	CA	Tomblinson	Hazel Loreta	23	Guerneville	CA
Kimes	Rufus Lee	21	Santa Rosa	IA	Jones	Georgana	18	Santa Rosa	CA
Kimes	Walter H.	21	Forestville	CA	Meredith	Blanche P.	18	Healdsburg	CA
Kimura	Tokizo	22	Santa Rosa	JPN	Kimura	Sakae	21	Santa Rosa	JPN
Kincaid	Edwin J.	28	Cloverdale	CA	Smith	Genevieve	24	Cloverdale	CA
King	Albert Roy	24	San Francisco	CA	Cordes	Ethel Lucy	24	San Francisco	CA
King	Andrew	28	Petaluma	CA	Gollnik	Lizzie	30	Petaluma	CA
King	Cecil Ray	29	Potter Valley	CA	Meade	Edna	19	Coyote Valley	CA
King	Charles W.	34	Monte Rio	ENG	Browning	Catherine L.	33	Monte Rio	CA
King	Chester James	23	Petaluma	CA	Starrett	Anna Letta	21	Guerneville	CA
King	David	35	Russian River Station	CND	Barnes	Annie	30	Cazadero	CND
King	E. Manuel	29	Sebastopol	CA	Emeral	Mary	20	Sebastopol	BER

	Groom					Bride			
Surname	Given Name	Age	Residence	BP	Surname	Given Name	Age	Residence	BP
King	Ernest F.	30	Petaluma	Pet	Sales	Geraldine	24	Petaluma	Pet
King	Fred	47	Santa Rosa	CND	Yates	Francis	42	Windsor	CA
King	George	65	Sebastopol	OH	Culver	Katherine	56	Sebastopol	OH
King	Horace Constable	25	Hoquiam, WA	ENG	Daniels	Zella	18	Healdsburg	CA
King	James	35	San Antonio Twp., Marin Co.	CND	Dahlmann	Augusta	28	Petaluma Twp.	CA
King	James	35	Chileno Valley	CND	Willis	Mabel	17	Petaluma	CND
King	John	23	Duncans Mill	CA	Moore	Amy L.	17	Duncans Mills	CA
King	John	36	Healdsburg	MI	Gibson	Nancy	23	Healdsburg	CA
King	John	32	Petaluma	CA	Bahr	Bertha	22	Petaluma	GER
King	John F.	29	Bodega	IA	Merryfield	Kittie	22	Bodega	MO
King	Joseph B.	26	Stony Point	CND	Cowles	Eva M.	19	Two Rock	CA
King	Joseph G.	28	Sebastopol	CA	Borges	Mary	18	Sebastopol	CA
King	Lochiel M.	24	San Francisco	CA	Wadsworth	Anna M.	21	Vineburg	CA
King	Theodore G.	25	the Laguna, Marin Co.	CA	Sales	Ida M.	24	Petaluma Twp.	CA
King	Thomas Riley	21	Healdsburg	CA	Strode	Theresa E.	20	Guerneville	CA
King	W. E.	24	Ukiah	CA	Gardner	Flora	18	Santa Rosa	CA
King	William	26	Bodega	CND	Adams	Lora Z.	19	Austin Creek, Ocean Twp.	CND
King	William	33	Guerneville		Blakley	Mary E.	17	Guerneville	
King	Willis James	23	Petaluma	CA	Perry	Gertrude M.	24	Petaluma	CA
King	Charles W.	21	Santa Rosa	IA	Campion	Kate	19	Santa Rosa	CA
Kingman	Ralph Elmer	37	Stony Point	WI	McNally	Ella	43	Petaluma	WA
Kingsbury	De Witt	23	San Francisco	CA	Pretorious	Mary	23	San Francisco	CA
Kingwell	Alfred Leslie	20	Cloverdale	CA	Weythman	Lucretia Elizabeth	17	Cloverdale	CA
Kingwell	B.	24	Howard Station	ENG	Beedle	Josephine	18	Howard Station	CA
Kingwell	William I.	23	Occidental	ENG	Collins	Clara E.	22	Occidental	CA
Kinley	Basil E.	21	Santa Rosa	CA	Gumes	Bessie V.	19	Healdsburg	MO
Kinley	Fielden	26	Santa Rosa	IA	Fassoth	Courdadena	20	Hawaii	HWI

	Groom					Bride			
Surname	**Given Name**	**Age**	**Residence**	**BP**	**Surname**	**Given Name**	**Age**	**Residence**	**BP**
Kinley	Newton B.	26	Santa Rosa	IA	Severy	Edna A.	25	Santa Rosa	CA
Kinne	Albert B.	33	San Francisco	KY	Dechenne	Rosa	32	Fulton	IL
Kinner	William G.	27	near Santa Rosa		Runyon	Annie	20	near Santa Rosa	
Kinney	John H.	27	West Oakland	IRL	Bueno	Maria	27	Vallejo Twp.	CA
Kinney	William S.	33	San Francisco	CND	Kittler	Rose J.	31	San Francisco	CA
Kinsey	Harvey C.	23	San Francisco	CA	Wyckoff	Emma	20	Ukiah	CA
Kinyon	Reuben H.	25	Vacaville	CA	Wheatley	Besse Maude	19	Santa Rosa	MO
Kirby	Charles F., Jr.	30	San Francisco	ENG	Baron	Julia Adeline	27	Santa Rosa	ENG
Kirby	Duncan J.	23	San Francisco	ENG	Lesser	Anita T.	22	San Francisco	CA
Kirkland	David J.	20	Bloomfield	IRL	Blake	Effie M.	20	Bloomfield	CA
Kirkland	Harry B.	23	Graton	CA	Nowlin	Lula L.	17		KS
Kirkland	Henry B.	27	Essex, CT	NY	Mays	Helen J.	21	Santa Rosa	CA
Kirkland	Joseph B.	41	Sausalito	Ontario CND	Wilson	Ettie Sarah	35	Hemet	CA
Kirkman	Claude J.	24	El Verano	IN	Perry	Elizabeth G.	21	El Verano	GER
Kirkpatrick	Josiah M.	66	Santa Rosa	NC	Moore	H. C., Mrs.	55	Santa Rosa	TN
Kirkpatrick	Josiah M.	58	Santa Rosa	NC	Calbreath	Maggie A.	52	Santa Rosa	VA
Kirkpatrick	Virgil	23	Healdsburg	CA	Louk	Katie	22	Oakland	CA
Kirsch	Henry	24	Santa Rosa	CA	Henrahan	Effie H.	22	Santa Rosa	CA
Kirstein	Max	29	San Francisco	GER	Vogel	Camilla A.	21	San Francisco	CA
Kirwan	Louis J.	35	San Francisco	FRN	Davis	Georgia M.	39	Santa Rosa	CA
Kirwan	Thomas D.	28	Berkeley	WI	Mosher	Lucile Ruth	25	San Francisco	OR
Kise	Philip	27	Windsor	CA	Myers	Emily	23	Windsor	NBW
Kise	Philip A.	23	Windsor		Myers	Katie	21	Windsor	
Kiser	Antone	23	Sonoma	CA	Stevens	Catherine M.	20	Sonoma	CA
Kiser	Nicklaus	25	Sonoma	SWT	Jakoba	Christina	19	Sonoma	SWT
Kiser	William	25	Petaluma	SWT	Infield	Josephine	17	Petaluma	SWT
Kisling	Frank	33	Sacramento	IA	Geary	Florence	27	San Francisco	MA
Kissam	William A.	30	Oakland	NY	Hussey	Anita	30	Oakland	CA

	Groom					Bride			
Surname	Given Name	Age	Residence	BP	Surname	Given Name	Age	Residence	BP
Kistler	Ray S.	41	Rock Island, IL	IL	Stowe	Anna F.	36	San Francisco	CA
Kistner	Lester Alfred	25	Guerneville	OR	Bever	Cleo Maud	18	Mercury	CA
Kistner	Loren T.	28	Santa Rosa	OR	Hicklin	Evelyn M.	18	Fulton	CA
Kivett	David W.	22	Santa Rosa	MO	Miller	Minnie	18	Healdsburg	IA
Kivett	Walter L.	27	Oakland	KS	Johnson	Rolla May	21	Oakland	WI
Kivi	Newton M.	25	San Francisco	CA	Capella	Corinne M.	22	Sebastopol	CA
Kjeldsen	Vernon Edward	18	Fort Bragg	CA	Gibbons	Rose Elliot	18	Santa Rosa	CA
Klaus	Charlie	24	Santa Rosa	MO	Filion	Mary	22	Santa Rosa	CA
Klaustermeyer	Charles F.	26	Santa Rosa	GER	Hefty	Amelia M.	20	Santa Rosa	CA
Kleeman	John	35	Timber Cove		Sper	Rosa	21	Timber Cove	
Klein	Christian	24	Petaluma	GER	Weishand	Margaretta	17	Vallejo Twp.	NE
Klein	Ernest E.	24	Guerneville	CA	Johnson	Cassie B., Mrs. (?)	27	Guerneville	CA
Kleiser	James H.	26	San Francisco	CA	Armstrong	Fannie	26	Santa Rosa	CA
Klemgard	James G.	24	Pullman, WA	WA	Eardley	Gladys	24	Berkeley	CA
Kline	S. R.	30	Petaluma	PA	More	Lena	22	Petaluma	CA
Klingler	George Adolph	24	San Francisco	CA	Gale	Ellen E.	22	San Francisco	CA
Klintworth	Edward	36	Oakland	WI	Michaelsen	Mary W.	38	Alexander Valley	GER
Kloustermeyer	Wm. J.	30	Flagstaff, Ariz. Territory	MO	Block	Lora	24	Healdsburg	MO
Knaak	August	28	Healdsburg		Funk	Lena	20	Healdsburg	
Knack	Frederick	37	Seattle	GER	McGregor	Agnes, Mrs.	30	Petaluma	SCT
Knaff	Henry Richard	48	Oakland	ENG	Tryon	Elizabeth	28	San Francisco	ME
Knapp	Charles Houry (?)	27	Bloomfield		McAlister	Martha Ann	18	Bloomfield	
Knapp	Gen W.	24	Bloomfield		Hamilton	Alice B.	18+	Stony Point	
Knapp	Marion O.	22	Point Arena	IN	Brown	Mary E., Mrs.	26	Healdsburg	CO
Knapp	Wm. D.	23	Santa Rosa Twp.	ID	Hawkins	Maud	21	Santa Rosa Twp.	CA
Knecht	Frederich	56	Mark West	SWT	Hunger	Maria, Mrs.	55	Mark West	SWT
Knecht	Tony	23	Windsor	CA	Frey	Anna	23	Santa Rosa	WA

	Groom					Bride			
Surname	**Given Name**	**Age**	**Residence**	**BP**	**Surname**	**Given Name**	**Age**	**Residence**	**BP**
Kneiss	Gilbert H.	22	Reno, NV	CA	Rayburn	Hannah E.	20	Los Angeles	KY
Kneppler	George H.	25	Martinez	CA	Roberts	Lulla G.	20	Cloverdale	CA
Knight	Bert P.	33	Los Angeles	RI	Arkland	Mabel E.	32	Los Angeles	KS
Knight	Francis Marion	35	Santa Rosa	IA	Baker	Roxie Dell	19	Santa Rosa	MO
Knight	George W.	21	Mount Olivet	CA	Barnes	May E.	20	Fulton	CA
Knight	Reginald S.	27	San Francisco	ENG	MacKenzie	Blanche	32	Camp Meeker	ENG
Knight	Russell H.	32	Shellville	CA	Cornish	Shirley F.	25	Glen Ellen	VA
Knipp	Ruscher A.	31	Santa Rosa	NY	Wheeler	Harriet S.	24	Santa Rosa	CA
Knock	Malcolm A.	28	Willows	CA	Moon	Carrie	23	Chico	CA
Knoles	Rollin C.	21	San Francisco	IL	Hulbert	Fannie O.	20	Santa Rosa	MI
Knolle	Frans J. B.	33	Sonoma	HLD	Soderberg	Alice	27	Sonoma	CA
Knott	Warren T.	28	Duncans Mills		Allen	Rebecca H.	20	Duncans Mills	
Knott	William	51	Santa Rosa	MD	Perry	Alice L.	51	Santa Rosa	IL
Knowles	Albert William	22	Sebastopol	CA	Palmer	Lou	22	Sebastopol	CA
Knowles	D. C.				Menefee	Marinda I.			
Knowlton	Cyrus Dexter	28	Petaluma	ME	Dahlmann	Alba Flora	24	Petaluma	CA
Knox	Josiah N.	53	Baker City, OR	OH	Cooper	Ella J.	30	Santa Rosa	CA
Knudsen	Conrad	26	Sebastopol	GER	Hansen	Josie	20	Sebastopol	GER
Knudson	Arthur J.	21	Santa Rosa	MN	Powers	Zelma V.	18	Santa Rosa	CA
Knudtsen	Sophus	25	Sebastopol	GER	Nissen	Henrietta	18	Sebastopol	GER
Knutsen	Isaac	36	San Jose	NRY	Miller	Rae	17	Crescent City	CA
Knutsen	Iver				Clawsen	Cynthia A.			
Koch	John J.	49	Healdsburg	KS	Morris	Anna M.	38	Healdsburg	CA
Koch	Leroy	26	Santa Rosa	PA	Norris	Emma	22	Santa Rosa	CA
Koch	William B.	33	Santa Rosa	CA	Nichols	Lillian Edith	29	Santa Rosa	MA
Kock	George A.	19	Santa Rosa	CA	DuBois	Hazel M.	18	Santa Rosa	CA
Koebeli	Rudolph	51	Santa Rosa	SWT	Bech (?)	Elisabeth	43	Santa Rosa	SWT
Koeboom	John Henry	51	Schellville	GER	Slade	Alma, Mrs.	38	San Francisco	WI
Koenig	Charles	45	Oakland	GER	Costigan	Mary Louise	27	Oakland	ME
Koenig	Frank	59	Santa Rosa	GER	Livernash	Elizabeth A.	32	Healdsburg	CA

	Groom					Bride			
Surname	Given Name	Age	Residence	BP	Surname	Given Name	Age	Residence	BP
Koenig	Frank	50	San Francisco	CA	Strickirt	Martha F.	34	San Francisco	GER
Koenig	William	40	San Francisco	GER	Schwartz	Margaretha	37	San Francisco	GER
Koffenstein	Jacob	33	Santa Rosa	RUS	Sauer	Carrie	35	Santa Rosa	RUS
Kohl	Stanley E.	24	Santa Rosa	IA	Nalley	Marion	21	Windsor	CA
Kohr	Robert L.	29	San Francisco	PA	Rose	Eldora	20	Lytton	CA
Kolb	August L.	23	Alexander Valley	MO	Johnson	Belle	20	Alexander Valley	MO
Kolb	Clifford A.	24	Healdsburg	CA	McDowell	Hazel E.	22	Healdsburg	CA
Kolliker	Fred	31	Sacramento	SWT	Young (?)	Minnie E.	25	Santa Rosa	IL
Kolm	Robert	34	San Rafael	Sfo	Huston	Estella	21	Alameda	NY
Konig	John	24	Santa Rosa	RUS	Isaak	Helena	20	Santa Rosa	RUS
Kopf	August J.	35	Santa Rosa	MN	Quinn	Frances M.	27	Santa Rosa	CA
Kopf	Carl L.	33	Santa Rosa	MN	Fick	Emma M.	26	Santa Rosa	NY
Korbel	Frank	31	Guerneville	BOH	Blaha	Catherine	21	Santa Rosa	BOH
Korbel	Leo V.	31	Korbel	CA	McNear	Miriam	23	Petaluma	CA
Kornmuller	Wilhelm	58	Petaluma	GER	Wenger	Selma	35	Petaluma	SWT
Koski	Matt	48	El Verano	Warsaw	Frandell	Mandi	42	El Verano	FIN
Koster	James	29	Petaluma	Seb	Martin	Alma	25	Petaluma	Pet
Kothgassner	Joseph M., Jr.	25	Cloverdale	CA	Reger	Marie A.	22	Cloverdale	CA
Kozminsky	Nicholas	24	San Francisco	CA	Duffey	Cassandra	23	Oakland	AL
Kraemer	Herman	40	Selma	MO	Combs	Frances	32	Rio Nido	CA
Kraft	Emil C.	28	San Francisco	IL	Perkins	Fay K.	17	San Francisco	CA
Kragel	Adam H.	23	San Francisco	NY	Belden	Grace A.	23	Santa Rosa	CA
Kraimer	Isaac	41	San Francisco		Hecht	Helen	21	San Francisco	
Kraus	Albert	32	Healdsburg	HUN	Moody	Viola	30	Healdsburg	CA
Krauss	Frederick G.	27	San Francisco	Sfo	Hilmer	Lizzie	22	Petaluma	Sfo
Krayenbuhl	John F.	28	San Francisco	MO	Rebscher (?)	Louise M.	29	San Francisco	CA
Kreidler	Carl W.	34	Oakland	GER	Bettencourt	Elvira S.	28	San Francisco	PRT
Kreis	Harry Gailord	21	Inglewood	ID	Jackson	Myrtle P.	22	Gardena	SD
Kreiss	Frederick W.	28	Redwood City	CA	McCormick	Alice	26	Woodside	CA

	Groom					Bride			
Surname	Given Name	Age	Residence	BP	Surname	Given Name	Age	Residence	BP
Kreitler	John H.	39	Petaluma	NY	Cornwell	Bessie Agnes	24	Petaluma	CA
Krenzer	Thomas C.	24	Richmond	NE	White	Loma A.	18	Sacramento	CA
Kretzmer	William J.	26	Richmond	CA	Carberry	Josephine M.	21	San Francisco	CA
Kreutzberg	Robert				Mangers	Ester May	17		
Kriedell	Fred W.	29	Guerneville	MN	Hayes	Freda M.	30	Santa Rosa	ENG
Kroncke	Henry Carl	25	Santa Rosa	CA	Staley	Ada Lavonia	22	Santa Rosa	OR
Kronke	Edward J.	32	Santa Rosa	CA	Gibson	Gladys J.	24	Santa Rosa	CA
Krough	Martin L.	31	Skaggs Springs	Sfo	Combs	Genevieve	17	Healdsburg	Hld
Krueger	Oscar Feasco	24	Healdsburg		Cook	Cassie	21	Healdsburg	
Kruse	August W. T.	20	Healdsburg	CA	McLean	Katie G.	19	Healdsburg	CA
Kruse	Charles C.	24	Bellevue	WA	Willey	Mamie E.	16	Santa Rosa	IL
Kruse	Charles G.	25	Fulton	CA	Baagoe	Carrie	22	Guerneville	DNK
Kruse	Fred G.	21	Bellevue	WA	McCombs	Luetta A.	17	Santa Rosa	NE
Kruse	Frederick Antonio	26	Healdsburg	CA	Hobson	Louise Jane	25	Healdsburg	CA
Kruse	H. A.	42	Mark West	CA	Davis	Gertrude L.	28	San Francisco	MO
Kruse	Herbert M.	22	Roseville	CA	Pfister	Nellie M.	19	Santa Rosa	CA
Kruse	Herbert M.	26	Santa Rosa	CA	Bullen	Clara J.	24	Santa Rosa	MI
Kruse	James H.	21	Healdsburg	CA	Ingalls	Emma	21	Healdsburg	CA
Kruse	James H.	26	Healdsburg	CA	McNeeley	Eva	24	Healdsburg	CA
Krutzberger	Fred	28	Monte Rio	CA	Short	Louise Amelia	28	Monte Rio	MO
Kryst	Charles	21	Sonoma	MD	Reichlin	Anna	21	Sonoma	CA
Kuchmann	Henry, Jr.	28	San Anselmo	CA	Waterman	Wylda S.	20	San Anselmo	IL
Kuck	Hans A.	23	Petaluma	GER	Hansen	Helga A.	19	Petaluma	CA
Kuechler	Harold J.	22	Sacramento	CA	Mackey	Verda E.	22	Sacramento	CND
Kuhi	Henry	30	Petaluma	CA	Brava	Edith	24	Petaluma	CA
Kuhn	Michael	36	Greenback, OR	FRN	Miller	Sophie	24	Petaluma	CA
Kuhule	Perry	24	Petaluma	IL	Eades	Nellie	23	Petaluma	CA
Kulberg	Andrew John	44	Petaluma	SWD	Walsh	Sarah Jane	25	Petaluma	IRL
Kunde	Kurt G.	23	Glen Ellen	CA	Cook	Alice Emme (?)	18	Santa Rosa	WA
Kunz	George E.	28	Healdsburg	VA	Mason	Mary C.	28	Healdsburg	CA

	Groom					Bride			
Surname	Given Name	Age	Residence	BP	Surname	Given Name	Age	Residence	BP
Kunzler	Edward Theodore	22	Point Arena	CA	Reynolds	Edna May	18	Point Arena	CA
Kunzler	Ora Archibald	25	Pt. Arena	CA	Donahoo	Ilma	23	Pt. Arena	CA
Kurlander	Maurice Aaron	23	Santa Rosa	CA	Griffith	Juanita	26	Santa Rosa	CA
Kurlander	Sidney	25	Santa Rosa	CA	Lawrence	Georgie May	18	Santa Rosa	CA
Kuster	Gerhard	43	San Francisco	IN	McDowell	Elsie	23	Petaluma	KS
Kuykendall	J. O.	26	Santa Rosa	OR	Noffsinger	Melvina E.	20	Santa Rosa	MO
Kuykendall	James O.	32	Seattle	OR	McCoy	Dollie	22	Petaluma	CA
Kuykendall	William Stark	31	Santa Rosa	OR	Ingram	Emma	25	Santa Rosa	CA
Kyburz	Alfred A.	25	Fulton	CA	Holloway	Florence M.	25	Fulton	MN
Kyle	John G.	32	Santa Rosa	CND	Cauckwell	Nancy M.	19	Santa Rosa	MO
Kynoch	Ransom	30	Novato	MI	Rodeck	Louise	24	Petaluma	CA
La Bossure	Louis	56	Santa Rosa	CND	McCreagh	May	43	San Francisco	CND
Labat	Jean	28	San Francisco	FRN	Bonnemazon	Catherine	26	San Francisco	FRN
Lacey	William F.	34	Fort Bragg	CA	Rose	Bessie Pearl	33	Petaluma	CA
Lackmann	H.	23	San Francisco	CA	Hollahan	Iva	19	Santa Rosa	IL
Lacoste	George J.	46	San Francisco	CA	Hautot	Marthe A.	34	San Francisco	FRN
Lacque	Clarence Andrew	20	Santa Rosa	CA	Beach	Jeannette	20	Santa Rosa	CA
Lacque	Edward F.	21	Petaluma	CA	Ducker	Ella Mae	24	Petaluma	CA
Lacque	Frank	22	Santa Rosa	CA	Weeks	Effie	20	Santa Rosa	ME
Laddish	H. J.	23	Berkeley	CA	Songey	Harriet M.	22	Berkeley	CA
LaDue	Earl Francis	27	Bellevue	CA	Leith	Kathleen Laurence	18	Bellevue	CA
LaDue	Valloise A.	29	Santa Rosa	CA	Wilson	H. Isabella	18	Santa Rosa	PA
Lafferty	Daniel H.	34	Santa Rosa	CA	Leddy	Lillian Ruth	29	Santa Rosa	CA
Lafont	Walter Thomas	25	Occidental	IL	Sturgeon	Irene	23	Occidental	CA
Lafranchi	Alfonso	25	Petaluma	SWT	Garzola	Lena Frances	21	Petaluma	CA
Lafranchi	Edward	20	Santa Rosa	AZ	Piezzi	Lucy	20	Santa Rosa	CA
Lafranchi	Frank	35	El Verano	SWT	Forni	Josephine	36	El Verano	SWT
Lafranchi	Fred L.	27	Nicasio	SWT	Dolcini	Zelma D.	26	Petaluma	CA
LaFranchi	Henry G.	26	Duncans Mills	CA	Scott	Hattie	20	Duncans Mills	CA

	Groom					Bride			
Surname	Given Name	Age	Residence	BP	Surname	Given Name	Age	Residence	BP
Lafranchi	John	28	Marshall	SWT	Confette	Eufemia	24	Marshall	ITL
Lafranchi	Joseph	36	Agua Caliente	SWT	Spaletta	Erminia	28	San Rafael	SWT
Lafranchi	Marino Joseph	22	Petaluma	CA	Peterson	Emily	19	Santa Rosa	CA
LaFranchi	Robert	29	Point Reyes	SWT	Albini	Ersilia	29	Point Reyes Station	ITL
Lafranconi	Frank	33	Santa Rosa	SWT	Scaroni	Adelina	26	Santa Rosa	SWT
Lafranky	Morris	21	Santa Rosa	SWT	Piezzi	Eliza	19	Santa Rosa	SWT
Lafrenz	Henry	21	Geyserville	GER	Teaby	Leonnora	22	Geyserville	IL
Lager	Phillip	27	San Francisco	RUS	Manuck	Minnie	22	El Verano	RUS
Lagger	Cesare	34	Sonoma	SWT	Kreutzer	Kate	43	Sonoma	SWT
Lagomarsino	George J.	20	San Francisco	CA	Cassini	Carrie	18	Santa Rosa	CA
LaGrant	Lucon	27	Petaluma		Carmady	Maggie	21	Analy Twp.	
Lahue	E. D.	41	Sebastopol	OH	Gross	Ida J.	33	Sebastopol	CA
Laird	Fred J.	30	Santa Cruz	CA	Kelley	Caroline L.	26	Petaluma	VT
Laird	H. Spencer				Logan	Harriet			
Laird	Thomas F.	25	Angels Camp	Angels Camp	Aiken	Mary Edith	18	Santa Rosa	CA
Lake	Alfred Edwin	29	San Jose	CA	Shelford	Susie Blanche	26	Cloverdale	CA
Lake	D. Delos	25	Healdsburg	MI	Good	Helen	25	Healdsburg	ENG
Lalanne	John	18	Healdsburg	CA	Hulbert	Julia A.	18	Santa Rosa	CA
Lalanne	Laurence Marius	24	San Francisco	FRN	Dutil	Jeanne Harriette	21	El Verano	NY
Lalanne	Louis	28	San Francisco	FRN	Mauregard	Marguerite	30	San Francisco	FRN
Lamay	Alfred	24	Sonoma Co.		McDonald	Isabelle	24	Sonoma Co.	
Lamb	George H.	23	Occidental	CA	Moranzoni	Edith A.	18	Occidental	CA
Lamb	Louis	30	Healdsburg		Fruitt (?)	Ellen	23	Healdsburg	
Lambert	Charles A.	25	Duncans Mill	CND	Leclerc	Emily	17	Duncans Mills	CA
Lambert	Edward	27	Healdsburg	CA	King	Jennie N.	16	Healdsburg	CA
Lambert	Frank	21	Duncans Mills	CA	Moore	Sarah Inza	16	Duncans Mills	CA
Lambert	Henry A.	23	Duncans Mills	CA	Moore	Zilla C.	17	Duncans Mills	CA
Lambert	John W.	26	Santa Rosa	CA	Rodgers	Julia	24	Healdsburg	CA

Groom					Bride				
Surname	**Given Name**	**Age**	**Residence**	**BP**	**Surname**	**Given Name**	**Age**	**Residence**	**BP**
Lambert	Lewis A.	33	Oakland	VT	Bowers	Bertha Blanche	33	Oakland	ME
Lambert	Richard	22	San Francisco		Long	Minnie A., Mrs.	29	San Francisco	
Lambert	Robert Franklin	22	Healdsburg		Niles	Lavania A.	19	Healdsburg	
Lambert	William A.	22	Suisun	CA	Vadon	Bertha E.	19	Cloverdale	CA
Lameneth	Jacob F.	52	Santa Rosa Twp.	GER	Priestly	Sophia	43	Santa Rosa	SAF
Lamore	Joseph Verrell	28	Los Angeles	CA	Morse	Marie L.	29	Los Angeles	OH
Lampson	Augustus	23	Glencoe	CA	Warren	Mary L.	19	Healdsburg	ME
Lampson	Chester William	23	San Bernardino	CA	Parrott	Marguerite Marion	20	Geyserville	CA
Lampson	Everett D.	27	Geyserville	CA	Caldwell	Ora Helena	20	Santa Rosa	CA
Lampson	Walter A.	21	San Francisco	CA	Kirkland	Frances M.	24	NY	MS
Lancaster	John	33	Petaluma	IA	Truitt	Eva	20	Healdsburg	CA
Lancaster	William				Daly	Maria			
Lance	Ora L.	31	Mansfield, WA	WI	Miller	Beulah G.	25	Fulton	KS
Landelin	Frank W.	23	Ukiah	CA	La Page	Cora M.	23	Ukiah	CA
Lander	Eugene	52	Santa Rosa	IL	Arnold	Margaret Elizabeth	32	Santa Rosa	IA
Landgrebe	Milton William	21	Berkeley	CA	Lanpher	Ruth Louise	19	San Anselmo	CA
Landi	Enrico	23	Healdsburg	ITL	Lencioni	Emma	17	Healdsburg	Hld
Landis	Arthur L.	23	Mark West	CA	Barnes	Cora	18	Fulton	CA
Landis	William A.	38	Agua Caliente	IA	Sericano	Julia A.	35	Agua Caliente	ITL
Lando	Frank	25	Healdsburg	CA	Treadwell	Alicia E.	16	Healdsburg	CA
Landree	Roy	20	San Francisco	MO	McCulloch	Eva	15	Santa Rosa	CA
Landresse	Charles Paul	48	San Francisco	CA	Kripp	Clara Betts	27	Sacramento	CA
Lane	Allen S.	26	San Francisco	CA	Harding	Edith M.	22	San Francisco	WA
Lane	Carlton A.	27	Santa Rosa	MN	Brooks	Edith Nellie	23	Santa Rosa	CA
Lane	Thomas	35	Ukiah	CA	Harris	Laura Jane	32	Sacramento	CA
Lane	Ernest	30	Napa	CA	St. Clair	Lettye	29	Napa	CA
Lane	Ernest	26	Santa Rosa	CA	Bailey	Hester Drew	25	Santa Rosa	KS
Lane	F. J.	24	San Francisco	NSC	Rogers	Mamie	22	Sonoma	CA

Groom					Bride				
Surname	Given Name	Age	Residence	BP	Surname	Given Name	Age	Residence	BP
Lane	Frank J.	23	Reno, NV	NV	Gossage	Jessie	18	Petaluma	CA
Lane	Howard A.	21	San Francisco	CA	Bozza	Phyllis Leigh	19	San Francisco	IL
Lane	J.	35	Guerneville	NY	Conklin	E. C.	39	Forestville	OH
Lane	James Albert	27	Portland, OR	MN	Toomey	Mary Ellnor	21	Healdsburg	CA
Lane	Joseph W.	23	Santa Rosa	CA	Robertson	Nellie	19	Santa Rosa	KS
Lane	Lonnie	25	San Francisco	IA	Cunningham	Alice M.	25	Santa Rosa	ENG
Lane	Louis M., Jr.	28	Calistoga	Sfo	Blanchard	Lizzie Eveline	19	Calistoga	NY
Lane	Richard E.	29	Alameda	MA	Montgomery	Frances	25	San Francisco	CO
Lane	Walter J.	35	Turlock	Sfo	McNally	Mary A.	29	Petaluma	CA
Lane	William J.	30	Richmond	CA	Williams	Clara C.	23	Santa Rosa	CA
Lanfear	James A.	25	Redwood City	NJ	Gilbert	Eleanor M.	25	Redwood City	WI
Lang	August B.	22	Trenton	CA	Burgess	Mary Ann	17	Mt. Olivet	CA
Lang	Henry A.	28	Petaluma	GER	Morgan	Grace E.	20	Petaluma	TX
Lang	Herman Charles	24	Windsor	CA	Gwin	Carrie Elizabeth	20	Windsor	CA
Lang	Robert A.	22	Stockton	WI	Turner	Frances A.	21	Stockton	MN
Lange	Niels Frederik	23	Petaluma	DNK	Latell	Elsie Elizabeth	18	Penngrove	CA
Langensand	Melchior	33	Sonoma	SWT	Daschwander	Francisca	23	Sonoma	SWT
Langero	Giovani	30	Fulton	ITL	Bonfigli	Nazarena	40	Fulton	ITL
Langlois	Robert Franklin	26	Sebastopol	IA	McFarlane	Elizabeth Robina	23	Sebastopol	CA
Langon	Michael O.	32	Fortuna	CA	Riddle	Marvele O.	30	Fortuna	CA
Langpaap	Max	30	San Francisco	AZ	Traeger	Orah Dell	27	Porterville	CA
Langsdorf	Charles	24	San Francisco	CA	Dellenbaugh	Madge	22	San Francisco	CA
Lankant	Carl M.	38	Sebastopol	NV	Schumacher	Carrie Theresa	27	Sebastopol	CA
Lanker	Albert	32	Petaluma	SWT	Schumacher	Mary	29	Petaluma	SWT
Lannom	Clarence Worton	31	Oakland	TN	Westover	Minnie Merle	27	Oakland	CA
Lantz	George F.	29	Honcut, Butte Co.	CA	Newbert	Della	25	Healdsburg	CA
Lapham	Matthew	53	Occidental	ENG	Welch	Effie C.	26	Occidental	MN
Lapham	William C.	23	Occidental	WI	Bones	Elsie D.	18+	Occidental	Soc
Lapum	Oscar Edwin	23	Peachland	CA	Livings	Flora Estella	22	Santa Rosa	IN

	Groom					Bride			
Surname	Given Name	Age	Residence	BP	Surname	Given Name	Age	Residence	BP
Large	Arthur R.	25	Petaluma	ENG	Quinn	Addie	17	Petaluma	CA
Larimer	Robert E.	52	Santa Rosa	PA	Berger	Clara Lee	39	Santa Rosa	WA
Lark	Newton Allen	27	Santa Rosa	Sfo	Rich	Bernise Irene	18	Santa Rosa	MI
Larsen	Albert O.	36	Petaluma	DNK	Anderton	Gertrude A.	23	Petaluma	OR
Larsen	John	38	San Francisco	DNK	Gibbs	Martha	40	San Francisco	MN
Larsen	Jorgen	25	near Bloomfield	DNK	Larsen	Maria Christine	20	Bloomfield	DNK
Larsen	Julius Anton	32	Santa Rosa	DNK	Barnes	Eliza Lownes	22	Santa Rosa	WA
Larsen	L. P.	27	Two Rock	DNK	Nielsen	Tine	26	Two Rock	DNK
Larsen	Peter L. N.	24	San Francisco	DNK	Henrichsen	Anna M.	20	San Francisco	GER
Larsen	Thomas A.	30	Modesto	NRY	Tunsen	Edith L.	18	Modesto	CA
Larson	Carl	44	El Verano	DNK	Nilson	Pauline	27	El Verano	NRY
Larson	John Benjamin	22	Petaluma	CA	Wittkowski	Frieda	18	Petaluma	GER
Larson	Rudolph Otto	25	Billings, MT	OR	Clavey	Dorothy Louise	24	Chicago	IL
Larson	Sven	41	Colusa	SWD	Lussier	Minnie I.	38	San Francisco	IL
Larsson	Gustaf Adolf	29	San Francisco	SWD	Johnson	Lillian May	20	Sonoma	CA
Lascuola	Frank P.	21	San Francisco	CA	Cordes	Wanda H.	21	San Francisco	CA
Lass	Peter	46	San Francisco	GER	Friedrichs	Mariechen	25	Santa Rosa	GER
Lassen	Chris	21	Petaluma	GER	Hansen	Frieda Elsie	18	Petaluma	CA
Latell	Harry	27	San Francisco	PA	Fair	Helen	22	San Francisco	OR
Latimer	Hugh N. N.	29	Windsor	CA	Kingsbury	S., Mrs.	39	Windsor	CA
Latimer	Lorenzo P.	35	San Francisco	CA	Phelps	Jennie E.	35	Santa Rosa	WI
Laton	Edward Lee	24	Guerneville	CA	Flarity	Sadie M.	21	Guerneville	IL
Lattanzi	Emil C.	39	Santa Rosa	ITL	Dal Poggetto	Elena	29	Santa Rosa	ITL
Lattin	Perry Raymond	23	Alexander Valley	NE	Combs	Clara Edna	18	Alexander Valley	CA
Laufenburg	George	54	Petaluma	CA	Byce	Eveline	47	Petaluma	CA
Laufenburg ?	George	20	Petaluma	CA	Hinshaw	Mattie	26	Santa Rosa	CA
Lauge	Walter Harry	23	San Francisco	GER	Moore	Ruby Freeman	18	Colusa	CA
Laughlin	A. P.	29	Windsor	MO	Yarbrough	Mattie	23	Guerneville	CA
Laughlin	Gail Everil	22	Healdsburg	MO	Wilson	Mildred Irma	18	Windsor	CA

	Groom					Bride			
Surname	**Given Name**	**Age**	**Residence**	**BP**	**Surname**	**Given Name**	**Age**	**Residence**	**BP**
Laughlin	Glen P.	21		CA	Mitchell	Margaret E.	21	Guerneville	CA
Laughlin	Grant A.	41	Mark West	CA	Finley	Abbie J.	31	Santa Rosa	CA
Laughlin	John M.	28	Santa Rosa	CA	Hall	Sara C.	27	Santa Rosa	CA
Laughlin	Joseph P.	55	Healdsburg	MO	Beardin	Mary E., Mrs.	42	Healdsburg	OH
Laughlin	Joseph W.	31	Healdsburg	MO	Litton	Mary L.	38	Healdsburg	MO
Laughlin	Lester	31	Healdsburg	CA	DeWitt	Ruby Ruth	17	Healdsburg	KS
Laughlin	Merton	21+	Windsor	CA	Tarwater	Ida	19	Mark West Springs	CA
Laughlin	Merton	33	Windsor	CA	Laughlin	Maesota	18	Healdsburg	MO
Laughlin	Perry Raymond	25	Healdsburg	CA	Archer	Grace Dorothy	21	Healdsburg	CA
Laughlin	R. L.	19	Windsor	CA	Lafferty	Lola F.	18	Windsor	CA
Laughlin	Samuel McKendry	22	Windsor	MO	Laughlin	Josephine	19	Windsor	CA
Laugridge	Leo J.	29	San Francisco	CA	Hoffman	Nell M.	26	San Francisco	IA
Lauman	John	30	Fulton	IL	Gesel	Anne	25	Guerneville	SWT
Laumann	Arthur H.	21	Fulton	CA	Thomas	Florence L.	18	Fulton	CA
Laumann	Frank E.	25	Fulton	CA	Meyer	Dorothy S.	20	Fulton	CA
Laurance	George A.	29	Ukiah	CA	Thomas	Cora	17	Santa Rosa	CA
Laurence	John H.	29	Petaluma	CA	Jewett	May	21	Forestville	CA
Laurent	Ernest	24	Melita	CA	Nonnon	Marie	24	San Francisco	BLG
Laurent	Julius B.	26	Melita	BLG	Francard	Julia	18	Melita	BLG
Laurin	Robert	34	San Francisco	ENG	Phillips	Martha	26	Healdsburg	CA
Lauritano	Edward	21	Santa Rosa	CA	Perazzo	Julia	18	Asti	CA
Lauritzen	Chrisitian	42	Petaluma	GER	Dahlmann	Clara	26	Petaluma	CA
Lauritzen	Jesse C.	36	Petaluma	GER	Claassen	May	25	Petaluma	GER
Lauritzen	Knudt Broder	26	Petaluma	GER	Harms	Edith Johanna	23	Petaluma	Sfo
Lauritzen	Lewis	20	Petaluma	CA	Ayers	Veryl D.	19	Petaluma	CA
Lauritzen	Kundt	28	Petaluma	GER	Zamaroni	Jennie	24	Petaluma	CA
Laursen	Peter C.	33	Salinas	DNK	Fredericksen	Anna K.	28	Racine, WI	IA
Lausten	Louis Mitchell	30	San Francisco	GER	Caltoft	Mary	26	Petaluma	CA

	Groom					Bride			
Surname	**Given Name**	**Age**	**Residence**	**BP**	**Surname**	**Given Name**	**Age**	**Residence**	**BP**
Lauteren	Ferdinand	61	Redwood Twp.		Cnopius	Antoniette Maria	22	Forestville	
Laux	John Frances	25	Petaluma	CA	Burns	Nellie T.	22	Petaluma	CA
LaValley	Elmer R.	33	Cloverdale	IA	Nydegger	Anna C.	22	Santa Rosa	CA
Lavell	William T.	25	Fulton	CA	Newlin	Laura D., Mrs.	32	Santa Rosa	Son
Laveroni	Dave	22	Sonoma	CA	Bassi	Julia	20	Petaluma	
Lavin	Joseph E.	28	Los Angeles	CA	Doran	Josephine E.	22	Santa Rosa	CA
Lavio	Dazio	29	Petaluma	ITL	Stefenoni	Maria	27	Petaluma	
Lawford	William E.	33	San Francisco	IDA	Sprague	Blanche	26	Sonoma	IL
Lawler	Howard T.	21	San Francisco	CA	Hoffmann	Verona	21	San Francisco	CA
Lawler	James	40	San Francisco	CA	Hoover	Louise Booth	22	San Francisco	TX
Lawler	John Gardner	28	Petaluma	CA	Burns	Carrie Mable	20	Petaluma	CA
Lawler	John, Jr.	23	Petaluma	Pet	Poehlmann	Helen Mary	23	Petaluma	Pet
Lawrason	Dinnie Fred	19	Irmulco, CA	MI	Drake	Clarica	16	Windsor	CA
Lawrence	Bert M.	27	Santa Rosa	CA	Kimble	Annie M.	22	Sebastopol	CA
Lawrence	Chester Earl	27	Vacaville	KS	Smyth	Edith	24	Napa	CA
Lawrence	Frank	35	Hanford	AZR	Olivera	Margaret	31	Oakland	CA
Lawrence	Frank	25	Santa Rosa		Bean	Harriet Newell	21	Santa Rosa	
Lawrence	George	51	Alviso	AZR	Green	Frances	21	Sebastopol	CA
Lawrence	George Edwin	29	Santa Rosa	MA	Elmore	Lois Merrill	26	Santa Rosa	CA
Lawrence	Henry E.	74	Petaluma	TN	Falkner	Amelia, Mrs.	52	Petaluma	
Lawrence	Horace	39	San Francisco	WI	Riley	Mary	23	San Francisco	MO
Lawrence	James W.	28	Sebastopol	MA	Clayton	Alice	24	Sebastopol	IA
Lawrence	James W.	40	Forestville	IL	McPeek	Mary I.	30	Cambridge, OH	OH
Lawrence	Joseph G.	25	Alviso	AZR	Lawrence	Francis Green	27	Sebastopol	CA
Lawrence	William H.	27	Santa Rosa	CA	Diaz	Isabelle E.	18	Santa Rosa	MA
Lawry	William	41	Santa Rosa	CA	Cameron	Lottie	38	Santa Rosa	ID
Lawson	Charles Garfield	36	San Jose	IN	Freitas	Edna Lillian	28	Palo Alto	CA
Lawson	Grover E.	22	Santa Rosa	CA	Adams	Mary L.	20	Preston	CA

	Groom					Bride			
Surname	**Given Name**	**Age**	**Residence**	**BP**	**Surname**	**Given Name**	**Age**	**Residence**	**BP**
Lawson	Grover Edward	19	Petaluma	CA	Ruggs	Ola	18	Petaluma	IA
Lawson	Ivan G.	21	Petaluma	CA	Linscott	Hazel	21	Point Arena	CA
Lawson	J. P.	21	Santa Rosa	MO	Rima	Tina L.	15	Santa Rosa	KS
Lawson	Jesse Herbert	29	Santa Rosa	CA	Akers	Blanche Louisa	23	Ukiah	CA
Lawson	Oliver Lester	23	Healdsburg	CA	Young	Mattie Isadora	28	Healdsburg	CA
Lawson	Perry Alexander	38	Santa Rosa	MO	Wagner	Mazie	21	San Francisco	CA
Lawson	Thomas	23	Santa Rosa	CA	Lewis	Cora	26	Windsor	CA
Lawson	Z. Bert	32	Cottage Grove, Lane Co., OR	MN	Rees	Nettie	19	Stacy, Douglas Co., OR	MO
Lay	Henry D., Jr.				Mulligan	Ellen J.			
Laymance	F. W.	24	Windsor	CA	Robinson	Mary E.	29	Sebastopol	IA
Laymance	Francis M.	36	Healdsburg	MO	Clark	Leona	30	Healdsburg	MO
Laymance	George Ebin	20	Healdsburg		Hatch	Blanche	19	Healdsburg	
Laymance	Henry J.	29	Healdsburg	CA	Bruner	Ada B.	20	Windsor	CA
Laymance	Henry J.	21	Sonoma Co.	CA	Morris	Emma Allice	19	Sonoma Co.	KS
Lazier	Donald C.	26	Geyserville	CND	Gould	Mabel	25	Santa Rosa	IL
Lazzaroni	Peter	25	Healdsburg	ITL	Esaia (?)	Jennie	21	Healdsburg	ITL
Le Baron	Harrison M.	59	Valley Ford	CND	Davis	Helen, Mrs.	52	Bismark, ND	CND
Lea	Clarence F.	33	Santa Rosa	CA	Wright	Daisy A.	32	Santa Rosa	CA
Leabo	Benjamin	26	Portland, OR	OR	Stoetz	Louisa	30	Portland, OR	CA
Leach	John W.	35	San Francisco	CA	Marall	Christine M.	28	Petaluma	CA
Leach	Roy H.	19	Vacaville	OK	Knipp	Winfred	19	Perdue, OR	OR
Leachman	Ream S.	29	Vallejo	KY	Muller	Anna	20	Vallejo	CA
Leahey	Martin E.	21	Healdsburg	MI	Richey	Ella E.	19	Healdsburg	CA
Leahy	John	30	San Francisco	CA	Hoyne	Bessie E.	37	San Francisco	CA
Leal	Frank Avila	23	San Francisco	CA	Silva	Annie	19	Santa Rosa	AZR
Leaner	Maurice	28	Oakland	AUS	Kronich	Hannah	21	Oakland	RUS
Leard	Charles M.	26	Healdsburg	CA	Bale	Loletta	22	Healdsburg	CA
Leard	J. B.	34	Healdsburg		Nooland	A. A.	24	Healdsburg	
Leard	Robert B.	25	Healdsburg	CA	Miller	Effie C.	22	Healdsburg	CA

Groom					Bride				
Surname	Given Name	Age	Residence	BP	Surname	Given Name	Age	Residence	BP
Leathe	Frank C.	27	Mill Valley	CA	Tobin	Alice M.	28	Mill Valley	CA
Leathers	G. N.	32	San Francisco	KY	Winters	Theresa I.	25	Petaluma	NY
Leathers	Harry Allison	26	Santa Rosa	PA	Morrill	Julia Marie	24	Santa Rosa	CA
Leavenworth	Randolph J.	30	San Francisco	CA	McBrown	Marie M.	29	Petaluma	CA
Leavitt	Albert Henry	26	Cloverdale	CA	Gotterba	Leona Inez	17	Cloverdale	CA
LeBallister	Thomas W.	21	San Francisco	CA	Sander	Ida D.	18	Sebastopol	CA
LeBaron	Adelbert J.	24	Santa Rosa	CND	Forsyth	M. Margaret	22	Santa Rosa	CA
LeBaron	C. A.	23	Valley Ford	CA	Johnson	Annie	22	Valley Ford	CA
LeBaron	Harrison M.	36	Valley Ford		Palmer	Sarah Emily	20	Valley Ford	
LeBaron	Harrison M., Jr.	21	Valley Ford	CA	Slattery	Frances	20	Bloomfield	CA
Lebech	Andreas	28	Petaluma	GER	Ketelsen	Freda	22	Petaluma	GER
Leber	Albert L.	24	Oakland	IL	Savage	Laura I.	24	Santa Rosa	CA
LeCarn	F.	30	San Francisco	CA	Torre	A. C.	28	Amador	CA
Lecchetti	Tony	35	Cloverdale	ITL	Gargini	Zaira	18	Cloverdale	ITL
Leclileiter	Joseph A.	27	San Francisco	CA	Bowen	La Verne	20	San Francisco	CA
Lecost	William A.				Stewart	Emeline E.			
Ledford	Clayton A.	35	Yorkville		England	Mary	18	Cloverdale	
Ledford	Frank M.	29	Yorkville	CA	Johnson	Ina B.	20	Geyserville	OR
Ledford	George Lee	31	Cloverdale	CA	Caughey	May	25	Cloverdale	CA
Ledford	J. H.	32	Yorkville	CA	Hayes	Mae	17	Yorkville	CA
Ledford	John Irvin	19	Cloverdale	CA	Capell	Ethel Pauline	17	Healdsburg	CA
Ledford	Leonard Dowler	20	Cloverdale	Soc	Hixson	Mildred Janette	17	Cloverdale	Soc
Ledford	William F.	37	Yorkville	CA	Larsen	Stella M.	18	Cloverdale	MN
Ledger	Guy Wallace	21	Wendling, Medocino Co	CA	Darr	Lena	18	Elk	CA
Lee	Alban	28	Sausalito	SD	Jones	Myrtle A.	23	Sausalito	MI
Lee	Charles A.	31	Tehachapi	IN	Perry	Ellen, Mrs.	28	Tehachapi	CND
Lee	Charles E.	28	Santa Rosa		Schutts (?)	Teresa L.	21	Santa Rosa	
Lee	Edward P.	47	San Francisco	MN	Blindhein (?)	Alma	30	San Francisco	NRY
Lee	George S., Jr.	31	Lower Lake	CA	Shaul	Velma Jessie	18	Lower Lake	CA

	Groom					Bride			
Surname	Given Name	Age	Residence	BP	Surname	Given Name	Age	Residence	BP
Lee	Olaf	21	Santa Rosa	CA	Gotrig	Stella Marie	16	Santa Rosa	ND
Lee	Richard A.	25	Fulton	KS	Voss	Anna K.	24	Mark West	CA
Lee	Rollen M.	28	Jamestown, NY	NY	McHarvey	Mary	28	Sonoma	CA
Lee	W. H.	30	Santa Rosa	MI	Casto	Mamie	27	Santa Rosa	CA
Lee	Walter	27	San Francisco	CO	Wood	Clara Edith	18	Santa Rosa	CA
Leech	Albert Ernest	27	Sonoma	AUT	Jacobs	Nettie Ellen	24	Healdsburg	CA
Leedy	Chester Clyde	26	Ukiah	MO	Maupin	Olive Pearl	30	Ukiah	CA
Leek	Charles E.	22	Mark West	IL	Van Winkle	Olive	19	Mark West	CA
Leephart	James H.	27	San Francisco	OH	Anderson	Nellie V.	26	San Francisco	KY
Leete	Orton R.	46	Santa Rosa	CT	Peddrazzi	Margaret	28	Santa Rosa	GER
LeFebvre	Eugene O.	27	Petaluma	CA	Adams	Jennie M.	24	Petaluma	CND
LeFever	Eugene	21	San Francisco	CA	Alonso	Ruth C.	18	San Francisco	CA
Leffler	Herman V.	25	San Francisco	CA	MacGregor	Mabel C.	28	Santa Rosa	CA
Leffmann	Julius W.	41	San Francisco	PA	Sykes	Lillian R.	25	Penngrove	ENG
Legg	Edward T.	21	Yorkville	CA	Pallady	Viola E.	18	Yorkville	CA
Legg	Samuel M.	27	Sonoma Co.	IA	Wall	Ella	20	Sonoma Co.	CA
Legg	Samuel M.	41	Windsor	IA	Pallady	Ida M.	34	Windsor	MO
Legg	W. H.	28	Forestville		McIntosh	Mary Ellen	22	Forestville	
Leggett	A. E.	26	Santa Rosa	IA	Ballou	Althea L.	19	Santa Rosa	CA
Leggett	Charles F.	23	Santa Rosa	CA	Wendt	Mollie	22	Santa Rosa	CA
Leggett	Elmer E.	26	Santa Rosa	CA	Wiley	Minnie H.	19	Green Valley	CA
Leggett	Henry B.	26	Santa Rosa	CA	Fulkerson	Nora C.	16	Santa Rosa	CA
Leggett	Raford Wesley	22	Santa Rosa	CA	Lukas	Lavana Ruth	20	Santa Rosa	CA
Leggett	William Alexander	28	Sonoma Co.	CA	Willey	Fannie B.	18	Freestone	CA
LeGoullon	L. C.	27	Palo Alto	PA	Remer	Bertha A.	19	Oakland	TX
Lehman	George	51	Santa Rosa	FRN	Bumford (?)	Mary I.	26	Santa Rosa	IA
Lehn	Charles	26	Santa Rosa		Adams	Emma	20	Petaluma	
Lehn	Charles				Strother	Joanna			
Lehn	Louis	27	Windsor	CA	Kennedy	Maggie	26	Windsor	NV

	Groom				Bride				
Surname	Given Name	Age	Residence	BP	Surname	Given Name	Age	Residence	BP
Leib	Jacob	33	Healdsburg	GER	Pugni	Ida	22	Vallejo	SWT
Leibert	Robert E.	24	Healdsburg	CA	Lelouarn	Celestine	21	Healdsburg	CA
Leiby	George	41	Sebastopol	FRN	Roberts	Katie, Mrs.	32	Santa Rosa	SWT
Leich	James L.				Virgil	Martha E.			
Leichter	Paul F.	29	Geyserville	Sfo	Hastings	Johnietta B.	19	Geyserville	TX
Leighton	Fred H.	27	Napa	NH	Hall	Grace E.	18	Healdsburg	CA
Leininger	Daniel W.	31	Chico	IL	Cordevant	Lilly	25	Healdsburg	CA
Leisen	William C.	19	Santa Rosa	Sfo	Leisen	Jennie, Mrs.	26	Santa Rosa	PA
Leiser	George	30	Sonoma	KS	Breitenbach	Emma Anita	25	Sonoma	CA
Leisinger	George Henry	36	Santa Rosa	PA	Proctor	Kate	31	Healdsburg	CA
Leithman	Louis L.	25	Oakland	CA	Williams	Lottie E.	18	Healdsburg	CA
Leithold	John V.	25	Woodland	IA	Moreland	Esther	20	Healdsburg	OR
Lelinger	August C.	21+	San Francisco	MO	Murphy	Mary Elizabeth	21+	Petaluma	Pet
Lelounarn	John	26	Healdsburg	CA	Terry	Della	17	Healdsburg	CA
Lemaihe (?)	Louis	22	Mill Valley	CA	Murphy	Myrtle	18	Monterey	ID
Lemay	Josiah	26	Mark West Springs	OR	Adams	Ellen	21	Santa Rosa	MO
Lemon	Joseph P.	25	Hanford	AZR	Ramos	Mary E.	21	Vine Hill	CA
Lemos	J. F.	25	Petaluma	PRT	Marshall	E. E.	23	Petaluma	PRT
Lemos	John B.	25	Cotati	PRT	DeBorba	Mary L.	17	Cotati	CA
Lencioni	Agostino	40	Healdsburg	ITL	Sbragia	Nanziata	27	Healdsburg	ITL
Lencioni	Henry	25	San Francisco	ITL	Alberigi	Ancilla	19	Healdsburg	CA
Lencioni	Domenico	21	Healdsburg	CA	Puccioni	Lena	20	Healdsburg	CA
Leneve	Edward	25	Healdsburg	OR	Cozad	Bertha M.	17	Healdsburg	CA
Lenhart	Lee R.	28	Santa Rosa	WI	Morse	Mary	22	Santa Rosa	IL
Lennard	Edward	37	San Francisco	CA	Downs	Annie	38	San Francisco	MO
Lennon	Edward Francis	48	Red Bluff	CA	Lewis	Annie A. Walter	43	Sebastopol	IN
Lent	D. A.	33	Petaluma	NSC	Gregory	Susie	18	Petaluma	CA
Lentz	Walter Edward	31	Santa Rosa	CA	Bedford	Elise	20	Santa Rosa	ENG
Leona	Frank J.	24	Santa Rosa	CA	Peck	Henerietta	26	San Francisco	CA

	Groom					Bride			
Surname	**Given Name**	**Age**	**Residence**	**BP**	**Surname**	**Given Name**	**Age**	**Residence**	**BP**
Leonard	James M.	24	Sutro, NV	MA	Hobart	Jessie Margaret	22	Santa Rosa	NV
Leonardi	Joseph	23	Santa Rosa	Monte-vedio, SAM	Burlando	Amelia	16	Santa Rosa	ITL
Leonardini	Paolo (Paul)	23	Santa Rosa	URG	Paravinni	Maria	30	Santa Rosa	ITL
Leonesio	Frank	22	San Rafael	CA	Silva	Lydia	20	San Rafael	CA
Leoni	Placido F.	34	Petaluma	SWT	Zanoni	Lena	21	Petaluma	SWT
Lepori	Peter	45	Sonoma	SWT	Lafranchi	Mary	50	Sonoma	SWT
Leppo	David Harrison	25	Santa Rosa	IA	McNear	Clara	21	Petaluma	CA
Leppo	O. Frank	27	Santa Rosa	IA	Spottswood	Minerva Belle	21	Santa Rosa	CA
Lerouge	Stephen A.	30	Ridgefield, WA	IL	Deputy	Isabelle	18	Battle Ground, WA	CA
Leroux	Arthur	21	Oakland	CA	Cottle	Ella	19	Geyserville	CA
Leroux	Robert	24	Cloverdale	CA	Peterson	Elsie	21	Alexander Valley	CA
Leroux	Walter George	26	Cloverdale	KS	Hall	Marion Belle	19	Pasadena	CA
Leslie	Charles W.	35	Bakersfield	CA	Hotchkiss	Anna	25	Healdsburg	KY
Less	Alexander S.	35	San Francisco	CA	Searl	Lotta	27	Philadelphia	KS
Lester	B. W.	26	Penngrove	RI	Rooney	Mary	22	Petaluma	IRL
Lestingue	Jean	55	Sonoma	FRN	Bertres	Marie, Mrs.	40	Sonoma	FRN
Leva	Leo Frank	30	San Francisco	ITL	Meineri	Edith A.	21	Cloverdale	CA
Levansaler	Russell J.	21	Vallejo	CA	Clarke	Agnes T.	20	Vallejo	CA
Levens	Harry Stocking	25	San Francisco	OH	Barboni	Celestina	23	Freestone	CA
Leveroni	Victor L.	31	Sonoma	CA	Bremer	Elmira G.	25	Sonoma	CA
Levey	Morris	39	Glen Ellen	CA	Bosch	Katherine	19	Vineburg	CA
Levich	George	34	British Columbia	ENG	Ruebenack	Ella A.	24	Sebastopol	MI
Levine	Abraham	32	Petaluma	RUS	Schachter	Mary	28	Petaluma	ROM
Levy	Alexander	34	San Francisco	CA	Von Pokrzywnicki	Hattie	19	San Francisco	GER
Levy	Harold Walter	30	San Francisco	CA	Creighton	Elizabeth M.	30	Seattle	MI
Levy	Joseph	47	San Francisco	FRN	Heine	Helen	24	San Francisco	CA
Levy	Robert	23	San Francisco	CA	Miller	Minnie D.	19	San Francisco	CA

	Groom					Bride			
Surname	**Given Name**	**Age**	**Residence**	**BP**	**Surname**	**Given Name**	**Age**	**Residence**	**BP**
Lewell	Luther Enloe	24	Berkeley	TN	Rambo	Esther Irene	21	Santa Rosa	CA
Lewis	Albert Ray	23	Cloverdale	Colusa Co.	Daniels	Nellie Estella	19	Cloverdale	OR
Lewis	Calvin McM.	62	Healdsburg	OH	Dodson	Minnie M.	38	Healdsburg	KS
Lewis	Charles Wadsworth	50	Petaluma	CA	Goodwin	Mary Elizabeth	50	Petaluma	MA
Lewis	Edwin	19	Santa Rosa	NE	Skinner	Pearl Ethel	15+	Santa Rosa	
Lewis	Harry D.	24	Graton	OR	DeRose	Lenora	19	Petaluma	CA
Lewis	J. F.				Van Allen	Emeline C., Mrs.			
Lewis	J. Hall	34	Half Moon Bay	CA	Bartlett	Frances Gertrude	23	Petaluma	ENG
Lewis	Jere	59	Healdsburg	OH	Wetherbee	Elizabeth C.	44	Healdsburg	MA
Lewis	John F.	26	Santa Rosa	CA	Fisher	Florence M.	23	Santa Rosa	CA
Lewis	Joseph Walter	33	Redding	IL	Pfost	Alice May	19	Ukiah	KS
Lewis	Ralph	25	Windsor	CA	Robbins	Cora	18	Windsor	CA
Lewis	Ray A.	21	Sacramento	CA	Wheeler	Alta	20	Sacramento	OR
Lewis	Saml. R.				Williams	Mary E., Mrs.			
Lewis	Samuel B.	30	Sonoma	KS	White	May E.	25	Kenwood	CA
Lewis	Washington J.	30	Bodega		Towner (?)	Adeline	19	Bodega	
Lezzeni	Joseph Andrew	26	Fairfax	CA	Raphael	Hazel Evelyn	25	San Francisco	Por
Libbey	William S.	29	Vallejo	WI	Willet	Nora M.	21	Vallejo	OR
Libby	George W.	24	Sebastopol	ME	Brown	Leila Emma	23	Santa Rosa	CA
Lichan	Arthur Lincoln	34	Kenwood	CA	Sutherland	Annie Beulah	22	Kenwood	CA
Lichau	Charles Fabian	24	Bloomfield	CA	Farrer	Jessie Catherine	20	Bloomfield	UT
Lichau	Edward P.	28	Penngrove	CA	Esler	Della	20	Petaluma	CA
Lichau	Ernest A.	30	Penngrove	CA	Whitaker	Julia H.	17	Santa Rosa	CA
Lichau	George	25	Oakdale	CA	Riebli	Annie	19	Penngrove	CA
Lichau	Henry P., Jr.	48	Penngrove	MA	Keithly	Lucy B., Mrs.	31	Rochester, MA	MA
Lichau	Henry Peter	78	Penngrove	GER	Stackhouse	Mary Elizabeth	36	Penngrove	NBW
Licht	George J.	30	San Francisco	NY	Underwood	Pearl Alphia	28	San Francisco	CA

	Groom					Bride			
Surname	**Given Name**	**Age**	**Residence**	**BP**	**Surname**	**Given Name**	**Age**	**Residence**	**BP**
Liddle	W. J.	41	Petaluma	CND	Green	Mary A.	23	Petaluma	PA
Liddle	William S.	30	Sebastopol	SCT	McVean	Martha M.	17	Sebastopol	KS
Liggett	Thomas, Jr.	22	Cloverdale	CA	Jenkins	Hulda	18	Marysville	OR
Light	Elisha	23	Chileno Valley	CA	Schlake	Lizzie	23	Novato	CA
Light	Wm. R.	24	Stony Point		Smith	Rosetta (?) J.	21	Two Rock	
Lightner	Raymond J.	20	Guerneville	AZ	Vascaressa	Henrietta M.	24	Guerneville	CA
Ligore	David Claude	44	San Francisco	TN	Cooney	Mary Eleanor	32	San Francisco	CA
Likins	James L.	22	Healdsburg	MO	Stapp	Dovey	21	Healdsburg	CA
Lile	Joseph A.	24	Cloverdale	MO	Ingram	Bell E.	23	Cloverdale	CA
Lincoln	Ulysses G.	31	Dunigans, Yolo Co.	CA	Adams	Abbie Mary	28	Upper Lake	CA
Lind	Aogost	29	Santa Rosa	RUS	Giles	Lizzie	22	Santa Rosa	MA
Lind	Charles W.	21	San Francisco	CA	Quackenbush	Luella D.	21	Santa Rosa	CA
Lindenbaum	Louis	44	San Francisco	AUS	Siegle	Sarah	35	Sonoma	RUS
Linderman	Clyde E.	50	Los Angeles	IL	Leef	Edith F.	43	Los Angeles	MD
Lindig	Charley D.	56	Santa Rosa	GER	Kramer	Regine	54	San Francisco	GER
Lindley	Charles	26	Santa Rosa	IL	Lewis	Nellie	21	Santa Rosa	WA
Lindner	John D.				Maule	Lucinda, Mrs.			
Lindon	Harvey J.	21	Vallejo	VA	Magnani	Eugenia M.	20	Vallejo	KS
Lindsay	Adin Arthur	25	Windsor	CA	Shuster	Ivy Irene	18	Duncans Mills	CA
Lindsey	Calvin				Barney	Ophelia			
Lindsey	Elon	37	San Francisco	WI	Lange	Catherine	33	San Francisco	CA
Lindsey	Frank	30	Santa Rosa	IL	Keenan	Anna	25	Santa Rosa	CND
Lindsey	William A.	38	Cloverdale	IL	Elden	Helena	24	Cloverdale	AZ
Lindsley	Alfred	41	Santa Rosa	NV	Rowan	Albertine	26	San Francisco	CA
Lindstrom	Charles Otto	46	Willows	SWD	Miller	Lois	26	Healdsburg	CA
Lindstrom	Henry F.	35	Gualala	SWD	Johnson	Mary Caroline	18	Stewarts Point	CA
Linebaugh	Abraham	37	Analy	TN	Millingtin (?)	Ollie	28	Santa Rosa	IA
Linebaugh	Charles	21+	Two Rock	Soc	Cunningham	Lillian N.	21+	Two Rock	Mac
Linebaugh	Columbus	23	Santa Rosa	IA	Hervey	Katie	17	Santa Rosa	MI

	Groom					Bride			
Surname	**Given Name**	**Age**	**Residence**	**BP**	**Surname**	**Given Name**	**Age**	**Residence**	**BP**
Linebaugh	Francis Elmer	23	Sebastopol	CA	Driver	Edith Katherine	18	Sebastopol	CA
Linebaugh	Robert	23	Sebastopol	CA	Berry	Gertrude	21	Sebastopol	CA
Linebaugh	Robert A.	44	Two Rock	CA	Robertson	Rose	23	Valley Ford	CA
Linebaugh	Robert A.	22	Analy Twp.		Lloyd	Emma May	19	Petaluma	
Linebaugh	Robert F.	20			Dunn	Daisy B.			
Linebaugh	William A.	31	Petaluma	CA	Nisson	Anna	24	Petaluma	CA
Lingenfelter	Charles H.	31	Santa Rosa	CA	Stearns	Ethel A.	23	Santa Rosa	CA
Linn	Allen McLeod	37	Mendocino City	SCT	Dakin	Eunice I.	30	Windsor	CA
Linoberg	Montague L.	25	Los Angeles	CA	Kahn	Estelle	19	Petaluma	CA
Linse	C. F.	23	Seattle	UT	Quade	Martha L.	21	Seattle	MN
Linser	Frederick W.	24	Richmond	CA	Bloom	Anna M.	33	Richmond	OH
Linsley	Winfield S.	33	Santa Rosa	MD	Hocker	Alice	22	Santa Rosa	CA
Linthicum	J. F.	51	Sacramento	VA	Peterson	Annie F.	34	Santa Rosa	MO
Linton	T. S.	24	Forestville	IL	Davis	Lydia A.	21	Forestville	CA
Linville	Clement R.	21	Santa Rosa Twp.	CA	Pocock	Eva	19	Calistoga	ENG
Linz	Adelbert G.	24	Santa Rosa	NY	Ward	Rosine T.	18	San Francisco	TX
Lippi	Dean Orlando	23	San Francisco	Sfo	Scatena	Eda Norma	21	Healdsburg	Sfo
Lippitt	Frank K.	41	Petaluma	CA	Lysnar	Edith E.	36	Petaluma	NZD
Lippold	Alfred E.	21	San Francisco	IN	Andrews	Lilian Grayce	21	Petaluma	CA
Lires	Ramon	33	San Francisco	SPN	Garcia	Marie Blasa	19	San Francisco	SPN
Liston	Van Wyck	22	Chicago	NY	Stewart	Edith J.	22	Santa Rosa	IL
Litchfield	Frank S.	23	San Francisco	CA	Haas	Vera R.	30	San Francisco	CA
Lithwin	August	24	Santa Rosa	GER	Wilson	Iva Selina	16	Santa Rosa	CND
Little	Wilbert James	19	Sebastopol	CA	Ward	Hattie May	18	Santa Rosa	CA
Litton	A. P.	23	Healdsburg	MO	Keys	Nellie	25	Forestville	CA
Litton	Bearse A.	27	Healdsburg	CA	Featherly	Fannie	30	San Francisco	CA
Litton	H. B.	21	Mendocino Twp.		Yarbough	Saddie	20	Redwood Twp	
Litton	Roy Burton	23	East Oakland	CA	Hildebrand	Lena Rivers	23	Santa Rosa	OR
Litton	William	26	Healdsburg	CA	Rackliff	Ella C.	20	Healdsburg	CA
Livernash	Edward J.	25	Healdsburg	CA	Overton	Jessie	26	Santa Rosa	CA

	Groom					Bride			
Surname	Given Name	Age	Residence	BP	Surname	Given Name	Age	Residence	BP
Livernast	John J.	22	Santa Ana	CA	Schultz	Elizabeth	22	Cloverdale	CA
Livingston	Charles	55	Sebastopol	MO	Dougherty	Lillian E., Mrs.	53	Sebastopol	NY
Livingston	Charles S.	29	Duncans Mill	IL	Taylor (?)	Elizabeth	23	San Rafael	MN ?
Livingston	Edward Perry	34	Garberville	CA	Nobles	Minnie Frances	20	Sonoma Co.	CA
Livingston	Harry Henry	27	Santa Rosa	MN	Russell	Isabelle Adelaide	18	Bellevue	NJ
Livingston	William Jesse	27	Santa Rosa	CA	Crow	Luella Rains	25	Santa Rosa	CA
Lloyd	Hubert T.	24	San Francisco	Chi	Cline	Jennie	21	Santa Rosa	CA
Lloyd	Louis A.	24	San Francisco	MS	Purvine	Jeannette D.	24	Petaluma	CA
Lloyd	Walter A. L.	31	Windsor	CA	Lake	Grace E.	24	Bloomfield	CA
Lobb	Lewis	23	Geyserville	WI	Gordon	Ruby Ethel	21	Geyserville	CA
Locatelli	Antonio	28	Fulton	ITL	Figini	Margherita	18	Fulton	ITL
Locatelli	Luigi	29	Windsor	ITL	Locatelli	Teresina	19	Windsor	ITL
Lochmer	Joseph K.	29	San Francisco	GER	Johnson	Emma	27	San Francisco	SWD
Lock	Charles	23	Rincon Valley		Cauckwell (?)	Mary E. C.	19	Rincon Valley	
Lock	Ernest Lawrence	23	Geyserville	CA	Buhl	Dorothy Inez	23	Santa Rosa	CA
Lock	William H.	31	Santa Rosa	ENG	Norris	Julia	30	Santa Rosa	ENG
Lock	Wm. H.	22	Santa Rosa	CA	Hornbuckle	Lulu J.	20	Santa Rosa	MO
Lockard	Joseph H.	39	Napa	NV	Batten	Sarah, Mrs.	43	Santa Rosa	CA
Locke	Albert	25	Santa Rosa	ENG	Butler	Lillian R.	19	Santa Rosa	Hon
Locke	Augustus Caldwell	23	Santa Rosa	CA	Loveland	Inez Lillian	18	Healdsburg	CA
Locke	George	26	Guerneville		Smith	Ada	19	Guerneville	
Locke	J. B.	24	Santa Rosa	CA	Feehan	Lizzie	24	Santa Rosa	CA
Lockhart	Archie	27	Santa Rosa	NE	Reid	Esther B.	24	Santa Rosa	CA
Lockhart	Robert	29	Mendocino Co.	IRL	Ritchie	Maggie J.	24	Freestone	IRL
Lockie	James S.	46	Cotati	SCT	McEwan	Maggie	30	Oakland	SCT
Lockwood	Frank B.	35	Sebastopol	CA	Dodenhoff	Edythe W.	23	Sebastopol	CA
Lockwood	Harry E.	34	San Francisco	CA	Rivers	Mabel	20	Santa Rosa	CO

	Groom					Bride			
Surname	Given Name	Age	Residence	BP	Surname	Given Name	Age	Residence	BP
Lockwood	James Otis	60	Lodi	OH	Sharp	Sara M.	58	Green Mountain, IA	MI
Lodge	David E.	31	Petaluma	CA	Noble	Lizzie	17	Petaluma	PA
Lodovico	Morgantine	35	Valley Ford	SWT	DeGiorgi	Giuseppina	32	Laguna, CA	SWT
Loftus	Thomas M.	22	San Francisco	CA	Harrison	Viola M.	17	San Francisco	CA
Loftus	William	36	Petaluma	CND	Murphey	Margarett L.	28	Petaluma	CA
Logan	Howard	24	Berkeley	NSC	Cashdollar	Algie B.	22	Two Rock	NY
Logan	John F.	35	Sebastopol	CA	Richey	Ellen May	25	Fresno	KY
Logan	Roy Sylvester	23	Healdsburg	IL	Dawkins	Lillian E.	22	Healdsburg	CND
Logan	Walter	61	Santa Rosa	SCT	Shulman	Lillie	46	San Francisco	HLD
Logue	James P.	24	San Francisco	CA	Rushton	Coovaa Oral	20	San Francisco	CA
Loiser (?)	Gustave A.	25	Healdsburg		Conger	Antoinette Isabel	16	Healdsburg	
Lomax	Walter B.	40	San Leandro	CA	Langenour	Irma R.	38	Palo Alto	CA
Lombardi	Guiseppe	26	Santa Rosa	ITL	Bertoli	Carmella	20	Santa Rosa	ITL
Lombardi	Joseph Augustus	25	San Francisco	ITL	Paolini	Mary Innocentia	22	Santa Rosa	ITL
Lombardi	Peter	26	Guernville	ITL	Bonaccorsi	Mary	18	Guerneville	Cazadero
Londen	Melville Charles	33	San Francisco	CA	Fields	Margaret	29	San Francisco	AUT
Loney	David M.	31	Grass Valley	CA	Busher	Marion Gladys	24	Sebastopol	OH
Long	Alfred G.	23	Healdsburg	CA	Hoffman	Louise A.	22	Healdsburg	MO
Long	Charles H.	24	Petaluma	KS	Willis	Mary Elizabeth	19	Petaluma	CA
Long	Charles H.	33	Petaluma	KS	Long	Mary E.	27	Petaluma	OR
Long	D. W.	31	Petaluma	CA	Mallen	Kate F.	22	Lakeville	CA
Long	Geo. W.	18			Davis	Mary E.			
Long	George	39	San Francisco	IL	Leathe	Alice May	39	Mill Valley	CA
Long	Harold C.	23	Healdsburg	CA	Garrison	Bertha B.	18	Santa Rosa	CA
Long	James N.	23	Santa Rosa	CA	Johnson	Della A.	18	Santa Rosa	CA
Long	John Suoddy? Beach	23	Healdsburg		Copple	Mary	19	Healdsburg	

	Groom					Bride			
Surname	**Given Name**	**Age**	**Residence**	**BP**	**Surname**	**Given Name**	**Age**	**Residence**	**BP**
Long	R. H.	27	Los Angeles	MO	Offuit	Ella	23	Petaluma	CA
Long	William Lile	22	Petaluma	CO	Napper	Maude Ethel	18	Petaluma	CA
Longley	John A.	25	Mountain View	MA	Dale	Clara E.	21	Geyserville	CA
Longsine	William M.	30	Santa Rosa	WI	Scott	Lottie	26	Hopland	MO
Lonkey	Lloyd C.	29	San Francisco	NV	Young	Ivy M.	29	San Francisco	MI
Loomis	Denton W.	45	Cloverdale	PA	Fenner	Sarah C.	23	Cloverdale	MI
Lopera	Rafael Riviera	37	Santa Rosa	SPN	Martines	Maria Lopes	24	Santa Rosa	SPN
Lopez	Charles Paul	23	Santa Rosa	CA	Burke	Anna Matilda	18	Upper Lake	CA
Lopus	Frank R.	24	Penngrove	CA	Peters	Mary	19	Petaluma	CA
Lopus	George E.	23	Penngrove	CA	Young	Cora B.	20	Windsor	CA
Lopus	Joseph	26	Penngrove	CA	Herbert	Frances H.	18	Cotati	CA
Lorange	John				Norsworthy	Hattie F.			
Lorenze	Albert D.	35	Oakland	IL	Ludwick	Elma	36	Oakland	NY
Lorenzen	Philip S.	33	Petaluma	GER	Rörden	Ricke G.	24	Petaluma	GER
Lorenzi	Luigi	41	Santa Rosa	ITL	Antonietti	Angelina	46	Santa Rosa	ITL
LoRomer	J. B.	45	Stockton	NY	Raab	Minnie G.	25	Stockton	
Lotti	A.	34	Cloverdale	ITL	Fienili	Rosa	29	Cloverdale	ITL
Lottman	W. B.	23	Sprauge, Lincoln Co, WA Terr.	CA	Eagleson	Anna May	19	Santa Rosa	CA
Loukemann ?	Richard	38	Occidental	GER	Robinett	Mary J.	23	Occidental	CA
Loukes	Harris Fisk	19	Petaluma	MI	Baldwin	Cora B.	18	Petaluma	KS
Louvis	Steven	28	San Francisco	GRC	Avila	Mary Ruth	19	Sebastopol	CA
Love	Francis	39	San Francisco	SCT	Donahue	Margaret	38	San Francisco	CA
Love	Wm.				Adams	Margaret, Mrs.			
Lovejoy	George P.	21+	Petaluma	CA	Bryant	Effie Lyle	18+	Petaluma	CA
Lovejoy	Robert T.	20	Covelo	CA	Ells	Inice R.	23	Covelo	CA
Loveland	E. A.	36	Cloverdale	IA	Hancock	Mary	26	Cloverdale	MO
Lovell	David J.				Bones	Elizabeth A.			
Lovell	Frank P.	24	Geyserville	CA	Gathergood	Della Clyde	23	Healdsburg	CA
Lovell	James T.	22	Guerneville	CA	Hopper	Eva Elizabeth	16	Guerneville	CA

	Groom					Bride			
Surname	Given Name	Age	Residence	BP	Surname	Given Name	Age	Residence	BP
Lovell	John	47	Fisherman's Bay	MO	Cox	Mary Catherine, Mrs.	54	Fisherman's Bay	IL
Lovell	John M.	30	Healdsburg	TX	Lovell	Sarah	20	Healdsburg	CA
Lovell	Kenneth Henry	21	Santa Rosa	CA	English	Norma Beulah	18	Santa Rosa	CA
Lovell	Walter G.	25	Healdsburg	CA	Hill	Mae	25	Cloverdale	CA
Lovell	William Ferdinand	23	Covelo	CA	Thompson	Lucy Myrtle	18	Covelo	CA
Lovell	William I.	26	Geyserville	CA	Williams	Daisy Dean	21	Geyserville	KS
Lovinggood	Harmon G.	34	San Francisco	GA	Musser	Edith E.	29	San Francisco	CA
Lovotti	F.	31	San Francisco	BUA	Lagomarsino	Rosa E.	21	Santa Rosa	CA
Low	William R.	59	San Francisco	SCT	Palmer	Jennie, Mrs.	43	Alameda Co.	CA
Lowary	Joseph F.	27	Santa Rosa	AL	McMenamin	Rosa	23	Santa Rosa	IRL
Lowe	Dawson	35	Two Rock Valley		Linebaugh	Mary Jane	19	Blucher Valley	
Lowe	George W.	59	Petaluma	ENG	Herges	Celia K.	47	San Francisco	GER
Lowe	Herbert E.	21	Berkeley	CA	Dryer	Bessie L.	22	Berkeley	TX
Lowe	Hugh O.	34	Sebastopol	IL	Whitney	Mabel L.	31	San Francisco	IA
Lowe	James Garrett	40	Belen, NM	KS	Shaughnessy	Margaret A., Mrs.	37	San Francisco	MA
Lowell	George R.	28	Sonoma	CA	Weber	Sophie A.	22	Sonoma	CA
Lower	John	18	Santa Rosa	OR	Doremus	Florence M.	21	Santa Rosa	NE
Lowery	James N.	36	Healdsburg	OH	Hatfield	Mary J., Mrs.	31	Healdsburg	CA
Lowery	Mansfield B.	23	Oleum	CA	Phillips	Henrietta C.	19	Freestone	CA
Lowery	Robert D.	22	Santa Rosa	CA	Fisher	Etta E.	20	Santa Rosa	VT
Lownes	John	21	Healdsburg	CA	King	Irene	18	Healdsburg	CA
Lowrey	Frederick D.	25	Honolulu	Honolulu	Parsons	Leila A.	21	Santa Rosa	CA
Lowrey	George A.	28	Healdsburg	CA	Patton	Lillian E.	18	Healdsburg	CA
Lowrey	George W.	27	Freestone	CA	Black	Jessie F.	24	Elkhart, IN	IN
Lowrey	Leroy	30	Rock Pile, Sonoma Co.		Dennis	Sarah E.	17	Rock Pile Ranch	

	Groom					Bride			
Surname	Given Name	Age	Residence	BP	Surname	Given Name	Age	Residence	BP
Lowrey	Robert L.	24	Gualala	CA	Cameron	Martha M., Mrs.	25	Santa Rosa	CA
Lowrey	Thomas J.	25	Freestone	CA	Wyllie	Beatrice	20	Freestone	CA
Lowry	Chas. E. C.	24	Santa Rosa	CND	Perrier	Katheen	20	Santa Rosa	ENG
Lowry	Herbert L.	23	Hume	GA	Armstrong	Florence	20	Santa Rosa	CA
Lowry	J. W.	58	Butler, Bates Co. MO	KY	Farmer	Rebecca W.	50	Santa Rosa	MO
Lowry	Nicholas M.				Hensley	Mary E.			
Lowry	Patrick Joseph	39	San Francisco	MA	Elias	Margaret Josephine	39	San Francisco	CA
Lucas	Jacob	24	Santa Rosa	RUS	Johnson	Allie	23	Santa Rosa	CA
Lucas	Joseph	24	San Bruno	CA	Reese	Emma, Mrs.	28	Napa	GER
Lucchesi	Alberto	21	Bulwinkle	CA	Petrini	Lena Lizzie	17	Hilton	ITL
Lucchesi	Enrico	26	Oakland	ITL	Del Fava	Gina	18	Healdsburg	ITL
Lucchesi	Francisco	32	Healdsburg	ITL	Paccini	Italia	17	Healdsburg	ITL
Luce	Chas. F.	29	Petaluma	OR	Martin	Amy	21	Petaluma	CA
Luce	Elmer E.	39	Santa Rosa	IA	Dickey	Bessie	28	Santa Rosa	CA
Luce	Elmer E.	36	Santa Rosa	IA	Lawsen	Cherrosette	20	San Francisco	MO
Luce	George Liddle	23	Santa Rosa	CA	McPeak	Edna Carl	23	Santa Rosa	CA
Luce	Guy R.	31	San Francisco	CA	Trunz	Josephine A.	25	San Francisco	CA
Luce	Hughbert S.	21	Santa Rosa	CA	Coy	Ethel A.	20	Occidental	CA
Luce	Jirah	42	Healdsburg	MA	Matheson	Nina R.	30	Healdsburg	CA
Lucero	Gilbert E.	21	Sebastopol	CA	Marshall	Mary I.	20	Sebastopol	CA
Luchesi	Angelo	28	San Francisco	ITL	Dinelli	Nonziatina	18	Santa Rosa	ITL
Luchetti	Agostino	29	Cloverdale	ITL	Cerruti	Rosi	27	Cloverdale	ITL
Luchetti	Giovani	33	Cloverdale	ITL	Cerruti	Dominica	25	Cloverdale	ITL
Luchsinger	Peter	49	Petaluma	SWT	Katharin	Agnes	42	Petaluma	SWT
Luciani	Pete	27	Guerneville	ITL	Vannucci	Algi	24	Guerneville	ITL
Ludtke	John Emil	28	Mount Eden	GER	Tomka	Meta Martha	18	Alameda	WI
Ludwig	J. Elmer	20	Santa Rosa	OH	Hopper	Rosa B.	19	Vallejo Twp.	CA

Groom					Bride				
Surname	Given Name	Age	Residence	BP	Surname	Given Name	Age	Residence	BP
Ludwig	Peter H.	30	Cloverdale	GER	Albee	May Edith	26	Cloverdale	USA
Ludwigs	George	40	Walla Walla	GER	Hunziker	Emma	20	Cloverdale	MS
Ludy	Herman	27	Petaluma	SWT	Griess	Caroline	23	Petaluma	GER
Luebberke	Benjamin H.	25	Windsor	MO	Cooper	Margaret E.	20	Windsor	CA
Lueger	Ernest	56	Sebastopol	GER	Horn	Anna	40	Santa Rosa	GER
Luff	Caleb B.	27	Petaluma	DNK	Dalton	Eva C.	24	Petaluma	CA
Lugo	John A.	23	Healdsburg	MEX	Babcock	Sylvania E.	21	Healdsburg	MO
Luhr	Lawrence E.	23	Oakland	CA	Glavin	Carmelita	22	Oakland	CA
Luisi	Leonardo	33	Healdsburg	ITL	Gandola	Mary A.	21	Healdsburg	ITL
Lukas	Chris A.	23	Sacramento	SD	Hadrich	Elsa Barbara	22	Santa Rosa	CA
Lukas	Israel	26	Santa Rosa	RUS	Pahud	Heloise	20	Santa Rosa	RUS
Lukeer	Charles R.	28	Woodland	MN	Archer	Nellie	16	Petaluma	CA
Lum	Tsai Yan	27	Berkeley	CA	Ming	Jennie Woo	25	Oakland	CA
Luman	William E.	24	Santa Rosa	CA	Cuyler	Anna H.	20	Santa Rosa	NY
Lumsden	Alexander Henry, Jr.	23	Petaluma	CA	Crawford	Mary Anderson	19	Petaluma	MEX
Lumsden	Charles William	19	Petaluma	CA	Ducker	Lottie Alice	18	Petaluma	CA
Luna	Frank	38	Healdsburg	CA	Dugan	Linda	35	Healdsburg	CA
Lunardi	Giovanni	38	Healdsburg	ITL	Vitali	Eleda	18	Healdsburg	ITL
Lund	Aage F.	26	Petaluma	DNK	Werenberg	Dorthea	22	Petaluma	DNK
Lund	August	27	Cloverdale	SWD	Cooper	Lillie May	19	Cloverdale	CA
Lund	Charles	39	San Francisco	SWD	Green	Carrie	32	Sonoma	CA
Lund	John Oscar	28	Oakland	PA	Hayes	Lillian	31	Sonoma	CA
Lundholm	Charles E.	29	Petaluma	WI	Bryan	Maud R.	20	Petaluma	AZ
Lundin	Carl Arthur	51	San Mateo	SWD	Poppic	Sarah Anna	35	Orland	RUS
Lundy	Harry	30	Fallon	IRL	Steele	Jennie	27	Marshall	CA
Luney	William	29	Santa Rosa	IRL	MacDonald	Vestina	20	Santa Rosa	SD
Lunger	Elmer S.	21	Occidental	CA	Bones	Ella Bessie	17	Occidental	CA
Lunger	Walter E.	24	Mesa Grande	CA	Weber	Ruth B.	22	Mesa Grande	AUT
Lunn	Fred C.	22	Alameda	CA	Karry	Alice M.	19	Alameda	CA

	Groom					Bride			
Surname	**Given Name**	**Age**	**Residence**	**BP**	**Surname**	**Given Name**	**Age**	**Residence**	**BP**
Lunney	Phillip	39	Yountville		Walters	Sianea (?)	22	Healdsburg	
Lunt	Arnold E.	21	Sausalito	CA	O'Leary	Isabella	19	Sausalito	CA
Lupton	Earl L.	26	Sebastopol	IL	Denman	Nellie A.	21	Petaluma	CA
Luque	Peter	29	San Francisco	FRN	Labastorde	Jennie	18	San Francisco	FRN
Lusk	William	54	Oakland	PA	Coe	Nannie T.	60	Oakland	AL
Lutgens	Henry Chas.	24	Sonoma	CA	Backer	Elizabeth	17	Sonoma	CA
Luth	Frederick Henry	27	Sebastopol	Oak	Fairclo	Carrie Martha	24	Sebastopol	Lak
Luttrell	Frank M.	23	Glen Ellen	CA	Weise	Hattie A.	22	Glen Ellen	CA
Luttrell	H. L.	23	Glen Ellen	CA	Law	Nettie M.	18	Glen Ellen	CA
Lutz	Carl	55	San Francisco	GER	Jorden	Mary A.	50	San Francisco	GER
Lyman	Chas.	26	San Francisco	PA	Thompson	Mattie M.	26	San Francisco	DNK
Lyman	Eugene	27	Sebastopol	CA	Jacobs	Myrtle	19	Bloomfield	UT
Lyman	James H.	31	Sebastopol	CA	Stephens	Oma E.	18	Santa Rosa	AR
Lyman	James H.	42	Sebastopol	CA	Lyman	Owa (?) E.	29	Santa Rosa	AR
Lyman	William J.	30	Blucher Valley	CA	Robertson	Bessie	22	Blucher Valley	CA
Lyman	William Wickam	23	San Francisco	FL	Gordon	Edna Isma	18	Fort Bragg	CA
Lynch	Bernard C.	24	Cotati	CA	Sills	Rhoda M.	18	Cotati	CA
Lynch	George L.	32	Amador City	MI	Tripp	Grace A.	31	Sebastopol	NY
Lynch	James M.	41	San Francisco		Mizer	Sarah P.	47	Santa Rosa	
Lynch	Robert Newton	31	Petaluma	PA	Riley	Elizabeth	18	Petaluma	IA
Lynch	William Allen	22	Petaluma	CA	Frahm	Hertha	20	Petaluma	IL
Lyon	Arthur J.	36	Goldfield, NV	ENG	Ware	Margaret	23	Santa Rosa	CA
Lyons	Cornelius P.	33	San Francisco	CA	Shadburne	Julia A.	26	Petaluma	NY
Lyons	James A.	35	San Francisco	CA	Nutting	Mable L.	37	San Francisco	CA
Lyons	John Joseph	35	Petaluma	Sfo	Silva	Mary E.	25	Petaluma	CA
Lyons	Thomas J.	36	San Francisco	CA	Kelso	Eunice O.	33	San Francisco	CA
Lytjen	Ludwig M.	33	Berkeley	DNK	Navoni	Johanna I.	28	Napa	CA
Lyttaker	Albert	22	Santa Rosa	CA	Garrison	Ellen M.	21	Santa Rosa	TX
Lyttaker	E. V.	22	Santa Rosa	CA	Dillon	Sarah M.	20	Santa Rosa	CA
Lyttaker	Will	23	Santa Rosa	CA	Dearing	Josie	21	Santa Rosa	CA

Groom					Bride				
Surname	Given Name	Age	Residence	BP	Surname	Given Name	Age	Residence	BP
Lytte	George W.	29	Guerneville	PA	Abrams	Nettie L.	22	Guerneville	CND
Maas	William George	22	San Francisco	CA	McNeil	Myrtle Adell	18	Geyserville	CA
Mabee	John	33	Petaluma	MN	Richardson	Nettie Gertrude	16	Petaluma	CA
Mac	M. B.	64	Santa Rosa	WI	Littell	Nellie, Mrs.	51	St. Louis, MO	OH
Mac Lean	Hector	27	Santa Rosa	SCT	Gilooly	Rose May	23	Santa Rosa	CA
Maccagno	Joseph	23	San Francisco	ITL	Bocca	Clementina	22	Glen Ellen	ITL
Maccario	Tony	21	Santa Rosa	CA	Pasero	Christine	21	Santa Rosa	ITL
MacDonald	Gilbert	31	Petaluma	IN	Piotrowski	Elizabeth M.	30	Petaluma	MO
Macdonald	Leonard C.	24	Oakland	CA	McDermott	Marie L.	24	Berkeley	CA
Macdonald	William	35	Oakland	SCT	Spurr	Grace J.	32	Napa	OR
Macedo	Antone Domingos	49	Oakland	PRT	Furtado	Emma	27	Oakland	PRT
Macerida/Macida	Marcallo	39	Bodega	ITL	Robba	Malgerita	37	Bodega	ITL
MacFarlane	Earl R.	31	San Francisco	CND	Thibadore	Jean M.	24	San Francisco	MA
MacGowan	Henry	21	Oakland	CA	Brown	Edna	18	Oakland	CA
MacGowan	Henry	22	Oakland	CA	Brown	Edna Catherine	18	Oakland	CA
MacGregor	Allan Peter	36	Santa Rosa	CND	Keaton	Martha Jane	28	Santa Rosa	CA
Mache	John A.	22	Bodega	ITL	Albini	Mary	17	Bodega	ITL
Mache	Steve A.	40	Cazadero	ITL	Silacci	Dora L.	28	Petaluma	CA
Mack	Charles Westly	31	Petaluma		Charnock	Amy	22	Healdsburg	
Mack	John	21	Franz Valley	CA	Nance	Grace A.	17	Franz Valley	CA
Mack	Richard	21	Windsor	CA	Conelly	May	20	Windsor	CA
Mack	William E.	23	Santa Rosa	IL	Du Commun	Lucille	23	Santa Rosa	CA
Mack	William, Jr.	25	San Francisco	CA	Church	Linnie	21	Petaluma	CA
MacKay	William	56	San Francisco	SCT	McFadyen	Isabel	43	San Francisco	CND
MacKenzie	Hugh Fraser	23	Berkeley	CA	Wisnom	Margaret	23	San Francisco	CA
Mackey	Edward	28	Graton	ID	Howard	Ruby S.	22	Graton	TX
MacKillop	David V.	25	Santa Rosa	CA	Isaak	Emma V.	18	Santa Rosa	CA
Maclay	Thomas	21+	Petaluma	Glasgow SCT	Wickershaw	Lizzie C.	21+	Petaluma	Pet
MacMurdo	Willis	33	Fort Bragg	PA	Riffe	Hazel Idella	28	Fort Bragg	CA

	Groom					Bride			
Surname	Given Name	Age	Residence	BP	Surname	Given Name	Age	Residence	BP
Macnair	Douglas	47	San Francisco	ENG	Glaszer	Gertrude J.	35	Sebastopol	CA
MacNevin	Wm. V.	31	San Francisco	CA	Denton	Carrie M.	24	Stockton	CA
Macphail	John R.				Munro	B. F.			
MacPherson	Stuart	39	Alameda	SCT	Jones	Jeannette, Mrs.	43	Alameda	CA
MacQuiddy	Oscar Lee	30	Oakland	CA	Dunn	Anna M.	25	Sonoma	CA
Macrina	Leo D.	24	Santa Rosa	PA	Poncetta	Rosie	19	Santa Rosa	CA
Macy	William C.	28	Windsor	NC	Looney	Nellie	19	Fulton	CA
Macy	William C.	37	Windsor	NC	Philpott	Helen Alzina Lordell, Mrs.	25	Windsor	NY
Maddalena	Charles J.	24	Petaluma	CA	Leibert	Lorraine E.	18	Petaluma	CA
Maddalena	John H.	22	Petaluma	OH	White	Isadora M.	20	Petaluma	OH
Maddelena	Fred	31	Petaluma	SWT	Sartori	Rina	27	Petaluma	SWT
Madden	Edward	36	Albion	OH	Richardson	Mary, Mrs.	54	Cloverdale	IL
Madden	William	33	Berkeley	CA	Davies	Rose E.	31	Berkeley	CA
Maddocks	Fred W.	23	Green Valley	CA	Marshall	Irene P.	24	Santa Rosa	CA
Maddocks	Harold F.	32	Graton	CA	King	Dorothy I.	21	Sebastopol	WA
Maddocks	Louis A.	21	Forestville	CA	Johnson	Hattie C.	22	Forestville	CA
Maddox	Samuel W.	18	Guerneville		Thompson	Laura M.	18	Guerneville	
Maddrell	Lepolde S.	46	San Francisco	ENG	Zell	Martha S.	45	Fetters Springs	GER
Maddux	Burt	29	Guerneville	CA	Wallin	Eva M.	32	Fulton	OR
Maddux	Harry W.	31	Oakland	MT	Clarke	Maybelle	18	Oakland	GA
Maddux	Joe Ferreira	24	Mark West	CA	Curry	Lizzie	22	San Francisco	
Maddux	Preston	28	Santa Rosa	CA	Sprague	Elsie L.	17	Santa Rosa	CA
Madeira	George D.	28	Healdsburg	NV	Fenno	Minnie	25	Healdsburg	CA
Madeira	George Madison	23	Healdsburg	CA	McLean	Ella A.	19?	Healdsburg	CA
Madeira	W. R.	28	Healdsburg	NV	Ward	Mary J.	24	Healdsburg	CA
Madero	Alvin	24	Santa Rosa	PRT	Nelson	Mary	22	Santa Rosa	CA
Maderous	Antone	25	Crockett	CA	Moniz	Marie Eugenia	24	Sebastopol	CA
Madison	J. Harry	25	Agua Caliente	CA	Rice	Charlotte L.	19	Agua Caliente	CA

	Groom					Bride			
Surname	Given Name	Age	Residence	BP	Surname	Given Name	Age	Residence	BP
Madison	James	23	Petaluma	Louisville, KY	Blain	Audrey Jane	17	Petaluma	Ray Co. MO
Madison	John Harold	21	Petaluma	CA	Silva	Alice May	19	Petaluma	CA
Madsen	Herbert H.	24	San Jose	CA	Kyle	Mildred Baxter	22	Santa Rosa	MI
Madsen	Neils G.	39	Paso Robles	DNK	Franzen	Augusta	38	San Francisco	SWD
Maffei	Gaetano	31	Valley Ford	ITL	Barella	Elena	24	Tomales	ITL
Maffei	Italo	32	San Francisco	ITL	Marcucci	Angelina	21	Sonoma	CA
Maffei	Luigi	31	Sonoma	ITL	Michalini	Corina	19	Sonoma	SWT
Maffia	Emilio	30	Tomales	ITL	Moreschi	Maria	19	Tomales	ITL
Maffini	Ernest	25	Santa Rosa	ITL	Barsi	Della	24	Mt. Olivet	CA
Mafia	Antoni	20	Bodega	ITL	Albini	Maria	18	Bodega	ITL
Magatelli	Antonio	25	Santa Rosa	ITL	Malogani	Sereno	18	Santa Rosa	CA
Magatelli	Domenico	21	Alpine Valley	ITL	Paroli	Domenica	18	Alpine Valley	CA
Magee	Thomas Wm.	50	Santa Rosa	IRL	Mobley	Anna Dorothea	50	Santa Rosa	GER
Magetti	Robert	24	Marshall	SWT	Baccala	Carrie	16	Sonoma Twp.	SWT
Maggart	Edward F.	25	San Francisco	MO	Aitken	Elenor M.	25	San Francisco	CA
Maggiora	Costantino Delbi (?)	28	Santa Rosa	ITL	Benedetti	Charlotte M.	20	Santa Rosa	CA
Maghetti	Henry A.	31	San Rafael	CA	Mehegan	Margaret U.	31	San Francisco	CA
Magona	Peter F.	30	Cambria	SWT	Filippini	Rose A.	22	Petaluma	CA
Magoon	Edward Oliver	20	Santa Rosa		Gentry	M. Alice	19	Santa Rosa	
Magoon	Wm. H.	38	Stony Point	IA	Bock	Kate	30	Stony Point	PA
Magri	Guiseppe	22	Santa Rosa	ITL	Cia	Antoinetta	31	Santa Rosa	ITL
Maher	William M.	27	Healdsburg	NM	Mason	Rossaline L.	22	Healdsburg	CA
Mahler	Henry J., Jr.	21	San Francisco	CA	Leahy	Lillian	19	San Francisco	CA
Mahlstedt	August	24	San Francisco	CA	Fochetti	Theresa	24	Sonoma	Soc
Mahoney	David I.	28	San Francisco	CA	Roche	Annie J.	26	San Francisco	CA
Mahoney	John M.	37	Petaluma	CA	Robinson	Pearl	27	Sebastopol	NE
Mahoney	William	30	near Petaluma	CA	Geaney	Mary	30	Petaluma	IRL
Mahony	H. C.	33	San Francisco	MT	Sexton	Marie A.	25	San Francisco	SD

	Groom					Bride			
Surname	**Given Name**	**Age**	**Residence**	**BP**	**Surname**	**Given Name**	**Age**	**Residence**	**BP**
Mailer	John A.	26	Santa Rosa	NE	Lewis	Katherine E.	24	Santa Rosa	WI
Maitoza	Manuel P.	22	Rodel, CA	PRT	Rose	Julia	21	Sebastopol	CA
Makee	George William	31	Clay	CA	Beckman	Emma Lena	29	Sebastopol	CA
Maker	Archie	26	Middletown	WI	Ellis	Mary Jane	18	Cloverdale	IL
Maksente	Victor S.	21	Ornbaun	CA	Scaramella	Rosie Rena	19	Point Arena	ITL
Malandra	Mauro	23	Santa Rosa	SWT	Verzasconi	Clotilda	20	Santa Rosa	SWT
Malaspina	Gustavo	28	Occidental	ITL	Rossi	Iside	19	Occidental	ITL
Malfante	Victor	24	St. Helena	ITL	Buschini	Maria	33	St. Helena	ITL
Maliard	Edwin	23	San Francisco	CA	Perry	Violet	19	Petaluma	CA
Mallory	George Brown	40	Petaluma	CA	Wade	Juniatta, Mrs.	40	Petaluma	CA
Mallory	Herbert W.	26	Santa Rosa	CA	Steger	Betty	23	Santa Rosa	CA
Mallory	Jacob T.	25	Santa Rosa	MO	Magnam	Anneta Estella	23	Santa Rosa	KS
Malm	Arthur Marian	28	Sebastopol	WA	DeWitt	Mary Lauvira ?	20	Healdsburg	KS
Malm	Carl	25	San Francisco	SWD	Johnson	Betty	27	Stockton	SWD
Malmgren (?)	Carl C. M.	29	Oakland	DNK	Harper	Margaretta W. V.	20	Berkeley	IRL
Malnati	Carlo	32	Occidental	ITL	Giovanni	Clara M.	21	Occidental	CA
Malnburg	Ira C.	23	Sacramento	CA	Rinker	Elizabeth	24	Sacramento	SD
Malof	John	22	Sebastopol	AZR	Matos	Minnie L.	20	Trenton	CA
Malone	James H.	27	Santa Rosa	OR	Johnson	Rebecca	20	Analy Twp.	CA
Malone	Joseph	36	Mountain View	CA	Carrigan	Agnes	26	San Francisco	CA
Maloney	James	29	Sonoma	IRL	Marmori	Stella	24	Sonoma	CA
Maloof	Charles	33	Santa Rosa	EGY	Panini	Carmelina	33	Santa Rosa	ITL
Maloof	John	29	Santa Rosa	SYR	Morchio	Eva	20	Santa Rosa	CA
Maloof	John	24	Vine Hill	SYR	Matus	Lena	21	Vine Hill	CA
Maltman	Francis D.	56	Healdsburg	NY	Bell	Amanda Lydia, Mrs.	60	Healdsburg	IN
Manch	Gottfried	28	Santa Rosa	RUS	Bollinger	Catherine	17	Santa Rosa	RUS
Mancini	Massimo	22	Forestville	ITL	Ginsti	Julia	16	Green Valley	CA
Mancini	Pietro	25	Santa Rosa	ITL	Rossi	Angelina	23	Santa Rosa	ITL

Groom					Bride				
Surname	Given Name	Age	Residence	BP	Surname	Given Name	Age	Residence	BP
Mane	Paul	23	Petaluma	MT	Vogel	Olga T.	24	Petaluma	CA
Maner	Marcellus	31	Alturia	IN	Paxton	Emza E.	28	Sacramento	MO
Mangiantini	Narciso	32	Sonoma	ITL	Catelani	Conchetta	32	Sonoma	ITL
Mangili	Henry G.	28	Petaluma	SWT	McLaughlin	Mary T.	28	Petaluma	Pet
Mangin	Eugene Louis	27	Petaluma	CA	Peloquin	Marie Louise	27	Petaluma	CND
Mangin	Eugene Louis	23	Oakland	CA	Fancher	Gladyst Maud	18	Petaluma	ND
Mangini	Jack	36	Napa	ITL	Ponzo	Margherita	36	Healdsburg	ITL
Mangini	Louis J.	24	Petaluma	CA	Hyland	Elizabeth J.	23	Petaluma	CA
Manies	Morrison	25	Vallejo	NC	Kelsey	Florence	31	Vallejo	KS
Mankins	Daniel E., Jr.	21	San Francisco	CA	Johnson	Juanita Ruth	22	San Francisco	CA
Mann	Edward H.	23	Agua Caliente	CA	Penning	Mary	17	Agua Caliente	IL
Mann	Frank B.	31	Windsor	CA	Bedwell	Annie Alberta	17	Windsor	CA
Mann	Guy Chester	22	Freestone	CA	Todd	Ruby Angeine	19	Freestone	CA
Mann	Ned Frase	27	Salida	CO	McNamee	Lenora Margarete	23	Selma	CA
Mann	Robert J.	20	Mendocino	CND	Critchfield	Lulu B.	18	Geyserville	Geyserville
Mann	T. W.	24	Petaluma	LA	Dolet	Helen A.	25	Petaluma	CA
Mann	Thomas L.	39	Glen Ellen	CA	Temple	Anna	19	Santa Rosa	CA
Manney	James F.	28	San Rafael	VT	Roach	Jennie E.	22	Petaluma	IL
Manning	James C.	37	Santa Rosa	OH	Cropley	Adella C.	33	Santa Rosa	CND
Manning	John	24	Bodega		Quinlan	Sarah	18	Bodega	
Manning	Lincoln	40	Clarksville, El Dorado Co.	CA	Bennett	Freda, Mrs.	35	Reno, NV	TX
Manouk	Charles	50	San Francisco	Smyrna	Harenisch	Agnes D. M.	30	San Francisco	GER
Mansfield	Col. L.				Whitlock	Sophia, Mrs.			
Manter	Benjamin H.	30	Hayward	CA	Kidd	Alta S.	28	Hayward	WV
Mantua	Julius	30	Bodega	ITL	Righetta	Elia	23	Bodega Corners	ITL
Manuel	George S.	47	San Francisco	IL	Krepps	Jennie L.	36	San Francisco	IA
Manuel	H. S.	22	Sonoma	CA	Baettge	Sophia	19	Sonoma	CA

	Groom					Bride			
Surname	**Given Name**	**Age**	**Residence**	**BP**	**Surname**	**Given Name**	**Age**	**Residence**	**BP**
Mapes	Ira C.				Hall	Sarah F.			
Mapes	L. Percy	21	Sebastopol	CA	Hansen	Sadie M.	20	Sebastopol	WY
Maple	Geo. M.	21	Santa Rosa	IL	Mapel	Belle	19	Sonoma	CA
Marall	Henry R.	21	Placer Co.	CA	Delmue	Mary J.	20	Placer Co.	NV
Marando	Frank Harry	28	Mt. Olivet	CA	Fowler	Della	18	Mt. Olivet	CA
Marble	Edward R.	27	Santa Rosa	CA	Allen	Hattie W.	23	Santa Rosa	CA
Marble	John H.	36	Petaluma	CA	Garrison	Grace E.	33	Petaluma	CA
Marcell	N. E.	25	Santa Rosa	CND	Donoven	Mally (?)	20	Santa Rosa	MA
Marchant	Frederick R.	25	Healdsburg	CA	Saul	Sallie Belle	22	Petaluma	CA
Marchetti	Nicoderro	31	Sebastopol	ITL	Viviani	Georgia	26	San Francisco	ITL
Marchisio	Delfino	30	Healdsburg	ITL	Wernecke	Katie	21	Healdsburg	GER
Marchisio	Enrico F.	21	San Rafael	CA	Wiser	Macel	20	Mill Valley	KY
Marci	Jerunoz	28	Santa Rosa	SWT	Malugani	Martina	20	Santa Rosa	SWT
Marci	Luca	27	Stony Point	SWT	Pomi	Anonziata	35	Stony Point	SWT
Marcollo	John	35	Santa Rosa	SWT	Fochetti	Caterine	26	Santa Rosa	SWT
Marcucci	Abromo	59	Agua Caliente	ITL	Gaddini	Elisabeth	50	Healdsburg	ITL
Marcucci	Faustino	29	Geyserville	ITL	Bertossi	Teresa	28	Geyserville	ITL
Marcucci	Oreste	28	Santa Rosa	ITL	Monticelli	Emma	20	Guerneville	Guerneville
Marcucci	Paul	23	Santa Rosa	ITL	Sani	Marie	23	Santa Rosa	ITL
Marcus	Carl Ralph	28	San Francisco	CA	Matzen	Ella	27	Petaluma	CA
Mardis	John Harvey	20	Santa Rosa	KS	Porcher	Marion Louise	18	Santa Rosa	San Luis Obispo
Mari	Ernesto	33	San Francisco	SWT	Domeniconi	Matilde	24	San Francisco	SWT
Maria	Jose	31	Point Reyes	PRT	Souza	Mary	21	Sebastopol	AZR
Marier	Edmund L.	28	San Francisco	UT	Hoffman	Gertrude L.	21	San Francisco	CA
Marin	George	25	San Francisco	ITL	Bin	Lena	18	Santa Rosa	ITL
Marin	Louis	26	Oakland	ITL	Martin	Aurore	25	San Francisco	RI
Maringo	Steven	23	Petaluma	CA	Baker	Lillian Emma	22	St. Helena	CA

	Groom					Bride			
Surname	**Given Name**	**Age**	**Residence**	**BP**	**Surname**	**Given Name**	**Age**	**Residence**	**BP**
Marino	Filippo	40	Tomales	ITL	Pozzi	Caterina	28	Tomales	SWT
Marinoni	Gaetano	40	Santa Rosa	ITL	Coregliano	Domencia	38	Santa Rosa	ITL
Marion	Angelo Nickoles	25	Petaluma	CA	Martin	Sarah Matilda	22	Petaluma	CA
Marion	Vernal Kennet	23	Petaluma	CA	Summ	Erna Georgia	21	Petaluma	CA
Mariotte	Paul A.	29	Oakland	CA	Law	Myrtle H.	22	Oakland	SD
Markham	Henry C.	52	Sebastopol	IA	Brodie	Annie, Mrs.	50	Sebastopol	MI
Markley	Albert E.	34	Petaluma	CA	Palmer	Nirma	20	Santa Rosa	CA
Markley	Thomas Cox	57	Santa Rosa	Charleston, SC	Smyth	Jennie Elizabeth	33	Santa Rosa	Soc
Markopulos	Antonio	24	Santa Rosa	GRC	Root	Hilda	19	Santa Rosa	CA
Marks	Harry	31	San Francisco	CA	Keller	Dora	29	San Francisco	UT
Marks	Thomas F.	48	Stony Point	PRT	Piezzi	Catherine D., Mrs.	49	Stony Point	Phl
Marks	Walter Randolph	21	Vallejo	CA	Washburn	Catherine Faith	20	Richmond	KS
Marks (?)	Julian	21	St. Helena	MEX	Cordova	Rosie	18	St. Helena	CA
Marlatt	Al	22	Santa Rosa	IL	Heather	Lizzie	18	Santa Rosa	OR
Marlatt	Charles E.	43	Ukiah	KS	McConihe	Ethel M.	32	San Francisco	NJ
Marlatt	Frank	22	Santa Rosa	IL	Heather	Kate	18	Santa Rosa	OR
Marlatt	Perry Edward	25	Oakland	IL	Udall	Lola Maud	25	Santa Rosa	IA
Maroni	George Joseph	22	Santa Rosa	CA	Lencioni	Theresa Josephine	18	Santa Rosa	CA
Maroni	Louis	29	Kenwood	ITL	Cassani	Ricca	16	Santa Rosa	ITL
Maroni	Peter	28	Santa Rosa	ITL	Gomberina	Rosa	17	Santa Rosa	Sfo
Marple	Robert J	24	Ukiah	CA	Roberts	Daisy E.	22	Ukiah	CA
Marquis	Thomas C.	42	San Francisco	CA	Schulz	Gertrude E.	30	San Francisco	PA
Marr	Clyde H.	29	San Francisco	ME	Martin	Mildred Mae	26	Healdsburg	CA
Marr	John A.	22	Colusa	CA	McMinn	Rosa	19	Santa Rosa	CA
Marra	Battista	28	Occidental	SWT	Maggini	Catterina	29	Bodega Corners	SWT
Mars	Charles	24	Healdsburg	CA	Poe	Ethel	19	Sebastopol	CA
Marsh	Arthur	23	Cotati	Soc	Cullen	Mary	18	Petaluma	CA

	Groom					Bride			
Surname	Given Name	Age	Residence	BP	Surname	Given Name	Age	Residence	BP
Marsh	Charles E.	24	Forestville	CA	Green	Lida	18	Vine Hill	CA
Marsh	Clarence Joseph	20	Cotati	CA	Sleeper	Ruth Severne	20	San Francisco	NY
Marsh	Ira M.	26	Freestone	MI	Gelhart	Mattie J.	19	Freestone	CA
Marsh	John P.	38	Santa Rosa	CA	Lagan	Katherine J.	24	Santa Rosa	IRL
Marsh	Robert Linus	29	Bloomfield	IA	Mayfield	Flora	28	Bloomfield	CA
Marshall	A. F.	43	Butte, MT	PRT	Abario	Rose S.	23	Petaluma	CA
Marshall	Adam, Jr.	31	Sausalito	CA	Mullikin	Arrilla J.	29	Sausalito	CA
Marshall	Aretus	27	Santa Rosa	CA	Plum	Elsie	15	Santa Rosa	CA
Marshall	Charles Wilson	21	Graton	CA	Bruce	Ruth Helen	18	Freestone	NE
Marshall	Cleveland H.	20+	Santa Rosa	MO	Davis	Pearl	18	Santa Rosa	NE
Marshall	Frank L.	23	Sebastopol	CA	Turner	May M.	18	Sebastopol	CA
Marshall	H. M.	28	Berkeley	CA	Smith	Gertrude E.	27	Santa Rosa	CA
Marshall	Harry Lee	27	Cloverdale	CA	Fisher	Lora Etta	29	Ukiah	MO
Marshall	James M.	21	Fallon, Marin Co.	CA	Steele	Margaret Mae	23	Tomales	NY
Marshall	Joseph Gilbert	28	Tomales	IRL	Mitchell	Susan	24	Tomales	IRL
Marshall	Manuel J.	27	Sebastopol	CA	Walters	Pearl	21	Sebastopol	OK
Marshall	Robert		Fisherman's Bay		Haupt	Louisa		Fisherman's Bay	
Marshall	Thomas	24	Oakland	CA	Bryn	Carrie	18	Oakland	IA
Marshall	Thomas H.	35	Oat Hill, Napa	GA	Winkler	Hattie L.	22	Green Valley	CA
Marshall	Thos. H.	31	Guerneville	GA	Pickle	Blanche	19	Guerneville	CA
Marshall	William	25	Green Valley	CA	Ames	Annie L.	19	Green Valley	CA
Martell	Joseph A.	30	San Francisco	CA	Ford	Lettie F.	27	Oakland	CA
Marten	John Edward	25	San Rafael	CA	Rosewarne	Elizabeth Serretta	24	San Rafael	UT
Martens	Dietrich W.	47	San Rafael	GER	Kelly	Emma M.	30	San Francisco	CA
Marties	Joseph F.	50	Healdsburg	PRT	Dyozenz?	Maria	36	Healdsburg	PRT
Martignoni	Walter	26	Oakland	CA	Lafranchi	Ollie	27	Petaluma	CA
Martin	Andrew William	44	Oakland	PA	Court	Ida Belle	48	Oakland	MI
Martin	Arthur J.	23	Geyserville	IA	Newbert	Margaret B.	21	Geyserville	CA

	Groom					Bride			
Surname	**Given Name**	**Age**	**Residence**	**BP**	**Surname**	**Given Name**	**Age**	**Residence**	**BP**
Martin	Charles J.	37	Geyserville	OH	Cummings	Hattie E.	24	Geyserville	CA
Martin	Charles L.	23	Alameda	MO	Jorgensen	Evelyn L.	22	Penngrove	CA
Martin	Christian J.	20	Windsor	CA	Daniels	Lorena F.	19	Windsor	MI
Martin	Dock	61	San Rafael	IN	Higgins	Minnie E.	47	San Rafael	IN
Martin	Dorchester E.	27	Santa Rosa		Rutledge	Mary E.	22	Santa Rosa	
Martin	Edgar	32	Healdsburg		McGaughey	Fannie G.	24	Healdsburg	
Martin	Edgar Laurens	24	Santa Rosa	CA	Gailor	Ima Edna	19	Santa Rosa	CA
Martin	Eugene E.	27	Healdsburg	TN	Brown	Hallie B.	21	Healdsburg	CA
Martin	Frances W.	20	Alameda	MO	Zumwalt	Berenice I.	19	Penngrove	CA
Martin	Frank F.	25	Petaluma	CA	Cadd	Lillian Rebecca	22	Healdsburg	CA
Martin	Frank M.	27	Sebastopol	MI	Litchfield	Mary E.	26	Sebastopol	IL
Martin	Frederick	38	Petaluma	CA	Cook	Beatrice Bidwell	24	Petaluma	OH
Martin	George A.	23	Windsor	IL	Pohley	Mary L.	19	Windsor	CA
Martin	Ira P.	21	Healdsburg	CA	Bellah	Mildred M.	20	Lytton Springs	CA
Martin	J. E.	24	Healdsburg	CA	Leard	Nettie A.	21	Healdsburg	CA
Martin	James	22	Bloomfield	CA	Kane	Minnie	19	Bloomfield	IRL
Martin	James C.	27	Healdsburg	TN	Bryant	Susan F.	16	Healdsburg	CA
Martin	James Delea	28	Petaluma	SCT	Buchanan	Effie	27	Petaluma	CA
Martin	Joe	23	Marshall	CA	Smith	Mary	33	Bodega	CA
Martin	John				Mathison	Ida E. J.	23		
Martin	John A.	28	Santa Rosa	IRL	Shields	Susan	25	Santa Rosa	IRL
Martin	John M.	52	Santa Rosa	AR	Meyers	Sussie	48	Santa Rosa	HUN
Martin	John Milton	19	Healdsburg	OH	Turner	Minnie L.	17	Kellogg	CA
Martin	John S., Jr.	33	Mendocino Twp.		Brown (?)	Nellie	18	Healdsburg	
Martin	Josiah	20	Healdsburg	OH	Lewis	Rebecca	19	Healdsburg	CA
Martin	Lauren M.	35	Guerneville	IA	Peterson	Edith V.	18	Guerneville	CA
Martin	Leopold	25	Lathrop, San Joaquin Co.	Mac	Zanini	Maria	25	Lathrop	SWT
Martin	Lewis	22	San Luis Obispo	CA	Brown	Marian		22 Petaluma	CA

| | Groom | | | | | Bride | | | |
Surname	Given Name	Age	Residence	BP	Surname	Given Name	Age	Residence	BP
Martin	Louis	39	San Francisco	FRN	Dormeau	Albertine	21	San Francisco	FRN
Martin	Manuel	26	Petaluma	WTS	Cuadro	Mary	22	Petaluma	CA
Martin	Merwin	23	San Francisco	NY	Gano	Maud	21	San Francisco	MN
Martin	Milo ?				Mathis?	Emma	28		
Martin	Milton	24	Healdsburg	OH	Frost	Corda	20	Healdsburg	CA
Martin	Oscar J.	32	Petaluma	CA	Kenison	Mabel E.	30	San Francisco	CA
Martin	Paul C.	23	Petaluma	CA	Gravatte	Katheryn F.	22	Petaluma	NJ
Martin	Rasmus	21	Petaluma	Soc	Thompson	Annie	19	Petaluma	OH
Martin	Robert A.	45	Santa Rosa	CA	Nichols	Sade Jane	30	Santa Rosa	CA
Martin	Robert Edward	35	San Francisco	NY	Berger	Flora Helen	37	San Francisco	KY
Martin	Russel Sage	18	Healdsburg	CA	Lyman	Francian V.	18	San Francisco	CA
Martin	T. J.	24	San Francisco	MO	Wall	Jennie	24	Cloverdale	NY
Martin	Van T.	20	Healdsburg	OH	Proctor	Laura Jane	24	Healdsburg	NV
Martin	Walter	31	Tomales	IRL	Deacon	Martha	30	Tomales	IRL
Martin	William Ira	20	Healdsburg		Stark	Rebecca Marilla	17	Healdsburg	
Martin	William S.	37	San Francisco	CA	Esterman	Elsa	25	San Francisco	NE
Martinelli	Fortunato	21	Geyserville	ITL	Chintelli	Jennie	15	Geyserville	ITL
Martinelli	Gildo P.	24	Petaluma	CA	Spottswood	Ada	23	Petaluma	CA
Martinelli	Ulesse	29	Duncans Mills	ITL	Casini	Emma	22	Duncans Mills	ITL
Martinelli	Ulysses J.	23	Lakeville	CA	Fillippini	Silvia O.	21	Petaluma	CA
Martinetti	Gabriele	21	Elk	Sar	Guenza	Carmelina	18	Elk	ITL
Martinez	Leonardo	28	Santa Rosa	SPN	Remesal (?)	Maria	18	Santa Rosa	SPN
Martinez	Sylvester	28	Sebastopol	PRT	Francisco	Mariana	21	Sebastopol	CA
Martini	Adolfo	23	San Francisco	ITL	Davini	Antonietta	18	Petaluma	ITL
Martini	Narciso	26	Trenton	CA	Vannucci	Florinda	21	Trenton	CA
Martino	Giovanni	59	Occidental	ITL	Amavisca	Matilda	38	Sebastopol	MEX
Martinoni	A. H.	29	Alameda	CA	Barboni	Mae	24	Petaluma	CA
Martola	H. A.	24	Oakland	AZ	Fox	Adeline M.	20	Oakland	CA
Martz	Roy	27	Guerneville	CA	Badger	Blanche H.	19	Sebastopol	CA
Martz	Samuel Anderson	75	Santa Rosa	VA	Allen	Cornelia	62	Santa Rosa	KY

| \multicolumn{5}{c|}{Groom} | \multicolumn{5}{c}{Bride} |

Surname	Given Name	Age	Residence	BP	Surname	Given Name	Age	Residence	BP
Marval	John	25	San Francisco	SAM	Rivera	Inocencesia	23	San Francisco	PUR
Marvin	John F.	29	Santa Rosa	MI	Owen	Mary M.	18	Santa Rosa	NV
Marx	Bert Franklin	30	San Francisco	PA	Dowling	Anna Katherine	25	San Francisco	TX
Marzolf	Charles Joseph	23	Petaluma	CA	Offutf	Ella May	20	Petaluma	CA
Marzolf	Frederick George	25	Petaluma	CA	Furlong	Kathryn A.	20	Petaluma	CA
Masa	Joe	41	Windsor	CA	Molf	Minnie, Mrs.	27	Santa Rosa	ASY
Maschetti	Ben	23	Santa Rosa	ITL	Esaia	Julia	17	Healdsburg	ITL
Mascho	Leland H.	28	San Francisco	MI	Jensen	Caroline	19	San Francisco	CA
Masciorini	Henry T.	25	Sevon (?) Point	CA	Petersen	Hattie	18	Petaluma	CA
Masconi	Pasquale	22	Healdsburg	ITL	Belli	Marguerite	17	Healdsburg	CA
Masgado	Jose				Werano	Wisenta, Mrs.			
Masher	John Ed				Mathews	Evy			
Masini	Sante	25	Cloverdale	ITL	Barzi	Angelina	22	Cloverdale	ITL
Maslin	Woolsey	29	Guatemala	CA	Saunders	Emma	29	Sonoma	CA
Mason	Chas. O.	23	Santa Rosa	CA	Cofer	Mary	22	Santa Rosa	CA
Mason	Craig M.	36	Santa Rosa	MO	Hendricks	Sadie D., Mrs.	35	Santa Rosa	VA
Mason	Ernest	27	Cloverdale	CND	Field	Kate	19	Cloverdale	CA
Mason	Frank L.	34	Guerneville	OH	Hitchcock	C. Elizabeth	15	Guerneville	CA
Mason	Fred B.	33	Guerneville	PA	Barham	Hattie L.	30	Guerneville	CA
Mason	George B.	25	Petaluma	KS	Baldwin	Mollie Dell	22	Petaluma	PA
Mason	George C.	26	Healdsburg	CA	Hassett	Carrie J.	19	Healdsburg	CA
Mason	James S.	31	Santa Rosa	ENG	Greensmith	Emily R. M.	26	Santa Rosa	ENG
Mason	James W.	25	San Francisco	CA	Parkin	Josie, Mrs.	27	San Francisco	CA
Mason	Marshall E.	24	Healdsburg	KY	Staples	Viola B.	20	Healdsburg	CA
Mason	Robt. A.	40	Skaggs Springs	KY	Tombs	Nellie M.	28	Skaggs Springs	CA
Mason	Troy F.	21	San Francisco	CA	Fiefer	Della E.	18	Santa Rosa	NV
Mason	William C.	38	Healdsburg	KY	Howard	Maud C.	22	Healdsburg	CA
Mason	William C.	40	Healdsburg	KY	Shohoney	Ethel, Mrs.	21	Healdsburg	KS
Mason	William H.	26	Santa Rosa	CA	McGinnis	Mary	20	Weiser, ID	IA
Massaini	Guiseppe	22	Melita	ITL	Pensa	Linda	22	Melita	ITL

	Groom					Bride			
Surname	Given Name	Age	Residence	BP	Surname	Given Name	Age	Residence	BP
Massei	Guido	25	San Francisco	ITL	Marcucci	Iris Marie	17	Santa Rosa	ITL
Massie	Fred B.	22	Grass Valley	CA	O'Brien	Annie	30	Sonoma	CA
Massimo	George	28	Santa Rosa	ITL	Asnip	Ellen	16	Santa Rosa	AUT
Massini	Giuseppe	29	Healdsburg	ITL	Scatina	Margherite	20	Healdsburg	CA
Massler	George	32	Trenton	GER	Messerle	Rosa	30	Santa Rosa	CA
Massoni	William J.	20	Healdsburg	CA	Davini	Bruna N.	18	Healdsburg	ITL
Mast	C. I.	19	Willits	CA	Smith	Kittie E.	22	Santa Rosa	CA
Mastai	Battista	30	Freestone	ITL	Ballati	Ursula	22	Freestone	ITL
Mastrado	Angelo	48	Guerenville	ITL	Benelli	Rosa	47	Guerneville	ITL
Mastrup	Andrew	26	Petaluma	CA	Hutchins	Violet	19	Santa Rosa	CA
Mastrup	Christian Theodore	26	Petaluma	CA	Bruhn	Nandina Rosina	17	Penngrove	GER
Matazzoni	Armando	22	San Francisco	ITL	Ottoboni	Lena Helen	22	Santa Rosa	CA
Matazzoni	Guiseppe	21	Santa Rosa	ITL	Baraldi	Leontina	27	Santa Rosa	ITL
Mates	George Adams	22	Hawthorn, Esmeralda Co., NV	CA	Peters	Anna Marie	22	Petaluma	CA
Mateson	Hans	41	Santa Rosa	NRY	McKean	Mary, Mrs.	47	Santa Rosa	IRL
Mather	William	25	Sebastopol	CA	Allen	Catherine	28	Sebastopol	CA
Mather	William Henry	37	Honolulu	IRL	Daywalt	Elizabeth	31	Santa Rosa	CA
Mathers	Wesley	27	San Francisco	Wdc	Schultes	Florence G.	18	Sebastopol	PA
Matheson	Charles J.	31	Navarro	CA	Brown	Erma B.	17	Philo	CA
Mathews	Alfred F.				Manning	Mary F.			
Mathews	Alvaro Brown	22	Petaluma	PRT	Veira	Mary Agnes	21	Petaluma	CA
Mathews	George I.	56	Cloverdale	WLS	Hall	Eliza	39	San Rafael	IRL
Mathias	Antoni B.	24	Petaluma	PRT	Dutro	Josephine M.	18	Petaluma	CA
Mathias	John B.	30	Petaluma	PRT	Raymond	Annie	30	Petaluma	CA
Mathiesen	Fred	27	Chileno Valley	GER	Wiegand	Mary	20	Petaluma	Two Rock
Mathiesen	Jesse C.	27	Merced	CA	Hoban	Ida N.	21	Walnut Creek	NY
Mathiessen	Henry A.	24	Petaluma	GER	Andersen	Theresa M.	26	Petaluma	GER

	Groom					Bride			
Surname	Given Name	Age	Residence	BP	Surname	Given Name	Age	Residence	BP
Mathis	Ephraim R.	33	Windsor	CA	Drake	Pearl A.	19	Windsor	CA
Mathis	Henry F.				Leek	Cyntha			
Mathisen	Dudley	25	Fulton	CA	Haigh	Ethel	25	Healdsburg	CA
Mathisen	Henry	28	Santa Rosa	CA	Mason	Clarrisa	18	Lakeport	CA
Mathisen	Jesse	32	Santa Rosa	CA	Dollar	Elsie Elma	17	Healdsburg	CA
Mathison	Hans Peter	34	Petaluma	DNK	Nilousen	Hanna M.	26	Petaluma	DNK
Mathorn	Perry D.	23	Healdsburg	IN	Lewis	Cashia S.	19	Healdsburg	CA
Matison	Frank M.	25	San Rafael	CA	Howard	Mabel C.	20	Occidental	CA
Matlock	Walter J.	24	Santa Rosa	PA	Stiles	Bertha M.	17	Sebastopol	CA
Matson	Arthur C.	26	Petaluma	IN	Kowski	Johanna Witt	20	Petaluma	GER
Matson	Carl E.	27	Santa Rosa	SWD	Smidberg	Ellen V.	22	San Jose	SWD
Matson	Hjalmar	38	San Francisco	SWD	Bentsen	Carola	29	Oakland	DNK
Mattei	Richard C.	29	Petaluma	CA	Winchell	Laura A.	34	Petaluma	CA
Mattei	Valenti C.	34	Petaluma	CA	Fredericks	Ida L.	32	Petaluma	CA
Matteri	Gottardo	26	Modesto	ITL	Poncia	Mary	18	Fallon	ITL
Matteri	John	25	Petaluma	ITL	Mazzucchi	Giuseppina	18	Petaluma	ITL
Matteri	Paolo	24	Valley Ford	ITL	Motti	Maddalena	18	Valley Ford	ITL
Matteri	Peter	37	Sebastopol	ITL	Mazzucchi	Giovanna	35	Sebastopol	ITL
Matteucci	Laurence	21	Santa Rosa	CA	Simoncini	Emma	17	Santa Rosa	Chi
Matthes	Charles C.	41	Cloverdale	GER	Ramsner	Marie R.	40	Cloverdale	AUS
Matthews	Alvin Wesley	24	San Francisco	CA	Barnett	Minnie Della	18	Sebastopol	CA
Matthews	Charles H.	43	Soda Rock	CA	Clark	Selina C., Mrs.	23	Soda Rock	CA
Matthews	Charles W.	61	Santa Rosa	MO	Wallace	Annie E.	48	Oakland	CA
Matthews	Charles W.	36	Healdsburg	MO	Barth	Mary E.	33	Windsor	NY
Matthews	Fred R.	21+	Sebastopol	CA	Estes	Fannie E.	20	Freestone	CA
Matthews	Frederic Hamilton	23	Garfield, UT	UT	Bowman	Estella May	20	Sebastopol	CA
Matthews	Hiram Walker	43	San Francisco	IA	Cusick	Helen Winifred	23	San Francisco	NY
Matthews	James L.	27	San Francisco	CA	Bassett	Lillian E.	23	San Francisco	IL
Matthews	James Overton	36	Petaluma	MO	Levilt	Mary Ward	29	Petaluma	
Matthews	John E.	28	Green Valley	CA	Parmeter	Mary L.	18	Green Valley	CA

	Groom					Bride			
Surname	**Given Name**	**Age**	**Residence**	**BP**	**Surname**	**Given Name**	**Age**	**Residence**	**BP**
Matthews	John W.	28	Healdsburg	CA	Johnson	Mattie E.	22	Healdsburg	MO
Matthews	O. P.	24	San Francisco	ENG	Hardesty	Susie	27	Los Angeles	OR
Matthews	Oscar F.	33	Santa Rosa	CA	Woodcock	Maud	26	Reno, NV	NV
Matthews	W. C.	29	Santa Rosa	CA	Finley	Leora M.	21	Bodega	CA
Matthews	Winfield Scott, Jr.	24	Sacramento	MI	Comstock	Cornelia	23	Santa Rosa	IL
Matthias	Henry G.	25	Healdsburg	WI	Wheeler	Frances L.	19	Santa Rosa	IL
Matthias	Manuel C.	29	Petaluma	CA	Rodgers	Catherine M.	24	Petaluma	CA
Matthiesen	Anton Ludwig	22	Kenwood	GER	Nielsen	Else Christine	25	Kenwood	GER
Mattiesen	Hermann	24	San Francisco	CA	Paul	Mabel	24	San Francisco	CA
Mattley	George	26	San Francisco	CA	Rodeck	Margaret	23	Petaluma	CA
Mattos	Arthur G.	29	Santa Rosa	PRT	Gomes	Alexandrina A.	27	Santa Rosa	PRT
Mattos	Joseph	37	Sebastopol	AZR	Barba	Joaquinna	38	Sebastopol	AZR
Mattos	Manuel B.	26	Petaluma	CA	Segueira	Maria	20	Petaluma	PRT
Mattson	Laurence A.	19	Geyserville	CO	Henderson	Myrtle May	19	Santa Rosa	CA
Mattson	Martin	26	Sonoma	SWD	Pihl	Jennie N.	18	Sonoma	DNK
Matzen	Edward	28	Petaluma	CA	Schlinkmann	Marie	28	Petaluma	IA
Mauck	Carl August				Nessen	Ana			
Mauerhan	John P.	23	San Francisco	CA	Johnson	Carolyn	21	San Francisco	CA
Maurer	Ed	25	North Yakima, WA	IL	Caldwell	Georgia	22	Santa Rosa	CA
Max	Albert	28	Cloverdale	GER	Martin	Susie	23	Cloverdale	MI
Maxwell	Ernest Edgar	21	Santa Rosa	CA	Taft	Georginia ? A.	19	Santa Rosa	NM
Maxwell	Frank Lawrence	26	San Francisco	KS	Hicks	Grace J.	24	Healdsburg	CA
Maxwell	Frank Washington	30	Healdsburg	OR	Gaskins	Minnie Maud	22	Healdsburg	CA
Maxwell	John R.	34	San Francisco	CA	Burns	Carrie Virginia	36	San Francisco	NY
Maxwell	Michael	35	San Francisco	GER	Wittmann	Maria	26	Santa Rosa	AUS
Maxwell	Watson B.	21	Santa Rosa	CA	Wagner	Frances M.	17	Santa Rosa	CA
Maxwell	William	30	San Francisco	IRL	McCarthy	Tillie	23	San Francisco	NY
Maxwell	William Albert	24	Petaluma	KS	Rodgers	Alvina Maria	19	Petaluma	CA
Maxzenti	Amanezio	40	Two Rock	ITL	Canepa	Clementina	36	Two Rock	SWT

	Groom					Bride			
Surname	Given Name	Age	Residence	BP	Surname	Given Name	Age	Residence	BP
May	Ernest Clarke	21	Sebastopol	WA	Driver	Emma Sarah	17	Sebastopol	CA
May	Henry C.	22	Sacramento	KS	Bach	Adeline W.	19	Petaluma	CA
Maybee	F. E.	45	Petaluma	MI	Peterson	Sophia	35	Petaluma	CA
Maybee	Frank E.	28	Petaluma		Johnson	Kitty	21	Petaluma	
Mayer	Edmond A.	22	Oakland	CA	Olsen	Ruth N.	22	Oakland	CA
Mayer	Frederic D.	23	Sonoma		Weyl	Nellie	18+	Sonoma	
Mayers	Irving	22	Lynn, Essex Co., MA	MA	Mills	Sadie Florence	23	Sacramento	GA
Mayes	Ernest E.	19	Healdsburg	CA	Beach	Della E.	17	Healdsburg	CA
Mayes	Ernest E.	32	Mill Valley	CA	Pezzie	Ethel	25	Santa Rosa	CA
Mayes	John H.	25	Santa Rosa		McMinn	Mary Frances	17	Fulton	
Mayfield	George W.	56	Santa Rosa	CA	Manville	Minnie E.	53	Santa Rosa	MO
Maynard	Harry H.	34	Petaluma	Sfo	Ficker ?	May	22	Petaluma	MO
Mayo	Larry G.	21	Berkeley	CA	Williamson	Dorothy E.	19	San Francisco	CA
Mays	John Burton	22	Santa Rosa	OR	Berry	Anna Belle	18	Santa Rosa	CA
Mays	Larkin B.	26	Cloverdale	OR	Carrie	Anna B.	23	Cloverdale	CA
Mayze	Joseph	23	Santa Rosa	CA	Peterson	Mabel Violet	18	Santa Rosa	CA
Mazza	Domenico	48	Sonoma	ITL	Proletti	Giovanna	30	Sonoma Twp.	ITL
Mazza	John	27	Sonoma	ITL	Arata	Angela	18	St. Helena	CA
Mazza	Joseph H.	28	Petaluma	CA	Filippini	Elvira Leretta	21	Petaluma	CA
Mazza	Ralph	38	Petaluma	SWT	Shepard	Oliva	17	Petaluma	NY
Mazza	Romildo Louis	30	Petaluma	CA	Soldati	Jennie Ida	18	Petaluma	CA
Mazzeri	Enrico	43	Santa Rosa	ITL	Ferraris	Annetta	37	Santa Rosa	ITL
Mazzoni	John	33	Bodega Port, Sonoma Co.	ITL	Lafranchi	Giema	23	Bodega Port	SWT
Mazzoni	Peter	40	Bodega	ITL	Mazzurchi	Angiolina	34	Bodega	ENG
Mazzotti	Ralph	26	Occidental	GER	Donati	Dosola	23	Occidental	ITL
Mazzucchi	Adorno	28	Santa Rosa	ITL	Bellotti	Mary	18	Santa Rosa	ITL
Mazzucchi	Martino	24	Tomales	ITL	Albini	Angela	18	Tomales	ITL
Mc?ammon	Joseph	25	Point Reyes	IRL	Hendren	Rebecca	22	Santa Rosa	IRL

	Groom					Bride			
Surname	Given Name	Age	Residence	BP	Surname	Given Name	Age	Residence	BP
McAbee	Frank	24	Watsonville	CA	Lile	Ethel	18	Cloverdale	CA
McAfee	Lorn Charles	28	Bellevue	CA	Wade	Bernice	25	Bellevue	CO
McAfee	Vernon	26	Santa Rosa	CA	Menne	Mary	24	Santa Rosa	CA
McAllaster	Anson D.	22	Graton	CA	Nielsen	Mattie	19	Santa Rosa	NE
McAllaster	Fred Shelby	27	Santa Rosa	CA	Lowrey	Florence E.	27	Santa Rosa	CA
McAllister	Floyd Stanley	27	San Francisco	CA	Hall	Evelyn Louise	25	Petaluma	Pet
McAllister	Kieth (?) M.	21	Healdsburg	CA	Phillips	Gertrude E.	17	Glen Ellen	WA
McAlpine	J. K.	27	San Francisco	CT	Smith	Florence A.	18	San Francisco	CA
McAnally	Robert W.	23	Oakland	MO	Meredith	Gladys L.	20	Healdsburg	CA
McAnear	Saml. F.	38	Sacramento	AR	Towne	Florence	30	Petaluma	CA
McAninch	Harry	28	Green Valley	CA	Wilson	Ella G., Mrs.	30	Green Valley	WI
McAskell	Angus H.	30	Petaluma	CA	Koch	Dorothy B.	22	Petaluma	CA
McAuley	George W.	32	Graton	KS	Rhodes	Clara M.	32	Graton	CA
McAuley	George William	23	Woodland	KS	Wirts	Elizabeth Bernice	19	Green Valley	CA
McBee	Nathan	21	Korbel's Mill		Newton	Jennie, Mrs.	21+	Korbel's Mill	
McBrayer	Arthur Lewis	34	Goldfield, NV	MO	Hale	Samantha Anise	35	Goldfield, NV	IL
McBride	David				Willard	Susan Alice			Jac
McBride	Murrie J.	25	Healdsburg	IA	Bell	Mary E.	22	Healdsburg	CA
McCabe	Arthur D.	33	Elko, NV	Carson, NV	Ehly	Lucile E.	27	San Francisco	TX
McCabe	John D.	23	San Francisco	NSC	Pollard	Jean	22	Cazadero	OR
McCabe	W. H.	22	Los Angeles	CA	Peugh	Erba M.	22	Guerneville	CA
McCallum	Alphonso	21	Ukiah	CND	Day	Lizzie	20	Ukiah	CA
McCammon	Robert	32	Pt. Reyes	IRL	Nichols	Sarah Margaret	32	Bloomfield	IRL
McCan	Francis A.	27	San Francisco	MN	Watkins	Annette A.	26	San Francisco	CA
McCandless	Robert	22	Howards	IRL	Zearns	Mary	28	Howards	CA
McCann	George				Lytaker	Anna			
McCann	Thomas F.	29	Windsor	AUT	Chambaud	Sadie	23	Santa Rosa	CA

	Groom					Bride			
Surname	Given Name	Age	Residence	BP	Surname	Given Name	Age	Residence	BP
McCann	William Charles A.	33	Mark West Springs	CA	Danhansen	Louise	21	Mark West Springs	CA
McCappin	John A.	35	Santa Rosa	CA	Staley	Ethyle M.	33	Santa Rosa	CA
McCarcy	Harry	31	Santa Rosa	IA	Gwaltney (?)	Myrtle Alice	21	Santa Rosa	MO
McCargar	H. S.	33	Petaluma	CND	Warner	Minnie E.	20	Petaluma	CA
McCarter	William Ernest	19	Ely	CND	Alden	Priscilla B.	17	Ely	OR
McCarthy	A. Marden	23	Berkeley	CA	Frank	Marie L.	23	Oakland	NV
McCarthy	David A.	38	Long Ridge, Trinity Co.	OR	McGuire	Mary Jane	30	Dixon	CND
McCarthy	Eugene G.	21	Healdsburg	CA	Fewel	Addie J.	21	Windsor	CA
McCarthy	Geo. J	22	Santa Rosa	CA	Hyde	Annie E.	20	Santa Rosa	CA
McCarthy	Timothy	48	Vallejo	IRL	Grabs	Lila B.	22	Standish, CA	CA
McCarthy	Will	23	Healdsburg	CA	Farrar	Theo	20	Healdsburg	CA
McCarty	Eugene G.	27	San Francisco	CA	Burger	Jessie	25	Boonville	CA
McCaslin	Reo W.	21	San Francisco	CA	Crist	Wilma L.	18	San Francisco	CA
McCaughey	Howard Cyril	24	Bodega	CA	Tibbetts	Elsie Maude	24	Bodega	CA
McCaughey	James				Carsen	Nancy			
McCauley	Thomas P.	29	San Francisco	WI	Church	Alice C.	23	San Francisco	CA
McCausland	James	47	Tomales		Kidder	Lizzie	23	Santa Rosa	
McCawley	L. E.	21	Santa Rosa	IL	Irvin	Maggie	21	Santa Rosa	CA
McCawley	Lucien E.	28	Santa Rosa	IL	Lukas	Emilie	20	Santa Rosa	CA
McChesney	Robert S.	41	San Francisco	PA	Davis	Ona M.	33	San Francisco	NE
McChristian	Owen A.	25	Sebastopol	CA	Greening	Nellie E.	23	Santa Rosa	CA
McChristian	Wm. E.	20	Sebastopol	Seb	Chenoweth	Viola T.	20	Occidental	Occidental
McClary	David Reid	24	Fruitvale	CA	Pedersen	Christine Jensine	22	Santa Rosa	MN
McClellan	Albert R.	42	Vine Hill	IL	Lynch	Tillie	41	Vine Hill	WI
McClellan	J. A. S.	28	Stewarts Point		Johnson	Lizzie	16	Stewarts Point	
McClelland	Buchanan	25	Santa Rosa	CA	Hudson	Elizabeth, Mrs.	29	Santa Rosa	PA
McClelland	Robert Henry	28	Eureka	CA	Myers	Alice R.	21	Eureka	CA

	Groom					Bride			
Surname	**Given Name**	**Age**	**Residence**	**BP**	**Surname**	**Given Name**	**Age**	**Residence**	**BP**
McClendon	William J.	50	Healdsburg	TX	Carter	Alice M.	25	Healdsburg	CA
McClish	James B.	24	Healdsburg	CA	Lodge	Hazel K.	21	Healdsburg	CA
McClish	James Blaine	18	Healdsburg	CA	Mothom	Claudia Alice	21	Healdsburg	CA
McClish	John M.	27	Healdsburg	CA	Hamilton	Georgia	25	Healdsburg	CA
McClish	Ralph	25	Healdsburg	CA	Thurman	Nellie	19	Healdsburg	CA
McClool	Thomas A.	36	Guerneville	MO	Cargile	Lucina	19	Forestville	CA
McCloskey	R. M.	27	San Francisco	CA	Nicholson	Catherine A.	22	San Francisco	CA
McCloud	Louis Clifford	29	Ukiah	CA	Clark	Mary E.	29	Tomales	CA
McCloud	William Elbert	22	Esparto, CA	CA	Samuel	Dorothy Viola	19	Capell, CA	CA
McClude	Roland R.	39	San Francisco	PA	Harman	Elizabeth	37	San Francisco	NZD
McClure	Isaac	49	Healdsburg	CA	Grasso	Mary	39	Healdsburg	NY
McClure	Walter	22	Forestville	CA	Hansen	Frances	19	Stony Point	CA
McClymonds	Vance	25	Oakland	CA	Ellis	Treasure Sterling	23	Petaluma	AUT
McCoffrey	Bernard	35	San Francisco	IRL	Wilson	Agnes	33	San Francisco	PA
McCollam	William	25	Guerneville	CND	Friend	Mary E.	20	Guerneville	OR
McColloch	Wilson	29	Bloomfield		Stainin (?)	Anie	25		
McCollum	William	24	Guerneville	CND	Friesia (?)	Mary E.	19	Guerneville	OR
McComb	Barron N.	23	Healdsburg		Bailey	Clara V.	20	Healdsburg	
McComb	George B.	27	NY	PA	Griffith	Lucille M.	19	NY	TN
McCombs	Aaron Cecil	32	Bellevue	IA	Sandberg	Olga Olivia	32	Bellevue	WI
McCombs	Charles W.	24	Santa Rosa	IA	Gillett	Elizabeth A.	24	Santa Rosa	CA
McCombs	Edward O.	24	Santa Rosa	IA	Vivarelli	Minnie	18	Santa Rosa	NE
McCombs	John F., Jr.	28	Turlock	NE	Barrett	Luella B.	20	Santa Rosa	KS
McCombs	Joseph Franklin	21	Santa Rosa	CA	Crowder	Erma May	17	Santa Rosa	CA
McCombs	William H.	24	Santa Rosa Twp.	IA	Rich	Eula S.	24	Santa Rosa Twp.	MI
McConnell	Frederick William	27	Healdsburg	CA	Hall	Gladys	23	Healdsburg	CA
McConnell	Hugh	38	Forestville	IRL	Svenson	Anna D.	36	Forestville	SWD
McConnell	Jesse C.	27	Windsor	IA	Hammerlund	Ada C.	21	Petaluma	SWD

	Groom					Bride			
Surname	Given Name	Age	Residence	BP	Surname	Given Name	Age	Residence	BP
McConnell	Joseph P.	54	Santa Rosa	OR	Wilt	Carolyn J.	38	Santa Rosa	DNK
McConnell	Mark	23	Santa Rosa	CA	Woodward	Lillian Pearl	18	Santa Rosa	IA
McConnell	William S.	26	San Lucas, Monterey Co.	MO	Alton	Mary Agnes	17	Fulton	NY
McConochie	Thomas S.	28	San Francisco	CA	Emmick	Minnie	31	San Francisco	MS
McCord	Arthur	34	Santa Rosa	CA	Gray	Minnie M.	34	Santa Rosa	CA
McCord	Charles	23		CA	Carrillo	Lulu	16		CA
McCord	Charles	30	Healdsburg	OR	McDonnell	Florence Evelyn	27	Healdsburg	CA
McCord	David C.	22	Healdsburg	IA	Combs	Leonore	20	Healdsburg	CA
McCord	Robert B. M.	28	Glen Ellen	MO	Bones	Electa Z.	30	Glen Ellen	CA
McCord	Rollin Burdette	21	Healdsburg	IA	Tully	Louise B.	19	Healdsburg	AZ
McCord	Smith	34	Santa Rosa	MO	Davidson	Zidana	29	Santa Rosa	CA
McCormack	Philip	27	Valley Ford	CA	Norton	Ellen	30	Valley Ford	IRL
McCormack	William H.	35	Coronado	PA	Stover	Lillian D.	30	Ross	CA
McCormack	Percival W.	29	Stockton	CND	Purvine	Lena Aletha	31	Petaluma	CA
McCormick	Chalmers	25	Fresno	CA	Hendrickson	C. Maud	23	Santa Rosa	MN
McCormick	Charles E.	21	St. Helena	CA	Bradbury	Eva	25	Healdsburg	KS
McCormick	Rodney	29	Altruria	CA	O'Hara	Emma E.	26	Altruria	
McCory	Gene L.				Fine	Caroline, Mrs.			
McCown	Albert E.	35	Bodega	CA	McCaughey	Edith	23	Bodega	CA
McCown	George M.	39	Garfield, Whitney Co., WA	MO	Boyd	Elizabeth L.	34	Bodega	CT
McCoy	Clyde	22	Petaluma	IL	Harrison	Margaret	22	Petaluma	NV
McCoy	David A.	48	Santa Rosa	OR	Dill	Matilda S.	50	Santa Rosa	MO
McCoy	Hugh				Combs	Amnada M. F.			
McCoy	John M.	27	Potters Mills, PA		Young	Emma	21	Sonoma	
McCracken	Frank B.	24	Healdsburg	CA	McClish	Jennie C.	21	Healdsburg	CA
McCracken	Geo. F.	27	Healdsburg	CA	Capell	Margaret E.	21	Healdsburg	CA
McCracken	Marshal N.	27	Healdsburg	CA	Thurman	Alice	19	Healdsburg	CA
McCracken	William J.	27	Healdsburg	CA	Archer	Nellie R.	17	Healdsburg	CA

| | Groom | | | | | Bride | | | |
Surname	Given Name	Age	Residence	BP	Surname	Given Name	Age	Residence	BP
McCraken	Alexander	35	Berkeley	SCT	Anthony	Anna M.	25	Healdsburg	NV
McCraney	Harrie E.	27	Oakland	CA	Condy	Mae E.	27	Oakland	CA
McCray	Armund W.	23	Cloverdale	MO (?)	Welley (?)	Nora	18	Cloverdale	CA
McCray	David W.	24	Guerneville	MO	Maddux	Gertrude E.	23	Guerneville	CA
McCray	Logan	23	Cloverdale	CA	Sinn	Carrie M.	26	Cloverdale	CA
McCray	William Lloyd	23	Lakeville	CA	Johnson	Ella F.	18	Lakeville	CA
McCray	William Lloyd	38	Monticello	CA	Collins	Marie	26	San Francisco	CO
McCrea	James Walter	25	Oakland	CA	Goodfellow	Thelma Marie	20	Santa Rosa	CA
McCready	Thomas	43	Bodega	CA	Black	Marie	40	San Francisco	CA
McCready	Thomas C.	26	Bodega	CA	Cockrill	Lora T.	20	Bloomfield	CA
McCrystle	Arthur B.	23	San Francisco	CA	Winslow	Geraldine M.	20	San Francisco	CA
McCue	Herbert E.	29	San Francisco	CA	Rossi	Alice M.	20	Roseville	CA
McCulley	T. A.	27	Santa Rosa	CA	Brockmann	Agnes M.	26	Santa Rosa	IA
McCulloch	Irvin Scott	23	Oakland	IN	Dovin	Elizabeth	21	Oakland	CA
McCulloch	James Henry	21	Ukiah	CA	Barham	Lucy	20	Santa Rosa	CA
McCulloh	Frank	25	Hornitos, Mariposa Co.	CA	Laughlin	Lizzie	26	Mark West	CA
McCune	William M.				Dickey	Parmelia			
McCustion	Bert James	24	Santa Rosa	CA	Trowbridge	Grace Tyler	24	Santa Rosa	CA
McCutchan	Fred E.	21	Napa	CA	Lucas	Metta	18	Geyserville	CA
McCutchan	Geo. F.	22	Windsor	IA	Pohley	Margaret		Windsor	CA
McCutchan	George F.	29	Windsor	IA	Meek	Mary L.	22	Windsor	CA
McCutchan	George Francis	40	Healdsburg	IA	Sorden	Mary	34	Healdsburg	KS
McCutchan	William H.	28	Windsor	CA	Ward	Ada E.	22	Windsor	MN
McCutchen	James B.	26	Windsor	CA	Bell	Geneva	17	Windsor	CA
McCutchen	Stanley S.	29	Petaluma	NE	Stout	Lizzie	24	Petaluma	IN
McDaniel	Albert Edwin	25	San Rafael	MD	Cramer	Nettie Louisa	20	San Rafael	IN
McDaniel	Edgar A.	22	San Francisco	UT	Reihl	Marie Madeline	19	San Francisco	CA
McDaniel	Levi J. M.	23	Colusa	CA	Griggs	Hattie C., Mrs.	29	Santa Rosa	CA
McDaniel	Victor G.	30	Santa Rosa	KS	Wright	Ruth E.	24	Santa Rosa	CA

	Groom					Bride			
Surname	**Given Name**	**Age**	**Residence**	**BP**	**Surname**	**Given Name**	**Age**	**Residence**	**BP**
McDermed	Joseph E.	25	Hayward		Lewis	Lydia Mary M.	21	Petaluma	CND
McDermott	Charles Henry	34	Santa Rosa	CA	Denny	Sadie Mae	25	Santa Rosa	CA
McDermott	William, Jr.	18	Petaluma	CA	Barnes	Mildred	16	Petaluma	CA
McDevitt	Edward	39	San Francisco	IRL	Murphy	Hannah	25	San Francisco	Sfo
McDill	S. F.	31	Biggs, Wasco Co., OR	IL	James	Allie	25	Santa Rosa	CA
McDonald	Albert S.	25	Hayward	CA	Laffey	Rose	16	Oakland	CA
McDonald	Alexander	61	Santa Rosa	CND	Mortimer	Anna May	56	Santa Rosa	NY
McDonald	Bernard John	25	San Francisco	CA	Noli	Olympia M.	20	San Francisco	NY
McDonald	Casey	24	Petaluma	CND	Butts	Nellie	18	Petaluma	KS
McDonald	Daniel	28	Petaluma		Gilbert	Amelia	28	Petaluma	
McDonald	Daniel	28	Petaluma		Gilbert	Amelia	19	Petaluma	
McDonald	Frank Andrew	32	San Francisco	MN	Catlin	Beatrice Lenore	23	Los Angeles	IA
McDonald	George Alfred	35	San Francisco	CA	Swadeling	Josephine Alden	26	Oakland	CA
McDonald	Glen	24	Petaluma	ND	Bugghard	Minnie	20	Santa Rosa	CA
McDonald	J. R.	50	Stanislaus		Cooper	Emma J.	25	Sonoma	
McDonald	James P.	57	Santa Rosa	NY	Brown	Lida E.	57	Santa Rosa	OH
McDonald	John	33	Marshall	IRL	Kelley	Maggie	23	Marshall	IRL
McDonald	Joseph F.	38	Eldridge	MA	Snieckpeper	Lillian D.	27	Eldridge	WI
McDonald	Mark L.				North	Ralphina			
McDonald	Mark L., Jr.	29	Santa Rosa	CA	Juilliard	Florence Isabelle	29	Santa Rosa	CA
McDonald	Marshall Bell	28	San Francisco	CND	Vier	Clara Ellen	23	Sebastopol	CA
McDonald	Robert J.	38	Petaluma	MA	Quant	Minnie Myrtle	39	Petaluma	CA
McDonald	Thomas J.	27	Santa Rosa	PA	Brittain	Ora C.	21	Santa Rosa	CA
McDonald	W. L.	27	Novato		Hayden	A. A.	26	Novato	
McDonald	William	27	Humboldt Co.	CND	Miller	Edith Maria	18	Cloverdale	IA
McDonald	William M.	32	Petaluma	CA	Moretti	Stella I.	22	Petaluma	CA
McDonald	William Vincent	23	San Rafael	Sar	Coul	Annie Laura	22	Petaluma	CA

	Groom					Bride			
Surname	Given Name	Age	Residence	BP	Surname	Given Name	Age	Residence	BP
McDonald	Winthrop G.	22	Palmyra, MO	MO	Moss	Minnie P.	19	Paris, MO	MO
McDonnell	Charles P.	32	San Mateo	PA	Hodgins	Kathyrn M.	24	San Francisco	NY
McDonnell	John Joseph	27	San Francisco	IRL	Hickey	Ella Berniece	29	San Francisco	CA
McDonnell	Joseph A.	29	San Francisco	PA	Ruffe	Pauline	20	San Francisco	FRN
McDonough	Joseph P.	26	Geyserville	CA	Powell	Mabel W.	21	Geyserville	CA
McDonough	Michael	30	Petaluma	VT	Stites	Sarah Effie	23	Geyserville	CA
McDonough	Michael	70	Geyserville	IRL	Baker	Susie R., Mrs.	53	Healdsburg	OH
McDougall	Edwin J.	25	Kenwood	ND	Streeter	Myrtle R.	21	Richmond	IL
McDowell	Frank	23	Penngrove	CA	Craig	Ethel	23	Penngrove	CA
McDowell	Harry E.	28	Petaluma	CA	Thompson	Ineaz M.	19	Vancouver, WA	WA
McDowell	James				Hoar	Addie E.	17		
McDowell	William A.	25	Healdsburg	CA	Craig	Bessie	23	Penngrove	CA
McDowell	Wm. J.				McLeod	Amy			
McElheny	Roy	21	Santa Rosa	CA	Fawcett	Margaret	21	Santa Rosa	ENG
McElwain	Arthur E.	46	Camp Meeker	WV	Whitcomb	Lelia A.	51	Camp Meeker	VA
McEntire	Ernest J.	36	Oakland	CA	Bullard	Iva Irene	35	Santa Rosa	WI
McEowen	John W.	40	Coalinga	KS	Wade	Daisy E.	33	Santa Rosa	MI
McFadden	George Reuben	22	Petaluma	NV	Coll	Edna G.	21	Petaluma	NV
McFadden	Joseph	62	San Francisco	IL	Birks	Elizabeth Richmond	62	Berkeley	CA
McFadden	Sandy	25	Petaluma	IRL	Seiss	Marie Martha	22	Petaluma	CA
McFadden	William H.	51	Sonoma	CND	Doherty	Sadie M.	35	Sonoma	MI
McFall	Frank	32	Guerneville	IL	Brown	Martha E.	19	Guerneville	CA
McFarland	James	26	Potter Valley		Morris	Lizzie	19	Ukiah	
McFarlane	Frederick George	26	Sebastopol	CA	O'Connor	Eleanor Inez	20	Santa Rosa	CA
McFarlane	James D.	22	Healdsburg	CDN	Broderson	Anna P.	19	Healdsburg	GER
McFarlane	Reginald L.	23	Healdsburg	CND	Seawell	Alice A.	20	Healdsburg	CA
McFarlane	Walter C.	20	Sebastopol	CA	Williams	Edna Merle	18	Sebastopol	CA
McFarling	Clarence H.	24	Cozzens	CA	Bruner	Edith M.	20	Windsor	CA

	Groom					Bride			
Surname	Given Name	Age	Residence	BP	Surname	Given Name	Age	Residence	BP
McFarling	John Stanley	21	Healdsburg	CA	Cook	May Adeline	17	Healdsburg	CA
McFeely	John	32	Calistoga	CA	Bishop	Effie	17	Calistoga	CA
McGarr	Frank	30	Dixon	CND	McFarland	Dora M.	30	Santa Rosa	IA
McGarvey	Laurence Thurman	19	Ukiah	CA	Yates	Pearl	20	Ukiah	CA
McGavin	William	28	Oakland	SCT	McDonald	Erma Eunice	28	Santa Rosa	CND
McGawim (?)	Frank P.	40	San Francisco	CND	Norton	Laura A.	49	San Francisco	CA
McGee	Edward William	26	Sebastopol	CA	Gambini	Edith Gladys	24	Sebastopol	CA
McGee	Thomas J.	33	Cloverdale	Boston	Donnelly	Kate	20	Cloverdale	Men
McGeein (?)	Roland J.	27	Santa Rosa	CND	Dietz	Gladys N.	22	Santa Rosa	NJ
McGeorge	Le Roy	24	Santa Rosa	IA	Hesseltine	Stella C.	23	Sebastopol	IA
McGhaney	Edward Jasper	24	Santa Rosa	ID	Johnson	Mae	20	Santa Rosa	CA
McGillwray	William	25	San Francisco	CA	Donair	Helen E.	19	San Francisco	CA
McGimsey	Charles L.	22	Anderson Valley	CA	Murray	Melinda O.	22	Healdsburg	CA
McGimsey	Charles L.	44	Throop, CA	CA	Keithley	Nora	39	Philo	IN
McGimsey	John Milton	25	Sonoma	Ukiah	Morris	Katherine Rice	23	Agua Caliente	Agc
McGimsey	Charles R.	27	Cottonwood, AZ	CA	Trondsen	Emily Rowena	23	Petaluma	CA
McGlauflin	Hallam C.	21	Petaluma	CA	Bond	Frances G.	21	Petaluma	CA
McGowan	James E.	29	San Francisco	OK	Staples	Charleen G.	21	San Francisco	MI
McGowen	A. L.	21	Santa Ana	TX	Evans	Ruby F.	17	Forestville	CA
McGrath	Basil William	40	Cloverdale	NV	Heselschwerdt	Amy Lillie	24	Santa Rosa	CA
McGrath	Patrick J.	29	Richmond	IRL	Bradley	Margaret	23	San Francisco	IRL
McGrath	Peter J.	31	San Francisco	CA	Clanton	Rebecca, Mrs.	34	San Francisco	NBW
McGregor	Franklin D.	24	Santa Rosa		Cooper	Elanor A.	18	Santa Rosa	
McGrew	Francis H.	19	Sebastopol	CA	Cole	Arcadia F.	18	Freestone	CA
McGrew	James Gale	21	Stony Point	CA	Dabney	Lida E.	19	Sebastopol	MO
McGrew	Samuel	65	Petaluma	WV	Wilsey	Sarah	35	Petaluma	NY
McGroghegan	John Thomas	30	Oakland	Sfo	Hihu (?)	Kathryn Bothwell	30	Oakland	Toronto CND
McGuire	I. N.	55	Santa Maria	MO	Horsley	Annie, Mrs.	53	Bloomfield	PA

	Groom					Bride			
Surname	**Given Name**	**Age**	**Residence**	**BP**	**Surname**	**Given Name**	**Age**	**Residence**	**BP**
McGuire	Jacob	22	Windsor	TX	McHall	Mary Ellen	22	Windsor	CA
McGuire	Laurence B.	43	Santa Rosa	KS	Vitale	Louisa	39	Santa Rosa	NY
McGuire	Nathaniel				Wilhoit	Mary Ellen			
McGuire	Oscar Alonzo	54	Colusa	CA	Parsons	Lavina J.	43	Petaluma	CA
McGuire	William J.	26	Oakland	CA	O'Leary	Blanche A.	23	Santa Rosa	CA
McGuire	William J.	41	San Francisco	ENG	Yancey	Laura Russell	39	Sacramento	OH
McGuire	Bert	19	Windsor	Lak	Bradshaw	Meita	18	Santa Rosa	Winters
McGuyre	William	24	Windsor	CA	McLeod	Margaret	22	Ukiah	SCT
McHale	William Anthony	24	Windsor	CA	Doughty	Margaret Elizabeth	23	Windsor	OR
McHatton	Robert L.	27	Sacramento	KY	Hood	Eva L.		Santa Rosa	CA
McHugh	George	21	Oakland	CA	Martin	Josephine G.	21	Sebastopol	CA
McHugh	John	25	Oakland	CA	McAlpine	Alice M.	21	Santa Rosa	CA
McIlree	Alexander	40	Mendocino City	OH	Russell	Eliza F.	41	Comptche	HLD
McIlwain	Alexander	35	Petaluma	IRL	Long	Maud R.	20	Independence, MO	MO
McIntosh	Andrew	37	Penngrove	SCT	Wood	Hellen	26	Oakland	SCT
McIntosh	Charles	28	Mark West	CA	Regan	Elizabeth	23	Mark West	CA
McIntosh	D.	31	Forestville	CA	Clark	Lennie	24	Forestville	CA
McIntosh	E. A.	38	Seattle	TN	Jones	Veta	26	Petaluma	OR
McIntosh	John O.	34	Forestville	CA	Henderson	Mamie	19	Forestville	MO
McIntosh	Richard Robert	39	Tiburon	CA	Hemsath	Jewel Hermina	23	Cloverdale	CA
McKay	Loran	35	Elk Grove	CND	Wilson	Elizabeth Ellen	31		CND
McKean	George F.	32	Guerneville	CA	Pool	Elizabeth	24	Guerneville	CA
McKeand	William J.	38	Lakeport	IN	Benner	Etta M.	31	Lakeport	CA
McKee	Harry B.	26	San Francisco	IA	Bird	Emma L.	23	Seattle	WA
McKee	Samuel	28	San Francisco		Bowse	Nellie F.	25	Santa Rosa	
McKee	William A.	35	Sebastopol	SC	Collins	Maud	32	Sebastopol	IL
McKenzie	James	63	Sebastopol	SCT	Banks	Susan R.	38	Forestville	OR

	Groom					Bride			
Surname	Given Name	Age	Residence	BP	Surname	Given Name	Age	Residence	BP
McKenzie	William H.	22	Fresno		Harie (?)	Carrie E.	18	Healdsburg	
McKibbin	Edward L.	25	Healdsburg	KS	Baker	Alma E.	20	Healdsburg	CA
McKibbin	George M.	28	Knob, CA	CA	Wanaka	Leona E.	23	Vallejo	CA
McKillap	Dugald	72	Petaluma	SCT	Allen	Huldah	55	Petaluma	MO
McKillop	Dugald	38		SCT	Ingrim	Delia	25		IL
McKillop	Harry C.	24	Petaluma	CA	Gibbons	Myrtle M.	19	Cloverdale	CA
McKillop	William D.	24	Weed, CA	CND	England	Elma L.	17	Healdsburg	CA
McKinlay	D. E.	23	Santa Rosa	CND	Hendley	Nannie V.	26	Santa Rosa	CA
McKinlay	James M.	22	Santa Rosa	CND	Glenn	Luella	18	Santa Rosa	CA
McKinley	Charles. C.	39	Los Angeles	KS	Utman	Hazel E.	23	Los Angeles	CA
McKinna	Frank	36	Sonoma	IRL	Sheridan	Alice	25	Sonoma	IRL
McKinney	George B.	31	Santa Rosa	OR	Murray	Annie E.	30	Santa Rosa	IL
McKinney	John H.	28	Santa Rosa	NBW	McPeak	Dora	30	Ukiah	CA
McKinney	Joseph Edward	41	Wheatland	CA	Senteney	Roxie May	31	Ukiah	CA
McKinnon	Alexander W.	30	San Francisco	CA	Wilson	Elizabeth Elsie	33	San Francisco	IN
McKinstry	George D.	45	Dixon	CA	Finley	Carrie Ann	45	Santa Rosa	CA
McKinstry	Henry H.				Fleming	Nancy M.			
McKnight	John	34	Santa Rosa	CND	Grimley	Eva	16	Santa Rosa Twp.	MO
McKune	Otis E.	29	Santa Rosa	KS	Head	Lulu M.	26	Sebastopol	CA
McLaren	Duncan T.	29	Stockton	CA	Willard	Nellie C.	25	Stockton	CA
McLaren	Henry Havelock	33	Duncans Mills	ME	DeCarly	Annie	21	Duncans Mills	CA
McLaren	Richard	29	Sebastopol	PA	McMillen	Cora	19	Fisherman's Bay	CA
McLaughlin	Alexander Douglas	22	San Francisco	CA	Julian	Victoria Susan	17	Petaluma	MN
McLaughlin	Bernard H.	27	San Francisco	MA	Wolf	Marie	19	Petaluma	SD
McLaughlin	Clarence Joseph	27	Sacramento	CA	Gillians	Alice	27	Sacramento	CA
McLaughlin	Oswald R.	25	Santa Rosa	CND	Parkins	Harriett E.	18	Santa Rosa	CA
McLaughlin	William Joseph	37	Petaluma		Shea	Alice Jane	33	Petaluma	CND

	Groom					Bride			
Surname	Given Name	Age	Residence	BP	Surname	Given Name	Age	Residence	BP
McLean	George Graham	27	San Francisco	CND	Washburn	Rose May	26	San Francisco	CA
McLean	Hector	34	Santa Barbara	MI	Carr	Ursula A.	32	Petaluma	WI
McLean	Walter N.	21	Healdsburg	CND	Piutt	Bertha F.	25	Healdsburg	IN
McLellan	David T.	33	Santa Rosa	CND	Reading	Lizzie	27	Nova Scotia	NSC
McLennan	James	26	Stewarts Point	CA	Batt	Faith Ray	22	Stewarts Point	WI
McLeod	Alfred W.	26	New West-minster, B. C.	CND	Temple	Ruth	26	Santa Rosa	CA
McMahan	Grover Cleveland	28	San Francisco	TX	Linkogel	Ledona Beatrice	32	San Francisco	IL
McMahon	James	32	Webster Grove, MO	MO	Osborne	Katherina	27	Mt. Olivet	IL
McMahon	John Henry	27	Healdsburg	CA	Spencer	Mabel M.	18	Healdsburg	CA
McManus	George E.	27	Graton	SD	Hopper	Bertha S.	19	Graton	CA
McMath	Ernest Burwell	20	Upper Lake	CA	Harrow	Della	20	Santa Rosa	WA
McMath	Sanford	43	Elmira, CA	CA	Renstrom	Ida M.	36	Santa Rosa	CA
McMichael	John William	21	Healdsburg	CA	Covey	Cashia Mary	17	Trenton	CA
McMichael	Rice F.	22	Healdsburg	TN	Yarbrough	Ethel B.	18	Hilton	CA
McMillan	Alexander	31	Oakland	MI	Palm	Hilda A.	37	San Francisco	SWD
McMillan	Harmon D.	24	Santa Rosa	CA	Cloer (?)	Vada	25	Santa Rosa	AR
McMillan	Wm. S.	34	Cloverdale	NY	Garrison	Carrie	25	Cloverdale	CA
McMillen	Edd	25	Stewarts Point	CA	Johnson	Myrtle	18	Stewarts Point	CA
McMillen	Hiram	29	Stewarts Point	IA	Miller	Sarah B.	23	Stewarts Point	CA
McMillen	James William	28	Strewarts Point	IA	Boyd	Ella Vinora	28	Stewarts Point	CA
McMillen	John J.	25	Stewarts Point	IA	Miller	Daisy M.	21	Stewarts Point	Ca
McMinamin	John	38	Sebastopol	IRL	Fitzgerald	Annie	19	Sebastopol	IRL
McMinn	J. A.	20	Alexander Valley	CA	Crisp	Sarah J.	26	Alexander Valley	CA
McMinn	Joseph	27	Santa Rosa	CA	Carlton	Ada B.	27	Santa Rosa	CA
McMullen	John	26	Alexander Valley	KS	Myers	Phoeby	18	Alexander Valley	CA
McMullen	Russell McGarvey	21	Petaluma	CA	McGovern	Clara Josephine	20	Petaluma	CA
McMullin	Joseph E.	25	Shellville	CA	Bates	Pauline C.	20	Sonoma	CA

	Groom					Bride			
Surname	**Given Name**	**Age**	**Residence**	**BP**	**Surname**	**Given Name**	**Age**	**Residence**	**BP**
McMullin	Thomas F.	33	Santa Rosa	CA	Johnson	California I.	36	Petaluma	CA
McMurray	R. W.	36	NY	CA	Gardanier	Carol	26	Cincinatti, OH	OH
McNab	Gavin	24	San Francisco	SCT	Davidson	Wilma	22	Petaluma	CA
McNabb	James Henry	64	Petaluma	IL	Carpenter	Adelia E.	56	Petaluma	IL
McNair	Elmer A.	29	Dixon	NY	Conyers	Iva	18	Santa Rosa	OR
McNair	James	38	Sacramento	IA	Peters	Ada May	23	Healdsburg	CA
McNally	Oscar	25	Ashland, ME	ME	Clark	Ella	22	Healdsburg	ME
McNally	Raymond Gregory	25	Petaluma	CA	Meyers	Carleen Marie	22	Petaluma	CA
McNally	Thomas Charles	21	Petaluma	CA	Camm	Charlotte Shepard	19	Petaluma	IL
McNamara	Bernard	46	Santa Rosa		Loughead	Maggie	40	Santa Rosa	
McNamara	Dan	34	San Pablo	MA	Silvia	Frances	19	San Pablo	CA
McNamara	James E.	29	Santa Rosa	CA	Trembley	Evelyn A.	21	Santa Rosa	CA
McNamara	James J.	37	San Francisco	IL	Sweitzer	Audrey M.	24	San Francisco	KS
McNamara	Thomas	21	San Francisco	IRL	Cullahan	May A.	21	San Francisco	IRL
McNeal	William E.	56	Santa Rosa	TN	Conne	Annie, Mrs.	48	Santa Rosa	CND
McNear	George Plummer	29	Petaluma	Pet	Denman	Ida Belle	27	Petaluma	Soc
McNear	John A., Jr.	21+	McNear, Marin Co.	Pet	Egan	Nellie V.	21+	Petaluma	Pet
McNeil	James F.	20	Petaluma	Pet	Krohn	Joeliene E.	18	Petaluma	CA
McNeil	James J.	25	San Francisco	MA	Nelson	Vera A.	22	San Francisco	CA
McNeil	John	44	San Francisco	MD	Butteer	Henriette	29	San Francisco	CND
McNeil	John	43	Agua Caliente	CA	Copperelmann	Laura	26	San Francisco	Sfo
McNeil	Justin Louis	21	Healdsburg	CA	Barnes	Edna Gay	23?	Healdsburg	CA
McNeil	Wilbur J.	33	Petaluma	MA	Barlow	Elizabeth L.	31	Two Rock	CA
McNeill	Wm. J.	28	Sebastopol	OR	Foley	Pearl O.	27	San Francisco	CA
McNiel	James F.	24	Petaluma	Boston	Parrish	Eliza Jane	17	Petaluma	Analy Twp.
McNulty	Charles Augustus	38	Santa Rosa	CA	Barnes	Myrtle Blanche	19	Santa Rosa	KS
McNutty	Edward Francis	42	Santa Rosa	CA	Olstad	Gunhild	26	Santa Rosa	NRY

	Groom					Bride			
Surname	**Given Name**	**Age**	**Residence**	**BP**	**Surname**	**Given Name**	**Age**	**Residence**	**BP**
McPeak	Charles E.	23	Cloverdale	CA	Henry	Lucile E.	23	Cloverdale	Men
McPeak	Harmon P.	23	Guerneville	CA	Sinclair	Tenia	20	Forestville	CA
McPeak	Jefferson P.	28	Ukiah	CA	Critchfield	Lulu	22	Ukiah	CA
McPeak	Mathew A.				McBee	Fetnie A.			
McPeak	William H.	22	Guerneville	CA	White	Jennie L.	19	Santa Rosa	CA
McPeak	William H.	33	Guerneville	CA	Mendenhall	Carrie P.	22	Santa Rosa	IA
McPhail	A. J.	30	Petaluma	CA	Gale	Mary Ella	28	Petaluma	CA
McPherson	August	26	Healdsburg	CA	Hoe	Elsie	23	Healdsburg	CA
McPherson	Bert	24	Cloverdale	CA	Smith	Rose	20	Alexander Valley	CA
McPherson	Charles W.	27	Cloverdale	CA	Hale	Nannie	19	Alexander Valley	CA
McPherson	Early	21	Healdsburg	CA	Ferguson	May	18	Alexander Valley	CA
McPherson	Ernest I.	21	Chico	CA	Baker	Atlanta	20	Santa Rosa	MO
McPherson	Hal	22	Healdsburg	CA	Johnson	Cora F.	24	Healdsburg	CA
McPherson	Harry Moore	20	Alexander Valley	CA	Beeson	Ella Frances	22	Alexander Valley	CA
McPherson	Leon	23	Cloverdale	CA	Capell	Elsie Aline	18	Dry Creek Valley	CA
McPherson	Perry Lewis	24	Cloverdale	CA	Brumfield	Margaret Jenette	19	Cloverdale	CA
McPherson	Thomas				Harden	Lucinda, Mrs.			
McPherson	Walter	21	Cloverdale	Soc	Allen	Belle	20	Cloverdale	CA
McPike	William F.	40	St. Helena	MO	Hopley	Juno Clarice	37	St. Helena	IA
McProud	Oscar C.	51	Santa Rosa	IN	Jackson	Delia	37	Santa Rosa	UT
McReynolds	Arthur	24	Santa Rosa	CA	Clegg	Grace	17	Santa Rosa	CA
McReynolds	Charles Newton	21	Bloomfield		Gregory	Mary Elizabeth	19	Bloomfield	
McReynolds	Dennis H.	23	Healdsburg	CA	Hinshaw	Amanda	21	Bloomfield	CA
McReynolds	Lewis M.	23	Bloomfield		Phariss	Alice	18	Bloomfield	
McReynolds	Melvin J.	26	Sebastopol	CA	Clegg	Alice	20	Santa Rosa	CA

	Groom					Bride			
Surname	Given Name	Age	Residence	BP	Surname	Given Name	Age	Residence	BP
McReynolds	R. E. L.	24	Valley Ford	CA	Dunwoody	Lizzie	22	Santa Rosa	
McReynolds	Samuel W.	28	Sebastopol	CA	Haley	Emma E.	25	Sebastopol	IA
McReynolds	Stephen				Olison	Georgianna, Mrs.			
McReynolds	Thos. A.				Harris	Ellen M.			
McSweeney	Daniel	35	San Francisco	IRL	McKay	Margaret	30	Freestone	IRL
McVay	Clarence L.	29	Petaluma	IA	Dudley	Daphne A.	17	Petaluma	CA
McVay	John A.	36	Petaluma	IA	Iffland	May L.	25	Petaluma	MI
McWilliams	Arthur C.	26	Santa Rosa	NE	Reeves	Caroline Helena	24	Santa Rosa	CA
McWilliams	Eslie B.	31	Healdsburg		Long	Lucy A. M.	23	Healdsburg	
McWilliams	George S.	43	Alexander Valley	IA	Seeman	Dora	28	Alexander Valley	GER
McWilliams	Hugh	31	Sacramento	SCT	Shaw	Georgie P.	21	Duncans Mills	CA
Meacham	Charles S.	26	Occidental	WI	Collins	Mary A.	22	Occidental	CA
Mead	Albert Miller	24	Santa Rosa	NV	Surryhne	Barbara Stuart	22	Santa Rosa	CA
Mead	Charles S.	27	Santa Rosa	CA	Reed	Mary	22	Healdsburg	WI
Mead	Fred Ryland	29	Santa Rosa	CA	Gist	Fannie Irene	25	Santa Rosa	CA
Mead	Wilson Henry	45	Santa Rosa	PA	Hewit	Rosanna	19	Santa Rosa	CA
Meador	Bert L.	31	Santa Rosa	CA	Farmer	Agnes	30	Santa Rosa	CO
Meador	George Frank	26	Graton	CA	Schindler	Lena Olive	24	Fulton	OR
Meads	Willia C.	26	Los Angeles	NY	Howard	Eleanor Adella	19	Santa Rosa	MO
Meagher	John F.	32	Petaluma	OH	Hardin	Nancy	32	Petaluma	CA
Meagher	Thomas	40	Petaluma	OH	Lowe	Annie	23	Petaluma	IL
Meaney	John	33	Petaluma	IRL	Kaiser	Laura Teresa	36	Petaluma	CA
Means	Thomas Jefferson	32	Fulton	CA	Bones	Lillie	20	Occidental	CA
Mecchi	Costantino	34	Asti	ITL	Passalacque	Amelia I.	18	Healdsburg	IL
Mecham	Harrison Carlos	39	Santa Rosa	ID	Peerman	Alice Elizabeth	39	Santa Rosa	MO
Mecham	Sherman A.	33	Santa Rosa	CA	Noonan	Alice R.	28	Santa Rosa	CA
Meck	William Edward	31	Healdsburg	WY	Hall	Laura Alice	31	Healdsburg	NE
Medeira	William	23	Healdsburg	NV	Cummings	Kate	19	Healdsburg	CA

	Groom					Bride			
Surname	**Given Name**	**Age**	**Residence**	**BP**	**Surname**	**Given Name**	**Age**	**Residence**	**BP**
Mediros	Frank	22	Oakland	CA	Haraldson	Elizabeth	18	Oakland	NY
Mee	Thomas H.	33	Etna Mills, Siskiyou Co.	CA	Lewis	Mary Elisabeth	33	Healdsburg	IN
Meek	Nathan T.	26	Windsor	CA	Young	Flora E.	26	Alexander Valley	NY
Meek	Thomas Barney	22	Healdsburg	WY	Cavers	Margaret I.	18	Healdsburg	CA
Meeker	Alexander H.	24	Occidental	Occidental	Dodge	Florence H.	18	Occidental	CA
Meeker	Godfrey Hinkley	22	Santa Rosa	CA	Dearborn	Ethel	19	Santa Rosa	CA
Meeker	John V.	20	Lytton	WA	Petersen	Clara	18	Alexander Valley	CA
Meeker	John V.	24	Graton	WA	Rieck	Mable M.	24	Salinas	CA
Meeker	Robert T.	23	Occidental	CA	Lapham	Ethel	22	Sebastopol	WI
Meeker	Stephen A.	58	Occidental	NJ	Menary	Kate G., Mrs.	48	Occidental	CA
Meeker	William J.	24	Occidental	NJ	Smith	Carrie B.	25	Occidental	MO
Meeks	Everett	22	Vallejo	CA	Petersen	Margaret Marie	23	Petaluma	CA
Meeks	George Lawson	26	Graton	CA	Palmer	Maud Elizabeth	26	Sebastopol	CA
Meeks	Robert G.	31	Green Valley		Branscomb	Sarah L.	18+	Green Valley	
Meeks	Walter B.	24	Sebastopol	CA	Woodworth	Rose E.	18	Cloverdale	CA
Meeks	Walter H.	46	San Francisco	CA	Harttrodt	Hilda J.	40	San Francisco	CA
Meese	Henry	32	Santa Rosa	GER	Mangold	Frederika	22	Santa Rosa	GER
Meeth	Paul J. W.	26	Daly City	MI	Redding	Eva Lee (?)	21	Kenwood	TX
Mego	Edward	26	Petaluma	Soc.	Sullivan	Ella	25	Petaluma	Soc
Megonigil	Eli	68	Windsor	MO	Wahrman	Augusta	46	Windsor	GER
Mehl	Walter A.	22	Portland, OR	OR	Lawson	Marion E.	21	Healdsburg	OR
Mehl	Carl Frederick	31	Petaluma	GER	Doelling	Eliza	30	Petaluma	IL
Meilicke	Carl H.	32	Winona, MN	MN	Stickel	Katie	36	Hagle, ID	SD
Meincke	Herman F.	39	San Francisco	CA	Vincent	Irene	26	San Francisco	CA
Meineri	Guy	20	Asti	CA	Costa	Lizzie	19	Sebastopol	CA
Meisner	Frank Gustave	28	Healdsburg	WA	Sawtell	Winifred	23	Healdsburg	MT
Meissner	Walter Charles	25	Fulton	PA	Smither	Ruby Pearl	21	Fulton	CA

| \multicolumn{5}{c|}{Groom} | \multicolumn{5}{c}{Bride} |

Surname	Given Name	Age	Residence	BP	Surname	Given Name	Age	Residence	BP
Meldi	Paul E.	22	San Francisco	ITL	Thorgood	Vera G.	18	Santa Rosa	UT
Melehan	Daniel John	25+	Petaluma	CA	Wiers	Mattie Theresa	19+	Petaluma	CA
Mell	A. William	32	San Francisco	HWI	Duncan	Helen	20	Healdsburg	CA
Mell	John W.	25	Healdsburg	HI	Duncan	Vella I.	20	Healdsburg	CA
Meller	Reginald D.	22	San Francisco	AUT	Chauvet	Henrietta M.	18	Glen Ellen	CA
Mellette	Randolph H.	67	Sebastopol	IN	Mantle	Susie L.	58	Santa Rosa	NY
Mello	Frank	24	Sebastopol	CA	Owens	Leeta	21	Santa Rosa	CA
Mello	Joseph	24	Sebastopol	CA	Green	Lenora	19	Sebastopol	CA
Mello	Louis	27	Vine Hill	Boston	Holmes	Minnie M.	19	Forestville	CA
Mello	William B.	23	Sebastopol	CA	Nielson	Lenora M.	18	San Francisco	CA
Mellow	Frank	28	Fresno	CA	Silva	Isabel	18	Cloverdale	CA
Melson	J. R.	32	Santa Rosa	AR	Swenson	Gyda S.	25	Santa Rosa	NRY
Melton	Newton				Dervin	Eliza	17		
Melton	Thomas	25	Petaluma	TN	Bean	Zella	28	Petaluma	IA
Melton	William				Barton	Nellie			
Mendelson	Isador	52	Oakland	OR	Clunan	Esther	34	San Francisco	CA
Mendenhall	Roy D.	24	Culdesac, ID	CA	Branstetter	Sylvia S.	20	Santa Rosa	MO
Mendonca	Antonio	26	Sebastopol	AZR	Green	Clara	23	Sebastopol	CA
Mendonca	Joseph J.	36	Petaluma	WTS	King	Mary F.	29	Petaluma Twp.	CA
Menefee	Campbell A.	60	Visalia	MO	Hall	M. Isadora	54	Healdsburg	CA
Menefee	John Wesley	40	Santa Rosa	MO	Smith	Sarah Eliza	28	Santa Rosa	IL
Menefee	Roderick E.	24	Oakland	CA	Mattaini	Mae Isabel	20	Berkeley	CA
Menefee	William Alfred	26	Santa Rosa	CA	Zeigler	Minnie Florence	23	Santa Rosa	OR
Menetrey (?)	Charles Louis	28	San Francisco	CA	Huffam	Hazel May	27	San Francisco	CA
Mengelt	George	26	Santa Rosa	SWT	Hemmy	Maria Ursula	28	Sebastopol	SWT
Menihan	Thos. M.	25	Healdsburg	CA	Hyde	Alicia A.	21	Santa Rosa	CA
Mentasta	Giovanni (John)	32	Sebastopol	ITL	Meineri	Adelaide	19	Asti	CA
Mentch	Hiram A.	45	Chicago	WI	Seyfferth	Ida	32	Chicago	GER
Mentz	Jack F.	23	Healdsburg	PA	Cromwell	Florence	18	Healdsburg	CA

	Groom					Bride			
Surname	**Given Name**	**Age**	**Residence**	**BP**	**Surname**	**Given Name**	**Age**	**Residence**	**BP**
Meranda	Howard E.	25	Healdsburg	MO	Blakesley	Lillie Maud	16+	Forestville	CA
Meranda	Robert	21	Forestville	IA	Morris	Bessie	18	Forestville	IA
Merchant	Thos. S.	40	Healdsburg	AUT	Hobson	Mary L.	25	Healdsburg	CA
Meredith	Cyrus N.	23	Russian River		German	Margaret E.	17	Russian River Twp.	
Meredith	Laurence Milton	28	Healdsburg	CA	Dibble	Jennie	28	Healdsburg	CA
Meredith	Milton L.	27	Healdsburg	CA	Greaver	Jennie	27	Guerneville	CA
Merga	Ambrose C.	21	Marshalls	ITL	Rovera	Marie T.	16	Calpella	FRN
Merga	Antonio	26	Valley Ford	ITL	Perottini	Rosa	16	Santa Rosa	ITL
Mergo	Charley	24	Fallon, Marin Co.	ITL	Marenghi	Mary	26	Valley Ford	SWT
Merlo	John	30	Santa Rosa	ITL	Garbarini	Louise	22	Santa Rosa	CA
Mero	Hedly L.	31	San Francisco	CA	Kahl	Bertha M.	34	San Francisco	CA
Merrill	George D.	38	Oakland	ME	Holman	Annie	35	San Francisco	FRN
Merrill	Grant P.	34	Woodfords, CA	CA	Stacey	Angie T.	28	Petaluma	UT
Merrill	John L.	22	San Francisco	TN	Newman	Nita Claire	22	San Francisco	CA
Merrit	Edson C.	32	Santa Rosa	IL	Olson	Edyth W.	29	Santa Rosa	KS
Merrithew	Robert	26	Santa Rosa	CA	Stevens	Helen E.	22	Santa Rosa	CA
Merritt	Carl B.	24	Tracy	CO	Hetzil	Mable K.	18	Berkeley	CA
Merritt	Edson C.	25	Santa Rosa	IL	Brush	Mame E.	25	Santa Rosa	IA
Mersereau	Paul, Dr.	70	Sonora	NY	Gregg	Mary P., Mrs.	50	Santa Rosa	NY
Mersfelder	William	22	San Francisco	CA	Hamilton	Nettie	18	Stony Point	CA
Mesa	Joseph	40	Healdsburg	CA	Allen	Annie K.	45	Healdsburg	CA
Meschi	Ostiglio	32	Healdsburg	ITL	Buchignani	Fannie	25	Geyserville	ITL
Messerer	Joseph R.	27	San Francisco	CA	Schadt	Marjorie	26	San Francisco	CA
Messner	Jacob F.	25	Ukiah	OH	Eperson	Fannie	24	Cloverdale	CA
Metcalf	John W., Jr.	21	San Francisco	CA	Murk	Mabel	18	Santa Rosa	CA
Metzger	Alfred V.	38	Healdsburg	IN	Leard	Dora	24	Healdsburg	CA
Metzger	George V.	28	San Jose	CA	Bowen	Elenore C.	22	San Jose	CA
Metzger	Joseph E.	38	Geyserville		Horner	Wilmos E.	28	Geyserville	
Metzler	J. A.	36	Alturas	OH	Williams	Mary L.	21	Alturas	MS

Groom					Bride				
Surname	Given Name	Age	Residence	BP	Surname	Given Name	Age	Residence	BP
Metzzer	Alfred E.	28	Santa Rosa	NY	Lundan (?)	Rose	19	Santa Rosa	TX
Meulenbrock	Leonard	30	Occidental	HLD	Evans	Lydia L.	30	Occidental	
Meyer	Benedikt	25	Shellville	SWT	Gisler	Kathrina	28	Shellville	SWT
Meyer	Bruno	38	Santa Rosa	GER	Hanks	Alice C.	42	Santa Rosa	VA
Meyer	Conrad N.	35	San Francisco	SWT	Keller	Winifred W.	21	San Francisco	CA
Meyer	Friedrich Wilhelm	70	Santa Cruz	GER	Kurtz	Henricki	61	Santa Rosa	GER
Meyer	Fritz	22	Healdsburg	GER	Brannum	Myrtle E.	18+	Healdsburg	CA
Meyer	George Homer	25	Oakland	CA	Menefee	Sarah Bell	19	Santa Rosa	CA
Meyer	Henry C.	24	San Francisco	CA	Silver	Veris A.	22	San Francisco	CA
Meyer	Jakob	32	Shellville	SWT	Gisler	Emma	22	Shellville	SWT
Meyer	Lawrence	27	Analy Twp.	Pet	Smith	Bertha G.	18	Green Valley	
Meyer	Lorenz				Miller	Elizabeth			
Meyer	Louis C.	26	Alexander Valley	SWT	Schifferli	Anna N.	26	Dry Creek	SWT
Meyer	Theodore	28	San Francisco	CA	LeMester	Lula A.	28	San Francisco	OR
Meyer	Walter	21	San Francisco	CA	Barker	Ruth	19	San Francisco	CA
Meyer	William J.	28	San Francisco	CA	Urton	Elsie S.	21	Sebastopol	CA
Meyer	William Jacob	25	Peachland	CA	Powers	Adelia	24	Peachland	CA
Meyers	Charles F.	20	Petaluma	CND	Mastin	Mary L.	18	Petaluma	IA
Meyers	Chas. H.	26	Petaluma	CA	Young	Maggie J.	25	Petaluma	CA
Meyers	Clarence M.	31	San Francisco	NJ	Spiro	Fannie J.	26	San Francisco	CA
Meyers	Henry	34	Los Angeles	GER	Abramsky	Katie	21	Santa Rosa	CA
Meyers	Herman C.	27	Stewarts Point	GER	Davidson	Alice L.	31	Stewarts Point	GER
Meyers	John C. E.	23	Geyserville	CA	Pedraita	Clara Irene	21	Geyserville	CA
Meyers	Ranie I.	35	Santa Rosa	MO	Ingram	Kezia	30	Santa Rosa	OR
Mezger	Adolph	29	Santa Rosa	GER	Steinhorst	Amelia	24	Santa Rosa	GER
Mezzera	Paul P.	27	Petaluma	ITL	Zanoni	Elvezia F.	18	Petaluma	CA
Mich	Mike, Jr.	26	San Francisco	AUS	Smith	Fannie	28	San Francisco	AUS
Michael	David Benj.	22	Healdsburg	CA	Boud	Effie	19	Healdsburg	
Michael	George W.	27	Healdsburg	Placer Co.	Crewdson	Dobey	18	Santa Rosa	Hld

	Groom					Bride			
Surname	Given Name	Age	Residence	BP	Surname	Given Name	Age	Residence	BP
Michael	George W.	26	Healdsburg		Miller	Nannie	18+	Healdsburg	
Michaelson	Otto Emil	26	Alexander Valley	DNK	Christoferson	Dina Marie	21	Dry Creek Valley	MN
Micheletti	Stefano	29	Geyserville	ITL	Buffi	Gina	16	Geyserville	ITL
Micheli	Adamo	23	Healdsburg	ITL	Micheli	Pia	19	Healdsburg	ITL
Micheli	Alfredo	26	San Francisco	ITL	Picchi	Pasquina	17	Santa Rosa	CA
Micheli	Alfredo	36	Healdsburg	ITL	Franceschi	Colomba	34	Healdsburg	ITL
Micheli	Charles				Miller	Margaret			
Micheli	Eisani	44	Cloverdale	ITL	Buffi	Rosaria	27	Cloverdale	ITL
Micheli	Giovani	23	Trenton	ITL	Bertolucci	Lieta	24	Trenton	ITL
Michelson	George L. F.	42	Windsor	CA	Grove	Edna M.	24	Windsor	CA
Michelson	Andrew P.	30	Oakland	CA	Ryan	Gertrude K.	23	San Francisco	CA
Michener	William Lewis	32	Oakland	CA	St. John	Florence Marion	24	Healdsburg	MI
Mickelsen	Mads Peter	27	Petaluma	DNK	Nisson	Christine Anna	17	Petaluma	CA
Mickelsen	Madsen	36	Two Rock	DNK	Nisson	Mary	33	Two Rock	CA
Middagh	Ezra Sypes	26	Petaluma	CND	Lane	Mary C.	26	Petaluma	Soc
Middagh	John R.	21	Petaluma	CA	Milton	Elizabeth May	17	Petaluma	CA
Middagh	Samuel	27	Petaluma	CND	Doss	Laura	22	Two Rock	CA
Middagh	William A.	27	Petaluma	CND	Bellingham	Maggie	23	Santa Rosa	CND
Middleton	Walter V.	21	Santa Rosa		Sutton	Annie	17	Santa Rosa	
Middling	Casper	23	San Francisco	MI	Fisher	Fannie	22	Santa Rosa	CA
Miebach	Hans	29	Cloverdale	GER	Woodard	Helen E.	25	Geyserville	OR
Mietzech	Charles E.	31	Santa Rosa	NY	Quinn	Margaret A.	28	Santa Rosa	CA
Mihan	Leo B.	25	Sausalito	CA	Schudsan	Amalia	30	Chicago	RUS
Milanesio	Virgilio	54	San Francisco	ITL	Vianesi	Angelina	48	San Francisco	ITL
Miles	Elmer Alfred	22	Hanford	CA	Goss	Pauline M.	22	Stockton	CA
Miles	William J.	29	Berkeley	CA	Van Winkle	Evalena	27	near Santa Rosa	CA
Mill	Clarence J.	25	Marysville	CA	Quintero	Florence	19	Sebastopol	CA

	Groom					Bride			
Surname	Given Name	Age	Residence	BP	Surname	Given Name	Age	Residence	BP
Millar	John W.	23	Santa Rosa	CA	Koch	Anna E.	20	Santa Rosa	CA
Millar	S. Arthur	32	Santa Rosa	CND	Simpson	Ivah	24	Santa Rosa	CA
Millee	C. T.	39	Lawrence, Nassau Co., NY	NY	Bolton	Emma M.	30	Lawrence, Nassu Co., NY	NY
Miller	Addison Charles	21	Santa Rosa	CA	Cheesborough	Mable Teresa	19	Los Angeles	MO
Miller	Benjamin F.	26	Pope Valley, Napa Co.	IL	Tunstall	Annie	19	Guerneville	CA
Miller	Carl L.	21	Healdsburg	CA	Yangling	May	20	Healdsburg	CA
Miller	Cecil Jesse	22	Ukiah	WA	Taylor	Orlean Martha	21	Chico	CA
Miller	Charles C.	29	Santa Rosa	GER	Gehlken	Anna	24	Santa Rosa	MO
Miller	Charles R.	32	Geyserville	MO	Leigh	Jennie	26	Geyserville	CA
Miller	Charlie V.	35	Santa Rosa	NE	Harris	Maud	29	Grass Valley	CA
Miller	Chas. S.	32	Napa	CA	Benson	Martha E.	27	Vallejo Twp.	IA
Miller	Clarence A.	22	Sebastopol	IA	Palmer	Edith B.	23	Sebastopol	CA
Miller	D. P.	31	Wapella, CND	SCT	Clements	Maude H.	24	Sonoma	CND
Miller	Daniel Erskin	30	Santa Rosa		Ayer	Lizzie	30	San Francisco	
Miller	David	40	Salt Point Twp.	IL	Beeson	Kate	20	Salt Point Twp.	CA
Miller	David A.	25	Ukiah	CA	Orr	Ora A.	25	Ukiah	CA
Miller	David W.	42	San Jose	MA	Pound	Jennie G.	23	San Jose	IA
Miller	E. H.				Mayse	Mary E.			
Miller	Elmer F.	24	Fresno	IA	Allen	Maggie E.	21	Sebastopol	Seb
Miller	Emerson Paris	28	Windsor	MO	Hanke	Beryl Andes	18	Windsor	CA
Miller	Francis W.	28	Stockton	FL	Blonquist	Amanda	27	Richmond	UT
Miller	Frank B.	31	Valley Ford	CA	Clark	Annie	25	Valley Ford	CA
Miller	Frank J.	44	Sebastopol	IA	Petersen	Carrie S.	30	Sebastopol	DNK
Miller	Frans Oskar Gustafson	33	Petaluma	SWD	Martin	Lauriana Vieira	28	Petaluma	PRT
Miller	Fred	24	Windsor	OR	Hart	Nora	18	Windsor	WI
Miller	Fred H.	22	near Napa	AR	Ferguson	Nora	18	Napa	AR
Miller	Frederick H.	27	Sacramento	CA	Gonzalez	Margaret F.	22	Santa Rosa	CA

	Groom					Bride			
Surname	Given Name	Age	Residence	BP	Surname	Given Name	Age	Residence	BP
Miller	Frederick William	42	Santa Rosa	ME	Pedigo	Retha Rosalie	32	Santa Rosa	CA
Miller	Garnet W.	50	Windsor	IN	Boehm	Annie	50	Windsor	GER
Miller	Geo. F.	60	Santa Rosa	GER	Tiede	Mary	33	Santa Rosa	IL
Miller	George	29	Cotati	NY	Greenslade	Ada Louise	20	Cotati	CT
Miller	George	50	Stewarts Point	IL	Jones	Carrie May, Mrs.	49	Stewarts Point	NY
Miller	George	29	Fisherman's Bay		Canway	Mary E.	20	Petaluma	
Miller	George B.	25	Healdsburg	MI	Sheffer	Delpha	29	Healdsburg	CA
Miller	George E.	24	Vacaville	CA	Johns	Stella L.	25	Hilton	CA
Miller	George R.	20	Sebastopol	IA	Meyer	Caroline L.	18	Sebastopol	CA
Miller	George W.	22	Healdsburg		Peters	Maggie J.	20	Healdsburg	
Miller	Harold K.	20	Healdsburg	MO	Comstock	Eleanor W.	19	Healdsburg	OH
Miller	Harry J.	26	Agua Caliente	OH	Richards	Ellen B.	18	Agua Caliente	CA
Miller	Henry H.	51	Sebastopol		Mitchel	Sarah	29	Sebastopol	
Miller	Henry Maurice	30	San Jose	IL	Whitaker	Elsie Day	30	Eureka	CA
Miller	J. F.	26	Santa Rosa	NE	Hudspeth	Exor	17	Sebastopol	CA
Miller	J. S., Dr.				Patten	Elizabeth			
Miller	Jacob B.	33	Santa Rosa	NY	Feltz	Elsie	25	Santa Rosa	CND
Miller	James Jesse	49	Ukiah	MO	English	Sadie, Mrs.	35	Ukiah	IL
Miller	James M.	56	Santa Rosa	OH	Miller	Martha M., Mrs.	52	Santa Rosa	IN
Miller	James P.	56	Healdsburg	CA	Meeks	Sarah L.	49	Sonoma Co.	CA
Miller	James Pierce	28	Santa Rosa	CA	Brown	Birdie Estella Neva	21	Green Valley	NV
Miller	James R.	22	Healdsburg	CA	Barnes	Ida M.	20	Healdsburg	MO
Miller	James Z.	30	Guerneville	IL	Mosely	Edith P.	19	Guerneville	MO
Miller	John	50	Santa Rosa	SCT	Tate	Feliciatadad, Mrs.	32	Santa Rosa	CA
Miller	John	25	Santa Rosa		Swan	Dora	18+	Santa Rosa	
Miller	John J.	36	Napa	CA	Lawrence	Louise A.	21	Petaluma	CA
Miller	John W.	32	Petaluma	IRL	Naughton	Annie	23	Petaluma	CA

Groom					Bride				
Surname	Given Name	Age	Residence	BP	Surname	Given Name	Age	Residence	BP
Miller	Joseph James	21+	Red Bluff	CA	Schoonover	Alice Edna	18+	Santa Rosa	MO
Miller	Leffler B.	22	Berkeley	CA	Porter	Dorothy Nell	23	Berkeley	CA
Miller	Louis E.	21	Oakland	CA	Gummeson	Grayce M.	18	Oakland	CA
Miller	Melvin Stanley	27	Upper Lake	CA	Wheeler	Grace Gertrude	23	Newman	OR
Miller	Oscar Paul	27	Santa Rosa	CA	Scott	Nora Edna	18	Santa Rosa	WA
Miller	Rasmus J.	26	Petaluma	GER	Hansen	Margretha S.	24	Petaluma	GER
Miller	Raymond F.	22	Lakeport	CA	Beattie	Edith I.	18	Hopland	CA
Miller	Raymond J.	22	Santa Rosa	CA	Berndt	Gladys	22	Santa Rosa	MI
Miller	Robert Lee	21	Ukiah	TX	Ellingwood	Bertha May	18	Ukiah	CA
Miller	Thomas B.	33	Santa Rosa Twp.	CA	Espey	Jessie L.	20	Santa Rosa Twp.	CA
Miller	Walter	24	Tulare	ND	Gemmill	Lillian J.	21	Healdsburg	CA
Miller	Will Henry	32	Geyserville	CA	Palmer	Clara May	21	Healdsburg	CA
Miller	William	26	Guerneville	CA	Eckman	Emma May	20	Guerneville	CA
Miller	William	22	San Francisco	CA	Reeves	Maud	19	San Francisco	KS
Miller	Wm. R.				Kelley	Emma A.	21		
Millerick	David	25	Petaluma	IRL	Hollenbarter	Mary	19	Petaluma	Sfo
Millerick	James G.	27	Petaluma	IRL	Focha	Annie	18	Petaluma	CA
Millerick	John	34	Tomales	IRL	Connell	Lizzie	20	Petaluma	IRL
Millerick	John	24	Petaluma	Cork Co., IRL	Landgren	Teresa	22	Petaluma	Pet
Millerick	Phillip	24	Petaluma	IRL	Summ	Amelia	22	Petaluma	CA
Millerick	William Dennis	22	Petaluma	Valley Ford	Brown	Hazel Violia	17	Petaluma	Stockton
Millett	William H.	24	Santa Rosa		Curter (?)	Mary J.	25	Santa Rosa	
Millington	Ira				Cook	Susan			
Mills	Allen Davis	20	Walnut Creek	CA	Brady	Julia May	16	Santa Rosa	CA
Mills	Asa H.	23	Sebastopol	CND	Scudder	Hattie L.	18	Sebastopol	CA
Mills	Charles E.	31	Santa Rosa	NY	Hodge	Minnie C.	30	Santa Rosa	OH
Mills	Don	33	Santa Rosa Twp.	CA	Hudson	Mary E.	21	Santa Rosa Twp.	CA

	Groom					Bride			
Surname	Given Name	Age	Residence	BP	Surname	Given Name	Age	Residence	BP
Mills	Easton	31	San Luis Obispo	CA	Singley	Gertrude E.	21	Petaluma	Pet
Mills	Edward C.	39	Lakeville	NY	Morris	Annie	25	Petaluma	Soc
Mills	Ernest M.	27	Santa Rosa	CA	Austin	Gula B.	18	Santa Rosa	TX
Mills	Fredrick W.	23	Healdsburg	CA	Gerow	Elsie E.	23	Healdsburg	CA
Mills	G. W.				Hatfield	Sarah M.			
Mills	Henry J.	36	Petaluma	CND	Shatto	Jennie	21	Sebastopol	KS
Mills	Hiram B.	17	San Francisco	CA	White	Mary Ellen	20	Upper Lake	CA
Mills	Jas. Byron	54	Sebastopol	CND	Tennant	Rose Anna	51	Sebastopol	CND
Mills	John	55	Bloomfield	ENG	Dodge	A. C., Mrs.	29	San Francisco	WA
Mills	Robert				Irwin	Paulina			
Mills	Robt.	26	Stewarts Point	CND	Irwin	Paulina A.	17	Fisk's Mill	CA
Mills	Roy Hudson	22	Santa Rosa	CA	Nagle	Helen Catherine	20	Santa Rosa	CA
Mills	William J.	39	Bloomfield	CND	Jones	Mary C.	21	Bloomfield	CA
Mills	William Leslie	24	Santa Rosa	NY	Winton	Flora A.	19	Santa Rosa	MI
Mills	Wm.	33	Santa Rosa	CND	Kohle	Minnie	21	Santa Rosa	CA
Millstead	Silas Augustus	33	Camp Meeker	VA	Stevens	Virginia Francis	18	Santa Rosa	CA
Milne	Donald	18	San Francisco	CA	Lapus	Marie	18	Penngrove	CA
Milne	Henry Clinton	21	Willits	Ukiah	Moxley	Roberta Blanche	18	Willits	Willits
Milner	Joseph B.	21	Petaluma	OR	Dahlmann	Gladys Marie	20	Petaluma	CA
Milton	John L.	25	Napa	IA	Hamerlund	Hilda	19	Petaluma	CA
Milty	Nicholas				Middleton	Emma			
Minaglia	John	25	Healdsburg	CA	Bachman	Sophia	22	Healdsburg	CA
Minahan	William T.	21+	Napa	CA	Millerick	Mary	18+	Petaluma	IRL
Minelli	Cesare	31	Sonoma	ITL	Decanini	Amanda	26	Sonoma	ITL
Miner	E. E.	43	San Francisco	NY	Buller (?)	A.	28	Bloomfield	CA
Miner	Edward P.	36	San Francisco	CA	Stinson	Elizabeth	27	San Francisco	ENG
Minetti	Charles L.	22	Sebastopol	FRN	Moran	Vola B.	20	Sebastopol	IL
Minghi	Guiseppe	26	Cloverdale	ITL	Pigoni	Assunta	20	Cloverdale	ITL
Mini	Olindo	32	Windsor	SWT	Binggeli	Rosa	32	Windsor	SWT

	Groom					Bride			
Surname	Given Name	Age	Residence	BP	Surname	Given Name	Age	Residence	BP
Minkel	William J.	23	El Verano	NY	McIntyre	Ella F.	22	Sonoma	CA
Minor	William Peter, Jr.	25	Stockton	MS	Lebaron	Laura Mabel	25	Santa Rosa	CND
Minsky	Nathan	30	El Verano	ENG	Sekolsky	Rose	25	El Verano	RUS
Minto	Lloyd R.	22	San Francisco	CA	Ford	Alice L.	18	San Francisco	CA
Minton	Wm. M.	35	San Francisco	NY	Levy	Felice	26	San Francisco	New Orleans
Minyard	Thomas D.	26	Fulton	MO	Reed	Jessie L.	19	Fulton	
	John	34	Petaluma	CA	Noriel	Lydia Bell	18	Santa Rosa	CA
Miranda	William Melvyn	23	Petaluma	Soc	Hollister	Anna Laura	25	Petaluma	Santa Barbara
Misener	Albert F.	34	Windsor	Jackson OH	McPeak	Minnie	21	Guerneville	CA
Misner	Horace W.	22	Petaluma	IL	Cardoza	Alice J.	22	Petaluma	CA
Mitchell	Benjamin F.				Isham	Tolitha Elizabeth			
Mitchell	Charles	44	San Francisco	KY	Sander	Mary	24	Sebastopol	CA
Mitchell	Claude D.	22	Ukiah	CA	Elliott	Marion G.	18	Ukiah	MA
Mitchell	F. M.	28	Upper Lake	CA	Bray	Louisa J.	23	Santa Rosa	CA
Mitchell	Floyd H.	39	San Francisco	MO	Dean	Sylvia G.	35	San Francisco	ENG
Mitchell	Frank S.	21	Healdsburg	CA	Weller	Margaret	18	Ukiah	CA
Mitchell	Harry	28	Healdsburg	ENG	Wiedemann	Minna Margaret	27	Healdsburg	WA
Mitchell	Harry T.	24	Healdsburg	CA	Jones	Geneva A.	20	Healdsburg	CA
Mitchell	J. Wright	50	Santa Rosa	OH	Wood	N. Pheobie	39	Santa Rosa	CA
Mitchell	James H.	27	Healdsburg	CA	Loe	Elvira R.	23	Healdsburg	MO
Mitchell	John	40	San Francisco	Worcester, MA	Equi	Teresa	23	Sonoma	Sfo
Mitchell	John H.	40	Santa Rosa	NY	Bonham	Mattie	23	Sebastopol	CA
Mitchell	Joseph				Webster	Charlotte E.			
Mitchell	L. W.	27	Sonoma	ME	Dunbar	M. A.	36	Sonoma	MI
Mitchell	Merle Ellsworth	29	San Francisco	IL	Stone	Genevieve Amelia	29	Santa Rosa	CA

	Groom					Bride			
Surname	Given Name	Age	Residence	BP	Surname	Given Name	Age	Residence	BP
Mitchell	Ralph Brown	27	San Francisco	CA	Clark	Grace Pitkin	26	San Francisco	LA
Mitchell	Robert A.	26	Chico	CA	Dickson	Adela	26	Santa Rosa	CA
Mitchell	Robert Henry	28	San Francisco	NC	Russell	Lena	23	Santa Rosa	MO (?)
Mitchell	W. J.	21	Windsor	CA	Kennedy	Annie E.	20	Windsor	CA
Mitchell	Wm. H.	21	Healdsburg		Hays	Anna M.	17	Healdsburg	
Mize	Cyril F.	25	Oakland	CA	Homerhouse	Alma Margaret	18	San Francisco	CA
Mize	Frederic	33	Santa Rosa Twp.	CA	Mize	Adeline N.	23	Santa Rosa Twp.	CA
Mize	Frederick	50	Santa Rosa	CA	MacDonald	Nellie M.	45	Santa Rosa	NY
Mize	Thompson	24	Santa Rosa		Edmiston	Annie	19	Santa Rosa	
Moad	Marshall M.	25	Los Angeles	CA	Harden	Edna Ursula	22	Santa Rosa	CA
Mobley	John Elmer	26	Santa Rosa	KY	Burger	Pearl J.	22	Santa Rosa	CA
Mobley	William H.	27	Sacramento	IA	Arnold	Lucile Frances	26	Santa Rosa	CA
Modesto	Rovere	31	Cloverdale	ITL	Frusendi	Mary	32	Chianti	ITL
Modini	D.	46	Petaluma	ITL	Campini	Carolina	35	Petaluma	SWT
Modini	James Laurence	32	Sonoma	CA	Livernash	Margaret Theresa	26	Sonoma	CA
Moe	William	23	Suisun	MN	James	Addie Virginia	19	Soledad	OR
Moenning	George	43	Berkeley	CA	Frontier	Clara	29	Oakland	CA
Moffett	L. L.	28	Oakland	MT	Chinnock	Jessie May	20	Sebastopol	OH
Moffit	Lewis	30	Petaluma	CT	Howard	Mignonette	27	Bloomfield	CA
Mohl	Emil	28	San Francisco	Sfo	Goetz	Lena	23	Petaluma	GER
Moiles	Theodore	28	Cordelia	MI	Risk	Nancy	21	Petaluma	IRL
Molinari	Giocommo	36	Petaluma	ITL	Maggioro	Maria Della	26	Petaluma	ITL
Moll	Albert Eugene	22	Petaluma	MN	Hardin	Esther Jimella	21	Petaluma	CA
Moller	Harry H.	21+	Petaluma	CA	Hickey	Lulu	19	Petaluma	CA
Moller	Henry, Jr.	21	Santa Rosa	CA	Mills	Sadie	17	Santa Rosa	CND
Moller	Michael C.	26	Petaluma	GER	Jorgensen	Christina	19	Two Rock	DNK
Molne	Cuthbert E.	23	Sebastopol	WA	Jewell	Eleanor F.	20	Sebastopol	MI
Moltzen	Albert Christian	24	Petaluma	OR	Rodgers	Anna Belle	27	Petaluma	CA

Groom					Bride				
Surname	Given Name	Age	Residence	BP	Surname	Given Name	Age	Residence	BP
Moltzen	Axel	23	Portland, OR	GER	Ekman	Sigrid	21	Petaluma	SWD
Moltzen	Thomas	22	Petaluma	CA	Yockey	Bessie	20	Petaluma	MI
Momsen	Charles F.	25	San Antonio Twp., Marin Co.	GER	Clausen	Anna D.	23	Petaluma	GER
Monett	Chauncey D.	26	Petaluma	NY	Houx	Edith Pearl	30	Petaluma	CA
Monez	Manuel P.	23	Vallejo	CA	Rodgers	Mary Edna	25	Vallejo	CA
Mong	George William	45	Tionesta, PA	PA	DeGroot	Flora	40	Santa Rosa	MO
Moni	Frank	52	Petaluma	ITL	Buzzini	Kate	45	Petaluma	SWT
Moniz	Frank P.	30	Sebastopol	CA	Silva	Frances M.	20	Sebastopol	CA
Moniz	Joseph S., Jr.	23	Sebastopol	CA	Felciano	Mary C.	20	Sebastopol	CA
Moniz	Manuel Joseph	29	Sebastopol	HI	Ramos	Josephine Matilda	27	Sebastopol	CA
Moniz	Tony G.	24	Sebastopol	CA	Moore	Alta	18	Santa Rosa	IL
Monk	Hans Julius	29	Bloomfield	DNK	Simansen	Gertrude Marie Dagmar	20	Bloomfield	DNK
Monks	John	54	Glen Ellen	ENG	King	Bertha F., Mrs.	49	Glen Ellen	ENG
Monotti	Eugene	43	Forestville	ITL	Baldi	Amelia	37	Forestville	ITL
Monroe	Harold H.	22	Melita	KS	McDonald	Mary Elizabeth	19	Santa Rosa	Por
Monroe	Peter	32	Cloverdale	CND	Taylor	Annie	27	Cloverdale	ENG
Monroe	Raymond	29	Santa Rosa	MA	Leggett	Della Z.	18	Santa Rosa	CA
Monroe	William Henry	58	Santa Rosa	IN	Waugh	Armina	49	Santa Rosa	OH
Monsen	Martin	34	Santa Rosa	NRY	Shibbetts	Grace Knick	19	Santa Rosa	OH
Monson	John C.	33	Oakland	DNK	Lemley	Laida F.	31	Oakland	WI
Montague	Frank P.	41	Alameda	MO	Hoagland	Nellie A.	40	San Francisco	CA
Montalon	Paul	23	San Francisco	FRN	Sabia	Camela	18	Asti	ITL
Montano	Constantin	37	San Francisco	ITL	Sermet	Marie L.	35	San Francisco	FRN
Monte	Tiziano	32	Windsor	ITL	Luiebberke	Flora	18	Windsor	MO
Montessoro	Pietro	27	Asti	ITL	Perazzo	Mary	20	Asti	CA
Montgomery	Elmer J.	38	San Francisco	WI	McCanse	Margaret F.	38	San Francisco	CND
Montgomery	George French	28	San Francisco	CA	Keener	Raphaella Acosta	26	San Francisco	FL

	Groom					Bride			
Surname	Given Name	Age	Residence	BP	Surname	Given Name	Age	Residence	BP
Montgomery	Raleigh Claude	27	Santa Rosa	TX	Silva	Louise Dalphine	24	Santa Rosa	CA
Montgomery	Robert B.	38	Santa Rosa	CO	Cave	Freda Marie	18	Santa Rosa	CA
Montgomery	Samuel M.	37	Sonoma	KY	Scheiderer	Helen M.	28	Sonoma	OH
Monti	Chester H.	20	Windsor	CA	Wilson	Iris V.	19	Healdsburg	CA
Montijo	Daniel	22	San Francisco	CA	Otterbeck	Evelyn M.	25	San Francisco	IL
Montna	Henry Lewis				Pina	Theresa			
Moodey	Ross Clarence	25	Santa Rosa	IL	LeBaron	Grace Eleanor	24	Santa Rosa	CND
Moody	Arthur W.	21	Geyserville	CA	Pitts	Ethel S.	20	Geyserville	IL
Moody	Clyde L.	21	Bloomfield	WA	Hansen	Bertha	17	Bloomfield	CA
Moody	Edward Elmer	28	Healdsburg	IL	Warren	Sarah B.	19	Healdsburg	NV
Moody	Frank L.	44	Santa Rosa	ME	Kubala	Rose A.	30	Los Angeles	TX
Moody	Harry E.	41	Portland, OR	TN	Bartlett	Ella M.	40	Portland, OR	NY
Moody	Logan	29	Geyserville	MN	Eslick	Daisy Belle	19	Healdsburg	AR
Moody	Wilfrid	27	Geyserville	CA	Petray	Mary E.	23	Geyserville	CA
Mooney	J. William	23	Geyserville	MA	Ray	Elsie K.	19	Lakeport	KS
Mooney	William O.	25	Oakland	CA	Olson	Mabel B.	24	Oakland	CA
Moore	Benjamin	33	Anderson Valley	CA	Murphy	Minnie A.	16	Knights Valley	CA
Moore	C. A.				Morgan	S. J.			
Moore	C. P.	54	Cloverdale	ME	Vassar	N. J., Mrs.	42	Cloverdale	IA
Moore	Charles	20	Healdsburg		Brown	Fannie	20	Healdsburg	
Moore	Charles M.	32	Napa	NE	Keyes	Mary	23	Napa	GER
Moore	Clement J. B.	48	Sebastopol		Carr	Mary T.	38	Sebastopol	
Moore	Francis M., Jr.	20	Sebastopol	KS	Clark	Frances H.	18	Sebastopol	CA
Moore	Frank E.	24	Healdsburg	CA	Malipeide	Rosie	19	Healdsburg	CA
Moore	Fred T.	30	Geyserville	CA	Blair	Huldah	18	Skaggs	WA
Moore	Friend Francis	23	Santa Rosa	KS	Ives	Amanda Louise Muller	23	Santa Rosa	Windsor
Moore	Geo. W.				Mize	Amanda			
Moore	George Henry	27	Santa Rosa	NE	Campbell	Ida Cynthia	23	Santa Rosa	CA

	Groom					Bride			
Surname	**Given Name**	**Age**	**Residence**	**BP**	**Surname**	**Given Name**	**Age**	**Residence**	**BP**
Moore	Gideon J.	25	Eureka	MI	Ashley	Mary A.	17	Bloomfield	
Moore	Harley La Verne	28	San Francisco	OH	Shelford	Wilda Mabelle	20	Healdsburg	CA
Moore	Harold S.	40	Petaluma	MN	Linebaugh	Anna G.	30	Sebastopol	CA
Moore	Harvey	21	Santa Rosa	MO	Mitchell	May A.	18	Santa Rosa	CA
Moore	James E.	38	Santa Rosa	CA	Butler	Bettie	24	Santa Rosa	KY
Moore	James Henry	66	Eugene, OR	IA	Powell	Elizabeth	39	Lakeport	IL
Moore	Jesse R.	29	Red Bluff	CA	Saylor	Florence M.	23	Occidental	CA
Moore	John	34	Sea View	IRL	Cawley	Maria	25	Sea View	IRL
Moore	John T.	32	Hesperia, San Bernardino Co.	CND	Hammond	Caroline	31	Petaluma	MN
Moore	Joseph H.	28	Santa Rosa	WIN	Williams	Lucy	25	Santa Rosa	PA
Moore	Leo A.	22	Oakland	CA	Highlander	Irma M.	23	Oakland	CA
Moore	Lewis? D.	32	Geyserville	CA	Sheffield	Cora	17	Geyserville	IL
Moore	Oliver C.	33	Philo	CA	Holmberg	Hilda A.	26	Philo	CA
Moore	Ray	26	Healdsburg	NY	Duncan	Vella Irene	19	Healdsburg	CA
Moore	Ray D.	20	Sebastopol	KS	Ross	Lodema O.	18	Sebastopol	CA
Moore	Robert W.	34	Santa Rosa	IL	McIntosh	Annie	24	Forestville	CA
Moore	Saml. C.				Carrillo	Mary Agnes			
Moore	Thomas B.	27	Duncans Mills		Richardson	Emogene	16	Duncans Mills	
Moore	Thomas B.				Richardson	Emogene	16		
Moore	Thomas W.	64	San Francisco	TN	Moore	Elizabeth	41	San Francisco	ME
Moore	Walter Shelby	30	Antioch	TX	Hagmayer	Beatrice Urania	25	Cloverdale	CA
Moore	Warren B.	22	Petaluma	CA	Huggard	Etta	23	Petaluma	CA
Moore	William	31	Sonoma		Parker	Ella	17	Sonoma	
Moore	William J.	24	Healdsburg	CA	Foster	Blanche	21	San Francisco	CA
Moore	William Washington	39	Yampa, Routt Co., CO	IL	Roberts	Edith	28	Yampa, Routt Co., CO	MN
Moorehead	Lee	29	Newman	CA	Hendrickson	Clara	18	Petaluma	GER
Moose	Edward Henry	22	San Francisco	IL	Blankstein	Belle	20	San Francisco	CA
Mora	Antone	46	Mt. Olivet	PRT	Lopes	Mary L.	43	Mt. Olivet	PRT

	Groom					Bride			
Surname	**Given Name**	**Age**	**Residence**	**BP**	**Surname**	**Given Name**	**Age**	**Residence**	**BP**
Mora	Laurence	26	Santa Rosa	AUS	Ariasi	Rose	18	Santa Rosa	CA
Morais	John P.	27	Santa Rosa	PRT	Brazil	Vetra A.	16	Santa Rosa	CA
Moralli	Bernardo	21	Bodega	ITL	Poncia	Mary	17	Bodega	ITL
Moran	Alexander	25	Electra, CA	CA	Lewis	Eva	24	Petaluma	CA
Moran	Jack Willis	25	Virgina City, NV	NV	Thompson	Heneretta	25	Ukiah	MN
Moran	James	30	San Francisco	MA	Ross	Georgia N.	30	San Francisco	
Moran	Joseph	24	Sebastopol	IL	Poole	Hattie	24	Sebastopol	MA
Morand	Charles Harrison	48	Rincon Valley	CND	Robertson	Lizzie	53	Rincon Valley	MO
Moranda	Charles S.	23	Santa Rosa	CA	Fees	Mattie Grace	16	Santa Rosa	CA
Moranda	Silva	29	Ferndale	CA	Criteser	Ella	27	Eureka	OR
Mordecai	William B.	20	Petaluma	CA	Gould	Hannah C.	18	Penngrove	MO
More	E. R.	25	Tacoma, WA	IL	Mills	Gertrude	27	Palo Alto	MN
Morehouse	Arthur L.	26	Geyserville	CA	Glass	Sarah, Mrs.	28	Geyserville	CA
Morehouse	J. W.	33	Napa	NY	Murbar	Mattie	24	Santa Rosa	CA
Morelli	Antonio	33	Occidental	SWT	Mazza	Josephine	18	Camp Meeker	ITL
Morelli	Giuseppe, Jr.	36	Occidental	ITL	Vanoni	Ermine	30	Occidental	SWT
Morelli	Lee G.	29	Occidental	SWT	Ferrari	Angelica	18+	Santa Rosa	CA
Morelli	Morvin Ulysses	20	Occidental	CA	Gonella	Florence Marie	17	Occidental	CA
Morelli	Orlando	30	Vallejo	NY	Canaveri	Louise	19	Santa Rosa	CA
Morenzoni	Joseph	35	Occidental	CA	Mache	Minnie L.	33	Valley Ford	CA
Moret	Elie H.	31	San Francisco	FRN	Chevallier	Marie	22	San Francisco	FRN
Moretti	Camillo P.	36	Santa Rosa	SWT	Ramatici	Linda B.	21	Petaluma	CA
Moretti	Joseph	28	Cazadero	ITL	Giaconi	Geovanina	19	Cazadero	ITL
Morey	Charles H.	48	Tonopah, Nye Co., NV	IL	Wood	Mae R.	36	Cloverdale	CND
Morey	Robert G.	49	Oakland	NY	Rainier	Ida M.	49	San Francisco	SWT
Morford	Edward Elmore	29	Santa Rosa	IA	Huntley	Birdie J.	23	Sebastopol	CA
Morgan	Carey	30	San Francisco	Jackson, MO	Barth	Mae	21	Los Angeles	Los Angeles
Morgan	Hugh				Warner (?)	Madova (?)	17		

| \multicolumn{5}{c|}{Groom} | \multicolumn{5}{c}{Bride} |

Surname	Given Name	Age	Residence	BP	Surname	Given Name	Age	Residence	BP
Morgan	John Albert	25	Healdsburg	TN	Barr	Maysel	19	Healdsburg	OR
Morgan	John Franklin	24	Oakland	CA	Collins	May Caroline	19	Santa Rosa	IL
Morgan	Patrick H.	25	Petaluma	IRL	Boyle	Sara Hilarita	16	Petaluma	CA
Morgan	Ross	30	Jackson	CA	Bodwell	Charlotte Elizabeth	30	Lakeville	CA
Morgan	Samuel Henry	23	Healdsburg	TN	Howard	Mary E.	19	Healdsburg	KS
Morgan	Samuel M.	40	Atlantic City, NJ	IA	Holst	Mary C.	27	Healdsburg	CA
Morgan	Thomas P.	23	Sebastopol	IA	Christie	Isabella J.	16+	Bellevue	CA
Morillo	Peter C.	40	Cloverdale	CA	Hooker	E. C., Mrs.	38	Cloverdale	IN
Morin	Frank L.	40	Healdsburg	CA	Cochran	Mattie J.	38	Oakland	NE
Morini	Frank	50	Santa Rosa	ITL	Shoemaker	Leonarda	36	Santa Rosa	HLD
Morini	Ubaldo	22	Cloverdale	ITL	Pacini	Ida	17	Cloverdale	CA
Morion	Louis	35	Petaluma	FRN	Orilley	Nellie	19	Petaluma	Soc
Moritz	Meyer	47	Oakland	LA	Stewart	Elizabeth	39	Oakland	CA
Morley	Virgil	21	Napa	CA	Greco	Immaculate	18	Napa	NY
Morniga	Lugi	36	Santa Rosa	ITL	Burnardi	Magareta	24	Santa Rosa	ITL
Morrell	Leonard	26	Fulton	CA	Smither	Wanda	17	Fulton	CA
Morrell	William L.	24	Occidental	CA	Stone	Grace E.	20	Occidental	CA
Morrice	Edward	27	Oakland	SCT	Lee	Ada A.	30	Hayward	CA
Morris	Alfred	22	Santa Rosa	NZD	Cook	Salome	37	Santa Rosa	CA
Morris	Anton	36	Vine Hill	AZR	Smith	Marie	26	Vine Hill	CA
Morris	Edward	35	Petaluma	ENG	Rodric	Carrie	32	Petaluma	PRT
Morris	Ernest	25	Petaluma	CA	Wagner	Alma	20	Petaluma	WA
Morris	George F.	24	Chicago	MO	Kinsel	Dorothy	23	Santa Rosa	MO
Morris	Harry B.	24	Sebastopol	CA	Howell	Albrnia C.	18	Sebastopol	CA
Morris	Henry	36	San Francisco	CA	Messing	Rebecca	25	San Francisco	TN
Morris	J. E.	29	Petaluma	CA	Partington	Mary Ellen Frances	17	Petaluma	CND
Morris	James	24	Santa Rosa	MI	Covert	Emma H.	22	Santa Rosa	CA
Morris	John	21+	Petaluma	NZD	Gallagher	Nellie Mae	21+	Petaluma	CA

	Groom					Bride			
Surname	**Given Name**	**Age**	**Residence**	**BP**	**Surname**	**Given Name**	**Age**	**Residence**	**BP**
Morris	John	59	Petaluma	ENG	Stewart	Lydia	59	Petaluma	PA
Morris	John Reuben	22	Forestville	CA	Archer	Rubie Isalene	19	Fulton	CA
Morris	Leslie Lenore	33	Freestone	CA	Potter	Hattie Isabel	31	Santa Rosa	CA
Morris	Roy	23	Forestville	IA	Elder	Emma	20	Forestville	OR
Morris	Rudolph A.	21	Santa Rosa	CA	Finale	Josephine	18	Santa Rosa	CA
Morris	Walter	34	Forestville	IA	Mason	Eva	27	Sebastopol	WY
Morris	Walter C.	19	Trenton	IA	Easter	Lucy J. (?)	21	Trenton	CA
Morris	Wm. H.	32	San Francisco	MO	Franklin	Blandine L.	16	Petaluma	CA
Morrison	Alvah Herbert	28	Santa Rosa	CA	Hesse	Rachel Elizabeth	18	Santa Rosa	CA
Morrison	Burk Guy	34	Skaggs	CA	Davis	Mary Warren	25	Geyserville	WY
Morrison	Francis George	25	Fisherman's Bay		Totton	Ella	23	Santa Rosa	
Morrison	George W.	41	Sacramento	MO	Steele	Etta	21	Roseville	CA
Morrison	Guy Bryan	28	Santa Rosa	CA	Doyle	Mary Ellen	22	Santa Rosa	NY
Morrison	John H.	58	Santa Rosa	SCT	Wagner	Julia	40	Santa Rosa	GER
Morrison	John J.	50	Ukiah	OH	Smith	Carrie	35	San Francisco	TN
Morrison	John M.	21	Fulton	CA	Monroe	Madalene	21	Sonoma	CA
Morrison	Lester	24	Healdsburg	CA	Garrett	Ida Hazel	21	Healdsburg	ID
Morrison	Thomas	61	Fulton	KY	Redenbaugh	Lydia E.	32	Santa Rosa	IA
Morrison	William	23	Berkeley	CA	Williams	Daisy P.	23	San Francisco	CA
Morrison	William L.	50	Graton	IL	Roberts	Ella G.	38	Graton	NE
Morrow	Harrison E.	30	Santa Rosa	CA	Blake	Ruth W.	20	Guerneville	OR
Morrow	Harrison E.	23	Santa Rosa	CA	Griffin	Mamie R.	20	Santa Rosa	UT
Morrow	James	30	Santa Rosa Twp.	IRL	McKee	Hattie Bailey	15	San Francisco	LA
Morrow	John	25	Petaluma		Rochford	Jennie	22	Petaluma	
Morrow	John A.	25	Modesto	WI	Ritz	Ada E.	24	Sonoma	WI
Morrow	Joseph A.	22	Guerneville	CA	Yancey	Emma B.	17	Healdsburg	CA
Morrow	Thomas J.	25	Petaluma	Ontario, CND	Moore	Ellen C.	25	Petaluma	Pet
Morrow	Wilford E.	36	Santa Rosa	CA	Fagan	Cora A.	36	Santa Rosa	CA

	Groom					Bride			
Surname	Given Name	Age	Residence	BP	Surname	Given Name	Age	Residence	BP
Morrow	Wm. H.	25	San Francisco	CA	Hinkle	Katherine Dillon	22	Petaluma	
Morse	Daniel G.	33	Cloverdale	IL	Young	Flora M.	16	Cloverdale	CA
Morse	Harry S.	31	San Francisco	WA	McFarlin	Lottie V.	35	San Francisco	IL
Morse	James Grant	22	Sebastopol	CA	Elphick	Annie M.	22	Sebastopol	CA
Morse	Stephen C.	36	Sebastopol	IL	Weeks	Frances E.	31	Sebastopol	IL
Morten	A. J.	38	Petaluma	MO	Morton	L. Permilia Louisa	42	Petaluma	IL
Mortenson	Hans	32	Santa Rosa	GER	Peterson	Etta	30	Santa Rosa	CA
Mortenson	Nicholas	32	Santa Rosa	GER	Hewitt	Mary Jane	23	Santa Rosa	CA
Mortimer	John K.	50	Santa Rosa	PA	Brady	Anna, Mrs.	45	Fairfield	NY
Mortimer	John K.	42	Santa Rosa	PA	Grant	Elizabeth	41	Oakland	OH
Morton	Charles	29	Sebastopol	CA	Brown	Della Louise	24	St. Helena	CA
Morton	Claude C.	37	Forest Knolls	OH	Gregory	Louise V.	24	Forest Knolls	LA
Morton	Dudley D.	26	San Francisco	CA	Wendt	Katherine B.	24	Santa Rosa	CA
Morton	Harris M.	54	Sacramento	CA	Schuhrer	Wilhelmine	61	Sausalito	GER
Morton	Henry	27	Benicia	CA	Stack	Lotta, Mrs.	32	Benicia	CA
Morton	John J.	31	Napa	CA	Brennan	Hetty	26	Napa	IRL
Morton	Martin Tuller	41	Sonoma	MA	Caldwell	Martha H.	23	Sonoma	MN
Morton	Nathaniel T.	28	San Francisco	Mec	Pomeroy	Eda	21	Sonoma Co.	Soc
Morton	Raymond A.	30	San Francisco	CA	Speyer	Catherine A.	30	Red Bluff	NY
Moseley	William W.	51	San Francisco	NY	Graves	Mary A.	45	Oakland	MO
Mosely	Gus	19	Guerneville	CA	Calcote	Eva Ethel	16	Guerneville	CA
Mosely	Irve Clyde	23	Guerneville	CA	Patterson	Pearl Elizabeth	17	Guerneville	CA
Moser	Charles E.	27	Santa Rosa	KS	Tew	Clara N.	27	Santa Rosa	CA
Moses	Isaac Newton	32	Duncans Mills		Breakes	Katie A.	23	Santa Rosa	
Moses	Meyer	31	San Francisco	Clv	Cochran	S.	27	San Francisco	Groveland, CA
Moses	Robert T.	25	Alameda Co.	CA	Olney	Mary Louise	22	Alameda	KS
Mosher	Frank	35	Oakland	ME	Gay	Mary E.	25	Oakland	MA

	Groom					Bride			
Surname	Given Name	Age	Residence	BP	Surname	Given Name	Age	Residence	BP
Mosier	Francis L.	43	Upper Lake	NE	Johnson	Anne	35	Upper Lake	CA
Mosna	Ezekiele	50	Healdsburg	AUS	Reinero	Mary Elenar	50	Santa Rosa	ITL
Mosna	John	19	Healdsburg	CA	Mitchell	Elisabeth	19	Healdsburg	CA
Moss	George W.	42	Sacramento	OR	Maguire	Ethel Adella	41	Sacramento	CND
Moss	James Marion	67	Sebastopol	TN	Kelly	Ida C., Mrs.	41	Sebastopol	CA
Moss	Lemuel A.	39	San Francisco	MI	Dahse	Johanna Dorothy	33	San Francisco	CA
Moss	Reginald G.	35	Berkeley	ENG	Heath	Budella W.	33	San Francisco	IL
Mossi	Achille	25	Cloverdale	SWT	Bassetti	Amelia	20	Cloverdale	CA
Mossi	Emilio	28	Petaluma	SWT	Dado	Guilietta C.	35	Petaluma	CA
Mossler	Frederick A.	28	Trenton	GER	Denner	Fulvia M.	24	Mt. Olivet	CA
Mothern	Fernando C.	20	Healdsburg	IN	Lewis	Sarah A.	20	Healdsburg	CA
Mothersole	Thomas H.	38	Talmadge, Mendocino Co.	ENG	Durkee	Caroline A.	25	Talmadge	CA
Mothorn	Pressley Perry	23	Healdsburg	CA	Luce	Marie Antoinette	23	Healdsburg	CA
Motroni	Herbert J.	22	San Francisco	CA	Bertoli	Stella M.	19	Santa Rosa	CA
Moulton	Page H.	40	Reno, NV	IL	Graham	Ivy E.	20	Cloverdale	CA
Mount	John Clayton	27	Petaluma	NY	Bowman	Bertha May	23	Petaluma	MI
Mountain	Floyd	22	Sebastopol	CA	Peyser	Amelia Augusta	22	San Francisco	CA
Mouyer	Louis	47	El Verano	FRN	Lourdeaux	Aline	46	Sonoma	FRN
Mowberry	Francis Walter	29	Cloverdale	CA	Fisher	May Stella	23	San Francisco	IA
Moy	John Daniel	24	San Francisco	CA	Vanoni	Ynez Dorothy	21	Geyserville	CA
Muat	William F.	20	Oakland	CHN	Weinberg	Emma A.	24	Oakland	CA
Much	Herbert N.	26	San Francisco	CA	Cnopius	Gertrude M.	24	Santa Rosa	CA
Muchway	Peter S.	22	Youngstown, OH	OH	Miller	Ruth M.	18	Pittsburg	CA
Mudget	Charles Austin	40	Coalinga	CA	Steele	Cora Lovina	29	Petaluma	CA
Mueller	Charles	36	Kellogg	GER	Pullen	Minnie, Mrs.	38	Kellogg	OH
Mueller	Frank	24	San Francisco	Sfo	Frese	Irene A.	22	Santa Rosa	CA
Muenzer	Anton	25	Santa Rosa Twp.	GER	Schalid	Julia	25	Santa Rosa	GER

	Groom					Bride			
Surname	Given Name	Age	Residence	BP	Surname	Given Name	Age	Residence	BP
Muenzer	John P.	26	Petaluma	CA	Schoningh	Marie A.	21	Petaluma	CA
Mueting	William F.	21	Santa Rosa	NE	Taylor	Effie J.	28	Santa Rosa	CA
Muff	John	50	Petaluma	SWT	Luckenbill	Elise	48	Petaluma	SWT
Mugler	Albert Miller	59	Santa Rosa	CA	Mugler	Frances Helen	48	Santa Rosa	CA
Muheim	Adolph A.	26	San Francisco	CA	Gomzenbach	Elizabeth I.	21	San Francisco	NY
Muir	Guy Edward	28	Willits	CA	Murphy	Dorothy Marie	22	Blocksburg, CA	CA
Mulford	George N.	21	Santa Rosa	NJ	Forsythe	Margaret	20	Sebastopol	CT
Mulhall	Henry John	25	San Diego	CA	Woodson	Pearl Alphia	24	Petaluma	CA
Mulhall	Thomas J.	27	Petaluma	NJ	Bolle	Sopha M.	26	Los Guilicos	CA
Mullan	Felix George	29	San Francisco	CA	Nelson	Jennie	27	San Francisco	IL
Mullen	James J.	34	San Francisco	NV	Kuehne	Clara	28	Riverside	FL
Muller	Daniel L.	60	Petaluma	HLD	Allen	Luella Rebecca	55	Petaluma	CA
Muller	Frank M.	23	Healdsburg	GER	Thistle	Lizzie	18	Healdsburg	CA
Muller	Frederick	29	San Francisco		Schuster	Barbara	21	Sonoma	
Muller	George A.	21	Oakland	CA	Engdol	Mabel E.	20	Oakland	CA
Muller	John				Bryant	Mary	17		
Muller	Joseph	24	Sonoma	SWT	Kieser	Agnes	24	Sonoma	SWT
Muller	Martin	41	Santa Rosa	GER	Nelson	Agnes	34	Santa Rosa	SWD
Mulligan	George Julian	36	Selma	CA	Feltes	May Caroline	24	Santa Rosa	CA
Mullikin	Andrew Frederick	23	Winters	KY	Saxe	Vella	23	Winters	CA
Mullin	Edwin F.	40	Greenview, CA	CA	Morrison	Alice J.	28	Healdsburg	CA
Mullins	Robert W.	33	San Francisco	NY	Grosgebaur	Louise A.	47	Fairfax	OR
Mumay	William	30	Guerneville	MI	Beebe	Maggie	17	Guerneville	CA
Munday	Martin E. C.	under 21			Linville	Pemelia			
Munday	Thomas O.	26	San Rafael	CA	Connelly	Mary K.	26	Occidental	CA
Mundee	George E.	28	Portland, ME	ME	Thomas	Grace E.	23	San Francisco	CA
Mundell	Jackson W.				Procise	Sarah J.	20		
Mundell	Oliver A.	32	Petaluma	KS	Bernardi	Inez M.	20	Santa Rosa	CA

	Groom					Bride			
Surname	**Given Name**	**Age**	**Residence**	**BP**	**Surname**	**Given Name**	**Age**	**Residence**	**BP**
Mundkowski	Clements Vincent	26	Santa Rosa	GER	Jacquet	Rosa Celestine	20	Santa Rosa	IL
Mundkowski	Hans A.	26	Shellville	GER	Guilfoyle	Margaret	18	Shellville	CA
Munfrey	William Osmund	30	Sonoma	Sfo	Dunn	Lillie Caroline	30	Sonoma	Son
Munk	William N.	24	Willits	CA	Barnwell	Gail	19	Willits	CA
Munn	Joseph L.	46	Garberville	MO	Ray	Robert M., Mrs.	39	Healdsburg	ENG
Munoz	Mariano	22	Santa Rosa	SPN	Martinez	Adoracion	18	Santa Rosa	SPN
Murbar	George	22	Santa Rosa	CA	Kinlock	May	18+	Santa Rosa	CA
Murchie	William T.	25	Cloverdale	NBW	Bale	Caroline	21	Healdsburg	CA
Murdock	J. W.	32	Guerneville	CND	Rickett	Clara	25	Forestville	IA
Murphey	Harry Bruton	26	Petaluma	CA	Offutt	Rieta J.	20	Petaluma	CA
Murphey	John J.	30	Santa Rosa	LA	Mould	Ella E.	24	Santa Rosa	CA
Murphey	William H.	42	Santa Rosa	LA	Redoine	Edith V. A.	38	Ukiah	NY
Murphy	Albert E.	28	Petaluma	CA	Cox	Florence M.	29	Cloverdale	CA
Murphy	Dennis	47	San Francisco	IRL	Carter	Mary	33	Sebastopol	CA
Murphy	Frank Edward	25	Camp Fremont	MA	Doss	Wilma Eloise	19	Santa Rosa	CA
Murphy	Frank J.	23	Guerneville	ME	Button	Theodosia C.	19	Santa Rosa	CA
Murphy	George B.	40	Petaluma	CA	Purvine	Alice	29	Petaluma	CA
Murphy	Henry	54	Antioch	NY	Turner	Bettie, Mrs.	35	St. Helena	CA
Murphy	Herman N.	28	Santa Rosa	IL	Polhemus	Louisa M.	27	Santa Rosa	CA
Murphy	J. R.	31	Petaluma	CT	Early	Mary L.	20	Petaluma	CA
Murphy	James E.	55	Petaluma	NY	Grimm (?)	Jeannie M.	36	Petaluma	CA
Murphy	John	26	Cloverdale	Geyser-ville	Tucker	Mona E.	23	Santa Rosa	Pet
Murphy	Lewis T.	25	Petaluma	Oakdale	Finerty	Katherine L.	21	Petaluma	Pet
Murphy	Osbort Louis	28	Sebastopol	MN	Dovey	Minnie Henrietta	26	Green Valley	CA
Murphy	Ralph Everett	24	Sonoma	IL	Thomas	Mabel Clare	23	Sonoma	CND
Murphy	Robert M.	25	San Francisco	CA	Jurgensen	Hermina F.	25	Petaluma	CA
Murphy	Wallace	20	Cloverdale	CA	Hiatt	Meta May	18	Santa Rosa	CA
Murphy	Walter Lewis	28	Sonoma	IL	Granice	Celia Celeste	24	Sonoma	CA

	Groom					Bride			
Surname	Given Name	Age	Residence	BP	Surname	Given Name	Age	Residence	BP
Murphy	William G.	21	Cloverdale	CA	Bush	Lillian P.	18	Cloverdale	CA
Murphy	Wm.	22	Knights Valley	CA	Sensibaugh	Armodale	16	Knights Valley	CA
Murphy	Wm. A.	28	Marshall	MO	McLaughlin	Mary	24	Petaluma Twp.	CA
Murray	Archibald Benjamin	21	San Rafael	Los Angeles	Warner	Maud	18	Sebastopol	CA
Murray	Byrd B.	18	Healdsburg	CA	Drake	Ada Verlina	17	Healdsburg	CA
Murray	Charles L.	22	San Francisco	CA	Burns	Mae	20	San Francisco	CA
Murray	Cleve	34	Cloverdale	CA	Capell	Lula Romona	20	Cloverdale	CA
Murray	Elmer J.	25	Healdsburg	MD	Lombardi	Lillien B.	24	Healdsburg	WY
Murray	George Willis	24	Oakland	CA	Johnson	Evelyne Marjorie	22	Petaluma	CA
Murray	Howard E.	34	San Francisco	MO	Hall	Alice M.	19	San Francisco	CA
Murray	James H.	37	Guerneville	TX	Perks	Lilly Bevins	33	Henderson, IA	
Murray	John	32	Bodega Corners	CA	Clark	Hattie	20	Valley Ford	CA
Murray	John A.	21	Forestville	CA	Stump	Jessie M.	19	Forestville	CA
Murray	Joseph	21	Cloverdale	CA	Scott	Ruth	19	Cloverdale	CA
Murray	Joseph	26	Cloverdale	CA	Murphy	Sallie	23	Cloverdale	CA
Murray	Paul	22	Cloverdale	CA	Archer	Laura	19	Fulton	CA
Murray	Perry L.	19	Windsor	CA	Drake	Maude A.	17+	Mt. Olivet	CA
Murray	Perry Leland	18	Healdsburg	CA	Howard	Juanita V. R.	16	Healdsburg	CA
Murray	Ruby E.	22	Santa Rosa	CA	Vanderkarr	Daisy M.	17	Santa Rosa	CA
Murray	Thomas	23	Cloverdale		O'Brien	Hattie	19	San Francisco	CA
Murray	Thomas Elmer	23	Boonville	CA	Crigler	Sally E.	23	Cloverdale	CA
Murray	Thos. B.	28	Cloverdale	CA	Capell	Ruby I.	20	Cloverdale	CA
Murray	William	34	Sonoma Twp.	IRL	Dowdall	Katie	24	Sonoma	CA
Murray	William	24	San Francisco	IRL	Dwane	Agnes	28	San Francisco	ENG
Murray	William Henry	46	Bodega	CA	Wing	Belle	46	Sebastopol	CA
Murrel	Sylvanus B.	33	Chicago	MN	Little	Beatrice G.	28	Chicago	MI
Murry	John P.	24	Geyserville		Morris	Leah Isabelle	15	Geyserville	
Murskey	Frederick A.	21	San Francisco	CA	Hary	Louise M.	21	San Francisco	CA

	Groom					Bride			
Surname	**Given Name**	**Age**	**Residence**	**BP**	**Surname**	**Given Name**	**Age**	**Residence**	**BP**
Musante	Louis S.	32	San Francisco	CA	Walker	Evelyn I.	29	San Francisco	CA
Muse	George W.	24	Santa Rosa	CA	Stump	Katie	17	Santa Rosa	CA
Musgrave	Albert	30	Wilfred	CA	Findlay	R. Christina	30	Wilfred	CND
Musgrave	Benjamin F.	30	Napa Junction	MO	Whitechurch	Julia E.	26	Santa Rosa	CA
Musselman	William T.	25	Santa Rosa	IN	Moore	Lulu E.	18	Santa Rosa	CA
Mussleman	Jesse A.	30	Santa Rosa	IN	Beckner	Carrie O.	22	Santa Rosa	CA
Mustain	Terry	32	San Francisco	NE	Kelleher	Rose C.	29	San Francisco	PA
Muther	Frank, Jr.	25	Santa Rosa	MO	Ewald	Frances	26	San Francisco	GER
Myer	Anthony R.	33	Petaluma	OH	Hall	Nellie	35	Petaluma	CA
Myers	Arthur W.	27	Healdsburg	WI	Pratt	Amy	22	St. Helena	CA
Myers	D. P	68	Windsor	PA	Bostick	Mary	46	Windsor	IN
Myers	Frank H.	24	Petaluma	Soc	Brownlee	Ida Mabel	23	Petaluma	San Jose
Myers	George	29	Salinas	MO	Woodcock	Lee	21	Santa Rosa	MO
Myers	Henry	22	Petaluma	PA	McNeill	Viola	19	Petaluma	CA
Myers	Henry J.	24	Petaluma	CA	Hannan	Margaret Grace	20	Petaluma	CA
Myers	Joseph J.	28	Healdsburg	WI	Harris	Grace J.	20	Healdsburg	CA
Myers	Joseph S.	25	Petaluma	CA	Goodwin	Alma R.	20	Petaluma	CA
Myhre	Olaf A.	28	San Francisco	NRY	Koller	Sanne H.	35	San Francisco	DNK
Myrick	H. R.	28	Petaluma	OH	Purvine	Alice	28	Petaluma	CA
Myring	W. H.				Taylor	Emily B.			
Myron	William	24	San Francisco	OH	Dowdall	Genevieve	22	Glen Ellen	CA

Other Heritage Books by the Sonoma County Genealogical Society, Inc.:

CD: *Sonoma County [California] Records, Volume 1*

Early School Attendance Records of Sonoma County, California, Beginning 1858

Early School Attendance Records of Sonoma County, California, Volume II: 1874–1932

Index and Abstracts of Wills, Sonoma County, California: 1850–1900

Index to Naturalization Records in Sonoma County, California, Volume 1: 1841–1906

Naturalization Records in Sonoma County, California, Volume II: 1906–1930

Index to The Sonoma Searcher: *Volume 16, No. 1 to Volume 28, No. 3*
(*Including Index to* The Sonoma Searcher: *Volume 1, No. 1 to Volume 15, No. 4, SCGS, August 1993*)

Index to Vital Data in Local Newspapers of Sonoma County, California, Volume 1: 1855–1875

Index to Vital Data in Local Newspapers of Sonoma County, California, Volume 2: 1876–1880

Index to Vital Data in Local Newspapers of Sonoma County, California, Volume 3: 1881–1885

Index to Vital Data in Local Newspapers of Sonoma County, California, Volume 4: 1886–1890

Index to Vital Data in Local Newspapers of Sonoma County, California, Volume 5: 1891–1899

Index to Vital Data in Local Newspapers of Sonoma County, California, Volume 6: 1900–1903

Index to Vital Data in Local Newspapers of Sonoma County, California, Volume 7: 1904–1906

Index to Vital Data in Local Newspapers of Sonoma County, California, Volume 8: 1907–1909

Index to Vital Data in Local Newspapers of Sonoma County, California, Volume 9: 1910–1912

Indigent Records in Sonoma County, California 1878 to 1926, Volume 1: The Indigents

Indigent Records in Sonoma County, California 1878 to 1926, Volume 2: Taxpayers Who Certified Indigent Need

Marriage License Affidavits, 1861–1921, Sonoma County, California, Volume I: A–F

Marriage License Affidavits, 1861–1921, Sonoma County, California, Volume II: G–M

Marriage License Affidavits, 1861–1921, Sonoma County, California, Volume III: N–Z

Marriage License Affidavits, 1861–1921, Sonoma County, California, Volume IV: Index to Bride's Surname

Militia Lists of Sonoma County, California, 1846 to 1900

Santa Rosa Rural Cemetery, 1853–1997

Sonoma County, California Cemetery Records, 1846–1921, Third Edition

Sonoma County, California Death Records, 1873–1905, Second Edition

Sonoma County California Reconstructed 1890 Census

The 1930 School Census of Sonoma County, California